W9-CMB-995

DK
67
.W6
1970

Wolfe
Soviet power
and Europe, 1945
1970

9335

DATE DUE

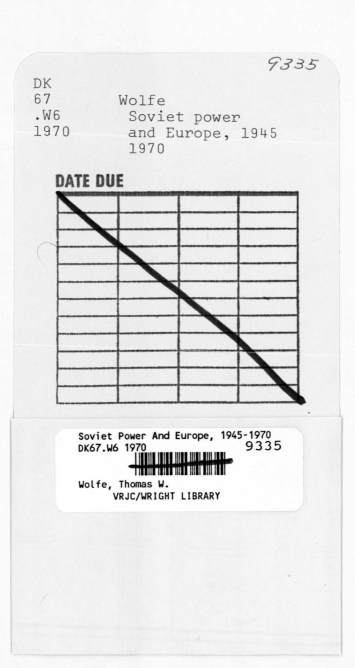

Soviet Power And Europe, 1945-1970
DK67.W6 1970   9335

Wolfe, Thomas W.
VRJC/WRIGHT LIBRARY

SOVIET POWER AND EUROPE
1945–1970

Thomas W. Wolfe

VERNON REGIONAL
JUNIOR COLLEGE LIBRARY

THE JOHNS HOPKINS PRESS
Baltimore and London

Copyright © 1970 by The RAND Corporation
All rights reserved
Manufactured in the United States of America

The Johns Hopkins Press, Baltimore, Maryland 21218
The Johns Hopkins Press Ltd., London

Library of Congress Catalog Card Number 74-111998
International Standard Book Number 0-8018-1166-X (clothbound)
International Standard Book Number 0-8018-1169-4 (paperback)

Originally published, 1970
Johns Hopkins Paperbacks edition, 1970

CONTENTS

Part Three

THE BREZHNEV–KOSYGIN PERIOD: ITS FIRST HALF-DECADE

To my wife

ACKNOWLEDGMENTS

In this book I have sought to provide a balanced appraisal of the evolution of Soviet policy toward both halves of a divided Europe in the postwar period from 1945 to 1970. Together with an analysis of the intermeshing political and military aspects of Soviet policy toward Europe during the long postwar rivalry between the Soviet Union and the United States in this key arena of international politics, the study seeks also to view Moscow's European policy in the framework of Soviet domestic developments and global interests, with particular attention to the changing Soviet–American strategic balance that has emerged in the late 1960's.

Although responsibility for the contents of the book is entirely mine, I owe much to the advice and support of colleagues and friends. Among those to whom I am especially indebted for intellectual stimulus and criticism are Marshall D. Shulman, Andrew W. Marshall, Fritz W. Ermarth, Richard V. Burks, Pierre Hassner, Richard Lowenthal, Philip E. Mosely, James L. Richardson, Malcolm Mackintosh, Arnold L. Horelick, Horst Mendershausen, Malcolm Toon, Hans Speier, and Llewellyn E. Thompson. Others without whose dedicated help the preparation of this book would not have been possible are Sibylle O. Crane, Eugenia Arensburger, Nadia Derkach, Carol Stacey, Dorothy E. Logsdon, Rosalie Fonoroff, Roberta Sharpe, Joseph M. Goldsen, Fred C. Iklé, John C. Hogan, and, not least, my wife, Elizabeth Ann.

The study was prepared as part of a continuing program of research undertaken by The RAND Corporation for United States Air Force Project RAND.

THOMAS W. WOLFE

Washington, D.C.

I

INTRODUCTION

To set the present study of postwar Soviet policy toward Europe in perspective, it may be useful in this introductory chapter to sketch some of the salient changes in the postwar political life of Europe and in the relationship of Europe to the two great outside powers that have helped to shape its destiny since the end of World War II.

Throughout most of the postwar period, the life of Europe was dominated by the East–West confrontation, which perhaps started out as a struggle between the Soviet Union and the United States to deny Europe to each other.[1] Each half of a partitioned Europe became, in a sense, as George Kennan once put it, the political and military province of a superpower peripheral to Europe proper.[2] The bipolarity of power in postwar Europe was brought home above all by the phenomenon of mutual nuclear deterrence, which, following the transient phase of the American atomic monopoly, served to stabilize the military division of Europe and, for a time, tended to immobilize its politics as well.

Meanwhile, however, the postwar status quo was being slowly and subtly undermined by forces of change at work both in the West and in the East. The revival of nationalism, which helped to set in motion what has sometimes been called the process of polycentrism, was probably the key element in the gradual breakdown of bipolarity on both sides of the European dividing line. In turn, the reassertion of nationalist interests in the politics of Europe was perhaps made possible by, more than anything else, the nuclear stalemate between the superpowers, which to many people seemed to dispel the threat that another great war might arise in Europe.

As Europe's own political life reawakened, it gradually became apparent that the opposing alliance systems led by the United States and the Soviet Union were evolving into something new, reflecting important if not fundamental shifts in the political climate of Europe on both sides of the river Elbe. Besides changes within the NATO and Warsaw alliances themselves, to which we shall come in a moment, perhaps the most significant development in European political life by the middle sixties was the belief, or at least the hope, that after more than two decades of the Cold War the two

[1] William H. McNeill, *America, Britain, and Russia: Their Cooperation and Conflict, 1941–1946* (London: Oxford University Press, 1953), pp. 758–60.
[2] George F. Kennan, "Europe in East-West Relations," *Survey* (January 1966): 126.

halves of a divided Europe were at last moving toward some sort of reconciliation.

Needless to say, this prospect was rudely shaken in August 1968, when the leaders of the Soviet Union chose to call upon Soviet arms to hold back the process of change in East Europe. Although it might be supposed that in the long run Soviet military intervention in Czechoslovakia, like that in Hungary twelve years earlier, would not mean the end of hopes of building bridges between the two parts of a partitioned continent, it could scarcely be doubted that the tenuous trend toward European reconciliation had been seriously interrupted by the Soviet action against Czechoslovakia.

To retrace briefly the paths by which, prior to the summer of 1968, the two halves of Europe had moved gradually away from the earlier rigidities of the Cold War era, let us consider first the case of Western Europe. Left prostrate by World War II and helped to its feet by the United States, Western Europe found its postwar partnership with America a mixed blessing. Among the rewards of this association one may cite the containment of the Soviet political-military threat to Western Europe, the phenomenal recovery of the European economy, and the emergence of various common institutions which to many Europeans seemed to bring nearer the vision of a united Europe.

At the same time, however, partnership with America not only brought to the surface many tensions inherent in the relationship between a superpower and its lesser partners, such as those which developed between the United States and France, but it also failed to offer to West Germany much promise of resolving unsettled problems left over from World War II, such as the painful issue of German reunification. Moreover, Western Europe's gross dependence on the United States for its military security gave rise to growing strains within the NATO alliance over questions of strategy and military policy, not to mention disturbing doubts in some quarters about the reliability of the American commitment to defend Europe under the conditions of the nuclear missile age.

With French withdrawal from the military structure of NATO, in 1966, and de Gaulle's open challenge to American leadership of the alliance, NATO seemed to have fallen on hard times. Its troubles were compounded by other developments, such as America's increasing preoccupation with the war in Vietnam and balance-of-payments problems, as well as a growing belief that Soviet military pressure upon the affairs of Europe was a thing of the past. In a sense, NATO's very success had prompted some of its beneficiaries to believe that it had outlived its usefulness, an idea the Soviet Union also sought to encourage. Others, persuaded that NATO had fulfilled its original purpose, thought that it should now seek a new role in the reconciliation of Europe, West and East. Thus, for one reason or another, despite its past contributions to the security of Western Europe, and with its twentieth anniversary less than a year away, NATO's future seemed clouded in the summer of 1968. Then came the rape of Czechoslovakia, one effect of which was doubtless to give NATO a new lease on life.

In East Europe, where Soviet power helped to bring Communist regimes into being in the wake of World War II, the passage of more than two decades also saw some profound changes. Tight Soviet domination of East Europe during Stalin's lifetime, though marred by Yugoslav defiance in 1948, had seemed to augur the creation in that historic buffer region of a unified economic and political system, ultimately destined to be incorporated into a Communist empire ruled from Moscow. What the Soviet leadership had not foreseen was that nationalism in East Europe would prove stronger, in some respects, than a common ideology. Gradually, in the period after Stalin's death, nationalist self-assertion began to spread in varying degree among Moscow's East European satellites. The first hint of impending trouble was furnished by the East German uprising in 1953, followed by the Hungarian revolt and the events in Poland in 1956, which provided dramatic evidence that the Soviet writ no longer ran unchallenged in East Europe. Thereafter, as the effects of Khrushchev's de-Stalinization campaign and the Sino–Soviet dispute caused growing disturbance within the Communist world, the East European regimes found new room for maneuver against the Soviet Union.

Well before the downfall of Khrushchev in late 1964, it became evident not only that nationalist trends in the East European countries were having a destructive impact on the notion of international Communist unity but also that they might undermine the foundations of Soviet hegemony in East Europe itself. In the face of these developments, the Soviet Union, through such multilateral economic and military instrumentalities as the Council for Economic Mutual Assistance (CEMA) and the Warsaw Pact, sought to forge closer ties among the East European states and to bind them securely to its own policy interests. Although these measures fell short of relieving the underlying tensions in relations with East Europe, they served, along with other factors, to emphasize that the Soviet Union had by no means ceased to exercise predominant power and influence in the affairs of the Warsaw bloc. The animosities of the Cold War, attenuated but not buried by the détente which set in after the Berlin and Cuban crises of the early sixties, skillful Soviet play upon East European fears of a resurgent Germany, and, above all, the Soviet military presence in East Europe, continued to place limits upon the ability of the East European countries to shape their own policies independent of Soviet priorities.

Khrushchev's successors found no formula for smoothing Soviet relations with other members of the Warsaw alliance. Indeed, the problems of maintaining discipline and unity within the bloc that had plagued the Kremlin in Khrushchev's time assumed new urgency for the Brezhnev–Kosygin leadership. Initially, it was Rumania that gave the new Soviet leaders the most trouble, not only challenging Soviet authority in economic, political, and military matters but also being the first to break ranks on a common Warsaw bloc policy toward West Germany. However, even Rumania's recalcitrance was overshadowed by the spirit of reform that began to manifest itself in Czechoslovakia early in 1968. Although Czechoslovakia was struck down by the Soviet Union, abetted by several of Moscow's more orthodox Warsaw Pact partners, the brief Czech reform experiment nevertheless seemed to reflect an underlying ferment in East Europe, with unpredictable consequences for Soviet hegemony in the region.

Before the Soviet blow fell upon Czechoslovakia in August 1968, it was often argued that the evolution of the two alliance systems in Europe presented some interesting parallels which might have a significant bearing on Europe's future. Each of the peripheral superpowers had begun to suffer a decline of authority within its alliance system, and in a sense, as the vitality of European politics grew, each alliance leader faced the somewhat comparable problem of not becoming irrelevant to Europe. There were those who felt that Europe, having experienced an internal revival of its own political life and ceased being the mere object of superpower politics, might be better able to work out its own destiny within a pan-European framework, particularly if the energies of the superpowers were increasingly to turn from the European scene to problems connected with the rise of China and with endemic ferment in the Third World.

Although it could be argued that the internal loosening of the two alliance systems meant that the old bipolar division of Europe was on the way out, it was less clear what might be on the way in. Some saw a compelling historical trend toward wider integration of Europe, despite the various setbacks suffered by proponents of European unification; others, a trend toward the return of a Europe of competing nationalisms. East–West reconciliation, either through European integration or through the recovery of national identity, was viewed as a hopeful and desirable prospect growing out of the rise of new political forces and the diffusion of the old bipolar order. Curiously, hardly anyone thought it likely that Europe might revert once more to the frozen bipolarity of the Cold War.

In the aftermath of the Soviet assault upon Czechoslovakia, much of this speculation on possible alternative paths of European development was left hanging in mid-air. Whatever their motives—fear that orthodox Communist rule could not survive in an atmosphere of relative freedom, concern that their military defenses might be breached by a westward-looking Czechoslovakia—the Soviet leaders not only had demonstrated that they would use naked force to reimpose their authority over the Warsaw alliance system, they also had spiked the possibility that Europe might begin to settle its own problems without participation by the superpowers; for their action, casting the shadow of Soviet arms over Europe once more and reviving the suspicions of the Cold War, could hardly help but draw the United States more fully back into Europe. Thus, in the process of stamping out the Czech reform experiment, the Soviet Union, unwittingly perhaps, made clear that it was

premature to think of a Europe independent of Soviet—and American—
power, let alone a reconciled Europe knit together by a unifying "European
idea." At best, what the Soviet action seemed to promise Europeans was
that they might again look forward to an indefinite period of bipolar alliance arrangements aimed at maintaining an uneasy status quo.

If it is difficult in present circumstances to imagine that Europe will
acquire sufficient freedom of maneuver to work out its own destiny without
the superpowers' influence—malign or benign—playing a significant role
in the process, the obverse is also true. The fortunes of the two superpowers
themselves are closely linked with Europe's future. Industrially, geographically, and politically the prime prize of the Cold War, Europe has been the
central arena of the power struggle between the Soviet Union and the
United States since World War II. No matter what course this global competition for influence and primacy eventually may take, what happens in
Europe will be an important, perhaps the most important, key to its outcome.

In the present study we shall be concerned with the two powers' struggle
over Europe primarily from the viewpoint of the Soviet Union. The aim here
is to examine the evolution of Soviet policy toward Europe, West and East
—with particular attention to the military and security dimensions of that
policy—within the framework of the foreign policy and political strategy
pursued by successive generations of postwar Soviet leaders, from Stalin
through Khrushchev to the collective oligarchy under Brezhnev and Kosygin.

It goes without saying, of course, that the military dimensions of policy
are but one aspect of the seamless web of political, economic, strategic, and
other considerations out of which the policy of the Soviet Union—or of any
major state in the modern world—is woven. In choosing to explore in some
depth the military and security aspects of Soviet policy toward Europe, the
author does not mean to suggest that these ingredients of Soviet policy are
somehow more important than the essentially political ends they are intended
to serve. However, there are several cogent reasons why the bearing of
Soviet military power upon the problems of Europe merits more than
casual treatment in this inquiry.

Not only did the political division of Europe after World War II spring
up along the boundary marking the limits of Soviet military penetration into
Europe but the threat of Soviet military power, as perceived in the early
years of the postwar period, had a great deal to do with bringing a Western
defense alliance into being. Much of the history of the two postwar decades
of the Cold War in Europe revolved around the establishment and build-up
of this alliance and its counterpart in the East. Finally, the stabilization of
the European military environment under the influence of these alliance
systems, which helped to exorcise the fear of war in Europe and facilitated
the revival of Europe's political life, also was accompanied by a growing
debate over the continued need for NATO defenses against a Soviet military
threat which, until August 1968—when Soviet tanks and planes broke the
back of a sovereign government in Prague—was widely presumed to be

dying, if not already dead. Because the extent to which this threat is indeed moribund promises to have an important bearing, not only upon the levels of NATO preparedness henceforth deemed necessary but also upon the prospects of working toward some sort of collective security arrangement in Europe, it has seemed appropriate in this study to inquire closely into the Soviet military stance toward Europe and the part it plays in the Soviet Union's European policy.

Most of the present three-part study is addressed to political-military developments during the past fifteen years—the decade of Khrushchev's rule and the half–decade after his successors came to power in late 1964. In the interest of continuity and perspective, however, some attention also has been given to the postwar years under Stalin, during which the lines of the Cold War were drawn in Europe. In recapitulating these earlier years, I do not wish to leap into the revisionist controversy over who started the Cold War, the responsibility for which doubtless rests with leaders on both sides of the postwar confrontation. It will be apparent, however, that my views diverge at many points from those of the New Left historians, whose revisionist criticism of postwar US policy[3] has sometimes inclined them also to washing Stalin clean of historical error—an absolution which not even Soviet historiography has been prepared to grant him.

Finally, while the major portion of this work is given over to a descriptive and analytical account of how Soviet postwar policy toward Europe has evolved up to now, one can hardly help speculating on the direction that Soviet power and purpose in Europe may take in the years immediately ahead. This too is a matter upon which the present study hopes to shed some light.

---

[3] The revisionism of the New Left represents a full swing of the pendulum from earlier revisionists of the Right who found fault with American policy for having allegedly "handed over" the fruits of World War II victory to Stalin.

Part One

THE POSTWAR PERIOD UNDER STALIN

II

STALIN'S POSTWAR POLICIES TOWARD EUROPE

Among the immediate consequences of World War II, which went far toward shaping the postwar environment in Europe, was the penetration of Soviet military power into Central and Eastern Europe and the employment of this military presence to serve a Soviet political strategy aimed at goals beyond the defeat of Nazi Germany. As Stalin said to a Yugoslav visitor, in April 1945: "This war is not as in the past; whoever occupies a territory imposes on it his own social system. Everyone imposes his own system as far as his army can reach. It cannot be otherwise."[1]

In postwar Europe, as the Soviet Union set out to consolidate its share of the victory over Germany, it became apparent that this prescription had indeed been put to work. Besides the obvious task of securing the Soviet position in occupied Germany, the Soviet armed forces were used to garrison other parts of Eastern Europe and to pave the way for subsequent absorption of this region into the Communist fold.

The Western allies were in no mood at war's end to contemplate the prospect of dislodging the Soviet armies by force. For all practical purposes, the Western partners acquiesced in the early postwar period to Soviet hegemony in Eastern Europe, if indeed they had not already recognized the Soviet Union's future claims to pre-eminent influence in this region while the war was still in progress.[2] Moreover, they had largely demobilized their own wartime forces within a year or so after the end of the war.

Under these circumstances, relatively modest Soviet forces would have apparently sufficed to safeguard Soviet gains and to shield the process of

[1] Milovan Djilas, *Conversations with Stalin*, trans. by Michael B. Petrovich (New York: Harcourt, Brace & World, Inc., 1962), p. 114.

[2] As early as the Teheran Conference at the end of 1943, the Western allies apparently gave Stalin the impression that he would have a free hand in Eastern Europe after the war, although they then regarded their assent to making East Europe a zone of Soviet operations as only a provisional military agreement. Churchill's celebrated "spheres of influence" conversation with Stalin in October 1944 also was interpreted by the latter as giving him the green light in Eastern Europe. At Yalta in 1945, some attempt was made, on paper at least, to hedge the concessions accorded Stalin in Eastern Europe, but they did not suffice to alter the de facto situation in which the massive presence of Soviet troops made Stalin the real arbiter of the region. One must add that there is still a great deal of ambiguity, which competing historical interpretations have not resolved, as to the extent to which the West during the war accepted a future Soviet hegemony in East Europe. See W. W. Rostow, *The United States in the World Arena* (New York: Harper & Brothers, 1960), pp. 101–8; John Lukacs, *A New History of the Cold War* (Garden City, N.Y.: Doubleday & Company, Inc., 1966), pp. 46–50; Ghita Ionescu, *The Break-Up of the Soviet Empire in Eastern Europe* (Baltimore, Md.: Penguin Books, 1965), pp. 12–16; H. Gordon Skilling, *The Governments of Communist East Europe* (New York: Thomas Y. Crowell Co., 1966), pp. 3–6.

revolutionary takeover in Eastern Europe. On the contrary, however, the Soviet Union chose to keep very substantial forces under arms. Precisely how large a Soviet demobilization took place in the early postwar years has never been positively established, owing to Soviet secrecy in such matters. Official Soviet statements claimed that large-scale reductions from the war-time peak of around 12,000,000 troops were carried out in several stages between 1945 and 1948,[3] but no figures were ever given until Khrushchev offered a set of retrospective statistics in January 1960. According to Khrushchev, the Soviet armed forces were reduced to a strength of 2,874,000 men by 1948, and by 1955 had been built up again to 5,763,000 after "provocation" from the West.[4]

The 1948 figure cited by Khrushchev generally has been regarded as understating the size of the regular military establishment in the early postwar years,[5] as well as excluding the then sizable armed security police force. Various Western accounts, some of which presumably reflected official estimates of the period, put the over-all size of the Soviet armed forces at approximately 4,000,000 men in the 1947–48 period.[6] Even if Khrushchev's lower figure of 2.8 million were to be accepted at face value, however, it

[3] See, for example, "Demobilizatsiia," Bol'shaia sovetskaia entsiklopediia (The Large Soviet Encyclopedia), vol. 13 (Moscow, 1952), pp. 652–53. The figure of around 12,000,000 for the war-time peak of the Soviet forces, which approximates that for the United States, has sometimes been set higher. Some Western accounts have placed Soviet strength under arms at war's end at 15,000,000 or more. See, for example, R. L. Garthoff, "What's Behind Soviet Disarmament?" Army Combat Forces Journal, vol. 6, no. 3 (October 1955): 24; Malcolm Mackintosh, Juggernaut: The Russian Forces, 1918–1966 (New York: Macmillan Company, 1967), p. 271.

[4] N. S. Khrushchev, "Disarmament Is the Path Toward Strengthening Peace and Ensuring Friendship Among Peoples," Pravda, January 15, 1960. In this speech Khrushchev gave figures purporting to show Soviet armed forces strength at selected intervals during a thirty-three-year period from 1927 to 1960. The complete set of figures he gave was as follows: 1927—586,000; 1937—1,433,000; 1941—4,207,000; 1945—11,365,000; 1948—2,874,000; 1955—5,763,000; 1960—3,623,000.

These figures, without amendment, have since remained the only tally of pre-1960 Soviet troop levels to be cited in Soviet sources. For a recent example, see Colonel N. Kozlov, "The Armed Forces of the USSR in the Period of the Building of Communism," Kommunist Vooruzhennykh Sil (Communist of the Armed Forces), no. 4 (February 1967), p. 77.

[5] There is a strong supposition that Khrushchev's January 1960 list of strength figures may have been politically colored to show the Soviet Union in a good light as compared with the West, since his statement was made in the context of claimed unilateral contributions to disarmament by the Soviet Union. Incidentally, while the 1948 figure was set lower than generally accepted Western estimates in order to underscore the Soviet contribution to disarmament immediately after the war, the figure given for 1955 was somewhat higher than what was thought to be the case by many Western observers. Doubtless, the interaction between Soviet force-level decisions and such develop-ments as the Korean War and the build-up of NATO in the 1949–55 period had resulted in an upward trend in over-all Soviet strength. Skepticism seems warranted, however, that the Soviet level had dropped as low as purported in 1948, especially since this would imply that Soviet forces had subsequently been more than doubled in size by 1955—a rearmament effort of far greater magnitude than suggested either by Soviet policy pronouncements or by Western estimates during the period concerned.

[6] A survey of numerous Western accounts of the Soviet military establishment during the five-year period between the end of World War II and the Korean War shows that a majority of American and European observers placed the over-all size of the Soviet armed forces at somewhere between four and five million men, exclusive of security troops, generally estimated at from 400,000 to 600,000. The ground forces, representing the backbone of continental Soviet military power during this essentially pre-nuclear phase of Soviet military development, were usually

would still suggest a considerable disparity between the postwar Soviet forces and those maintained by any of the principal Western powers. By 1947, for example, the US armed forces were down to about 1.4 million, where they remained until after the start of the Korean War in June 1950, while British and French forces were somewhat smaller.[7]

Whatever the actual over-all level of the Soviet military establishment may have been in the early postwar period, it is quite clear that a large combined-arms force of Soviet ground troops and tactical support aircraft was left in place in occupied Germany and elsewhere in East Europe. Numbering close to thirty divisions and well upward of a half-million men,[8] the equivalent of a Soviet wartime *front*, this Soviet force loomed formidably against the fewer than ten loosely co-ordinated British, French, and American divisions that garrisoned Western Europe in 1947–48. Moreover, this forward deployment of Soviet military power at the threshold of Western Europe remained relatively constant in size thereafter, being reduced only marginally during the next two decades.

It was this visible Soviet military presence in Europe, backed by additional forces of substantial, though perhaps exaggerated, size in the bordering territory of the USSR itself, which initially gave rise to serious concern in the West that an "imbalance of forces" existed that might prejudice the postwar security of Europe. One might add that the early postwar image of a massive Soviet military machine poised at the threshold of Europe was not entirely the product of estimates of the forces kept actively under arms. It also was shaped by such factors as the large trained reserves which the Soviet military training system continued to produce annually after the war. The induction rate of new age-classes into the armed forces, releasing a roughly equivalent number of trained men into the reserves, was estimated in 1949 at about 750,000 per year,[9] which would have permitted rapid mobilization of forces comparable in size to those raised at the peak of World War II.

---

bracketed somewhere between 2.5 and 4 million men. See, for example, "World Military Survey," *New York Times*, May 12, 1947; "Armies of the World," *Britannica Book of the Year*, Walter Yust, ed. (Chicago–Toronto–London: Encyclopaedia Britannica, Inc., 1948), p. 75; ibid. (1949), p. 73; Hal D. Stewart, "The Russian Army Today," *Armored Cavalry Journal* (September–October 1947): 35; Jerry S. Addington, "The Postwar Russian Army," *Field Artillery Journal* (March–April 1949): 81; Colonel Louis B. Ely, *The Red Army Today* (Harrisburg, Pa.: Military Service Publishing Company, 1949), pp. 3, 126; "Stärke der russischen Wehrmacht" (The Strength of the Russian Armed Forces), *Schweitzer Artillerist*, no. 9 (September 1949): 107; B. H. Liddell Hart, "The Red Army: A Searching Analysis of Russian Men and Tactics," *Ordnance* (July–August 1949): 25–28; T. Norwid, "Sovjets stridskrafter" (Soviet Armed Forces), *Folk och Försvar*, no. 8 (1950): 17–20.

[7] The precipitous reduction of the US military establishment also was reflected in American defense budgets, which dropped from a 1945 figure of $81.2 billion to $14.4 billion in 1947 and to $11.7 billion the following year.

[8] See Ely, *The Red Army Today*, p. 166; "Die Sowjetbesatzungstruppen in Ostdeutschland" (The Soviet Occupation Troops in East Germany), *Allgemeine Schweizerische Militärzeitschrift* (General Swiss Military Review), no. 5 (May 1951): 366–67; Hanson W. Baldwin, *The Great Arms Race* (New York: Frederick A. Praeger, Inc., 1958), p. 36. Mackintosh, *Juggernaut*, p. 271, places the total number of Soviet troops kept in Europe outside the USSR in the early postwar years at about one million.

[9] Ely, *The Red Army Today*, p. 14.

Much of the impetus for the subsequent rearming of Western Europe undoubtedly derived, in one way or another, from an underlying fear that postwar Europe lay exposed to preponderant Soviet conventional power. Why then should Stalin have decided to keep under arms what appeared to be unreasonably large forces, when a less formidable image of Soviet military power might have allayed Western concern and helped to alter profoundly the climate of postwar relations between the Soviet Union and its wartime allies? Obviously, there is no simple answer to this question. Perhaps we can best approach it by reviewing some of the salient factors that seem to have conditioned Soviet policy toward Europe during the postwar years of Stalin's rule.

Stalin's Perception of the Postwar Scene

In the fullness of time, history may provide answers to all the questions it poses, as Max Beloff has observed,[10] but it does not tell us much about the possible outcome of the lost opportunities with which it is strewn. One such lost opportunity was doubtless the failure of the Soviet Union and the West to establish a mutually acceptable set of relationships in the world which emerged from World War II. If there is little point in speculating on what might have been, it is at least appropriate to note that in the first years after World War II Stalin chose a policy course which not only prejudiced the possibility of postwar collaboration with the West but which also served to unite the West in opposition to his aims.[11] That Western attitudes and statesmanship also contributed to the breakdown of wartime unity and helped to give rise to what was to become the Cold War goes without saying; however, to recognize this is not to embrace the thesis—expounded by some writers of the so-called "revisionist" school—that Stalin stands in the eyes of history as the injured party, put upon by erstwhile allies bent on humiliating the Soviet Union and depriving it of the rightful fruits of victory.[12]

[10] Max Beloff, " 'Twixt Knowledge and Illusions," book review in *Problems of Communism* (July–August 1966), p. 50.

[11] J. M. Mackintosh, *Strategy and Tactics of Soviet Foreign Policy* (London: Oxford University Press, 1962), p. 17; Leopold Labedz, "Twenty Years After," *Survey*, no. 58 (January 1966): 9.

[12] The revisionist thesis, expounded in the United States largely by historians of the New Left, lays full responsibility for the Cold War upon the US "containment" policy fathered by George F. Kennan and allegedly imposed without justification upon "an almost mortally wounded Soviet Union" which after the war had only "sought compensation for her major and decisive role in the destruction of Hitler's armies." The quoted words are D. F. Fleming's from his "Is Containment Moral?" *Annals of the American Academy of Political and Social Science* (hereafter cited as *Annals*) (November 1965): 19. Although avowedly meant to challenge the conventional view that American policy in the Cold War was essentially a response to Soviet expansionism, the revisionist argument often goes far beyond trying to restore "balance" in the apportionment of blame for the Cold War. In its more extreme forms, it attempts to depict postwar US policy as the product of a chauvinist-rightist mentality intent at every turn upon snuffing out "a rising movement for social justice" in the world, leaving the implication—whether intended or not—that Soviet and Communist policy amounts to a defense of social justice against American power. Among exponents of the more extreme revisionist viewpoint, see Fleming, *The Cold War and Its Origins, 1917–1960*, 2 vols. (Garden City, N.Y.: Doubleday and Company, 1961); David Horowitz, *The Free World Colossus: A Critique of American Foreign Policy in the Cold War* (New York: Hill and Wang,

Many interpretations of Stalin's motives have been offered. They tend to fall into two categories: those stressing his desire to exploit the postwar situation in order to make positive gains for Soviet policy on the one hand; and those emphasizing his concern to ward off anticipated threats to Soviet security on the other. In the first category, for example, is the view that Stalin, sensing that the floodgates of social and political upheaval after the war would not remain open forever, decided he must make the most of a transitory period for revolutionary advance, even at the cost of alienating his wartime allies.[13] Or, as a variant interpretation, the collapse of Germany left a power vacuum in the heart of Europe which Stalin was cynically prepared to fill,[14] the main restriction upon his expansionist urge being what, in George Kennan's phrase,[15] "the amiable indulgence of the Western powers," would tolerate.

In the second category, by contrast, Stalin was said to be primarily concerned to stave off anticipated efforts by the Western powers to undo his wartime gains, and he therefore sought to forestall them by militant consolidation of Soviet control over territories occupied by the Red Army.[16] A variant explanation, which contrives to fit into both categories, holds that Stalin was prone to disguise his expansionist aims as security guarantees, and that, in fact, as he understood it, there was little difference between the extension of Communist rule and the enhancement of Soviet security.[17] There is also, of course, the revisionist argument that Stalin wished to preserve the wartime alliance and co-operation with the West and that he adopted a tough line in East Europe only after being confronted with Western demands that

1965). Somewhat more moderate versions of the revisionist viewpoint may be found in William A. Williams, *The Tragedy of American Diplomacy* (Cleveland, Ohio: World Publishers, 1959); Gar Alperovitz, *Atomic Diplomacy: Hiroshima and Potsdam* (New York: Vintage Books, 1967); Ronald Steel, *Pax Americana* (New York: Viking Press, Inc., 1967). For discussion of some of the pros and cons of the revisionist effort to rewrite the history of the Cold War, see Arthur Schlesinger, Jr., "Origins of the Cold War," *Foreign Affairs* (October 1967): 22–52; Christopher Lasch, "The Cold War, Revisited and Re-Visioned," *New York Times Magazine*, January 14, 1968, pp. 26 ff.; and Letters to the Editor, especially that of John Lukacs, himself a Cold War historian critical of both the conventional and revisionist schools, ibid., February 4, 1968, pp. 12–14.

[13] See, for example, Paul E. Zinner, "The Ideological Bases of Soviet Foreign Policy," *World Politics* (July 1952): 497–99; Melville J. Ruggles, *The Soviet Image of the United States*, The RAND Corporation, P-418, July 9, 1953, pp. 8–9; George Waskovich, "The Ideological Shadow of the USSR," *Annals* (September 1950): 45–46.

[14] See George B. de Huszar, "Use of Satellite Outposts by the USSR," *Annals* (September 1950): 158; Wilfred Knapp, "Cold War Origins," *Survey* (January 1966): 153–54.

[15] George F. Kennan, *American Diplomacy, 1900–1950* (Chicago, Ill.: University of Chicago Press, 1951), p. 136.

[16] This interpretation of an essentially reactive Soviet policy has been carefully spelled out by Marshall D. Shulman, *Stalin's Foreign Policy Reappraised* (Cambridge, Mass.: Harvard University Press, 1963), pp. 13–18, 258–59.

[17] See Frederick C. Barghoorn, "The Soviet Union Between War and Cold War," *Annals* (May 1949): 1; Alexander Bregman, "The Polish Question," *Survey* (January 1966): 165. For a concise analysis which takes into account both the security aspect of Soviet postwar objectives in East Central Europe and the significance of this area as a basis for expansive operations, see Zbigniew K. Brzezinski, *The Soviet Bloc: Unity and Conflict* (Cambridge, Mass.: Harvard University Press, 1960), pp. 4–6.

the Soviet Union give up its "hard-won military positions" under the "clear threat of preventive war."[18]

Perhaps many of these elements entered in one degree or another into Stalin's perception of the international scene in the early postwar years when, as McGeorge Bundy has described it, Stalin seemed bent upon squandering the "reservoir of good will" he had inherited from the wartime years of partnership with the West.[19] In any event, without trying to exhaust the sources of Stalin's motivation, one may identify several factors that seem to have had a particular bearing upon his military policy decisions at this period.

The frame of mind which led Stalin to interpret the postwar diplomacy of the Western powers as confirmation of ingrained hostility to the Soviet Union[20] was probably one of the chief factors that underlay his decision to maintain large military forces. A desire to stake out a protective belt of territory to cover the Soviet Union's traditionally vulnerable frontier with Europe was probably another factor that led Stalin to keep substantial Soviet forces deployed in Central and Eastern Europe. Stalin's reluctance to remove these forces from their wartime lodgement in Eastern Europe may also have been due to the belief that local resistance to satellization of the area would otherwise present serious problems. His awareness that the postwar presence of military forces in Europe would help determine its future political boundaries may also have stayed him from a hasty decision to bring his troops home. Another key element in Stalin's perception of the postwar scene—and perhaps one which weighed most heavily of all in his military policy decisions—was the possibility that American involvement in Europe might threaten not only the Soviet Union's wartime gains but also its prospects for future political advance.

Initially, Stalin may have hoped, or even expected, that the United States would in fact disengage itself from postwar Europe, as suggested by President Roosevelt's comment at Yalta in 1945 that he "did not believe that

---

[18] See, for example, Horowitz, *The Free World Colossus*, pp. 46, 247, 254–55; Williams, *The Tragedy of American Diplomacy*, p. 229; P. M. S. Blackett, *Atomic Weapons and East-West Relations* (New York: Cambridge University Press, 1956), p. 86. It should be noted that there is an important distinction between the view that Stalin's moves were motivated by a concern to forestall anticipated Western efforts to contest his domination of East Europe, and the revisionist contention that he set out to secure control over East Europe only after making unrequited offers to co-operate with the West. The interaction of mistrust and suspicion on both sides was much too complex to admit such a pat explanation.

[19] McGeorge Bundy, "The Test of Yalta," *Foreign Affairs* (July 1949): 618. See also James F. Byrnes, *Speaking Frankly* (New York: Harper & Brothers, 1947), p. 71.

[20] The extent to which Stalin was, on the one hand, the prisoner of an ideology which led him to regard the capitalist West as an unappeasably hostile adversary, or, on the other hand, a cold political realist who weighed his dealings with that adversary in essentially power terms, is a question which defies precise answer. In any event, the ideological element seems to have been pervasive enough to make it doubtful whether any policy approach from the Western powers, so long as they remained capitalist democracies, could have hoped to set Stalin's suspicions at rest. As Arthur Schlesinger has noted, this is a point which the revisionist critique of Western policy tends to gloss over. See *Foreign Affairs* (October 1967): 47.

American troops would stay in Europe much more than two years."[21] For many reasons, including the prospect of gaining a free hand to deal with the question of postwar Germany's political future, an American withdrawal from Europe would certainly have seemed to be in the Soviet interest. In connection with the German question, the Soviet Union in the spring of 1946 rejected a US proposal for what would have amounted to a twenty-five-year alliance to insure the disarmament of Germany.[22]

Presumably, Soviet objections rested on the fact that such an agreement would have given the United States a lasting foothold in Europe and a continuing voice in German affairs, whereas an American return to isolationism would have left Germany little choice but to accept the Soviet alternative for its future. Indeed, the latter expectation probably lent support to an initial Soviet policy favoring German unity, on the grounds that political capture of a reunified Germany was possible. As long as there was a prospect that the political forces in Germany opposing dismemberment of the country could be mobilized to support a Soviet alternative, the Soviet Union was willing to consider the idea of reunification;[23] when this prospect evaporated with the inability of the Socialist Unity Party (SED) to capitalize on reunification sentiment, so did Soviet interest in ending the de facto division of Germany. However, up to the time of Stalin's death, at least, the idea that a reunified Germany would tend to disrupt Western unity and thus serve Soviet policy ends was kept alive by Stalin himself, as we shall see.

Despite the fact that American disengagement from Europe must have been a desideratum high on Stalin's priority list, his maneuvering for position toward the end of the war and in the early postwar period was scarcely calculated to encourage it. Of course, it is only fair to recognize that Stalin's policies evolved in the context of a mutual decay of confidence on both sides, a process fed by conflicting Western and Soviet conceptions of what was necessary to insure postwar security and a sound peace.[24] However, one

[21] Herbert Feis, *Churchill, Roosevelt, Stalin* (Princeton, N. J.: Princeton University Press, 1957), p. 531.

[22] For a discussion of Soviet resistance to this proposal, which Secretary of State Byrnes had first broached to Molotov in September 1945 and which was taken up again in 1946, see Byrnes, *Speaking Frankly*, pp. 125, 171–76. See also Philip E. Mosely, "Soviet-American Relations Since the War," *Annals* (May 1949): 207.

[23] How long after the war Stalin seriously held to the belief that Communist control could be extended over the whole of Germany is a matter of some dispute. As Marshall Shulman (*Stalin's Foreign Policy Reappraised*, p. 19) has noted, Stalin in 1946 predicted that all of Germany would fall under Communist domination, whereas two years later Stalin is quoted by Djilas as saying that Germany would remain divided. The argument that Stalin wavered back and forth on the postwar prospects for Communist control of all of Germany, as well as on the desirability of dismemberment or reunification, has been advanced by other observers. See, for example, Walter Laqueur, *Russia and Germany: A Century of Conflict* (Boston, Mass.: Little, Brown and Company, 1965), pp. 271, 274–75.

[24] It should be noted that there were significant Anglo-American differences over how to secure the peace, as well as the deeper division between these Western partners and the Soviet Union. In general, the prevailing US view ran toward what Schlesinger identifies ("The Origins of the Cold War," p. 26) as the "universalist" conception for assuring world order through international organizations, while the British preference expressed by Churchill lay in the direction of a "spheres-

can but remark that Stalin helped to defeat his own purposes. Skeptical that the Soviet Union might find security through the international machinery of a United Nations, suspicious of US advocacy of self-determination for East Europe, Stalin set out to work his will there unilaterally, above all in the test case of Poland,[25] and thereby stirred forebodings in the West about Soviet intentions which virtually precluded the possibility of a prompt American exodus from the postwar European scene.

Although Stalin's moves—from those involving East Europe and Germany to his demands for revision of the Montreux Convention and his territorial claims on Turkey—certainly had the effect of blighting the Big Three spirit of co-operation,[26] they did not necessarily mean that Stalin was indifferent to the need for allaying the growing suspicions of his wartime allies. Indeed, he demonstrated more than once that he was anxious not to provoke a Western reaction that might jeopardize his plans for setting up a system of Soviet-controlled states in East Europe. One such instance was the withdrawal of Soviet troops from northern Iran in the spring of 1946, in response to President Truman's warning,[27] a gesture suggesting that Stalin was neither prepared for nor wished to invite a showdown with the United States which could arrest the latter's hoped-for return to isolationism.

Another instance was Stalin's quiet advice to Communist leaders in France and Italy to refrain from trying to seize power immediately after the war, though his caution in this regard may have stemmed no less from wanting to lull US apprehensions than from his appreciation, as expressed later to the Belgrade Politburo, that the way the war ended—i.e., without Soviet forces reaching France and Italy—had "unfortunately" made it impossible for the Soviet Union to establish "people's democracies" in those countries.[28] A third example of Stalin's desire to avoid giving the West an excuse for action which might jeopardize the Soviet foothold in southeastern Europe came in connection with Greece, following the proclamation of the Truman Doctrine in March 1947. As Milovan Djilas has disclosed,

---

of-influence" solution resting on the balance of power. At some points, the Churchillian view probably came closer to Stalin's thinking than what Anthony Eden described as the "exaggeratedly moral" character of US policy.

[25] For a useful analysis of the reasons why Poland's fate was critical to whether there would be postwar co-operation among the victorious wartime powers or competition between them over Germany, see Martin F. Herz, *Beginnings of the Cold War* (Bloomington, Ind.: Indiana University Press, 1966), pp. 38–63. See also, Rostow, *The United States in the World Arena*, pp. 109–10 ff.

[26] André Fontaine has offered a somewhat mordant view of how the spirit of co-operation came to be undermined. Stalin, he suggests, gained the impression that the wartime Western leaders were "weaklings and hypocrites forever ready to yield to pressure and happy to settle for empty promises." On the basis of this estimate, he went about achieving his ends in a way which contributed largely to subsequent Western doubt about "the usefulness of trying to negotiate with a partner in such flagrant bad faith." See Fontaine's *History of the Cold War*, English translation (New York: Pantheon Books, 1968), p. 256.

[27] See John C. Campbell, *Defense of the Middle East: Problems of American Policy* (New York: Frederick A. Praeger, Inc., 1960), p. 33.

[28] *The Soviet–Yugoslav Dispute*, Royal Institute of International Affairs, London, November 1948, p. 51.

Stalin grew alarmed lest the guerrilla uprising in Greece "endanger his already-won positions," leading him to insist in early 1948 that it be called off.[29]

Precisely when the possibility of maintaining Big Three unity and a collective approach to the problems of the peace was lost, if indeed it was ever in the cards, no one can say with certainty. Perhaps it was in Poland in the troubled year of 1944,[30] or perhaps it was sometime in the period between Yalta in February 1945 and Potsdam six months later,[31] when the military deployments at war's end began to congeal into what was to become, in Walter Lippmann's words, "the political boundary of two hostile coalitions."[32] By the end of 1946, certainly, the prospects for postwar co-operation no longer appeared very encouraging. Early in the year—a month before Churchill's Iron Curtain speech in Fulton, Missouri—Stalin had delivered his celebrated February 9 election speech in Moscow, which, along with similar ominous statements made later by Andrei Zhdanov,[33] publicly reintroduced the assumption of deep-rooted conflict with the West and foreshadowed a return to the doctrine of a world divided into two hostile camps. Throughout the remainder of 1946, increasing Soviet truculence in the series of futile negotiations aimed at drafting peace treaties with Germany and Austria did not augur well for the future.[34]

Even so, the situation might have been salvaged in the early months of

[29] Djilas, *Conversations with Stalin*, pp. 182–83. For an informative appraisal of this question, see D. George Kousoulas, "The Truman Doctrine and the Stalin–Tito Rift: A Reappraisal, Twenty Years Later," paper presented at the Institute for Sino-Soviet Studies, The George Washington University, November 14, 1967, pp. 2–5.

[30] In the view of William H. McNeill, one of the ablest historians of the wartime Big Three relationship, failure "to achieve a peaceable settlement of the Polish problem in the first seven months of 1944 may well be considered the turning point in the history of the Grand Alliance. Although a semblance of harmony was re-established at Yalta in February 1945, that harmony was never translated into deeds. Despite all later efforts to mend the breach between East and West, the bad blood created in Poland in 1944 proved the beginning of the end." See his *America, Britain, and Russia: Their Cooperation and Conflict, 1941–1946* (London: Oxford University Press, 1953), p. 433.

[31] Both orthodox and revisionist historians are generally agreed that this was a critical period in the deterioration of the wartime relationship. The revisionist viewpoint, however, tends to put somewhat heavier stress on this period, citing such things as Truman's coming to office after Roosevelt's death; the influence of Harriman, Byrnes, Forrestal, Vandenberg, and other so-called hard-liners on the new President; the cutting off of Lend-Lease and denial of loans to Russia, and the first successful atomic test, as factors responsible for a shift of American policy which assertedly left Stalin no alternative but to look after his interests unilaterally. See, for example, Fleming, *The Cold War and Its Origins*, pp. 207–87; Horowitz, *The Free World Colossus*, pp. 31–54; Alperovitz, *Atomic Diplomacy*, pp. 19–187.

[32] Walter Lippmann, *The Cold War* (New York: Harper & Brothers, 1947), p. 36.

[33] Election speech by I. V. Stalin, February 9, 1946, *Pravda*, February 10, 1946; Speech by Andrei Zhdanov on the twenty-ninth anniversary of the October Revolution, *Pravda*, November 7, 1946; A. A. Zhdanov, "The 29th Anniversary of the Great Socialist Revolution; Speech at the Commemorative Meeting of the Moscow Soviet on November 6, 1946," *Bol'shevik*, no. 21 (November 1946): 1–13.

[34] Robert D. Warth, *Soviet Russia in World Politics* (New York: Twayne Publishers, Inc., 1963), pp. 327–31. See also Alvin Z. Rubenstein, *The Foreign Policy of the Soviet Union* (New York: Random House, 1960), pp. 202–14.

1947, for the United States was still seeking conceptual moorings for its postwar policy toward the Soviet Union,[35] and the door was kept at least partly open for co-operation with the Russians in Europe. According to some observers, the conclusive turning point in postwar Soviet–US relations probably came with failure of the March 1947 Conference of Foreign Ministers in Moscow to reach a settlement on Europe,[36] a failure which coincided with and, in the opinion of some critics,[37] could be blamed upon the Truman Doctrine speech of March 12. Or, it might be argued that the Marshall Plan initiative of June 1947 represented still one more chance to find a way out of the impasse in which the World War II victors found themselves. The Soviet Union had been invited to participate in this general program for the reconstruction of all Europe and had even sent Molotov to Paris on June 28, 1947, with a bevy of advisors to look the plan over. However, after two days, the Soviet delegation pulled out, and Stalin also forbade the governments of Poland and Czechoslovakia to take part in the European Recovery Program (ERP). To many observers, this was the irreversible turning point which marked the postwar division of Europe and the beginning of the Cold War.[38]

Militant Pressures of the Zhdanovist Period

Had Stalin's rejection of the Marshall Plan as a possible avenue to the restoration of East–West understanding and co-operation stopped there, the Cold War might subsequently have taken a less frigid course. What happened, however, was that the Marshall Plan became one of the targets of a militant campaign of Soviet pressure against Europe which unfolded in 1947–48 following the founding meeting of the Cominform in Warsaw in October 1947, where Zhdanov enunciated the policy line for the period that was to bear his name.[39] As even the sharpest critics of Anglo–American postwar policies concede,[40] the Communist attack against the Marshall Plan, upon which the economic revival of West Europe depended, lent substance to fears of sabotage and subversion aimed at preparation for a political offensive against the war-weakened European countries.

[35] The appearance of George F. Kennan's famous "X" article on "The Sources of Soviet Conduct" in *Foreign Affairs* (July 1947) is generally taken to mark the juncture at which a rationale for postwar US policy toward the Soviet Union had begun to jell. For an excellent discussion of the conceptual moorings of US policy in this period, see Seyom Brown, *The Faces of Power: Constancy and Change in United States Foreign Policy from Truman to Johnson* (New York: Columbia University Press, 1968), pp. 31–52.

[36] Rostow, *The United States in the World Arena*, pp. 208–9.

[37] Horowitz, *The Free World Colossus*, p. 76. See also Howard K. Smith, *The State of Europe* (New York: Alfred A. Knopf, Inc., 1949), pp. 118–23.

[38] See Louis J. Halle, "The Turning Point," *Survey*, no. 58 (January 1966): 168–76.

[39] The period and the policies associated with it are frequently known as the *Zhdanovshchina*. The speech which launched it may be found in Andrei Zhdanov, *The International Situation* (Moscow: Foreign Languages Publishing House, 1947).

[40] See Horowitz, *The Free World Colossus*, p. 81.

Other aspects of the new phase of Soviet militancy inaugurated under Zhdanov's nominal sponsorship only helped to reinforce such fears. In addition to speeding up the consolidation of Soviet control in East Europe, Soviet policy in this period was marked also by attempts of the French and Italian Communist parties to bring down their governments through strikes and mass movements, by the coup in Czechoslovakia, by efforts to bring the "renegade" Tito to heel, and by initiation of the Berlin blockade.[41] Amongst these developments, perhaps the Communist takeover in Czechoslovakia in February 1948 and the Berlin blockade had the most powerful impact, sending a shudder through Western Europe and helping to overcome the apathy in many quarters which had greeted the Brussels plan for Western European Union, announced by Ernest Bevin in January 1948. This was especially true in Scandinavia, where there had been little enthusiasm for projected European defense plans until the Czech coup brought a change of mind leading to the participation of Norway and Denmark. Apparently, also, it was the Berlin blockade which tipped the scales for Truman, leading him to give the go-ahead for commitment of American military power to the defense of Europe.[42]

Whether the aggressive phase of Soviet policy in the Zhdanovist period was undertaken in the belief that it might actually result in the political collapse of Western Europe, or merely to test the outer limits of Soviet influence over postwar Europe, is a question which perhaps can never be answered. Clearly, however, it did convey to many people in the West and their governments the impression that the Soviet Union was seeking to extend its dominance to all of Europe, and upon this perception Western policies for the defense of Europe were founded.[43] From Stalin's viewpoint, in turn, whatever his basic intentions may have been, the militancy of the Zhdanovist program was such that he would hardly have felt it expedient for the Soviet Union to lower its military guard until the Western response became known. Indeed, Stalin could not rule out the possibility that he might have a new war on his hands. Although no Western government was seriously considering this form of response to Soviet pressures in the late forties, some voices

---

[41] For various accounts of the Zhdanovist phase of Soviet policy, which began with Zhdanov's Cominform speech in Warsaw in October 1947 and ended shortly after his death on August 31, 1948, see Franz Borkenau, *European Communism* (New York: Harper & Brothers, 1953), pp. 519–42; Shulman, *Stalin's Foreign Policy Reappraised*, pp. 14–20; Rubinstein, *The Foreign Policy of the Soviet Union*, pp. 215–16; Knapp in *Survey* (January 1966): 153–58; and Evelyn Anderson, "Germany in the Cold War," ibid., pp. 177–86.

[42] See Brown, *The Faces of Power*, p. 12.

[43] Whether groundless or not, the fears of Soviet expansion generated in the West during the period of Zhdanovist militancy were an undeniable contribution to the Cold War, which the revisionist school of historians finds it difficult to explain away, for if indeed Western policy was influenced by such fears, was it not then a policy of response after all? The customary revisionist argument to demonstrate that fear of Soviet expansion was not a motivation behind Western, and specifically US, policy is that American leaders, sharing an estimate attributed to George Kennan, were confident of the imminent collapse of Soviet power and hence could not have been genuinely worried about Soviet expansion. See Williams, *The Tragedy of American Diplomacy*, pp. 179–80; Horowitz, *The Free World Colossus*, pp. 254–57.

VERNON REGIONAL
JUNIOR COLLEGE LIBRARY

in the West, including that of Bertrand Russell, had been urging nothing less than preventive war.[44]

In this connection it is worth recalling that Zhdanov believed that the West was in the throes of a deep economic crisis which it might try to solve in characteristic "capitalist" fashion by means of war. According to some analyses of the Zhdanovist program, the policy of revolutionary action against the West was therefore to be regarded as the prelude to a probable war; in short, a preparatory program calculated to disrupt and weaken further a hostile West already rent by economic woes.[45] Whether such an estimate of the likelihood of war actually lay behind the militancy of the *Zhdanovshchina*, or whether, as a close reading of Zhdanov's remarks on the threat of a "new war" might suggest, he was employing Communist militancy as a way to demonstrate that the Soviet Union would not allow itself to be intimidated by the prospect of another war,[46] is again a matter of speculation.

In any event, at a time in the early postwar period when Stalin himself was presumably not very sanguine about the outcome of a new war, as his rather bleak comments on the subject in the Soviet–Yugoslav dispute correspondence would suggest,[47] the importance of maintaining the strongest military posture he could muster, in the event war should materialize, was doubtless not lost upon him. While the Western reaction to the pressures of the *Zhdanovshchina* fell far short of resort to war, and thus should have allayed any anxiety Stalin may have felt on that score, the main features of the Western policy which took shape at this time certainly brought Stalin no great comfort.

American acceptance of responsibility in 1947 for aiding Greece and Turkey under the Truman Doctrine, the launching of the Marshall Plan in the same year, the Anglo–American airlift to counter the Berlin blockade in 1948, and finally the formation of NATO and the establishment of a West German government in 1949, all served to demonstrate that the first militant phase of postwar Soviet European policy had proved unproductive. Not only had the Soviet Union failed to strengthen its influence over the war-weakened countries of Western Europe but it had alarmed them to the point that they began to think seriously of taking further measures for their collective defense. Moreover, these developments also made it unmistakably clear to Stalin by the late forties that the United States had a deep interest in the fate of Western Europe and that it had emerged as a major rival to the Soviet Union upon the European scene.

[44] For a lucid discussion of the restraint which prevailed among Western leaders at the time of the Western nuclear monopoly when voices like Lord Russell's were being raised in favor of preventive war, see Richard H. Rovere, "Reflections: A New Situation in the World," *New Yorker*, February 24, 1968, p. 45.

[45] For the most explicit interpretation along this line, see Borkenau, *European Communism*, pp. 523–24.

[46] See especially Zhdanov speech in *Bol'shevik* (November 1946), p. 12.

[47] *The Soviet–Yugoslav Dispute*, p. 36.

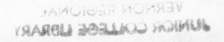
VERNON REGIONAL
JUNIOR COLLEGE LIBRARY

At this juncture, when there was no longer any doubt that the harsh pressures of Soviet European policy in the Zhdanov period had produced results unpalatable from the Soviet viewpoint, Stalin adopted a somewhat less militant general policy line toward the West. Before taking up this policy shift in the latter years of Stalin's rule, however, let us look briefly at certain prior developments in Eastern Europe, where, during the period of Communist takeover from 1945 to 1949, Stalin managed both to achieve some significant successes for Soviet policy and to sow the seeds of subsequent difficulties with which his successors were left to contend.

Postwar Communist Takeover in Eastern Europe

In 1945 the defeat of Germany had left the Soviet Union virtually unchallenged in Eastern Europe, where it became Stalin's task to translate into practical political arrangements the Soviet Union's new position of influence. Although there may be some question whether Stalin's aim from the outset was to impose the Soviet system throughout East Europe, he clearly meant to keep it under Soviet control, if for no other reason than to prevent it from again becoming the staging area for an invasion of the Soviet Union. In Stalin's view, "friendly" East European states bordering the Soviet Union were necessary to insure this fundamental security objective, and only countries with Communist regimes could be regarded as safe and dependable friends.[48] At the same time, however, Stalin also apparently saw the wisdom of not plunging into the manufacture of Communist revolutions in the East European countries. Rather, during the first year or two after the war, he was satisfied to close off the region gradually from Western influence and to set in motion a transitional stage of takeover.

As some observers affirm, Stalin's interest in asserting Soviet strategic and economic claims in Eastern Europe may have taken precedence at this time over the immediate establishment of Communist regimes.[49] Other reasons also may have counseled against proceeding too rapidly toward outright communization of the region: A respite was needed for reconstruction at home; time was required to undermine potential opposition and to consolidate Soviet control in Eastern Europe itself; and, as previously noted, there was the prob-

---

[48] C. E. Black, "Soviet Policy in Eastern Europe," *Annals* (May 1949): 153; Joseph Rothschild, *Communist Eastern Europe* (New York: Walker and Company, 1964), pp. 6–7. Whether Stalin's thinking went beyond the establishment of friendly Communist states on the Soviet Union's borders to a more ambitious conception under which East Europe would eventually be incorporated into the Soviet Union itself—i.e., whether he envisaged East Europe as part of a Soviet-dominated interstate system or its absorption into a universal Soviet state—is a question which remains unanswered. So far as the testimony of Stalin's actions goes, as distinct from what may have been his ultimate ambitions, he was apparently satisfied to allow the neighboring East European states to stay outside the federative framework of the Soviet Union—unlike his previous treatment, for example, of the Baltic states. See Hajo Holborn, "Russia and the European Political System," in Ivo J. Lederer, ed., *Russian Foreign Policy: Essays in Historical Perspective* (New Haven, Conn.: Yale University Press, 1962), p. 414.

[49] See, for example, Isaac Deutscher, *Russia After Stalin* (London: Hamish Hamilton, 1953), p. 79; Ionescu, *The Break-Up of the Soviet Empire*, pp. 18–19.

period, 1945 to 1949, could be judged a good deal more successful than Soviet policy toward Western Europe during the same years. Communist regimes responsive to Stalin's authority, with the conspicuous exception of that in Yugoslavia, had been placed in power without provoking immediate danger of Western intervention. These regimes were being increasingly bound to Moscow by political, economic, and military ties. Deviationism had reared its head among some East European Communists, to be sure, but only the better to be lopped off. On the surface, at least, Stalin's techniques for exercising Soviet control through the secret police, party channels, and the armed forces seemed to be weathering the test of the takeover years.

Not far beneath the surface, however, issues and forces were stirring with which the methods of Stalinism were to prove inadequate to cope after Stalin himself was gone. National pride, popular resentment toward Soviet economic exploitation and "cultural imperialism," fears among party cadres for their personal security and dissatisfaction with the "degeneration of Party life," growing doubt among both indigenous populations and their Communist regimes that doctrinaire Soviet methods and Soviet experience were relevant models for the societies of Eastern Europe—these were among the factors that combined to generate mounting pressure against the lid which Stalin had clamped upon the life of the region.[57] Moreover, even though the Western states had not been moved to resist directly the Stalinist takeover of Eastern Europe, developments here had certainly given additional stimulus to the unprecedented economic and military measures for the strengthening of Western Europe that had been initiated since 1947. Aware perhaps that the smoldering problems of Eastern Europe might ignite at the same time that trends toward greater unity among the Western powers were becoming increasingly evident, Stalin responded by adopting a new and somewhat less militant policy line toward the West.

Policy Shift in the Latter Years of Stalin's Rule

The new policy line, which evolved gradually in the period between Zhdanov's death on August 31, 1948, and the May 1949 lifting of the Berlin blockade, was aimed essentially at disrupting the growth of Western cohesion and common defense efforts through "Peace Movement" tactics and play upon political divergencies in the West.[58] Slightly reminiscent of Soviet "Popular Front" tactics of the mid-thirties, the new Soviet line sought political collaboration with intellectual and anti-war bourgeois elements in the West without the encumbrance of formal party coalitions that had characterized the earlier Popular Front period.

At the center of Soviet efforts to rally anti-war social forces in support of Soviet policies was the backing given the Peace Movement, which Com-

---

[57] See Brzezinski, *The Soviet Bloc*, pp. 138–46; Ionescu, *The Break-Up of the Soviet Empire*, pp. 33–39.

[58] Shulman, *Stalin's Foreign Policy Reappraised*, pp. 80–103, 131–38, passim; Mackintosh, *Strategy and Tactics of Soviet Foreign Policy*, pp. 64–65.

munist parties at the November 1949 meeting of the Cominform were directed to make the "pivot" of their "entire activity."[59] Among focal points of the political and propaganda campaign carried on through the Peace Movement were attacks upon German remilitarization, efforts to link the newly emerging and nonaligned nations with a worldwide "anti-imperialist" front, and attempts to reduce the political advantages to the West of its atomic monopoly by arousing popular feeling against the use of nuclear weapons. The latter effort assumed its most dramatic form in the Stockholm Appeal—a massive signature-collecting maneuver tied to the simple slogan: "Ban the Bomb!"

The Peace Movement aspects of Soviet policy seem to have been based on the expectation that Western governments could be deprived of popular support by exploitation of anti-war sentiment. As Soviet commentary in *Izvestiia* put it in April 1949: "The Soviet emphasis on the cleavage between the plain peoples of the United States and Britain and the warmongers . . . reflects the hope that popular resentment against war will cause the Western governments to modify their programs, thus establishing the prerequisites for the possibility of new high-level efforts to resolve world tensions."[60] Such rather thinly veiled attempts to put public pressure upon the Western governments were accompanied by other hints in late 1949 and early 1950 of Soviet interest in settlement of differences by high-level negotiation.[61] Although no summit talks were arranged, Stalin at least managed to get across the idea that he was now prepared to seek an abatement of Cold War tensions in Europe. His attitude on this point was further signaled by authoritative statements in the Soviet press that Soviet policy was based on "the inevitability of the coexistence for a protracted period of the two systems—socialism and capitalism."[62]

Thus, the new face of Soviet policy presumably meant that Stalin had come to recognize the need for an interlude of reduced Soviet pressures against Europe. As we have already suggested, this change of approach probably appeared necessary not only to arrest growing trends toward Western unity but also to permit closer attention to the Soviet position in Eastern Europe, where—despite the accelerated process of satellization during the Zhdanov period—incorporation of the region into the Soviet sphere had not proved altogether smooth. Doubtless, still another cogent reason for Stalin's interest in a breathing spell was the need to buy time for a major Soviet technological-industrial effort aimed at producing a favorable long-term shift in the balance of power.

There is, however, more than a touch of irony in the fact that while Stalin evidently believed that a relaxation of Cold War tensions in Europe would best serve Soviet ends, developments in the period from abandonment of the

[59] *Cominform Bulletin*, November 29, 1949, p. 1.

[60] *Izvestiia*, April 24, 1949, as cited by Shulman, *Stalin's Foreign Policy Reappraised*, p. 100.

[61] For discussion of these hints, see Shulman, *Stalin's Foreign Policy Reappraised*, pp. 115–16.

[62] A. Leont'ev, "On the Peaceful Coexistence of the Two Systems," *Pravda*, March 28, 1950. See also Shulman, *Stalin's Foreign Policy Reappraised*, p. 116.

Zhdanovshchina in 1949 to Stalin's death in early 1953 brought no real sense of relief from Soviet pressure in Western Europe. On the contrary, events during this period—which included the Soviet Union's first atomic test, the establishment of a Communist regime in China, and the invasion of South Korea by Communist forces from the north—had quite the opposite effect, serving, among other things, to heighten the shadow which Soviet military power had cast over Europe during the preceding few years.

Although the emergence of the Soviet Union as a nuclear power eventually was to have more fundamental and far-reaching implications for European security, it was the outbreak of the Korean War in 1950 that had the most immediate effect in robbing Stalin's Peace Movement tactics of conviction and in persuading the West that it could not afford to lower its guard. Undertaken apparently at Soviet initiative[63] without due appreciation for its impact on the Western world—especially in the wake of China's succumbing to Communist power—the Korean War was viewed both in the United States and Europe as the opening round of a new aggressive phase of Soviet policy, leading to a widespread belief that it might next be Europe's turn to be subjected to Communist military pressure. Whatever Stalin's military plans may have been—and, as we shall see, they were evidently directed far less toward an actual invasion of Europe than toward creating the impression that Europe was a hostage to Soviet arms—this perception of a renewed threat from Soviet military power alarmed Europe and undoubtedly had a lot to do with transforming NATO from little more than a declaration of purpose into a going military alliance.[64]

For example, the process of turning over the Western European Union's nascent defense activities to NATO was greatly quickened under the impetus of the Korean War. Measures taken in the first couple of years after the June 1950 invasion of South Korea included the activation of SHAPE, which became operational under General Eisenhower in 1951; the admission of Greece and Turkey to NATO in 1952; and, in the same year, the establishment of the Lisbon force goals for NATO and the working out of treaty terms for the European Defense Community (EDC) under which West German rearmament was initially intended to be carried out. Subsequent hitches developed in implementing some of these measures, to be sure. The EDC was

---

[63] The origins of the Korean War are still somewhat obscure, but the available evidence suggests that the war was essentially Soviet-inspired, and that the Soviet Union found itself obliged to rely on the Chinese to salvage a venture which the North Koreans, in a proxy role, were originally expected to be able to carry off without difficulty. See Allen S. Whiting, *China Crosses the Yalu* (New York: Macmillan Company, 1960), pp. iv–v, 124–26; Raymond L. Garthoff, "Sino-Soviet Military Relations," *Annals* (September 1963): 81–93; Philip E. Mosely, *The Kremlin and World Politics* (New York: Vintage Books, 1960), pp. 323–35; and the present author's *The Soviet Union and the Sino-Soviet Dispute*, The RAND Corporation, P-3203, August 1965, p. 41. For a contrary view, arguing that the North Korean attack was probably ordered by Kim Il-Sung after provocation by the Rhee government, and without Moscow's knowledge, see Fleming, *The Cold War*, pp. 604–8, and Horowitz, *The Free World Colossus*, p. 121.

[64] Robert E. Osgood, *NATO: The Entangling Alliance* (Chicago, Ill.: University of Chicago Press, 1962), p. 74.

sidetracked, after signing of the treaty in 1952, and its purpose salvaged only by the Paris Agreements a couple of years later. The Lisbon force goals, which envisaged the build-up of large conventional forces as a counterpoise to Soviet conventional strength, were never met. But at the same time, a spur was given both to planning for a NATO atomic capability in conjunction with reduced conventional force goals and to the build-up of external US strategic nuclear delivery capabilities.[65]

In the meantime, of course, the Soviet Union in turn was obliged to give sober thought to its own further military preparations, especially in light of the stimulus given by the Korean War to the build-up of American strategic power. Thus, the interacting spiral of what has been termed "mutual anxiety and rearmament,"[66] which had been set in motion during the earlier postwar years, continued to take on momentum as the decade of the fifties began, fed no doubt by distrust on both sides of the provisional line that had been drawn across Europe and by events elsewhere in the world, particularly the Communist takeover of the Chinese mainland and the Korean War.

Stalin and the German Question

Other aspects of Stalin's new policy line in the early fifties also contributed to keeping alive Cold War anxieties in Western Europe. Amongst these, from both a theoretical and a practical standpoint, perhaps Stalin's latter-day approach to the question of Germany proved to be least reassuring to the Western allies. On the theoretical plane, Stalin's thinking on the future role of Germany found expression in his treatise *Economic Problems of Socialism in the USSR*, issued on the eve of the Nineteenth Party Congress in October 1952. Among other things, this document summed up the views on international affairs toward which Stalin had been moving in his latter years. Curiously enough, although this work offered the estimate that war between the Soviet Union and the West was less likely than new wars among the capitalist countries themselves[67]—thus, in effect, backing away somewhat from the "two hostile camps" concept which had provided the doctrinal underpinning for the period of the *Zhdanovshchina*—it did not thereby succeed in conveying a benign image of Soviet intentions. Rather, it came to be looked upon as the prescription for a policy aimed at provoking dissension, or possibly even war, among the Western countries which had welcomed a defeated Germany into their midst.[68]

[65] Ibid., pp. 61, 68–98. See also Timothy W. Stanley, *NATO in Transition: The Future of the Atlantic Alliance* (New York: Frederick A. Praeger, Inc., 1965), pp. 38–47, passim.

[66] Shulman, *Stalin's Foreign Policy Reappraised*, p. 26.

[67] Joseph Stalin, *Economic Problems of Socialism in the USSR* (New York: International Publishers, 1952), pp. 28–29.

[68] For such an interpretation of the foreign policy intent behind Stalin's 1952 theoretical analysis, see H. Achimow, "The General Line of Soviet Policy in Europe," *Bulletin of the Institute for the Study of the History and Culture of the USSR* (Munich: March 1954): 7–15. For a useful analysis of the domestic policy implications of Stalin's last work, see Wolfgang Leonhard, *The Kremlin Since Stalin* (New York: Frederick A. Praeger, Inc., 1962), pp. 36–39.

That Germany should be very much at the center of Stalin's thinking was not, of course, surprising. Indeed, the prospect of German recovery and the direction in which a resurgent Germany might turn her energies could scarcely fail to be of central concern to any Soviet leader. In his 1952 treatise, Stalin predicted that Germany would again arise as a great power, just as she had done "within the space of some 15 to 20 years after her defeat" in World War I, and that as a consequence of attempting to "break out of American bondage," Germany would bring on a new war.[69] (Japan was cast in a similar role by Stalin.)

While there is no reason to suppose that Stalin took lightly the possibility that Germany might prove to be the catalyst of a new war into which the Soviet Union could be drawn, it is less clear how he hoped to avert such a prospect. Perhaps, as suggested above, he believed that the trouble-making potential of a resurgent Germany could be turned against the West by an adroit Soviet diplomacy, despite what must have been a somewhat unhappy recollection of the failure of prewar Soviet diplomacy to keep Hitler's attention focused westward. Or, alternatively, he may have counted upon finding an approach to the German question which would neutralize West Germany as a prospective military partner of the NATO powers and perhaps enable the Soviet Union to gain a controlling hand in German affairs. That Stalin may even have been prepared to reverse the de facto Soviet preference for a divided Germany in order to find such an alternative is suggested by the controversial Soviet proposal of March 10, 1952, which preceded by several months Stalin's *Economic Problems of Socialism in the USSR* and which gave rise in the West to a still unsettled debate over a possible "lost opportunity" to achieve German reunification.

In brief, this proposal dropped previous Soviet insistence on a totally disarmed Germany and raised the prospect of unification in return for neutralization and the liquidation of foreign military bases on German territory.[70] Among features of the proposal, besides the key one that a unified Germany must not enter any coalition or military alliance directed against the Soviet Union, were provisions that "organizations hostile to democracy and the cause of maintaining peace" should be prohibited in Germany, and that the national armed forces and military production permitted in Germany must be kept within limits to be established by a peace treaty. Such provisions, which could be construed as giving the Soviet Union the opportunity for exerting strong influence upon the internal political life of a united Germany, as well as control over its armaments, helped to make the proposal unpalatable to many quarters in the West, and especially to the Adenauer government. The

[69] Stalin, *Economic Problems of Socialism*, pp. 29–30.

[70] Details of the proposal contained in the Soviet note of March 10, 1952, to the three Western powers may be found in Clarence W. Baier and Richard P. Stebbins, eds., *Documents on American Foreign Relations, 1952* (New York: Harper & Brothers, 1953), pp. 250–51. The note and its accompanying proposal was published in *Pravda*, March 11, 1952.

latter argued not only that a neutral Germany deprived of the protection of the Western alliance would be exposed to Soviet military pressure and political subversion, but that Western negotiation on a double-edged proposal like that put forward by the Soviets would in effect be risking "the substance of West German security for the shadow of reunification talks."[71]

Some seven months of diplomatic maneuver between Moscow and the West followed the Soviet overture on Germany, with the Western powers accusing the Soviet government of dodging the question of free elections as an essential first move toward reunification, while the Soviets charged that the issue of free elections was only intended to divert discussion away from the Soviet proposal.[72] Although the end result was that the West declined to negotiate on the Soviet proposal of March 1952, tending to regard it primarily as a tactical maneuver or "delaying bid" to forestall the ratification of EDC rather than a genuine "bargaining bid" on reunification, this view was challenged by both some of Adenauer's domestic political opponents and later by other Western critics.[73] The burden of this criticism (which also was extended subsequently to Western reaction to Soviet negotiating initiatives in 1954 and 1955 when the Paris Agreements involving Germany's participation in NATO were up for ratification)[74] comes down to the point that since the West failed to test Stalin's proposal by actual negotiations, it must remain an open question whether a genuine opportunity for German reunification was lost.

Granting that neither skeptics nor proponents of the "lost opportunity" thesis can be proved right concerning the *bona fides* of Stalin's March 1952

[71] For an excellent examination of the pros and cons of the March 1952 proposal from the viewpoint of Western and especially German diplomacy, as well as a balanced judgment on the "lost opportunity" thesis itself, see James L. Richardson, *Germany and the Atlantic Alliance: The Interaction of Strategy and Politics* (Cambridge, Mass.: Harvard University Press, 1966), pp. 24–37. See also Shulman, *Stalin's Foreign Policy Reappraised*, pp. 191–94.

[72] Shulman, ibid., p. 193. The Soviets also claimed that Western refusal to conclude a German peace treaty was "in violation of the decisions reached at Teheran, Yalta, and Potsdam." See *Pravda*, April 23, July 8, 1952.

[73] Among accounts critical of Western diplomacy for not having followed up the Soviet proposals are: Melvin Croan, "Reality and Illusion in Soviet-German Relations," *Survey* (October 1962): 18, and Coral Bell, *Negotiation from Strength* (New York: Alfred A. Knopf, Inc., 1963), pp. 105, 214. See also discussion of the persistence of the "lost opportunity" viewpoint among some opposition political elements in West Germany, in Walter Laqueur, "Thoughts at the Wall," *Encounter* (August 1962): 66. Soviet sources also have continued to allude to such West German sentiments. A book on the German question, published in 1966, for example, cites accusations that Adenauer sacrificed a "favorable opportunity" to attain reunification by turning down the "peace loving initiative of the Soviet government" in favor of West German remilitarization and entry into NATO. In the same Soviet account, however, the United States is pictured as the principal seat of opposition to the March 1952 proposal, rather than Adenauer. See P. A. Nikolaev, *Politika Sovetskogo Soiuza v germanskom voprose, 1945–1964* (Policy of the Soviet Union on the German Question, 1945–1964) (Moscow: Izdatel'stvo "Nauka," 1966), pp. 168–85. See also *Mezhdunarodnye otnosheniia posle vtoroi mirovoi voiny* (International Relations After the Second World War), N. N. Inozemtsev, chief ed., 3 vols., prepared by the Institute of World Economics and International Relations of the USSR Academy of Sciences, (Moscow, 1962–65), esp. vol. 2 (1963), pp. 585–87.

[74] See chap. V, pp. 74–80.

proposal, one may observe that the motivations behind it could well have been compatible with both the "delaying bid" and "bargaining bid" interpretations. With respect to the former, Stalin had every reason for seeking a tactical device to delay, and if possible to forestall, implementation of the then-projected European Defense Community, under which West Germany would have taken a long first step toward participation in the Western defensive system. That Stalin may also have been prepared to bargain seriously over reunification if other obstructive tactics failed to block this unwelcome step is somewhat less obvious, but by no means incompatible with his prior outlook on the German question; as may be recalled, he had earlier in the postwar period leaned toward the notion of a unified Germany drawn politically into the Soviet orbit.[75]

The key question from Stalin's viewpoint in 1952 would seem to have been whether in trading off reunification for abandonment of West German rearmament under EDC, he would be risking the further revival of a nationalistically oriented Germany that might eventually defy Soviet control and align itself with Western "imperialism," whatever its treaty obligations. How Stalin appraised this risk, one can only speculate. Given West German apprehensions that a unified and neutral Germany bereft of Western support would prove vulnerable to Soviet influence, especially under conditions of an American military withdrawal, Stalin may well have felt that the chances of a bad bargain were minimal. Moreover, the expectation of growing capitalist "contradictions" spelled out in Stalin's last theoretical treatise may have encouraged him to believe that the effect of German reunification would merely be to deepen differences within the West, thus further reducing the prospect that Germany might find a new home in an integrated Western community.

On the other hand, considering the problem of Soviet interests with respect to East Germany, there is certainly some question whether Stalin could have seriously entertained the possibility of German reunification in the circumstances prevailing in 1952. That is to say, prospective gains in terms of keeping West Germany out of NATO and stimulating Western disunity may have been outweighed by the jeopardy to a Communist regime and to the Soviet Union's own position in East Germany that reunification would have entailed. The fact that a new forced-draft program for the "construction of socialism" in East Germany was adopted in July 1952, even while an exchange of notes on Stalin's March proposal was still underway between Moscow and the West, lends plausibility to the argument that Stalin had never really expected his reunification offer to bear fruit.[76]

Whatever Stalin's expectations were in 1952, however, is somewhat beside the point in light of Western refusal to explore the bargain he may have had in mind. So far as the immediate object of sidetracking the EDC was con-

---

[75] See pp. 14–15 above.

[76] See Shulman, *Stalin's Foreign Policy Reappraised*, p. 193; Evelyn Anderson, "East Germany," *Survey* (June 1962): 97. See also Laqueur, *Russia and Germany*, pp. 277–78.

cerned, the results were mixed. The West went ahead with signature of the European Defense Treaty on May 27, 1952, but later failed to follow through with it as originally planned—thus perhaps justifying to some extent Stalin's belief in the divisive potential of German rearmament. In a larger sense, however, his latter-day policy on the German issue accomplished less than he had probably expected. For its net effect was not so much to accelerate Western "contradictions" connected with the revival of Germany as to sharpen suspicions in the West that Stalin hoped to capitalize upon Germany's recovery to split the Western alliance itself.

III

POSTWAR SOVIET MILITARY POLICY UNDER STALIN

Turning more closely now to the evolution of Soviet military policy during the latter forties and the early fifties, two basic considerations had tended to become paramount on Stalin's military agenda. The first, given the fact of deepening US involvement in Europe and the American lead in nuclear age technology, was the problem of finding a way to deter the United States from either exploiting potential unrest in Eastern Europe or reacting in a dangerous fashion to Soviet political moves calculated to play upon divergences within the West. In essence, this problem bore upon the immediate situation confronting the Soviet Union in Europe, and had to be met by whatever means were immediately available.

The second problem was the longer-range task of steering the Soviet Union through an indefinite period of vulnerability while efforts were made to whittle down the initial nuclear advantage of the West and to provide the Soviet Union with modern arms. Calling for heavy commitment of Soviet scientific and industrial resources, this undertaking was aimed essentially at altering the over-all power balance in favor of the Soviet Union.

Stalin's Military Policy Approach

Postwar Soviet military policy under Stalin was partly the product of necessity and partly the result of Soviet preoccupation with Europe as the decisive arena in which the power contest between the Soviet Union and the advanced industrial nations of the West would be played out.[1] Both of these elements were evident in the approach taken to the military problems growing out of the Soviet Union's postwar rivalry with the United States—the first intercontinental adversary of major stature in Soviet history.

The most immediate problem on Stalin's military agenda, that of imposing adequate restraint upon so powerful an opponent as the United States, posed serious difficulties for Soviet policy, particularly when the US atomic lead was accompanied by an advantage in strategic delivery forces that appeared likely to persist for some time. From the Soviet viewpoint, the United States was inherently hostile, and any restraint on its part therefore would be largely the result, not of American good will, but of the pressure the Soviet armed

[1] See Bernard S. Morris, "Soviet Policy Toward the West," in Adam Bromke and Philip E. Uren, eds., *The Communist States and the West* (New York: Frederick A. Praeger, Inc., 1967), pp. 21–24; Marshall D. Shulman, *Stalin's Foreign Policy Reappraised* (Cambridge, Mass.: Harvard University Press, 1963), pp. 10–11; Zbigniew Brzezinski, *Alternative to Partition* (New York: McGraw-Hill Book Company, 1965), pp. 76–77.

forces could exert against the United States, or—in the last analysis—of the
price they could exact in the event of war.[2]

Here, however, the Soviet difficulties became apparent. The kind of continental military power at the disposal of the Soviet Union was ill-suited
to bringing direct pressure to bear on the United States, and if war should
come, waging it to a successful conclusion against a nuclear-armed transoceanic adversary whose sources of power lay beyond Soviet reach. If the
United States was to be deterred from pressing its nuclear advantage, the
Soviet forces at hand would have to do the job, and the place where they
could best be brought to bear was obviously Europe. By keeping substantial
elements of its conventional combined-arms forces deployed in the European
theater, and by taking care not to dispel the impression that they were prepared for a rapid advance to the Atlantic, the Soviet Union could in effect
hope to make Western Europe a hostage for American good behavior.[3] Moreover, the same forces that could threaten America's allies also provided in-

[2] One should observe, no matter how the Soviets may have viewed the question, that US
restraint was every bit as much self-imposed as it was the product of Stalin's doing. A further
word on American restraint is in order here. The idea of postponing a showdown with the Soviet
Union, even during the period of US atomic monopoly when it was no secret that the Russians
were on their way to acquiring their own bomb, was the underlying concept which informed
American policy. In turn, the postponement of a showdown was based far more deeply on the
hope that time might heal differences and bring a mellowing change in the Soviet system than
upon the notion of buying time in order to prepare the United States for delivering a final crushing ultimatum to the Soviet Union to give in or be destroyed—as the "revisionist" thesis runs.
The fatal flaw in the revisionist argument is that during the very period in which the US nuclear
monopoly might have been exploited to do so, the United States did not in fact rush to build up
nuclear forces of the magnitude required to make a policy of ultimatum possible. Neither, of
course, did it build up US conventional forces.

[3] It can be argued that in the late forties and early fifties, the Soviet leadership had not yet
articulated a specific concept of "hostage Europe," as Khrushchev was to do later when threatening
to drop nuclear weapons on countries which lent their territory to American military purposes.
However, it seems to the author that the hostage notion was implicit in the Soviet outlook from
the beginning. No one wanted another war in Europe, least of all the Europeans, but including
the United States and the Soviet Union also. This very fact, however, gave added weight to the
implied threat that Europe might be fought over once more, should US policy "provoke" the
Soviet Union into use of its continental military power. In this sense, certainly, Europe was made
a hostage for US good behavior. A direct Soviet threat to evict the US forces from the European
continent might also have made the United States cautious, but again—since the United States had
the means to retaliate directly against the Soviet Union—the principal deterrent effect of such a
threat upon US behavior would have lain in the accompanying damage to and possible loss of
Europe. Had the United States been indifferent to the fate of Europe, of course, then the Soviet
Union could not have expected to sway American conduct by threats to European well-being. But
this hardly seems to have been the case, for the welfare and survival of industrial Europe were
high on the postwar list of American priorities—if indeed, not the very objects over which the
Cold War arose.

It may be noted, incidentally, that the "hostage" notion has come to be applied in a quite different context in Europe. Many Europeans have regarded American troops stationed in Europe as
hostages guaranteeing that the United States would be automatically involved in the event of a
Soviet attack on Europe, a situation presumed to deter such an attack. For treatment of this aspect
of the question, see Herman Kahn and William Pfaff, "Our Alternatives in Europe," *Foreign
Affairs* (July 1966): 588, 590; Testimony by Professor Thomas C. Schelling in *The Atlantic Alliance*, Hearings Before the Subcommittee on National Security and International Operations of the
Committee on Government Operations, United States Senate, Eighty-ninth Congress, Second Session, May 19, 1966, Part 3 (Washington, D.C.: US Government Printing Office, 1966), pp. 96–97.

surance against defections in East Europe, and they stood ready to guard against a resurgence of West Germany—a prospect with visceral connotations for most Russians, and one that apparently was never far from Stalin's thoughts.

Such considerations as these, in conjunction with a continental military tradition, help to explain why the Soviet Union under Stalin continued to place a high premium on preserving strong European theater forces even after the militant Zhdanovist phase of Soviet European policy had been abandoned. Lacking as yet the means to adopt a strategy of nuclear deterrence, a concept which had already begun to take shape in the United States,[4] Stalin had no choice, at least for the time being, but to rely on Russia's traditional theater forces as the primary instrument of Soviet military policy. Although the task of inhibiting the United States from exploiting its nuclear status was also approached through other avenues, such as systematic use of the Stockholm Appeal and the worldwide peace movement, Stalin's main recourse in the military field lay in making the threat of Soviet land power against Europe the counterpoise to US nuclear power.[5] This circumstance was to have a number of rather far-reaching consequences which Stalin may not have foreseen.

In contrast with the US military posture, which enabled the United States to begin the practice of deterrence in the early years of the nuclear age by the threat of strategic retaliatory attack against a few vital centers in the Soviet Union, the Soviet military posture lent itself to deterrence only if the threat of Soviet invasion and occupation of Western Europe were made to seem credible. Thus, Stalin could hardly afford to deflate military programs and preparations that lent some substance to the threat of a Soviet sweep across Europe. On the contrary, the Soviet Union now gave fresh attention to training and equipping its theater forces for campaigns in Europe, with priority going to those forces already deployed in East Europe.

While one result of these programs was doubtless to enhance the credi-

[4] There is perhaps some question whether the concept of nuclear deterrence, as it is generally understood today, was yet a well-developed notion in US strategic thinking in the late forties. However, there were certainly many precursors to the later full-blown concept. As early as May 1945, for example, General Lauris Norstad and General H. H. Arnold had spoken of the need to develop modern weapons and forces "required to pose a warning to aggressors in order to deter them from launching a modern, devastating war." In January 1948, in *Survival in the Air Age*, Report by the President's Air Policy Commission, Washington, D.C., p. 12, it was stressed that the ability to deter any threatening power by holding out the prospect of retaliation of the utmost violence was critical to US security.

[5] The extent to which a Soviet land-power threat against Europe was a conscious element in the creation of a Soviet posture of deterrence remains a matter of varied interpretation. Many factors which cannot be ascribed necessarily to logical calculation helped to account for the large Soviet deployment against Europe, such as images of past incursions from the West and bureaucratic tendencies which perpetuated a Soviet orientation toward European problems. For an essay containing useful caveats on the question of trying to fit the Soviet military posture into a purely "rational" model of decision-making, see James R. Schlesinger, *European Security and the Nuclear Threat Since 1945*, The RAND Corporation, P-3574, April 1967, especially pp. 18–19.

bility of a Soviet capacity to overrun Europe to the Atlantic,[6] another was to stir apprehension in the West as to the intentions behind the Soviet military posture. Perhaps Stalin intended no more than to discourage the West, primarily the United States, from unwelcome interference in the affairs of the Soviet bloc he was then in the process of consolidating. Or perhaps he felt that a Soviet policy backed by the authority of Soviet arms might bring substantial political gains in a Western Europe still weak and disunited. Certainly, Stalin was not eager to see an enfeebled Europe recover its strength.

What happened, however, largely ran counter to Stalin's interests. Western uncertainty about Soviet intentions—stemming in part from what was perceived as a Soviet posture of readiness to use massive conventional forces against Western Europe—led not only to a gradual build-up to US strategic power, it also contributed to the affirmation of greater political solidarity among the countries of Western Europe and gave additional impetus to the planning for the common defense of Europe which had brought NATO into being in 1949.

With respect to Soviet military development in general, another effect of Stalin's persistent endeavor to improve Soviet capabilities for theater warfare in Europe was to help prolong the dominance of a continental military tradition in the Soviet strategic outlook. The priority placed during Stalin's lifetime upon the role of the combined-arms forces in the European theater persisted well into the period of Khrushchev's rule, when, as we shall see later, Soviet military thought was still grappling with the problem of establishing the relative priority of military preparations geared essentially to a European land-war strategy and those associated with the strategy for a new kind of war against a powerful, transoceanic adversary.

This is not to say, of course, that Stalin was indifferent to the military-technical revolution which ushered in the nuclear age, or that he was resigned to permanent acceptance of a purely continental military posture for the Soviet Union. Indeed, he had come early to recognize the need for breaking the US atomic monopoly, and even during the wartime years, before the success of the American nuclear weapons program was yet assured, he had sanctioned the start of a Soviet weapons program.[7] Casual though he may

---

[6] Malcolm Mackintosh, *Juggernaut: The Russian Forces, 1918–1966* (New York: Macmillan Company, 1967), p. 271. See also Shulman, *Stalin's Foreign Policy Reappraised*, p. 23; Ralph Haswell Lutz, "The Changing Role of Iron Curtain Countries," *Annals of the American Academy of Political and Social Science* (September 1950), p. 25.

[7] Precisely when the Soviet leadership under Stalin decided to embark upon a nuclear weapons program, as distinct from earlier work of Soviet scientists in the general field of nuclear physics, has been until recently a matter of informed speculation. Arnold Kramish of The RAND Corporation, the author of the first painstaking examination of the Soviet atomic program published in the West, placed this decision not later than the fall of 1943. See his *Atomic Energy in the Soviet Union* (Stanford, California: Stanford University Press, 1959), pp. 100, 106, passim. In August 1966 a Soviet physicist, Igor N. Golovin, gave the first Soviet disclosure on this subject, placing the decision for a program to build an atomic bomb in the summer of 1942. Golovin also reported that Soviet scientists were ordered to accelerate their efforts after the United States exploded its

have been upon hearing of the US atomic breakthrough from President Truman at Potsdam in July 1945,[8] Stalin was clearly determined that the Soviet Union should not be left behind in the technological revolution which this achievement heralded.

As the record testifies, Stalin bent great efforts to make the Soviet Union a nuclear power. These involved both weapons development programs and a diplomatic-propaganda campaign to avoid international constraints, such as those implied by the Baruch proposal, upon unilateral Soviet activity in atomic development. In August 1949, following earlier claims that Soviet scientists had solved the secret of the atomic bomb, the Soviet Union exploded its first known atomic device,[9] and slightly less than four years later, its first thermonuclear device.

Whether Stalin's determination to acquire nuclear weapons was matched from the start by a parallel resolve to develop delivery capabilities that would pose a direct threat to the American homeland is somewhat less clear. However, both the technological record and our occasional second-hand insights into Stalin's decisions[10] testify to the fact that he had begun to give thought to the need for long-range delivery means at least by the time that Soviet

---

first atomic bomb at Alamogordo on July 16, 1945. *New York Times*, August 19, 1966. According to other retrospective Soviet accounts, the first Soviet graphite reactor constructed under the leadership of I. V. Kurchatov went into operation in December 1946. This event, another of the key milestones on the way to development of the first Soviet atomic bomb, had been estimated by Kramish (*Atomic Energy in the Soviet Union*, p. 114) as occurring in the fall of 1947. See article, "First Soviet Atomic Reactor," *Izvestiia* (January 1967).

[8] Harry S. Truman, *Memoirs, I: Years of Decision* (Garden City, N.Y.: Doubleday & Co., Inc., 1955), p. 416. See also Kramish, *Atomic Energy in the Soviet Union*, pp. 71, 78, 85. An interesting sidelight on Stalin's reaction is given in Marshal Zhukov's memoirs. Zhukov tells us that Stalin did indeed appreciate the significance of Truman's Potsdam revelation about the American atomic bomb, and that Stalin remarked to Molotov that evening that he was going to tell Kurchatov (the physicist in charge of Russia's atomic program) "to step things up." Marshal G. K. Zhukov, *Vospominanie i razmyshlenie* (Reminiscences and Reflections) (Moscow: Novosti Press Agency, 1969), p. 713.

[9] The first *known* Soviet atomic test on August 29, 1949, could presumably have been preceded by earlier testing before the US test detection system went into operation. Molotov, for example, claimed in November 1947 that the Soviet Union already "possessed the secret of the atomic weapon," though he did not, significantly, claim that it had yet been tested. See Kramish, *Atomic Energy in the Soviet Union*, pp. 121–23.

[10] One such insight was furnished by a Soviet technical officer who defected in 1948 and reported that Stalin and Malenkov had taken a personal interest in pushing plans for development of long-range bombers. See G. A. Tokaev, *Stalin Means War* (London: George Weidenfeld & Nicolson, Ltd., 1951), pp. 93–95, 97–105, 113–18; Asher Lee, *The Soviet Air Force* (London: Gerald Duckworth & Co., Ltd., 1950), p. 177. Another such insight was furnished in testimony by Colonel Stig Wennerstroem, the Swedish spy for the Soviet Union, who claimed that the Soviet leadership had taken a "bold decision" in 1949 and 1950 to build long-range rockets which "could bring, e.g., the USA under fire." See *The Wennerstroem Spy Case: How It Touched the United States and NATO; Excerpts from the Testimony of Stig Eric Constans Wennerstroem, a Noted Soviet Agent*, translation prepared for use of the Committee on the Judiciary, United States Senate (Washington: US Government Printing Office, 1964), p. 95. The commander of the Soviet strategic missile arm, describing its development in a July 1967 article, stated that missile R&D programs were carried out parallel to the nuclear development program in the early postwar years. Marshal N. Krylov, "The Strategic Rocket Troops," *Voenno-istoricheskii zhurnal* (Military-Historical Journal), no. 7 (July 1967): 20.

success in the atomic weapons field was in sight, in the latter forties. There is thus no question that credit for initiating programs of research and development that ultimately gave the Soviet Union aircraft and missile delivery systems of intercontinental range does belong to Stalin.

Although these developments served to vindicate Stalin's technological foresight, his grasp of the strategic and political implications of nuclear age weaponry has often been judged unkindly. Both Western and Soviet writers, for example, have held Stalin largely responsible for the tardiness with which Soviet military thought accommodated itself to the revolution in military affairs brought on by the nuclear age.[11] Some of his Soviet critics have not only charged that he seriously impeded the "creative development" of Soviet military theory by converting his own World War II strategic experience into fundamental and unalterable laws, such as the "permanently operating factors" in warfare, they have also condemned him for "the harm he wrought in all areas of our work connected with strengthening and perfecting the combat might of the Soviet armed forces."[12]

Without discounting the negative influence that Stalin's attitudes may have had on Soviet military thinking and preparations at the dawn of the nuclear age, it would seem only fair to judge his outlook in light of the circumstances in which the Soviet Union found itself at that time. The USSR had just begun to acquire a small atomic capability; it was still distinctly inferior in this respect to the United States. From Stalin's viewpoint, the immediate aim of Soviet policy was to avoid being either attacked or intimidated by a stronger opponent.

In these circumstances, it made some sense to depreciate publicly the military and political significance of nuclear weapons and to promulgate a doctrine stressing that the Soviet Union's large conventional forces, together with the Communist system's advantage in political morale, would ensure victory if war should come. To have encouraged open discussion of such matters as the potentially disastrous consequences of surprise attack with nuclear weapons when only the adversary possessed means adequate to mounting this kind of attack would hardly have helped Soviet morale, to say the least.

[11] For some representative Western commentary on the critical revisions in Soviet military thought which followed Stalin's death, see H. S. Dinerstein, *War and the Soviet Union: Nuclear Weapons and the Revolution in Soviet Military and Political Thinking* (New York: Frederick A. Praeger, Inc., 1959), pp. 36–63; Raymond L. Garthoff, *Soviet Strategy in the Nuclear Age* (New York: Frederick A. Praeger, Inc., 1958), pp. 61–91; J. M. Mackintosh, *Strategy and Tactics of Soviet Foreign Policy* (London: Oxford University Press, 1962), pp. 88–104; Thomas W. Wolfe, *Soviet Strategy at the Crossroads* (Cambridge, Mass.: Harvard University Press, 1964), pp. 26–37. Among pertinent Soviet commentary, see Colonel I. Korotkov, "The Development of Soviet Military Theory in the Postwar Years," *Voenno-istoricheskii zhurnal*, no. 4 (April 1964): 39–50; Major Generals S. N. Kozlov and M. V. Smirnov, Colonels I. S. Baz and P. A. Sidorov, *O sovetskoi voennoi nauke* (On Soviet Military Science), rev. ed. (Moscow: Voenizdat, 1964), pp. 50, 204–8, 293–94; Marshal V. D. Sokolovskii et al., *Voennaia strategiia* (Military Strategy), 2nd ed. (Moscow: Voenizdat, 1963), p. 9.

[12] Kozlov et al., *O sovetskoi voennoi nauke*, pp. 50, 204. Soviet criticism of Stalin's influence on wartime and postwar military developments is discussed more fully in chapter IV of the present study.

By the same token, it was logical for Stalin not to indulge in the practice of nuclear blackmail or to raise the spectre of mutual nuclear destruction—phases of Soviet diplomacy which were left to his successors to cultivate after the Soviet Union had attained somewhat greater nuclear capabilities.[13] Had Stalin lived until Soviet technology and production of modern weapons reached the stage attained in Khrushchev's time, he might have sought to manipulate these developments for psychological and political effect, much as Khrushchev was to do. One might note, parenthetically, that the Chinese later took a page from Stalin's book by adopting rather similar attitudes at a comparable stage in their own nuclear infancy.[14]

Whatever the ultimate verdict may be as to Stalin's appreciation of the strategic and political implications of nuclear age weaponry, there is no question that his decisions to concentrate Soviet resources heavily upon development of modern weapons systems were of seminal importance. Certainly, he prepared the ground for subsequent major changes in Soviet strategic thinking and force posture. Let us return at this point, however, to Soviet military developments as they related to Europe during the last few years of Stalin's life.

Modernization of Forces Deployed against Europe

The years from 1949 to Stalin's death in 1953 brought important developments in the Soviet military posture, but at the same time they illustrated that requirements for theater warfare in Europe still had first call on Soviet military resources and planning. As new programs were undertaken to modernize and improve the Soviet military establishment[15]—a process that gained momentum coincident with the Korean War and the beginning of serious efforts in Western Europe in 1951 to organize an integrated NATO force under General Eisenhower[16]—the Soviet forces deployed against Europe were among the first whose re-equipment and training received attention.

[13] It is true, of course, that Malenkov first sounded the theme of mutual destruction in March 1954, before the Soviet atomic arsenal and associated delivery capabilities had grown greatly beyond the level of a year earlier at the time of Stalin's death. However, the Soviet Union in the meantime had exploded a thermonuclear device which heralded a much greater destructive potential in the future. Moreover, Malenkov's March 12, 1954, statement on the prospect of "destruction of world civilization" was judged politically premature by his colleagues, who forced him to recant a month later. See Dinerstein, *War and the Soviet Union*, pp. 102–3, 112–13.

[14] For an interesting argument on the relationship between strategic attitudes and the various stages of nuclear capability in the Soviet and Chinese cases, see George H. Quester, "On the Identification of Real and Pretended Communist Military Doctrine," *Journal of Conflict Resolution* (June 1966): 172–78.

[15] The first major reorganization of the postwar Soviet forces, following the demobilization process which brought these forces down from a wartime peak of 12 to 15 million men and some 500 divisions to a standing level of around 4 million men and 175 divisions, was undertaken in 1948. This program served essentially to reconstitute the forces organizationally, but left them still basically equipped with World War II matériel. It was followed by a second major round of programs beginning about two years later which not only included further organizational changes but also the introduction of new equipment of postwar design and training in its use. It is this second major phase of postwar reorganization that is referred to here.

[16] General Eisenhower took command of SHAPE, the international headquarters of NATO, in February 1951, after which serious steps were taken in NATO to work out joint defense plans and

The "ready-made spearhead" of these forces, to use Field Marshal Montgomery's description, was composed of around thirty Soviet divisions stationed in the East European countries, twenty-two of them in East Germany. An additional, though less visible, force of some fifty to sixty Soviet divisions was estimated to stand behind this spearhead in the western military districts of the USSR itself.[17] The six field armies and the supporting tactical air army making up the combat core of the Group of Soviet Forces in Germany (GSFG) were generally understood to be blue-ribbon formations, among the best in the Soviet armed forces.[18]

Although the numerical strength of the GSFG apparently remained fairly constant in the early fifties (at around 400,000),[19] the quality of this force was notably improved by the programs of reorganization and re-equipment carried out during the period under the command of General Vasilii Chuikov, who was later to become a marshal and commander of the Soviet ground forces. The main improvements in the field armies of the GSFG lay in increasing their battlefield mobility and firepower by motorizing their transport and strengthening their armored elements, then still largely equipped with modified versions of the T-34 tank and self-propelled guns of World War II design,[20] although the follow-on T-54 tank began to appear in late 1952–

---

to provide commensurate forces. While the original European army concept under the aegis of the European Defense Community (EDC) did not come to fruition as proposed, nevertheless the actual build-up of the international NATO force under alternative arrangements followed during the succeeding years. For a summary of this period of birth pains in NATO's history, see Timothy W. Stanley, *NATO in Transition: The Future of the Atlantic Alliance* (New York: Frederick A. Praeger, Inc., 1965), pp. 43–50.

[17] Field Marshal Viscount Montgomery, "Statement on Current Soviet Military Capability," dated April 20, 1954, as published in *U.S. News and World Report*, vol. 36, no. 23, June 4, 1954, p. 45. Drew Middleton, *The Defense of Western Europe* (New York: Appleton-Century-Crofts, Inc., 1952), pp. 34, 61; Blair Bolles and Francis O. Wilcox, *The Armed Road to Peace: An Analysis of NATO*, Headline Series, Foreign Policy Association, no. 92 (March–April 1952): 46–48; "Military Affairs," *Bulletin of the Institute for the Study of the History and Culture of the USSR* (hereafter cited as *Bulletin*), vol. 1, no. 8 (Munich: November 1954): 29. A useful summary of the strength and deployment of Soviet forces in this period may be found in Mackintosh, *Juggernaut*, pp. 271–75.

[18] The presence in the GSFG of many units at various levels bearing the elite designations of "Guards" or "Shock" formations testified to its select character. See Middleton, *The Defense of Western Europe*, p. 34. The six field armies of the GSFG, varying in size from three to five divisions, were the 3rd Shock Army, the 3rd and 8th Guards Armies, and the 1st, 3rd, and 4th Mechanized Armies. The 24th Air Army, the tactical air element of the combined-arms forces in East Germany, also drew upon the best personnel and equipment available. See "Soviet Forces in Europe," *An Cosantóir*, Dublin, vol. 12 (December 1952): 573–75. See also Mackintosh, *Juggernaut*, p. 272.

[19] Middleton, *The Defense of Western Europe*, p. 61. In light of Khrushchev's retrospective claim in 1960 that the over-all level of Soviet forces increased by about 2.9 million men from 1948 to 1955 (see chapter II, fns. 4 and 5), some of this increase might logically have been expected to occur in the forces deployed in East Europe during the early fifties while the Korean War was in progress. However, no substantial increase in Soviet force levels in Europe was reflected in Western estimates of this period. The inference is that the fluctuation in over-all strength was by no means as large as Khrushchev alleged, and/or that any strength build-up which may actually have taken place was mainly among Soviet forces other than those deployed in Europe.

[20] See discussions by R. M. Ogorkiewicz, Fritz Bayerlein, and Harold J. Gordon in B. H. Liddell Hart, ed., *The Soviet Army* (London: Weidenfeld and Nicolson, Ltd., 1956), especially pp. 303–6, 315–16, 363. For interesting commentary on the important wartime role of the T-34 tank

53. Under Chuikov, the GSFG's twenty-two divisions (ten mechanized, eight tank, and four motorized infantry divisions) were also put through a rigorous training program. At the same time, the introduction of early-generation jet aircraft into units of the Twenty-fourth Air Army in East Germany was rapidly stepped up in the early fifties, so that by the end of 1952 the estimated 1,700 aircraft of this organization included around 500 MIG-15 jet fighters and 211 IL-28 jet light bombers.[21] The MIG-17, successor to the MIG-15, began to appear the following year,[22] having first shown up toward the end of the Korean War, where Soviet jet fighter aircraft had been tested in combat against the F-86 and other American designs.

Along with these developments in the GSFG in the early fifties, somewhat similar changes in training and re-equipment took place in the two smaller groups of Soviet forces in Eastern Europe: a northern group based in Poland, and a southern group including the Soviet occupation forces in Austria and along the lines of communication through Hungary and Rumania. Accounting for upward of 100,000 men and seven or eight divisions, together with tactical air elements, these forces, too, could be regarded as part of the combined-arms spearhead poised against Western Europe.

European Orientation of Initial Soviet Nuclear Delivery Forces

Interestingly enough, the continental orientation of Soviet military preparations remained in evidence when nuclear weapons were initially introduced into operational Soviet forces in the early fifties, after the Soviet Union had turned the atomic corner with its first test explosion in 1949. It later became known that Soviet energies at this time were also being devoted to development of modern heavy bomber aircraft (such as the BISON jet bomber and the BEAR turboprop bomber)[23] that could threaten the United States directly, once they began to appear in operational units, from the mid-fifties onward. Nevertheless, the bulk of the initial Soviet effort to fashion a nuclear delivery capability went into delivery forces that were oriented essentially toward Eurasian operations rather than intercontinental strategic missions.

The aircraft with which these delivery forces were mainly equipped—IL-28 jet light bombers in tactical aviation units; TU-4 piston medium bombers

---

and its variant, the T-34/85, see also Alan Clark, *Barbarossa: The Russian-German Conflict, 1941–1945* (New York: The New American Library, Inc., 1966), pp. 188–90, 223, 326, 411, 456. While the wartime T-34 and the postwar T-54 medium tanks were the backbone of the Soviet armored forces until the T-55 and T-62 came along after Stalin's day (around 1958 and 1962, respectively), the Soviets also produced many other models, including several versions of the JS (Stalin) heavy tank.

[21] *An Cosantóir* (December 1952): 575.

[22] See Robert A. Kilmarx, *A History of Soviet Air Power* (New York: Frederick A. Praeger, Inc., 1962), p. 229; William Green and Roy Cross, *The Jet Aircraft of the World* (New York: Hanover House, 1955), p. 31.

[23] Kilmarx, *A History of Soviet Air Power*, pp. 252–53. The nicknames for Soviet aircraft such as BISON, BEAR, and BADGER derive from a descriptive system of identification adopted by NATO, and are not employed by the Soviets themselves.

copied from the US B-29; and, later, TU-16 BADGER jet medium bombers in long-range aviation units[24]—were best suited, in view of their range limitations, to bringing nuclear firepower to bear against Europe and overseas bases around the periphery of the Eurasian land mass. Equipment limitations, lack of forward bases, delay in developing refueling techniques for intercontinental missions, and other considerations of a technical and operational nature probably accounted in part for the orientation of Soviet nuclear delivery forces toward medium-range Eurasian operations in Stalin's time. However, this pattern of Soviet development also was no doubt influenced by a military tradition in which intercontinental strategic bombing concepts had not hitherto won a firm hold, as well as by the general focus of Soviet attention upon the European politico-military arena, to which we had occasion to refer earlier.

It must be recognized, of course, that Soviet medium bomber aircraft like the TU-4 or the subsequent TU-16 BADGER jet bomber, if regarded as an expendable weapon system for one-way employment, would have increased the early Soviet intercontinental delivery potential against the United States. Whether the Soviets so regarded them at the time is an open question. In the late fifties, after introduction of air refueling and development of forward arctic bases,[25] it could be argued that at least part of the numerically large Soviet medium bomber force might serve as an intercontinental supplement to the small force of BISON and BEAR heavy bombers, which at that time (prior to the build-up of an ICBM force) represented the principal long-range delivery threat against the North American continent. However, in Stalin's lifetime these developments still lay ahead, again suggesting that in the early fifties Soviet strategic delivery capabilities were still basically oriented toward medium-range operations in the Eurasian area.

Parenthetically, although the Soviet Union did not acquire operational ballistic missile systems until after Stalin's time, the pattern of placing greater initial emphasis on European than on intercontinental targets tended to repeat itself in the missile era. Here again, while part of the Soviet effort went into the gradual build-up of ICBM submarine-launched missile forces that could pose a direct threat to the United States, the main weight of the early Soviet strategic missile deployment in the western border regions of the USSR consisted of medium- and intermediate-range missiles (MRBM and IRBM) suitable primarily for coverage of targets in the NATO European

[24] Ibid., pp. 230–31, 253; Garthoff, *Soviet Strategy in the Nuclear Age*, pp. 177–78. While Stalin lived, the Soviet long-range air arm (known as *dal'niaia aviatsiia*) depended mainly on the TU-4, copied from American B-29's which had made emergency landings in the Soviet Far East during the war. Large numbers of TU-4 aircraft were built in the Soviet Union in the late forties and early fifties before jet bombers of Soviet design became available. Although the TU-4 piston bomber lacked the characteristics necessary for modern intercontinental delivery tasks, it did serve the important function of providing an interim bomber with which Soviet long-range units could be trained for strategic operations, in which they had comparatively little wartime experience. As noted earlier, Stalin himself is reported to have been vitally interested in efforts to develop the new Soviet strategic bomber arm. See fn. 10 above.

[25] See Asher Lee, ed., *The Soviet Air and Rocket Forces* (New York: Frederick A. Praeger, Inc., 1959), pp. 18–19; Kilmarx, *A History of Soviet Air Power*, pp. 253, 258.

area. We shall take up this subject more fully later, in dealing with the Khrushchev period.

Revival of the East European Armed Forces

In the latter years of the Stalinist period, an important corollary to the strengthening of the Soviet military posture against Europe was the process of rebuilding the armed forces of the Soviet Union's East European satellites. This process began in 1949, after the first postwar years, during which the fortunes of the badly disorganized national armies of the East European states were at a low ebb.[26] By 1949, with Communist regimes now firmly in power in these countries, Stalin evidently decided the time had come to rehabilitate and expand their military forces,[27] perhaps in line with a general plan to add the military potential of East Europe to the Soviet forces already opposing the West, or, at the very least, with a view to integrating the satellite armies more closely into the Soviet system of control in East Europe. As noted in the preceding chapter, the Soviet Union had completed a series of bilateral defense treaties with East European countries in 1948, which doubtless provided another reason for the military rehabilitation program undertaken in the years 1949–53.

During this period the heterogeneous structure of the various national forces was modified to conform to the Soviet organizational pattern, widespread personnel purges were carried out on grounds of both political reliability and professional efficiency, and large missions of Soviet officers took over staff and, in some cases, command responsibility for retraining the East European forces.[28] At the same time, coincident with the modernization program underway in the Soviet Union's own forces, the satellite military establishments began to receive sizable quantities of Soviet arms and equip-

[26] For an examination of the low fortunes of the Eastern European armies during the period of Communist takeover from 1945 to 1949, see *The Soviet Takeover of Eastern Europe* (Cambridge, Mass.: Center for International Studies, Massachusetts Institute of Technology, 1954), especially the treatment in chapter VI, "The Police and the Army." See also Ithiel de Sola Pool et al., *Satellite Generals: A Study of Military Elites in the Soviet Sphere* (Stanford, Calif.: Stanford University Press, 1955), pp. 12–17, passim; Raymond L. Garthoff, "The Military Establishment," *East Europe* (September 1965): 2–12.

[27] One observer has placed the first steps in the rehabilitation of the East European armies in March 1949, shortly before the signing of the North Atlantic Treaty. At this time, according to E. Hinterhoff, the Soviet Union secretly set up a bureau to oversee the satellite armies and Bulganin was sent to East Europe to speed up plans for their integrated development. This was also the time when the Soviet Union made Marshal Rokossovskii the Minister of Defense in Poland, indicating Soviet interest in maintaining close control over the military rehabilitation process. See E. Hinterhoff, "The Military Potential of the Warsaw Pact," *East and West*, vol. 2, no. 7 (1956): 22.

[28] For accounts of the process of rebuilding the East European armed forces after the picture changed in 1949, see Leland Stowe, "Satellites in Arms," *Life*, December 17, 1951, pp. 99–106; *The Soviet Takeover of Eastern Europe*, chapter VI; Middleton, *The Defense of Western Europe*, pp. 74–83; J. M. Mackintosh, "The Satellite Armies," in Liddell Hart, ed., *The Soviet Army*, pp. 439–51; Garthoff, in *East Europe* (September 1965): 6–13.

ment. While much of this was less up to date than the newest matériel being introduced into Soviet units, it at least laid the basis for the standardization of equipment and procedures that was to be carried further in later phases of joint Soviet–East European military arrangements under the Warsaw Pact.

The results of this initial program of rebuilding the armed forces of the satellite countries during the Stalinist period were impressive in numerical terms, even if less so in other respects. By 1953 these forces had attained a strength of around 1,500,000 men,[29] providing a total number of divisions estimated variously at from sixty-five to eighty,[30] of which perhaps less than half were well enough trained and equipped to be of some combat significance. The reorganization of the East European forces along Soviet lines also included the air forces of these countries. However, the Soviet Union evidently was less interested then in the immediate improvement of the indigenous air forces than in the development of airfields and air defense warning facilities in the area for the use of Soviet air elements.[31] Modernization of the East European air forces and their integration into the Soviet air defense system were largely deferred until after the Korean War; they began at about the same time that major organizational and equipment changes were undertaken in the Soviet air defense system itself.[32]

In the case of Hungary, Rumania, and Bulgaria—countries which had been on the Axis side in World War II—the build-up of forces in the 1949–53 period involved violation of their peace treaty obligations.[33] Poland and Czechoslovakia, on the other hand, were not similarly bound by treaty to limit the size of their forces. East Germany, the principal remaining participant in the military rehabilitation of the satellite forces, presented a special case. The German Democratic Republic (GDR), which had been set up in the Soviet zone of Germany in October 1949, after the Soviet Union had failed to block the formation of a West German government, originally had at its disposal the nucleus of a military establishment in the form of the "Bereitschaften" (special Alert Units), created in 1948. By 1950—well before the new West German state possessed any semblance of a military establishment—this East German force, which was supplemented by sea and air police components, had reached a strength of some 50,000 men. Two years later it was renamed the "Kasernierte Volkspolizei" (People's Police in Garrison—KVP). By 1953, following further reorganization, the

[29] Garthoff, in East Europe (September 1965): 13.

[30] See Middleton, The Defense of Western Europe, p. 183; Stowe, in Life, December 17, 1951, p. 106; Mackintosh, in The Soviet Army, pp. 441–48; Bulletin (November 1954): 22. The wide range of estimates concerning the number of East European divisions in the early fifties reflected the uncertainty at that time about what was going on in East Europe. Partly, the tally of divisions was obscured by the process of reorganization then in full swing. In retrospect, it seems likely that the lower bracket of figures was closer to the mark.

[31] An Cosantóir (December 1952): 575; Middleton, The Defense of Western Europe, p. 81.

[32] Kilmarx, A History of Soviet Air Power, p. 262; Field Marshal Montgomery, in U.S. News and World Report, June 4, 1954, p. 45.

[33] See J. M. Mackintosh's discussion in Liddell Hart, ed., The Soviet Army, p. 439.

KVP had attained a strength of about 100,000 men and seven infantry divisions.[34] Its eventual transformation into a National People's Army came after Stalin's time, in early 1956, and coincided with the formal admission of East Germany into the Warsaw Pact.

On the whole, the rehabilitation and build-up of the East European satellite forces in Stalin's last years can be regarded as a process still far from complete at the time of his death. Both the reliability and the military efficiency of these forces posed major question marks to the Soviet Union. Military integration of the Eastern bloc countries with Soviet forces in the area made little progress under the bilateral arrangements that prevailed at the time, except perhaps in the field of air defense. Certainly, the Stalin period produced no joint framework for co-operative military activity comparable to that which Khrushchev was to encourage after the Warsaw Pact came into being,[35] as we shall see. For all practical purposes, the Soviet Union up to and beyond the end of the Stalin era counted essentially upon its own military forces to carry the burden of any military undertakings in Europe in which the Soviet Union might become involved.[36] At the same time, it must be recognized that Stalin did set in motion important changes which during the next decade led to the development of a substantial East European military potential.

Before leaving the subject of Soviet military policy under Stalin, let us turn briefly to two other major elements of the Soviet military posture to which Stalin found it expedient to devote greatly increased attention. These were the Soviet Union's naval forces and the country's air defense system.

Soviet Naval Expansion under Stalin

During World War II, the Soviet navy had played no major role in the world's oceans, but had been used mainly for support of the seaward flanks of the Soviet ground forces and for defense of Soviet coastal areas.[37] Much

[34] Mackintosh, *Strategy and Tactics*, p. 29; Garthoff, in *East Europe* (September 1965): 11. Some accounts hold that original plans for the East German armed forces envisaged the building of a much larger force of seventeen to twenty-four divisions from the hard core Bereitschaften units, but that these plans were scaled down owing to doubts about the reliability of East German personnel and other factors. See Pergent, "Forces et potentiel militaires de l'URSS," *Allgemeine Schweitzerische Militärzeitschrift* (General Swiss Military Review) (1956): 333–34; Stowe, in *Life*, December 17, 1951, p. 100.

[35] The Soviet contention has been that the postwar bilateral agreements "played a big part in strengthening the defense capacity of the socialist countries," but that they proved "insufficient" for this purpose after West Germany's inclusion in NATO, and hence the Warsaw Pact was created to meet the need for "collective action" against the "growing military threat" of NATO. See A. A. Grechko, *Voenno-istoricheskii zhurnal* (May 1965): 21–22; unsigned article, "The Armed Forces of the Socialist Countries and Their Military Alliance—Guarantee of Peace and the Security of Nations," *Kommunist Vooruzhennykh Sil* (Communist of the Armed Forces), no. 13 (July 1965): 66.

[36] See by the present author, *The Evolving Nature of the Warsaw Pact*, The RAND Corporation, RM-4835-PR, December 1965, pp. 3–5.

[37] The Soviet navy's role of protecting the seaward flanks of the Red Army has been described by Soviet naval leaders as its "main and most important task" in World War II. See Admiral I. S.

as in the days of Imperial Russia, the Soviet leaders had looked to their naval forces to serve the strategic interests of an essentially landlocked continental power, with the result that Soviet naval operations had been confined for the most part to enclosed waters such as the Baltic and the Black Sea.[38]

The great change in the strategic landscape brought about by World War II, however, resulted in a new Soviet emphasis on the importance of sea power. The Soviet Union now found itself facing a coalition that included the leading Western maritime powers and, moreover, was characterized by the growing link between the United States and Western Europe. In these circumstances, Stalin and his professional advisors evidently came to the conclusion that the Soviet navy must be prepared for essentially the same mission that the German navy had set for itself in two world wars: namely, in the event of another war, to interdict American supplies and military forces bound for Europe.

In preparing the postwar Soviet navy for its new mission, the main effort in the last few years of Stalin's rule was concentrated on building up a large submarine fleet. Contrary to popular impression, this postwar submarine program did not begin from scratch. Thanks to an impressive construction effort in the latter thirties, the Soviet Union had entered World War II with a fleet of about 220 submarines, the largest force in the world at the time.[39] Although this force lacked a long-range, ocean-going capability and failed to distinguish itself in the war,[40] it did provide the basis for the postwar program of modernization and expansion which began in the late forties, drawing in part on German submarine technology and boats acquired by way of reparations.[41] By the time of Stalin's death in 1953, the Soviet navy possessed an underseas fleet in excess of 300 submarines, of which about half

---

Isakov, *The Red Fleet in the Second World War* (London: Hutchinson & Co., 1944), p. 16; Admiral V. Alafuzov, "On the Nature of Naval Operations," *Voennaia mysl'* (Military Thought), no. 8 (August 1946): 19–20.

[38] See Commander M. G. Saunders, ed., *The Soviet Navy* (New York: Frederick A. Praeger, Inc., 1958), pp. 4, 12, 26, 43, 127; David Woodward, *The Russians at Sea: A History of the Russian Navy* (New York: Frederick A. Praeger, Inc., 1966), pp. 14, 206–8; Garthoff, *Soviet Strategy in the Nuclear Age*, p. 196.

[39] Admiral N. G. Kuznetsov, wartime commander of the Soviet navy, states in his memoirs that the Soviet Union had about 218 submarines in 1941. See "Reminiscences: Before the War," *International Affairs*, no. 2 (February 1967): 94. Western sources have customarily estimated Soviet submarine strength before the war at about 250. As is often the case, numbers alone were probably misleading with regard to the wartime Soviet submarine fleet. Of the approximately 220 submarines on hand in 1941, only about 170 to 200 were actually serviceable, although this number was still greater than any other power possessed at the start of the war. Germany, for example, began the war with less than 30 ocean-going U-boats and attained a peak strength of about 220 during the war itself. By the end of the war, owing to attrition and generally poor management, the number of Soviet submarines in commission was down to around 100. See Woodward, *The Russians at Sea*, pp. 204, 227, 229; Saunders, *The Soviet Navy*, pp. 158, 169, 176; Hanson W. Baldwin, *The Great Arms Race* (New York: Frederick A. Praeger, Inc., 1958) p. 25.

[40] Saunders, *The Soviet Navy*, pp. 158, 176; Woodward, *The Russians at Sea*, p. 212.

[41] Saunders, *The Soviet Navy*, pp. 143, 159.

were modern ocean-going types of long and medium range, and Soviet shipyards were turning out new boats at an impressive rate.[42]

While this ambitious submarine program might be considered the logical response of a continental power to superior Western naval strength, with a particular eye to the strategic problem of interdicting sea communications between the United States and Europe, the Soviet naval expansion under Stalin did not stop there. At the strong urging of the Soviet naval leadership under Admiral N. G. Kuznetsov, who became head of the separate Ministry of the Navy set up in early 1950,[43] the Soviet Union also embarked upon a major program of surface-ship construction,[44] centered mainly on building up its strength in cruisers and destroyers. At the close of World War II, the Soviet Union had about three cruisers and twenty to thirty destroyers of prewar vintage.[45] By 1953 the output of Soviet shipyards plus a few units handed over by the former Axis powers had boosted Soviet strength to around fifteen cruisers and sixty destroyers, and additional construction, including eight of the new Sverdlov class cruisers, was on the way.[46]

To judge by the scope it had attained by 1953, this surface-ship program reflected a critical decision at a time when postwar economic reconstruction and modernization of other elements of the armed forces were making heavy demands on Soviet resources. Whether the decision actually meant that the Soviet Union intended to challenge the surface domination of Western naval power remained unclear, for, as we shall see, the program of surface-ship construction was to be curtailed considerably not long after Stalin's death.

Even in its original conception, however, the program conspicuously failed to include plans for building up one element of naval power in which the United States held a long lead, namely—aircraft carrier forces. Although

[42] Sampson Low, *Jane's Fighting Ships, 1953–1954* (London: Marston & Co., Ltd., 1954), p. 312; *An Cosantóir* (December 1952): 575; Field Marshal Montgomery, in *U.S. News and World Report*, June 4, 1954, p. 45; Saunders, *The Soviet Navy*, pp. 164–65; Woodward, *The Russians at Sea*, p. 229. Estimates of new Soviet submarine production went as high as fifty to seventy annually, but this seems somewhat above the sustained level achieved, judging from the eventual size of the force.

[43] Throughout its existence, the Soviet navy has alternately come under a separate naval ministry or been merged at the ministry level with other services under a single Ministry of Defense. The re-establishment of a separate Ministry of the Navy in February 1950 lasted until Stalin's death three years later, since which time there has been a single Ministry of Defense (*Ministerstvo oborony*). For a listing of the various changes in the status of the navy at the ministry level, see Raymond L. Garthoff, *Soviet Military Doctrine* (Glencoe, Ill.: The Free Press, 1953), pp. 361, 411.

[44] In a sense, the postwar surface-ship program represented continuation of a program laid down in the late thirties but interrupted by World War II. For a Soviet discussion of this prewar program, which had been stimulated by Soviet naval impotence during the Spanish Civil War in 1936, see Admiral N. G. Kuznetsov, "Reminiscences: Before the War," *International Affairs*, no. 12 (December 1966): 94–95. The best account in English of the prewar Soviet naval construction program and of the factors which led Stalin to undertake it is to be found in Robert W. Herrick, *Soviet Naval Strategy: Fifty Years of Theory and Practice* (Annapolis, Md.: United States Naval Institute, 1968), pp. 28–46. Herrick's volume became available only after this chapter of the present study was written.

[45] See Woodward, *The Russians at Sea*, p. 227.

[46] *Jane's Fighting Ships, 1953–1954*, pp. 301–8; Mackintosh, *Juggernaut*, p. 274.

there had been occasional advocacy of carrier construction in Soviet naval circles before and after World War II,[47] some observers have attributed Soviet failure to develop carrier forces to the legacy of "enclosed-sea" thinking— the same sort of outlook, essentially, that had caused Mussolini to conclude that there was no place for carriers in an Italian fleet which would be operating largely in Mediterranean waters within range of land-based aircraft.[48] Perhaps some such notion, fortified by the belief that carriers had become more vulnerable with the advent of nuclear weapons,[49] did indeed enter into Soviet naval planning decisions.

In any event, neither under Stalin nor later under Khrushchev were decisions made to compete with the West in carrier forces. Rather, the principal Soviet response to the carrier threat took the form of building a land-based naval air arm, together with submarines and a variety of mobile surface forces for torpedo and missile operations against carriers.

The Problem of Air Defense

Another important element of the Soviet military posture that called for greatly increased attention during the postwar reconstruction of the Soviet armed forces under Stalin was the air defense system, known as the PVO.[50] During World War II, there had been relatively little need to develop defenses against strategic air attack, for the limited capabilities of Goering's Luftwaffe in this field of air warfare had been largely dissipated in the Battle of Britain early in the war. Consequently, the Soviet Union emerged from the war with what was at best a rudimentary system of air defense.[51] Given the vast destructive possibilities of strategic air attack posed by the advent of nuclear weapons, however, it soon became obvious that urgent measures had to be taken to improve the Soviet air defense system.

[47] See Garthoff, *Soviet Strategy in the Nuclear Age*, pp. 200–2. An interesting account of Soviet failure to include aircraft carriers in the prewar naval construction program is given in Admiral N. G. Kuznetsov's memoirs. Kuznetsov indicates that carriers were deleted from the program on Stalin's personal instruction, even though expert naval opinion favored them. Stalin's prejudice against carriers again apparently ruled them out in the later postwar program. Kuznetsov suggests, "with benefit of hindsight," that it was a mistake not to have provided for carriers as an element of Soviet sea power. See the installment of his memoirs in *International Affairs*, no. 12 (December 1966): 95. The author is indebted to Robert Herrick, one of the West's best-informed students of Soviet naval affairs, for pointing out Soviet sensitivity to Kuznetsov's admission that the Soviet Union should have built carriers but failed to do so. In two separate Russian language versions of the Kuznetsov memoirs (one published serially in the magazine *Oktiabr'* and the other in book form), treatment of the carrier issue differs, with the latest corrected explanation being that carrier construction was not vetoed in the prewar program but only postponed because of technical and other difficulties. A full account of the carrier issue may be found in Herrick's *Soviet Naval Strategy*, pp. 10, 31–36, 58, 68–69, 122–23, 147–51. See also further discussion of the carrier issue in chapter VIII.

[48] See Woodward, *The Russians at Sea*, p. 205.

[49] Garthoff, *Soviet Strategy in the Nuclear Age*, p. 202.

[50] PVO (*protivovozdushnaia oborona*) is the Russian abbreviation for air defense forces, which include anti-aircraft troops and fighter aircraft units. They are also now charged with anti-missile and anti-satellite defense. For a Soviet description of the PVO system, see *Bol'shaia sovetskaia entsiklopediia* (The Large Soviet Encyclopedia), vol. 35 (2nd. ed., Moscow, 1955), pp. 122–24.

[51] See Asher Lee, "Strategic Air Defense," in Lee, ed., *The Soviet Air and Rocket Forces*, p. 120.

Initially, the air defense potential of the PVO was clearly unimpressive. Its chief assets were a small interceptor force of about a thousand fighter aircraft of World War II vintage and a considerable amount of anti-aircraft artillery,[52] and neither was suitable for defense against bomber operations conducted at high altitude or in conditions of poor visibility. The PVO fighter units shared air defense responsibilities with an approximately equal number of fighter regiments of the naval air arm, based in coastal areas.[53] Additional fighter aircraft in tactical or "frontal" aviation units, amounting to about half of the estimated active Soviet inventory of 15,000 combat aircraft,[54] were also theoretically available for air defense tasks in an emergency. A visual warning service existed in some areas, but for the most part the Soviet Union was still without a radar warning network throughout its wide expanse of territory. Thus, although some of the elements of a nationwide air defense system were at hand, its over-all potential was poor, owing not only to inherent limitations of the aircraft available but also to lack of electronics equipment for warning and control, and to generally inadequate arrangements for co-ordination of the air defense system as a whole.[55]

In the early postwar years, vigorous, though somewhat uneven, efforts were undertaken to remedy these shortcomings. Competitive programs among Soviet aircraft designers yielded several jet-fighter prototypes, of which the most notable, the MIG-15, made its debut in December 1947.[56] Thanks in part to importation of the latest British jet engine technology, the MIG-15 was shortly thereafter placed in mass production and eventually reached a total output of some 15,000, more than that of any other Soviet jet fighter.[57] This aircraft, and the improved MIG-17 that appeared several years later, near the end of the Korean War, remained the backbone of the PVO interceptor force—and of tactical fighter units as well—until the Soviet Union's first supersonic fighter, the MIG-19, came along after Stalin's day.[58] In terms of numbers, the conversion to jet fighters of the MIG family proceeded very rapidly during the last years of the Stalinist period. In 1951 about 20 per cent of the Soviet fighter units had been re-equipped with jet types; by the end of 1953, the changeover was virtually complete,[59] including the whole of the PVO interceptor force, whose strength had been increased since 1948 to more than 2,000 aircraft.

At the same time that such intensive Soviet efforts were going into the development and production of jet fighters, in the late forties and early

[52] Asher Lee, *The Soviet Air Force*, pp. 51, 199; Kilmarx, *A History of Soviet Air Power*, p. 179.

[53] Lee, *The Soviet Air Force*, p. 199.

[54] Kilmarx, *A History of Soviet Air Power*, p. 226.

[55] Lee, *The Soviet Air Force*, pp. 198-99.

[56] William Green, "The Development of Jet Fighters and Fighter Bombers," in Lee, ed., *The Soviet Air and Rocket Forces*, pp. 138-39.

[57] Kilmarx, *A History of Soviet Air Power*, p. 230.

[58] Ibid., p. 141 and pp. 227-30, and Richard E. Stockwell, *Soviet Air Power* (New York: Pageant Press, Inc., 1956), pp. 35-55, for additional details of the intensive Soviet jet fighter development effort in the late forties and fifties.

[59] Marshal Montgomery, in *U.S. News & World Report*, June 4, 1954, p. 45.

fifties, serious attention was being devoted to overcoming the technical backwardness of the Soviet electronics industry, upon which the ultimate creation of a modern air defense system would heavily depend. By borrowing freely from foreign technology and experience (even to the point of copying some defects in Western equipment), the Soviet electronics industry managed to meet many of the essential requirements for setting up a nationwide radar warning network and other facilities for a co-ordinated air defense system.[60] During the last years of the Stalinist period, as noted previously, steps were also taken to extend the area of early-warning coverage into the satellite countries of Eastern Europe—adding an air-age dimension, as it were, to the historic role of this region as a defensive buffer zone against a possible land invasion from the West.

Despite impressive technical progress and the large-scale operational training and deployment of PVO forces achieved under Stalin, the Soviet air defense system still suffered from serious deficiencies at the time of his death. Among the more glaring of these was a poor capability for coping with night and all-weather operations of the kind that Western strategic bomber forces could be expected to mount in case of war. This shortcoming was the product of many factors, including inadequate GCI (ground-controlled intercept) facilities; shortage of all-weather fighter aircraft (only one all-weather design, the Yak-25, was developed in the Stalinist period, and virtually all of the MIG fighter force in the early fifties was configured solely for good-visibility operations); and lack of training under adverse weather conditions. Moreover, the great expanse of Soviet territory itself, offering diverse approaches to incoming bombers, was likely to place a severe burden upon an air defense system that was still plagued with growing pains.[61]

Although the task of defending the Soviet Union against possible strategic attack clearly remained far from solved at the close of the Stalinist period, it would be unfair to lay the blame wholly at Stalin's door. Not only was this task formidable to begin with but it was subject to new orders of change as the unceasing duel between modern offensive and defensive means of strategic warfare went forward. As Stalin's successors were to learn, the problems of defense against aircraft delivery forces were soon to be overtaken by those of defense against missile attack. Indeed, there was something almost Sisyphean about the effort to build effective strategic defenses in an age when offensive delivery means seemed able always to keep a jump ahead of the defense—a situation which, of course, might always be changed by some new turn in technology. But the Soviets kept trying, and where Stalin left off his successors picked up. It certainly can be said that he laid the groundwork for further reorganization of the Soviet air defense system and for the introduction of surface-to-air missiles that took place after he was gone.

60 Lee, *The Soviet Air and Rocket Forces*, pp. 120–22.
61 Lee, *The Soviet Air Force*, p. 199.

IV

THE STALINIST LEGACY: A BALANCE SHEET

By the end of the Stalinist period, the Soviet Union had passed through almost a decade of postwar reconstruction and massive concentration upon industrial and military growth. The balance sheet for this period was by no means clear-cut, however, and, even in retrospect, historical judgments differ widely on the question of Stalin's services to Soviet policy. In particular, so far as the subject of this study is concerned, there has been considerable controversy among Western observers as to whether Soviet policy toward Europe reached a dead end in the latter years of Stalin's rule as a result of his intransigent methods and lack of new ideas, or whether it was already shifting toward the more varied and flexible line that was to be pursued by Stalin's successors, most notably, Khrushchev.

Not only in the West, however, have differing interpretations been placed on the policy record of the Stalinist years, postwar as well as earlier. In the Soviet Union itself, "de-Stalinization" under Khrushchev and, more recently, the partial rehabilitation of Stalin's reputation have produced variant evaluations of his services to Soviet society, including his contribution in foreign policy and military affairs. Before going on to examine the Soviet Union's European policy after Stalin's death, therefore, it may be useful to look briefly at some of the retrospective judgments—both Western and Soviet—of Stalin's performance in those fields, particularly where they bear on areas germane to this study.

Western Appraisal of Stalin's Policies

The time is undoubtedly distant when anything like a unanimous historical judgment will be passed on Stalin, who, as Walter Laqueur has put it, will probably be compared by some future generation of historians with his most outstanding contemporary, Adolf Hitler, as either the hero or the villain of the totalitarian age.[1] Whatever may be the ultimate assessment of Stalin's place in history, one may note that judgments in the West have already gone through several cycles with respect to his merits as the architect of Soviet policy. Broadly speaking, the fashion during most of his lifetime was to regard him as a masterful leader, who, despite moral and intellectual shortcomings, managed Soviet affairs successfully within the context of

[1] Walter Laqueur, *Russia and Germany: A Century of Conflict* (Boston: Little, Brown and Company, 1965), p. 290.

the totalitarian system he had helped to construct. Following his death, and in the new perspective afforded by anti-Stalinist revelations within the Soviet Union itself, it became a good deal more common to deflate his accomplishments and to find him guilty of bungling and mismanaging Soviet interests at home and abroad. More recently, as the Stalinist period has receded in time, a somewhat more balanced view of his achievements and failures has begun to emerge. On the whole, however, seen in terms of the state of affairs existing at the time of his death, Stalin's policy performance still tends to receive rather poor marks from many Western observers.

Critical assessments of Stalin's conduct of Soviet affairs often have suggested that Stalin in his last years had run dry of new ideas on foreign and domestic policy and tended toward "the reliving of old situations and to the reemployment of old devices rather than to the recognition of the realities of a new day."[2] This view of a man grown rigid and inflexible in the autumn of his life may not be wholly in accord with evidence that Stalin wavered between intransigence and a last-minute return to the strategic and ideological flexibility of a peaceful coexistence line.[3] In terms of results, however, it could be argued that his policies yielded a cumulative list of setbacks, in both foreign and domestic fields, which saddled his successors with more than a fair share of problems.

In foreign policy, for example, Stalin had signally failed to achieve such major objectives as breaking up the Western alliance or altering the military-strategic balance in favor of the Soviet Union. His European policy, in particular, had helped to harden the Cold War division of Europe and had left the Soviet Union bogged down in a political-military confrontation with a Western coalition to which the economic and military resources of the United States were being increasingly committed.[4] Moreover, Stalin's approach had not only failed to block the formation of a West German government or to neutralize Germany in other ways, but had helped to drive West Germany into the arms of NATO.[5] In this respect, critics could observe that the theoretical guidelines for Soviet policy laid down in Stalin's *Economic Problems of Socialism in the USSR* had defeated their own purpose and proved to be out of tune with the basic trends of the early fifties. Instead of profiting from a split in the Western camp over Germany's revival, as predicted in Stalin's testamentary contribution to Soviet foreign policy, the Soviet Union

[2] George F. Kennan, *Russia and the West Under Lenin and Stalin* (Boston, Mass.: Little, Brown and Company, 1961), p. 386. See also Bertram D. Wolfe, *Khrushchev and Stalin's Ghost* (New York: Frederick A. Praeger, Inc., 1957), pp. 47–48.

[3] See Marshall D. Shulman, *Stalin's Foreign Policy Reappraised* (Cambridge, Mass.: Harvard University Press, 1963), pp. 260–63; J. M. Mackintosh, *Strategy and Tactics of Soviet Foreign Policy* (London: Oxford University Press, 1962), p. 71; Philip E. Mosely, *The Kremlin and World Politics* (New York: Vintage Books, 1960), pp. 337, 453–54.

[4] Mackintosh, *Strategy and Tactics*, pp. 61–68; James L. Richardson, *Germany and the Atlantic Alliance: The Interaction of Strategy and Politics* (Cambridge, Mass.: Harvard University Press, 1966), p. 115.

[5] Laqueur, *Russia and Germany*, p. 273; Shulman, *Stalin's Foreign Policy Reappraised*, pp. 72–73.

found itself facing a situation in which Western plans were moving ahead to draw Germany more intimately into arrangements for the defense of Europe.

Even in Eastern Europe, where Soviet policy under Stalin had a good deal more to show for itself at the time of his death, the picture was by no means altogether rosy. Despite Stalin's seemingly tight grip on the life of this region, trends were at work beneath the surface which would confront his successors with the realization—already foreshadowed by Yugoslavia's defection from the Cominform camp—that Stalinist methods for Soviet control over East Europe were proving increasingly inept.[6]

On the other side of Stalin's foreign policy balance sheet, as even the most severe of his critics could scarcely deny, were some very substantial achievements. Not the least of these, however unpalatable to the Western powers with which he had allied the Soviet Union in World War II, was Stalin's postwar success in establishing Communist regimes almost everywhere that the Soviet armed forces had set foot.[7] Mainland China's fall to communism, though not, strictly speaking, a feather in Stalin's own cap, was nevertheless an event of enormous significance to world politics, for which Stalin, as putative leader of the international Communist movement, could take at least some vicarious credit. In the field of national security policy, the programs initiated under Stalin which later boosted the Soviet Union to the status of a nuclear superpower, as well as those which kept Soviet armies entrenched at the doorway to Western Europe, were accomplishments of no mean scale. They not only served as a virtual guarantee that the Soviet Union no longer need fear a traditional land invasion from the West; they also, among other things, gave the men who were to follow Stalin into the Kremlin a much greater capability for exerting pressure upon the politics of Europe and for influencing events on a global scale than any previous generation of Russian leaders had ever enjoyed.[8]

At the same time, however, even such developments in the latter years of Stalin's rule as the Soviet Union's acquisition of nuclear weapons and the strengthening of its capabilities for theater warfare in Europe were not without contradictory results. Although doubtless underscoring a determination to yield no ground to US power and influence, these developments still left the Soviet Union in a power position inferior to that of the United States. Indeed, the irony of the situation from Stalin's viewpoint was that, despite his best efforts to catch up, the military programs he launched for this pur-

[6] Zbigniew Brzezinski, *The Soviet Bloc: Unity and Conflict* (Cambridge, Mass.: Harvard University Press, 1960), pp. 138–50, and *Alternative to Partition* (New York: McGraw-Hill Book Company, 1965), pp. 1–29.

[7] Mackintosh, *Strategy and Tactics*, pp. 70–71. In Central Europe, the conspicuous exception to this rule was Austria, but this was a special case, in which joint occupation by the Western powers enabled Austria to remain non–Communist. See H. Gordon Skilling, *The Governments of Communist East Europe* (New York: Thomas Y. Crowell Co., 1966), p. 3.

[8] See Thomas W. Wolfe, *Soviet Strategy at the Crossroads* (Cambridge, Mass.: Harvard University Press, 1964), p. 21.

pose, taken together with the Soviet miscalculation of Western reaction to the Korean War, had the immediate effect of spurring efforts in the West for the common defense of the NATO area.[9] In sum, from the outcome of Stalin's performance in foreign policy and defense it can be argued that he mismanaged Soviet policy to the extent of prompting the West to close ranks against the Soviet Union—the very thing his policies ostensibly were meant to avoid.

In the domestic policy field, with which our review of the Stalinist period is not directly concerned, Western assessments critical of Stalin's record are many. Although the positive side of his domestic policy performance has not gone unrecognized—and in this regard his role in transforming the Soviet Union into a strong industrial power is generally seen as his "real and lasting merit" in history[10]—the negative side has dominated most Western appraisals of Stalin's internal rule. Here, too, one finds the argument, applied also to his conduct of foreign policy, that toward the end of his regime he ran out of fresh ideas and therefore began to turn the clock back to the harsher features of his earlier years. The tightening of police repression and the apparent preparations for a new round of purges, foreshadowed by the "Doctors' Plot" of January 1953, were among the sterile aspects of his latter-day domestic policy upon which the argument rests.[11]

Seen from a different perspective, however, Stalin's legacy in the fields of foreign and domestic policy can be appraised somewhat less negatively—in terms of the objectives he sought to attain—than when his policies are judged mainly by relatively short-term results. With regard to foreign policy, for example, it can be argued that Stalin took a long view of the situation. What some have perceived as policy stagnation and failure to achieve the weakening of the Western alliance may, from a long-term viewpoint, appear as a prudent policy of gaining time during which Stalin banked on exploiting potentially divisive tendencies in the West, while seeking to overcome the vulnerabilities of the Soviet military-industrial position.[12]

Viewed in this light, Stalin's European policy was by no means inconsistent with what he understood to be the correlation of forces and the underlying political trends at work in the postwar world. If the short-term result of Soviet policy was to alarm Europe and to give impetus to its rearmament, this was the unavoidable price to be paid for strengthening the power position of the Soviet Union; in the long run, the revival of underlying antag-

[9] See Shulman, *Stalin's Foreign Policy Reappraised*, p. 26.

[10] See Laqueur, *Russia and Germany*, p. 295.

[11] For accounts of the Doctors' Plot, the Voznesenskii case, and other aspects of Stalin's internal rule during the latter years of his regime, see Robert Conquest, *Power and Policy in the USSR: The Study of Soviet Dynastics* (New York: St. Martin's Press, 1961), pp. 95–191; Boris I. Nicolaevsky, *Power and the Soviet Elite: "The Letter of an Old Bolshevik" and Other Essays*, Janet D. Zagoria, ed. (New York: Frederick A. Praeger, Inc., 1965), pp. 111–14.

[12] See Merle Fainsod, *How Russia Is Ruled* (Cambridge, Mass.: Harvard University Press, 1953), pp. 286–88; Mosely, *The Kremlin and World Politics*, p. 360; Shulman, *Stalin's Foreign Policy Reappraised*, pp. 9, 21, 25.

However, the first clear attribution to Stalin of past mistakes in Soviet foreign policy came only at the Twentieth Party Congress, where both Khrushchev and Mikoyan spoke out against the departed dictator.[20] The different grounds on which Stalin's conduct of foreign policy drew criticism, as first broached at the Twentieth Party Congress and amplified subsequently, are summarized below. It may be noted, incidentally, that the Soviet gravamen against Stalin parallels in at least some respects the points raised by many Western critics.

One of the general charges against Stalin was that he developed a faulty perception of the outside world which led him, especially toward the end of his life, into arbitrary and erroneous theoretical formulations that "fettered" the foreign policy of the Soviet Union and deprived it of necessary "flexibility." Mikoyan adumbrated this line of criticism at the Twentieth Party Congress when he asserted that Stalin's *Economic Problems of Socialism in the USSR* had provided an erroneous theoretical analysis of the economy of modern capitalism (having failed, for example, to explain the phenomenon of growth in capitalist production in many countries since the war) and, by inference, had hampered a proper policy course toward the capitalist world. Mikoyan also criticized the disbanding under Stalin of the Institute of World Economy and World Politics and of the Moscow Institute of Eastern Studies as steps that deprived the leadership of appropriate studies at a time when they were greatly needed, and thus contributed to faulty assessment of the international situation.[21]

Another theoretical error of Stalin's guiding treatise with an adverse bearing on policy formulation, to which later Soviet criticism made reference, was its stress on the "inevitability of war among capitalist states under modern conditions"—a proposition singled out as an example of its "erroneous and questionable theses."[22] Incorrect ideological formulas were said to be contained also in the well-known *History of the CPSU—Short Course,* an indoctrination manual first published in 1938 and later attributed to Stalin. After Khrushchev had criticized it in his secret speech of 1956, this manual was replaced by a new one-volume party history, published in 1959.

Typical perhaps of the post-Stalin references to the generally negative effects upon Soviet foreign policy of Stalin's "subjective and dogmatic" theoretical assessments was that given by the authors of a major Soviet work on international relations. Stalin's assessments, they said, "hindered the development of Marxist theory on questions of international relations, led to an alienation between theory and foreign policy practice and in the end resulted in an un-

return to the practices and policies of the Stalinist period, and had resisted bringing up Stalin's mistakes at the Twentieth Party Congress in 1956. *Pravda*, October 29, 1961.

[20] In his speech before the Twentieth Party Congress, Anastas Mikoyan stated that the Soviet government had previously acknowledged some past Soviet foreign policy mistakes under Stalin, but he failed to offer specific references. *Pravda*, February 18, 1956. In general, the public record prior to the Twentieth Party Congress does not reveal open condemnation of Stalin's policies.

[21] *Pravda*, February 18, 1956.

[22] See article on "Stalin," *Bol'shaia sovetskaia entsiklopediia* (Large Soviet Encyclopedia), 2nd ed., vol. 40 (Moscow, 1957), p. 422.

acceptable situation." Not unexpectedly, in a work written while Khrushchev was at the helm, he was given credit, together with the party and its "Leninist" Central Committee, for having "accomplished a great deal to eliminate everything which under the conditions of Stalin's personality cult fettered the foreign policy of the USSR, interfered with effective implementation of its basic principles, and deprived it of needed flexibility and initiative."[23]

Besides criticism of Stalin for theoretical mistakes that led to "alienation between theory and foreign policy practice," another general charge was that his practical leadership was faulty, and that his one-man decisions—sometimes his failure to make decisions—adversely affected Soviet relations with other countries. Linked with this complaint about Stalin's conduct of foreign policy was the further charge that his style of leadership contributed to an aggravation of international tensions "fraught with great danger." These general themes were first sounded at the Twentieth Party Congress by Khrushchev, who said:

> ...the leadership practice which came into being during the last years of Stalin's life became a serious obstacle in the path of Soviet social development. Stalin often failed for months to take up some unusually important problems, concerning the life of the Party and the state, whose solution could not be postponed. During Stalin's leadership our peaceful relations with other states were often threatened, because one-man decisions could cause and often did cause, great complications.[24]

Later, in defending his own de-Stalinization campaign at the Twenty-second Party Congress, in October 1961, Khrushchev observed that this return to "Leninist principles" of leadership had averted a worsening of the Soviet Union's international position. Failure to restore the Leninist leadership principles which Stalin's cult of personality had violated, Khrushchev said, "would have led to a weaker position for the Soviet Union in the world arena, and to a worsening of relations with other countries, which would have been fraught with serious consequences."[25]

Precisely what the serious consequences of Stalin's alleged mismanagement of Soviet foreign policy might have been has seldom been spelled out in critical assessments of his performance. However, from claims that his successors took steps necessary to "reduce international tension" and to "assure that the conduct of Soviet foreign policy would take full account of the concrete particulars of the situation and the actual correlation of forces,"[26] it may be

---

[23] Inozemtsev, *Mezhdunarodnye otnosheniia*, vol. 2, p. 55.

[24] Khrushchev's Speech at the Twentieth Party Congress, as cited in *Khrushchev and Stalin's Ghost*, p. 236.

[25] Report by Comrade N. S. Khrushchev, First Secretary of the Central Committee, October 17, 1961. *Pravda*, October 18, 1961.

[26] Inozemtsev, *Mezhdunarodnye otnosheniia*, vol. 2, p. 58. For an enumeration of tension-reducing steps taken by Stalin's successors, such as initiatives toward terminating military action in Korea and Indochina, and calling of the 1955 Geneva Summit Conference, see ibid., vol. 1, p. xxx; "Soviet Foreign Policy," in *Diplomaticheskii slovar'* (Diplomatic Dictionary), vol. 3 (Moscow: Izdatel'stvo politicheskoi literatury, 1964), pp. 200–1.

inferred that Stalin's leadership was seen as increasing the danger of open conflict with the West at a time when détente was called for. As one Soviet account put it, in summing up the achievements of the post-Stalin leadership between 1953 and 1955: "Thanks to the consistent peaceful foreign policy of the countries of the socialist camp, the tension in international relations, fraught with great danger, was replaced by a certain détente."[27]

It should be observed here that even during the period of de-Stalinization, and especially toward its end, Soviet criticism sought to avoid the pitfall of condemning Soviet foreign policy wholesale in the process of pointing up Stalin's faults. It was said, for example, that although Stalin had caused "some damage" to Soviet relations abroad, he "could not, however, change the essence and the general line of Soviet foreign policy which the Party and the people developed and implemented."[28] Or, as stated in a 1964 evaluation of Stalin's foreign policy role (which also, incidentally, contained a pat-on-the-back for Khrushchev's particular brand of summitry):

> The success of Soviet foreign policy could have been even greater if I. V. Stalin had not repeatedly violated Leninist standards in his leadership of internal and foreign policy. Stalin shunned the necessary political contacts with the government leaders of other countries. He alienated many political friends of the USSR by his dogmatic stand on many questions of international affairs.[29]

Although most negative references to Stalin's legacy in the field of foreign policy were cast in rather general terms, specific problems and mistakes were occasionally identified. Perhaps the frankest criticism was devoted to Stalin's responsibility for the worsening of relations with other socialist states, particularly with Yugoslavia.[30] Khrushchev, it may be recalled, while not absolving Tito of blame, singled out Stalin's belief that the "shaking of [his] little finger" would bring about Tito's downfall as a mistake for which the Soviet Union "paid dearly."[31]

Soviet relations with underdeveloped countries were another matter that Stalin was said to have handled badly, with criticism centering especially on his allegedly narrow view of revolutionary opportunities in the colonial world. Though Stalin was credited with "belatedly" recognizing the collapse of the colonial system, critics asserted that he underestimated the potential of the "national bourgeoisie" in the developing countries as an ally of the "world proletariat" in the struggle with imperialism.[32]

---

[27] Inozemtsev, *Mezhdunarodnye otnosheniia*, vol. 2, p. 56.

[28] Ibid., vol. 1, p. 106.

[29] *Diplomaticheskii slovar'*, vol. 3, p. 200.

[30] Ibid., p. 202; Inozemtsev, *Mezhdunarodnye otnosheniia*, vol. 1, pp. 103–4; *Bol'shaia sovetskaia entsiklopediia*, 2nd ed., vol. 40 (1957), p. 423.

[31] See Khrushchev's Twentieth Party Congress speech, in *Khrushchev and Stalin's Ghost*, p. 200. See also Khrushchev's 1958 speech at the Fifth Congress of the SED (Socialist Unity Party) in East Berlin, in N. S. Khrushchev, *K pobede v mirnom sorevnovanii s kapitalizmom* (Toward Victory in Peaceful Competition with Capitalism) (Moscow: Gospolitizdat, 1959), p. 425.

[32] See report of V. M. Khvostov, in *Vsesoiuznoe soveshchanie o merakh uluchsheniia podgotovki nauchnopedagogicheskikh kadrov po istoricheskim naukam, 18-21 dekabria 1962 g.* (All-Union

Stalin's judgment with respect to decisions which led to the launching of the Korean War in 1950 was never questioned, even at the height of the de-Stalinization campaign; however, tardiness in recognizing that this venture should be brought to an end in order to lessen international tension and reduce the danger of another world war was presumably laid at his door, for among the steps credited to his successors in liquidating the harmful consequences of the personality cult was the termination of the Korean War.[33]

The signing of the State Treaty with Austria, in 1955, was another corrective step credited to the post-Stalin leadership. Although Molotov was usually singled out as the chief obstruction to an earlier solution of the Austrian question, Stalin was also, by implication at least, blamed for delaying the treaty with Austria, which, according to a representative Soviet account, brought to a close "one of the most acute and complex questions of the entire postwar decade and one which had adversely affected relations between states."[34]

Criticism of Stalin occasionally acknowledged that relations with Turkey suffered through mistakes committed by Soviet diplomacy under Stalin in the early postwar period. Two issues said to have brought about a deterioration in relations with Turkey were the Soviet demand, in 1946, for review of the Montreux Convention and the territorial claims of Georgia and Armenia upon Turkey. Although still holding to the view that these moves were partly justified by Soviet security needs, the critics conceded that Stalin's "erroneous diplomatic actions" contributed unnecessarily to a bad situation, which his successors corrected in May 1953.[35]

With regard to the Soviet policy toward West Germany, no critical references to Stalin appeared during the de-Stalinization period. Only the fact that diplomatic relations were established with Bonn after Stalin's death testified to the possibility that Stalin's stance toward West Germany also may have been considered among the liabilities in foreign policy that he left to his successors.

Stalin's Military Role as Presented during "De-Stalinization"

In the process of de-Stalinization, Soviet criticism dealt harshly with Stalin's record in the military domain, both in connection with his leadership in World War II and as regards his influence upon the postwar development of Soviet military thought and policy. The general direction which this criticism took was signaled by Khrushchev's denunciation of Stalin at the Twentieth Party Congress in 1956. Here the disastrous losses and other "grievous conse-

---

Conference on Measures To Improve the Preparation of Scholarly-Pedagogical Cadres of the Historical Sciences) (Moscow: Izdatel'stvo "Nauka," 1964), pp. 395–96. An informative discussion of the tactical deficiencies attributed to Stalin with regard to the underdeveloped countries is to be found in Thomas B. Larson, "The Transient Hero in the USSR," unpublished monograph, Washington, D.C., June 1966, pp. 36–37.

[33] *Diplomaticheskii slovar'*, vol. 3, p. 201.

[34] Inozemtsev, *Mezhdunarodnye otnosheniia*, vol. 2, pp. 56, 636–37.

[35] Ibid., vol. 1, pp. 254–55. See also *Pravda*, July 19, 1953; Khrushchev speech of December 29, 1955, before the Supreme Soviet, *Pravda*, December 30, 1955.

quences" visited upon the Soviet Union during the initial phases of the German attack in World War II were blamed on Stalin as the results of his having ignored warnings of Hitler's plans, delayed modernization and re-equipment of the Soviet armed forces, and decimated the country's military leadership during the purges of the late thirties.[36] Stalin's immediate reaction to the early Soviet reverses was pictured, in highly unflattering terms, as one of despair, epitomized by his statement: "All that which Lenin created we have lost forever." Rounding out this picture of a demoralized Stalin, Khrushchev charged that "Stalin for a long time actually did not direct the military operations and ceased to do anything whatever."[37]

Even after Stalin "returned to active leadership" upon the urging of other Politburo members, his conduct of the war, according to Khrushchev, was marked by lack of "understanding of the real situation" and by interference with operations "which could not help but result in huge personnel losses."[38] Furthermore, since Stalin considered himself a "genius," he never acknowledged "any mistake, large or small . . . in the matter of theory and in his practical activity." It would therefore be necessary, Khrushchev concluded, "to reevaluate many wartime operations and to present them in their true light."[39]

In fact, such a re-evaluation had already begun in Soviet professional military circles, as made evident by the publication in 1955 of several groundbreaking articles in the journal *Military Thought*. These not only questioned the sanctity of such Stalinist military dogmas as the "permanently operating factors" of warfare in a postwar world, where the factor of surprise nuclear attack had taken on new significance, but they also drew attention to the "distortion of actual military events" in the war itself which the adulatory official historical literature of the Stalinist period was said to have fostered.[40] After Khrushchev, in 1956, lent his authority to the denigration of Stalin, Soviet historians and military theorists found themselves a good deal freer to dismantle the military genius of the dead generalissimo. The ensuing re-

---

[36] Text of Khrushchev's speech in *Khrushchev and Stalin's Ghost*, pp. 166–74.

[37] Ibid., p. 176.

[38] Ibid., p. 178.

[39] Ibid., p. 182.

[40] Among the more notable iconoclastic articles of 1955 were the following: Marshal P. Rotmistrov, "On the Role of Surprise in Modern War," *Voennaia mysl'* (Military Thought), no. 2 (February 1955); editorial, "On Certain Problems of Soviet Military Science," ibid., no. 3 (March 1955); "On Results of the Discussion on the Nature of the Laws of Military Science," ibid., no. 4 (April 1955); Colonel General P. Kurochkin, "Victory of Soviet Military Art in the Great Patriotic War," ibid., no. 5 (May 1955). The forerunner of these revisionist articles was one by Major General N. Talenskii in the September 1953 issue of *Voennaia mysl'* (of which he was then editor), entitled "On the Question of the Laws of Military Science." Although obliquely critical of some of Stalin's ideas, Talenskii in 1953 merely sowed the seeds of what was later to become a revisionist movement. For references to the above-cited articles in *Voennaia mysl'*, see H. S. Dinerstein, *War and the Soviet Union*, rev. ed., (New York: Frederick A. Praeger, Inc., 1962), pp. 36–64, and Matthew P. Gallagher, *The Soviet History of World War II: Myths, Memories and Realities* (New York: Frederick A. Praeger, Inc., 1963), pp. 133–36.

writing of history had many undertones of the rivalry between party and military in which each sought to establish its wartime merits now that Stalin had been toppled from his pedestal.[41] This subject, however, goes beyond our present review of the treatment accorded Stalin himself.

One critical theme adumbrated by Khrushchev, upon which many subsequent accounts enlarged, was that Stalin's "gross miscalculation" of the "political-military situation" had been responsible for Soviet military failures at the beginning of the war.[42] An interesting variation on this theme, which some military writers later employed as an apparent polemical device against Khrushchev, was the charge that Stalin had been guilty of formulating a false "objective law" that the aggressor power would always be better prepared than the defender.[43] A third aspect of criticism touching upon Soviet war preparedness under Stalin concerned the point that prewar Soviet policy had left the Soviet Union threatened by a two-front war, while allowing it to remain politically isolated. This was occasionally mentioned in a way that implied criticism of Stalin's foresight;[44] usually, however, the issue was presented in terms suggesting that prewar Soviet policy was intended to gain time—a view reflecting some credit on Stalin, even though he may not have made the best use of time gained, as Khrushchev had asserted.

Stalin's image as the infallible strategic architect of Soviet victory during the war itself was another casualty of the reappraisal of wartime Soviet history. In addition to the broad claim that the party and the military had pulled the country through the peril in which Stalin's leadership had helped to place it,[45] a theme for which Khrushchev had given the cue, many of Stalin's strategic and operational conceptions, once pictured as the product of brilliant pre-planning, were presented as, in fact, improvisations designed to conceal mistakes or to account for developments that had not been foreseen. Thus, the Stalinist doctrine of "strategic defense" was no longer to be regarded as skillfully planned to create the conditions for a crushing "counteroffensive," but to be explained rather as the hasty rationale for initial defeats and enforced "withdrawal operations" that resulted in the "abandonment of extensive terri-

[41] For a discerning account of the post-Stalin reappraisal of the history of the war, see Gallagher, *Soviet History of World War II*, pp.128–75.

[42] See, for example, editorial, "The Masses, the Party, and the Leaders in the Struggle for Communism," *Kommunist*, no. 5 (April 1956): 24; P. N. Pospelov, ed., *Istoriia Velikoi Otechestvennoi voiny Sovetskogo Soiuza* (History of the Great Patriotic War of the Soviet Union), 6 vols. (Moscow: Voenizdat, 1960–65), vol. 1, pp. 415–16, 473–79, vol. 2, pp. 10, 46–50; Inozemtsev, *Mezhdunarodnye otnosheniia*, vol. 1, p. 14; P. N. Pospelov et al., *Velikaia Otechestvennaia voina Sovetskogo Soiuza, 1941–1945; kratkaia istoriia* (Great Patriotic War of the Soviet Union, 1941–1945: Short History) (Moscow: Voenizdat, 1965), pp. 58–59.

[43] For such accusations, see Colonel V. Konoplev, "On Scientific Foresight in Military Affairs," *Kommunist Vooruzhennykh Sil*, no. 24 (December 1963): 33; Colonel S. I. Krupnov, *Dialektika i voennaia nauka* (Dialectics and Military Science) (Moscow: Voenizdat, 1963), p. 40; Marshal V. D. Sokolovskii et al., *Voennaia strategiia* (Military Strategy), 2nd ed. (Moscow: Voenizdat, 1963), p. 9. See also Wolfe, *Soviet Strategy at the Crossroads*, pp. 89, 278.

[44] See Pospelov, *Velikaia Otechestvennaia voina—kratkaia istoriia*, p. 20.

[45] See, for example, Marshal Malinovskii's Armed Forces Day speech, *Pravda*, February 23, 1957.

tory to the enemy." As for the doctrine of the "counteroffensive," while it was to be recognized as "an unavoidable form of strategic operations during the war," its problems had not been worked out beforehand, nor did it deserve being raised to the level of a dogmatic principle, as Stalin contrived to represent it.[46]

Since critical attacks on Soviet prewar preparedness or on the actual conduct of the war under Stalin raised delicate questions concerning the extent to which others in the party and military leadership might find themselves tarred with the same brush, the revision of World War II history was a somewhat delicate maneuver of apportioning blame and credit for the events of the war years, a process from which Stalin's military reputation emerged tarnished but not altogether blackened.[47] The war, after all, had been won, and even detractors of Stalin's services could hardly deprive him of some share of credit for the victory. With regard to Stalin's postwar influence upon Soviet military affairs, however, Soviet criticism proved even less generous than toward his wartime record, perhaps because Khrushchev and "modernist-minded" elements among the political and military leadership felt that even after Stalin's death, the heavy hand of his orthodoxy was still retarding the country's realistic adaptation to the new conditions of the nuclear age.

In general, Stalin's positive contributions to Soviet military development from 1945 until his death in 1953 were largely passed over in silence, while the negative aspects of his influence were accentuated. In this period, according to one critical account, not only was "historical truth about the war trampled upon for Stalin's advantage," but, still worse, "the cult of personality adversely affected the development of military-theoretical thought."[48] Such important new concepts as the critical nature of the initial period in a modern war and the greatly increased significance of surprise attack with atomic weapons were neglected, owing to Stalin's depreciation in 1946 of the atomic bomb as a "serious force" and to his dogmatic insistence that his "five permanently operating factors" should remain at the center of theoretical study.[49]

[46] Sokolovskii, *Voennaia strategiia*, p. 9. Essentially similar accusations that the doctrines of "strategic defense" and the "counteroffensive" had served to cover miscalculations and mistakes in Stalin's management of the war had been made as early as 1955 in the previously mentioned articles in *Military Thought*. See also Pospelov, *Istoriia Velikoi Otechestvennoi voiny*, vol. 1, pp. 439, 441.

[47] For a discussion of the complications involved in apportioning blame and credit for the events of the war years, see Gallagher, *The Soviet History of World War II*, especially pp. 135–46. An example of the attempt to strike a balance with respect to Stalin's wartime services was provided by an editorial in 1959 on the eightieth anniversary of Stalin's birth. The editorial noted that while he "rallied and mobilized . . . the Soviet people for defense of the homeland," he had "at the time made serious errors which . . . had the gravest consequences." *Pravda*, December 21, 1959.

[48] Colonel I. Korotkov, "The Development of Soviet Military Theory in the Post-War Years," *Voenno-istoricheskii zhurnal* (Military-Historical Journal), no. 4 (April 1964): 40–41. For a more detailed analysis of Korotkov's account, see Thomas W. Wolfe, "Some New Developments in the Soviet Military Debate," *Orbis* (Fall 1964): 550–56.

[49] Ibid. Stalin's comment on the atomic bomb which critics cited had been made in his reply of September 24, 1946, to a published letter by a Soviet military historian, Colonel E. A. Razin. Stalin wrote: "I do not believe the atomic bomb to be as serious a force as some politicians tend to regard it. Atomic bombs are intended to intimidate the weak-nerved, but they cannot decide

Other writers also condemned Stalin, not only for holding back "creative" work in the "realm of military theory"—where even his most insignificant remarks were often declared to be "discoveries of genius" and were straight-away converted into "the important laws"—but also for the "harm he wrought in all areas of our work connected with strengthening and perfecting the com-bat might of the Soviet armed forces."[50] As noted earlier, the last accusation was hardly fair to Stalin, during whose rule research and development pro-grams were initiated that were to culminate in the acquisition of nuclear weap-ons and delivery systems, and thus certainly contributed to the strengthening of the Soviet armed forces. On the other hand, there was probably more sub-stance to the complaint that in the early postwar years, even as military-tech-nical work on new weapons was going forward, Soviet military theory under Stalin continued to lag behind events.

The Partial Rehabilitation of Stalin's Image

After the ouster of Khrushchev in 1964, a trend toward partial restoration of Stalin's image became evident in the Soviet Union, but it proceeded by fits and starts and was not accompanied by any formal party declaration re-scinding the process of de-Stalinization.[51] The new trend was marked by the less severe portrayal of Stalin, but it stopped well short of a major rehabilita-tion. The fact that a new target of criticism now presented itself in the person of the deposed Khrushchev may have had something to do with the tempering of the anti-Stalinist campaign. So too, the new treatment of Stalin may have reflected a subtle internal contest in party ranks between de-Stalinizers and neo-Stalinists.[52] But perhaps the most obvious explanation for efforts to pre-sent a more balanced picture of Stalin lay in concern that excessive criticism of the Stalinist past had tended to reflect on the Soviet Union as a whole, and was responsible, furthermore, for the disturbing ideological implication that a "personality cult" could distort the whole Marxist–Leninist process of "socialist construction."

This concern, which had begun to be evident before Khrushchev's removal,[53]

---

the outcome of a war...." The five "permanently operating factors" which, according to his critics, Stalin "dogmatized" to the detriment of creative new thinking in the postwar period, were: stability of the rear; morale of the army; quantity and quality of divisions; armaments; and organizing ability of commanders. Occasionally, a sixth factor was added—adequate reserves.

[50] Major Generals S. N. Kozlov and M. V. Smirnov, Colonels I. S. Baz and P. A. Sidorov, *O sovetskoi voennoi nauke* (On Soviet Military Science), rev. ed. (Moscow: Voenizdat, 1964), pp. 50, 204–6, 293–94. See also Sokolovskii, *Voennaia strategiia*, p. 9.

[51] The principal party document which had initially laid down guidelines for de-Stalinization was a Central Committee pronouncement of June 30, 1956, "On the Overcoming of the Cult of Personality and Its Consequences," *Pravda*, July 2, 1956. There was some speculation prior to the Twenty-third Party Congress, in April 1966, that a new, formal enactment might be published in the place of this document, but none was forthcoming.

[52] See Sidney I. Ploss, *To the Twenty-third Congress of the Soviet Communist Party*, Foreign Policy Research Institute, University of Pennsylvania, October 8, 1965. This subject will be dis-cussed further in chapter XI.

[53] See the discussion on pp. 57–58 above.

became more explicit in 1965 as a number of party officials deplored excessive attacks upon the cult of personality,[54] and historians and other writers set about the task of undoing the ideological damage of such attacks.[55] Typical of the approach taken was a *Pravda* article in October 1965 by a prominent educational official, S. Trapeznikov.[56] "Historical experience," he wrote, "shows that the strategy of Marxist–Leninist parties" has conformed "to the needs of the world development," although "with regard to tactics . . . no revolutionary party is safe from mistakes and shortcomings." Such mistakes, which arose under the "Stalin personality cult" and were "exposed and criticized" by the Soviet Communist party, "wrought considerable harm upon the cause of socialist construction." However, Trapeznikov argued, the personality cult was neither "a logical outcome of the nature of the socialist system" nor could it "alter the character" of the system. Therefore, he concluded, it was incorrect to portray things "only in terms of phenomena of the personality cult, thereby obscuring the heroic efforts of the Soviet people in building socialism."

Other Soviet writers, in search of a formula to prevent criticism of the Stalinist past from conveying a dark picture of Soviet accomplishments, suggested that the very term, "the period of the personality cult," should be dropped. Thus, in a *Pravda* article in January 1966, three Soviet historians found fault with the works of some of their colleagues in which this "erroneous, non-Marxist term, was widely used." The resultant "exaggeration of the role of one person," they charged, "led to the belittling of the heroic efforts of the Party and the people in the struggle for socialism and to the impoverishment of history."[57]

With regard to Stalin's foreign policy role, the effort to revise his image once more and bring him down to life size has seemed to be aimed more at minimizing the negative influence of his leadership upon Soviet policy than at dwelling upon his positive achievements. True, there has been some tendency to cite him again as an authority on questions of Marxism-Leninism,[58] and to speak approvingly of his conduct of foreign policy, as when he is said to have seen through the "tactics of the Western powers" who sought to "shift the blame for noncooperation" after World War II upon the Soviet

---

[54] One of these officials was N. G. Egorychev, First Secretary of the party organization for the city of Moscow, who expressed his views in March 1965. See Larson, "The Transient Hero in the USSR," p. 3.

[55] In April 1965, for example, the issue of a revised interpretation of the cult of personality became a heated item of business at a conference of some 600 Soviet writers and philosophers in Moscow. See ibid., pp. 3–4.

[56] "Marxism-Leninism—Firm Foundation of Development of the Social Sciences," *Pravda*, October 8, 1965. The author, S. Trapeznikov, was head of the CPSU Central Committee's Department of Science and Educational Institutions.

[57] E. Zhukov, V. Trukhanovskii, and V. Shunkov, "High Responsibility of Historians," *Pravda*, January 30, 1966.

[58] See, for example, P. N. Fedoseev, *Dialektika sovremennoi epokhi* (Dialectics of the Modern Epoch) (Moscow: Izdatel'stvo "Nauka," 1966), pp. 24, 247.

Union.[59] For the most part, however, as in the treatment of Stalin's efforts to stave off the war, reappraisal of his foreign policy leadership has tended to emphasize the complexity of the situations with which he had to deal rather than crown Stalin himself with fresh laurels.[60]

Much the same can be said of the reappraisal of Stalin's role in military affairs, although here the tendency to speak of his positive merits, particularly during the wartime years, has been somewhat greater. In fact, the partial rehabilitation of Stalin's image under the Brezhnev–Kosygin regime began with his role in World War II, and most of the attention given thus far to refurbishing his reputation has continued to center on his performance during the war.

The process of presenting Stalin's wartime services in a somewhat kinder light than at the height of the de-Stalinization campaign became publicly evident in the spring of 1965, when Leonid Brezhnev, in a May 8 "Victory Day" speech, referred to Stalin's "tremendous work" as head of the State Defense Committee in organizing the Soviet war effort.[61] This re-evaluation of Stalin by one of the top figures in the new regime had been foreshadowed in April 1965 by Marshals Konev and Bagramian, among others. The former attributed to Stalin a "certain positive role" as a military leader, and the latter, while not absolving Stalin of "obvious errors," said it was "unjust" to accuse him of failure to prepare the country against aggression.[62]

As other voices were heard, the question of Soviet preparation for the war and the setbacks suffered at its outset came up repeatedly. Indeed, the refurbishing of Stalin's wartime reputation seemed in some sense incidental to an effort to judge these chapters of Soviet history somewhat less negatively than had been the fashion during de-Stalinization,[63] an effort in which, as we shall

[59] As, for example, in the book by P. A. Nikolaev, *Politika Sovetskogo Soiuza v germanskom voprose, 1945–1964* (Policy of the Soviet Union on the German Question, 1945–1964) (Moscow: Izdatel'stvo "Nauka," 1966), p. 115.

[60] A case in point arises in connection with the rationale offered for signing of the Nazi–Soviet nonaggression pact of August 1939, long an issue of considerable sensitivity in Soviet historical writing. The earlier tendency to allow Stalin to shoulder the blame for the failure of Soviet policy to ward off Hitler's attack has been dropped, leaving Stalin in a much better position historically. As the reviewer of a new Soviet history in 1966 put it, in the "extremely complex international situation" prevailing at the time, the Soviet Union "was forced to accept the German offer to sign a nonaggression pact. In doing this, it managed to escape the trap into which the creators of Munich politics were trying to entice it, and was able to avoid a war on two fronts: with Germany and Japan." G. Deborin, "Lessons of History and the Present," a review of the book *Istoriia vneshnei politiki SSSR 1917–1945 gg.* (History of USSR Foreign Policy, 1917–1945), *Pravda*, May 9, 1966. See also A. Grylev, "The Lessons of the Past War Tell Us: Be Alert and Improve Combat Readiness," *Krasnaia zvezda*, June 22, 1967.

[61] "The Great Victory of the Soviet People; Comrade L. I. Brezhnev's Report," *Pravda*, May 9, 1965.

[62] Marshal Konev interview, *Sovetskaia Rossiia* (Soviet Russia), April 16, 1965; Marshal Bagramian interview, *Literaturnaia gazeta* (Literary Gazette), April 17, 1965.

[63] Although it may be a long time, if ever, before a fully informed appraisal of Soviet unpreparedness and setbacks at the outset of the war becomes available, it is worth noting the explanation offered by a prominent British student of Soviet affairs, Malcolm Mackintosh. In a recent historical study of the Soviet armed forces, Mackintosh observes that when the German attack came, in June 1941, the Soviets were caught in the process of reorganizing and re-equipping their forces

see, some commentators appeared reluctant to join. Incidentally, even those who were treating Stalin more leniently were not inclined to speak positively of his postwar influence on Soviet military affairs.[64]

Among the exponents of reappraisal, two somewhat different lines of approach were discernible. The first approach stressed that "the causes of the failures of the Soviet armed forces at the beginning of the war were complex and varied," and, therefore, even though mistakes had occurred, it was improper to place the blame at a single door.[65] Exponents of the second approach went further toward revising unfavorable depictions of the Soviet war effort. Thus, they took the position that it was altogether inappropriate to fasten upon certain failures early in the war, for to do so was tantamount to accepting the "false version" of the war, peddled by "bourgeois" writers, to the effect that "the USSR was unprepared to repel fascist aggression and that its victory over Hitlerite Germany was a 'pure accident.' "[66] While not urging that wartime mistakes be expunged from the record altogether, expositors of this line chose to emphasize that the party and government had foreseen the danger threatening the country and had taken the steps to meet it that led to victory.[67]

Within both approaches to a reappraisal of the wartime period, the treatment of Stalin himself varied; some accounts either did not mention him at all or simply listed him noncommittally along with other members of the wartime leadership,[68] while others bestowed credit upon him, as in this passage from a *Krasnaia zvezda* article of May 1967: "The Supreme Commander,

---

after the unhappy lessons of the Finnish campaign, which had ended fifteen months earlier. The confusion attending this process, coupled with Stalin's political miscalculations and a belief shared by both political and military leaders that the Soviet armed forces could not be taken by surprise, is seen by Mackintosh as the chief cause of the difficulties in which the Soviet Union found itself. See his *Juggernaut: The Russian Forces, 1918–1966* (New York: Macmillan Company, 1967), pp. 129–34.

[64] One of the reasons that the military remained cold toward Stalin's postwar performance may relate to the fact that, after the war, Stalin cracked down on the military leadership to discourage such war heroes as Zhukov, Novikov, Kuznetsov, and others from taking advantage of their wartime prestige. The cowed state in which Stalin kept the military leadership is suggested by the virtual absence of any high-level promotions in the armed forces from 1946 until 1953. Only in the last year of his life did Stalin show some signs of relenting in his attitude toward leading military figures, like Zhukov, and even this change of heart was more than offset by fear within senior military ranks that the Doctors' Plot foreshadowed a new round of purges which might fall heavily upon the military leadership. See discussion in Mackintosh, *Juggernaut*, pp. 276, 284–85.

[65] General A. Epishev, "Glorious Feat," *Izvestiia*, May 9, 1966; Marshal Ivan Bagramian, "The Great Patriotic War," *Soviet Life* (August 1967): 19–20.

[66] Grylev, in *Krasnaia zvezda*, June 22, 1967; P. A. Zhilin and V. Makarov, "The Memoirist and History," *Krasnaia zvezda*, May 30, 1967.

[67] For an example of this approach, see "Fifty Years of the Great October Socialist Revolution; Theses of the CPSU Central Committee," *Pravda*, June 25, 1967.

[68] Among articles touching upon the question of leadership in the war, which to some extent refurbished Stalin's role by no longer linking him personally with errors of commission or omission, see: Marshal V. D. Sokolovskii, "The Great Moscow Battle," *Pravda*, December 1, 2, 3, 1966; Marshal I. S. Konev, "Great Feat of the People," *Krasnaia zvezda*, December 5, 1966; Marshal M. V. Zakharov, "The Dawn of Victory," *Izvestiia*, December 5, 1966; S. Shatilov, "The Dnieper Battle," *Krasnaia zvezda*, May 18, 1967.

I. V. Stalin, displayed great firmness; his leadership of military operations was on the whole correct and his merits in this field were numerous."[69]

An occasional kind word for Stalin cropped up also in the reminiscences of military leaders who had once suffered indignities at his hands. Marshal K. K. Rokossovskii, for example, recounted how, during the critical battle on the approaches to Moscow, he reported by phone to the Kremlin and "heard the calm, unruffled voice of the Supreme Commander," whose "personal attention" to the course of the battle proved "very significant."[70] Marshal G. K. Zhukov, himself restored to partial grace in 1965 after having gone into eclipse under both Stalin and Khrushchev in turn, also recalled favorably some of his wartime dealings with Stalin. Thus, he defended Stalin (and, incidentally, himself) against charges made during the Khrushchev period that Berlin could have been taken sooner in 1945 had it not been for errors of judgment and indecision by Zhukov and Stalin.[71] Another military leader who dug back in his memory for a happier picture of Stalin was his one-time crony Marshal S. Budennyi, who recalled Stalin's decision to hold a ceremonial parade in Moscow on November 7, 1941, when the Germans were knocking at the city's gates, as a "courageous" stroke which marked the psychological watershed in the war.[72]

In the face of this general tendency, from early 1965 on, to remove some of the tarnish from Stalin's wartime image, there were some exceptions to the practice of playing down his mistakes and putting a gloss on Soviet failures in the early period of the war. A particularly sharp example of such dissent appeared in the September 1966 issue of the *Military-Historical Journal*, in an article offering a comprehensive critique of the Soviet literature on military operations in 1941. Deploring the fact that objective analysis of the mistakes of the last war was not possible under Stalin, the author of the article, P. Maslov, insisted that military historians had an obligation to examine the miscalculations of the country's political and military leadership for their educational value. "Today," he said, "it is important to know not only who made mistakes, and the type of errors committed, but also how to prevent them from occurring in the future."[73]

Apart from arguments of the sort advanced in print by Maslov, the pros and cons of toning down criticism of Stalin apparently were at issue on other

[69] Zhilin and Makarov, in *Krasnaia zvezda*, May 30, 1967.

[70] Marshal K. Rokossovskii, "Reminiscences: On the Volokolamsk Approaches," *Voenno-istoricheskii zhurnal*, no. 11 (November 1966): 50.

[71] Marshal G. K. Zhukov, "The Advance on Berlin," *Voenno-istoricheskii zhurnal*, no. 6 (June 1965): 12, 15, 16–19. In his full-length memoirs, completed in 1968, Zhukov went still further in depicting Stalin's positive attributes as a wartime leader. Marshal G. K. Zhukov, *Vospominanie i razmyshlenie* (Reminiscences and Reflections) (Moscow: Novosti Press Agency, 1969), pp. 279–82, 291–98.

[72] Marshal S. Budennyi, "Legendary Parade," *Izvestiia*, November 7, 1966. See also similar article by Iurii Zhukov, "Red Square: 1941," *Pravda*, November 5, 1966.

[73] P. Maslov, "Literature on Military Operations in the Summer of 1941," *Voenno-istoricheskii zhurnal*, no. 9 (September 1966): 92–95.

levels of discussion. For example, a dispute reportedly erupted among military historians and other scholars who had met privately in Moscow in early 1966 to discuss a book by Professor A. M. Nekrich that was bitterly critical of Stalin's performance in World War II. The lines of this dispute, according to the accounts available, were drawn between those pressing for further exposure of Stalin's errors and those anxious to close the archives on the Stalinist period.[74] A certain amount of continued sniping at Stalin's wartime reputation was evident also in the published memoirs of various Soviet public figures. Admiral N. G. Kuznetsov, former head of the Soviet navy, and Professor V. S. Emel'ianov, a scientist prominent in the atomic field, were among those who spoke with critical candor of Stalin's faulty decisions,[75] while Marshal Zhukov tempered his charitable recollections of Stalin with the dry comment that "unfortunately, he sometimes made decisions which did not answer to the situation."[76]

To some extent, the continuing differences over the question of Stalin's wartime services probably were related to internal controversy over the larger question of how far to carry the general rehabilitation of Stalin. This issue apparently grew sharper in the months preceding the Twenty-third Party Congress, in April 1966, as suggested, among other things, by a reported letter to the Kremlin from twenty-five leading Soviet scientists and intellectuals warning that "any attempt to whitewash Stalin" at the Congress held the danger of stirring "serious dissension within Soviet society" and the international Communist movement.[77]

Such protests, symptomatic perhaps of the sensitivity of the Stalinist issue, may have helped to head off an impending move to formalize Stalin's re-

[74] An account of the February 16, 1966, meeting of historians at the Marxist-Leninist Institute in Moscow was originally published in the Italian left-wing journal *La Sinistra*, reportedly from a transcript circulated in Moscow, and later appeared in the Russian emigré weekly *Posev* (The Sowing), no. 2, January 13, 1967, pp. 3–5. While the authenticity of the account cannot be verified, the reported lines of argument tally closely with exchanges to be found in the Soviet press itself. The book in question by Professor Nekrich, published in 1965, was entitled *1941, 22 iiunia* (1941, June 22). For a searching analysis of the Nekrich affair, including a translation of the book, see Vladimir Petrov, *"June 22, 1941": Soviet Historians and the German Invasion* (Columbia, S.C.: University of South Carolina Press, 1968).

[75] Two separate accounts by Admiral N. G. Kuznetsov drew return fire in 1967 for his having dealt too harshly with Stalin and having given an "exaggerated" picture of "confusion and irresponsibility which allegedly reigned in the system of leadership of the USSR armed forces." These accounts were a set of memoirs entitled "Pered voinoi" (Before the War), appearing in *Oktiabr'*, no. 8 (August 1965), no. 9 (September 1965), and no. 10 (October 1965); and a book, *Nakanune* (On the Eve) (Moscow: Voenizdat, 1966). Kuznetsov's critics were Zhilin and Makarov, *Krasnaia zvezda*, May 30, 1967. Professor Emel'ianov's unflattering recollection of Stalin, which appeared in the literary journal *Novyi mir* in January and February of 1967, concerned a decision by the dictator, who had cowed his professional advisors into silence, to adopt a "miracle method" of armoring tanks, which proved worthless. See *New York Times*, April 18, 1967.

[76] Marshal G. K. Zhukov, "Reminiscences: The Moscow Counteroffensive," *Voenno-istoricheskii zhurnal*, no. 10 (October 1966): 85.

[77] See "Soviet Intellectuals Hit Stalin 'Reprieve,' " *Christian Science Monitor*, March 21, 1966; Eric Bourne, "Intellectual Protest Gains in USSR," ibid., March 28, 1966; Peter Grose, "Moscow Takes a Third Look at Stalin," *New York Times*, November 6, 1966. See also discussion of Soviet intellectual protest in chapter XI.

habilitation at the Twenty-third Party Congress, but this remains a matter of speculation. In any event, the Congress came and went without coming to grips with the unfinished problem of defining Stalin's place in Soviet history. So, too, in November 1967, when the fiftieth anniversary of the Soviet Union called forth innumerable commentaries on a half-century of Soviet history, no appraisal of Stalin's role therein was offered.[78] By the fall of 1968, after reformist ferment in East Europe had led the Soviet regime to redouble its efforts to enforce conformity on its own intellectual community, a growing tendency to applaud Stalin's "iron will" began to appear in the wartime reminiscences of some military leaders who had written disparagingly of him only a year or so before.[79] Again in 1969, Stalin's birthday anniversary on December 21 was marked for the first time in many years by a commemorative article which spoke favorably of his role as a Communist "theoretician," although it also noted that he had committed serious political errors "during the latter period of his life," thus implying that his reputation was not yet fully restored.[80]

Whether with the passage of time Stalin will fare better or worse historically is not, however, a matter to be pursued further here. Rather, let us return to the state of affairs at the time of Stalin's death. His successors were obliged to deal with the situation as he left it in early 1953. How they, and particularly Khrushchev, chose to treat Stalin's policy legacy in the next decade within the constraints and opportunities that lay before the Soviet Union is the question to which we now turn.

[78] Prior to the anniversary celebration in November 1967, there were signs of a continuing tussle over how far to carry Stalin's rehabilitation. See *Posev*, no. 28, July 14, 1967, pp. 1–2; Paul Wohl, "Soviet Critic of Stalin Ousted by Communists," *Christian Science Monitor*, July 29, 1967; "Red Press Reminisces and Takes a Hard Line," *Washington Post*, August 9, 1967; Paul Wohl, "New Criticism Sweeps Soviet Secret Police," *Christian Science Monitor*, August 17, 1967; "The Responsibilities of Military Historians: An Interview with the Institute of Military History of the USSR Ministry of Defense, Major General P. A. Zhilin," *Krasnaia zvezda*, August 24, 1967.

[79] One of those who, in the "conformity climate" of 1968, wrote more approvingly of Stalin was Admiral Kuznetsov, in a continuation of his earlier wartime memoirs. Another was General S. M. Shtemenko, chief of staff of the Warsaw Pact armed forces. See "Soviet Officer Eulogizes 'Iron-Willed' Stalin," *Washington Post*, August 12, 1968.

[80] "On the 90th Anniversary of the Birth of I. V. Stalin," *Pravda*, December 21, 1969.

Part Two

THE KHRUSHCHEV ERA

VERNON REGIONAL
JUNIOR COLLEGE LIBRARY

VERNON REGIONAL
JUNIOR COLLEGE LIBRARY

V

DEVELOPMENT OF SOVIET EUROPEAN POLICY
UNDER KHRUSHCHEV

In the main, Stalin's passing, in March 1953, did not basically affect the priority he had assigned to the development of Soviet economic and military power, nor did it change the Soviet Union's Cold War objectives in Europe with respect to the neutralization of Germany, blocking the further build-up of NATO defenses, and preventing potential defections from the East European bloc. His demise did, however, open the way for notable innovations in the style and manner in which policy objectives were to be pursued; in the field of military affairs, it released an internal debate over nuclear age concepts that was to precipitate significant changes in Soviet military preparations under Khrushchev.

One might note that there is by no means universal agreement with the view expressed here that what took place after Stalin's death was essentially a shift in tactics, leading to the employment of more subtle and flexible means to attain the same old objectives. It has been argued, by way of exception to this view, that basic Soviet objectives were called into question as soon as Stalin left the scene, a development that was exemplified by Malenkov's effort during his premiership, in 1953–54, to alter the traditional order to economic priorities so as to give greater emphasis to the growth of light industry and the satisfaction of consumer needs at the expense of heavy industry and the military. In a sense, it is probably true that Malenkov's light-industry policy marked the beginning of movement away from the Stalinist past. But it was hardly a radical break with the economic priorities of the past, given the relatively modest shift of resources proposed.[1] Moreover, Malenkov's policy was promptly repudiated by his opponents in the struggle for Stalin's succession. Khrushchev and his backers used this issue, along with charges that Malenkov lacked nerve in conducting Soviet foreign policy, in their successful effort to unseat Malenkov in early 1955.[2]

The argument that more than a mere tactical shift in Soviet behavior ensued after Stalin's death has also been put forward on somewhat broader grounds than those indicated above. Thus, for example, it has been held that

[1] Philip E. Mosely, *The Kremlin and World Politics* (New York: Vintage Books, 1960), pp. 397–98.

[2] Boris I. Nicolaevsky, "Malenkov's Heyday and Deposition," *New Leader*, August 12, 1957, pp. 6–8; J. M. Mackintosh, *Strategy and Tactics of Soviet Foreign Policy* (London: Oxford University Press, 1962), pp. 88–90; Arnold L. Horelick and Myron Rush, *Strategic Power and Soviet Foreign Policy* (Chicago, Ill.: University of Chicago Press, 1966), pp. 26–30.

the transition from Stalinism to the "revisionism" of the Khrushchev period actually reflected a fundamental change in the Soviet outlook—a departure from the old Marxist–Leninist orthodoxy that was to result in the dilution of its original, radical goals and the adaptation of its means to new conditions. Some of the major steps undertaken by Khrushchev from 1956 on, including his de-Stalinization program, his revision of such enshrined doctrinal tenets as the inevitability of war with the capitalist countries, and his stress on the general line of "peaceful coexistence," have been interpreted as symptoms of a long-term, secular change in the character of Soviet communism rather than as tactical modifications.

I do not quarrel with the general proposition that the Soviet Union has undergone important changes, nor with the specific thesis that it has exhibited tendencies in the course of time toward what may be called "deradicalization" of the original revolutionary ethos.[3] In other words, the Soviet Union has edged in practice toward accommodation with the existing world order while continuing to pay lip service to the old goal of demolishing it. The extent of "deradicalization" of the Marxist–Leninist outlook in the Soviet Union and the implications of this phenomenon for Soviet behavior on the world scene doubtless merit close attention. To explore these issues further, however, would carry us well beyond the compass of the present chapter.[4]

Suffice to say here that, while deep-seated forces of change may have been stirring in Soviet society in the early fifties, they apparently exercised a less compelling influence upon the post-Stalin leadership at that time than did tactical and immediate policy interests.[5] Certainly, the immediate problems of Soviet policy toward Europe in the early fifties were tackled in a way more suggestive of shifts in tactical approach than of a fundamental realignment of Soviet objectives.

New Style in Soviet Policy of the Mid-Fifties

Some signs of a new flexibility in the conduct of Soviet European policy began to appear even before the transitional succession struggle between Georgii Malenkov and Nikita Khrushchev was resolved in the latter's favor. Perhaps the most notable evidence of a new tactical approach to old problems was provided by a series of Soviet proposals, in 1954 and early 1955, in which various alternative plans for an all-European collective security system were linked with suggestions for a settlement of the German question—the chief object in both cases apparently being to persuade the West to give up

[3] For a scholarly analysis of the phenomenon of "deradicalization," which draws certain parallels between Soviet experience and that of the German Social–Democratic movement earlier in this century, see Robert C. Tucker, "The Deradicalization of Marxist Movements," paper presented at the 62nd annual meeting of the American Political Science Association, New York, September 10, 1966.

[4] Some aspects of Khrushchev's transitional role in a changing Soviet society are treated in chapter X. For a stimulating discussion of the general question of change in the Soviet system, see the series of articles on this theme by Zbigniew Brzezinski, Michel Tatu, Merle Fainsod, Frederick C. Barghoorn, and others in *Problems of Communism*, from November–December 1965 through July–August 1967. See also the essays on various aspects of change in the Soviet system in Allen Kassof, ed., *Prospects for Soviet Society* (New York: Frederick A. Praeger, Inc., 1968).

[5] See Mosely, *The Kremlin and World Politics*, pp. 438, 454.

the idea of mutual defense arrangements in which West Germany would have a role.

The first set of these proposals was advanced by V. M. Molotov in January–February 1954 at the Berlin conference of the Council of Foreign Ministers, which had been convened to deal with the question of peace treaties for Germany and Austria. Molotov tabled a draft proposal for a collective security system embracing both West and East European states, but tentatively excluding the United States (along with the Chinese People's Republic) except in "the capacity of observers."[6] On the question of Germany, Molotov rejected the Western demand that a peace treaty be concluded with an all-German government formed on the basis of free elections. He countered with Soviet conditions of a peace conference at which Germany would be represented by a coalition government, giving equal status to the Bonn government and the East German Communist regime, prior to the holding of elections throughout Germany.[7] Like meetings of the Council of Ministers in Stalin's day, the conference ended without East–West agreement on how to settle the problem of a vanquished Germany.[8]

In the months following this fruitless meeting, while the EDC treaty was under climactic debate in Western parliaments, Soviet diplomacy came up with several modified versions of the proposals linking a peace settlement on Germany with calls for a conference on European security.[9] One of these, offered in a Soviet note of March 31, 1954, included a novel suggestion, soon to reappear in the language of the Warsaw Treaty, that NATO be widened to take in the Soviet Union and some of the East European countries.[10] The reluctance of the West to act upon this suggestion, incidentally,

[6] *Pravda*, February 11, 1954. Text of the draft General European Treaty on Collective Security proposed by Molotov on February 10, 1954, may be found in *Department of State Bulletin*, February 22, 1954, pp. 269–70. A Soviet account of the February 10 proposal and the USSR's other 1954 collective security proposals, stressing that they were met by Western "obstructionist tactics" in the form of "the so-called 'Eden Plan,' " are given in *Mezhdunarodnye otnosheniia posle vtoroi mirovoi voiny* (International Relations After the Second World War), N. N. Inozemtsev, chief ed., 3 vols., prepared by the Institute of World Economy and International Relations of the USSR Academy of Sciences (Moscow, 1962–65), vol. 2 (1963), pp. 590–94.

[7] *Pravda*, February 2, 1954. See also *Foreign Ministers Meeting, Berlin Discussions, January 25–February 18, 1954*, State Department Publication 5399 (Washington, D.C.: US Government Printing Office, 1954), pp. 218, 225; Ivison S. Macadam, ed., *The Annual Register of World Events: A Review of the Year 1954* (London: Longmans, Green and Co., 1955), pp. 156–59, 192.

[8] The last notable attempt to reach a peace treaty settlement on Germany in these joint negotiations during the Stalinist period had been in June 1949, at the sixth session of the Council of Foreign Ministers in Paris, where Vyshinskii sought to restore the principle of four-power control over the whole of Germany. See Marshall D. Shulman, *Stalin's Foreign Policy Reappraised* (Cambridge, Mass.: Harvard University Press, 1963), pp. 73–75; Robert D. Warth, *Soviet Russia in World Politics* (New York: Twayne Publishers, Inc., 1963), p. 363; Dean Acheson, *Sketches from Life of Men I Have Known* (New York: Harper & Brothers, 1961), pp. 13–16.

[9] Mackintosh, *Strategy and Tactics*, p. 85; Macadam, *Annual Register of World Events*, p. 192; Warth, *Soviet Russia in World Politics*, p. 427.

[10] It should be observed that in the same note of March 31, 1954, in which the USSR suggested its own entry into NATO, it also reversed its previous stand that the United States should be excluded from an all-European security pact. See P. A. Nikolaev, *Politika Sovetskogo Soiuza v germanskom voprose, 1945–1964* (Policy of the Soviet Union on the German Question, 1945–1964) (Moscow: Izdatel'stvo "Nauka," 1966), p. 190.

was later to be cited as proof that NATO was "an aggressive military organization, directly aimed against the Soviet Union and other socialist countries."[11]

Rejection of the EDC treaty by the French Assembly in August 1954 brought momentary satisfaction in Moscow, where the French decision was hailed as "an important event in the political history of Europe."[12] However, the speedy conclusion of the Paris Agreements less than two months later enabled the Western governments, including France, to surmount French failure to ratify the EDC,[13] and the Soviet Union was abruptly confronted once more with the problem of blocking West German participation in NATO defense arrangements. Since the Paris Agreements of October 1954 were not to go into effect until May 5, 1955, Soviet diplomacy devoted itself in the interim to a further effort to discourage their implementation.

This effort took several forms, including threats to abrogate the Anglo–Soviet and Franco–Soviet treaties of 1942 and 1944[14] and a new series of proposals for conferences on collective security and German reunification.[15] In late November 1954, the Soviet Union convened a truncated "European Security Conference" in Moscow that was attended only by countries of the Soviet bloc. At the close of this conference, on December 2, 1954, it was announced that the participants had agreed to form an Eastern bloc counterpart to NATO if the Paris Agreements were ratified.[16] Most significantly, in its last-ditch campaign against the Paris Agreements in late 1954 and early 1955, the Soviet Union shifted its position on the vexing issue of German elections, indicating that it was prepared to discuss the "holding of free all-German elections" and the "reunification of Germany on a peace-loving and democratic basis," provided the West would refrain from ratifying the Paris Agreements.[17]

---

[11] Ibid.

[12] *Pravda*, September 9, 1954.

[13] Texts of the Paris (and London) Agreements of October 1954 which made possible West Germany's entry into NATO, along with the protocols of the WEU (Western European Union) binding Germany not to undertake manufacture of atomic and certain other weapons, may be found in Peter V. Curl, ed., *Documents on American Foreign Relations, 1954* (New York: Harper & Brothers, 1955), pp. 107–24, 145–65. For two quite different commentaries on the rapid conclusion of the Paris Agreements in the brief period between September 28 and October 23, 1954, see Timothy W. Stanley, *NATO in Transition: The Future of the Atlantic Alliance* (New York: Frederick A. Praeger, Inc., 1965), pp. 48–50; and Richard J. Barnet and Marcus G. Raskin, *After 20 Years: Alternatives to the Cold War in Europe* (New York: Random House, 1965), pp. 34–35.

[14] *Pravda*, December 17, 21, 1954. These threats were subsequently carried out.

[15] The first of these proposals, calling on October 23, 1954, for a four-power conference in the following month on German reunification and creation of a collective security system, was followed in rapid order by further proposals on November 13, December 2, 1954, January 15, and February 8, 1955. *Pravda*, October 24, November 14, December 3, 1954, January 16, February 10, 1955. See also Nikolaev, *Politika v germanskom voprose*, pp. 211–18.

[16] *Pravda*, December 3, 1954. See also Boris Meissner, ed., *Der Warschauer Pakt* (The Warsaw Pact), vol. 1 in the series *Dokumente zum Ostrecht* (Documents on Eastern Law) (Cologne, Germany: Verlag Wissenschaft und Politik, 1962), pp. 1–7.

[17] See, in particular, the Soviet proposals of October 23, November 13, 1954, and February 8, 1955. *Pravda*, October 24, November 14, 1954, February 10, 1955.

Thus, as in the case of Stalin's March 1952 reunification proposal, the Soviet Union again called for abandonment by the West of the NATO concept of common defense as the price for a peace treaty that would settle the future status of Germany. Whereas Stalin, however, had merely hinted at free elections, the collective leadership shared by Malenkov and Khrushchev now held out the prospect, at least briefly, that all-German elections were within grasp if the West cared to pay the price.

Were one tempted to second-guess history, this juncture might be identified as another lost opportunity[18] for finding a basis of agreement on Germany that could have altered the course of the Cold War. As matters turned out, however, the problem of a divided Germany remained unresolved. The West declined to dismantle its security structure as the down payment on the possible reunification of Germany and went ahead with the Paris Agreements, while the Soviet Union for its part displayed little real interest in sacrificing the East German Communist regime upon the altar of reunification.[19] Although, at the Geneva Summit Conference of July 1955, both sides went on record as favoring free elections to unite Germany,[20] they manifestly remained deadlocked on the essential issue of what kind of Germany they would settle for. Before the year was out, Khrushchev had indicated that the Soviet Union would "not agree to a solution" at the expense of the GDR,[21]

[18] One of these cases, the frequently-cited "lost opportunity" of March 1952, has been discussed (see pp. 28–31 above). Another instance of a possible abortive path to German reunification arose immediately after Stalin's death in 1953, when a group of Ulbricht's opponents within the Socialist Unity party (SED) allegedly conspired to take over the SED as a prelude to dissolving the Ulbricht–Grotewohl regime. This challenge to Ulbricht by the Rudolf Herrnstadt–Wilhelm Zaisser group may have been encouraged by elements within the Soviet leadership, as suggested by some former SED officials. See, for example, Fritz Schenk, *Im Vorzimmer der Diktatur; 12 Jahre Pankow* (In the Antechamber of Dictatorship; 12 Years of Pankow) (Cologne–Berlin: Kiepenheuer & Witsch, 1962), pp. 192, 213–14. See also Robert Conquest, *Power and Policy in the USSR: The Study of Soviet Dynastics* (New York: St. Martin's Press, 1961), p. 221; Wolfgang Leonhard, *The Kremlin Since Stalin* (New York: Frederick A. Praeger, Inc., 1962), pp. 70–73; Boris I. Nicolaevsky, *Power and Soviet Elite: "The Letter of an Old Bolshevik" and Other Essays*, Janet D. Zagoria, ed. (New York: Frederick A. Praeger, Inc., 1965), p. 126.

Retrospective Soviet accusations against Beria for having plotted to give up East Germany after Stalin's death (see N. S. Khrushchev speech of March 8, 1963, before Soviet Writers and Artists, *Pravda*, March 10, 1963; *New York Times*, March 11 and 16, 1963) have in turn suggested that he may have been the anonymous Soviet patron of the Herrnstadt–Zaisser group. Whether the aim of this group was to steer East Germany toward incorporation into a new, unified all-German state, with the consequent possibility of loosening its ties with the Soviet Union, remains historically obscure, as does the question whether the Soviet collective leadership during the period of internal maneuvering immediately after Stalin's death actually would have condoned a policy that would have amounted to a "sellout" of the East German Communist regime. In any event, the Soviet leadership reacted to the June 1953 workers' uprising in East Germany by quickly concluding that it was necessary to suppress any further tendencies toward undermining the Ulbricht–Grotewohl regime.

[19] See Melvin Croan, "Reality and Illusion in Soviet-German Relations," *Survey* (October 1962): 20–21.

[20] The Geneva Directive of the Heads of Government of the Four Powers to the Foreign Ministers, July 23, 1955, may be found in *Documents on Germany, 1944–1961* (Washington, D.C.: Committee on Foreign Relations, US Senate, Government Printing Office, 1961), pp. 184–95.

[21] See Khrushchev's remarks in East Germany on July 26, 1955, while he was on his way back to Moscow from the Geneva Summit Conference. *Pravda*, July 27, 1955.

and Molotov had formally restated Soviet opposition to "the mechanical merging of the two parts of Germany through so-called free elections."[22]

For all practical purposes, Soviet diplomacy in the two-year interval between Stalin's death and Malenkov's resignation in February 1955 met with scant success in Europe, although it did achieve a triumph of sorts at the Geneva Conference on Korea and Indochina, in mid-1954, by helping to bring the war in Indochina to a close on terms which included creation of the new Communist state of North Vietnam.[23] This achievement, coupled with liquidation of the deadlocked Korean armistice talks, could be regarded as a useful dividend of the new maneuverability that Stalin's successors had introduced into Soviet Asian policy.[24] In Europe, however, Soviet policy had failed rather conspicuously to meet its prime objective in this period—that of forestalling the inclusion of West Germany in NATO defense arrangements.

Despite this major setback, which may have contributed to Malenkov's being displaced by Nikolai Bulganin,[25] Soviet diplomacy in Europe struck out along several new paths in 1955, now under the emergent leadership of Khrushchev. The precise point at which Khrushchev achieved dominant control over Soviet foreign policy is not altogether clear, but he was probably well on the way toward it by the end of 1954, before Malenkov's forced resignation on February 8, 1955. Khrushchev's increasing influence in foreign affairs was evident, for example, in October 1954, when he turned up in Peking as the Soviet leader who was to deal with Mao Tse-tung on the already delicate issue of Sino–Soviet relations. In mid-1955, at the Geneva summit meeting, where Khrushchev emerged as the chief Soviet spokesman despite Bulganin's presence as the nominal head of government, it was apparent that he had become the principal architect of Soviet foreign policy. He probably did not gain undisputed control of Soviet foreign and domestic policy, however, until he had eliminated the so-called "anti-party group" in mid-1957.[26]

At any rate, it became apparent soon after Malenkov's removal that Khrushchev's ebullient personal style was bringing a new vigor to the conduct of Soviet diplomacy. In the spring of 1955 the Soviet Union injected a fresh note into its European policy approach by reviving talks on the long-stalled

[22] See Molotov's reply at the Geneva Foreign Ministers' Conference to the Western proposal of November 4, 1955, on reunification of Germany by free elections. *Pravda*, November 9, 1955.

[23] For a summary of the Geneva Conference of April–July 1954 on Korea and Indochina, and the pertinent agreements which it produced, see Macadam, *Annual Register of World Events*, pp. 159–63, 456–68. See also Allan B. Cole, ed., *Conflict in Indo-China and International Repercussions: A Documentary History, 1945–1955* (Ithaca, N.Y.: Cornell University Press, 1956).

[24] Soviet accounts have, in fact, pointed to the liquidation of the Korean War and the results of the 1954 Geneva Conference on Indochina as examples of the success achieved by Soviet foreign policy after it had overcome "the negative consequences of the Stalinist cult of personality." See Inozemtsev, *Mezhdunarodnye otnosheniia*, vol. 1, p. xxx; vol. 2, p. 63.

[25] See Mackintosh, *Strategy and Tactics*, pp. 86–87.

[26] For detailed accounts of Khrushchev's rise to power, see Myron Rush, *The Rise of Khrushchev* (Washington, D.C.: Public Affairs Press, 1958), especially pp. 6–39; Lazar Pistrak, *The Grand Tactician: Khrushchev's Rise to Power* (New York: Frederick A. Praeger, Inc., 1961); Carl A. Linden, *Khrushchev and the Soviet Leadership, 1957–1964* (Baltimore, Md.: The Johns Hopkins Press, 1966), pp. 22–89.

problem of Austria. The relative ease with which past obstacles to agreement were cleared away came as a pleasant surprise to most participants, and the successful conclusion of the Austrian State Treaty on May 15, 1955, awakened hopes that a rift in the Cold War clouds over Europe might be in sight. Under the terms of the Treaty,[27] the Soviet Union—in return for permanent Austrian neutrality—gave up a forward military base in Central Europe, an unprecedented step suggesting that Stalin's political heirs had overruled the probable advice of the Soviet General Staff on this subject.[28] On the other hand, in withdrawing from its postwar military salient in the Soviet-occupied portion of Austria, the Soviet Union had reaped the strategic dividend of creating a neutral wedge some 500 miles deep between West Germany and Italy, thereby in effect splitting the area of Western defense in two. As one astute observer put it, "what the Paris Agreements had joined together," less than six months before, "the State Treaty, at least partly, put asunder."[29]

Simultaneously with conclusion of the Austrian State Treaty, which Soviet commentary pictured as an example for West Germany to ponder,[30] the Soviet Union made another move, which took the edge off some of the more optimistic expectations of a break in the Cold War climate. On May 15—one day before the Austrian State Treaty was signed in Vienna—another treaty ceremony was held in Warsaw, where the Soviet Union and six East European Communist governments signed the documents that brought into existence the Warsaw Pact.[31] This step, taken in avowed response to West Germany's entry into NATO, marked the formal emergence of rival military alliance systems in postwar Europe. Although the Warsaw Treaty at its inception was largely a diplomatic countermeasure which, as we shall see later, brought little immediate change in the military potential of the Eastern bloc, it did have the incidental effect of providing a new legal basis for the presence of Soviet military forces in Hungary and Rumania, including most of the forces to be withdrawn from Austria under the State Treaty.[32]

[27] *New York Times*, May 16, 1955. It may be noted that the treaty signed at Schoenbrunn Palace in May 1955 did not differ greatly from terms which had been worked out in 1949 but which Stalin had refused to formalize.

[28] See Mackintosh, *Strategy and Tactics*, p. 105.

[29] William Lloyd Stearman, *The Soviet Union and the Occupation of Austria* (Bonn: Siegler and Co. [circa 1960]), pp. 162–63. This work provides an excellent and well-documented analysis of developments which led to the conclusion of the Austrian State Treaty, and of the implications of the treaty itself for Soviet policy.

[30] Ibid., p. 165. See also comments by Molotov at the signing of the State Treaty (*New York Times*, May 16, 1955).

[31] *Pravda*, May 15, 1955. Original signatories of the Warsaw Treaty on Friendship, Cooperation and Mutual Assistance, besides the Soviet Union, were Poland, Czechoslovakia, Hungary, Rumania, Bulgaria, and Albania. East Germany formally joined in January 1956, and Albania ceased to be an active participant after March 1961. Besides the Warsaw Treaty itself, the other major document signed on May 14, 1955, was a "Resolution on the Formation of a Unified Command of the Armed Forces."

[32] The Soviet forces evacuated from Austria (their withdrawal was completed in September 1955) were relatively small, totaling around 50,000 men, and comprising, in addition to headquarters and air elements, less than two full divisions. Presumably, most of the units withdrawn from Austria were relocated in Hungary, which was to remain the principal base area for Soviet

On the heels of the above-mentioned moves, Soviet diplomacy under Khrushchev displayed another facet of its new style in the summer of 1955 when the Geneva Summit Conference was convened to discuss the problems of Europe. This conference, which grew in part out of the cordial atmosphere established during the negotiations for an Austrian treaty,[33] afforded the first opportunity for Khrushchev to deal face-to-face with the Western heads of government, though nominally he did not yet hold office.

Neither the "friendly" exchange at the summit in July nor the ministerial conference that followed in the fall of 1955[34] yielded tangible progress on such problems as German reunification, a European security treaty, or disarmament. However, the atmosphere of détente which prevailed at Geneva, superficial though it may have appeared to critics of this new brand of summit diplomacy,[35] was to persuade many people that the Cold War had passed its peak. Under the influence of the Geneva thaw and other developments of the mid-fifties—the opening of an intensive round of East–West disarmament negotiations and Soviet announcement of unilateral troop reductions in 1955;[36] the establishment in September 1955 of Soviet-West German diplomatic relations; the return during the same year to Finland of the Porkkala naval base; the denunciation of Stalin at the Twentieth Party Congress in early 1956; and the much-publicized "friendship" visits of Bulganin and Khrushchev to India and Britain in 1955 and 1956—sentiment grew in Western Europe that not only the rigors of the Cold War but the Soviet military threat to Europe had finally begun to subside.

This emergent optimism was dealt a hard blow in the fall of 1956 by the eruption of virtually simultaneous crises in the Middle East and in Eastern Europe, both of which produced tensions at odds with the notion of a durable détente. In the Suez case, East–West tension rose sharply on November 5, when the Soviet Union, in a note to the British government and in a radio broadcast, threatened to intervene militarily and hinted that Soviet rockets might

---

forces stationed in the "Southern Tier" of the Warsaw Pact alliance system. See Mackintosh, *Strategy and Tactics*, p. 106; Stearman, *The Soviet Union and the Occupation of Austria*, p. 133.

[33] The original suggestion for a summit conference came from Winston Churchill in May 1953, but the idea did not take hold until the change of Soviet attitude on an Austrian treaty helped to remove the conditions which President Eisenhower had set on attending such a meeting. The immediate proposal for the Geneva Summit Conference came in a Western note of May 10, 1955, to which the Soviet government agreed on May 26. Final arrangements for the July conference were settled on June 13. One of the Soviet conditions for the Geneva meeting was that there should be no discussion of East European affairs or of international communism. The four agreed-upon items on the agenda were German reunification, European security, disarmament, and means to improve East–West contacts. See Paul E. Zinner, ed., *Documents on American Foreign Relations, 1955* (New York: Harper & Brothers, 1956), pp. 171–76; *Department of State Bulletin*, Washington, D.C., July 4, 1955, pp. 20–21.

[34] *The Geneva Meeting of Foreign Ministers, October 27–November 16, 1955*, Department of State Publication No. 6156, Washington, D.C., November 30, 1955.

[35] See, for example, James Reston in *New York Times*, April 15, 1956; Michael T. Florinsky, "The USSR and Western Europe," *Current History* (February 1957): 79–80.

[36] See *Documents on Disarmament, 1945–1959*, Department of State (Washington, D.C., 1960), vol. 1 (1945–56), pp. 630–39, vol. 2 (1957–59), p. 780; Joseph Nogee, "The Diplomacy of Disarmament," *International Conciliation* (January 1960): 256–57; Thomas W. Wolfe, *Soviet Strategy at the Crossroads* (Cambridge, Mass.: Harvard University Press, 1964), pp. 233–44.

be used against Britain and France—a threat that was answered on November 6 by an American warning that such an attack would provoke US retaliation.[37] Foreshadowing what was later to become Khrushchev's standard rocket-rattling practice in crisis situations, the missile threat against Britain and France came at a time when the Soviet Union had only begun to deploy a few medium-range missiles in the western USSR and had not yet tested its first ICBM.[38] Its missile inventory was therefore still far too limited to lend much substance to Khrushchev's threat, which probably had less to do with terminating the Suez affair than had US diplomatic arm-twisting in London and Paris. Nevertheless, the introduction of Soviet missile diplomacy in the Suez case added a new dimension to the Cold War tensions with which postwar Europe had learned to live.

During the Hungarian revolt, which immediately preceded the Suez crisis, there was no comparable possibility of intervention from the West. Thus, although East–West tensions also rose over the events in Hungary, they did not carry the overtones of a possible nuclear missile clash that were briefly introduced into the Suez crisis. On the other hand, as in the case of the East German uprising in the summer of 1953, Soviet reaction to the Hungarian revolt of 1956 did demonstrate[39] that, when necessary, the Soviet Union would enforce its controls in Eastern Europe through the local use of Soviet military power.

Despite the dual impact of Suez and Hungary upon hopes of a détente in Europe, neither crisis in the fall of 1956 marked a conclusive end to the period of the Geneva thaw. The motion still persisted in varying degree that a mellowing of Soviet policy under Khrushchev could be expected, offering hopeful prospects of liquidating some of the worst Cold War obstacles to East–West understanding. Indeed, the surprising defiance of Soviet authority in Hungary (and Poland), which could be interpreted as one of the logical consequences of de-Stalinization, helped to sustain the belief that Khrushchev might find himself too busy putting his own house in order to have either time or inclination to exert new Soviet pressures upon Western Europe. The next phase of Khrushchev's European policy, however, was to have the effect of dampening such expectations for at least the time being.

---

[37] For analysis of Soviet threats during the Suez crisis, see Mackintosh, *Strategy and Tactics*, pp. 186–90; Hans Speier, *Soviet Atomic Blackmail and the North Atlantic Alliance*, The RAND Corporation, RM-1837, December 1956, especially pp. 23–42.

[38] The development of the Soviet missile posture under Khrushchev is treated more fully in chapter VIII.

[39] There are numerous accounts of the manner in which the Soviet Union put down the Hungarian rebellion and dealt with the Polish challenge at about the same time. See, for example, Raymond L. Garthoff, *Soviet Military Policy: A Historical Analysis* (New York: Frederick A. Praeger, Inc., 1966), pp. 155–72; Paul Kecskemeti, *The Unexpected Revolution* (Stanford, Calif: Stanford University Press, 1961); George Mikes, *The Hungarian Revolution* (London: Andre Deutsch, 1957); Tibor Meray, *Thirteen Days that Shook the Kremlin* (New York: Frederick A. Praeger, Inc. 1959); Melvin J. Lasky, ed., *The Hungarian Revolution* (New York: Frederick A. Praeger, Inc., 1957). For a Soviet version see A. Belokon and V. Tolstikov, *The Truth About Hungary* (Moscow: Foreign Languages Publishing House, 1957); S. Krushinskii et al., *Chto proizoshlo v Vengrii* (What Happened in Hungary) (Izdatel'stvo "Pravda," 1956).

Resumption of Pressure Tactics by Khrushchev in 1957

General recognition that the Geneva interlude was not the harbinger of a lasting thaw in Europe followed the resumption of pressure tactics, beginning in the latter fifties, after Khrushchev had fully established his political primacy at home by quashing the so-called "anti-party group" in June 1957.[40] The pressures that Khrushchev chose to exert took a variety of forms which not only testified to his versatile touch as a practitioner of power politics but were also to have the net effect, during the next five years, of casting the shadow of Soviet military power once again across the European scene.

Among the first moves signaling the resumption of a Soviet political offensive against Western Europe was the launching, in 1957, of a vigorous diplomatic and propaganda campaign evidently intended to take advantage of strains that had arisen within the Western alliance as a result of the Suez crisis. This campaign began while Khrushchev was also in the process of mending the damage dealt to the unity of the Soviet bloc itself by the events in Hungary and Poland in the fall of 1956. Khrushchev's fence-mending efforts within the Soviet bloc included a "unity" meeting of East European Communist leaders in Budapest in January 1957 and a series of discussions with East European delegations in Moscow, as a result of which the Soviet Union, in 1957, concluded new bilateral agreements with its various Warsaw Pact allies. These agreements incorporated economic concessions as well as status-of-force arrangements aimed at blunting East European resentment against the Soviet military presence in the area.[41] At this time, Khrushchev also courted Peking's support for Soviet policy in East Europe, although strains in Sino–Soviet relations were already showing.

The political offensive that was put in motion against the West while these internal bloc repairs were going on had at least two apparent objectives: to drive a wedge between the West European countries and the United States; and to head off steps that would put nuclear weapons at the disposal of NATO forces in Europe, particularly those which might be deployed in Germany. In neither case did Khrushchev have cause to be happy with the results achieved by Soviet diplomacy.

The Soviet campaign to promote a division between Europe and America was touched off in February 1957 by Dimitri T. Shepilov, then still enjoying his short-lived tenure as Soviet Foreign Minister. In a speech to the Supreme

---

[40] For accounts of Khrushchev's successful showdown with the "anti-party group" of Molotov, Malenkov, Kaganovich, and others, in which the support of Marshal Zhukov and the military was an important factor in Khrushchev's favor, see Rush, *The Rise of Khrushchev*, pp. 80–81; Conquest, *Power and Policy in the USSR*, pp. 330 ff.; Roger Pethybridge, *A Key to Soviet Politics: The Crisis of the Anti-Party Group* (New York: Frederick A. Praeger, Inc., 1962), pp. 89–90, 103–6, 128–32. See also T. W. Wolfe, *The Soviet Military Scene: Institutional and Defense Policy Considerations*, The RAND Corporation, RM-4913-PR, June 1966, pp. 18–19.

[41] See Mackintosh, *Strategy and Tactics*, pp. 192–97; Zbigniew Brzezinski, "The Organization of the Communist Camp," *World Politics* (January 1961): 183–86; Richard F. Staar, "The East European Alliance System," *U.S. Naval Institute Proceedings* (September 1964): 34–36; Meissner, *Der Warschauer Pakt*, pp. 27–80, 129 ff.

Soviet, followed by Soviet notes to the Western powers, Shepilov declared that the US stand during the Suez crisis and the promulgation of the "Eisenhower Doctrine" for the Middle East meant that the United States had set out to undermine traditional British and French interests.[42] Subsequently, a shower of Soviet notes to various European governments, including the Scandinavian countries, played on the theme of the danger to peace inherent in their relationships with the United States and suggested that they assert their "independence" from American "domination" and seek closer relations with the Soviet Union.[43] These suggestions, by and large, proved unconvincing to the recipients, in whose minds the harsh suppression of Hungarian efforts to throw off Soviet domination was still fresh.

Perhaps the failure of the Soviet wedge-driving tactics was best illustrated by the restoration of Anglo–American harmony at the March 1957 Bermuda Conference of Prime Minister Macmillan and President Eisenhower, and by the meeting of the NATO Council at Bonn, in May 1957, where important decisions were taken to confirm the unity of the Western alliance and to register its resolve to go ahead with measures for strengthening NATO's military potential. This is not to say that differences between the United States and the European members of the Western alliance, or among the Western European countries themselves, had ceased to be existent; it meant, simply, that Soviet efforts to inflame them in the post-Suez, post-Hungary environment had not been very successful. The European allies did not rise to the suggestion that they should seek their destiny in closer association with the Soviet Union; nor did the opposite tack that Khrushchev tried during this period, when he hinted to the United States that the two superpowers should deal directly with each other on basic international security issues, over the heads of the European countries,[44] yield much progress toward the goal of separating Europe from America.

The Soviet attempt to fan popular opposition to the nuclear arming of NATO forces in Europe fared no better. It ran the gamut from propaganda for cessation of nuclear testing[45] and proposals like that of the Rapacki Plan

[42] See "Questions of the International Situation and Foreign Policy of the Soviet Union; Report by USSR Minister of Foreign Affairs D. T. Shepilov," *Pravda*, February 13, 1957.

[43] See, for example, "Message from the Chairman of the USSR Council of Ministers N. A. Bulganin to the Federal Chancellor of the Federal German Republic Konrad Adenauer," *Pravda*, February 12, 1957; "Message from the Chairman of the USSR Council of Ministers N. A. Bulganin to H. C. Hansen, Prime Minister of Denmark," *Pravda*, March 31, 1957; "Message from the Chairman of the USSR Council of Ministers N. A. Bulganin to Prime Minister Einar Gerhardsen of Norway," *Pravda*, March 27, 1957; "Message from the Chairman of the USSR Council of Ministers N. A. Bulganin to Prime Minister Harold Macmillan of Great Britain," *Pravda*, April 24, 1957; "Message from the Chairman of the USSR Council of Ministers N. A. Bulganin to the Chairman of the French Republic Council of Ministers Guy Mollet," *Pravda*, May 21, 1957.

[44] See, for example, an interview with Turner Catledge of *The New York Times* in which Khrushchev stated that major world problems could best be settled by direct agreement between the two most powerful states, the Soviet Union and the United States. *New York Times*, May 11, 1957.

[45] This propaganda was turned on full force after the Soviet Union, during the March–August 1957 session of the UN Disarmament Commission Subcommittee in London, had revived earlier pro-

for an atom-free zone in Central Europe[46] to warnings that European governments which permitted nuclear bases on their territory took the risk of having
their countries destroyed in case of war.[47] Indeed, it was in this campaign
that the concept of European vulnerability to the "country-busting" potential
of nuclear weapons, which had been foreshadowed by the Soviet missile threats
against Britain and France in the Suez crisis, was explicitly introduced into
government notes and elite statements. General reminders that the Soviet
Union possessed weapons with which entire countries could be "wiped from
the face of the earth" were coupled with more specific warnings to designated
NATO countries, including West Germany and Great Britain, that they would
have "no chance of survival" in the event of war.[48] Despite this vigorous
Soviet campaign of persuasion and intimidation, however, the Western alliance went ahead with plans, which had been endorsed by the NATO Council
in May 1957,[49] to introduce American-controlled nuclear weapons into NATO
forces in Europe.

Khrushchev's Attempt to Turn Soviet Missile Technology to Political Advantage

The pressure tactics against Europe in the latter fifties were closely related to Khrushchev's efforts during this period to press Soviet successes in
missile and space technology into the service of Soviet politics. These efforts,
which began in earnest upon the heels of the Soviet Union's initial ICBM
and Sputnik launchings, in the autumn of 1957,[50] have in retrospect been

posals for cessation of nuclear tests. The formal Soviet proposal for an immediate cessation of tests
was introduced on June 14, 1957, although the Soviet delegate Valerian Zorin had brought the
question up in March as a riposte to the Eisenhower–Macmillan Bermuda statement that continued
nuclear testing was required for "the security of the free world." See *Documents on Disarmament,
1945–1959*, vol. 2, pp. 772–774, 791; Mackintosh, *Strategy and Tactics*, p. 200.

[46] The Rapacki Plan, first proposed by Poland on October 2, 1957, and offered in an amended
version on February 14, 1958, after Polish–Soviet consultation, called for a nuclear-free zone to
include the two Germanys, Poland, and Czechoslovakia. The amended version, drawn to meet
Western objections that Europe's security would still be threatened by the "large and widely
deployed military forces of the Soviet Union," included provisions for reduction of conventional
forces as well as denuclearization. See *Documents on Disarmament, 1945–1959*, vol. 2, pp. 889,
936, 944, 1023–25; Lincoln P. Bloomfield, Walter C. Clemens, Jr., and Franklyn Griffiths,
Khrushchev and the Arms Race: Soviet Interests in Arms Control and Disarmament, 1954–1964
(Cambridge, Mass.: M.I.T. Press, 1966), pp. 131, 148–51, 158.

[47] See, for example, Bulganin's comment in a letter to President Eisenhower in December 1957,
Documents on Disarmament, 1945–1959, vol. 2, p. 921.

[48] For various Soviet statements along this line in the fall of 1957 and 1958, see Horelick and
Rush, *Strategic Power*, pp. 48–49; Mackintosh, *Strategy and Tactics*, p. 207.

[49] In its communiqué of May 3, 1957, the NATO Council took note of a Soviet campaign to
"induce public opinion in various member countries to oppose the modernization of defense forces,
and to weaken the principle of collective security in NATO." One of the objects of this campaign,
the communiqué averred, "was to ensure for Soviet forces a monopoly of nuclear weapons on the
European continent." See Final Communiqué, in Paul E. Zinner, ed., *Documents on American
Foreign Relations, 1957* (New York: Harper & Brothers, 1958), pp. 73–75.

[50] The first report on successful testing of a Soviet ICBM was made on August 26, 1957. This
report was followed shortly by the placing into orbit of the first satellite, Sputnik I, on October 4,
1957. For a listing of all Soviet spacecraft launchings up to the beginning of 1966, see *Soviet*

interpreted by some analysts as a bold exercise in strategic bluffing.[51] Others have questioned this thesis, arguing that Khrushchev at best merely stumbled upon the idea of boasting of Soviet missile prowess after the West overreacted to its own fears of a "missile gap."[52] Whether Khrushchev deliberately set out to practice studied deception or whether he slipped into the habit of missile diplomacy by accident, the fact remains that he advanced strategic claims which, for a time, carried sufficient conviction to have a marked impact upon the foreign and domestic policies of many countries.

Relying partly on the visible and "authentic" evidence of Soviet technological accomplishment and partly upon implications of operational capabilities that could not readily be verified because of Soviet secrecy practices, Khrushchev sought to persuade the world that the Soviet Union had tipped the balance of strategic power in its favor by scoring a major breakthrough in the missile field. The detailed pattern of missile claims and related strategic threats through which Khrushchev wove an image of rapidly growing Soviet strategic power in the years 1957–61 need not be reconstructed here.[53] Suffice it to say that during this period the notion of a "missile gap" gained wide credence, reinforcing Khrushchev's assertions—which reached their peak in 1959 and early 1960—that the strategic balance had shifted to the advantage of the Soviet Union.[54]

Although later reassessments by Western officials indicated that the Soviet Union had actually deployed only "a handful" of ICBMs by 1961,[55] the

Space Programs, 1962–1965; Goals and Purposes, Achievements, Plans, and International Implications, Staff Report Prepared for the Use of the Committee on Aeronautical and Space Sciences, US Senate, December 30, 1966, 89th Congress, 2nd Session, Government Printing Office, Washington, D.C., 1966, pp. 529–33.

[51] This view, based on a searching and detailed analysis of Khrushchev's strategic claims and his attempts to trade upon them in the foreign policy arena, is argued in Horelick and Rush, *Strategic Power and Soviet Foreign Policy*.

[52] Among critical appraisals of the Horelick–Rush thesis, which argue on one basis or another that Khrushchev did not in fact undertake a studied exercise in strategic deception, see R. T. Rockingham Gill, *East Europe* (October 1966): 47; Elizabeth Young, "The Persistence of Some Myth or Other of Soviet Superiority," *Bulletin of the Atomic Scientists* (December 1966): 26–28.

[53] See Horelick and Rush, *Strategic Power*, pp. 35–102.

[54] At the Twenty-first Party Congress, in January 1959, Khrushchev offered the authoritative doctrinal assessment that a favorable shift in the balance of power had finally been achieved, as a result of which the danger of war had decreased and the triumph of socialism in the USSR was irreversible. In January 1960, in a memorable speech to the Supreme Soviet, he laid out his military policy guidelines based on the new strategic capabilities claimed for the Soviet Union. In between, he advanced various claims on the theme of the Soviet Union's improved strategic position. See Horelick and Rush, *Strategic Power*, pp. 54–60; *Khrushchev on the Shifting Balance of World Forces*, US Senate Document No. 57, Legislative Reference Service of the Library of Congress, Washington, D.C., September 1959. See also commentary in U.S. Editors' Analytical Introduction to V. D. Sokolovskii et al., *Soviet Military Strategy* (Englewood Cliffs, N.J.: Prentice–Hall, Inc., 1963), pp. 24–27.

[55] "Department of Defense Statement on U.S. Military Strength," April 14, 1964, cited by Horelick and Rush, *Strategic Power*, p‍. 37. The only specific figures ever given by Khrushchev for the number of Soviet long-range missiles were interpolated in a speech in East Germany on January 19, 1963. At that time, after withdrawal of Soviet medium-range missiles from Cuba, Khrushchev said the United States was still covered by 80 to 120 other missiles, by which he presumably meant ICBMs. If this statement properly conveyed the size of the Soviet ICBM force in 1963, it implies that the force had been considerably smaller when Khrushchev was claiming strategic superiority several years earlier.

impression current at the time of the missile-gap scare was that the Soviet Union had vaulted into a substantial lead in the build-up of ICBM forces. For example, a *New York Times* article in January 1959, based on interviews with informed sources, estimated that Soviet ICBM strength would reach 100 by 1960 and 500 the following year, compared with much smaller figures for the United States.[56] Other reports of the period likewise credited the Soviet Union with having gained a commanding headstart in the field of intercontinental ballistic missiles.[57] While Western strategic planners and decision-makers were by no means prone to equate such a "missile gap" with a general Soviet military ascendancy over the United States,[58] whose long-range bomber forces remained a potent element of strategic power, public opinion in the Western world tended to be much less discriminating. As a 1960 survey of several West European countries put it, "Popular opinion has seemingly concluded from Soviet boasts of superiority and American admissions of a temporary 'missile gap' that the United States is not only currently militarily inferior to the USSR but will continue to be so for the next decade or two as well."[59]

The first cracks in the edifice of Khrushchev's strategic claims appeared after the U-2 incident in May 1960. This event not only raised questions about the efficacy of Soviet defenses, which had failed to prevent previous flights, but also suggested that the Soviet Union would not have suffered such flights in silence had its strategic posture been as formidable as pictured. Moreover, the U-2 incident was a reminder that the United States had set itself the task of resolving the uncertainties about the Soviet missile deployment on which Khrushchev's strategic claims rested. That the intelligence resources of the West were adequate to this task became apparent when, in the fall of 1961, responsible American officials began publicly to express confidence that no missile gap existed after all and that the United States continued to enjoy a wide margin of strategic superiority.[60]

---

[56] *New York Times*, January 12, 1959. See also John F. Kennedy, *The Strategy of Peace*, Allan Nevins, ed. (New York: Harper & Brothers, 1960), p. 184.

[57] See, for example, Thomas R. Phillips, Brigadier General, USA (Ret.), "The Growing Missile Gap," *Reporter* (January 1959): 10–16; interview with Wing Commander Asher Lee, RAF, "To Set You Straight on Russia's Rockets," *U.S. News and World Report*, July 20, 1959, pp. 46–49; General Pierre Gallois, "The Space Race," *Réalités* (English edition), no. 110 (January 1960): 10–13.

[58] See, for example, commentary by Dr. Herbert F. York and Admiral Arleigh Burke, respectively, in *U.S. News and World Report*, September 28, 1959, pp. 64–66, and no. 8, February 22, 1960, pp. 45–47.

[59] *Free World Views of the US–USSR Power Balance*, United States Information Agency, R-54-60, August 29, 1960, p. 5, cited in Horelick and Rush, *Strategic Power*, p. 64. Figures from the opinion surveys conducted by USIA are also given by Horelick and Rush, showing that, in four of the five European countries polled, a heavy percentage thought that the USSR was ahead in relative military strength.

[60] A speech by Deputy Defense Secretary Roswell Gilpatric on October 21, 1961, was the first in what turned out to be a series of assurances by high-ranking US spokesmen that, as a result of both improved intelligence and the acceleration of the United States' own missile programs, the strategic balance could still be confidently understood to favor the United States. About a month earlier, some press reports had begun to hint at revised estimates of the Soviet missile inventory.

As the record of Khrushchev's exercise in missile boasting indicates, the assurance with which he advanced claims of Soviet superiority declined perceptibly after the U-2 affair and the public references of US officials to revised estimates of the Soviet missile posture.[61] Khrushchev's confidence in the political efficacy of the Soviet strategic posture no doubt was shaken also by his failure to force the West out of Berlin in the renewed crisis there in the summer of 1961, a matter we shall come to presently. By late 1961 and early 1962, he and other Soviet spokesmen were on the defensive, offering as a new formula the idea of "strategic parity," with the suggestion that "equal forces" should be translated politically into "equal rights and opportunities."[62] This more circumspect treatment of US strategic capabilities was matched by Khrushchev's increasing tendency to trim back doctrinaire Marxist–Leninist assertions of Communist victory in the event of war. Indeed, from mid-1960 on—roughly the time that the shock of the U-2 episode made itself felt—Khrushchev had begun to revise the Soviet declaratory stand on the consequences of a nuclear war: He no longer insisted that it would result in the collapse of the capitalist order only, but admitted that it would exact a fearful toll on both sides.[63] He had thus come back full circle to Malenkov's position of 1953, to which at the time he had been opposed.

Khrushchev's strategic claims in the four years from 1957 to 1961 not only failed in the end to convince his adversaries that the Soviet Union had gained the upper hand in global military power; they also had what from Khrushchev's viewpoint was the unwelcome effect of stimulating the United States to throw its immense resources more fully than before into the missile race. The question therefore arises: Why did Khrushchev not take more effective steps to translate early Soviet advantages in missile technology into an operational ICBM force large enough to give substance to Soviet claims, or, failing this, why did he persist in advancing such claims prematurely?

See *New York Times*, October 21, 1961; Joseph Alsop in *Washington Post*, September 25, 1961. For the best account of steps leading to official American assessments of the strategic balance in 1961, see William W. Kaufmann, *The McNamara Strategy* (New York: Harper & Row, Inc., 1964), pp. 38–41, 49–50, 65–66, 108–9, 253–55.

61 See Horelick and Rush, *Strategic Power*, pp. 72–86.

62 Khrushchev in July 1961 and Marshal Malinovskii in January 1962 were among the expositors of the new formula of strategic parity, to be equated with equal political leverage. The Soviet insistence on "equal" political returns from the respective strategic postures of the two sides can be regarded as a form of Soviet protest against Western refusal to budge on the Berlin issue. *Pravda*, July 9, 1961, January 25, 1962. See also discussion in Horelick and Rush, *Strategic Power*, pp. 87–98.

63 The beginning of Khrushchev's shift in public utterances to the theme of the mutual destructiveness of nuclear war goes back to his speech at the UN General Assembly in September 1959, but he began to pay it more explicit attention in statements in July and October 1960, at the time that one of his favored military publicists, Major General Nikolai A. Talenskii, was saying in various publications that a nuclear war "will lead to such an increase in human losses on both sides that its consequences for the human race can be catastrophic," and that "nuclear-missile war is not only extremely dangerous to the party under attack but is also suicidal for the aggressor." See "An Irrefutable Conclusion Drawn from History," *Kommunist*, no. 7 (May 1960): 37; "Modern War: Its Nature and Consequences," *Mezhdunarodnaia zhizn'*, no. 10 (October 1960): 37. See also discussion in Horelick and Rush, *Strategic Power*, pp. 78–79.

On the first point, technical and operational problems relating to the Soviet Union's early-generation ICBMs, which will be discussed in a subsequent chapter, were probably in part responsible for the slow pace of the initial ICBM build-up, perhaps along with economic factors.

The second point poses a more subtle set of considerations. Khrushchev at first may have thought only that Soviet advances in missile-space technology offered opportunities for political exploitation that it would be wasteful to pass up, such as the chance to weaken the confidence of America's European allies in US pledges to protect them. His natural exuberance, combined with his impatience to bring the top leaders of the West to a new summit meeting which would help to confirm his own status as the head of a great power strong enough to shape the settlement of major international issues, also may have led Khrushchev to offer an inflated picture of the Soviet Union's strategic power position. Later, he may himself have fallen victim, in a sense, to the psychology of the missile gap, coming to believe that the self-confidence of the Western world was so shaken that a vigorous missile diplomacy together with "Bolshevik fortitude" would precipitate a general political retreat by the West.

Whatever his motivations may have been, the key to Khrushchev's persistent attempts to derive political advantage from his strategic claims of the 1957–61 period undoubtedly lay in his estimate of the danger of war. On this score, despite occasional tendentious charges that the West was preparing for a "preventive" attack against the Soviet camp, Khrushchev apparently felt that the likelihood of war had greatly declined. In particular, he seems to have thought it quite unlikely that the United States would start a war that would put his claims to the test.[64] The Hungarian experience of 1956, when, despite some prior lip service to the doctrine of "rollback," the United States displayed its disinclination to make Hungary a *casus belli,* may have helped to confirm this belief. Subsequent situations in which Soviet missile threats were brandished—for example, the Turkish–Syrian tension in October 1957 and the Quemoy Straits crisis of August–September 1958—also passed without eliciting exceptionally dangerous reactions from Western leaders, whose "responsible" behavior thus served to reassure Khrushchev both that Soviet deterrence was working and that he was keeping within safe limits.[65] Further-

[64] Mackintosh, *Strategy and Tactics,* p. 277; Horelick and Rush, *Strategic Power,* p. 106; Wolfe, *Soviet Strategy at the Crossroads,* pp. 117, 287, fn. 27. See also Malcolm Mackintosh, "Three Détentes: 1955–1964," in Eleanor Lansing Dulles and Robert Dickson Crane, eds., *Détente: Cold War Strategies in Transition* (New York: Frederick A. Praeger, Inc., 1965), p. 109.

[65] The somewhat ambiguous character of the backing which Khrushchev offered to Communist China in the Quemoy Straits crisis of 1958 suggests that Khrushchev did not feel he was courting a high risk of war. Although Khrushchev warned President Eisenhower on September 18, 1958, that the Soviet Union would retaliate with nuclear weapons in the event of a US nuclear attack against China, this warning—according to subsequent charges by Peking—was merely a gesture, which came only after it was clear "that there was no possibility that a nuclear war would break out." See "Statement by Spokesman of the Chinese Government: A Comment on Soviet Government's Statement of August 21," September 1, 1963, in *Peking Review,* no. 36, September 6, 1963, p. 13.

more, Khrushchev's Camp David discussions with President Eisenhower, in 1959, seem to have persuaded him that the United States harbored no designs for a military attack on the Soviet Union. As for the possibility that war might arise from the acts of "irresponsible" leaders or "madmen"—a danger to which Khrushchev occasionally alluded[66]—he may have felt that the deterrence of irrational behavior could be served as well by the image of formidable Soviet retaliatory power as by its substance, and more cheaply by the former.

That some of Khrushchev's associates, and particularly the military leadership, entertained misgivings about the position in which the Soviet Union would find itself if deterrence should break down for one reason or another is amply documented, as we shall see. Khrushchev himself, however, evidently felt that there was little chance of his bluff being called, or, if it were, that he could control the ensuing risk of war. In this, events proved him right. Where Khrushchev erred most conspicuously in his use of missile diplomacy was in thinking that it would be easier to wrest major concessions from the West than actually proved to be the case—or, as Horelick and Rush have put it, he found that the Western "threshold of concession" was too high to be overcome without creating situations in which the risk of war might indeed get beyond control.[67]

The Soviet Campaign against Berlin, 1958–61

In Europe, the case of Berlin stands as the prime example of the miscarriage of Khrushchev's belief that the forbidding image of Soviet strategic power, together with local pressures, would bring the West to concede positions previously impervious to Soviet diplomatic assault. Following the failure of Soviet policy in 1957 and early 1958 to forestall the nuclear arming of NATO and to win acceptance for Rapacki-type denuclearization proposals, as well as the Soviet Union's continued inability to obtain Western recognition of the East German Communist regime, Khrushchev evidently decided to make Berlin the specific target[68] of his efforts to convert the successes of Soviet technology into meaningful political gains.[69]

Precisely what gains Khrushchev may have hoped to achieve by his campaign against Berlin remains a matter of surmise. His most likely objective seems to have been to induce the Western powers to yield their rights in

[66] For example, in connection with his November 1958 ultimatum on Berlin, and in his January 1960 speech to the Supreme Soviet, *Pravda*, January 15, 1960.

[67] Horelick and Rush, *Strategic Power*, p. 115.

[68] Khrushchev's decision to launch a political offensive against Berlin may have been influenced by the state of Sino–Soviet relations as well as by European policy considerations. In the aftermath of Khrushchev's visit to Peking in August 1958 and the Quemoy Straits crisis in September, Peking may have raised new questions as to Khrushchev's staunchness as a Communist leader, adding another reason for him to demonstrate that he could be tough toward the West.

[69] See Jean Edward Smith, *The Defense of Berlin* (Baltimore, Md.: The Johns Hopkins Press, 1963), pp. 157, 165. This work furnishes a thorough account of Khrushchev's campaign against Berlin, as well as of earlier Soviet efforts under Stalin to force the West from Berlin.

Berlin without offering military resistance. Western surrender of a position as pivotal as West Berlin would doubtless have opened up a number of attractive prospects from Khrushchev's viewpoint; they included its creating an acute sense of insecurity and betrayal in West Germany while helping to repair the instability of the East German regime; lending new weight to Soviet influence over Central European affairs; slowing down the momentum of economic and defense integration in Western Europe; undermining European confidence in the American commitment; and, not least, demonstrating the emergence of a new balance of power, under which the West would have to be prepared to make further concessions on disputed issues.[70]

Onset of the Berlin Crisis

The formal launching of Khrushchev's campaign against Berlin, which was preceded by several months of local harassment and increased diplomatic pressures for a summit conference,[71] came on November 27, 1958, when the Soviet Union laid down a six-month deadline for radical changes in the four-power status of Berlin that would end the occupation rights of the Western powers and transform West Berlin into a "demilitarized free city."[72] This demand, accompanied by the threat that the Soviet Union was prepared to seek an independent solution of the Berlin problem, precipitated a crisis that was to endure at varying degrees of intensity for the next four years.

Needless to say, Soviet accounts of the origin and development of the Berlin crisis differ markedly from Western views of the same events. As treated in two recent Soviet studies,[73] published since the ouster of Khrushchev, the crisis arose because the West refused to recognize the "existence of two sovereign states" in Germany and insisted on maintaining West Berlin as an "advanced post of NATO" for conducting activities intended to "undermine the position of the GDR."[74] The Soviet note of November 27, 1958, as pictured in these works was a "compromise proposal" which the Western powers then "twisted" around, interpreting it as an ultimatum and declaring that they were prepared to hold Berlin by armed force.[75] Thereafter, the "feverish military preparations" of the West created "a situation of extreme tension," making

[70] For an excellent analysis of Soviet objectives and interests in Europe, as suggested by Soviet behavior in the Berlin crisis, see James L. Richardson, *Germany and the Atlantic Alliance: The Interaction of Strategy and Politics* (Cambridge, Mass.: Harvard University Press, 1966), pp. 301–13.

[71] Smith, *The Defense of Berlin*, pp. 155–62.

[72] The Soviet demands were presented in a speech by Khrushchev on November 10, 1958, and in subsequent diplomatic notes sent to the Western powers on November 27. The Soviets called for establishment of a "demilitarized free city" of West Berlin within six months, and stipulated that, if the Western powers turned down the Soviet proposal, the Soviet Union would unilaterally act to restore full sovereignty to the East German government over land, water, and air, which would mean giving it control over access to Berlin. For Khrushchev's speech of November 10 and the Soviet note of November 27, see *Documents on Germany*, pp. 339–43, 348–63. See also *The Soviet Note on Berlin: An Analysis*, Department of State Publication No. 6757, Washington, D.C., January 1959.

[73] The Soviet accounts in question are to be found in Inozemtsev, *Mezhdunarodnye otnosheniia*, vol. 3, pp. 198–211; and Nikolaev, *Politika v germanskom voprose*, pp. 268–95.

[74] Inozemtsev, *Mezhdunarodnye otnosheniia*, pp. 198–99.

[75] Ibid., p. 204; Nikolaev, *Politika v germanskom voprose*, pp. 269–73.

it necessary for the Soviet Union and its Warsaw Pact partners to adopt measures which "successfully repulsed the imperialist attacks."[76] Although blaming the West for provoking and keeping alive the long crisis, the Soviet accounts nevertheless admit that it was "thanks to the Soviet proposal" of November 1958 that "the German question again became the focus of international politics."[77] We shall return to these Soviet versions of the Berlin crisis later; for the moment, let us pick up the situation as it developed in 1959.

The first phase of the crisis subsided in 1959 after the three Western governments, despite differences among themselves over tactics for meeting the Soviet challenge to Berlin,[78] had made clear that the proposed Soviet solution of the Berlin problem was unacceptable[79]—a position emphatically endorsed by the people of West Berlin themselves in the city's elections in December 1958.[80] Although by March 1959 Khrushchev was obliged to withdraw his six-month ultimatum,[81] he did not come away altogether empty-handed. Among other things, the crisis helped to bring about the Foreign Ministers Conference in the spring and summer of 1959, at which the issues of Germany and European security were reopened and agreement was reached on a Big Four summit meeting in May 1960.[82]

The draft treaty on Germany proposed by the Soviet Union at the Geneva Foreign Ministers Conference was patently designed to open West Germany to Communist penetration while barring Western influence in East Germany. Among its provisions were the following: (1) All "revanchist and revisionist" activities in West Germany were to be banned, but the Communist party and associated groups were to enjoy "unhampered activity" there; (2) no all-German elections were to be held, and in any "confederation" formed between West and East Germany both sides were to have "equal" representation, despite a three-to-one population ratio in favor of West Germany; (3) any future steps toward reunification could be undertaken only by negotiation between the separate German governments; (4) Berlin was to become a "free city," with foreign troops to be withdrawn within an agreed time period.[83]

---

[76] Inozemtsev, *Mezhdunarodnye otnosheniia*, pp. 198, 209; Nikolaev, *Politika v germanskom voprose*, p. 288.

[77] Inozemtsev, *Mezhdunarodnye otnosheniia*, p. 205.

[78] For a discussion of Western differences over handling of the Berlin situation and their resolution, see Richardson, *Germany and the Atlantic Alliance*, pp. 314–36.

[79] For a penetrating study of the first phase of the crisis precipitated by Khrushchev's speech of November 10, 1958, see Hans Speier, *Divided Berlin: The Anatomy of Soviet Political Blackmail* (New York: Frederick A. Praeger, Inc., 1961). See also Richardson, *Germany and the Atlantic Alliance*, pp. 264–71; Smith, *The Defense of Berlin*, pp. 181–98; Eleanor Lansing Dulles, "Berlin —Barometer of Tension," in Dulles and Crane, *Détente*, pp. 121–37.

[80] In these elections, the Communists were overwhelmingly rejected, the SED receiving less than 2 per cent of more than 1,700,000 ballots cast, and Major Willy Brandt was returned to office as a result. See Smith, *The Defense of Berlin*, pp. 187–88.

[81] Soviet retreat from the six-month ultimatum began with a Soviet note of March 2, 1959, and speeches by Khrushchev in East Germany on March 7 and 9. See *Documents on Germany*, pp. 414–36.

[82] A full documentary record of the Geneva Foreign Ministers' Conference of May 11– August 5, 1959, may be found in *Documents on Germany*, pp. 456–83.

[83] For a text of the Soviet draft treaty, see *Department of State Bulletin*, March 9, 1959, pp. 337–43.

The first phase of the Berlin crisis also proved useful to Khrushchev by boosting his prestige and helping to pave the way for his much-publicized visit to the United States and his Camp David meeting with President Eisenhower in the autumn of 1959. At Camp David, Khrushchev obtained Eisenhower's agreement to reopening negotiations on Berlin the following year,[84] along with the President's acquiescence in the Soviet contention that the Berlin situation was "abnormal"—an admission which may have led Khrushchev to believe that he would be able to exact major concessions in a new round of negotiations.[85] In the months following Khrushchev's American visit, US–Soviet relations were conducted in the relatively amicable atmosphere of what was called the "spirit of Camp David."

During this period of partial détente, the Ten-Nation Disarmament Conference was convened in Geneva to take up new proposals for General and Complete Disarmament (GCD), the first of which had been presented by Khrushchev at the United Nations General Assembly in September 1959,[86] and preparations were completed for the Paris summit meeting at which Khrushchev was expected to reopen the question of a Berlin settlement. However, this interlude of comparative calm was shattered in early May 1960 by the U-2 incident, after which the summit parley in Paris was broken off by Khrushchev, on May 18, without having led to any further top-level consideration of the Berlin problem. For all practical purposes, therefore, Soviet diplomacy in the period of the "Camp David spirit" produced no more in the way of tangible Western concessions on Berlin than had the preceding period of Soviet pressures.

From the break-up of the Paris meeting to the following spring, a time in which a new American administration came into office, the Berlin issue remained outwardly in a relatively quiescent phase, marked less by direct Soviet pressures against the Western position than by East German harassments, which the Soviet Union presumably could call off if they threatened to get out of hand.[87] That Khrushchev had not given up the idea of forcing the West to abandon its position in Berlin was evident, however, in January 1961, when he said that the Western powers must realize that ". . . sooner or later the occupation regime in this city will come to an end. It is necessary step by step to continue bringing the aggressive imperialist circles to their senses, to compel them to reckon with the real situation. If they balk, we will take decisive measures."[88]

[84] Documents on Germany, pp. 585–86; New York Times, September 28, 29, 1959.

[85] For a discussion of this aspect of the Camp David meeting, see Smith, The Defense of Berlin, pp. 210–11; Richardson, Germany and the Atlantic Alliance, pp. 272–73. For a general analysis of the negotiating technique of "normalizing" an acknowledged situation of "abnormality," which is highly relevant to Khrushchev's approach to the Berlin problem, see Fred C. Iklé, How Nations Negotiate (New York: Harper & Row, Inc., 1964), pp. 28–33.

[86] New York Times, September 19, 1959.

[87] See Smith, The Defense of Berlin, pp. 222–29; Richardson, Germany and the Atlantic Alliance, pp. 278–79.

[88] This statement was made in Khrushchev's January 1961 report on a conference of world Communist parties in Moscow in November 1960. See "For New Victories of the World Communist Movement," Kommunist, no. 1 (January 1961): 22.

Among factors which apparently persuaded Khrushchev that a new attempt to force a Berlin settlement was in order were internal developments in East Germany, where enforced collectivization and intensified political controls over the population had resulted in a stepped-up flow of refugees to the West.[89] Also, as Khrushchev had an opportunity to see the new American administration in action, its setback after the Bay of Pigs incident, in the spring of 1961, may have strengthened his belief that the time was ripe for a new squeeze on Berlin.[90]

Second Phase of the Berlin Crisis, 1961

After meeting with the new American President, John F. Kennedy, in Vienna in June 1961 and presenting him there with a fresh statement of Soviet proposals on Germany and Berlin,[91] Khrushchev resumed the Soviet campaign against the Western position in Berlin, setting a new deadline for a settlement by the end of the year. This deadline was laid down in a major television speech, on June 15, in which Khrushchev reported on the Vienna meeting. He wanted everyone to understand "correctly," he said, that "the conclusion of a peace treaty with Germany cannot be put off any longer; a peace settlement in Europe must be attained this year." In another speech, six days later, he reaffirmed the Soviet position that a separate peace treaty would be signed with East Germany by the end of the year if the West refused to accept an all-German treaty.[92]

The renewal of the Berlin crisis in mid-1961 brought a new surge of tension as the exodus of refugees from East Germany swelled to record proportions of 20,000 to 30,000 per month. As during the confrontation of 1958–59, when he had threatened that Soviet rockets would "fly automatically" if the West sent tanks to Berlin to maintain its position there by force,[93] Khrushchev again invoked the spectre of possible war.[94] In return, President Kennedy pledged in an address on July 25 that, if necessary, the United States would fight over Berlin; with regard to the alleged untenability of the Western

---

[89] See Philip Windsor, *City on Leave: A History of Berlin, 1945–1962* (New York: Frederick A. Praeger, Inc., 1963), pp. 221–23.

[90] See Richardson, *Germany and the Atlantic Alliance*, p. 279.

[91] The *aide-mémoire* handed to President Kennedy at Vienna on June 4, 1961, was published a week later in the Soviet press. In it, the Soviet government demanded the speedy conclusion of a German peace treaty and the conversion of West Berlin into a "free city" with termination of Western occupation and access rights. Complete text in *Pravda*, June 11, 1961; see also *Documents on Germany*, pp. 642–45. The *aide-mémoire* itself contained no time deadline, which was laid down by Khrushchev shortly after the Vienna meeting. Incidentally, the previously-cited Soviet accounts of the Berlin crisis, written after Khrushchev fell into political limbo, contain no personal mention of Khrushchev or of his Vienna meeting with Kennedy.

[92] *Pravda*, June 16 and 22, 1961.

[93] See Khrushchev's remarks to Averell Harriman during an interview on June 23, 1959, as reported by Harriman in *Life*, July 13, 1959, p. 33.

[94] See, for example, Khrushchev's speech of June 21, in which those whom he accused of wishing to make the Berlin question a "test of strength" were warned that "if you really threaten us with war, we do not fear such a threat; if you unleash a war, this will mean suicide for you." *Pravda*, June 22, 1961. See also James Reston's account of the Khrushchev–Kennedy meeting in Vienna, where, as Reston put it, "Khrushchev had bullied [the President] and threatened him with war over Berlin." *New York Times Magazine*, November 15, 1964, p. 126.

military position in Berlin, he observed that "any dangerous spot is tenable
if men—brave men—will make it so."[95]

During the mounting crisis of 1961, both sides engaged in a series of interacting moves to increase their military readiness and to signal their determination to the other party. Among measures taken by the United States and its
NATO allies were: President Kennedy's announcement on May 25 of a $3.4
billion increase in defense expenditures; his elaboration, on July 25, of a
series of steps to strengthen US conventional capabilities and to improve the
US strategic posture, including a 225,000-man increase in the armed forces,
authorization to call up additional reserves, procurement of non-nuclear matériel, retention in service of B-47 bombers earmarked for retirement, and upgrading of the alert status of the strategic bomber forces; the dispatch in
August, following the raising of the Berlin Wall, of a US army battle group
to Berlin and of modest French and British reinforcements to West Germany;
Vice President Johnson's demonstrative visit to Berlin, on August 18, and
General Lucius Clay's temporary resumption of command there shortly afterward; the further call-up of US reserves and dispatch of additional troops
and tactical aircraft to Europe in September; and the staging of two NATO
exercises (Check Mate I and II) in Central Europe and the Mediterranean
area in the same month.[96]

On the Soviet side, the measures taken included: the announcement on
July 8, 1961, of a 3.1 billion ruble increase in the defense budget and suspension of the troop-cut program which Khrushchev had inaugurated in January 1960; Marshal Ivan S. Konev's recall from retirement, on August 10,
to take command of Soviet forces in Germany; the closing off of East Berlin
with the start of the Wall on August 13; the staging, in mid-August, of a
field exercise featuring the simulated use of tactical nuclear weapons, to which
foreign military attachés in Moscow were invited; the publication, on August
30, of a decree retaining in service conscripts due for annual release; the
resumption of nuclear testing on September 1 with a test series in the Arctic,
including a much-publicized "supermegaton" weapon; the first publicly announced meeting of Warsaw Pact defense ministers in Moscow on September
8–9; and, following this, in early October, the first large-scale joint Warsaw
Pact field maneuvers in which Soviet, Polish, East German, and Czechoslovak
forces participated.

It is a matter of some interest that, from all these measures, two have
been singled out in retrospective Soviet accounts of the Berlin crisis as having
had the most significant effect on its outcome. The first was the Soviet Union's
Arctic test series involving supermegaton weapons. It was said to have
demonstrated graphically that the "military superiority" that the West "still

[95] "Report to the Nation on the Berlin Crisis by President Kennedy, July 25, 1961," *Documents
on Germany*, pp. 694–701.

[96] For fuller accounts of the politico-military measures taken by the contending sides during the
1961 phase of the Berlin crisis, see Smith, *The Defense of Berlin*, pp. 235–325; Richardson,
Germany and the Atlantic Alliance, pp. 282–90; Garthoff, *Soviet Military Policy*, pp. 115–20.

possessed in the middle fifties" no longer held good, and thus to have had a "sobering effect" on the Western leaders, who did not dare "to risk unleashing a military conflict with the Soviet Union in the autumn of 1961" and were obliged instead to seek a peaceful way out of the crisis through talks with the Soviet Union. The second measure hailed as a significant stroke for the Communist side was the erection of the Berlin Wall, said to have "demonstrated the changed relationship of forces in Germany and the growth of the international authority and prestige of the GDR."[97]

No doubt, sealing off of East Berlin on August 13 did represent the high point of the Berlin confrontation of 1961. Although the Wall was essentially a defensive device to relieve the acute refugee problem of the GDR, and one which subsequently came to be regarded by many on both sides as a stabilizing factor,[98] at the time it had the character of a provocative move that could have touched off a military clash had the Western powers chosen to challenge it forcibly. What the Soviet response in such a case would actually have been remains, of course, an unanswerable question. It is worth noting, however, that the Soviet Union's concern over a possible Western military reaction to the fait accompli of the Berlin Wall seems to have remained acute for at least two months. Between mid-August and about mid-October of 1961, a period during which Soviet military demonstrations reached their peak, many of the top Soviet military leaders joined in a concerted speech-making campaign, stressing such themes as the increased danger of "imperialist attack" and measures being taken by the Soviet Union and its Warsaw Pact partners to ensure against being caught unprepared as in 1941. Besides its intended deterrent effect upon the West, this campaign appears to have had the internal function of conditioning the people for a period of heightened danger while reassuring them that the Soviet armed forces were prepared to cope with any situation.

Whether the private views of the Soviet military were as confident as their public utterances is not so clear. In this connection, the behind-the-scenes "revelations" of Colonel Oleg V. Penkovskiy, since given some support by Soviet charges that Khrushchev's "subjective" military judgments had endangered the country's security, are of some interest. According to Penkovskiy, Khrushchev was prepared to take military action if "anything unfortunate" should occur after the signing of a German peace treaty or the building of the Wall, but the private sentiment in the higher circles of the military was that Khrushchev was taking a "big risk," and that his Berlin moves might involve the Soviet Union in a major war for which it was not ready.[99]

---

[97] Nikolaev, *Politika v germanskom voprose*, pp. 290, 293–94; Inozemtsev, *Mezhdunarodnye otnosheniia*, p. 211.

[98] For an argument contesting the view that the Berlin Wall had a stabilizing effect, see Melvin Croan, "Bonn and Pankow: Intra-German Politics," *Survey* (April 1968): 78–80.

[99] *The Penkovskiy Papers*, Introduction and Commentary by Frank Gibney, translated by Peter Deriabin (Garden City, N.Y.: Doubleday and Company, Inc., 1965), pp. 207, 220, 244. In the present writer's opinion, offered elsewhere in this study and in separate commentary (e.g., his review of *The Penkovskiy Papers* in *Journal of Modern History* [June 1966], pp. 236–38),

Perhaps the closest that things came to a military test was a day-long confrontation of American and Soviet tanks on opposite sides of a Berlin checkpoint, on October 27, but by that time the crisis had already begun to subside. In fact, the collapse of the 1961 Soviet campaign against Berlin had been signaled some days earlier, on October 17, when Khrushchev, in his keynote speech to the Twenty-second Party Congress, lifted the deadline he had imposed in June for a German peace treaty. Although he did not abandon his professed intention to conclude a German peace treaty "with or without the Western powers," he now said that, if the West showed a readiness to settle the German problem, he would "not in that case absolutely insist on signing the peace treaty before December 31, 1961"—thereby in effect taking himself off the hook with regard to the deadline.[100]

Thereafter, despite such desultory Soviet pressures as the harassment of commercial air traffic in the Berlin air corridor in early 1962, Khrushchev's second campaign against Berlin gradually petered out.[101] Once again he had tried, and failed, to force the Western powers into a peace treaty that would have terminated their presence in Berlin and wrung from them recognition of the Communist regime in East Germany. This failure was doubtless one of the factors that led to Khrushchev's next and most spectacular venture in missile diplomacy, a year later in Cuba.[102]

Berlin and the Cuban Missile Crisis of October 1962

By way of demonstrating that the problems of European security cannot be readily isolated from conflicts occurring in other parts of the world, we might say that the campaign which Khrushchev launched against Berlin in November 1958 was finally halted in Cuba in October 1962. Although it

---

Khrushchev's actual performance during the various crises in which he was an actor does not bear out the allegation of his propensity to take large risks. Rather, while he was prone to get into ticklish situations, his conduct became basically cautious when the risks were manifestly great.

[100] *Pravda*, October 18, 1961.

[101] Smith, *The Defense of Berlin*, pp. 330–37. See also George Bailey, "The Gentle Erosion of Berlin," *Reporter*, April 26, 1962, pp. 15–19.

[102] During the months of 1962 preceding the Cuban crisis in October, the problem of Berlin continued to receive Soviet attention, although deadlines for settlement were no longer laid down. In April, Khrushchev told Gardner Cowles that he was "optimistic" about the prospects of an understanding on Berlin (*Pravda*, April 27, 1962). The following month, however, an article in *Pravda* (May 3, 1962) charged that the West was abandoning a "flexible" policy on Berlin; it cited President Kennedy's comment on the prospect of Western resort to nuclear weapons in the event of a massive Soviet attack on Europe (*Saturday Evening Post*, March 31, 1962, p. 11) as an attempt to apply pressure on the Soviet Union with regard to Berlin. In June, during a trip to Rumania and upon return to Moscow, Khrushchev again threatened to conclude a separate peace treaty with East Germany and demanded withdrawal of Tripartite troops (*Pravda*, June 20 and 26, 1962). In July, Khrushchev proposed that troops from small countries of NATO and the Warsaw Pact should replace the occupation forces of the Tripartite powers (*Pravda*, July 11, 1962); and in August the Soviet Union announced that it had "abolished" the post of Soviet military commandant in Berlin as a move to end four-power "co-operation" (*Pravda*, August 23, 1962). These various Soviet pronouncements served to keep alive the idea during early and mid-1962 that a new crisis over Berlin might be impending.

is unnecessary for our purposes to dwell in detail upon the circumstances attending the Cuban missile episode,[103] several points should be made concerning its place in Khrushchev's search for a solution to the Berlin impasse and other important problems confronting him in the early sixties.

The decision to deploy a force of Soviet-manned missiles to Cuba, evidently taken sometime in the spring of 1962, appears to have resulted mainly from the cumulative frustrations of policy setbacks suffered by Khrushchev during the previous three or four years. They included not only the failure of Soviet pressure tactics to obtain concessions from the West on such specific pivotal issues as Berlin but also the deflation of Khrushchev's hopes that a diplomacy backed by the exploits of Soviet missile and space technology would weaken the resolution of the Western alliance and erode its confidence in the protective commitments of the United States. On the contrary, Khrushchev found that by early 1962 the parallel collapse of his Berlin offensive and of the "missile-gap" myth was serving to reinforce the assurances of American officials that the West still enjoyed an ample margin of strategic superiority. Moreover, he was now in the increasingly uncomfortable position of knowing what his adversaries only suspected and what some of his own military men had feared: namely, that he had been overambitious in trying to gain more political mileage from Soviet missiles than the actual strategic balance warranted. Beyond this, of course, Khrushchev was confronted in early 1962 by growing criticism of his strategic leadership from the Chinese wing of the world Communist movement,[104] and in Cuba itself Castro was pressing for some form of tangible Soviet commitment to the defense of the first Communist regime to be established in the Western Hemisphere.[105]

All of these factors evidently contributed in some measure to Khrushchev's belief that the covert emplacement of Soviet missiles in Cuba, followed by their unveiling at an appropriate moment, perhaps in connection with a new

[103] Among detailed accounts of the Cuban missile episode, see Arnold L. Horelick, "The Cuban Missile Crisis: An Analysis of Soviet Behavior and Calculations," *World Politics* (April 1964): 363–89; Roger Hilsman, "The Cuban Crisis: How Close We Were to War," *Look*, August 25, 1964, pp. 17–21; Elie Abel, *The Missile Crisis* (Philadelphia, Pa.: J. B. Lippincott Company, 1966); Theodore C. Sorenson, *Kennedy* (New York: Harper & Row, Inc., 1965), pp. 667–718. See also Horelick and Rush, *Strategic Power*, pp. 126–56.

[104] Following Khrushchev's open attack on the Albanian Communist leadership at the Twenty-second Party Congress, in October 1961, which was in part an attempt to force the Chinese to give up their opposition to Soviet policy, Peking's protests against Khrushchev had begun to take on a sharper character. See William E. Griffith, "Albania: An Outcast's Defiance," *Problems of Communism* (May–June 1962): 3. See also Thomas W. Wolfe, *The Soviet Union and the Sino-Soviet Dispute*, The RAND Corporation, P-3203, August 1965, pp. 12–26.

[105] Although on two occasions Castro has been publicly promised the "protection" provided by Soviet-based ICBMs (see Khrushchev speech, *Pravda*, July 9, 1960, and Soviet government statement on Cuba, *Pravda*, September 11, 1962), Cuba had not been admitted to the Warsaw Pact, and in the absence of this and any other formal Soviet commitment to Cuba's defense, Castro may have been looking for a way to nail down Soviet backing of his regime. Whether it was Castro or Khrushchev who took the initiative in proposing the emplacement of medium-range Soviet missiles in Cuba has never been made clear, but the move undoubtedly suited Castro's need for a more tangible Soviet commitment.

round of negotiations on Berlin,[106] would dramatically strengthen the Soviet Union's position and repair his own prestige.

The Cuban ploy, it should be noted, differed in at least one important respect from Khrushchev's earlier ventures in missile diplomacy, which had depended essentially upon making inflated Soviet strategic claims credible to the West.[107] The force of some forty MRBM and IRBM launchers dispatched to Cuba[108] would have narrowed in one quick stroke the actual margin of the US advantage in strategic forces, for it would have had the effect, as Raymond Garthoff has pointed out, of transforming readily available missiles of 1,100- to 2,200-mile range into "ersatz" intercontinental missiles.[109] In terms of the Soviet Union's then-existing first-strike salvo capability against targets in the United States, this would have meant an increase of almost 50 per cent.[110]

Although, in a strictly military sense, the initial batch of Soviet missiles deployed to Cuba was insufficient to reverse the strategic balance and to put the Soviet Union in a position where it could with impunity contemplate a first strike against the United States, the additional threat posed by these missiles was certainly calculated to act as a powerful new brake upon US freedom of action. Had installation of the initial missile sites at the southern flank of the United States gone without challenge, there would have been a prospect of increasing their numbers to degrade still further the American strategic posture. Whatever the ultimate effect of the Cuban missile deployment might have been militarily, however, it can hardly be doubted, as President Kennedy was to observe later, that it "would have politically changed the balance of power."[111]

From Khrushchev's viewpoint, certainly, the conjunction of political and military advantages that might accrue to the Soviet Union from the "end-run" deployment of missiles to Cuba must have been exceedingly attractive—enough so to have offset any qualms about the risks of such a project. Indeed, in light of the somewhat dismal results achieved by Soviet pressure tactics in Europe in the preceding years, one wonders what persuaded Khrushchev to feel confident that he could get away with a still bolder challenge in the Caribbean at the very doorstep of the United States.[112] At any rate, he tried.

[106] That Khrushchev counted upon calling for new Berlin negotiations after the US elections in November—by which time the Soviet missiles would have been ready for unveiling had they not been discovered by US aerial reconnaissance—seems to have been made quite clear in Gromyko's talk with President Kennedy on October 18. See Abel, *The Missile Crisis*, pp. 74–77.

[107] Horelick and Rush, *Strategic Power*, p. 140.

[108] For details on the MRBM and IRBM launching sites, see Briefing by John Hughes of the Defense Intelligence Agency, *Department of Defense Appropriations for 1964*, Hearings before a Subcommittee of the House of Representatives Committee on Appropriations, 88th Congress, 1st Session, 1963, Part I, p. 7.

[109] Garthoff, *Soviet Military Policy*, p. 120.

[110] Ibid., p. 122.

[111] *Washington Post*, December 18, 1962.

[112] One thing that seems clear is that Khrushchev badly misjudged the staunchness of the United States and its President, perhaps on the basis of the Bay of Pigs affair in April 1961 and his meeting with President Kennedy in Vienna in June 1961. As Khrushchev remarked to Robert

What happened is history. Without going into the details of the showdown that followed President Kennedy's television address of October 22, suffice it to say that Khrushchev was obliged to withdraw his missiles and IL-28 bombers, taking the line of retreat left open to him by the United States.[113] Although Khrushchev salvaged something from the wreckage of the Cuban episode by claiming, with some justice, that he had acted to avert the danger of a nuclear war,[114] he had plainly suffered a major defeat. Militarily, the Cuban missile gambit not only failed as a shortcut method of altering the strategic balance, but it also served to reconfirm American superiority. Politically, it deprived Khrushchev of any leverage for another squeeze on Berlin[115] and gave Western Europe renewed confidence in American pledges of protection. At the same time, the United States found that in a vital crisis arising in its own hemisphere its European allies were prepared to stand fast by their alliance commitments.[116]

From Khrushchev's personal standpoint, the Cuban missile showdown was undoubtedly a chastening experience. He showed little disposition thereafter to invite further tests of will, although he did not entirely abandon the habit of brandishing his missiles. His power position survived the immediate shock of the Cuban crisis, but the multiple embarrassments of this episode very likely contributed in some measure to his political downfall two years later. As regards Soviet policy, the Cuban missile showdown marked a definite turning point under Khrushchev's leadership. During the next two years, the need to recover from the damaging after-effects of the Cuban crisis converged with other difficulties at home and abroad, prompting Khrushchev to seek a breathing spell in Soviet relations with the West.

Frost and other foreign visitors prior to the Cuban showdown, it was his belief that Americans had become "too liberal to fight." For further relevant comment on this point, see Abel, *The Missile Crisis*, pp. 35–36, and Bernard Brodie, *Escalation and the Nuclear Option* (Princeton, N.J.: Princeton University Press, 1966), pp. 48–49.

[113] Garthoff, *Soviet Military Policy*, p. 122.

[114] See, for example, Khrushchev's Berlin speech of January 16, 1963, in defense of his Cuban policy. *Pravda*, January 17, 1963.

[115] It may be noted that, during the Cuban crisis itself, there was concern in many quarters in the West that Khrushchev might move either against the exposed Western salient in Berlin or elsewhere to recoup the losses suffered from his setback in Cuba. (See Brodie, *Escalation*, p. 29.) The Soviet view that this would have been a dangerously provocative step was later expressed by Gromyko, who said in December 1962 that the Cuban crisis had "made many people think how the whole matter might have developed if still another crisis in Central Europe had been added to the critical events around Cuba." *Pravda*, December 14, 1962.

[116] In this connection, let it be recalled that de Gaulle, though already on the way to becoming the most severe European critic of American policy, offered his unequivocal support to the United States at the height of the crisis. See Abel, *The Missile Crisis*, pp. 112–13.

VI

RETURN TO DÉTENTE TOWARD THE END OF
THE KHRUSHCHEV DECADE

Twice before—during the Geneva thaw of 1955 and again in the 1959–60 Camp David interlude between the crises over Berlin—the Soviet Union under Khrushchev had found it expedient to introduce a détente into its relations with the United States and other NATO powers. The third Soviet venture upon the path of détente, during Khrushchev's last two years in the Kremlin, went somewhat further than either of the previous ones, although it remains far from clear whether the détente approach of 1963–64 rested mainly upon relatively short-term, tactical considerations or upon factors of more enduring character.

In the broadest sense, perhaps, the origins of détente between the Soviet Union and the West in all three cases lay in mutual recognition of the destructiveness of nuclear war and a desire on both sides to reduce the risk of its occurrence. At the same time, however, neither side was prepared to equate détente with cessation of the political struggle. From the Soviet viewpoint, in particular—both during the Khrushchev era and since then—détente has tended to be a temporarily expedient and somewhat accentuated form of the general line of "peaceful coexistence," a line that expressly permits continuance of political, ideological, and economic struggle while steering clear of the danger of nuclear war.[1]

Khrushchev's renewed interest in an easing of Soviet relations with the West in 1963–64 was undoubtedly spurred most immediately by the failure of the Cuban missile gambit in the autumn of 1962. However, other factors,

---

[1] The concept of "peaceful coexistence" has been variously defined at different periods as the Soviets have tried to find a formula combining both co-operation and conflict with non-Communist states. It has never meant the cessation of conflict, however, as Soviet expositors themselves have taken pains to point out. Khrushchev, for example, described peaceful coexistence as "a form of intense economic, political, and ideological struggle of the proletariat against the aggressive forces of imperialism in the international arena." ("For New Victories of the World Communist Movement," *Kommunist*, no. 1 [January 1961]: 21–22.) As reiterated in a *Pravda* article following Khrushchev's fall, "peaceful coexistence means striving to exclude war, and primarily world war, as a means of solving interstate disputes and conflicts, but this by no means denotes rejection of the struggle against colonialism and imperialism." (Article by Observer, "For the Liquidation of Colonialism and the Triumph of Peace," *Pravda*, October 25, 1964.)

For useful commentary on the concept of peaceful coexistence, see Wladyslaw W. Kulski, *Peaceful Coexistence* (Chicago: Henry Regnery Company, 1959), especially pp. 127–37; Robert C. Tucker, *The Soviet Political Mind* (New York: Frederick A. Praeger, Inc., 1963), pp. 201–22; Richard V. Allen, *Peace or Peaceful Coexistence* (Chicago, Ill.: American Bar Association, 1966), especially pp. 75–108.

some of which had prompted him to gamble upon the Cuban "shortcut" in the first place, contributed to Khrushchev's readiness to pursue a policy of détente in these two years.[2]

Factors Bearing on Khrushchev's Interest in Détente

Among these factors perhaps the most significant in the strategic context of the early sixties was the existence of a military balance adverse to the Soviet Union, and the question of what to do about this situation. Although the Soviet Union's military posture provided what might be termed a credible "minimum" deterrent, Moscow's political bargaining power was in danger of being eroded by a growing US advantage in strategic forces, which had been dramatically underscored by the Cuban missile fiasco.

After Cuba, Khrushchev faced essentially two broad choices with respect to improving the strategic position in which the Soviet Union found itself. One was to plunge forthwith into an accelerated strategic arms race with the United States, despite the obvious drawback that an overt race with an adversary whose resources greatly outmatched those of the Soviet Union might well fail to improve the relative Soviet position. The other possibility was to seek ways of slowing down the competition, a choice which, even though it implied temporary acceptance of the position of second-best also promised to keep the strategic gap from widening further. For a variety of reasons, Khrushchev chose the second alternative. At the same time, by sanctioning such tributary measures as a stepped-up military research and development effort he evidently sought to fend off internal criticism and to provide the Soviet Union with the option to resume the strategic race if and when more favorable conditions presented themselves.

A second major factor in Khrushchev's desire for a rapprochement with the West following the Cuban debacle was the state of the Soviet economy in 1963–64. Without going into the details of the Soviet economic performance, one need only note here that cumulative problems on the economic front had deepened in the early sixties. They included a marked decline in the rate of economic growth, which, according to the best Western estimates, had dropped from an annual rate of between 6 and 10 per cent in the previous decade to less than 3 per cent in 1962–63, partly under the impact of the agriculturally disastrous year 1963.[3] Combined with increasing demands on

[2] For a judicious assessment of the various interacting factors which influenced the Soviet leadership to seek a détente in the 1963–64 period, see Lincoln P. Bloomfield, Walter C. Clemens, Jr., and Franklyn Griffiths, *Khrushchev and the Arms Race: Soviet Interests in Arms Control and Disarmament, 1954–1964* (Cambridge, Mass.: M.I.T. Press, 1966), especially pp. 244–50, 267–87. See also Malcolm Mackintosh, "Three Détentes: 1955–1964," and T. W. Wolfe, "Impact of Khrushchev's Downfall on Soviet Military Policy and Détente," in Eleanor Lansing Dulles and Robert Dickson Crane, eds., *Détente: Cold War Strategies in Transition* (New York: Frederick A. Praeger, Inc., 1965), pp. 112–20, 282–84, 298–303.

[3] See estimates by the US Central Intelligence Agency, reported in *New York Times*, January 8, 1964, and report released by Senator Paul H. Douglas, *Annual Economic Indicators for the USSR*, Materials Prepared for the Joint Economic Committee, 88th Congress, 2nd Session, US Government

Soviet resources to meet a rising level of consumer expectation, to revive the faltering agricultural sector, and to support defense and space programs this slowdown in the economic growth rate certainly sharpened the perennial problem of resource allocation with which the Soviet leadership once again found itself confronted in the aftermath of Cuba.

One effect of these competing pressures upon the country's resources was to generate an internal policy debate—not without antecedent in Soviet history—in which the issue tended to be whether to give priority to defense and heavy industry needs or to the requirements of domestic economic growth.[4] Khrushchev evidently sought to strike a workable balance between these two choices, but found it necessary to favor a policy of holding down Soviet military expenditures and promoting the growth of the civilian economy[5]—a course that suggested the wisdom of a conciliatory posture in foreign affairs.

Sino–Soviet discord was another important element that bore upon Khru-

---

Printing Office, Washington, D.C., February 1964, pp. 93, 98. See also Thomas W. Wolfe, *Soviet Strategy at the Crossroads* (Cambridge, Mass.: Harvard University Press, 1964), pp. 20, 265; the excellent discussion in Bloomfield et al., *Khrushchev and the Arms Race*, pp. 225–33; *Current Economic Indicators for the USSR*, Materials Prepared for the Joint Economic Committee, 89th Congress, 1st Session, US Government Printing Office, Washington, D.C., June 1965, pp. 11–15.

[4] See *Khrushchev and the Arms Race*, p. 230; Sidney I. Ploss, *To the Twenty-third Congress of the Soviet Communist Party*, Foreign Policy Research Institute, University of Pennsylvania, Philadelphia, Pa., October 8, 1965, pp. 44–45. See also Thomas W. Wolfe, *The Soviet Military Scene: Institutional and Defense Policy Considerations*, The RAND Corporation, RM-4913-PR, June 1966, pp. 70–71.

[5] For a concise description of Khrushchev's attempts to strike a balance between military expenditures and his domestic economic program, see *Khrushchev and the Arms Race*, pp. 229–32. See also Carl A. Linden, *Khrushchev and the Soviet Leadership, 1957–1964* (Baltimore, Md.: The Johns Hopkins Press, 1966), pp. 164–201. The question of how much retrenchment in military spending, if any, was finally achieved by Khrushchev is clouded by the well-known discrepancy between published Soviet budget figures and actual military outlays. The last published defense budget of the Khrushchev period, for calendar year 1964, was 13.3 billion rubles, a reduction of about 5 per cent from the 1963 budget (*Izvestiia*, December 15, 1963). Western estimates, however, generally place actual Soviet outlays at one-third or more above the published figures. See, for example, Abraham S. Becker, *Soviet Military Outlays Since 1955*, The RAND Corporation, RM-3886-PR, June 1964; Timothy Sosnovy, "The Soviet Military Budget," *Foreign Affairs* (April 1964): 448, 493; J. G. Godaire, "The Claim of the Soviet Military Establishment," in *Dimensions of Soviet Economic Power*, Part I, *The Policy Framework*, Joint Economic Committee, 87th Congress, 2nd Session, US Government Printing Office, Washington, D.C., 1962, pp. 33–46; Morris Bornstein, "A Comparison of Soviet and United States National Product," in *Comparisons of the United States and Soviet Economies*, Joint Economic Committee, 86th Congress, 1st Session, Part II, US Government Printing Office, Washington, D.C., 1959, pp. 377–95.

The presumption that Khrushchev's policies during 1963–64 had, or promised shortly to have, a retarding effect on actual military outlays rests largely on the controversial long-range plan for development of the Soviet economy which was partially unveiled just before Khrushchev's downfall. A summary account of this proposed plan as outlined by Khrushchev was published on October 2, 1964 ("On Main Directions for Drawing Up the Plan for Development of the National Economy in the Next [Plan] Period," *Pravda*, October 2, 1964). It called for downgrading of past emphasis on heavy industry and for more rapid development of consumer industry, while stating that the country's defenses were already at "a suitable level." This evidently was interpreted by some of Khrushchev's opponents as an indication that defense requirements might be slighted under his proposed long-range plan. For more detailed discussion, see Wolfe, "Impact of Khrushchev's Downfall," in *Détente: Cold War Strategies in Transition*, pp. 284–85.

shchev's disposition to adopt a posture of accommodation toward the West. Although Moscow's competition with Peking for leadership of the international Communist movement made it awkward in some respects for the Soviet Union to show an unseemly interest in "collaboration" with the "capitalist adversary," other factors tended to reduce this inhibition against détente. One of the more important of these was probably a dawning Soviet appreciation, sharpened by Peking's relentless determination to acquire nuclear weapons, that China posed an emergent political and military threat with disturbing long-term implications for the Soviet Union itself. In a more immediate sense, the rapid deterioration of Sino–Soviet relations in late 1962 and 1963, following Chinese charges of Soviet "capitulation" in Cuba, may have helped remove any lingering reluctance in Moscow to risk alienating Peking by moving toward détente with the West.

For that matter, the Soviet Union could expect to turn the advocacy of détente to some advantage in the polemics with Peking. Not only might Moscow embarrass Peking by portraying its intransigence as a danger to peace in the nuclear age,[6] but it could try to convince the Chinese that a détente-oriented environment would make it more difficult for the West to oppose "national-liberation" struggles in the so-called "Third World" and thus would actually advance the fortunes of the world revolutionary movement.[7] Still another motive for utilizing the politics of détente in the rivalry with Peking was Khrushchev's apparent desire to gain time in which to repair his own leadership position vis-à-vis Peking, as made evident, especially in the year or so before his fall, by his persistent efforts to organize a conference of Communist parties at which to expel China from the ranks of the world Communist camp.[8]

While Khrushchev's interest in détente after the Cuban fiasco thus arose to an important degree out of his need to deal with such problems as the unfavorable strategic balance, internal economic difficulties, and the trouble-making propensities of Peking, it was by no means entirely the product of

[6] Khrushchev, for example, did so in a speech in East Germany in January 1963 ("Speech by Comrade N. S. Khrushchev at the VI Congress of the Socialist Unity Party of Germany," *Pravda*, January 17, 1963). See also Morton H. Halperin, *Sino-Soviet Relations and Arms Control* (Cambridge, Mass.: East Asian Research Center, Center for International Affairs, Harvard University, 1966), pp. 25–26, 38; *Khrushchev and the Arms Race*, pp. 220, 275; Alexander Dallin et al., *The Soviet Union, Arms Control, and Disarmament* (New York: School of International Affairs, Columbia University, 1964), pp. 262–63.

[7] The argument that Soviet détente moves could aid the "national-liberation" movement was closely linked with a similar argument previously advanced on behalf of Soviet disarmament proposals. A. I. Mikoyan, for example, declared in March 1962 that Soviet disarmament proposals would facilitate the "national liberation struggle" by stripping the "imperialists of the means of resisting the revolutionary actions of the proletariat and the peasantry" ("Speech by Comrade Mikoyan," *Pravda*, March 15, 1962). The same theme was frequently repeated in subsequent years. See, for example, V. Shestov, "Disarmament Problems Today," *International Affairs*, no. 11 (November 1965): 54; O. Grinev, "Before the Ninth Round at Geneva," *Izvestiia*, February 23, 1966. For additional commentary on this point, see T. W. Wolfe, "Soviet Attitude Toward Arms Control and Disarmament," *Temple Law Quarterly*, vol. 38, no. 2 (Winter 1965): 127; *Khrushchev and the Arms Race*, p. 238.

[8] See J. F. Brown, "East Europe: The Soviet Grip Loosens," *Survey* (October 1965): 17.

adversity. With regard to Europe, the opportunity to reap positive political advantage from the pursuit of a more conciliatory line appears to have impressed Khrushchev greatly, although here, too, elements of antagonism continued to be interwoven with those of accommodation.

Among the salient features of the European situation which lay before Khrushchev in early 1963 was the manifest development of significant fissures in the NATO alliance and of a realignment of interests among the major partners. Differences between the United States and France over NATO strategy and de Gaulle's go-it-alone policies had been gathering momentum since 1958, except for brief interludes during the Berlin and Cuban crises. De Gaulle's press conference of January 14, 1963, not only brought these differences into the open but his veto of British entry into the Common Market on that occasion highlighted another serious issue dividing the NATO partners.[9] At the same time, the signing of the Franco–German treaty of cooperation in early 1963, while regarded with certain misgivings in Moscow, also had the virtue in Soviet eyes of creating a "two-power bloc" within the Western alliance that might further strain its fabric.[10]

In Germany the chances for developments disruptive of Western unity also seemed somewhat brighter. For example, not only was the problem of nuclear sharing becoming a more vexing issue in Germany's relations with her NATO allies, especially the United States, but also Adenauer's impending retirement opened the possibility of a reorientation of policy under his successors. All of these trends in early 1963, suggestive of serious "contradictions" beneath the surface of the Western alliance, tended to revive Soviet hopes, dormant since Stalin's latter days, that the capitalist system was entering a new stage of crisis.[11] Even the apparent progress of the Common Market as an instrument to promote Western European economic growth and political unity, a development to which Khrushchev had given pointed attention in 1962,[12] did not altogether dispel the impression that internal differences were growing sharper among the Western countries.

The important thing from the Soviet viewpoint—and here Khrushchev evi-

[9] *New York Times*, January 15, 1963. See also Henry A. Kissinger, *The Troubled Partnership* (New York: McGraw-Hill Book Company, 1965), pp. 86–88; Cecil V. Crabb, Jr., "The Gaullist Revolt Against the Anglo-Saxons," *Annals of the American Academy of Political and Social Science* (hereafter referred to as *Annals*) (January 1964): 15–23; Horst Mendershausen, *A View of U.S.–European Relations in 1964*, The RAND Corporation, RM-4334-PR, November 1964, pp. 2–3, 10–11, 26–29.

[10] See Alvin Z. Rubinstein, "The Soviet Image of Western Europe," *Current History* (November 1964): 283. For commentary on the ambivalent Soviet attitude toward Franco-German co-operation, see Zbigniew Brzezinski, "Russia and Europe," *Foreign Affairs* (April 1964): 432, 441–42.

[11] See Richard Lowenthal, "The End of an Illusion," *Problems of Communism* (January–February 1963): 1–10.

[12] See, for example, two of Khrushchev's speeches in May 1962, in *Pravda*, May 29, 31, 1962. In these speeches, Khrushchev took the line that the Common Market was more of a threat to newly "liberated" countries than to a "powerful force" like the Soviet bloc, but the vehemence of his attack on the Common Market suggested that it had also become a matter of concern to the Soviet Union.

dently drew profit from his own and Stalin's earlier mistakes—was to avoid threatening behavior at this juncture, which might only alarm the NATO partners and prompt them to close ranks once again. Indeed, positive steps to erase the sense of threat that had gathered over Europe during the period of the Berlin and Cuban crises might serve better than mere passivity on the part of Moscow to promote disarray in NATO and to provide new openings for Soviet diplomacy. In short, the opportunity to capitalize on growing strains within the Western alliance was another powerful incentive for Khrushchev to adopt a policy of détente.

Finally, Khrushchev's interest in easing relations with the West happened to coincide with a parallel Western interest in achieving a more stable set of East–West relationships. Although it is not our purpose here to explore in depth the pattern of Western motivation in favor of a détente, it doubtless stemmed in part from sober reflection on the Cuban confrontation, which, while it had paid off handsomely, was hardly to be recommended as a routine model for the future conduct of US–Soviet relations. Whatever its other wellsprings may have been, Western readiness to turn over a new leaf in East–West relations—which found its most graphic expression in President Kennedy's "Strategy for Peace" speech at American University in June 1963[13]— was a necessary complement to Khrushchev's movement toward détente.[14]

Beyond this conjunction of interest, one might add, was the tendency of the Kremlin leadership under Khrushchev's influence to sort out the "good guys" from the "bad guys" within leadership groups in the West, or, in the Soviet idiom, to distinguish between "moderate-sober" and "aggressive-adventuristic" elements within what hitherto had generally been treated uniformly as "bourgeois ruling circles."[15] This recognition of diversity in the

In the spring and summer of 1962 Khrushchev also had displayed his concern over the relatively poor performance of COMECON, the East European counterpart of the Common Market, and at that time took a number of measures intended to strengthen it. See Brown, *Survey* (October 1965): 16, 17; Brzezinski, *Foreign Affairs* (April 1964): 432; Rubinstein, *Current History* (November 1964): 285. It may be noted that Soviet concern over the unifying effect of the Common Market rested not on economic grounds alone. There has been a continuing Soviet belief that any movement toward European unity constitutes a threat to the Soviet Union; hence the long-standing tendency of Soviet policy to equate Soviet security with European disunity. For an earlier Soviet expression of the view that postwar attempts to promote Western unity are comparable to Hitler's efforts to " 'unify Europe' against the USSR," see S. Beglov, " 'European Commonwealth' —A Threat to Peoples' Peace and Security," *Kommunist*, no. 2 (January 1954): 72–73.

13 "Text of Kennedy's Address Offering 'Strategy of Peace' for Easing the Cold War," *New York Times*, June 11, 1963. For an analysis of President Kennedy's address, see Walter C. Clemens, Jr., ed., *Toward a Strategy of Peace* (Chicago, Ill.: Rand McNally and Company, 1965), pp. 1–19.

14 It should be recalled that before Kennedy's American University speech, in the first two years of his administration, there had been tentative US gestures toward détente, which Khrushchev had chosen largely to ignore in pressing the 1961 campaign against Berlin and embarking on the Cuban missile venture a year later. The tendency to forget that Khrushchev became a staunch partisan of détente only after having passed up the first opportunities in this direction is noted in James L. Richardson, *Germany and the Atlantic Alliance: The Interaction of Strategy and Politics* (Cambridge, Mass.: Harvard University Press, 1966), p. 92.

15 For an analysis of the Soviet tendency under Khrushchev to differentiate among elements of the bourgeois "ruling class," and of changes in this practice after Khrushchev's departure, see

Western leadership, however artificially defined, had several noteworthy implications in terms of the Soviet movement toward détente.

In a purely instrumental sense, it helped to cushion criticism from such diehard Communist purists as the Chinese, for détente-oriented dealings with the bourgeois adversary could be justified as efforts to undermine the domestic position of rabidly anti-Communist Western leaders while improving that of less hostile ones.[16] The notion of exploitable differences within Western leadership élites was also congenial to the hope of being able to manipulate intra-NATO suspicions; by playing upon the search for accommodation between the Soviet Union and the United States, for example, the Kremlin might hope to foster European mistrust of American motives and thus stimulate destructive feuds within the Western alliance.[17] In a less cynical sense, however, Khrushchev's perception of "reasonable" forces at work within Western leadership circles, particularly in the other great superpower, may also have led him to believe—contrary to his Marxist–Leninist upbringing—that he could establish even with the bourgeois adversary a mutual understanding upon the basis of which movement toward a stable condominium arrangement of some sort might be possible.

Steps toward Détente

It was against this background of diverse problems, pressures, and expectations, then, that in late 1962 and early 1963 Khrushchev took a number of specific steps toward détente. Most of these lay initially in the field of arms control, suggesting that, while Khrushchev was eager to create an atmosphere conducive to slowing down the arms race, he was by no means prepared to plunge headlong into détente with radical proposals for the settlement of basic political issues. Perhaps the first tentative sign of a softer Soviet approach came in December 1962 with a shift in the Soviet position on inspection arrangements for a comprehensive nuclear test ban.[18] Although prospects for a compre-

---

William Zimmerman, "Soviet Perceptions of the United States," in Alexander Dallin and Thomas B. Larson, eds., *Soviet Politics Since Khrushchev* (Englewood Cliffs, N.J.: Prentice-Hall, Inc., 1968), pp. 165–70, 173. See also Vernon V. Aspaturian, "Foreign Policy Perspectives in the Sixties," ibid., pp. 143–48; *Khrushchev and the Arms Race*, pp. 210–14, 272.

[16] See, for example, F. Burlatskii, "Concrete Analysis—The Most Important Requirement of Leninism," *Pravda*, July 25, 1963; "The Present International Situation and the Foreign Policy of the Soviet Union; Report by Comrade N. S. Khrushchev on December 12, 1962, at the Session of the USSR Supreme Soviet," *Pravda*, December 13, 1962.

[17] See G. F. Hudson, "Soviet Soft Line Toward the West," *Current History* (October 1963): 232; Alastair Buchan, "The Changed Setting of the Atlantic Debate," *Foreign Affairs* (July 1965): 579; *A View of the U.S.-European Relations in 1964*, pp. vii, 32–35. For a discussion of the roots of Bonn's fears that the United States might barter away German interests, such as reunification, for the sake of agreement with the Soviet Union, see also Jean Edward Smith, *The Defense of Berlin* (Baltimore, Md.: The Johns Hopkins Press, 1963), pp. 316–19.

[18] On December 19, 1962, in a letter to President Kennedy, Khrushchev modified the Soviet position against on-site inspection by saying that the Soviet Union would agree to "two or three" such inspections per year under a comprehensive test ban treaty. (US Arms Control and Disarmament Agency, *Documents on Disarmament, 1962*, vol. 2 [July–December 1963], p. 1241.) A few days earlier, Soviet readiness to accept "two or three" automatic seismic stations on Soviet territory to control an underground test ban had been made known. See *Khrushchev and the Arms Race*, pp. 187–88.

hensive test ban treaty evaporated in the spring of 1963, when discussions in the conference of the Eighteen Nation Disarmament Committee (ENDC) at Geneva on this and other arms control matters again bogged down,[19] progress toward another series of agreements was being registered elsewhere in quiet talks between Soviet and Western officials.

The first product of these talks to see the light was the Washington–Moscow "hot-line" agreement, signed on June 20, 1963. On July 2, Khrushchev made known the Soviet Union's readiness to conclude a partial test ban agreement on terms acceptable to the West,[20] and soon thereafter three-power negotiations on a treaty were opened in Moscow, where, by curious coincidence, a delegation from Peking was also present for separate talks aimed (without success) at patching up the Sino–Soviet quarrel.[21] The cordial and relatively brief three-power negotiations, during which the Soviet side dropped an initial attempt to link the test ban with a NATO–Warsaw bloc nonaggression pact, culminated in the signing of a limited test ban treaty on August 5, 1963,[22] an event greeted with widespread, though by no means universal, approbation.[23]

While the test ban treaty provided the most graphic single sign that a new season of détente had opened in 1963, other evidence of a more conciliatory Soviet posture toward the West was also forthcoming. By June 1963, Soviet jamming of Voice of America broadcasts had virtually ceased; during the same month, President Kennedy's American University speech elicited laudatory

---

[19] *Khrushchev and the Arms Race*, pp. 188–89. In an interview with Norman Cousins in April 1963, Khrushchev asserted that he had with difficulty persuaded his colleagues to agree to three on-site inspections for a comprehensive test ban treaty, only to be made "to look foolish" when the United States declined to accept a limit of three inspections. See "Notes on a 1963 Visit with Khrushchev," *Saturday Review*, November 7, 1964, pp. 16–21, 58–60.

[20] "Speech by Comrade N. S. Khrushchev at a Meeting in Berlin on July 2, 1963," *Pravda*, July 3, 1963.

[21] The Sino–Soviet interparty talks began in Moscow on July 5 and were "suspended" without result on July 20, 1963. *New York Times*, July 6 and 21, 1963. The likelihood that the talks would fail to bring about a reconciliation had been foreshadowed, however, by the prior exchange of two highly acrimonious letters—the Chinese "25 Points" document of June 14 to the CPSU and the latter's "Open Letter" reply of July 14. These letters may be found in *Peking Review*, no. 25, June 21, 1963, and *Pravda*, July 14, 1963, respectively. See also Thomas W. Wolfe, *The Soviet Union and the Sino-Soviet Dispute*, The RAND Corporation, P-3203, August 1965, pp. 6–7; William E. Griffith, *The Sino-Soviet Rift* (Cambridge, Mass.: M.I.T. Press, 1964), pp. 154–62.

[22] *New York Times*, August 6, 1963. The treaty was initialed on July 25, but was not signed until August 5.

[23] In the West, the treaty met with scant enthusiasm in Bonn and with lofty disregard in Paris; for that matter, it also received a mixed reception in the United States. On the other hand, outright denunciation came from Peking, which condemned the test ban treaty as an example of Soviet capitulation to the United States and as a plot between the two powers to preserve a nuclear duopoly to "contain" China. *Peking Review*, no. 32, August 9, 1963. A Soviet document in 1963 accounted for Peking's attitude in the following words: "It appears that the Chinese government can by no means forgive the Soviet Union for not providing China with samples. of atomic weapons. The wish to have the atomic bomb in its hands by any means is the moving force behind the Peiping campaign against the treaty banning nuclear experiments." Cited in *Soviet Space Programs, 1962–1965: Goals and Purposes, Achievements, Plans, and International Implications*, Staff Report prepared for the use of the Committee on Aeronautical and Space Sciences, US Senate, 89th Congress, 2nd Session, December 30, 1966, US Government Printing Office, Washington, D.C., 1966, p. 522.

comment from Moscow;[24] and, in the fall, previous US–Soviet differences on the uses of outer space were ironed out to the extent of permitting two understandings in this area under United Nations auspices—the UN resolution of October 17 against placing nuclear weapons in orbit,[25] and an agreement, on November 22, on various legal principles applicable to space exploration.[26]

Apart, however, from this cluster of agreements and pledges—to which one more was to be added before Khrushchev's downfall: a simultaneous pledge by Soviet, US, and British leaders, in April 1964, to cut back unilaterally the production of fissionable materials[27]—there was little tangible evidence that the onset of détente had cleared the way for resolution of more deep-seated differences between the Soviet Union and the West. These differences persisted over a wide range of issues, as was apparent in the arms control field itself, where initially the test ban treaty had generated considerable optimism.

Following a speech by Khrushchev on July 19, 1963, at the beginning of the détente, while the Moscow test ban talks were in progress, the Soviet Union put forward a number of disarmament proposals at the ENDC in Geneva and elsewhere.[28] Except for certain modifications of the Soviet position aimed at Moscow's retention of a "nuclear umbrella" during the process of general disarmament and for a suggested freeze on military budgets, most of these dealt with partial measures relating to Europe, among them the frequently reiterated proposal for a NATO–Warsaw bloc nonaggression pact; measures to prevent surprise attack, including the reciprocal stationing of Soviet–Western troop observers at control posts in both parts of Germany; and a reduction of forces in the two Germanys.

At the ENDC discussions in Geneva, where Soviet and Western negotiators argued the merits of their respective positions, it soon became apparent that neither side was prepared to make substantial concessions for the sake of chalking up new, symbolic contributions to détente. The prospect of reaching wider agreement here was not appreciably heightened by the Soviet Union's presumption that its own proposals provided the only basis for negotiation.[29] Furthermore, Soviet propaganda to the effect that those proposals had pro-

---

[24] The Kennedy address was published in full in the Soviet press (*Pravda* and *Izvestiia*, June 13, 1963), and Khrushchev commended it publicly two days later (*Pravda*, June 15, 1963).

[25] *New York Times*, October 17 and 18, 1963.

[26] Ibid., November 22 and 23, 1963. See also *Khrushchev and the Arms Race*, pp. 191–92. Features of both this agreement and the resolution against nuclear weapons in orbit were to be incorporated several years later in the space treaty negotiated at the United Nations in December 1966. *New York Times*, December 9, 1966.

[27] *New York Times*, April 21, 1964. In November 1965, the Joint Atomic Energy Committee of the US Congress reported that there was no evidence that the Soviet Union had in fact cut back the production of fissionable materials (*New York Times*, November 25, 1965).

[28] "A Meeting of Soviet–Hungarian Friendship; Speech by Comrade N. S. Khrushchev," *Pravda*, July 20, 1963; Soviet memorandum on "Measures Intended To Lessen the Arms Race and To Decrease International Tension," presented to the ENDC on January 18, 1964, *Izvestiia*, January 29, 1964. See also *Khrushchev and the Arms Race*, pp. 191, 242.

[29] See, for example, Interview with A. A. Gromyko, *Izvestiia*, March 3, 1964; M. L'vov, "Topsy-Turvy Logic," ibid., April 2, 1964; "Barrier on Arms Raised by Soviet," *New York Times*, June 24, 1964.

voked a tense inner struggle among NATO's members[30] suggests that they may have been designed as much with an eye to sowing dissension as to finding new areas of agreement. Although formal negotiations were pursued in Geneva off and on throughout the détente period, by the spring of 1964 the ENDC sessions had settled down to unproductive discussion, with familiar charges of obstructionism coming from both sides.[31]

Outside the forum of formal arms control negotiations, Khrushchev found it useful, as the détente unfolded, to promote what he sometimes described as a "policy of mutual example" or "negotiation by example." A representative instance of this approach came in December 1963, when he announced that the Soviet Union intended to reduce its military budget for 1964 by about 4 per cent and that it was considering a unilateral cutback of Soviet troop levels.[32] Although this action may have been prompted in part by internal military-economic considerations, upon which we shall elaborate later, it was immediately held up by Khrushchev as a token of the Soviet Union's good intentions and an example to the United States.[33]

Khrushchev's advocacy of "negotiation by example" can be interpreted variously as a matter of making a virtue of necessity, or of exploring a possible alternative to negotiations of a more formal character.[34] It probably also had the purpose, however, of putting the West on the defensive at a time when Khrushchev was suing for détente. To allow the diplomatic initiative to pass to the West at such a time would doubtless have seemed to him tantamount to inviting his adversaries to exploit the situation to their advantage.

A similar purpose may be seen in such initiatives as Khrushchev's letter, in early January 1964, to all heads of governments, proposing renunciation of force in the settlement of territorial disputes.[35] Besides serving notice on NATO, and especially West Germany, not to mistake détente overtures as an invitation to violate the territorial integrity of the GDR, this proposal was probably also aimed in part at China, whose irredentist assertions concerning Soviet territory in the Far East were now being injected into the Sino–Soviet quarrel.[36]

[30] *Khrushchev and the Arms Race*, p. 197. Soviet commentary similarly played upon the theme that signing of the test ban treaty also had precipitated a "crisis in NATO." See K. Lavrov, "The Jubilee of Crises," *Izvestiia*, May 30, 1964.

[31] *Khrushchev and the Arms Race*, pp. 190, 192, 199.

[32] *Izvestiia*, December 15, 1963; *Pravda*, December 16, 1963.

[33] Ibid. Soviet statements on the exemplary virtues of the announced Soviet budget reduction ignored the fact that it had been preceded by the initiative taken a few days earlier by the new Johnson administration in the United States to close a number of military installations and to lower the US military budget. Wolfe, *Soviet Strategy at the Crossroads*, pp. 45, 270.

[34] *Soviet Strategy at the Crossroads*, p. 45. See also *Khrushchev and the Arms Race*, p. 243; Arnold L. Horelick and Myron Rush, *Strategic Power and Soviet Foreign Policy* (Chicago, Ill.: University of Chicago Press, 1966), p. 155.

[35] "Message from N. S. Khrushchev, Chairman of the USSR Council of Ministers, to Heads of State of Countries of the World," *Pravda*, January 4, 1964. The letter had been sent out a few days before its publication in *Pravda*.

[36] It is not clear precisely when Chinese territorial claims entered the Sino–Soviet dispute. According to Mao Tse-tung in an interview with a group of Japanese socialists, which was published in the Japanese weekly *Sekai Syuho* on August 11, 1964, he had raised the question of Mongolia with Khrushchev and Bulganin in 1954, the same year in which Peking published a

Various aspects of the Soviet military stance in 1963–64 likewise seemed meant to convey the message that the West should not try to stretch the limits of détente too far. Although we shall return to this subject in greater detail, two cases in point may be mentioned here. One was the stepped-up Soviet effort during this period to integrate the Warsaw Pact armies more closely with Soviet forces in East Europe, which had the dual effect of warning both the East European countries and NATO not to count upon the détente for a loosening of Soviet control over East Europe. The other was a persistent attempt to enhance the credibility of the Soviet strategic deterrent in Western eyes. This took the form of advertising Soviet strategic capabilities in more technically sophisticated terms than previously, to the accompaniment of a propaganda patently meant to disabuse the United States of any idea that it could count upon a successful first strike or could expect to draw political advantage from its strategic position vis-à-vis the Soviet Union.[37]

Khrushchev's resolve to avoid the potential pitfalls of détente was perhaps most clearly manifested, however, in his policy toward Europe. While his passage along the path of détente led him into limited agreements with the United States in some fields, and to the tacit acceptance of a kind of truce on such disputed Cold War issues in Europe as that of Berlin, he stopped well short of surrendering the political initiative on the European scene to his Western adversaries. If anything, he deployed his diplomatic resources against Europe with an eye to taking advantage of the vulnerabilities which the tension-easing atmosphere of détente had helped to expose within the Western alliance itself. At the same time, however, the growing complexity of the Soviet Union's relations with Europe and the United States intruded into the détente picture, presenting Khrushchev with a number of competing and often contradictory policy choices, and making it difficult for him to decide just how the problems troubling NATO might be exploited. Before seeing what the record has to tell us about the policies he chose to pursue, it may be useful to look briefly at a few of the larger complexities that confronted Khrushchev in 1963–64 with regard to Soviet policy toward Europe and the United States.

Contradictory Policy Choices Confronting Khrushchev

Perhaps the most fundamental dilemma facing Khrushchev after almost two decades of the Cold War was to decide whether the Soviet Union would prefer

---

textbook showing a large part of Soviet Asian territory as belonging historically to China. In 1963 Peking began to warn that at some future date the return of territory annexed by Imperial Russia might be sought. Mao's 1964 interview with the Japanese socialists introduced the irredentist issue more explicitly, and drew from Moscow the warning that any attempt to recarve the map of the world according to the "Peking recipe" could lead to "the most dangerous consequences." Among other pertinent exchanges on the subject, see Chou En-lai's speech commenting on Khrushchev's proposal to renounce force in settling territorial disputes (New China News Agency broadcast, April 25, 1964); editorial, "Apropos the Conversations of Mao Tse-tung with a Group of Japanese Socialists," *Pravda*, September 2, 1964. See also Allen S. Whiting, "A Brief History," in Clement J. Zablocki, ed., *Sino–Soviet Rivalry* (New York: Frederick A. Praeger, Inc., 1966), p. 11.

[37] Wolfe, *Soviet Strategy at the Crossroads*, p. 48.

to have the United States in or out of Europe. At first glance, the answer would seem obvious, for had not the central aim of postwar Soviet policy in Europe always been unmistakably clear: to bring about the withdrawal of the American presence and to detach the United States from its commitments to the defense of Europe? However, as some observers have pointed out,[38] this aim had subtly collided at times, particularly after Khrushchev came to power, with a second and somewhat more tolerant Soviet attitude toward the American presence. Although not easily defined, this attitude would seem to rest on the basic reckoning that a decline of American influence in Europe would mean the rise of German dominance, and that, instead of seeking to evict the Americans from Europe, it might be preferable for the Soviet Union to co-operate with the United States—either to achieve a new European settlement or to stabilize the status quo, that is to say, a divided Germany embedded in a divided Europe.[39]

The ambivalence of Soviet policy with respect to the American presence in Europe carried over to the attitude toward NATO as well. On the one hand, the disintegration of NATO was a major Soviet objective, to be sought through such avenues as detaching the United States from Europe, driving a wedge between Germany and her allies, and encouraging the independent aspirations of de Gaulle. On the other hand, the value of NATO as a mechanism for restraining Germany was not wholly lost upon the Soviet leadership, despite its reluctance to accept entirely the American argument—advanced, for example, in connection with the Multilateral Force (MLF)—that a Germany bound more closely into the NATO system and thus insulated against a return to extreme nationalism actually would be in the Russian interest.[40] Nor, for that matter, was the Soviet leadership unaware that NATO's existence, portrayable as a "threat" to the Eastern bloc,[41] provided welcome cement for its own alliance system, serving in particular to justify the maintenance of the Warsaw Pact military coalition. Although not necessarily a permanent instrument of Soviet policy, this coalition nevertheless performed a

[38] See, for example, Pierre Hassner, "Polycentrism in the East and in the West: Meeting Point of the Two Evolutions?" a paper presented at East–West conference of the Atlantic Institute in Rome, October 1966, p. 31; Brzezinski, Foreign Affairs, April 1964, pp. 441–442.

[39] Hassner, "Polycentrism in East and West," p. 31. See also Max Frankel, "The Twilight of NATO," New York Times Magazine, December 5, 1965, p. 188; Zbigniew Brzezinski, Alternative to Partition (New York: McGraw-Hill Book Company, 1965), p. 86.

[40] See Alastair Buchan, The Multilateral Force: An Historical Perspective, Adelphi Papers, No. 13, The Institute for Strategic Studies, London, October 1964, p. 14; Zbigniew Brzezinski, "Moscow and the M.L.F.: Hostility and Ambivalence," Foreign Affairs (October 1964): 127, 131–33.

[41] See, for example, Colonel E. Fedulaev, "The Missile-Nuclear Arms Race in NATO Countries —a Threat to Peace," Kommunist Vooruzhennykh Sil (Communist of the Armed Forces), no. 17 (September 1963): 84–85. With the tendency of Soviet media in late 1963 and early 1964 to dwell on the growing contradictions within NATO, the image of the NATO "threat" became somewhat diluted. The line generally taken was that, despite contradictions between "sober-minded" and "aggressive" groups within NATO, the danger that the latter might get the upper hand dictated vigilance and high readiness on the part of the Warsaw alliance. For a typical example of this approach, see T. Fedorov, "The Call of the Times and NATO," Mezhdunarodnaia zhizn' (International Affairs), no. 2, February 1964, pp. 44–50.

useful cohesive and control function in the increasingly "polycentric" political environment of Eastern Europe in the early sixties.

Another array of contradictory choices confronting Khrushchev as he sought to deal with the increasingly complex problem of Soviet relations with Europe during the 1963–64 détente was connected with Soviet policy toward Paris and Bonn. There was, first of all, the problem of what to do about arresting the phenomenon of Franco–German reconciliation, a process which, though it seemed to be turning slightly sour, might have unfavorable effects upon Soviet hegemony in East Central Europe if it proved successful.[42] Beyond the matter of whether to abet or oppose the softening of traditional Franco–German enmity, there was also the question of what policy the Soviet Union should pursue toward France and Germany individually.

With respect to France, the temptation was obviously great to court de Gaulle and encourage his resistance to US leadership in Europe, thereby fanning the growing crisis within NATO. But there were several offsetting considerations. For one thing, the Soviet Union harbored certain reservations about de Gaulle's Olympian design for a "Europe to the Urals," which not only impinged rather ambiguously upon the Soviet Union itself but implied the ultimate liquidation of the Communist regimes of East Europe.[43] In more immediately practical terms, Soviet courtship of de Gaulle might cause the United States and Germany to draw more closely together and strengthen German influence within the Western alliance, a development Moscow did not welcome. Moreover, a widening of the breach between France and her Western allies could prejudice Soviet attempts to seek areas of mutual understanding with the United States, whose power and influence in the last analysis outweighed those of France on the global scale, if not on the European scale as well.

With regard to Germany, the choices facing Khrushchev doubtless had still more significant ramifications than with respect to France, if only because the German problem, as always, loomed so large in Moscow's view of Europe.[44] Here, the underlying tugs on Soviet policy apparently ranged from fear and suspicion of Germany on the one hand to hopes of seducing her on the other. The first of these attitudes counseled a continuing hard line toward Germany, consonant with the aim of keeping Germany divided and with playing upon European anxieties about a German resurgence, especially at the prospect of a nuclear-sharing role for Bonn within NATO. On the other hand, however, Soviet hopes of winning Germany over, dormant perhaps for some time, may have come to life under Khrushchev. The trump card for Germany's seduction was in his hands, as he could hold out to her the prospect of reunification,[45] provided this could be managed without too obvious infidelity toward the GDR. Since any settlement of the German prob-

[42] See Brzezinski, *Foreign Affairs* (April 1964): 441.
[43] Ibid.
[44] See Hudson, *Current History* (October 1963): 234.
[45] See Richardson, *Germany and the Atlantic Alliance*, p. 368.

lem involving reunification would inevitably call for Bonn to abandon NATO—a move even more certain to wreck the alliance than de Gaulle's restiveness[46]—the temptation to use his trump card with Germany to this end would have been difficult for Khrushchev to disregard.

All these separate strands of Soviet policy choices probably led ultimately to the question of what the basic Soviet relationship to Europe should be. Was the familiar equation, European disunity equals Soviet security, still the best foundation for Soviet policy? Or was the commitment to a policy predicated on European fragmentation due for serious re-examination? In short, was it not possible that a stable Europe which made progress toward a reconciliation of its divisions, including that of Germany, might in the long run prove to be in the larger interest of the Soviet Union—even if it meant giving up the hope that Western Europe would ever succumb to the appeal of communism?

These, then, were some of the primary, and in many respects contradictory, considerations that competed for dominance as Khrushchev, in the last two years of his tenure, played out his role as the architect of the Soviet Union's European policy. What does the record show to have been his preferences and his performance?

Khrushchev's Varied Policy Approaches

On the whole, Khrushchev appears to have settled upon no single line of policy. Rather, he chose to experiment with several approaches, testing them out as he went along. This lent a certain inconsistency, if not uncertainty, to his policy performance, and perhaps partly justified the subsequent charges of his peers that he had been an "erratic" and "subjective" leader. His personal preference, for example, seemed to lie in seeking to deal directly with American leaders,[47] giving the impression that he was chiefly interested in trying to stabilize the division of Europe through some form of understanding or "joint sponsorship" with the United States. At the same time, he was plainly unwilling to pass up opportunities for reducing American influence in Europe, especially those afforded by de Gaulle's anti-American bent and by Bonn's growing nervousness lest German interests be sacrificed for the sake of greater East–West détente. Thus, as we shall see in a moment, Khrushchev not only kept open the options of dealing separately with France and West Germany but he also went fishing in the troubled waters of the intra-NATO policy debate.

Among the vexing issues of strategic and diplomatic policy within NATO that invited Khrushchev's attention were those connected with the control and sharing of nuclear weapons within the alliance, at the root of which lay the question of Germany's future role in NATO's nuclear arrangements. In

---

[46] See Terrence Prittie, "Again the Issue of the Two Germanys," *New York Times Magazine*, August 16, 1964, p. 61. For a view suggesting that NATO might not fall apart if Bonn should opt out, see Fred Warner Neal, "The Unsolved German Settlement," *Annals* (January 1964): 153.

[47] See *Khrushchev and the Arms Race*, p. 249.

fact, Soviet preoccupation with the problem of preventing Bonn from attaining nuclear partnership in NATO was no doubt the most consistent feature of Soviet European policy during the 1963–64 détente.

The immediate target against which Khrushchev aligned his sights in this period was the project for creation of a NATO multilateral nuclear force, or MLF, the antecedents of which went back to exploratory proposals, in 1960, for a jointly shared NATO nuclear force.[48] The Soviet Union, of course, had consistently made known its opposition to these and all other co-operative schemes that it believed could gain Germany access to nuclear weapons. Indeed, while Franco–German collaboration was at its height, the Soviet Union voiced concern that France might, unwittingly or otherwise, help Bonn over the nuclear doorstep.[49] France's own "independent" nuclear deterrent, the force de frappe, though sometimes criticized by Soviet commentators, was generally treated as a much less serious threat to Soviet security than the possibility that French nuclear aspirations might play into the hands of the West Germans and facilitate their access to atomic armaments.[50]

By the autumn of 1963 the MLF project evidently had begun to displace collaboration between Bonn and Paris in Soviet eyes as the most likely route to Germany's acquisition of nuclear weapons.[51] For some months the United States had been pressing its European allies for a decision on the MLF proposal,[52] and in October 1963 NATO met to discuss the matter. From that time forward the Soviet Union brought increasing propaganda fire to bear against the MLF, warning the West that its adoption would not only obstruct progress toward further East–West agreements and make it necessary for the Warsaw Pact countries to take "appropriate measures" in return but would also increase the danger of nuclear war.[53]

[48] Buchan, The Multilateral Force, pp. 4–5. See also Raymond H. Dawson, "What Kind of NATO Nuclear Force?" Annals (January 1964): 31, 37; Robert E. Osgood, NATO: The Entangling Alliance (Chicago, Ill.: University of Chicago Press, 1962), pp. 232–34.

[49] See, for example, Soviet Government Statement, "The 'Bonn-Paris Axis' Is an Instrument of Revanchism," Pravda, September 19, 1962; V. Shatrov, "Trip of the French President Beyond the Rhine," Mezhdunarodnaia zhizn', no 10 (October 1962): 108. Soviet concern on this score later subsided, as it became clear that de Gaulle meant to preserve his own independent force de frappe without any idea of nuclear sharing with Bonn.

[50] For a fuller treatment of this question, see Thomas W. Wolfe, Soviet Commentary on the French "Force de Frappe," The RAND Corporation, RM-4359-ISA, January 1965, especially pp. 5–6.

[51] Ibid., pp. 26–27. In early 1964, however, Soviet sources were still saying that "the efforts to build a French force de frappe and the MLF project are both evidence of a growing threat to peace and security in Europe." See N. Matveyev, "Western Europe: Asset or Liability in the Struggle for Peace?" International Affairs, no. 1 (January 1964): 54.

[52] Buchan, The Multilateral Force, pp. 5–7; Dawson, Annals (January 1964): 38.

[53] See, for example, G. Deinichenko, "The NATO Pirate Fleet," Izvestiia, September 28, 1963; "Conversation Between N. S. Khrushchev and the Participants of the Third World Journalist Meeting on October 25, 1963," Pravda, October 27, 1963; Boris Leont'ev, "Time Accelerates the Flow of Events," Krasnaia zvezda, January 1, 1964; "Dangerous Actions Which Threaten Peace: Note of the Soviet Government [dated July 11] to the Government of the U.S.A.; Note of the Soviet Government [dated July 11] to the Government of the FRG," Pravda, July 13, 1964; and Vneshniaia politika Sovetskogo Soiuza i mezhdunarodnye otnosheniia; sbornik dokumentov; 1964–

Some of this hostility toward the MLF had a certain ritualistic character, as suggested later by the fact that it continued unabated even after the MLF project had been obviously shelved.[54] Nevertheless, Soviet opposition to the MLF, as to variant proposals for multinational or multilateral nuclear forces in NATO,[55] seems to have stemmed from fear that any such project would pave the way for Germany's eventual acquisition of nuclear weapons.[56] Even short of actual acquisition, the Soviet Union apparently believed that closer German participation in NATO nuclear matters would strengthen Bonn's political and military influence to the detriment of the Soviet Union's long-term interests.[57]

Besides the adamant resolve to bar Bonn's path to any sort of nuclear partnership in NATO, as subsequently underlined in the spun-out negotiations over a nonproliferation treaty, there were other reasons for Khrushchev's vigorous campaign against the MLF. One of these was the opportunity to play upon East European antipathies toward Germany by linking the anti-MLF campaign to the image of a "revanchist" Germany, and thus to allow the Soviet Union to enhance its influence in East Europe by assuming the role of protector against an alleged German peril.[58] A somewhat analogous aim to keep alive traditional anti-German sentiments in the West was doubtless involved also. Perhaps a third consideration, of no little weight from Khrushchev's viewpoint, was the hope of exacerbating US–German relations by impeding the MLF project; for one of the MLF's manifest purposes was to restore confidence between Bonn and Washington (to give the former warranty that its interests would not be ignored during the détente search for US–Soviet agreements, and to reassure the latter that German policy would not be reoriented from the NATO and Atlantic framework toward either Gaullism or even a Soviet–German rapprochement).[59]

1965 gody (The Soviet Union's Foreign Policy and International Relations: Collected Documents, 1964–1965) (Moscow: Izdatel'stvo Instituta mezhdunarodnykh otnoshenii, 1966), pp. 25–31.

[54] The peak of the anti-MLF campaign came in early 1965, by which time the project was already virtually moribund. Although not formally buried until 1967, the MLF project appeared to have expired in late 1966 with the adoption of nuclear consultative arrangements in NATO (New York Times, December 15, 1966).

[55] For a concise explanation of the difference between "multinational" and "multilateral" proposals, see Buchan, The Multilateral Force, p. 3.

[56] The main burden of Soviet arguments against NATO nuclear forces or other nuclear-sharing arrangements, was that "no matter what form they might ultimately take," they would open the path to the nuclear arming of West Germany. A summary of the Soviet position emphasizing this point is given in D. E. Mel'nikov and D. G. Tomashevskii, eds., Mezhdunarodnye otnosheniia posle vtoroi mirovoi voiny (International Relations After the Second World War), vol. 3 (1956–1964) (Moscow: Politizdat, 1965), pp. 307–9.

[57] See, for example, V. Nekrasov, "The Vicious Circle of 'Atlantic' Policy," Pravda, December 27, 1963; Iurii Zhukov, "Prisoners of Dangerous Illusions," Pravda, February 18, 1964; D. Umanskii, "Revanchism and the Atlantic Policy," Krasnaia zvezda, March 13, 1964; V. Petrov, "Of Those Who Crave for Revenge," International Affairs, no. 3 (March 1964): 9, 12.

[58] See Stephen S. Rosenfeld, "Moscow Reports Dip in MLF Interest But Regards Project Still a Threat," Washington Post, January 25, 1965; John C. Campbell, American Policy Toward Communist Eastern Europe: The Choices Ahead (Minneapolis, Minn.: University of Minnesota Press, 1965), p. 21.

[59] Buchan, The Multilateral Force, pp. 8–9.

This sort of fishing in troubled waters, as we have said, was not without its drawbacks from the Soviet viewpoint. Blocking the MLF, for example, though it might disturb US–German relations, could at the same time revive German interest in much closer ties with France, thereby raising once more the possibility not only of nuclear collaboration between Paris and Bonn but also of a political co-operation that might prove embarrassing to the maintenance of Soviet control over Central Europe. Partly to insure himself against this potentially unfavorable consequence of Soviet opposition to the MLF, and for other, larger reasons of long standing, Khrushchev found it useful in the 1963–64 détente period to pursue separate policies toward Paris and Bonn, emphasizing to each, although on somewhat different grounds, the advantages of improved relations with the Soviet Union.

Renewed Flirtation with France

Khrushchev's interest in keeping the door open for a Franco–Soviet rapprochement as one of several alternative lines of Soviet policy toward Europe antedated the 1963–64 détente by a number of years. His visit to France in March 1960, for example, had been hailed in the Soviet press as the advent of a new era in Soviet–French relations, providing among other things the occasion for Khrushchev's remark that "the path to peace in Europe lies in alliance and friendship between the Soviet Union and France."[60] This flirtation with France frequently foundered, however, not only on such abrupt issues as the break-up of the Paris summit meeting of May 1960 but also on such persistent obstacles as Franco–German reconciliation, which Moscow sometimes chose to interpret as "collusion" for "rebuilding the aggressive might of German militarism,"[61] and on Soviet ambivalence toward de Gaulle himself. The latter was alternately condemned and lauded by a Soviet leadership that evidently found him a disconcerting figure and viewed him with a mixture of mistrust and respect not unlike that prevalent in many Western capitals.[62]

In late 1963, at an appropriate interval after having disapproved of de Gaulle's opposition to the test ban treaty, Khrushchev renewed his courtship of France and in early 1964 sent his high-ranking Presidium colleague Nikolai Podgornyi on a goodwill mission to Paris, to be followed several weeks later by Alexei I. Adzhubei, Khrushchev's son-in-law and editor of Izvestiia.[63] In the course of these visits, de Gaulle himself was reportedly invited to visit the Soviet Union, an invitation he took up, however, only after Khrushchev's successors were in office.

The personal cultivation of de Gaulle was accompanied by a general Soviet line toward France that sought to widen the differences between Paris

60 *Pravda*, March 23, 1960.

61 Rubinstein, *Current History* (November 1964): 283.

62 Ibid. See also Wolfe, *Soviet Commentary*, pp. 28–29.

63 Podgornyi visited France from March 3 to March 7; Adzhubei, from March 30 to April 14 (*New York Times*, March 3, 7, 31, April 14, 1964).

and Bonn on the one hand and between Paris and Washington on the other. One of the themes frequently invoked by Soviet spokesmen was that France and the Soviet Union were natural allies and should act in concert to curb German nuclear rearmament and hegemony in Europe. Another prominent line was that the more forcefully France asserted her "great-power independence" against American leadership in NATO the easier it would be to solve Europe's problems. A third theme warned that the United States was threatening the interests of France in the underdeveloped world, while in Europe the German industrial potential in conjunction with German "revanchism" posed a dangerous threat to France. A warning to the effect that Germany would remain a source of trouble until her boundaries were fixed was often coupled with approval for de Gaulle's "realism" in recognizing the permanence of the Oder–Neisse boundary.[64] There was, however, one rather striking omission in these tributes to de Gaulle's "realism": Soviet spokesmen remained silent on his stubborn opposition to negotiating under pressure on the question of Berlin and a German peace treaty—a stand which probably helped to explain his surprisingly constant hold on German sentiment.[65]

It may be putting it too strongly to say that Soviet overtures to de Gaulle rested on the expectation that France would sooner or later prove to be the Achilles heel of NATO. Also, despite Soviet references to a natural community of interests between Moscow and Paris, there was little to suggest that Khrushchev was prepared to anchor Soviet policy on the premise that France might be treated as an equal to the Soviet Union in dealing with the problems of Europe. Evidently, however, he was persuaded that de Gaulle's ambitions would prove on balance more embarrassing to his Western partners than to the interests of the Soviet Union. Down to the time of Khrushchev's deposition, in the fall of 1964, this view of the situation continued to shape Soviet policy toward France. Khrushchev's successors were merely to pick up where he left off.

Unfinished Exploration of a New Policy toward Germany?

Khrushchev's overtures toward Bonn and the objectives he had in mind during the last two years of his tenure present a much more intricate and speculative case than his fairly straightforward bid for warmer relations with France. Khrushchev may actually have sought nothing more earth-shaking than some "normalization" of relations with the new Bonn regime which succeeded Adenauer in the fall of 1963. Or, as certain curious but incomplete bits of evidence permit one to speculate, he may have been exploring a radical change of policy, the implications of which could have been a contributory factor in his political downfall.

[64] See Wolfe, *Soviet Commentary*, pp. 2–3; Rubinstein, *Current History* (November 1964): 282–83.
[65] Hudson, *Current History* (October 1963): 233; Crabb, *Annals* (January 1964): 17.

In either case, Khrushchev's exploration of a new pattern of relations with Bonn was carried out in a rather low key, often difficult to discern above the din of a generally hostile line toward West Germany, which manifested itself in the steady stridence of the anti-MLF campaign and other Soviet propaganda aimed at reinforcing the image of German "revanchism."

Before going into the evidence which suggests that Khrushchev was actually searching for alternative lines of approach to the German question, we may find it useful to review some of the factors likely to have impressed upon him, in the course of the 1963–64 détente, the desirability of such a search.

To begin with, as noted earlier, the old policy of trying to impose a settlement of the German question upon the Western allies had proved less than fruitful, and, after the confrontations in Berlin and Cuba, it had been suspended without any positive new approach to take its place. Nor were the largely negative reflexes from Moscow which passed for policy toward Germany proving very productive. Not only was the general resurgence of West Germany going unchecked, but Bonn appeared, at least in the autumn of 1963, to be on the verge of attaining some sort of nuclear status. As for the Ulbricht regime in East Germany, its internal economic and political difficulties were at best mending only slowly, and its dismay at the failure of the earlier Berlin campaign to yield the stabilizing benefits of formal international recognition was now apparently impelling it to press anew for the long-promised separate treaty with the Soviet Union.[66]

Against this background of unchecked West German resurgence and East German malaise, which was in effect what the Soviets had to show for a policy based on the idea of keeping Germany divided, Khrushchev could well have felt that the time had come to re-examine the merits of a policy aimed toward German reunification. Compelling arguments could doubtless be advanced both for and against such a radical shift. Although Khrushchev may not have been prepared to break completely with the status quo, for reasons we shall suggest later, let us for the moment consider some of the pros and cons of a policy change that would have involved proffering a reunification deal to West Germany.

Among arguments in favor of such a shift, perhaps the following would have seemed particularly important. First, a reunified Germany—denuclearized as part of the price of reunification—would pose a less serious threat to the Soviet Union in the long run than a resurgent West German state whose attainment of nuclear status might otherwise appear to be merely a matter of time. Second, since the neutralization of Germany would also be part of the

---

[66] East German pressure for a separate peace treaty may be inferred from the fact that Khrushchev found it necessary a few months later to conclude the Soviet–GDR friendship treaty, even though, as we shall see, it came at a somewhat awkward time with respect to his overtures to Bonn for a meeting with Erhard. Various signs of disquiet within the Ulbricht regime over Khrushchev's intentions (see fn. 96 below) suggest that Pankow may have put priority on concluding a treaty as a means of cramping Khrushchev's style. For pertinent comment on general factors inducing the East Germans to exert pressure for changes in a status quo that denied them the privileges of diplomatic recognition, see Richardson, *Germany and the Atlantic Alliance*, p. 312.

price, the Soviet Union could count with confidence on the collapse of NATO, once a neutral Germany had been obliged to withdraw. Third, although the economic and political weight of a unified Germany would doubtless grow, such a Germany—with her nuclear teeth pulled, her ties with the West loosened, and her irredentist claims renounced—would stand little chance of resisting Soviet influence and might in fact move appreciably closer to the Soviet Union.[67] Fourth, in the new equilibrium established in East Central Europe, an independent, though neutral, unified Germany would remain worrisome enough to small allies of the Soviet Union, such as Poland and Czechoslovakia, to keep them aware of their dependence on Moscow for comfort and security.

On the other hand the most telling objection to moving away from a policy of keeping Germany divided would doubtless have been that the Soviet Union had already invested far too much political capital and prestige in the new Communist order in East Germany to contemplate abandoning the status quo for the uncertain benefits of reunification. Second, it was by no means clear that the Ulbricht regime could be persuaded to co-operate in its own dismantlement without exposing the Soviet Union to the stigma of having "sold out" a Communist regime to serve its own great-power interests. Third, the unfavorable reflections upon the Soviet Union's position in Eastern Europe and its leadership within the Communist world generally would be the more severe as Peking probably would seize upon the situation as a further sign of Moscow's perfidy and unfitness to lead the world Communist movement.

Finally, there was always the possibility that Germany, though neutralized, might not stay tamed, so that the end result of a radical Soviet policy shift could be to have reconstituted a powerful and independent state without the restraints and limits imposed by the status quo. Indeed, even if a reunified Germany were ultimately to embrace communism—an unlikely prospect at best—the Soviet Union might well find it uncomfortable to share the European stage with another Communist state potentially powerful enough to become a rival in Europe, as had China on the Asian flank.

Which set of arguments on the question of reunification may have seemed the more persuasive to Khrushchev it is impossible to say. Given the tendency of political leaders to prefer grappling with known difficulties rather than invite unknown hazards, however, Khrushchev would perhaps have shied away from such a radical departure as that involved in engineering a full-fledged reunification deal. In 1956 he had said to some French visitors that the reality of seventeen million Germans under Communist rule was preferable to the imponderables of seventy million Germans in a neutralized

[67] Hassner, "Polycentrism in East and West," p. 31. For a useful marshaling of factors weighing both for and against Soviet interest in a unified Germany, with the balance tending toward the negative, see *Germany and the Atlantic Alliance*, pp. 353–57. See also Brzezinski, *Alternative to Partition*, pp. 85–88; Wolfgang Bretholz, "The Soviet Union and the German Question," *Bulletin*, Institute for the Study of the USSR, Munich (April 1964): 6–7.

state.[68] He may have felt much the same way in 1963–64. If so, a policy of partial accommodation toward the Federal Republic may have held more appeal for Khrushchev than reunification.

Seen in the context of détente, for example, a new approach that went no further than probing for better relations with Bonn might have appeared as a way to promote the idea of mutual troop reductions in Europe, to take some of the steam out of the MLF nuclear-sharing scheme, and—of no small moment in view of Khrushchev's ambitious economic plans at home—to open up the prospect of obtaining large credits and other economic-technical benefits from West Germany. Furthermore, a policy of partial accommodation with Bonn might also have eased some of the problems of the Ulbricht regime. Not only could Bonn be pressed to relax its anti-Ulbricht stance as the price of improved relations with Moscow, for example, but it could perhaps be obligated to deal with East Germany on a basis that could be construed as de facto acceptance of the concept of two sovereign states.

To come now to the actual record of Khrushchev's overtures toward Bonn, it is evident that sometime between the fall of 1963 and mid-1964 he began to explore the new situation created by Adenauer's retirement and the establishment of the Erhard government on October 16, 1963.[69] At first, there was little outward sign that Bonn under Erhard–Schroeder would receive less hostile treatment from Moscow than while Adenauer was still at the helm.[70] Despite some cautious optimism in the Western press that Khrushchev might be disposed to reciprocate the "policy of movement" espoused by the Erhard–Schroeder team, thus opening fresh possibilities for settlement of the German problem,[71] his initial tack seemed designed to put the leaders of the new government on the defensive.

In early March 1964, for example, after Bonn had published a policy report which, among other things, broached the need to resolve the reunification question as a prerequisite for genuine East–West reconciliation, Mos-

---

[68] See Melvin Croan, "Reality and Illusion in Soviet–German Relations," *Survey*, no. 44/45 (October 1962): 20.

[69] Konrad Adenauer retired as Chancellor on October 15, 1963, but stayed on one day until the new government headed by Ludwig Erhard was installed (*New York Times*, October 16, 1963).

[70] In the fall of 1963, before Adenauer's retirement, the Soviet Union had consistently attacked Bonn, not only on the familiar grounds of German ambition to acquire nuclear weapons but also for Bonn's position toward East Germany. In August 1963, for example, the Soviet government rejected Bonn's right to speak for all of Germany (*Pravda*, August 27, 1963), and in an interview with Drew Pearson, Khrushchev asserted that unification of Germany was out of the question "unless agreed between the two German governments" (*Washington Post*, August 22, 1963). On October 12, a few days before Adenauer's retirement, the Soviet government issued its version of a purported proposal from Adenauer to Khrushchev in 1962 for a "10-year truce" on the German problem. The point of the Soviet statement was apparently to emphasize that a truce was unacceptable because it would delay the conclusion of a peace treaty with the GDR even if other "reasonable opportunities" for settlement of the German problem had been exhausted. See *Izvestiia*, October 13, 1963, and *New York Times*, October 12, 1963.

[71] See, for example, Alfred Friendly, "Clearing Atmosphere May Permit Probing of German Problem," *Washington Post*, January 1, 1964.

cow assailed the new leadership in terms as harsh as any ever visited upon Adenauer. Charging that Bonn's professed desires for peaceful settlement of disputed problems were worthless unless backed by deeds, a TASS statement went on to assert that Erhard's existing programs could not lead to "normalization" of relations with the USSR, that West Berlin "never was and never will be part of the FRG," and that the rise of a "new Hitler" in West Germany could not be ruled out.[72] Later in March, still apparently bent on keeping Bonn off balance with respect to the issue of reunification, the Soviet government said in a note to Bonn that it rejected "once again" the right of the Federal Republic to "speak on behalf of the whole of Germany."[73]

The Ulbricht regime, too, seemed intent on blunting the new government's initiative toward reopening the unification question. In the first months after Erhard had become Chancellor, Ulbricht showed increasing sensitivity to any inference that Bonn's hopes of ending the division of Germany meant that it alone had the interests of all the German people at heart. Indeed, in an interview with the editor of the West German magazine *Der Stern,* Ulbricht sought to demonstrate that Bonn's partnership with the West was less compatible with unification of the two German states than his own regime's relationship with the Soviet Union.[74] Although Ulbricht undoubtedly shared the Soviet Union's interest in placing Bonn on the defensive over the reunification issue, his motives were not necessarily entirely parallel. He also had to guard against the possibility that the Soviet Union might change its position acknowledging the existence of two separate and sovereign German states.

Even while Moscow's public attacks on the West German government and its policies continued unabated, however, the first private Soviet overtures toward the new Bonn leadership had apparently begun by the spring of 1964. It later became known, for example, that in mid-March the Soviet Ambassador to Bonn, Andrei A. Smirnov, met quietly with Chancellor Erhard for a "reasonable" discussion of Soviet–German relations, and that shortly thereafter discreet Soviet soundings began on the possibility of an Erhard–Khrushchev meeting.[75] At about the same time, various outward signs began to point to a less intransigent Soviet attitude toward Bonn: in late March, steps were taken for closer economic co-operation, including the establishment of a Krupp representative in Moscow and preparations for negotiating a new trade agreement;[76] in April a delegation of Soviet journalists, whose account of an interview with Erhard appeared in *Izvestiia,* reported that they had

---

[72] TASS, "To Learn Lessons from the Past," *Pravda,* March 8, 1964. See also Henry Tanner, "Moscow Castigates Bonn: Sees Risk of New Hitler," *New York Times,* March 8, 1964.

[73] The Soviet Government Note of March 23, 1964, to Bonn (*New York Times,* March 23, 1964).

[74] A report of this interview was carried in *Pravda,* December 4, 1963.

[75] See Henry Tanner, "Moscow and Bonn," *New York Times,* August 2, 1964; Sydney Gruson, "U.S. Said To Back Erhard Meeting with Khrushchev," ibid., May 12, 1964.

[76] See Paul Wohl, "Bonn-Moscow Ties Expand," *Christian Science Monitor,* April 30, 1964.

carried away a "positive impression" from their meeting with the new German Chancellor.[77]

The next significant outward indication of Khrushchev's interest in some "normalization" of relations with West Germany came, curiously enough, in connection with what appeared to be, on the surface at least, an important gesture of Soviet solidarity with the East German regime. On June 12, 1964, in Moscow, Khrushchev and Ulbricht signed a twenty-year treaty of friendship, mutual aid, and co-operation.[78] This pact was ostensibly a substitute for the separate peace treaty that Khrushchev had threatened to conclude during the 1958–61 period of recurrent crises over Berlin, and which Ulbricht had ardently desired in order to win for his regime the seal of international recognition. Although the new treaty of friendship probably gave Ulbricht some comfort by guaranteeing the "integrity" of the GDR's borders and by reaffirming that German reunification could only be achieved through agreement between the two "sovereign German states," it fell far short of conferring upon the GDR the status it had sought to gain through a formal peace treaty. Indeed, the basic relationship between the GDR and the Soviet Union was left essentially unchanged by the friendship pact,[79] which also stipulated that rights and obligations stemming from previous four-power agreements on Germany, including the Potsdam agreement, would remain unaffected.

Inasmuch as this last proviso reversed Moscow's earlier contention that the four-power agreements were outmoded, its effect was not only to dampen East German aspirations for untrammeled sovereignty but also to give tacit reassurance to the Western powers that no new challenges to existing Allied rights, such as access to Berlin, were in the wind.[80] This indication that the Soviet–GDR friendship treaty signaled no fresh round of tension-producing demands upon the West,[81] added to the fact that the substance of the treaty was unlikely to be intolerably offensive to the Federal Republic, gave grounds for interpreting it as designed to allay East German anxieties about a possible shift of Soviet policy while leaving the Soviet Union free to explore a new pattern of relations with Bonn.

Khrushchev's intention not to let the Soviet–GDR treaty stand in the way

---

[77] "Meeting in Badenweiler," *Izvestiia*, April 21, 1964.

[78] Full text in *Pravda*, June 13, 1964.

[79] The Soviet–GDR friendship treaty provided no additional security guarantees beyond those already given in the 1955 Warsaw Treaty, nor did it alter the tutelary relationship of the Soviet Union toward the GDR by providing any new basis for the legitimacy of the Ulbricht regime. As one commentator said about the failure of the friendship pact to formalize the legitimacy of the GDR, "the commonlaw marriage everyone has known about for 20 years was made public but the Soviet Union has not yet taken East Germany to the altar." See Katherine Clark, "Treaty's Text Eases Tension in West Berlin," *Washington Post*, June 14, 1964.

[80] See Moscow dispatches by Henry Tanner, *New York Times*, June 13, 1964, and Henry Shapiro, *Washington Post*, June 14, 1964.

[81] One possible exception to the treaty's avoidance of demands that could disrupt the status quo was its Article 6, stating that West Berlin was to be considered "an independent political entity." While this signified that demands to convert West Berlin into a "free, demilitarized city" were not being abandoned, the point was not spelled out in the treaty itself. It was mentioned, however, in the communiqué accompanying the treaty.

of diplomatic overtures toward Bonn was immediately evident in Soviet encouragement of the idea of a Khrushchev–Erhard meeting. A few days before the signing of the Soviet–GDR pact, for example, while Ulbricht was being entertained in the Soviet Union, the Soviet Embassy in Bonn let it be known publicly that Chancellor Erhard, too, would be welcome in Moscow; in an interview with a West German newspaper, an Embassy official stated that "Premier Nikita S. Khrushchev would be very glad to receive Dr. Erhard in Moscow," adding that "such a visit could produce a significant contribution to the solution of the German question through reunification."[82] A short time later, at a Kremlin rally following the signing of the friendship treaty, Khrushchev slipped some further words of encouragement for Bonn into his speech by saying: "We hail the efforts of all sober-minded people of West Germany directed at improving relations and developing peaceful co-operation between our states."[83]

Evidence of Soviet diplomatic probing for an Erhard–Khrushchev meeting, at which the two leaders might be expected to explore the future course of Soviet–German relations, continued to accumulate in mid-summer 1964. For one thing, Khrushchev proved to be in no hurry to obtain ratification of the Soviet–GDR friendship treaty, thereby suggesting that he preferred to keep this issue on the shelf while angling for an invitation to Bonn. Then, in July, Khrushchev's son-in-law Alexei Adzhubei, who had but recently returned from a goodwill visit to France, was sent off on a similar mission to West Germany at the head of a delegation of Soviet journalists.[84] His twelve-day tour, during which he made several well-publicized bids for better understanding between Moscow and Bonn,[85] included a private talk with Dr. Erhard, at which agreement "in principle" reportedly was reached for a meeting later in the year with Khrushchev.[86]

Snubbed by Ulbricht in Berlin on his way home, Adzhubei returned to his post as editor of *Izvestiia*, in whose pages a serial account of his West German visit appeared in early August.[87] Although Adzhubei's account for home consumption was less amicably flavored than his remarks to audiences in West Germany, it nevertheless conveyed a picture of a German leadership whose mentality was changing toward greater "realism" and whose "perception of the contemporary world" was becoming "more reasonable."[88] For

---

[82] See Paul Wohl, "What East German Treaty Means," *Christian Science Monitor*, June 17, 1964.

[83] Khrushchev speech at rally in Kremlin Palace of Soviets (*Pravda*, June 13, 1964).

[84] The Soviet press announced briefly on July 19, 1964, that Adzhubei and his party had arrived in West Germany the day before at the invitation of a group of West German newspaper editors (*Izvestiia, Pravda*, July 19, 1964).

[85] See Henry Tanner, "Moscow and Bonn," *New York Times*, August 2, 1964; Paul Wohl, "Adzhubei Bids For Bonn Amity," *Christian Science Monitor*, August 8, 1964. Soviet press coverage of the twelve-day Adzhubei visit was confined to brief bulletins while the trip was in progress; a full first-hand report of the trip came only after Adzhubei's return to Moscow.

[86] See Tanner dispatch, *New York Times*, August 2, 1964.

[87] The Adzhubei articles appeared under the heading "We Saw West Germany" in *Izvestiia* on August 9, 11, 13, and 16, 1964. In addition to Adzhubei, they were signed by V. Lednev, N. Polianov, and E. Pral'nikov.

[88] *Izvestiia*, August 9, 11, 1964. The relatively favorable image of West German leaders painted

Soviet readers, accustomed to a much harsher image of Germany's leaders, this conciliatory note doubtless constituted a clear hint that some change was in the air.

In early September, after Khrushchev had made a hurried trip to Prague to consult with the foreign ministers of the Warsaw block states,[89] it was disclosed that he had expressed his readiness to visit Bonn—thus to become the first Soviet premier ever to go to West Germany. Announced in Bonn on September 3, the visit was tentatively set for some time in December, pending a formal invitation and other incidental arrangements.[90] Although it now appeared that the path had been cleared for him to embark on a new and possibly portentous venture into personal diplomacy, developments in the course of September and early October suggested that Khrushchev's overtures toward Bonn had aroused serious concern and opposition within his own regime.

The first intimation of internal opposition came on September 6, only three days after the announcement of plans for the meeting with Erhard, when an official of the West German Embassy in Moscow was doused with liquid mustard gas, presumably by members of the Soviet secret police.[91] It may have been in retaliation for something connected with the victim's duties, and quite unrelated to internal Soviet opposition to Khrushchev; but the timing of the mustard-gas incident strongly implied that it was a provocation intended to stir up ill feeling that could obstruct plans for the Khrushchev visit to Bonn. Indeed, it had precisely this effect, at least temporarily. Bonn rejected the first Soviet reply to its protest and made known that no formal invitation would be extended to Khrushchev until the incident was satisfac-

---

by Adzhubei had been partially anticipated by the report of an earlier Soviet newspaper delegation to Bonn, in April 1964. (See fn. 77 above.) Adzhubei, however, was careful not to go overboard in assessing a changed mentality among West German leaders. At one point, for example, he observed that "Bonn is at a crossroads," and that it could not be predicted which "tendencies will prevail—common sense or recklessness." He also put emphasis on respect for Soviet power as the basis for changing and more reasonable German attitudes; at the same time, he conceded that such attitudes were to be found "among people of various political, social, and economic positions in the Federal Republic of Germany." Later references in *Pravda* to Adzhubei's assessment shifted this proposition, as we shall see presently, to imply that reasonable attitudes had not yet penetrated into the Bonn political arena.

[89] See David Binder, "Khrushchev Talks with Czech Chief," *New York Times*, September 1, 1964; C. L. Sulzberger, "Khrushchev's Watch on the Rhine," ibid., September 21, 1964. According to charges from Peking some days later, East German representatives were not invited to take part in this meeting. (See fn. 96 below.)

[90] Arthur J. Olsen, "Khrushchev States Readiness To Visit Bonn on Invitation," *New York Times*, September 4, 1964; Harry B. Ellis, "Moscow Timing: Bonn Takes Notice," *Christian Science Monitor*, September 5, 1964.

[91] The mustard-gas attack on Horst Schwirkmann, identified by Bonn sources as a security technician at the West German Embassy in Moscow, was presumed to be the work of the Soviet secret police if only because no other category of Soviet citizens would normally dare to carry out such a brutal assault upon an official representative of a foreign country. Schwirkmann's evident success in foiling Soviet wiretap attempts against the Embassy premises would have marked him as a logical victim for retaliation, permitting his attackers to justify their action on "professional" grounds in the event that they should be called to account by higher political authorities. See Arthur J. Olsen, "German Called Intrigue Victim," *New York Times*, September 15, 1964.

torily explained. Only after a second and somewhat conciliatory Soviet note to Bonn, on October 13, did it appear that the matters were about to be patched up.[92] By that time, of course, Khrushchev's downfall was only hours away.

Apart from the mustard-gas episode, there were other hints in September of gathering internal opposition to Khrushchev's planned trek to Bonn. One of the issues arose around the Soviet–GDR friendship treaty, ratification of which had been delayed for three-and-a-half months while Khrushchev was angling for an invitation to Bonn. On September 25 a recommendation for ratification was made public in Moscow. Although the timing alone might have passed unnoticed, the *Pravda* announcement added to the significance of this move by placing prominent emphasis upon the role of the treaty as a barrier to the aspirations of "West German militarism and revanchism," including "revanchist plans to swallow up the German Democratic Republic."[93] The suggestion that Khrushchev's overtures to Bonn had stimulated concern in some Soviet circles over a possible deal at the expense of the GDR was strengthened during the next few days, when successive *Pravda* editorials warned that "anyone who thinks that improvement of relations between the USSR and West Germany can be achieved in the slightest degree at the expense of the interests of the GDR is deeply mistaken."[94]

Meanwhile, Peking had openly alleged that a "criminal political deal" was in the making in connection with Khrushchev's projected visit to Bonn, aimed at "buying the GDR from the Soviet Union."[95] Obviously calculated to play upon East Germany's uneasiness about Khrushchev's visit,[96] the

---

[92] See Arthur J. Olsen, "Bid to Khrushchev Delayed by Bonn," *New York Times*, October 4, 1964; Bonn dispatch, "Attack on German Regretted by Soviet," ibid., October 14, 1964. The first West German protest on September 14 drew a brusque and unapologetic Soviet reply. A second protest elicited an expression of regret on October 13 that was conciliatory in tone, though still short of an apology. The fact that the second Soviet reply—couched in terms calculated to put Khrushchev's visit back on the track—was delivered on the very eve of his downfall suggests that knowledge of the conspiracy against him had not filtered down to the bureaucracy in the Ministry of Foreign Affairs.

[93] "In the Interest of the People's Peace and Security," *Pravda*, September 25, 1964. This announcement also alluded to the favorable assessment of some West German public figures which Adzhubei had given a month earlier in *Izvestiia*. It did not challenge the assessment directly, but it drew a somewhat sharper distinction than Adzhubei between nonpolitical and political figures, noting that among the former there were some "sober-minded and reasonable figures," and adding the hope that such people would "gain the upper hand in the Bonn political arena."

[94] Editorial, "A Great Goal Unites Us," *Pravda*, September 27, 1964. See also "Our Goal—Friendship and Peace," ibid., September 26, 1964.

[95] See Seymour Topping, "China Says Soviet Views Bonn 'Deal'," *New York Times*, September 9, 1964; "Red China Says Soviets Plot East German Sellout," *Washington Post*, September 9, 1964. Details of Peking's charges, which were aired in *Jen-min Jih-pao* (People's Daily) on September 8, 1964, may be found in *Peking Review*, no. 37, September 11, 1964, pp. 18–19.

[96] Even before announcement of the planned visit, East German disquiet was evident over the possibility that the GDR might be bypassed by Khrushchev's personal diplomacy. An editorial in *Neues Deutschland*, August 9, 1964, for example, had asked whether it could be called sensible "if a certain person should ... open the door to the burglar who had once broken into his own house." Peking cited this statement, as well as the exclusion of GDR leaders from Khrushchev's early September Prague meeting with East European foreign ministers, as evidence of East German concern that Khrushchev was planning to double-cross the GDR. See *Peking Review*, September 11,

Chinese charges included reference to rumors that West German leaders were prepared to offer Khrushchev "large trading credits" in return for Soviet "political concessions," and some Chinese commentary compared the alleged deal with the 1938 Munich pact between Hitler and Chamberlain.[97]

In early October, at the very time the internal Kremlin conspiracy to unseat Khrushchev was evidently coming to a head, new signs appeared that some of Khrushchev's Presidium colleagues had become alarmed at the implications of his projected visit to Bonn, and had found it expedient to quiet East German anxieties about a possible sellout. One of these colleagues, Leonid I. Brezhnev, showed up for the fifteenth anniversary celebration of the GDR in East Berlin, where, on October 6, he delivered a speech stressing that "the Soviet Union has always stood and will also in the future stand by the side of the GDR."[98] Another Presidium leader, Mikhail A. Suslov, speaking in Moscow the day before, had taken up the sellout theme even more directly, declaring that friendly Soviet–GDR relations "are not for sale, even if all the gold in the world were offered for them."[99]

Several days later, on October 14, it was Suslov who reportedly acted as chief spokesman for Khrushchev's opponents in the Central Committee session at which the Soviet leader was deposed.[100] At that point, a curtain of sorts descended on the question of Khrushchev's visit to Bonn, which had become an abortive project to be filed away with history's other unfinished business. What kind of "deal" with Bonn, if any, Khrushchev may have been contemplating and the extent to which its implications may have counted among the many other factors responsible for his ouster[101] cannot be determined from the record available to date.

The foregoing brief recital of developments attending Khrushchev's overtures to Bonn during the final year of his tenure does suggest, however, that he may have been toying with a policy shift that his colleagues found undesirable under the circumstances then prevailing. In light of the efforts that his

---

1964, p. 19. It is worth noting, incidentally, that a year earlier, in 1963, when Soviet policy was still markedly hostile toward Bonn, Peking had tried to stimulate East German fears that the Soviet Union was prepared to sacrifice the GDR in order "to curry favor with the United States." At that time, the GDR accused Peking of trying to sow dissension between the GDR and Moscow. See "German Reds Assail China," *New York Times*, August 29, 1963; Andrew Gyorgy, "East Germany," in *Eastern European Government and Politics* (New York: Harper & Row, Inc., 1966), p. 133.

[97] *Washington Post*, September 9, 1964.

[98] Speech by L. I. Brezhnev, *Pravda*, October 7, 1964.

[99] "The Banner of the GDR—Peace, Democracy, Socialism," *Pravda*, October 6, 1964.

[100] See dispatches by Henry Tanner, "Soviet Is Preparing Explanation on Shift," and "Rifts Preceded Khrushchev Fall," *New York Times*, October 21 and 22, 1964. See also "Details Given on Khrushchev's Fall," *Washington Post*, November 30, 1964 (reprinted from *Observer*, London).

[101] For an informed and useful examination of factors that entered into Khrushchev's ouster, see the series of commentaries by several leading analysts of Soviet affairs in *Problems of Communism* (January–February 1965): 1–32; (May–June 1965): 37–45; and (July–August 1965): 72–76. See also Linden, *Khrushchev and the Soviet Leadership*, pp. 203–20; Edward Crankshaw, *Khrushchev: A Career* (New York: Viking Press, 1966), pp. 272–87; Martin Page, *The Day Khrushchev Fell* (New York: Hawthorn Books, Inc., 1965), pp. 50–94. Further discussion of Khrushchev's downfall will be found in chapter X.

colleagues made just before his ouster to allay East German anxieties, they
may even have suspected Khrushchev of being willing to abandon the concept of two Germanys in favor of an alternative other than a single Communist state—the point upon which all previous proposals for a settlement
of the German question had foundered. The policy toward Germany adopted
by Khrushchev's successors—which, incidentally, did not involve a sharp
reversal of Khrushchev's general policy line, even though the matter of a
top-level visit was quietly dropped for the time being—is a subject to which
we shall give further attention. It is time now to return to a more detailed
examination of the specifically military policy problems and reforms which
had a bearing on the Soviet Union's European policy during the Khrushchev
era.

VII

MILITARY POLICY ISSUES AND REFORMS OF
THE KHRUSHCHEV ERA

For a variety of reasons, the military policy issues with which the Soviet leadership was confronted during Khrushchev's rule proved to be considerably more complex than those of the earlier postwar period. Under Stalin, Soviet military policy had been oriented in a relatively straightforward way toward two primary tasks: the first and most urgent, to break the American nuclear monopoly; the second, to hold Europe hostage to the preponderant conventional military power of the Soviet Union while the first task was being accomplished.

By contrast, Khrushchev found it necessary to deal not only with the unfinished business of the Stalinist period but also with a host of new problems that arose out of the military-technical revolution and the increasingly complex political environment in which Soviet affairs at home and abroad were conducted during the decade of his rule. In this, the first of three chapters dealing with various aspects of Soviet military policy and posture as the Khrushchev era unfolded, we shall look briefly at some of the major problems and considerations which were to shape the general evolution of Soviet military policy under Khrushchev, especially those pertaining to the place of Western Europe in Soviet strategy.

Impact of the Nuclear Age on Uses of Military Power

Among the broad general problems of the Khrushchev era, perhaps none presented more fundamental perplexities at both doctrinal and operative levels of Soviet policy than that of translating Soviet military power into effective political power in a nuclear world, where the machinery of power itself had taken on awesome new dimensions of destructiveness. In a sense, the Khrushchev period was one of wrestling with the paradox that while military power was acquiring an ever increasing coercive potential the constraints upon its use also grew apace, as technology tended to multiply the risks and thus to narrow the opportunities for turning military power to political advantage. Although this was a universal paradox which did not confront the Soviet leadership alone,[1] it proved to have particularly damaging effects upon the

---

[1] One should note that, although the constraints upon the use of modern military power have grown, this does not say that it no longer counts in international life. Indeed, the very essence of the problem is that military power in its modern forms has introduced confusion and uncertainty

doctrines of a Marxist–Leninist leadership élite schooled to take a tough-minded view of force and violence as agents of sociopolitical change.

While Communist doctrine of the prenuclear age neither embraced the notion of violence for its own sake nor stressed, except for brief intervals, the spread of revolution by Red bayonets,[2] it did regard war as the legitimate "midwife" of revolution. The experience of two world wars seemed to confirm this diagnosis, for it was after each of these wars that communism enjoyed its greatest expansion in the world.[3] In a nuclear environment, however,

---

into the customary conduct of politics. The world is in the process of trying to work out new rules of the game. For perceptive analyses of this subject, see Klaus Knorr, *On the Uses of Military Power in the Nuclear Age* (Princeton, N.J.: Princeton University Press, 1966); Thomas C. Schelling, *Arms and Influence* (New Haven, Conn.: Yale University Press, 1966). See also the excellent essay by Thornton Read, *Military Policy in a Changing Political Context*, Center of International Studies, Princeton University, December 1964, especially pp. 1–19, 38–73; and Urs Schwarz, *American Strategy: A New Perspective* (New York: Doubleday and Co., 1966), pp. 61 ff.

[2] In the early days of the Soviet regime, up to around 1924, considerable attention was given by Soviet theorists, both military and political, to elaborating a doctrine of military exploitation of what was at that time expected to be the imminent collapse of the capitalist countries. Under some of the conceptions advanced, the Red Army would be given the double task of defending the Soviet regime at home and of coming to the aid of proletarian revolutionaries seeking to overthrow their governments abroad. There were a number of attempts in the early twenties to put the doctrine of revolution by bayonet into practice, following collapse of the Bela Kun Communist regime in Hungary in 1919 before the Red Army could be dispatched to help consolidate it. These attempts included the establishment of the short-lived "Soviet Republic of Gilan" in Iran in 1920 and the abortive campaign against Poland in the same year. The Red Army was also employed, more successfully, to establish Communist rule in Georgia in 1921, and as an instrument for setting up "People's" governments in Outer Mongolia and Tannu Tuva at about the same time. Thereafter, the practice of revolution by bayonet declined, until it was partly revived by Stalin in the case of Finland and the Baltic countries on the eve of World War II. But by that time Stalin was probably acting as much in what he conceived to be the great power interests of the Soviet Union as in the service of an abstract notion of spreading the revolution by Soviet arms. Stalin's use of the Soviet military presence in East Europe after World War II to help underwrite the Communist takeover in that region was the last and most impressive manifestation in his time of the original notion of the Red Army's revolutionary role.

In light of the lengthy evidence, one can hardly dismiss the point that Soviet thought has remained hospitable to the idea that the armed forces should be prepared, if the occasion arises, to ensure the triumph of "historical truth" by helping to accelerate the historical process. Operatively, however, this notion has generally been applied with care, especially since the advent of the nuclear age.

For useful discussion of some of these points, see Raymond L. Garthoff, "Military Influences and Instruments," in Ivo J. Lederer, ed., *Russian Foreign Policy: Essays in Historical Perspective* (New Haven, Conn.: Yale University Press, 1962), pp. 252–57; Michel Garder, *A History of the Soviet Army* (New York: Frederick A. Praeger, Inc., 1966), pp. 46–58, 72–73; John Erickson, *The Soviet High Command* (London: St. Martin's Press, 1962), pp. 84–111.

[3] As late as 1959, Communist doctrine continued to recognize openly the historical dependence of communism on war, although by that time the revisionist view of revolution as no longer "obligatorily linked with war" had begun to circulate more widely. A concise statement of the historical link between war and revolution can be found in an authoritative doctrinal manual published in 1959 as the successor to Stalin's' celebrated *Problems of Leninism*. It reads: "Up to now historical development adds up to the fact that revolutionary overthrow of capitalism has been linked each time with world wars. Both the first and second world wars served as powerful accelerators of revolutionary explosions." O. V. Kuusinen, ed., *Osnovy Marksizma-Leninizma* (Foundations of Marxism-Leninism) (Moscow: Gospolitizdat, 1959), p. 519. For a fuller discussion of the place of war in Communist theory, see Thomas W. Wolfe, *Communist Outlook on War*, The RAND Corporation, P-3640, August 1967.

another world war began to look much too dangerous to perform the function of enhancing the conditions for a third wave of Communist advance. Moreover, a new constraint fell also upon the lesser forms of revolutionary conflict, as a small war might escalate into a larger nuclear conflagration which could jeopardize the Soviet system itself.

Symptoms of a doctrinal crisis growing out of the Soviet leadership's appreciation of this situation first came to the surface with Malenkov's short-lived thesis, in 1954, that a nuclear war could result in the "mutual destruction" of both capitalist and Communist society.[4] If this were so, then the long-held Communist dogma of the inevitability of an eventual war to the finish between the capitalist and Communist systems was patently the counsel of despair. Khrushchev himself initially opposed Malenkov's unorthodox and unsettling assertion, but later, having established his own leadership credentials, he progressively came around to views essentially similar to those of his discredited colleague.

Khrushchev's first step in this direction was his revision, in 1956, of the Leninist tenet on the inevitability of war, on the grounds that the growing strength of the Communist camp made it possible to avert war even though "imperialism" retained its aggressive character.[5] This doctrinal revision, which provided the theoretical underpinning for Khrushchev's advocacy of peaceful coexistence as the safest and most reliable form of class struggle in the international arena, also reflected a leaning toward the concept of deterrence, around which Khrushchev's military policy was to be largely fashioned.

Another revisionist tendency that manifested itself under Khrushchev was the gradual erosion of the dogma of inevitable Communist victory, should a new world war somehow occur. Although Khrushchev neither fully nor consistently embraced the "no victory" notion promulgated by some Soviet

[4] *Pravda*, March 13, 1954.

[5] This revision was enunciated by Khrushchev at the Twentieth Congress of the CPSU in 1956, where the Soviet leadership first recognized in a formal sense that nuclear weapons had undermined some of the fundamentals of traditional Communist doctrine. This was also the occasion for Khrushchev's "secret" speech denouncing Stalin.

It should be noted that some temporary shifts from the doctrine of the *inevitability* of war to to one of the *avoidability* of war had preceded Khrushchev. At the Seventh World Congress of the Comintern in August 1935, for example, in connection with the Popular Front line of that period, Georgii Dimitrov enunciated the thesis that war was preventable. (See G. Dimitroff, *The United Front: The Struggle Against War and Fascism* [New York: International Publishers, 1938], pp. 133, 174.) The Second World War tended to puncture the avoidability thesis advanced by Dimitrov. After World War II, Stalin, in his *Economic Problems of Socialism in the USSR* (1952), shifted attention to intercapitalist "contradictions" as stronger than those between capitalism and socialism (see discussion on pp. 27–31 above), thus implying that war was most likely to arise among capitalist countries. However, Stalin did not rule out the possibility that such a war would involve the Soviet Union, and he did reaffirm that it would be necessary to abolish imperialism in order to "eliminate the inevitability of war." For an analysis which distinguishes sharply between Soviet doctrine on the inevitability of intercapitalist wars and of wars between the opposing systems, see Frederick S. Burin, "The Communist Doctrine of the Inevitability of War," *American Political Science Review* (June 1963): 334–54.

publicists during his tenure,[6] the logic of his occasional admissions that nuclear war might mean mutual annihilation seemed to argue that he placed little stock in the doctrinaire formula of inevitable Communist victory.

A related sign of a doctrinal crisis over the political implications of modern weaponry during the Khrushchev period was the controversy as to whether the Leninist thesis on war as an instrument of politics, which had originally found its way into Lenin's thinking via Clausewitz[7]—still retained its validity under conditions of the nuclear age. Internal debate on this question in the general press and professional journals tended to find Soviet military writers persistently defending the validity of Lenin's dictum that war is a continuation of politics and an instrument of policy, while some political writers openly argued that in the nuclear age the formula should be changed to "War can be a continuation only of folly."[8] Again, Khrushchev himself stopped short of outright repudiation of Lenin's formula. His public remarks on the implausibility of erecting communism on the radioactive rubble of a nuclear war, however, seemed to reflect a personal belief that the Leninist link between war and politics was no longer tenable.[9]

These various departures from orthodoxy—best epitomized perhaps by the Soviet statement, in July 1963, that "the atomic bomb does not adhere to the class principle"[10]—were roundly challenged by the Chinese Communists in the many-sided quarrel between Moscow and Peking. Although we need not retrace here the lengthy exchange of polemics over Marxist–Leninist doctrine on war and politics,[11] it should be noted that this phase of the Sino–Soviet

[6] Among those who gave wide public currency to this notion was Major General Nikolai A. Talenskii, later to be attacked by some Soviet military writers for having spread such a "fatalistic" view. For references to Talenskii's statements, see chapter V, especially fn. 63.

[7] For illuminating discussions of the influence of Clausewitz on Lenin and Stalin, who were both keen readers of the German military thinker, see Byron Dexter, "Clausewitz and Soviet Strategy," *Foreign Affairs* (October 1950): 41–55; Henry A. Kissinger, *Nuclear Weapons and Foreign Policy* (New York: Harper & Row, Inc., 1957), pp. 340–44; Edward Mead Earle, "Lenin, Trotsky, Stalin: Soviet Concepts of War," in *Makers of Modern Strategy: Military Thought from Machiavelli to Hitler* (Princeton, N.J.: Princeton University Press, 1948), p. 337. See also Edward M. Collins, *War, Politics and Power* (Chicago: Henry Regnery & Co., 1962), especially the Introduction.

[8] Boris Dimitrev, "Brass Hats: Peking and Clausewitz," *Izvestiia*, September 24, 1963. For a description of the Soviet debate over the war as an instrument of politics, see T. W. Wolfe, *Soviet Strategy at the Crossroads* (Cambridge, Mass.: Harvard University Press, 1964), pp. 70–78.

[9] See, for example, Khrushchev's speech to the USSR Supreme Soviet on the international situation, *Pravda*, December 13, 1962.

[10] The full statement read: "The atomic bomb does not adhere to the class principle; it destroys everybody within range of its devastating force." ("Open Letter of the Central Committee of the Communist Party of the Soviet Union," *Pravda*, July 14, 1963.)

[11] In this exchange of polemics, a recurrent theme from the Soviet side was the alleged tendency of the Chinese leaders to regard war as "an acceptable and, in fact, the only means of settling contradictions between capitalism and socialism." The Chinese were accused of risking a nuclear holocaust by dogmatic interpretation of Lenin's views on war as an instrument of policy. The Soviets also coupled attacks on the Chinese "paper tiger" thesis, as applied to both nuclear weapons and the United States, with warnings that one must act in the nuclear age on a "sober estimate of actual forces." See, for example, M. A. Suslov's speech at the Central Committee Plenum,

quarrel spilled over into a running dispute over the soundness of the military theories espoused by each side. A long series of arguments from the Chinese and their adherents centered on charges that Soviet thinking was too pre-occupied with the problems of nuclear war, and that this "nuclear fetishism" with its lopsided emphasis on "technology over man" helped to account for the failure of Soviet military policy to serve the needs of the world revolutionary movement.[12] Criticism of Soviet military theory not only cited its allegedly "disastrous effects" on "the military activities of the socialist countries" but was used even in attempts to drive a wedge between Khrushchev and the Soviet military elite, as when the Chinese declared: "Khrushchev's whole set of military theories runs completely counter to Marxist–Leninist teachings on war and the army. To follow his wrong theories will necessarily involve disintegrating the army."[13]

The Soviet side responded with its own arguments, some of which were directed *ad hominem* against Mao and his pretensions as a strategist. Peking was reminded that the countries of the Communist camp itself, as well as "national-liberation" movements, lived under the protection of Soviet nuclear power, and that the real turning point in modern history had come when the Soviet Union broke the nuclear monopoly of the West.[14] The Chinese were

---

February 14, 1964, *Pravda*, April 3, 1964; Khrushchev's speech in Berlin, January 16, 1963, *Pravda*, January 17, 1963; editorial, "Let Us Strengthen the Unity of the Communist Movement in the Name of the Triumph of Peace and Socialism," *Pravda*, January 7, 1963.

The Chinese, in turn, while denying that they were courting war, argued that it cannot be ruled out while imperialism exists, and that to dwell on its horrors is only to discourage the revolutionary ardor and will-to-fight of the masses. The Chinese asserted categorically that, if nuclear war should come, it would end with the triumph of world communism. They charged that the Soviet Union had permitted itself to be awed into "capitulationism" toward the West through fear of nuclear war, and that it had failed to exploit its military power in a political sense to advance the interests of the Communist camp as a whole.

Polemics aside, the chances are that neither party to the dispute was any more eager than the other to invite a nuclear war, but that they differed essentially in their estimates of how far it was safe to go in exerting pressure upon the West without serious risk of precipitating war.

For a condensed account of these polemics on the question of war in the nuclear age, see Thomas W. Wolfe, *The Soviet Union and the Sino-Soviet Dispute*, The RAND Corporation, P-3203, August 1965, pp. 17–26. For fuller accounts, see Donald S. Zagoria, *The Sino–Soviet Conflct, 1956–1961* (Princeton, N.J.: Princeton University Press, 1962), especially pp. 154–72; Alice Langley Hsieh, *Communist China's Strategy in the Nuclear Era* (Englewood Cliffs, N.J.: Prentice-Hall, Inc., 1962), pp. 83–99. See also Morton H. Halperin, "Chinese Nuclear Strategy," *China Quarterly* (January–March 1965): 85.

[12] Among relevant Chinese comments, see "Two Different Lines on the Question of War and Peace," *Peking Review*, no. 47, November 22, 1963; "The Proletarian Revolution and Khrushchev's Revisionism," ibid., no. 14, April 1964; Kao Ko, "Road to Victory in the National Liberation War," *People's Daily*, July 31, 1963; Lu Chih-chao, "Examination of the Question of War Must Not Run Counter to the Marxist–Leninist Viewpoint on Class Struggle," *Red Flag*, August 15, 1963; General Lo Jui-ching, "Commemorate the Victory Over German Fascism," *Red Flag*, May 10, 1965. For a pithy North Vietnamese criticism, see Hoang Van Thai, "It Is Necessary To Hold Fast to the Party Military Line and Check the Revisionist Influence in the Military Sphere," *Hoc Tap*, Hanoi, no. 4, April 1964.

[13] *Peking Review*, November 22, 1963, p. 13.

[14] See Soviet government statement, *Pravda*, September 21, 1963; D. Vol'skii and V. Kudriavtsev, "Practical Reality and the Fantasies of the Splitters," *Krasnaia zvezda*, October 10, 1963; Colonel P. Trifonenkov, "The Most Pressing Problem of the Present Day and the Adventurism of

accused of inviting war on the basis of military theories that would pit man-power against nuclear weapons, and the Maoist belief that war can be won even though "modern techniques of war are ignored" was branded as "naive, to say the least, if not criminal."[15] In the course of the polemics, however, the Soviets, while criticizing the Chinese for trying "to impose their limited experi-ence and corresponding theories as a guide for all,"[16] did eventually come around to at least the partial admission that their own military theory had not fully faced up to the problems posed by small wars and "national liberation" conflicts.[17]

Deterrence Alone or Strategic Superiority?

Beneath the doctrinal ferment caused by awareness of the destructiveness of nuclear war, and apart from the polemics with Peking, lay practical ques-tions of great import for the shaping of Soviet military policy. Perhaps the knottiest of these questions for Khrushchev was this: could the Soviet Union continue to live, as it had for some time past, in a position of strategic infe-riority to its major adversary?

At the outset of his administration, Khrushchev faced the unpleasant fact that US strategic power had expanded rapidly under the stimulus of the Korean War.[18] In the Soviet military and political consciousness, partly as a result of Khrushchev's own efforts to free strategic thinking from the sterility into which it had fallen under Stalin, there was a heightened sense of the poten-tially disastrous consequences of a surprise nuclear attack upon the Soviet Union.[19] On the other hand, even as these considerations bespoke the need

the Chinese Dogmatists," *Kommunist Vooruzhennykh Sil* (Communist of the Armed Forces), no. 21 (November 1963): 23–28; Trifonenkov, "War and Politics," *Krasnaia zvezda*, October 30, 1963; Colonels I. Sidel'nikov and V. Zmitrenko, "The Modern Epoch and Defense of the Victories of Socialism," ibid., September 19, 1963; "Brass Hats, Peking and Clausewitz," *Izvestiia*, Sep-tember 24, 1963; Major General N. Ia. Sushko and Major T. Kondratkov, "War and Politics in the Nuclear Age," *Kommunist Vooruzhennykh Sil*, no. 2 (January 1964): 16–23.

[15] Major General S. Kozlov, "Against Dogmatism and the Distortion of Marxist-Leninist Teach-ing About War," *Narodna Armiya* (People's Army), broadcast on Sofia radio, October 8, 1963.

[16] Ibid. See also Raymond L. Garthoff, "A Soviet Critique of China's 'Total Strategy'," *Reporter*, May 19, 1966, pp. 48–49. This article discusses a blistering criticism of Chinese military theory which appeared in the October 1963 issue of *Voennaia mysl'* (Military Thought), a Soviet profes-sional journal of restricted circulation.

[17] Colonel I. Korotkov, "On the Development of Soviet Military Theory in the Post-War Years," *Voenno-istoricheskii zhurnal* (Military-Historical Journal), no. 4 (April 1964): 48. See also Thomas W. Wolfe, *Trends in Soviet Thinking on Theater Warfare, Conventional Operations, and Limited War*, The RAND Corporation, RM-4305-PR, December 1964, pp. 52–54. (The latter mon-ograph appears in essentially the same form as a chapter in John Erickson, ed., *The Military-Technical Revolution: Its Impact on Strategy and Foreign Policy* [New York: Frederick A. Praeger, Inc., 1966], pp. 52–79.)

[18] By 1955, for example, as a result of greatly increased emphasis by the Eisenhower adminis-tration in the post-Korean period on the development of the Strategic Air Command, American strategic bomber forces had increased to around 1,300 aircraft capable of missions against the Soviet Union. A forward base system to improve the operational employment of B-47 medium jet bombers, which at that time made up the bulk of the US strategic force, had also been developed.

[19] For examination of doctrinal revisions in the period following Stalin's death which reflected an awakened Soviet sense of the implications of surprise attack in the nuclear age, see Herbert S.

for great exertions to improve the Soviet strategic posture, Khrushchev was already moving toward the belief, expressed doctrinally in his revision of the thesis of inevitable war, that nuclear deterrence had begun to reduce the likelihood of a major war. In the late fifties, this confidence in deterrence was apparently fortified by Khrushchev's growing private conviction that the United States had no intention of initiating a nuclear attack on the Soviet Union.[20]

In circumstances in which long-term concern over a widening imbalance between Soviet and American strategic forces was thus partly offset by the absence of any immediate fear of attack, the Soviet leadership was obliged to weigh the relative merits of an essentially deterrent strategic posture for the Soviet Union versus a posture that would ensure Soviet superiority in the event deterrence failed and it became necessary to fight a war. It was here that the doctrinal debate as to whether nuclear weapons had made war politically obsolete ceased to be merely an academic issue and became a practical consideration bearing upon Khrushchev's policy approach.

If, on the one hand, there were still a prospect that war could be won or lost in a meaningful sense, it might be worth the effort to strive for a war-winning strategy and for superior forces commensurate to this task. Undesirable as a nuclear war might be, and despite the great pains which should be taken to avoid it, there would still be a sense in which winning would be politically preferable to losing any war that might occur. But if, on the other hand, there were no longer any victor and vanquished in a nuclear war, the advisable course might be quite different, particularly at a time when the Soviet Union's economic resources for support of a massive strategic arms build-up compared unfavorably with those of its adversary. In terms of Soviet military policy, the best solution then might well be to pin all hopes on a strategy of deterrence and to settle for something less than strategic superiority, that is to say, for strategic forces sufficient to maintain credibility but still clearly inferior to those of the adversary in any showdown that might take place.

Khrushchev's course, adopted perhaps reluctantly, lay in the latter direction. Although he brought about a substantial improvement in Soviet strategic forces, as we shall see presently, and although commitment to a doctrine calling for Soviet military-technological superiority over the West persisted throughout his tenure (with at least ritual adherence from Khrushchev himself),[21] his policies in effect amounted to settling for a second-best strategic posture. At the same time, however, Khrushchev sought to compensate in several ways for falling short of the doctrinal desideratum of Soviet superiority. One such way was to support a vigorous program of military research and

---

Dinerstein, *War and the Soviet Union*, rev. ed. (New York: Frederick A. Praeger, Inc., 1962), pp. 28–64, 167–214; Raymond L. Garthoff, *Soviet Strategy in the Nuclear Age*, rev. ed. (New York: Frederick A. Praeger, Inc., 1962), pp. 84–91. See also chapter IV, pp. 59–62 above.

[20] The question of Soviet views on the likelihood of war during the Khrushchev period is discussed further in the closing section of this chapter.

[21] On the issue of military superiority, see Wolfe, *Soviet Strategy at the Crossroads*, pp. 79–90.

development, recognized both in Khrushchev's time and by those who came after him as the indispensable technological base upon which any effort to attain strategic superiority would ultimately depend.[22] Another and more spectacular compensatory step, hastily abandoned under pressure, was Khrushchev's attempt to alter the strategic equation by deploying missiles to Cuba. Still another device was to cultivate an image of Soviet strategic power that went somewhat beyond what the substance of the strategic balance would justify. As our earlier discussion indicated,[23] Khrushchev's attempts to obtain political leverage from an inflated image of Soviet missile power foundered after the Berlin and Cuban crises; however, his missile showmanship undoubtedly did have the incidental effect of enhancing the deterrent aspect of the Soviet strategic posture that evolved during the latter 1950's and early 1960's.

From the standpoint of Soviet policy, neither the military nor the political worth of the strategic posture attained during these years could be judged solely in terms of its deterrent value, as Khrushchev himself was certainly made aware. On military grounds, forces that looked ample for deterrence were not necessarily adequate to win a war, if it should come to that. Soviet military leaders, professionally concerned with how to wage a war successfully once the shooting started, were naturally somewhat uneasy about a military policy design such as Khrushchev's, with what seemed to many of them its one-sided emphasis on the deterrent effect of missiles at the expense of the all-around strengthening of the armed forces.[24] Even if deterrence was to be

[22] For some typical expressions in Khrushchev's time of the view that technology and a vigorous research and development program provide the key to attaining military superiority, see Marshal R. Ia. Malinovskii, *Bditel'no stoiat' na strazhe mira* (Vigilantly Stand Guard Over the Peace) (Moscow: Voenizdat, 1962), p. 23; Marshal A. A. Grechko, "On a Leninist Course," *Krasnaia zvezda*, December 22, 1963; Marshal S. S. Biriuzov, "New Stage in the Development of the Armed Forces and Tasks of Indoctrinating and Training Troops," *Kommunist Vooruzhennykh Sil*, no. 4 (February 1964): 19. In a statement issued soon after Khrushchev's ouster, Alexei Kosygin, one of the new collective leaders, gave emphasis to the cardinal role of science and technology in supporting the power position of the USSR, although he did not specifically address himself to the issue of military superiority. See "On Improving the Management of Industry, Perfecting Planning and Strengthening Economic Incentives in Industrial Production," report by A. N. Kosygin to Central Committee Plenary Session, *Pravda*, September 28, 1965. Perhaps the most explicit Soviet treatment, in the post-Khrushchev period, or the role of technology in achieving military superiority was that by Lt. Colonel V. Bondarenko, "Military-Technical Superiority— The Most Important Factor for Reliable Defense of the Country," *Kommunist Vooruzhennykh Sil*, no. 17 (September 1966): 7–14.

For an informed Western account of technological competition as a phenomenon affecting the outcome of future wars, hot or cold, see Brig. General Robert C. Richardson, III, USAF, "Defense on the Technological Front: Anticipate the Attack," *Air Force* (June 1966): 98–102.

[23] See chapter V, pp. 84–99, above.

[24] Reservations on the part of Soviet military men about Khrushchev's overemphasis on deterrence became more pointed after his removal from power. However, a good deal of the military resistance to Khrushchev's reforms while he was still on the scene turned in one way or another on this question. For discussions of the subject, see Wolfe, *Soviet Strategy at the Crossroads*, pp. 34, 76, 130–52, 168–71; and Raymond L. Garthoff, *Soviet Military Policy: A Historical Analysis* (New York: Frederick A. Praeger, Inc., 1966), pp. 58–60.

Apart from the military's questioning of Khrushchev's deterrence-oriented philosophy, which could be explained on the grounds of professional concern with being better prepared to fight a war, if necessary, there was also a tendency in other quarters, perhaps unintended, to voice views

the primary criterion,[25] its credibility rested to an important extent on the Soviet Union's willingness to face the possibility of a war and on the capability of its armed forces to wage it at many levels of conflict—factors which professional military men felt Khrushchev was inclined to overlook. Beyond the controversial issue whether military preparations should be aimed primarily at deterrence or at improving capabilities for fighting a war if deterrence should fail, Khrushchev's military policies stirred up internal debate and questioning on other grounds.

Unsettling Effects of Khrushchev's Reforms

In essence, Khrushchev was a reformer, bent upon wrenching a traditionally conservative military bureaucracy out of its accustomed groove and forcing it to reorganize in line with the technological facts of life, as he saw them. His military policies brought about an appreciable shift of resources from conventional theater forces to strategic forces, and were accompanied on the conceptual level by a similar shift from almost exclusive preoccupation with continental land warfare to a new emphasis on the problems of intercontinental strategic war. Although these reforms were undoubtedly welcomed by some professional officers, they were plainly disturbing to others, particularly among the old-line commanders, whose careers had been forged in the great land campaigns of World War II. Throughout Khrushchev's tenure, his policies met with varying resistance from conservative marshals who felt, among other things, that his "one-weapon" emphasis on ballistic missiles was being carried too far.[26] Some of the military programs he adopted apparently reflected the need to strike a satisfactory compromise with that internal opposition as much as they did his own direct preferences.

Khrushchev's problems did not end, however, with his failure to see eye to eye with his marshals on the military merits of the Soviet strategic posture; he was also beset by questions pertaining to its political worth. On two important counts Khrushchev probably felt that Soviet military power adequately met the needs of Soviet policy: it served to ensure Soviet security by deterring the adversary from a deliberate military attack on the Soviet Union, and to inhibit dangerous political initiatives from the West. But apart from these

which were at variance with Khrushchev's expressed confidence in deterrence. For example, Soviet literature on disarmament often questioned the stability of "mutual deterrence." See V. A. Zorin, ed., *Bor'ba Sovetskogo Soiuza za razoruzhenie, 1946–1960 gody* (The Soviet Union's Struggle for Disarmament, 1946–1960) (Moscow: Izdatel'stvo Instituta mezhdunarodnykh otnoshenii, 1961), pp. 83–85; D. V. Bogdanov, *Iadernoe razoruzhenie* (Nuclear Disarmament) (Moscow: Izdatel'stvo Instituta mezhdunarodnykh otnoshenii, 1951), p. 75.

[25] A succinct statement of the Soviet military leadership's view of the requirements for deterrence was given by Marshal Malinovskii in 1962. Soviet military strength, he said, ought to be such as "to instill doubts about the outcome of a war planned by the aggressor, to frustrate his criminal designs in embryo, and if war becomes a reality, to defeat the aggressor decisively." ("The CPSU Program and Problems of Strengthening the Armed Forces of the USSR," *Kommunist*, no. 7 [May 1962]: 15.) For a sophisticated Western view of deterrence, which stands in some contrast to this statement, see Read, *Military Policy in a Changing Political Context*, pp. 12–19.

[26] See Wolfe, *Soviet Strategy at the Crossroads*, pp. 168–71.

essentially deterrent functions, the contributions of Soviet military power as a political instrument were less than clear under the constraints of the nuclear age.

Was the Soviet military posture adequate, for example, to support an assertive political strategy that would force the West into retreat on major political issues, particularly in the European arena, where the vital interests of the advanced industrial countries were sharply drawn? And how well could the Soviet military machine, as constituted, perform what might be called the counterdeterrent function[27] of discouraging Western military resistance to Communist attempts at political and proxy warfare in the underdeveloped Third World?

On both scores, Khrushchev's experience yielded little cause for satisfaction. With regard to Europe, as our earlier discussion brought out, the Soviet military posture lacked sufficient authority to wring important concessions from the Western powers, and Khrushchev was eventually obliged to discard an assertive policy line in favor of détente. The situation proved hardly better, from Khrushchev's standpoint, with respect to the political worth of Soviet military power in advancing communism in the underdeveloped countries. Here, despite frequent assertions from Moscow that Soviet nuclear missile power now provided a protective umbrella under which national revolutionary struggles might progress without "imperialist" interference, Communist gains were spotty at best. One may suppose that this was a particularly embarrassing disappointment to Khrushchev, not only because it left him vulnerable to Chinese charges of incompetence as a world revolutionary leader but also in light of his own apparent belief that the underdeveloped world—in the throes of transition from its former colonial status—offered a promising arena for undermining Western influence and attaching the emerging countries politically and economically to the Soviet bloc.

"National Liberation" Wars and the Constraint of Escalation

Khrushchev's most widely noted statement as to the promising prospects for Communist advance in the former colonial countries of the underdeveloped world appeared in his report on the 1960 World Conference of Communist Parties in Moscow.[28] This report was interpreted in the West as signaling the start of a new, aggressive phase of Soviet policy in the underdeveloped world in which Soviet support of revolutionary wars and insurgencies was expected to increase dramatically. Soviet policy proved more restrained than expected, in part perhaps because of such factors as Sino–Soviet differences over revolutionary tactics in the emerging nations, the danger of escalation that was pointed up by the sobering lessons of the Cuban missile confrontation, and economic and other difficulties which made a period of détente appear desir-

[27] See Garthoff, *Soviet Military Policy*, pp. 110–11.
[28] N. S. Khrushchev, "For New Victories of the World Communist Movement," *Kommunist*, no. 1 (January 1961): 3–37.

able to the Soviet leadership. In addition, Soviet policy-makers apparently differed among themselves on many ideological and practical problems of formulating a cohesive policy line toward the newly developing countries. A substantial literature on this subject during the Khrushchev period revealed considerable controversy on such questions as the appropriate Soviet attitudes toward the "national bourgeoisie" and local Communist parties in the emerging countries, the effect of various forms of Soviet aid, the opportunities for the new states to break away from the "world system of imperialism," and the prospects of their transition from "national democracy" to socialism.[29]

Of all the factors concerned, however, the escalation danger stands out as the principal thorn in Khrushchev's side. The constraint imposed by possible escalation of local revolutionary conflicts into global nuclear war—a concern which grew into a rather rigid doctrine of "inevitable escalation" in Khrushchev's time—seems to have had a strongly inhibiting effect upon direct Soviet support of the so-called "national liberation struggles." Khrushchev talked a strong line of support for such movements, but when concrete cases arose which might have involved the Soviet Union in a direct confrontation with US military power, he generally refused to tender Soviet aid in any form that would have entailed the unpredictable danger of widening war.[30]

Partly as a reaction to Chinese accusations that the Soviet Union was defaulting on its obligations to the national liberation movement, and partly to counteract a growing impression in the West that the Soviet Union was loath to act in local conflict situations because of fear of escalation, an attempt was made toward the end of Khrushchev's tenure to modify the rigid declaratory position on escalation. This was accompanied, as we shall see later, by a number of measures to improve military capabilities for the support of local conflicts far from the continental base of Soviet military power. However, down to the end of Khrushchev's time, Soviet policy on the support of local conflicts in the Third World, including the war in Vietnam, remained comparatively restrained, stopping short especially of such concrete steps as the commitment of Soviet military forces in those situations.

Perhaps the chief innovation in military policy that Khrushchev introduced

---

[29] For some representative Soviet analyses bearing on these points, see A. Beliakov and F. Burlatskii, "The Leninist Theory of the Socialist Revolution and the Present," *Kommunist*, no. 13 (September 1960): 14–15; G. Kim, "On the Government of National Democracy," *Aziia i Afrika segodnia* (Asia and Africa Today), no. 10 (October 1962): 5; V. I. Pavlov and I. B. Redko, "A Government of National Democracy and the Transition to Noncapitalist Development," *Narody Azii i Afriki* (Peoples of Asia and Africa), no. 1 (January 1963): 34–39; B. Minskii, "Creative Marxism and the Problems of the National Liberation Revolutions," *Mirovaia ekonomika i mezhdunarodnye otnosheniia* (World Economics and International Relations), no. 2 (January 1963): 65–67; G. Starushenko, "Through General Democratic Transformation to Socialist Transformation," *Kommunist*, no. 13 (September 1963): 106–8; I. Potekhin, "On 'African Socialism,'" *International Affairs*, no. 1 (January 1963): 75–76. For a perceptive analysis of the Soviet search for ways of exploiting revolutionary opportunities in the Third World, see Uri Ra'anan, "Moscow and the 'Third World,'" *Problems of Communism* (January–February 1965): 22–31.

[30] See Thomas W. Wolfe, *The Soviet Military Scene: Institutional and Defense Policy Considerations*, The RAND Corporation, RM-4913-PR, June 1966, pp. 105–8.

to advance Soviet influence in selected areas of the Third World was that of acting as a major arms vendor to the United Arab Republic, Indonesia, Syria, Iraq, India, Afghanistan, Algeria, and Somalia, among others. Beginning in 1955 with the export of arms to Egypt, the Soviet Union, which had previously confined itself to furnishing military equipment and associated technical training to other Communist countries within the Soviet bloc,[31] embarked on a policy of extending such assistance to non-Communist countries disposed, in varying degree, to follow an anti-Western line. By the time of Khrushchev's fall, in 1964, this program had resulted in the extension of around $3 billion worth of arms aid to thirteen countries, an amount nearly half that of all Soviet economic aid furnished to countries in the underdeveloped world in the same period.[32]

Whereas, in the first years of the program, Soviet aid consisted mostly of either obsolescent or surplus armaments, it subsequently came to include up-to-date items of first-line equipment, such as advanced jet fighters and bombers, armored vehicles, electronics gear, and surface-to-air missiles.[33] Although, in terms of enlisting the recipient states on the Soviet side in the Cold War, the program yielded mixed benefits at best—as the example of Indonesia, in particular, was later to demonstrate—it did have effects potentially significant for the Soviet Union's future political-military maneuverability in widely dispersed areas of the world. Among other things, by introducing its military instructors and technicians into the recipient countries and bringing them into contact with local power elites, the arms-aid program marked a notable departure from the continental isolation to which the Soviet Union's military establishment had previously been accustomed.

[31] Although, up to 1954–55, postwar Soviet arms aid had gone almost exclusively into strengthening the Communist bloc, it should be noted that the precedent for such aid to countries in the "outside" world had been set in earlier periods of Soviet history. Its recipients had been, among others, China, following the Sun Yat-sen–Joffe agreement of January 26, 1923; assorted warlords in North China in the mid-twenties; Chiang Kai-shek's Kuomintang China at various interludes in the late twenties and, from 1937 on, during the war with Japan; Sinkiang in the early thirties; and the Turkey of Kemal Ataturk during the war against Greece, in the early twenties. Among other accounts, see Garthoff, in Lederer, *Russian Foreign Policy*, pp. 257–62; Allen S. Whiting and General Sheng Shih-ts'ai, *Sinkiang: Pawn or Pivot?* (Ann Arbor, Mich.: Michigan University Press, 1948), pp. 10–90, 102–10, 265; Peter H. S. Tang, *Communist China Today* (Washington, D.C.: Research Institute on the Sino-Soviet Bloc, 1961), p. 33; Robert C. North, *Moscow and the Chinese Communists* (Stanford, Calif.: Stanford University Press, 1963), p. 183; Louis Fischer, *The Soviets in World Affairs* (Princeton, N.J.: Princeton University Press, 1951), vol. 1, p. 391, vol. 2, pp. 633–77.

[32] See Stephen P. Gibert, "Wars of Liberation and Soviet Military Aid Policy," *Orbis* (Fall 1966): 840; Hearings before the Committee on Foreign Affairs, US House of Representatives, 88th Congress, 1st Session (May 8, 1963), p. 733; (May 20, 1963), pp. 1116, 1132; (May 27, 1963), p. 1315; *Foreign Assistance Activities of the Communist Bloc and Their Implications for the United States*, Special Committee to Study the Foreign Aid Program, US Senate, Study No. 8, 85th Congress, 1st Session (March 1957, July 1957).

While a small amount of the approximately $3 billion worth of arms aid extended during the decade after 1955 was furnished by or channeled through some of the East European countries, most notably Poland and Czechoslovakia, the bulk of the program was carried by the Soviet Union.

[33] Gibert, in *Orbis*, pp. 853–58.

Portent of a Stronger NATO

Let us turn now to some of the key considerations bearing on the Soviet Union's military posture toward Western Europe under Khrushchev. High on Khrushchev's agenda from the outset was the need to check the further strengthening of NATO, especially plans for associating West Germany more closely with the defense of Europe, which had taken on fresh impetus in the aftermath of the Korean War. This particular problem, as we have seen, proved no more susceptible to solution than in Stalin's day. Although Soviet diplomacy under Khrushchev sought through a variety of avenues to undermine West Germany's entry into NATO, possibly even at the political expense of permitting all-German elections in return for a neutralized Germany,[34] it failed to achieve its objectives. In May 1955, early in the Khrushchev period, West Germany was taken into NATO. In response, the Warsaw alliance was set up.[35] But this Soviet countermove hardly altered the unpalatable fact that the way had been cleared for West German rearmament to begin.

The portent of a stronger NATO as a result of a German defense contribution was further driven home to Khrushchev in the next couple of years by a series of steps designed to put the NATO forces in Europe on an atomic footing. These steps, prompted largely by a shortfall in NATO's conventional force goals which not even a planned German contribution of twelve divisions promised to remedy, unfolded gradually between 1954 and the end of 1957. Studies in NATO[36] and other preparatory measures[37] led, in December 1954, to a major revision of NATO strategy looking toward reliance upon tactical atomic weapons for the defense of Europe against what was regarded as an overwhelming Soviet superiority in manpower.[38] This trend in NATO plan-

[34] See previous discussion of the disputed question whether Soviet offers on Germany in late 1954 and early 1955, like the earlier celebrated "lost opportunity" note of March 1952, represented serious bargaining bids or merely delaying tactics, pp. 27–31, above.

[35] See pp. 75–79.

[36] Among the more widely noted pioneering studies conducted in NATO on reorganization of NATO's forces and strategy for employing tactical nuclear weapons was that prepared in 1954 under the direction of General Alfred M. Gruenther, then SHAPE commander-in-chief. See "NATO Experts Under General Gruenther Complete Secret Report on Atomic Role in Warfare," *New York Times*, July 25, 1954, and speech by Gruenther on September 29, 1954, in *Department of State Bulletin*, October 18, 1954, pp. 562–66. See also John P. Leacacos, "Techniques for Atomic War: NATO Experts Map Some Drastic Changes in Tactics to Prepare the West for a New Kind of Fighting," *Providence (R.I.) Sunday Journal*, September 19, 1954.

[37] Measures preparatory to adoption of tactical nuclear weapons as an integral part of NATO's military establishment included the amendment, in 1954, of the US Atomic Energy Act of 1946 (the McMahon Act) to permit sharing of pertinent operational information on nuclear weapons with America's NATO allies. See Robert E. Osgood, *NATO: The Entangling Alliance* (Chicago, Ill.: University of Chicago Press, 1962), pp. 107–8.

[38] For detailed accounts of the revision of NATO strategy in 1954 and the steps subsequently taken to implement it, see Osgood, ibid., pp. 102–46; Roger Hilsman, "NATO: The Developing Strategic Context," in Klaus Knorr, ed., *NATO and American Security* (Princeton, N.J.: Princeton University Press, 1959), pp. 23–29; James L. Richardson, *Germany and the Atlantic Alliance: The Interaction of Strategy and Politics* (Cambridge, Mass.: Harvard University Press, 1966), pp. 39–61 and passim.

ning, which was accompanied by Secretary Dulles' modification, in 1955, of his earlier doctrine of massive retaliation by US strategic forces,[39] was capped in 1957 by concrete arrangements for incorporating American-owned and -controlled nuclear weapons in the NATO arsenal in Europe.[40]

NATO's movement toward a posture of atomic readiness, a development which threatened to reduce the value of Soviet conventional superiority in Europe upon which Stalin had long relied, came at an awkward transitional time for Khrushchev. Not only was he still in the process of consolidating his political power at home and seeking a more flexible approach to foreign policy problems abroad, but in the military field, too, he was becoming increasingly aware of the need for a major overhaul of the armed forces and a review of the nuclear age doctrine. This awareness was doubtless sharpened by the appearance of tactical nuclear armaments in NATO and, associated with it, the possibility of nuclear sharing arrangements involving West Germany.[41] Certainly, these questions, along with other interrelated considerations, helped to shape the program of military reforms toward which Khrushchev was feeling his way between 1955 and 1960.

During this period, the task of creating a strategic deterrent force, left unfinished at the end of the Stalin era, was in the forefront of Khrushchev's military policy concerns. This meant, among other things, that, unless he was

[39] Secretary of State John Foster Dulles had set forth the original "massive retaliation" policy of the Eisenhower administration in his speech of January 12, 1954 (*New York Times*, January 13, 1954). It is sometimes forgotten that Dulles amended this doctrine in March 1955 when he expounded a "less-than-massive" retaliation policy. Calling for use of small nuclear weapons against military targets rather than city-destroying weapons, the amended doctrine foreshadowed that enunciated, almost a decade later, by Secretary of Defense Robert S. McNamara at Ann Arbor in June 1962. See Elie Abel, "Dulles Says U.S. Pins Retaliation on Small A-Bomb," *New York Times*, March 16, 1955. The 1955 Dulles comments on the desirability of establishing limitations on nuclear warfare were made in a general context not applying directly to Europe. But in an article two years later he linked the notion specifically to the defense of Europe (see "Challenge and Response in United States Policy," *Foreign Affairs* [October 1957]: 30–33).

[40] Implementation of the 1954 NATO strategy required that the United States be willing to make tactical nuclear delivery vehicles available to its European allies, even though retaining control of warheads for them. Arrangements to this end were worked out in the course of 1957 after a US offer, in April, to furnish tactical missiles to some of the European countries and the NATO Council's endorsement, in May, of the introduction of American-controlled nuclear weapons into NATO forces in Europe. A long-term plan—MC70—covering, among other things, NATO's tactical nuclear requirements, was drawn up also at this time. American readiness to satisfy European requests for tactical nuclear capabilities was increased toward the end of 1957 by US interest in securing European approval for the stationing of Thor and Jupiter IRBMs in Europe as an interim counter to the successful development of a Soviet intercontinental missile, the first test of which had taken place in August 1957. See Richardson, *Germany and the Atlantic Alliance*, pp. 49–50; Osgood, *NATO: The Entangling Alliance*, pp. 117–18; Hans Speier, *German Rearmament and Atomic War* (Evanston, Ill.: Row Peterson & Co., 1957), pp. 220–21.

[41] Contrary to Soviet accusations that West Germany was eager to participate in NATO's tactical nuclear arrangements in order to acquire outright possession of nuclear weapons, the issue whether to equip the Bundeswehr with tactical nuclear delivery systems (for which the warheads were to remain under US control) aroused bitter political controversy in Germany, which continued after the Adenauer government had decided in favor of this step in March 1958. It was only after Khrushchev's threat to Berlin, in November 1958, that the Social Democratic party's and other internal opposition to Adenauer's policy on this issue abated. See Richardson, *Germany and the Atlantic Alliance*, pp. 48–62; Osgood, *NATO: The Entangling Alliance*, pp. 126–30.

prepared to reverse priorities in midstream, the problem of coping with the new NATO strategy of tactical nuclear response would have to be met within the framework of military preparedness measures already underway. Moreover, Soviet nuclear technology then was still concentrating on the development of strategic weapons, and apparently lagged well behind the United States in developing smaller tactical weapons at the lower end of the nuclear spectrum.[42] Putting Soviet European theater forces straightaway on a tactical atomic footing to match NATO programs was, therefore, not yet feasible, but would have to wait until strategic force requirements were more nearly satisfied.

On the other hand, a further build-up of Soviet conventional forces, which by 1955 had already reached their postwar peak in the wake of the Korean War,[43] could hardly have appeared to Khrushchev an appropriate answer to a NATO nuclear threat. Not only would additional troops be of marginal value in light of the large existing theater force establishment, but, in order to meet the costs of modernizing and strengthening the Soviet strategic delivery and defense forces, Khrushchev actually needed to free some of the resources tied up in the maintenance of these massive conventional forces.[44] He was thus more interested in reducing their size than in expanding them. Also, the increasingly apparent fact that NATO itself was going to fall far below the ambitious conventional force goals set at Lisbon in 1952[45] doubtless

[42] See Hanson W. Baldwin, "Some Atomic Facts," *New York Times*, October 28, 1954. American tests directed toward the development of tactical weapons had been conducted as early as 1951, five years before the Soviet Union apparently began to test atomic warheads for tactical purposes. See also Arnold Kramish, *Atomic Energy in the Soviet Union* (Stanford, Calif.: Stanford University Press, 1959), pp. 124, 126; Osgood, *NATO: The Entangling Alliance*, pp. 105, 385 fn. 8.

[43] According to figures given by Khrushchev in January 1960, the Soviet armed forces had reached a strength of 5,763,000 men in 1955. See chapter II, fn. 4, and further discussion in chapter VIII.

[44] It should be noted, however, that resources used to support the theater forces were at best only partly convertible to meeting requirements for the development of strategic offensive and defensive systems. The latter depended primarily upon the productive capacity of certain advanced sectors of the economy, such as chemicals, nonferrous metals, and sophisticated branches of engineering, while the theater forces were supported mainly by the more traditional heavy industry and munitions sectors. Modern strategic systems were thus more in direct competition with advanced industrial technology and skills needed for expanding new growth sectors of the economy than with the resources of traditional industry, which supported the theater forces. To meet the build-up of strategic forces, Khrushchev, therefore, could not expect to free resources directly simply by cutting back the theater forces. To the extent that industry generally was still suffering from manpower shortages (a result of the demographic trough following World War II), there was something to be gained, however, from reducing the manpower level of the theater forces. For an informative analysis of the convertibility problem involved here, see John P. Hardt, *Choices Facing the Soviet Planner*, reprint series no. 7 (Washington, D.C.: Institute for Sino-Soviet Studies, The George Washington University, January 1967), pp. 25–28.

[45] The NATO Council meeting at Lisbon in February 1952 had adopted a 96-division goal, including reserves, for NATO's ground forces. By the mid-fifties, the skeptical European reaction to this goal had made it fairly clear that it would not be attained. In 1954, at the time the strategy of tactical nuclear response was proposed, the goal slipped to thirty combat-ready divisions, and in the MC-70 plan adopted in 1957 it was set at the same figure, with the hope of having sixty additional reserve divisions. In actual strength, NATO at this time had less than twenty effective

reassured Khrushchev that Soviet conventional forces could be trimmed back somewhat without harm. Meanwhile, Soviet missile technology in the latter fifties was coming along fast, and this new element in the strategic picture held promise of greatly enhancing the Soviet deterrent posture. Khrushchev was later to find that he had overestimated the bargaining power of his missiles, but this was not yet apparent in the 1955–60 period, when his major military policy revisions were taking shape. At this time, the deployment of an MRBM force that could hold Europe under threat of strategic attack had already begun, supplementing bomber forces also equipped and in training for strategic nuclear strikes against Europe. Furthermore, first-generation ICBMs, initially tested in the fall of 1957, seemed to be in the immediate offing—giving Khrushchev some grounds for the missile euphoria which apparently colored his outlook for a time.

Indeed, Khrushchev was then banking heavily on the Soviet headstart in missile technology as an answer to NATO's emergent tactical nuclear posture in Europe. In particular, his reaction to plans for equipping the West German armed forces with tactical nuclear delivery vehicles—a step which the Soviet Union insisted upon describing as the "atomic arming of the Federal Republic"—was apparently prompted by the belief that the Soviet Union's nuclear missile power would have a sobering effect upon Bonn. In April 1957 a Soviet note warning Bonn against the Bundeswehr's participation in NATO's tactical nuclear arrangements reminded Germany of her vulnerability to Soviet nuclear weapons: "One can easily see that Western Germany, whose territory would become the target of the most powerful and concentrated blows of these weapons, would be destroyed, would become one big cemetery."[46]

As noted in our earlier discussion, Khrushchev bent more than one string to his policy bow, seeking through diplomacy and disarmament proposals in 1957–58 to dissuade the European countries from going along with NATO plans for stationing tactical nuclear weapons in Europe. The Rapacki Plan and related proposals for a nuclear free zone in Europe were vigorously pressed during this period, and intense diplomatic activity went into fostering suspicion between Germany and her NATO allies.[47] However, these efforts did not succeed in blocking NATO's nuclear plans[48] and were followed by Soviet pressure tactics with the renewed squeeze on Berlin in November 1958.

While Soviet diplomacy was thus shifting gears from the phase of arms con-

---

fighting divisions. By the beginning of the Kennedy administration, in 1961, the proposed level was thirty active and thirty reserve divisions. See Osgood, *NATO: The Entangling Alliance*, p. 118; Richardson, *Germany and the Atlantic Alliance*, p. 39; Hilsman, in Knorr, *NATO and American Security*, p. 31.

[46] Soviet government note of April 27, 1957, *Pravda*, and *Izvestiia*, April 28, 1957.

[47] See chapter V, pp. 83–84.

[48] Although Khrushchev's own efforts to impede NATO's adoption of a tactical nuclear posture proved to no avail, he at least had the subsequent satisfaction of observing that NATO itself was unable to work out acceptable forms of nuclear sharing or to agree upon the role of tactical nuclear weapons in NATO strategy, thus creating divisive issues from which the Soviet Union might hope to profit. See also fn. 52 below.

trol proposals to the less subtle campaign of pressures against Berlin, Khrushchev went ahead with his own plans for the reform and reorganization of the Soviet armed forces. Although these plans resulted in part from the increasingly global competition with the United States, they also reflected a continuing preoccupation with the Soviet Union's military stance toward Europe.

Khrushchev's New Military Policy Approach

Khrushchev, though reform-minded, was still influenced to some extent by a military tradition that called for the maintenance of superior Soviet strength in the European arena.[49] Much of the Soviet military bureaucracy was even more strongly set in this mold. Later, when the nuclearization and missile programs he had in mind in connection with his military policy reforms were further along, Khrushchev could begin to rethink the need for a large conventional military presence in Europe, even though, as we shall see, the technical possibilities for a marked change in the Soviet stance apparently were to be outweighed by other considerations. However, in the period of which we are now speaking, from around 1955 to 1960, Khrushchev's immediate problem was how to revamp the Soviet military posture without weakening its grip upon Europe.

The answers toward which he gradually progressed in that time were laid out formally in his celebrated presentation to the Supreme Soviet, on January 14, 1960, where he coupled the unveiling of a "new look" military policy with disarmament proposals aimed at the then forthcoming Ten-Nation Disarmament Conference in Geneva.[50] Incidentally, Khrushchev also used this occasion to revive the threat of a separate peace treaty with East Germany, an issue which had been soft-pedaled since his meeting with President Eisenhower at Camp David in the fall of 1959.

In the speech before the Supreme Soviet, spelling out his view of the requirements for a Soviet defense policy and structure in the nuclear missile age, Khrushchev said that nuclear weapons and missiles had become the main elements in modern war and that many types of traditional armed forces were rapidly becoming obsolete. He noted the probable decisiveness of the initial phase of any future war, implying that a nuclear war would be of short duration. At the same time, he asserted that a large country like the Soviet Union, even though attacked first, would always be able to survive and retaliate if it took care to disperse and camouflage its own strategic striking forces. Expressing confidence that the "imperialist camp" was deterred by Soviet military might, he then capped this presentation of his basic strategic ideas by announcing that the Soviet armed forces would be reduced about one-third,

[49] See Curt Gasteyger, "Modern Warfare and Soviet Strategy," *Survey* (October 1965): 48; J. M. Mackintosh, *Strategy and Tactics of Soviet Foreign Policy* (London: Oxford University Press, 1962), pp. 203–6.

[50] "Disarmament Is the Path Toward Strengthening Peace and Ensuring Friendship Among Peoples." N. S. Khrushchev's Report at the Session of the USSR Supreme Soviet, *Pravda*, January 15, 1960.

from 3.6 million to 2.4 million men. This reduction, he went on to say, meant no loss of combat capability, since nuclear firepower would more than make up for the manpower cut.

In a sense, one may say that the new military policy disclosed by this landmark speech and subsequent steps meant that Khrushchev had turned to a "technological solution" in the defense domain somewhat similar to that previously favored for the United States and NATO by the Eisenhower administration. With respect to Europe, the chief difference was that, whereas American nuclear technology made it possible for NATO in the late fifties to shift to greater reliance on tactical nuclear delivery systems, in the Soviet case the initial emphasis perforce lay upon the threat of massive retaliation against NATO Europe with strategic nuclear weapons.

This was only a temporary lag, however, for Khrushchev's new policy envisaged "nuclearizing" the theater forces as rapidly as Soviet technology and supplies of nuclear material would permit. Even so, after development and acquisition of a family of tactical weapons for battlefield use picked up tempo in the early sixties, Soviet doctrine was slow to admit that tactical weapons might be used in Europe without there being also a strategic nuclear exchange. In fact, the mere possibility of a nuclear exchange limited to tactical weapons was conceded only after Khrushchev had dropped out of the picture, by which time the European military environment had changed considerably.

There is more than a touch of irony in the fact that Khrushchev held steadfast to the view that any warfare in Europe would be likely to escalate to the broadest nuclear dimensions,[51] even after internal NATO differences over military strategy had plainly revealed widespread dissatisfaction with the dependence upon prompt nuclear response implicit in the 1954-57 NATO doctrine.[52] From the early sixties on, the arguments of the Kennedy adminis-

[51] Khrushchev's views on this point were frequently expressed by him, and although they were doubtless uttered for their deterrent effect, they also seemed to reflect his own personal conviction. In March 1961, for example, he said that neither side could be expected "to concede defeat before resorting to the use of all weapons, even the most devastating ones" (Pravda, March 8, 1961). For earlier statements in a similar vein, see Pravda, November 29, 1957; January 15, 1960; July 11, 1962. Khrushchev's last comment on the subject prior to his ouster was made in an interview with Lord Thompson in August 1964, when he said: "The trouble is, the losing side will always use nuclear weapons in the last resort to avoid defeat.... If a man thinks he's going to die he'll take any steps" (Sunday Times, London, August 16, 1964).

[52] The introduction of increasing numbers of ground- and air-launched tactical weapons in NATO was not accompanied by agreement on their role in NATO strategy, their control, or a doctrine for their employment. In the late fifties and early sixties, the NATO strategy of 1954 came under growing criticism in both Europe and the United States, which led to efforts by the Kennedy administration (only partly successful) to revise NATO's posture and policy. For some of the more widely-voiced criticisms of the 1954 strategy, see F. O. Miksche, The Failure of Atomic Strategy (New York: Frederick A. Praeger, Inc., 1958), especially pp. 11–136; Malcolm W. Hoag, "The Place of Limited War in NATO Strategy," in Knorr, NATO and American Security, pp. 98–126; Alastair Buchan, NATO in the 1960's (London: Weidenfeld & Nicolson, 1960), pp. 34–101; B. H. Liddell Hart, Deterrent or Defence (New York: Frederick A. Praeger, Inc., 1960), pp. 17–26; Henry A. Kissinger, The Necessity for Choice (New York: Harper & Brothers, 1960), pp. 101–59; F. W. Mulley, The Politics of Western Defence (London: Thames & Hudson, 1962), pp. 10–18, 49–118; Osgood, NATO: The Entangling Alliance, pp. 102–211.

tration for a build-up of NATO conventional forces and a shift to a strategy of flexible response that would have the effect of raising the nuclear threshold in Europe provided additional fuel for NATO's internal debate,[53] but apparently made little dent in Khrushchev's professed views on the danger of escalation.

Indeed, one may say that Khrushchev himself undermined the case of Western critics who feared that American advocacy of a conventional build-up in NATO would weaken deterrence. With rather more of an eye on NATO's growing nuclear arsenal[54] than an ear for its strategy debate, Khrushchev continued to believe that the main emphasis of NATO's planning lay in reliance upon nuclear weapons.[55] In this particular belief he had the support of Soviet professional military opinion until near the end of his tenure. But this is to anticipate our later discussion of specific trends in Soviet thinking on the probable character of any theater warfare that might occur in Europe. Let us return first to some of the other developments bearing upon the European aspects of the new military policy approach that emerged under Khrushchev's leadership in the late fifties and early sixties.

Compromise on Theater-Force Reforms

Resistance to some of Khrushchev's ideas by traditionalist marshals, as well as the pressure of events like the Berlin crisis of 1961, brought about various modifications in the military policy prospectus outlined by Khrushchev in January 1960.[56] In particular, the measures actually taken under Khrushchev with regard to the Soviet theater forces bore the mark of compromise rather

---

[53] For accounts of this debate, representing viewpoints both sympathetic to and critical of the new line of NATO strategy espoused by the United States, see Osgood, *NATO: The Entangling Alliance*, pp. 212–74; Helmut Schmidt, *Defense or Retaliation: A German View* (Edinburgh: Oliver & Boyd, 1962), pp. 13–20, 62–112, 182–205; Thomas C. Schelling, "Nuclear Strategy in Europe," *World Politics* (April 1962): 421–32; Timothy W. Stanley, "NATO's Nuclear Debate: Washington's View," *Reporter*, July 5, 1962, pp. 19–21; William R. Kintner and Stefan T. Possony, "NATO's Nuclear Crisis," *Orbis* (Summer 1962): 217–43; Charles J. V. Murphy, "NATO at a Nuclear Crossroads," *Fortune* (December 1962): 85–87, 214–25; Malcolm W. Hoag, "Nuclear Policy and French Intransigence," *Foreign Affairs* (January 1963): 286–98, and "Rationalizing NATO Strategy," *World Politics* (October 1964): 121–42; Henry A. Kissinger, "NATO's Nuclear Dilemma," *Reporter*, March 28, 1963, pp. 22–37; William W. Kaufmann, *The McNamara Strategy* (New York: Harper & Row, 1964), pp. 102–34; Richardson, *Germany and the Atlantic Alliance*, pp. 73–87, 159–223; Bernard Brodie, *Escalation and the Nuclear Option* (Princeton, N.J.: Princeton University Press, 1966), pp. 9–23, 25–41.

[54] In 1963, for example, Secretary McNamara stated that the tactical nuclear strength of NATO's armies in Europe had increased by 60 per cent between 1961 and 1963. He gave no specific numbers, but said that "thousands of US warheads" were deployed in Europe. Speech to the Economic Club, New York, November 18, 1963, in *Department of State Bulletin*, December 16, 1963, p. 919.

[55] To some extent, the arguments of the NATO disputants may have tended to cancel each other out, with one group, including many Germans and the French, arguing for "automaticity" of nuclear response as the best guarantee of deterrence, while the other side urged "controlled response" and a "pause" calculated to maintain a "firebreak" between conventional and nuclear hostilities. For Khrushchev, the safest conclusion evidently was that it would be best not to provoke a test of which of these contending strategies would prevail.

[56] Wolfe, *Soviet Strategy at the Crossroads*, pp. 30–34.

than of his personal preference. Had the logic of Khrushchev's preferences prevailed, his idea of substituting nuclear firepower for manpower—a notion explicitly advanced in his January 1960 policy presentation—might have been translated into measures for the wholesale dismantling of conventional theater forces, including those deployed in Europe. As it turned out, the measures taken were far less radical.

Several troop reductions did occur under Khrushchev, and from time to time there was a minor thinning out of the theater forces deployed in forward positions in Central and East Europe, changes which we shall treat in detail in the next chapter. The personnel cuts in these forces, however, were largely in connection with organizational reforms accompanying the introduction of new weapons and did not alter their significance as a combat "spearhead" poised against Europe. For the most part, the paring of the oversized theater force establishment was accomplished at the expense of second-line formations based in the interior military districts of the Soviet Union.

Moreover, while this retrenchment was going on the basic integrity of the ground forces and their supporting tactical air armies—which together comprised the combat backbone of the theater forces—was kept intact, and the validity of the combined-arms doctrine under which they operated was emphatically reindorsed. The most radical reform which did occur—and here was the heart of the compromise between Khrushchev and the professional advocates of strong theater forces—was a series of programs, taking up where Stalin had left off, to modernize the theater forces by equipping and training them for fast-moving operations under nuclear conditions. In the process of "nuclearizing" the theater forces, as described in 1961 by Soviet Minister of Defense Marshal Malinovskii,[57] stress was placed on developing greater battlefield mobility and firepower, while the massive use of conventional artillery on which these forces previously depended was supplanted to a considerable extent by tactical missiles employing nuclear and other mass-destructive warheads, as well as by nuclear-armed tactical aircraft.

In short, rather than reduce the theater forces to a small appendage of the Soviet military establishment, limited essentially to mopping-up operations in the wake of nuclear blows delivered by the strategic striking forces, Khrushchev through his reforms in effect endowed the theater forces with dual capabilities for both conventional and nuclear warfare and left them to play a continuing role as a central element of Soviet military power. In so doing, Khrushchev moved, at least part way, toward recognizing the arguments of those who feared that his excessive emphasis upon strategic deterrence would prove harmful to the Soviet Union's war-fighting preparedness and might even vitiate the country's deterrent posture itself.

Lest it be supposed that all parties were pleased with this outcome, however, let it be observed that some of Khrushchev's military critics continued to suggest that he had gone overboard in streamlining the theater forces, espe-

[57] Report of R. Ia. Malinovskii to Twenty-second Party Congress, *Pravda*, October 25, 1961.

cially in the event that these forces were called upon to conduct extensive or prolonged conventional campaigns, for which their increasing reliance on nuclear firepower might leave them poorly prepared.[58]

Shifts in Soviet Policy on the Warsaw Pact

Interwoven with the question of theater-force planning under Khrushchev was the development of Moscow's policy toward its Warsaw Pact allies in Eastern Europe.[59] This policy went through two rather distinct phases during the Khrushchev decade. In the first phase, lasting about five years after the formation of the Warsaw Pact in May 1955, the military contributions of the East European armed forces apparently carried little more weight in Soviet planning than had been the case in Stalin's day. Apart from the improvement of joint air defense arrangements in Eastern Europe,[60] the Soviet Union made no major effort to weld the Warsaw Pact into an integrated military alliance, being content to treat it largely as a political and propagandistic answer to the inclusion of West Germany in NATO.

During the first five years of the Pact's existence, for example, little attention was given to the problems of conducting modern theater warfare on a coalition basis; no joint exercises were held; and the Joint Command of the Warsaw Pact,[61] headed by a Soviet officer, remained mostly a paper organization with even less real work on its hands than the Political Consultative Committee, the Pact's policy organ.[62] The latter seems to have functioned less as a genuine policy-making body than as a forum for presentation of the Soviet policy line of the moment. The rare meetings of the Pact's formal organs further tended to bear out the supposition that its symbolic political role

[58] See Thomas J. Wolfe, *Soviet Military Power and European Security*, The RAND Corporation, P-3429, August 1966, p. 21. See also chapter VIII, pp. 177–78, and chapter IX.

[59] For a fairly detailed listing of both Western and Communist literature on the origin and development of the Warsaw Pact, see Thomas W. Wolfe, *The Evolving Nature of the Warsaw Pact*, The RAND Corporation, RM-4835-PR, December 1965, pp. 30–31. This paper may also be found under the title of "The Warsaw Pact in Evolution" in Kurt London, ed., *Eastern Europe in Transition* (Baltimore, Md.: The Johns Hopkins Press, 1966), pp. 207–35.

[60] During the late fifties, after formation of the Warsaw Pact, the Soviet Union gave renewed attention to improving the air defenses of East Europe by providing the Warsaw Pact countries with surface-to-air (SAM) missiles, more modern interceptors, and so on, but comparable modernization of the East European ground forces lagged somewhat behind in this period.

[61] Besides the Joint Command itself, the only other element of the Warsaw Pact command structure that has been mentioned publicly is the Staff of the Joint Armed Forces, composed of representatives of national general staffs and seated in Moscow. On the political side, two subsidiary organs of the Political Consultative Committee were provided by the Treaty—a Permanent Commission which was to deal with foreign policy questions, and a Joint Secretariat. See Colonel S. Lesnevskii, "Military Cooperation of the Armed Forces of the Socialist Countries," *Kommunist Vooruzhennykh Sil*, no. 10 (May 1963): 72.

[62] For comment by a knowledgeable ex-Polish officer on the dormant state of the Warsaw Pact joint military staff in the 1955–58 period, see Pavel Monat, with John Dille, *Spy in the U.S.* (New York: Harper & Row, 1962), pp. 188–89. The Political Consultative Committee was somewhat more active, although it met only three times during the first five years of the Pact: in January 1956, May 1958, and February 1960. (According to statements at the first meeting, the Committee was supposed to meet not less than twice yearly.) *Izvestiia*, January 29, 1956, May 27, 1958, February 5, 1960.

initially counted more heavily in Soviet thinking than its co-operative military aspects.

There was, to be sure, some progress toward military integration during the early years of the Warsaw Pact, representing essentially the continuation of trends that had begun in the latter part of the Stalinist period, and manifesting itself in the standardization of weapons and local arms production along Soviet lines; adoption of Soviet organizational forms and field doctrine; and a broad definition of the military tasks falling to the several national armies.[63] There was also some co-ordination of disarmament policy, as reflected in the moves for partial troop reductions and withdrawals endorsed at the May 1958 meeting of the Political Consultative Committee.[64] However, while the armed forces of the various Pact states served such obvious purposes as providing support for the Communist regimes in East Europe and meeting certain traditional needs for national prestige, they were hardly counted upon to bear much of the burden of any military undertakings in which the Warsaw Pact might become involved—a responsibility that still rested mainly upon the Soviet Union's own military forces.

Furthermore, even though a sense of common purpose may have lain behind the Warsaw alliance at its formation, the path to closer military co-operation between the Soviet Union and the East European countries was not smoothed by events in the treaty's early years. The crushing of the Hungarian rebellion in 1956 by the Soviet army not only tarnished the image of a socialist military alliance based on common goals but also left room for friction and for disagreement as to how far a treaty, ostensibly meant to counter NATO, might be stretched to cover Soviet policing actions in Eastern Europe.[65] It was probably the need to ease such friction that prompted the Soviet Union to negotiate a series of bilateral "status-of-forces" agreements with the various East European countries in 1956 and 1957.[66]

Soviet policy toward the Warsaw Pact entered a second phase under Khrushchev around 1960–61, roughly coincident with rising tension in Europe

---

[63] Zbigniew Brzezinski, "The Organization of the Communist Camp," *World Politics* (January 1961): 198–99; Richard F. Staar, "The East European Alliance System," *U.S. Naval Institute Proceedings* (September 1964): 36–37; Raymond L. Garthoff, "The Military Establishment," *East Europe* (September 1965): 14. See also unsigned article, "The Armed Forces of the Socialist Countries and Their Military Alliance—Guarantee of Peace and the Security of Nations," *Kommunist Vooruzhennykh Sil*, no. 13 (July 1965): 67.

[64] The May 1958 meeting of the Political Consultative Committee was the most substantial session of this body during the Warsaw Pact's first five years. It dealt with decisions on withdrawal of Soviet troops from Rumania, troop reductions by the East European countries, and organizational questions concerning the joint forces. See *Izvestiia*, May 27, 1958.

[65] The Soviet Union took the position that its military intervention in Hungary in 1956 was justified under the terms of the Warsaw Pact, a view occasionally disputed by the Poles and Hungarians. See W. Morawiecki, "On the Warsaw Pact," *Sprawy Miezynarodowz* (International Affairs), no. 5 (1958): 29; Lesnevskii, *Kommunist Vooruzhennykh Sil* (May 1963): 73; Garthoff, *East Europe* (September 1965): 16; Wolfe, *Soviet Strategy at the Crossroads*, p. 317. Among the bilateral Soviet agreements, the only one that contains a "safety clause" under which Soviet forces could presumably intervene to maintain security is the treaty of March 12, 1957, with the GDR. See Staar, *U.S. Naval Institute Proceedings* (September 1964): 35.

[66] Agreements were negotiated with Poland (December 1956), the GDR (March 1957), Rumania (April 1957), and Hungary (May 1957). See chapter V, p. 82.

over Berlin and with the deterioration of Sino–Soviet relations on the other side of the world. The Soviet Union now began to stress closer military co-operation with the East European countries, and measures were initiated to improve the collective military efficiency of the Pact forces.[67] Over the next few years, the new policy line had the general effect of upgrading the Warsaw Pact publicly in terms of the common defense of the Communist camp. More specifically, it served to elevate the importance of the military contribution of non-Soviet Pact countries in over-all Soviet planning; to extend the mission of the East European forces from primary emphasis on air defense to a more active joint role in defensive and offensive theater operations; and to promote joint training and re-equipment of the Pact forces commensurate with their apparently enlarged responsibilities.

Among the military features of the new policy on the Warsaw Pact was the practice of holding well-publicized joint maneuvers. The first of these took place in October 1961, with Soviet, East German, Polish, and Czechoslovak forces participating.[68] During Khrushchev's tenure, seven such major joint exercises were carried out, mostly involving the so-called "Northern Tier" of the alliance.[69] Extolling these joint training activities, Marshal Grechko stated in 1964 that their "great importance" lay in their contribution to "the further growth of the combat might of our joint armed forces, to higher stand-ards of training, to better co-ordination of forces and staffs, and to the elabora-tion of common views on methods of nuclear and conventional warfare."[70]

Along with joint exercises, which presented such departures from tradition as the mingling of troops from various East European countries on one anoth-er's soil, went a substantial program for the re-equipment and modernization of the East European armed forces. Beginning in the early sixties, the program focused mainly on the ground forces and their supporting air strength, which in the preceding years had received lower priority in equipment than air defense forces. The program included the replacement of older T–34 tanks with more modern T–54 and T–55 tanks, provision of anti-tank missiles and self-propelled guns, and introduction of newer fighter-bomber models of such aircraft as the MIG–21 and the SU–7.[71]

The main object of this modernization process was to improve the conven-

[67] See Wolfe, *The Evolving Nature of the Warsaw Pact*, pp. 7–11.

[68] The initial Warsaw Pact joint field exercise, which followed a meeting of the Pact's defense ministers in Warsaw in September 1961, was undoubtedly prompted by the need for a show of strength and unity in connection with the summer-long Berlin crisis of 1961, but it set the pattern for subsequent joint training and maneuvers.

[69] A listing of locations, dates, and participants for the joint exercises of the Khrushchev period, as well as for those during the first four years of the Brezhnev–Kosygin regime, will be found in chapter XVII. Together with Soviet forces, the Northern Tier countries (Poland, the GDR, and Czechoslovakia), frequently described as the "first strategic echelon" of the Pact, participated in more of these exercises than did the remaining (Southern Tier) countries, Hungary, Rumania, and Bulgaria.

[70] Marshal A. A. Grechko, interview in supplement to *Novosti* (News), February 26, 1964. See also similar remarks by Grechko in "The Military Alliance of the Fraternal Nations," *Voenno-istoricheskii zhurnal*, no. 5 (May 1965): 24.

[71] Garthoff, *East Europe* (September 1965): 14. See also *Voenno-istoricheskii zhurnal* (May 1965): 24, and *Kommunist Vooruzhennykh Sil*, no. 13 (July 1965): 68.

tional capabilities of the East European forces, but an important exception occurred when, around 1964, the Soviet Union began to furnish potential nuclear delivery systems to the other Warsaw Pact countries in the form of tactical missiles with ranges up to about 150 miles.[72] Although nuclear warheads for these missiles presumably remained in Soviet hands, the acquisition of missile delivery systems by the East European armed forces and their participation in simulated nuclear exercises marked a significant step toward possible nuclear sharing at some future time.[73]

The steps taken in accord with Khrushchev's revised policy toward the Warsaw Pact seemed calculated to serve a number of purposes beyond the ostensible one of strengthening Pact capabilities for conducting joint military operations in the European theater. Politically, the accent on closer integration apparently was meant to convey an image of Soviet bloc solidarity and to promote greater cohesion within the Warsaw Pact in the face of "polycentric" trends that had become increasingly manifest in East Europe by the early sixties.[74] Evidently, Khrushchev saw in the Warsaw Pact a potentially useful organizational instrument through which to offset such tendencies and to help maintain discipline and political unity within the Soviet bloc. In this regard, he may have hoped that cultivation of joint arrangements in the military sphere would accomplish what the multilateral Council for Economic Assistance (CEMA) had failed to do by way of drawing the bloc closer together. Set up originally in 1949 and reactivated after the disruptive events of the fall of 1956, this body had not proved particularly successful as a unifying political instrument, whatever its economic benefits may have been.[75]

In terms of the internal debate over defense policy that was going on in the

[72] See Wolfe, *The Evolving Nature of the Warsaw Pact*, pp. 10–11.

[73] Precisely when Soviet decisions were made to take this initial step toward possible nuclear sharing within the Warsaw Pact is not clear. As early as May 1958, in his speech at the Political Consultative Committee meeting in Moscow, Khrushchev accused NATO of planning "to arm West Germany with atomic weapons" and declared that the Warsaw Treaty states were "compelled by force of circumstance to consider deploying missiles in the German Democratic Republic, Poland, and Czechoslovakia." The first public confirmation that threats to make missiles available to other Warsaw Pact members had been carried out came in mid-1964, when Soviet-made tactical missiles were displayed by Polish forces in Warsaw. See ibid., p. 11.

[74] Among accounts discussing the development of "polycentric" trends in Eastern Europe, see George F. Kennan, "Polycentrism and Western Policy," *Foreign Affairs* (January 1964): 171–83; Richard V. Burks, "Perspectives for Eastern Europe," *Problems of Communism* (March–April 1964): 73–81; Zbigniew Brzezinski, "Russia and Europe," *Foreign Affairs* (April 1964): 428–44; Jeanne Kuebler, "Changing Status of Soviet Satellites," *Editorial Research Reports*, April 22, 1964, pp. 283–99; Richard Lowenthal, "Has the Revolution a Future?" *Encounter* (January 1965): 3–16, and (February 1965): 16–21; John M. Montias, "Communist Rule in Eastern Europe," *Foreign Affairs* (January 1965): 331–48. See also relevant articles in William E. Griffith, ed., *Communism in Europe*, vols. 1 and 2 (Cambridge, Mass.: M.I.T. Press, 1964–66).

[75] Disagreements within CEMA had begun to arise in 1961, about the time Khrushchev turned to the Warsaw Pact as a unifying instrument, and had emerged into the open by 1963, with Rumania leading the complaints against Soviet economic policy. See Michael Kaser, *COMECON: Integration Problems of the Planned Economies* (London: Oxford University Press, 1965), pp. 77–107; Montias, *Foreign Affairs* (January 1965): 332–33; Burks, *Problems of Communism* (March–April 1964): 74–79; Vaclav E. Mares, "East Europe's Second Chance," *Current History* (November 1964): 772–79; William E. Griffith, "The Revival of East European Nationalisms," paper presented at 5th International Conference on World Politics, Noordwijk, The Netherlands, September 1965.

Soviet Union in the early sixties, the new policy line toward the Warsaw Pact gave Khrushchev an additional rationale for trimming back Soviet theater forces on the grounds that a larger share of the European military burden and its costs could now be borne by Moscow's partners.

Despite the tendency under Khrushchev to encourage the other Warsaw Pact forces to stand on their own feet—a tendency underscored at least symbolically by the occasional practice of placing joint exercises under the nominal command of a non-Soviet military man[76]—there was no suggestion in professional military circles that the improved caliber of East European forces would actually justify a reduction in the Soviet Union's own theater-force requirements. Soviet military literature continued to take it as axiomatic that in wartime the other Warsaw Pact forces would be largely subordinated to direct Soviet command,[77] which did not testify to a high degree of confidence in either their performance or their reliability were they to operate on an autonomous basis.

Although it thus remained unclear in Khrushchev's day how far the Soviet Union was prepared to go in granting greater responsibility to East European forces that might prove unreliable in a pinch, the new policy had important implications for the Soviet Union's political and military flexibility in the future. For example, a policy permitting the withdrawal of some Soviet troops from Europe would provide telling leverage in disarmament and European security negotiations, and might even offer the prospect of throwing NATO into disarray by ostensibly reducing the Soviet threat to Western Europe. By the same token, should the possibility of a military collision between the USSR and China become a serious concern, Moscow would find it convenient to be in a position to shift some forces from Europe to the Far East. During Khrushchev's tenure, however, the necessity for such a redeployment of Soviet forces apparently did not assume serious weight in military policy decisions.[78]

Contradiction between Military and Political Strategy

The general proposition that the changing character of its relations with the Warsaw Pact countries might moderate the Soviet Union's long-felt need to keep substantial military forces in Europe brings us back to what were probably some of the most vexing and complex questions bearing on the Soviet military posture toward Europe in Khrushchev's time. One of these was the implicit contradiction between a Soviet military policy aimed at holding Western Europe hostage in order to deter the United States, and a political strategy

---

[76] Wolfe, *The Evolving Nature of the Warsaw Pact,* p. 23. See also chapter XVII.

[77] See Wolfe, *Soviet Strategy at the Crossroads,* pp. 211–12.

[78] Although rumors of minor Soviet military adjustments along the Sino–Soviet border began to appear as early as 1963, the question of possible troop shifts on a significant scale did not assume prominence until after Khrushchev had left the scene. See Wolfe, *The Soviet Union and the Sino–Soviet Dispute,* pp. 47–49, and Raymond L. Garthoff, "Sino–Soviet Military Relations, 1945–1966," in Garthoff, ed., *Sino–Soviet Military Relations* (New York: Frederick A. Praeger, Inc., 1966), pp. 98–99.

seeking to detach the United States from its European allies, which, if successful, would obviously reduce the latter's value as hostages.[79] Underlying this
contradiction was the unresolved question, mentioned earlier, whether Khrushchev thought it in the best interest of the Soviet Union to seek "co-operation" with the United States in maintaining a divided Europe or to work toward the eviction of American power from Europe.

Thanks to what has been called the military-technological revolution, Soviet
military power under Khrushchev developed in a way that made it at least
technically possible for the Soviet Union to practice nuclear deterrence against
the United States without having to maintain large theater forces with which
to threaten Europe. Yet despite this fundamentally new factor (which meant
that, in terms of deterrence, there was no longer any need to treat Western
Europe as a hostage for American good behavior), a large Soviet military
presence remained deployed in Europe and was only marginally reduced from
time to time. Khrushchev's policy thus perpetuated the postwar contradiction
between Soviet military and political strategy in Europe.

One way of resolving the paradox would have been to withdraw Soviet
forces from Europe and to "decouple" the threat to Europe posed by the
massive MRBM force in the Western USSR. Such lifting of the siege under
which Western Europe, figuratively speaking, had been living would have
removed the ostensible basis for an American military presence on the continent. Had the Soviet Union's interests, as Khrushchev saw them, extended
no further than to bringing about American disengagement from Europe and
deterring a possible US-supported attack on the USSR, this course logically
should have appealed to the Soviet leadership.

Why was it not taken? The simplest answer is that the Soviet Union's perception of its interests was apparently not such as to permit a radical lifting
of its military threat against Europe; a military posture revamped to provide
only a direct deterrent against the United States would not have afforded the
Soviet Union the leverage it desired upon European politics, especially those
of a resurgent Germany. But this answer falls short of explaining why the
Soviet Union under Khrushchev tended to duplicate the military capability it
had marshaled against Europe, a course it surely did not take in a fit of absent-
mindedness. And yet, Khrushchev's military policy, rather than replacing
Stalin's, in effect overlapped it,[80] so that the old threat geared predominantly
to land warfare continued alongside the new nuclear threat, most graphically
embodied in the large medium-range missile force targeted on Western Europe.

[79] See Anne Sington, "Peaceful Engagement in Europe," *NATO Letter* (December 1966): 22.
Another aspect of the contradictory position in which the Soviet Union found itself has been
pointed out by Philip Windsor, who notes that, if the Soviets were to make a limited military
move against Europe to demonstrate that the United States was unable to protect her European
allies, this too, if successful, would undermine the hostage value of Europe as a supplementary
deterrent against the United States. *Western Europe in Soviet Strategy*, Adelphi Papers, no. 8,
Institute for Strategic Studies, London, January 1964, p. 5.

[80] The author has profited from discussion of this and other relevant points with James L.
Richardson, whose own analysis may be found in his *Germany and the Atlantic Alliance*, pp. 124 ff.

Although a more ambitious answer that would account for these circumstances must be largely a matter of conjecture, let us try to assemble some of the apparent reasons for the course that Khrushchev actually found it expedient to follow, remembering first of all that his military policy was the product of many compromises—with economic and strategic realities, with technology, with tradition and institutional inertia, with the prejudices and vested interests of his marshals, and with political purposes that sometimes pulled in diverse directions.[81]

Duplication of the Soviet Military Threat against Europe

From a strategic and economic standpoint Khrushchev apparently realized that the Soviet Union stood little chance of winning an outright numbers race with the United States in intercontinental delivery forces. If the attainment of a superior strategic posture thus seemed out of effective reach for the indefinite future, a more modest deterrent posture against the United States and a continuation of a formidable threat to Europe may have appeared to Khrushchev as the best combination available to him. Technical factors could have added weight to this conclusion, since it was a lengthier and more difficult task for Soviet technology to develop satisfactory operational ICBM systems than medium-range missiles suitable for use against Europe. The latter point was underlined, in a sense, by Khrushchev's 1962 adventure in Cuba, which was intended among other things to convert some of his plentiful supply of medium-range missiles into "ersatz" ICBMs.

The influence of Russian history, such as the experience of past invasions from the West and especially the bitter memory of Nazi Germany's onslaught upon the Soviet Union, doubtless entered the picture along the way, reinforcing a determination to keep superior Soviet forces deployed against Europe. Khrushchev himself, as we noted earlier, was by no means immune to the voice of tradition in this respect, and his principal innovation was to propose that new technology take over more of the task previously borne by Soviet manpower. That Khrushchev's reforms went only part way in replacing the conceptions that had governed in Stalin's time may have been due in part to institutional inertia and to the resistance of conservative marshals with a vested interest in seeing the theater forces maintained on a strong footing. However, the explanation probably also lies in a congruence of other military and political considerations that argued in one way or another for redundant Soviet capabilities: strong theater forces as well as a large MRBM force.

Militarily, the case for redundant forces arose mainly out of Soviet views on the requirements for general war. The prevailing prudential view of the

---

[81] Khrushchev, of course, was not alone among the contemporary leaders of great powers in being obliged to settle for policies which represented a compromise among many conflicting pressures and interests. For interesting commentary on this point, see Samuel Huntington, *The Common Defense* (New York: Columbia University Press, 1961), p. 51.

military command, with which Khrushchev found it necessary to compromise, was that after initial missile strikes, large theater forces would be needed to consolidate victory and occupy Europe.[82] Outside the context of the conduct of a general war, redundant forces could also be justified in terms of deterrence, the thrust of the argument being that a Soviet Union inferior to the United States in global strategic power had to make doubly sure that her military posture against Europe would be taken seriously. The special problem of Germany also argued for a Soviet military policy of double insurance. Although denial of a German role in NATO nuclear-sharing arrangements continued to be high on Khrushchev's list of priorities, as the campaign against the MLF proposal in the last years of his regime attested, there was always the possibility that Soviet diplomacy might not be able to bar the nuclear door to Bonn. In this event, the compound threat of local Soviet military strength and a large missile force targeted upon Germany would provide a healthy margin of insurance against any tendency of Bonn to step out of line, politically or militarily.

Second thoughts about the advisability of downgrading the Soviet posture for conducting limited non-nuclear operations in the European theater provided a further argument for the principle of military redundancy in Europe. This became apparent toward the end of the Khrushchev regime, when, as we shall see later, Soviet military theorists began to examine more closely the implications of the Kennedy administration's strategy of "flexible response," aimed among other things at raising the nuclear threshold in Europe.

The missile build-up against Europe, moreover, could serve as a backstop for Soviet policy if future political developments were to lead to mutual troop withdrawals in Europe, or even to radical changes in alliance arrangements, such as a possible US military disengagement from NATO. In such a case, a large MRBM force based on Soviet territory would continue to give the Soviet Union an enormous bargaining advantage over Europe and would provide an answer to any small national deterrent forces (like France's *force de frappe*) that might remain in Europe. Even if the French and British were to pool their nuclear delivery arms in a combined nuclear force of purely European character, possibly with German participation, the massive threat of hundreds of Soviet missiles trained on the constricted territory of these countries would surely negate the value of such a force, especially as a counter to any Soviet move against a European state.[83]

Politically, a number of arguments could be made for the Soviet Union's maintaining a strong local military presence despite the build-up of medium-range strategic missile units in the western USSR. Apart from the general political leverage to be derived from having a tangible reminder of Soviet military power deployed in the heart of Europe, perhaps the most persuasive point was the advantage of the Soviet Union's unmistakable local superiority around

[82] See Wolfe, *Soviet Strategy at the Crossroads*, pp. 110–15, 139–46, 172–76.
[83] See Richardson, *Germany and the Atlantic Alliance*, p. 131.

Berlin—a card not to be given up lightly without major political concessions from the West. Another argument for keeping a manifest military presence in Eastern Europe may have had little to do with Soviet policy toward the West, but rather may have reflected a continuing need to command respect for Soviet interests from countries within the Warsaw Pact itself. However, since this was essentially a police function and could have been performed with relatively few troops, given the Soviet Union's geographic proximity, it would hardly seem to account in more than a marginal sense for the large Soviet combat deployment in the area.

Soviet Position on the Likelihood of War

To conclude this discussion of factors bearing on the evolution of Khrushchev's military policy, let us look briefly at Soviet thinking on the nature and likelihood of a war involving the Soviet Union—a question that obviously would have an important influence on the military preparations deemed necessary by the Soviet leadership. Soviet belief in the utility of intensive theoretical analysis of war[84]—its causes, forms, functions, likelihood, and so on—has led to a vast, and by no means wholly consistent, literature on the subject, which cannot be reviewed in detail here. What is pertinent to the present discussion is that, in the Khrushchev period, this Soviet literature had come to posit the "theoretical possibility" of three types of wars—general world war, imperialist war, and a third category that included national liberation wars.[85] Throughout Khrushchev's time, the main focus of Soviet attention lay upon the problems of a possible world war, which in the Soviet view would see the "imperialist and socialist camps" pitted against each other in widespread theaters of action, of which the central and most decisive one would be in Europe. Although under both Lenin and Stalin the possibility had sometimes been raised of an "intercapitalist" world war from which the Soviet Union might stand apart,[86] by Khrushchev's day it had become a firm tenet of Soviet doctrine that any world war would be fought, on a nuclear basis and for unlimited ends, between rival "socialist" and "imperialist" coalitions.[87]

The Soviet typology of wars under Khrushchev tended to become less precise with respect to the categories of "imperialist war" and "national libera-

[84] For a discussion of the Soviet belief that only from the starting point of intensive theoretical analysis of war can proper policies be developed to prepare the country for the eventuality of war, see Wolfe, Soviet Strategy at the Crossroads, pp. 110–11. See also Thomas W. Wolfe, Soviet Military Theory: An Additional Source of Insight Into Its Development, The RAND Corporation, P-3258, November 1965, pp. 24–49.

[85] For Soviet views of these various types of wars, see Marshal V. D. Sokolovskii et al., Soviet Military Strategy, with Analytical Introduction and Annotations by H. S. Dinerstein, L. Gouré, and T. W. Wolfe of The RAND Corporation (Englewood Cliffs, N.J.: Prentice-Hall, 1963), pp. 282–83; Khrushchev's report on the Eighty-one-Party Moscow Conference, in Kommunist, no. 1 (January 1961): 17–19; Colonel General N. A. Lomov, Sovetskaia voennaia doktrina (Soviet Military Doctrine) (Moscow: Izdatel'stvo "Znanie," 1963), p. 21.

[86] See Thomas W. Wolfe, Communist Outlook on War, The RAND Corporation, P-3640, August 1967, pp. 18–23.

[87] For basic features of the Soviet image of a future world war, see Wolfe, Soviet Strategy at the Crossroads, pp. 111–15.

tion war," the difference between the two being mainly one of political definition: that is, an imperialist war would be an "unjust" war waged by an imperialist power against a colonial country, while a national liberation war
would be a "just" war waged the other way around. Although the continued
occurrence of such small wars in underdeveloped countries was considered in
Khrushchev's time to be much more likely than the outbreak of a general war,
far less theoretical attention was devoted to the smaller wars than to the problem of general world war.

For our inquiry, the salient question is how seriously the Soviet leaders
during that period regarded the likelihood of general war—a conflict which
by Soviet definition would involve a clash of the rival military coalitions confronting each other in Europe. One finds it difficult to judge what the rock-
bottom estimate of this danger in the course of the Khrushchev decade may
have been, for not only did Soviet propaganda against the West blow hot and
cold on the danger-of-war issue as international crises waxed or waned, but
the issue was also colored by the exigencies of internal Soviet politics and by
the dispute between Moscow and Peking.[88] Nevertheless, two contrasting
trends of thought were evident, reflecting a somewhat ambivalent attitude
toward the likelihood of war.

On the one hand was the fairly persistent tendency, rooted perhaps in an
ideologically tinted view of Western intentions, to argue that the West was
bent upon attacking the Soviet camp if a favorable moment should arise. In
the early years of the Khrushchev regime, at a time when Soviet military
theorists were beginning to dwell upon the implications of surprise nuclear
attack, this line of argument frequently took the form of charges that the
United States was counting on surprise attack to ensure the success of a "preventive" war against the Soviet Union.[89] As one authoritative Soviet appraisal put it in 1959, US policies and the conception of a "massive surprise
blow" were "pregnant with serious danger of war."[90] This strand of argument
continued into the early sixties, particularly in military writing, where stress on
the ever-present danger of war appeared with the persistency of a well-learned
reflex.[91]

[88] Ibid., p. 116.

[89] Although Khrushchev himself, as well as other Soviet leaders, often spoke of the US "policy
of strength" as an aggressive effort to intimidate the Soviet Union and one which could lead to
war, and although Khrushchev asserted that "the imperialists have never abandoned their hopes
of destroying the first socialist state" (see, for example, Khrushchev's Minsk speech of January 22,
1958, and his interview of June 11, 1958, with an Australian journalist, in N. S. Khrushchev,
For Victory in Peaceful Competition with Capitalism [New York: E. P. Dutton & Co., 1960],
pp. 33, 491; see also Bulganin's letter of January 8, 1958, to President Eisenhower, TASS dispatch
and *New York Times*, January 10, 1958), direct charges of US plotting of "preventive war" were
customarily left to lesser propaganda media and, occasionally to military spokesmen. On the other
hand, not all military commentators took an indiscriminate view of US policy. For example, Lt.
General S. Krasil'nikov, in a radio broadcast on March 9, 1958, stated: "Of course, the Soviet
Union does not confuse the utterances of the supporters of a preventive war with the official policy
of the United States."

[90] Kuusinen, *Osnovy Marksizma-Leninizma*, pp. 489–90.

[91] See Wolfe, *Soviet Strategy at the Crossroads*, pp. 116–17.

On the other hand, however, there was cumulative evidence as the Khrushchev period unfolded that the danger-of-war issue was becoming more a matter of ritual than one of imminent concern, and especially that the formula of "surprise attack—preventive war" as a serious possibility was less prominent in Soviet thinking. Among such evidence, upon which we have remarked earlier, was Khrushchev's revision in 1956 of the thesis of inevitable war, indicating a growing confidence in the durability of mutual nuclear deterrence. Alongside this erosion of a long-standing doctrinal tenet was Khrushchev's apparent belief, dating from his personal contacts with President Eisenhower and reinforced later by his dealings with President Kennedy, that the emergence of "sober-minded" elements within the US leadership had greatly reduced the possibility of a deliberate attack on the Soviet camp.[92] Toward the end of the Khrushchev period, some Soviet military theorists (although not all) began to moderate their concern about surprise attack, conceding that improvements in warning capabilities and strategic posture could reduce the feasibility of achieving surprise and hence tend to discourage an attack from being attempted.[93]

With regard to Europe itself, Soviet thinking during Khrushchev's rule produced no visible expectation that war might occur there independently of war on a global scale. In neither the political nor the military discourse of the Soviet Union was there significant dissent from Khrushchev's frequent contention that any hostilities in Europe, where the vital interests of the great powers were closely intermeshed, were highly likely to escalate to general nuclear war.[94] Furthermore, the image of a surprise attack on the Soviet Union, the "scenario" of general-war outbreak most frequently cited by Russian military theorists, was generally anchored in Europe. While it was

[92] See the discussion of this point in chapter VI, pp. 105–6. Although the Soviet image of President Kennedy on the whole was relatively benign, there were some exceptions. For example, the revised Sokolovskii volume included a reference to President Kennedy's statement in early 1962 that under certain conditions the United States might initiate the use of nuclear weapons. This was construed as "a direct indication that the United States is preparing for the surprise use of nuclear weapons in unlimited fashion against the socialist countries." Marshal V. D. Sokolovskii et al., *Voennaia strategiia* (Military Strategy), 2nd ed. (Moscow: Voenizdat, 1963), p. 351. For President Kennedy's statement, made in the context of a possible massive assault on Europe by Soviet forces, see Stewart Alsop, "Kennedy's Grand Strategy," *Saturday Evening Post*, March 31, 1962, pp. 11, 13.

[93] For discussion of these Soviet views on the diminishing feasibility of surprise attack, see Wolfe, *Soviet Strategy at the Crossroads*, pp. 63, 253–54. There were Soviet writers, however, who continued to dwell on both the dangers and opportunities presented by surprise attack. Some stressed that Soviet forces could not be sure of advanced warning, and hence had to be ready for action "in minutes or seconds." See Colonel S. Lipitskii, "Activity of an Aggressor in the Period When War Threatens," *Voenno-istoricheskii zhurnal*, no. 8 (August 1963): 11–24. Other writers departed from the usual approach of casting the Soviet Union as the recipient of a surprise enemy blow, emphasizing instead the advantages to be gained if the enemy were taken by surprise. See, for example, Colonel S. A. Tiushkevich, "Necessity and Chance in Warfare," *Kommunist Vooruzhennykh Sil*, no. 10 (May 1964): 40–44. For fuller discussion of this changing treatment of surprise attack by Soviet writers, see Wolfe, *Soviet Military Theory: An Additional Source of Insight*, pp. 15–21.

[94] See fn. 51, above.

conceded that such an attack could result from escalation of a local conflict elsewhere, it was most often pictured as arising out of a period of crisis in Europe. In this connection, we may recall that during the Geneva conference on surprise attack in late 1958, the Soviet delegation devoted more attention to the problems of preventing surprise attack in the European context than to those associated with intercontinental strategic strikes.[95]

Summing up this brief review of Soviet attitudes of the Khrushchev period on the likelihood of war, one may say that professional military opinion tended to give the benefit of the doubt to the assumption that the danger of war was ever-present, whereas the political leadership seemed relatively confident that war was unlikely, short of extreme provocation, which it was the business of the Soviet Union's "peaceful coexistence" policy to avoid. Khrushchev's candid comment in the spring of 1962 that threats of war from both sides had the effect of canceling each other out and stabilizing the situation was perhaps suggestive of his private outlook on the likelihood of a major military conflict, especially in Europe.[96] Indeed, one might argue that, if he had, in fact, entertained a high expectation of war, he would probably have sanctioned considerably larger and more urgent military preparations than were made while he was responsible for Soviet security.

Having said this, one should add a qualification with regard to the concern that a resurgent Germany might one day draw the United States and the Soviet Union into war. On this score, Khrushchev, no less than other Soviet leaders before and since his time, seems to have harbored suspicions that were never fully laid to rest, even though a purely rational calculus might have argued that the odds were hopelessly stacked against Germany in any conflict which might arise in Europe in the nuclear age. The constancy of this concern, expressed in the dogma of West German "revanchism," rather than any concrete alarm about the likelihood of a war, seems to have been the common denominator upon which each generation of Soviet leaders since World War II has based its determination to prepare the Soviet Union for a possible war in Europe.

[95] The conference "To Study the Practical Aspects of Reducing the Possibility of Surprise Attack," held in Geneva from November 10 to December 18, found the Western and Soviet delegations largely talking past each other. For documents and proposals pertinent to this Conference, see *Documents on Disarmament, 1945–1959*, vol. 2 (1957–59), US Department of State, Washington, D.C., 1960, pp. 1126, 1129, 1145, 1222–24, 1227, 1230–1339, 1351–60.

[96] See Wolfe, *Soviet Strategy at the Crossroads*, p. 117.

VIII

CHANGES IN THE SOVIET MILITARY POSTURE
UNDER KHRUSHCHEV

According to an account of the postwar development of the Soviet armed forces published in the Soviet Union toward the end of the Khrushchev period, the chief characteristic of the years between 1945 and about 1954 was the effort to develop and master the new technology of the nuclear missile age, while the main feature of the following decade was the process of incorporating the new weapons into the armed forces, along with an appropriate doctrine for their use.[1] Although to some extent these two phases of development tended to overlap, one can say that historically it fell to Khrushchev to preside over the second process—that of introducing new instruments and concepts of modern warfare into the armed forces.

The great watershed in this process of assimilation came around 1960, when Khrushchev's new military policy, based on the primacy of strategic retaliatory power, was formally unveiled. We have reviewed some of the salient considerations that led up to this policy, as well as those which subsequently helped to modify it in various respects, especially with regard to the Soviet military stance toward Europe. Now, we shall consider more specifically the changes in the size and character of the armed forces themselves that took place during the Khrushchev decade. In the next chapter, we shall examine significant trends in Soviet thinking on theater warfare in Europe during the same period.

Debate Over the Size of the Theater Forces

Given the historically dominant role of land power in the Soviet military tradition, it is not surprising that Khrushchev's efforts to revamp the Soviet military establishment in accord with technological developments of the nuclear missile age should have brought him into frequent collision with the

[1] Colonel I. Korotkov, "The Development of Soviet Military Theory in the Postwar Years," *Voenno-istoricheskii zhurnal* (Military-Historical Journal), no. 4 (April 1964): 40–44. Another Soviet account, which fixes 1954 as the beginning of a second period of postwar development in which "military-theoretical thought began to work out new problems of warfare associated with the development of missiles and nuclear weapons," may be found in a work by Major Generals S. N. Kozlov and M. V. Smirnov and Colonels I. S. Baz and P. A. Sidorov, *O Sovetskoi voennoi nauke* (On Soviet Military Science), rev. ed. (Moscow: Voenizdat, 1964), pp. 209–15. This work also identified a third period, beginning in 1960 with Khrushchev's enunciation of a new Soviet military doctrine. For a more detailed discussion of these Soviet accounts, see Thomas W. Wolfe, *Soviet Military Theory: An Additional Source of Insight Into Its Development*, The RAND Corporation, P-3258, November 1965, pp. 24–30.

advocates of strong theater forces. These forces, representing principally the ground forces with supporting tactical aviation and coastal sea forces, were the numerically preponderant element of Soviet military power, and hence the logical target of manpower-saving reforms sponsored by Khrushchev. Although Khrushchev did in fact manage to achieve a very substantial cutback in the over-all size of the theater or general-purpose forces,[2] his reforms were, in a sense, the product of compromise. Thus, as mentioned earlier, his policy led to preparing the theater forces for nuclear warfare in addition to their previous, conventional role, and, despite over-all manpower reductions, the practice of keeping a large theater-force presence deployed in Central and Eastern Europe remained basically unchanged.

During the first five years or so of his rule, while he was feeling his way toward the "new look" military policy of 1960, Khrushchev managed to avoid open controversy over his evolving view that modern technology should make it possible to pare down an oversized traditional military establishment without endangering Soviet security. Indeed, despite the increasing emphasis given to Soviet strategic nuclear power, there was as yet little sign of a serious assault upon the established belief in the importance of large ground armies, even in the nuclear era. Such authoritative military spokesmen as Marshal Zhukov, prior to his dismissal in late 1957, continued to look upon nuclear weapons as supplementary to the operations of the traditional forces, whose primacy went unquestioned.[3] It was only after the promulgation of the new military policy of 1960 had caused a parting of the ways between Khrushchev and traditionalist elements among the military leadership that the debate over the size of the armed forces emerged into the open.

The course of this debate, which was intimately interwoven with both the economics and politics of Soviet defense, has been described elsewhere by the present writer.[4] Suffice to say here that the debate involved, on one side, a "modernist," future-oriented school which leaned generally toward Khrushchev's position, with its emphasis on missile forces over the larger theater ground forces, and on the other side, a "traditionalist" school which reaffirmed

[2] The term "theater forces" as used here corresponds approximately to what in current American usage are called "general purpose forces," described according to the broad mission they perform rather than by the formal organizational components from which they are drawn. In a formal organizational sense, the Soviet armed forces consist of five major branches or force components, plus a variety of administrative and technical services and miscellaneous commands. The five major branches are the ground, naval, air, air-missile defense, and strategic missile forces. Generally speaking, the ground forces provide the bulk of the "theater forces," along with tactical aviation and coastal sea units. For more detailed discussion of the formal organization of the Soviet armed forces, see Raymond L. Garthoff, *Soviet Strategy in the Nuclear Age* (New York: Frederick A. Praeger, Inc., 1958), pp. 41–46; Department of the Army, *Soviet Russia: Strategic Survey*, Pamphlet 20-64, Washington, D.C., December 1963, pp. 173–88.

[3] Representative statements of Marshal Zhukov's views before he was dismissed as Minister of Defense, in November 1957, may be found in *Pravda*, August 7, 1956, and *Krasnaia zvezda*, March 23, 1957. For an examination of the views of other Soviet military leaders in this period, see Garthoff, *Soviet Strategy in the Nuclear Age*, pp. 149–66, and Thomas W. Wolfe, *Soviet Strategy at the Crossroads* (Cambridge, Mass.: Harvard University Press, 1964), pp. 153–55.

[4] Wolfe, *Soviet Strategy at the Crossroads*, pp. 139–52.

the need to maintain massive armies prepared for combined-arms operations on a continental scale. Adherents of the modernist outlook pressed for radical adaptation of modern technology to military affairs, and suggested that this approach might lighten the strain on resources—that quality, so to speak, could replace quantity. The traditionalists, on the other hand, argued that technology had actually increased the need for multimillion-man armies to replenish the enormous potential losses of nuclear warfare, and some conservatives, like Marshals Rotmistrov[5] and Chuikov, buttressed their case by citing NATO's efforts in the early sixties to build up stronger conventional ground forces "in the decisive area of Europe."[6]

By the end of the Khrushchev decade, neither the modernist nor the traditionalist outlook had gained uncontested ascendancy; rather, what might be described as a "centrist" viewpoint, representing a compromise between the two, tended to prevail. Even so, by early 1964, conservatives like Marshal Rotmistrov had become more vocal, pointing to the danger that "calculations based on the anticipated results of using a single new type of weapon alone can lead to erroneous conclusions," and expressing concern that exaggerated emphasis on missiles threatened to cripple the "creative development" of other forces and of Soviet military theory in general.[7]

The practical consequences of the modernist–traditionalist debate, so far as the issue of massive armies was concerned, were registered in the several troop reduction programs carried out during the Khrushchev decade. In general, these programs fell into two phases. Between 1955 and 1960, before opposition to his new military policy began to crystallize, Khrushchev reduced Soviet troop levels on several occasions without evoking noticeable protest from the military leadership. In the second phase, however, during the military policy debate of the early sixties, Khrushchev's cutback proposals ran into growing resistance from the massive-army lobby among the Soviet marshals.

Context in Which Troop Reduction Proposals Arose

Before reviewing the history of Khrushchev's programs for troop cutbacks, it may be useful to recall briefly the interplay between Soviet military and disarmament policy in the mid-fifties. Along with the need to make additional manpower available for the Soviet economy, it was the strategic situation of the mid-fifties and Khrushchev's efforts to deal with it through a combination of military policy reforms and disarmament proposals that largely formed the context in which measures for manpower cutbacks were initiated.

[5] Marshal P. A. Rotmistrov, a hero of tank warfare in World War II and a military scholar, had been one of the first open critics of Stalinist military doctrine in the mid-fifties. As the Khrushchev period unfolded, Rotmistrov moved gradually from a "progressive" to a "conservative" position, taking the lead among senior marshals in criticizing Khrushchev's tendency to stress strategic missile forces at the expense of the traditional ground and air forces. See Wolfe, *Soviet Strategy at the Crossroads*, pp. 168–69, 301.

[6] Marshal V. I. Chuikov, "Modern Ground Forces," *Izvestiia*, December 22, 1963.

[7] Marshal P. Rotmistrov, "Military Science and the Academies," *Krasnaia zvezda*, April 26, 1964.

As matters stood in early 1955, near the beginning of the Khrushchev period, the strategic situation confronting the Soviet Union called for remedial action. The Korean War had been followed by a major build-up of US strategic delivery forces and the extension of an overseas network of American bases, bringing home more forcefully than ever to the Soviet leadership the potential consequences of a nuclear war. In Europe, the portent of a stronger NATO had been raised by the imminent rearming of Germany and plans for stationing tactical nuclear weapons in the NATO countries. Although Soviet military power had not been neglected and the US nuclear monopoly had been broken, the strategic situation from the Soviet viewpoint was nevertheless deteriorating. Not only did these circumstances counsel a fresh foreign-policy approach designed to lower international tensions and slow down the momentum of Western defense preparations, but Khrushchev himself in early 1955 was in a position where new initiatives promised to buttress his personal bid for leadership.

Precisely at this juncture, in May 1955, the Soviet Union put forward a major two-stage disarmament proposal, more ambitious in scope than anything proposed since World War II. It called for measures which, when completed (by the end of 1957), would leave the major powers with a fixed level of conventional forces and no nuclear weapons or foreign bases.[8] Had it been accepted, this proposal would have cleared the board of those aspects of Western military power that were causing the Soviet leadership the most concern.

First and foremost, the Soviet Union would have eliminated the threat of US strategic nuclear power, as well as the impending tactical nuclear threat in Europe. Second, the withdrawal of US forces to America (where it was proposed they be kept to a level of 1,500,000 men) would effectively have marked the end of NATO. Third, German rearmament would have been nipped in the bud. Finally, Soviet conventional superiority on the Continent, although scaled down, would have been safeguarded, with French forces of 650,000 men, separated by the English Channel from British forces of equal size, the principal remaining elements of Western military power on the Continent to face Soviet forces of 1,500,000 plus the East European armies.

This proposal, rejected by the Western powers, was followed by others which illustrated the correlation between the changing strategic situation and Khrushchev's emergent military policies. In 1956, for example, as Soviet nuclear capabilities were growing and Khrushchev's ideas of substituting "firepower for manpower" began to take shape, the Soviet Union turned anew to a proposal for reducing conventional arms as the prelude to efforts toward agreement on nuclear disarmament.[9] Although this proposal again failed to lead to a disarmament agreement, Khrushchev went ahead with a troop-reduction program of his own, thus suggesting that, in making his proposal,

---

[8] For details of the May 1955 Soviet proposal, see US Department of State, *Documents on Disarmament, 1945–1959*, vol. 1 (1945–56) (Washington, D.C., 1960), pp. 456–66.

[9] Ibid., pp. 603–7.

he had hoped to turn to account in the disarmament market steps that he intended to take anyway in connection with his military reforms.[10] Let us look now at the troop cutback measures which Khrushchev sponsored: first, as they affected the over-all manpower levels of the Soviet armed forces and, second, as they impinged upon the size of the theater forces deployed against Europe.

Impact of Khrushchev's Troop Reduction Programs

The first of the troop demobilization programs under Khrushchev was initiated in 1955, around the time of the Geneva "thaw," and continued roughly over the next two years, until May 1957.[11] According to Soviet claims, it resulted in a cut of 1,840,000 men from the 1955 peak of 5.7 million.[12] This reduction, Soviet spokesmen said, was undertaken to ease international tension and to free manpower for the Soviet economy. It was presented to the world as a unilateral Soviet initiative, although, in fact, the United States in December 1954 had announced a program for the gradual reduction of its post-Korean military manpower strength from 3.2 million to 2.8 million men by June 1956.[13] The Soviet troop cutback of 1955–57 was to involve, according to Moscow's statements,[14] the disbanding of "63 divisions and independent brigades"; since no further breakdown of this figure

[10] For further discussion of this question, see *Soviet Strategy at the Crossroads*, pp. 232–34; Malcolm Mackintosh and Harry Willetts, "Arms Control and the Soviet National Interest," in Louis Henkin, ed., *Arms Control Issues for the Public* (Englewood Cliffs, N.J.: Prentice-Hall, Inc., 1961), pp.149–51.

[11] The initial step in Khrushchev's troop reduction program, for which no specific figures were given in the *Pravda* announcement of July 19, 1955, was the transfer to the reserve of a number of men equal to the number of troops to be withdrawn from Austria under the State Treaty of May 1955. As indicated earlier (pp. 79–80, fn. 32), Western estimates put this number at something like 50,000. Later in 1955, the Soviet government announced that the armed forces would be reduced by a total of 640,000 men by December 15, 1955, a figure that included those already covered by the earlier announcement (*Pravda*, August 13, 1955). The continuation of the troop reduction program in 1956 and the early months of 1957 accounted for a further claimed reduction of 1,200,000 men, bringing the total for the 1955–57 period to 1,840,000 men. For sources see fn. 12, below.

[12] "Statement by the Soviet Government on the Disarmament Problem, May 14, 1956," *Documents on Disarmament, 1945–1959*, vol. 1, p. 638; "Soviet Memorandum Submitted to the Disarmament Subcommittee: Implementation of Partial Disarmament Measures, April 30, 1957," ibid., vol. 2, p. 780. These Soviet statements claiming a reduction of 1,840,000 men in the 1955–57 period gave no figures for the strength level of the armed forces when the reductions began or at the time they were completed. Not until Khrushchev's speech of January 14, 1960, was the starting figure of 5.7 million disclosed. *Pravda*, January 15, 1960.

[13] *New York Times*, December 21, 1954. Under the program announced by Secretary of Defense Charles E. Wilson in 1954, the US Army was to be reduced from nineteen to eighteen combat divisions, and its five training divisions were to be abolished. At the time, five of the US combat divisions were in Europe, where they were committed to remain. Subsequently, the reduction of US ground forces went beyond the Wilson program; by the end of the Eisenhower administration, the army was down to 875,000 men and fourteen divisions, of which three were below the strength required for combat. The downward trend in the strength and number of divisions of the ground forces was reversed only after the Kennedy administration came into office, when a build-up of the army to 1,000,000 men and sixteen combat-ready divisions was authorized. See William W. Kaufmann, *The McNamara Strategy* (New York: Harper & Row, 1964), pp. 34, 67–68.

[14] *Documents on Disarmament, 1945–1959*, vol. 1, p. 638.

was given, it was left obscure how many combat divisions, as distinct from smaller brigades and other miscellaneous formations, were to be deleted from the theater forces' order of battle.

The second over-all troop reduction program under Khrushchev took place in 1958-59, in connection with the widely publicized withdrawal of some Soviet forces from Eastern Europe, including those stationed in Rumania.[15] Smaller than the cutback of 1955-57, this demobilization program involved 300,000 men, according to Khrushchev's figures, bringing the total strength of the armed forces down to 3.6 million men by January 1960.[16] No indication was given of the number of divisions or other formations that may have been disbanded as a result of this manpower cutback.

The third troop reduction program under Khrushchev, announced in his January 1960 speech to the Supreme Soviet, was intended to reduce the manpower level of the armed forces from 3.6 to 2.4 million over the next couple of years.[17] As we have noted, this program helped to set in motion an internal policy debate over the size of the armed forces which continued through the remainder of Khrushchev's tenure. The program itself was suspended during the Berlin crisis of 1961, when only about half of the projected 1.2 million cut had been made, and there were indications that over-all manpower levels rose at least temporarily as the crisis prompted the retention in service of draftees normally due for discharge into the reserve in the fall of the year.

Khrushchev suggested on several occasions that the suspension of the troop cutback program was to be only temporary,[18] until international tensions had eased, and in fact he made good his word. In December 1963, while promoting a policy of "mutual example" in furtherance of his quest for détente,[19] Khrushchev launched his fourth and final troop cut proposal, stating that the Soviet Union was considering "the possibility of some further reduction in the numerical strength of our armed forces."[20] No figures were given for the contemplated reduction, although it may well have been aimed at bringing troop levels down to the goal of 2.4 million men set by Khrushchev in January 1960. Whether this final proposal had ever got beyond the "possible" category in the face of internal opposition to Khrushchev's policies was unclear at the time that the Soviet leader was forced out of the picture in the fall of 1964. Subsequently, there was some ambiguous evidence that the proposal had been at least partly implemented before the new leadership, in early 1965, began to reassess Soviet force-level requirements in light of the worsening of the international situation brought on by the war in Southeast Asia.

Altogether, as based on Soviet statements, Khrushchev's troop reduction

[15] TASS report, *Pravda*, January 27, 1958; Khrushchev speech at the May 1958 meeting in Moscow of the Warsaw Pact's Political Consultative Committee, *Pravda*, May 27, 1958.

[16] *Pravda*, January 15, 1960.

[17] Ibid.

[18] Khrushchev speech to graduates of Soviet military academies on July 8, 1961, *Pravda*, July 9, 1961; Khrushchev television address of August 7, 1961, *Izvestiia*, August 9, 1961.

[19] See chapter VI, p. 109.

[20] *Izvestiia*, December 15, 1963.

programs between 1955 and the fall of 1964 resulted in a cumulative cutback of approximately one-half in the over-all manpower strength of the armed forces—from 5.7 million to something on the order of 3 million. With respect to the thinning out of the theater forces deployed in Europe, however, the net results during this period appear to have been less impressive.

No aggregate Soviet figures were ever given on how many troops were withdrawn from Eastern Europe as a consequence of Khrushchev's reduction programs. Piecemeal statements indicated a withdrawal of 30,000 troops from East Germany in 1955, and another 41,000 in connection with the demobilization program of 1958, along with 17,000 from Hungary and an unannounced number from Rumania.[21] Presumably, the third reduction program, launched in 1960, involved some troop withdrawals from Eastern Europe, but no specific claims to this effect were linked either with the 1960 program or with Khrushchev's final proposal of December 1963. So far as Soviet statements go, therefore, only 89,000 troops are specifically accounted for as having been withdrawn during Khrushchev's time, with a further number probable but indeterminate. Since withdrawals were at least partially balanced by temporary build-ups of Soviet strength in Eastern Europe in connection with such crises as that of Hungary in 1956 and Berlin in 1958–61, the net figure for Soviet forces deployed in Europe is likely to have remained near the half-million mark at which it stood at the start of the Khrushchev period. On the basis of the data disclosed by the Soviets themselves, it certainly seems clear that the over-all cutback of around 50 per cent in the manpower levels of the Soviet armed forces during Khrushchev's time was not reflected in a proportionate reduction of the Soviet military presence in Europe.

This brings us to the complicated question of Western assessments of the changing Soviet troop levels, particularly the vexing problem of tallying up the number and quality of Soviet divisions immediately on hand, or readily available, for employment against NATO in Europe.

Western Reappraisal of the Theater-Force Balance

At the beginning of the Khrushchev period, Western appraisals were in general agreement that the Soviet Union had around 4 million men under arms, not counting several hundred thousand MVD security troops and border guards.[22] The ground forces were estimated to number about 2.5 million, with 175 divisions. Of these, twenty-eight to thirty divisions were generally believed

---

[21] See *Documents on Disarmament, 1945–1959*, vol. 1, p. 638; TASS report, *Pravda*, January 7, 1958; Khrushchev speech at Warsaw Pact meeting, *Pravda*, May 27, 1958.

[22] For some representative Western assessments in 1954–55, see Field Marshal Viscount Montgomery's "Statement on Current Soviet Military Capability" dated April 20, 1964, as published in *U.S. News and World Report*, June 4, 1954, p. 45; Lt. Colonel John Baker White, "The Armies of Communism," *Army Combat Forces Journal* (March 1954): 33–36; N. Galay, "Military Affairs: Mobilization and Demobilization," *Bulletin of the Institute for the Study of the History and Culture of the USSR* (September 1955): 40–41; R. L. Garthoff, "What's Behind Soviet Disarmament," *Army Combat Forces Journal* (October 1955): 24. See also chapter II, pp. 10–11.

to be deployed in Eastern Europe, facing NATO forces of less than twenty divisions on the central front.[23] Another sixty to seventy Soviet divisions in Western Russia, it was estimated, provided the back-up for the European theater, with the remaining divisions spread out elsewhere along the Soviet borders, in the Far East, and in the interior. Tactical air units with some 10,000 aircraft, about one-fourth of which were based in Eastern Europe, were thought to be available for battlefield support of the ground formations.[24]

These large standing forces of 4 million men were estimated to have remained fairly constant in size throughout the latter years of the Stalinist period, including the Korean War.[25] If Khrushchev's figure of 5.7 million in 1955 is taken at face value, those Western estimates, made in 1954–55, turn out to have been on the low side by almost 2 million, suggesting that a larger Soviet build-up took place during the Korean War period than had been suspected.[26]

On the other hand, it appears in retrospect that Western estimates tended to lag somewhat behind in their awareness of the downward trend in over-all Soviet manpower levels that was set in motion by Khrushchev's troop reduction programs after 1955. Throughout the latter fifties, they continued to adhere to the familiar Western assessment of approximately 4 million men and 175 divisions for the Soviet Union, and it was only following Khrushchev's unprecedented revelation of past and present Soviet strength levels, in January 1960, that these time-honored figures began to be publicly reappraised in the West.[27] Even so, Khrushchev's over-all figure of 3.6 million men for 1960 did

23 Mackintosh and Willetts, in *Arms Control Issues for the Public*, p. 150; Hanson W. Baldwin, *The Great Arms Race* (New York: Frederick A. Praeger, Inc., 1958), p. 36; Robert E. Osgood, *NATO: The Entangling Alliance* (Chicago, Ill.: University of Chicago Press, 1962), p. 118.

24 Robert A. Kilmarx, *A History of Soviet Air Power* (New York: Frederick A. Praeger, Inc., 1962), pp. 266, 268. See also Garthoff, *Soviet Strategy in the Nuclear Age*, p. 57; Asher Lee, "A Review of Red Air Power," *Contact* (March 1954): 3–5. The total number of Soviet military aircraft at the start of the Khrushchev period, in 1955, was generally put at 19,000 to 20,000 in Western estimates.

25 Garthoff, in *Army Combat Forces Journal* (October 1955): 24. See also Colonel Louis B. Ely, "A General Assessment," in B. H. Liddell Hart, ed., *The Soviet Army* (London: Weidenfeld and Nicolson, 1956), pp. 207–8.

26 For an earlier comment suggesting that the figures divulged by Khrushchev in January 1960 may have exaggerated an upward trend in over-all Soviet strength levels during the Korean War period, see chapter II, fn. 5. The inference is that Khrushchev wished to demonstrate for disarmament propaganda purposes that Soviet forces were dramatically hiked up to the 5.7 million level in response to Western moves during the Korean War. While some Soviet build-up undoubtedly occurred during the Korean period, the starting point was probably higher than the 2.8 million cited by Khrushchev for 1948.

27 Among the better-known Western sources of public information on Soviet military developments to reflect this process of reappraisal in 1960 was the annual *Military Balance* publication of the Institute for Strategic Studies in London. This publication, noting Khrushchev's announced figure of 3.6 million men for the Soviet armed forces as a whole, offered the estimate that the ground forces were down to a level of 2,240,000 men by 1960, with 135 active line divisions of varying strength and 40 cadre divisions. See *The Communist Bloc and the Free World: The Military Balance, 1960* (London: Institute for Strategic Studies, November 1960), pp. 2–4 (hereafter cited as *Military Balance, 1960*). Western commentary in general accepted Khrushchev's disclosure of Soviet manpower levels and his plans for further Soviet force reductions as indicating a need for Western reappraisal, but also pointed out that even after the proposed reduction the Soviet Union would still possess much larger land forces than any Western power. See *Times*, London,

not fall far below the standard Western measurement.[28] Khrushchev did not, however, divulge figures for the number of Soviet divisions to be affected by his reforms, and around this question arose much of the controversy in the West in the early sixties as to how large and how effective the Soviet theater forces might actually be.

Without attempting to retrace the details of this controversy, by 1963–64, toward the end of the Khrushchev period, a new image of what might be called the "divisional gap" between Soviet forces and those of NATO had emerged from a series of Western reappraisals of the military balance in Europe.[29] The familiar picture of massive Soviet superiority in continental theater forces was now replaced by one crediting the Soviet Union with forces of distinctly more modest proportions and with capabilities against NATO which, while "significant," were deemed "far from overwhelming."[30] Although much of the estimating process upon which this new image rested was not open to public scrutiny, thus leaving room for a certain amount of understandable skepticism, the revised appraisal was generally believed to approximate the realities of the situation in the early sixties more closely than did the old.

By the end of the Khrushchev decade, in 1964, according to the new Western estimates, the over-all strength of the Soviet armed forces was pegged at

---

January 15, 1960, and *Manchester Guardian Weekly*, January 21, 1960. For more detailed discussion of the European reception given Khrushchev's speech, see E. W. Schnitzer, *West European Comments on Soviet Posture as Presented in Khrushchev's Speech of January 14, 1960*, The RAND Corporation, RM-2557, March 22, 1960.

[28] A "crossover" point between the Western estimate of 4 million men and the descending Soviet strength level indicated by Khrushchev probably occurred around 1959, while Khrushchev's second troop reduction program was in progress. Prior to this, however, Western estimates in the late fifties erred on the low side—a point that has been overlooked in a good deal of uninformed commentary to the effect that the West consistently overestimated the size of the Soviet armed forces.

It is also of interest that, between 1955 and 1960, when the Soviet armed forces were presumably being reduced by a cumulative total of 2.1 million men, the officially announced military budgets for those years showed no commensurate drop. From 1955, when the announced budget stood at about 107 billion rubles, the annual budget declined to only 96 billion rubles in 1960. (The figures are given in "old" rubles, in effect in 1955, before a 10:1 devaluation of the ruble took place.) The explanation, assuming that the Soviet data can be taken at face value, would seem to be that, even though pay and maintenance costs for military manpower were going down substantially, expenditures for new equipment and modernization of the armed forces during the same period were rising sharply, thus canceling out most of the difference.

[29] The lead in official questioning of the then prevailing view of the theater force balance in Europe was taken in the early sixties by members of the Kennedy administration, partly to dispel the impression that Soviet forces were so far superior numerically that any attempt to build up NATO's conventional strength would be a waste of effort. See, for example, Paul H. Nitze, address before the Cleveland Council on World Affairs, March 2, 1963, *New York Times*, March 3, 1963; Cyrus R. Vance, address before the Southern Governors' Conference, August 20, 1963, *New York Times*, August 21, 1963; Robert S. McNamara, address before the Economic Club of New York, November 18, 1963, *Department of State Bulletin*, December 16, 1963, pp. 914–21. For a general discussion of how criticism of the traditional image of Soviet ground forces strength developed within the Kennedy administration, see Kaufmann, *The McNamara Strategy*, pp. 82–88. See also John G. Norris, "West Divided on Just How Big Soviet Army Is," *Washington Post*, September 23, 1963.

[30] See Kaufmann, *The McNamara Strategy*, p. 87.

somewhere between 3.3 and 3.1 million men,[31] of which approximately 2 million were in the ground forces. The total number of divisions, it was now generally agreed, was about 140,[32] but opinion diverged as to how many of these were at full strength and ready for combat.[33] Since Soviet military writers themselves indicated that ground-force units in peacetime fell into three different categories of strength readiness,[34] the question hinged on the numbers to be found in each category—figures which, to no one's surprise, Soviet sources failed to supply. A sifting of various published Western estimates yields the following approximations: In the first category, at or near full combat strength, from sixty to seventy divisions; in the second group, at a medium level of readiness permitting them to be brought up to strength on fairly short notice, from forty to fifty divisions; and the remainder in a third category of low-strength cadre divisions, which would require a considerable period of mobilization.[35]

Along with this revised tally of Soviet divisions, the Western estimates of the early sixties also reflected a sizable reduction in the tactical aviation strength available for support of theater operations. From around 10,000 aircraft in the mid-fifties, tactical aviation was cut back by more than half, to about 4,000, according to the revised estimates,[36] a large part of the reduction apparently having taken place around 1960 in conjunction with the growing reliance upon tactical and mid-range strategic missiles under Khrushchev's new military policy. The wholesale retirement of the increasingly obsolescent IL-28 jet light bomber in the early sixties contributed notably to the cutback of Soviet tactical air strength,[37] including that deployed in East Germany and Poland, which by 1964 was thought to have fallen to around 1,200 aircraft, of the more advanced types.

[31] As pointed out earlier, over-all Soviet strength levels in 1964 following Khrushchev's December 1963 proposal for a fourth round of manpower cuts may have been in a state of flux. The range of figures cited here from 3.3 to 3.1 million reflects published Western appraisals covering the period in question. See, for example, McNamara's speech before the Economic Club, *Department of State Bulletin*, December 16, 1963, p. 918; and the Institute for Strategic Studies, *Military Balance, 1963–1964*, p. 3, *1964–1965*, pp. 5–6, and *1965–1966*, p. 2.

[32] During 1964, published Western estimates on the total number of Soviet divisions varied between 150 and 140, with the latter figure tending to become generally accepted by the fall of the year. Whether this reflected an actual Soviet reduction of ten divisions during the year, or merely a new awareness of a reduction process that had been going on over a longer period, is one of the difficult questions that cannot be answered from the available data.

[33] For an exchange between two Western analysts of Soviet affairs which brings out divergent views on this question, see R. T. Rockingham Gill, "The New East-West Military Balance," *East Europe*, no. 4 (April 1964): 3–8, and Philip Windsor, "The East-West Military Balance," and a rejoinder by Gill, ibid., no. 7 (July 1964): 22–23.

[34] See, for example, Marshal V. D. Sokolovskii et al., *Soviet Military Strategy*, with Analytical Introduction and Annotations by H. S. Dinerstein, L. Gouré, and Thomas W. Wolfe of The RAND Corporation (Englewood Cliffs, N.J.: Prentice-Hall, 1963), p. 433.

[35] For a useful tabular summary giving a chronological picture of changes in Soviet manpower strength, number of divisions, etc., see Lincoln P. Bloomfield, Walter C. Clemens, Jr., and Franklyn Griffiths, *Khrushchev and the Arms Race* (Cambridge, Mass.: M.I.T. Press, 1966), p. 100.

[36] *Military Balance, 1963–1964*, p. 4, and *1965–1966*, p. 3.

[37] Gill, *East Europe* (April 1964): 6. As noted in chapter III, p. 40, the strength of the Soviet Twenty-fourth Tactical Air Army in East Germany in the early fifties was estimated at around 1,700 aircraft.

In purely numerical terms, the new estimates of a scaled-down Soviet theater-force establishment lent themselves to the proposition that the balance of
conventional military power in Europe between NATO and the Warsaw bloc
was no longer tilted heavily against the West. From a manpower standpoint
alone, NATO ground forces in Europe looked much better off than before—
2.2 million men compared with a Warsaw Pact total of about 3 million,[38] or,
counting only Soviet forces deployed in Eastern Europe itself plus the armies
of the other Warsaw Pact members, a paper balance of 2.2 million against
about 1.5 million in NATO's favor. From the standpoint of divisions, the
situation in 1964 also looked somewhat less discouraging for NATO than it
had ten years earlier. NATO forces in Central and Northern Europe stood at
the equivalent of about twenty-five divisions, compared with Soviet forces
now down to twenty-six divisions in Eastern Europe.[39] In Southern Europe
and Turkey, NATO had an additional twenty-nine divisions. On the other side
of the ledger, however, there were about sixty East European divisions to be
taken into account, along with an approximately equal number of Soviet divisions presumed to be stationed in Western Russia, as the back-up for theater
operations in Europe. Thus, only if other factors were to alter the sheer arithmetic of divisions could it be said that NATO's relative position in Europe
had improved very much.

This contention was advanced, on several grounds, in connection with Western reappraisal of the military balance in Europe. Some of the points raised,
however, seemed to cut both ways, one of them being the question of the Soviet
mobilization and reinforcement potential. Given the relative parity in the
number of NATO and Soviet combat-ready divisions immediately at hand in
Europe itself, together with an apparent edge for NATO in numbers and
quality of tactical aircraft,[40] the prospect of the Soviet Union's bringing
superior theater-force strength to bear in the event of conflict in Europe
hinged critically on its ability to move suitable reinforcements across Eastern
Europe from the USSR proper.

By the standard yardstick of "uninterrupted mobilization," published Western estimates generally credited the Soviets with a reinforcement potential of

[38] McNamara's speech to the Economic Club, *Department of State Bulletin*, December 16, 1963,
p. 918.

[39] *Military Balance, 1963–1964*, p. 5. Of the twenty-six Soviet divisions in Eastern Europe,
twenty were in East Germany, four in Hungary, and two in Poland. The NATO forces in Central
and Northern Europe, which came to the "equivalent" of twenty-five divisions in 1964 (before the
addition of two more German divisions), were apportioned as follows: German, ten; US, six;
British, two and one-third; French, two; Belgian, two; Dutch, two; Canadian, one brigade group.

[40] See McNamara speech, *Department of State Bulletin*, December 16, 1963, p. 918; Nitze speech
to the Cleveland Council on World Affairs, *New York Times*, March 3, 1963; Gill, *East Europe*
(April 1964): 7. NATO in 1964 had about 3,500 tactical aircraft in Europe, compared with
somewhat less than 1,500 Soviet tactical aircraft based in Eastern Europe. Both sides possessed
adequate airfield facilities to permit rapid build-up of these forces from the United States and the
USSR, respectively. The above numerical edge for NATO in tactical aircraft did not take into
account, however, some 2,500 tactical types which were available to the East European members
of the Warsaw Pact.

from forty-five to fifty-five additional divisions in thirty days, compared with a Western potential of less than twenty additional divisions.[41] Critics, however, questioned both the idea that Soviet mobilization would proceed on an "uninterrupted" basis and the assumption that sufficient numbers of under-strength Soviet divisions could be brought to combat readiness rapidly enough to make such a substantial reinforcement schedule feasible.[42] Furthermore, by the time the Soviet theater-force establishment as a whole could be built up to full combat readiness—an effort requiring four to six months in the judgment of some Western spokesmen[43]—it was thought probable that any major conflict in Europe already would have escalated to the nuclear level. As this would create an entirely different situation, in which NATO would no longer be competing on a conventional basis, the Soviet Union's potentially greater capability for theater reinforcement would have lost much of its meaning.

A second point relevant to reappraisal of the theater-force balance centered on the contribution that the East European armies could be expected to make in the event of military operations in Europe. Since these forces added up to a substantial total of some sixty divisions[44] and were, moreover, already in place in the European theater, how seriously to take them was a significant question. The answer, however, was elusive at best.

On the one hand, it had become apparent by 1964 that under Khrushchev's revised policy toward the Warsaw Pact considerable effort was being invested to improve the military value of the East European forces and to integrate them more closely into Soviet planning.[45] Thus, it no longer seemed prudent to assume that they might prove more of a liability than an asset to the Soviet Union. On the other hand, from the standpoint not only of territorial location and military effectiveness but also of reliability and responsiveness to Soviet direction, it was evident that these forces still varied greatly from one country to another.[46] It therefore remained an open question whether the Kremlin could count on more than a fraction of the sixty-odd East European

---

[41] *Military Balance, 1963–1964*, p. 5; Neville Brown, *Strategic Mobility* (New York: Frederick A. Praeger, Inc., 1964), p. 245; James L. Richardson, *Germany and the Atlantic Alliance* (Cambridge, Mass.: Harvard University Press, 1966), p. 120.

[42] See, for example, Gill, *East Europe* (April 1964): 6, and (July 1964): 23; Kaufmann, *The McNamara Strategy*, pp. 83–87.

[43] Speech by Cyrus R. Vance, August 20, 1963, *New York Times*, August 21, 1963. See also statements cited by Rockingham Gill, *East Europe* (April 1964): 6.

[44] *Military Balance, 1963–1964*, pp. 7–9. As in the case of Soviet divisions, the East European divisions were maintained at varying levels of strength and readiness. It was generally thought that at best no more than half of the East European divisions were in a combat-ready status.

[45] Ibid., p. 7. See also discussion of these trends in Wolfe, *Soviet Strategy at the Crossroads*, pp. 210–16, and in chapter VII, pp. 148–52, of the present study.

[46] Generally speaking, the East European countries of the Northern Tier—East Germany, Poland, and Czechoslovakia—accounting for slightly more than half of the East European divisions, appeared better situated and more immediately motivated to play a useful part in Soviet theater planning than the Southern Tier countries of Hungary, Rumania, and Bulgaria. See Gill, *East Europe* (April 1964): 5; *Military Balance, 1963–1964*, p. 5; Melvin Croan, "Moscow and Eastern Europe," *Problems of Communism* (September–October 1966): 64.

divisions for prompt use alongside the Soviet forces in any major campaign on the main front in Central Europe.[47]

A third factor that tended to diminish the Soviet bloc's potential advantage over NATO in numbers of divisions, and one which was perhaps given more emphasis than anything else in the Western reappraisal of 1963–64, was the relative combat power ascribed to individual divisions on the two sides. Neither Soviet nor East European divisions in the average case were on a par with Western types in manpower strength, firepower, logistics "tail," and other attributes that added to sustained combat ability or staying power. Although any "index of combat effectiveness" devised to compare Soviet divisions with their NATO counterparts was bound to be somewhat artificial and subject to many qualifications, it was generally accepted that a single US division (with a "division slice" of about 60,000 men compared to a Soviet slice of 15 to 20,000) was at least the equivalent of one and one-half to two Soviet divisions.[48] Non-US NATO divisions, though in general they had less depth than the American, were also larger than the Soviet formations. Translated into rough comparative terms, this meant that a NATO force of twenty-seven frontline divisions (the level attained in the course of 1964 with the addition of two German divisions) should be regarded as the equivalent of about forty divisions for the other side—an exercise in comparison which

[47] In this connection, one informed Western analyst, noting the difficulty of determining whether the East European divisions should be regarded as an asset or a liability to the Soviet Union, offered as a "reasonable adjustment" the view that from sixteen to eighteen of the East European divisions on hand might initially be employed for offensive operations on the central front along with Soviet forces, making the combined Warsaw bloc D-day threat on this front something on the order of forty to forty-five divisions. See Timothy W. Stanley, *NATO in Transition: The Future of the Atlantic Alliance* (New York: Frederick A. Praeger, Inc., 1965), pp. 247–48.

[48] Obviously, comparison of Soviet and Western formations was fraught with many difficulties, not only on technical grounds but in light of such subjective factors as combat morale, motivation, and leadership. Nevertheless, in the present instance, some rough parameters were available, beginning with divisional manpower strength. Soviet divisions in 1964, following the "streamlining" of their organization in connection with Khrushchev's military reforms of the early sixties, consisted of three types: motorized rifle, 11,000 men when at full strength; tank, 9,000 men; and a few airborne divisions of about 7,000 men each. American infantry and armored divisions, by comparison, had a manpower strength of 16,000, and West German divisions about 19,000. In such categories of major equipment as armored personnel carriers, anti-tank weapons, and electronics gear, the larger US divisions greatly outnumbered the smaller Soviet divisions, although in tanks and organic field artillery they were only fractionally ahead. At one remove from the combat division itself, in combat and logistics support personnel directly supporting divisional combat activity, the United States had an advantage of almost nine to one. Other, less immediate rear-area support personnel were also more numerous on the US side, providing in all a "division slice" of about 60,000 men, as compared with 15–20,000 for the Soviets. (The "division slice" is the over-all strength of a force divided by the number of divisions; in other words, it is the combat division plus its rear-area support.) On such comparative data rests the notion that a single US division should be credited with a combat and staying power from one and one-half times to twice that of a Soviet division. For further discussion and sources of these comparative figures, see Neville Brown, *Strategic Mobility*, pp. 208–12, and "The Armies in Central Europe," *Journal of the Royal United Service Institution* (November 1963): 341–48; Colonel Irving Heymont, "The Division Slice," *Military Review* (October 1962): 64–67; Richardson, *Germany and the Atlantic Alliance*, pp. 119–20; Stanley, *NATO in Transition*, pp. 248, 269–73; *Military Balance, 1963–1964*, p. 5.

appreciably narrowed the margin of conventional power between NATO and the opposing forces in Central Europe.

"Nuclearization" of Soviet Theater Forces

It seems a bit incongruous in retrospect that in the early sixties, while a Western reappraisal of the military situation in Europe was taking place centering mainly on the relative improvement of NATO's position with respect to the balance of conventional forces, accelerated measures were underway on the Soviet side to enhance the nuclear capabilities of the Soviet theater forces themselves. Indeed, Khrushchev's program for the reorganization and modernization of these forces had been largely completed, and they were now on a nuclear footing somewhat comparable to that which NATO had set out to attain some years earlier. Here, let us turn attention briefly to some of the principal changes in the character and composition of the Soviet theater forces that Khrushchev's program brought about.

The process of "nuclearizing" the theater forces, as described by Marshal Malinovskii and other Soviet military leaders,[49] involved streamlining them for fast-moving operations in a battlefield environment in which both sides were expected to employ nuclear weapons. Essentially, this meant that a number of traditional Soviet arrangements for the massive employment of men and weapons in land warfare campaigns were either modified or eliminated. Both combat formations and supporting elements were affected by changes whose basic aim it was to increase the firepower and mobility of the theater forces while permitting a reduction in their size.

The principal innovation with respect to firepower was the incorporation of tactical nuclear weapons at various levels of command within the theater forces,[50] down to the division level.[51] These weapons depended for delivery

[49] Marshal R. Ia. Malinovskii at the Twenty-second CPSU Congress, *Pravda*, October 25, 1961. In this speech, Soviet Minister of Defense Malinovskii said that reorganization of the Soviet military establishment, including the theater ground forces, had been "completed in the main." However, the process of reorganization apparently continued during the next few years, as indicated by various public references to it in the Soviet press. See, for example, Marshal R. Ia. Malinovskii, *Bditel'no stoiat' na strazhe mira* (Vigilantly Stand Guard Over the Peace) (Moscow: Voenizdat, 1962), pp. 40–41; Marshal Sokolovskii, *Soviet Military Strategy*, pp. 341–44; Colonel General S. M. Shtemenko, "Ground Forces in Contemporary War and Their Combat Preparation," *Krasnaia zvezda*, January 3, 1963; Colonel P. Astashenkov, "The Main Force of the Ground Forces," *Sovetskii patriot* (Soviet Patriot), January 16, 1963; Marshal V. Chuikov, "Modern Ground Forces," *Izvestiia*, December 22, 1963.

[50] The accounts cited in fn. 49, representing but a sampling of the voluminous Soviet literature on the subject, all stressed that the main firepower of the ground forces had shifted to "tactical missile formations and units" which would deliver nuclear weapons.

[51] Details of the distribution and the types of tactical nuclear weapons in the Soviet theater forces customarily are not discussed in the publicly available Soviet literature. However, occasional mock exercises witnessed by foreign observers have cast some light on the subject. The simulated use of tactical nuclear weapons by a Soviet division was demonstrated, for example, at the time of the Berlin crisis of 1961, at a tactical battlefield exercise staged near Moscow on August 17 for the benefit of Western observers. See *New York Times*, August 18, 1961. In general, the tactical nuclear weapons developed by the Soviet Union were of somewhat higher yields in the early sixties than those at the disposal of the United States. See, for example, *Military Balance, 1963–*

mainly upon rockets and tactical missiles with ranges from about 10 to 300 miles, the launchers for which were mounted on tank chassis or other special-tracked vehicles.[52] Tactical aircraft in the air armies assigned to the theater forces also provided delivery means for tactical nuclear weapons. This shift to nuclear weaponry was accompanied by a considerable reduction in conventional artillery, the massive use of which on a "hub-to-hub" basis for preparation of frontal breakthroughs had been one of the hallmarks of Soviet theater operations in World War II.[53] Despite the new reliance upon nuclear weapons to provide the main firepower of the theater forces, their conventional firepower was not neglected, according to Marshal Malinovskii, who stated in 1961 that improvements in conventional weapons had made possible a four-fold increase over the firepower of a typical rifle division of early postwar vintage.[54]

The chief contribution to improving the mobility of the theater forces and their capabilities for rapid exploitation of nuclear strikes doubtless lay in measures taken to streamline their organizational structure and to put them on a fully motorized basis. By 1964, the theater ground forces had been pared down to an estimated 140 divisions, including some 80 motorized rifle divisions, about 50 tank divisions, and 7 airborne divisions.[55] Although these

1964, p. 5; Neville Brown, *Journal of the Royal United Service Institution* (November 1963): 342. By 1963 Soviet professional military discussion revealed that increased attention was being devoted to the value of "small and very-small yield nuclear weapons," although no details were given of Soviet activity in the development of weapons at the low end of the nuclear spectrum. See Colonel General S. M. Shtemenko, "Scientific-Technical Progress and Its Influence on the Development of Military Affairs," *Kommunist Vooruzhennykh Sil*, no. 3 (February 1963): 22; Major General I. Anureev, "Physics and New Weapons," *Krasnaia zvezda*, November 21, 1963.

[52] *Military Balance, 1963–1964*, p. 5. The delivery range of rockets and tactical missiles in Soviet ground force detachments was said by Marshal Malinovskii to be "from several to hundreds of kilometers." *Pravda*, October 25, 1961. From the late fifties on, the military parades held in Moscow's Red Square in connection with major national holidays consistently featured several models of tactical rockets and missiles mounted on carrier vehicles for mobile field use. These included a short-range rocket known as FROG (NATO's descriptive designation), which was employed at division level; a tactical ballistic missile of 150-mile range labeled SCUD, which apparently was at the disposal of higher levels of command in the theater forces; and a cruise missile known as SHADDOCK, with a range up to 300 miles, served by crews from tactical air army units. See *Military Balance, 1965–1966*, p. 5; Michel Garder, *A History of the Soviet Army* (New York: Frederick A. Praeger, Inc., 1966), p. 199.

[53] See Raymond L. Garthoff, *Soviet Military Doctrine* (Glencoe, Ill.: Free Press, 1953), pp. 304–5; B. H. Liddell Hart, *The Soviet Army*, p. 292. For Soviet treatment of the role of artillery in World War II, see I. S. Prochko, *Artilleriia v boiakh za rodinu* (Artillery in Battles for the Motherland) (Moscow: Voenizdat, 1957), pp. 164–298; Marshal K. Kazakov, "Soviet Artillery," *Soviet Military Review*, no. 10 (October 1965): 18–20.

[54] *Pravda*, October 25, 1961. For a detailed discussion of conventional weapons in Soviet divisions, see Neville Brown, *Journal of the Royal United Service Institution* (November 1963): 341–48.

[55] *Military Balance, 1965–1966*, p. 4; Garder, *History of the Soviet Army*, p. 198. Up to the late fifties, before the full impact of Khrushchev's troop reduction and reorganization programs was felt, there had been, in addition to airborne divisions, three basic divisional types: tank, mechanized, and rifle (or infantry) divisions. Only some of the latter were motorized. Part of the streamlining process was to eliminate the mechanized category, combining such divisions with rifle divisions to put these on a fully motorized basis. The result was a standard motorized rifle division, which was in effect a semi-armored division.

reorganized divisions were smaller in authorized manpower levels than their predecessors,[56] their combat mobility was enhanced by an increase in the proportion of tanks and armored personnel carriers (APCs) relative to manpower. Under the new organizational structure, the motorized rifle division at full establishment strength had about 210 medium tanks and the tank division about 375 medium and heavy tanks, with from 350 to 400 APCs for both types of divisions.[57] Reflecting both the traditional Soviet predilection for strong tank forces and a fresh theoretical appraisal of the value of armored formations for battlefield operations in a nuclear environment,[58] the modernization program included introduction of a new T–62 medium tank, which from about 1963 on gradually replaced the celebrated T–54 in frontline units.

The more fully mobile but smaller Soviet divisions which emerged from the modernization program in the early sixties represented the building blocks, so to speak, of larger combat formations for field operations of the theater forces. The established organizational pattern for these larger field formations was retained essentially unchanged with respect to both major ground forces commands and the air armies of "frontal" or tactical aviation which were to provide air support for theater operations.[59] In accord with previous Soviet organizational concepts, the principal field command under which theater-force formations would operate in wartime continued to be known as the "Front"—a flexible organization of variable composition designed to conduct theater operations independently or in conjunction with neighboring Fronts.[60]

[56] The authorized manpower levels to which the Soviet divisions were reduced are given in fn. 48 above. In 1960, prior to the reorganization in question, the rifle division had a full-establishment strength of 12,000, and the tank division, 10,500. It should be noted that these figures are for authorized establishment strength, not actual strength, which, as previously discussed, was maintained at varying levels according to the readiness category involved. See *Military Balance, 1960,* p. 4.

[57] *Military Balance, 1965–1966,* p. 4. See also Kenneth R. Whiting, *The Development of the Soviet Armed Forces, 1917–1966,* Air University Documentary Research Study, Maxwell Air Force Base, Alabama, 1966, p. 89.

[58] See, for example, Marshal Sokolovskii, *Soviet Military Strategy,* pp. 342, 414; Marshal P. Rotmistrov, "Modern Tanks and Nuclear Weapons," *Izvestiia,* October 20, 1962; Major General S. N. Kozlov et al., *O Sovetskoi voennoi nauke,* p. 340. Khrushchev himself, it may be noted, evidently did not fully share the Soviet military's high opinion of the role of tanks in modern warfare. Thus his comment after a visit to a training area near Moscow, in September 1964, where he had just witnessed a demonstration of new anti-tank weapons: "It hurt. After all, we are spending a lot of money to make tanks. And if . . . a war breaks out, these tanks will burst into flames even before they reach the battleline." Speech to World Youth Forum, September 19, 1964, TASS International Service, September 21, 1964.

[59] Soviet tactical aviation, known as *frontovaia aviatsiia* (Frontal Aviation), traditionally the oldest and numerically largest combat arm of the Soviet Air Forces, was organized into a number of frontal or tactical air armies, each equipped to provide fighter cover, ground support, interdiction, and reconnaissance in support of ground operations. Customarily, a tactical air army was subordinate to the senior ground commander in its sector of operations. A discussion of these organizational arrangements, which were not altered by the reforms of the Khrushchev period, may be found in Garthoff, *Soviet Strategy in the Nuclear Age,* pp. 52–54.

[60] During World War II, the various "Fronts" (the term is the same in both English and Russian) were the main field commands of the fighting forces, directly subordinate to the *Stavka,* or Staff of the Supreme High Command, in Moscow. This direct Stavka–Front relationship ob-

A holdover from the Soviet experience of World War II, the typical Front organization as visualized in the sixties would consist of several combined-arms and tank armies,[61] a tactical air army, tactical missile units, an airborne formation,[62] and a variety of support elements.[63]

Fronts, however, would become active operating organizations only in wartime; their peacetime equivalents were to be found either in the military district commands within the Soviet Union itself or in the Groups of Soviet Forces deployed abroad in Eastern Europe.[64] Of the latter, the Group of Soviet Forces in Germany (GSFG) was by virtue of its forward location both the most readily visible and probably the best-trained and -equipped

tained everywhere but in the Far East, where, because of the distance from Moscow, a Far Eastern Command was created to stand between the *Stavka* and the Fronts. See Sokolovskii, *Soviet Military Strategy*, pp. 489–93. As described by another Soviet military leader, Lt. General V. Zlobin, the wartime Front was a "distinct operational organization of the armed forces in a theater of war," which conducted its operations either independently or jointly with other Fronts. Cited by Garthoff, *Soviet Military Doctrine*, p. 209.

The Sokolovskii volume indicates that essentially the same Stavka–Front system as was used in World War II would be revived in wartime, but it does not make clear whether individual Fronts in the European theater would be controlled directly from Moscow or through an intermediate command level, such as that potentially represented by the Soviet commander-in-chief of the joint Warsaw Pact forces.

[61] The two standard types of Soviet ground armies retained during Khrushchev's reorganization programs were the "combined-arms army" (*obshchevoiskovaia armiia*), which usually consisted of several motorized rifle divisions and one or two tank divisions, and the "tank army" (*tankovaia armiia*), containing several tank divisions only. In addition to combat divisions, these two basic types of armies had, of course, attached to them artillery, tactical missile, anti-tank, and anti-aircraft units, as well as such other support groups as signal units, and engineers. For a more detailed organizational breakdown of these two types of armies, see Captain Walter Lukens, "The Soviet Army Today," *Army Information Digest* (April 1963): 34–35.

[62] Depending on a given Front's location and mission, it might have one or more airborne divisions for paradrop and airlanding operations. The airlift was provided by Aviation of Airborne troops (*aviatsiia desantnykh voisk*), later renamed Military Transport Aviation (*voennaia transportnaia aviatsiia*). See Garthoff, *Soviet Strategy in the Nuclear Age*, pp. 46, 53.

[63] Logistics support for a Front would be provided by a network of rear area units (*tylovye chasti i podrazdeleniia*), headed by a deputy for rear services on the staff of the Front commander. Besides supply, repair, transport, medical, and associated functions performed by the rear services organization, additional types of support would be rendered by signal, engineer, intelligence, chemical, and other specialized units. For Soviet comment on logistical support systems and concepts under conditions of modern warfare, see Colonel General F. M. Malikhin, "The Combat Rear in Modern Battle," in P. M. Derevianko, ed., *Problemy revoliutsii v voennom dele* (Problems of the Revolution in Military Affairs) (Moscow: Voenizdat, 1965), pp. 159–66; Marshal Sokolovskii, *Soviet Military Strategy*, pp. 440–44; Lt. General M. Novikov, "Combat Logistics Today," *Soviet Military Review*, no. 5 (May 1966): 39–42.

[64] The Military Districts (*voennyi okrug*), of which there are fifteen, are peacetime territorial commands within the Soviet Union charged with training, mobilization, and other functions. In wartime, depending on their location, some of them presumably would be converted into Fronts as active forces or reserves for the theaters of operations. Similarly, the three Groups of Forces stationed outside the Soviet Union (in East Germany, Poland, and Hungary) would probably become Fronts in a wartime situation. Whether they would take orders directly from Moscow or through an intermediate command set up to control the joint Warsaw Pact forces in the European area is not clear from published Soviet sources (see fn. 60). For a general description of the Soviet system of Military Districts and their functions, see Garthoff, *Soviet Strategy in the Nuclear Age*, pp. 48–50.

prototype of a Front in the peacetime theater-force establishment of the Soviet Union.

The modernization program of the Khrushchev period left the GSFG with improved combat capabilities as well as with a number of shortcomings. As to strength, it stood in 1964 at twenty divisions—ten tank and ten motorized—generally thought to be close to their full authorized manpower level.[65] Evidently, such personnel economies as took place within the GSFG were achieved through a thinning out of various headquarters and support elements rather than at the expense of the combat units. Measures taken to re-equip the ground and air components of the GSFG,[66] together with frequent field training exercises, doubtless gave this prototype Front its superior firepower and mobility—the objectives sought by the modernization program. At the same time, however, the revamping of the GSFG with an eye to improving its capabilities for the kind of fast-moving theater warfare prescribed by the Soviet Union's nuclear age doctrine[67] also created its own problems. Some of these arose out of the sheer complexity of conducting and controlling theater operations under the conditions likely to be encountered on a nuclear battlefield. Others, on the contrary, had to do with the possibility that nuclear weapons might not be used at all, which raised the prospect of a protracted conflict fought with conventional arms.

In the latter case, in particular, the GSFG's position probably looked less than satisfactory to those among the Soviet marshals who had championed the concept of massive theater forces, for the streamlining of these forces had been accomplished at a cost in staying power. This was due at least in part to the tendency to put supporting elements on an austere peacetime basis[68]—a practice acceptable perhaps so long as the campaign envisaged was brief, but

---

[65] *Military Balance, 1963–1964*, p. 5, and *1965–1966*, p. 4.

[66] The most impressive of these measures was, of course, the introduction of tactical missile units, whose appearance in the GSFG was accompanied by some reduction of conventional artillery. Whether nuclear warheads for these missiles were stockpiled in East Germany or kept in rear depots for dispatch to field units in time of emergency was a question upon which Soviet spokesmen shed no light. Other measures affecting ground elements of the GSFG included the re-equipment of divisions to improve their cross-country mobility and river-crossing capabilities. Along with the introduction of the new T-62 medium tank, modern anti-tank weapons, such as the SNAPPER and SWATTER missiles were added, and field defenses against aircraft were strengthened by both mobile surface-to-air missiles and new AAA guns. At the same time that such measures as these were being taken in the ground forces elements of the GSFG, the Twenty-fourth Tactical Air Army in East Germany was gradually refitted with more advanced jet aircraft, including the MIG-21 FISHBED and SU-7 FITTER for interceptor and fighter-bomber roles, and the supersonic light bomber BREWER to replace the aging IL-28 BEAGLE. See *Military Balance, 1965–1966*, pp. 3–5.

[67] Soviet theater warfare doctrine will be discussed in the next chapter.

[68] Although the GSFG, by virtue of its location, probably was treated more generously than some forces in less exposed areas, the high ratio of combat over support personnel in the GSFG indicated that it did not escape the general austerity in supporting elements. (See fn. 48 for a discussion of this point.) As noted in 1962 by the authors of the Sokolovskii treatise, the majority of the rear elements of armies and fronts were kept at low peacetime strength, only to be "deployed or formed during mobilization." *Soviet Military Strategy*, p. 444.

one which might prove risky if strong and sustained opposition should be encountered. Although shortcomings in logistical back-up could be offset somewhat by the prepositioning of military stocks in East Germany and by the adoption of such techniques as portable pipelines,[69] the question remained whether deficiencies in supporting units and reserves might not turn out to be critical in the event of protracted campaigning.

Thus, even though the reforms of the Khrushchev period resulted in placing the theater forces on a better footing for waging nuclear warfare, they also had effects which were disturbing to some Soviet professional military men. In particular, Khrushchev's military critics apparently feared that his manpower economies and the increasing reliance of the theater forces on nuclear firepower might leave these forces inadequately prepared if they should be called upon to conduct extensive conventional campaigns in Europe. These concerns, as we shall see later, were to enter into a reappraisal of the Soviet theater-force posture under Khrushchev's successors.

Growth of Soviet Strategic Delivery Forces

As the legatee of Stalin's unfinished efforts to raise the Soviet Union to the status of a global nuclear power, Khrushchev found it necessary to devote much attention to the further development of Soviet strategic delivery means and a concomitant political-military philosophy. We have already examined the considerations which helped shape Khrushchev's strategic philosophy;[70] here we shall look briefly at changes that occurred in the Soviet strategic delivery forces themselves during the decade of his rule.

At the time Khrushchev came to power, in the mid-fifties, the strategic bomber program initiated under Stalin had reached a phase that demanded important decisions for the future. Soviet aircraft designers had come up with a new medium jet bomber, the TU–16 or BADGER, and two intercontinental heavy bombers, the pure-jet BISON and the turboprop BEAR.[71] The latter two aircraft were first publicly displayed in 1954 and 1955, respectively.[72] The salient question before Khrushchev was how large a procurement program for these new aircraft the Soviet Union should embark upon. Broadly speaking, he faced three choices: (1) an all-out effort to overtake the United States in intercontinental bomber forces; (2) a minimum effort to provide the Soviet Union with at least a token intercontinental threat against the United States; and (3) a compromise effort, combining a modest intercontinental capability against the United States with a larger, medium-bomber threat against America's European allies and its overseas bases.

[69] Ibid., p. 443.

[70] See especially chapter V, pp. 84–88, and chapter VII, passim.

[71] As noted previously, such names as BADGER, BISON, and BEAR are descriptive NATO designations for Soviet aircraft, not terms employed by the Soviets themselves. The BADGER (TU-16) and the BEAR (TU-95) were designed by Tupolev; the BISON (M-4), by Miasishchev.

[72] See Kilmarx, A History of Soviet Air Power, p. 252; Garthoff, Soviet Strategy in the Nuclear Age, p. 178; US Department of Defense release, May 13, 1955, New York Times, May 14, 1955.

For many reasons, not the least of which may have been Khrushchev's expectation that ballistic missile technology offered the most promising way to offset the large US lead in strategic bomber forces,[73] the third alternative was the one chosen. In the latter fifties, a modest force of 150 to 200 heavy bombers of the BISON and BEAR types was incorporated into the Soviet strategic air arm, and at the same time upward of 1,000 BADGER medium jet bombers were added to its operational inventory to replace the TU–4 piston bomber of Stalin's day.[74] Although less than 10 per cent of the Soviet procurement program for strategic jet bombers went into heavy bombers of intercontinental range, thus faulting Western estimates of the mid-fifties that by 1959 the Soviet Union might have from 600 to 700 long-range heavy bombers in operational units,[75] it is worth noting that the build-up of the Soviet strategic air arm[76] between 1955 and 1960 brought it fairly close to parity in total numbers of modern strategic aircraft with its American counterpart, SAC.[77]

[73] Although Khrushchev may have banked on the Soviet headstart in missile technology as a *future* means to offset the US lead in strategic delivery forces, it should be noted that, at the time that he had to preside over crucial decisions concerning the size and composition of the Soviet strategic bomber program in the mid-fifties, it was not yet clear how soon operationally suitable ICBMs might be available to the Soviet Union. If Khrushchev had decided to forgo a significant bomber-building program altogether, he would have exposed the Soviet Union to the risk of a lengthy hiatus in which it would have possessed no modern strategic delivery capability at all. Indeed, there was a longer delay in converting Soviet missile technology into operational forces than Khrushchev himself had evidently expected. In a sense, therefore, his decision to procure large numbers of strategic bombers, even if basically a stopgap measure rather than one founded on serious expectations of overcoming the US bomber lead, proved to be prudent. Incidentally, the notion that the economic burden of a bomber race was the critical factor in Khrushchev's choice of programs does not seem borne out by the record. Although the claim on resources was certainly a constraint, the production effort that went into strategic bombers was quite large—in fact, not far behind that of the United States. The anomaly in the Soviet case was that so much of this effort was devoted to building up a medium-range BADGER force, rather than intercontinental heavy bombers. Some of the reasons for this disproportion are suggested in the text.

[74] Kilmarx, *A History of Soviet Air Power*, pp. 253–54; *Military Balance, 1960*, p. 3. See the earlier discussion of the Soviet bomber programs initiated under Stalin in chapter III, pp. 40–42. Incidentally, in addition to an operational inventory of more than 1,000 BADGERS in the strategic air arm, the naval air arm, too, was supplied with several hundred BADGERS during the Khrushchev period.

[75] In 1959, for example, Secretary of Defense McElroy said in testimony before the Senate Subcommittee of the Committee on Appropriations: "Three years ago it was estimated that by 1959 the Soviet Union could have about 600–700 BISON long-range jet bombers in operational units. But it is now known that they built only a fraction of that number." Cited by Kilmarx, *A History of Soviet Air Power*, p. 325, fn. 27.

[76] In Soviet usage, the strategic air arm was known as *dal'niaia aviatsiia* (Long-Range Aviation). It was composed of several Long-Range Air Armies. Garthoff, *Soviet Strategy in the Nuclear Age*, p. 53.

[77] In 1960 the over-all bomber strength of *dal'niaia aviatsiia* was about 1,500 aircraft, compared with around 1,800 for SAC. In both forces, the build-up of heavy bombers began around the same time in 1955, but the US B-52 program turned out to be about three times the size of the Soviet program for BISONS and BEARS. The narrowing of the over-all disparity in numbers was largely due to a reduction of SAC's B-47 medium-bomber strength by several hundred aircraft beginning in the late fifties, and to the build-up of the Soviet medium-bomber BADGER force during the same period. After about 1960, the size of the BADGER force leveled off, although phasing out of the American B-47s continued. In the early sixties, introduction of small numbers of a

This approach toward over-all numerical parity was not, of course, translatable into comparable intercontinental delivery capabilities. Both before and after 1960, the United States not only maintained at least a three-to-one margin over the Soviet Union in long-range bomber types (mostly B–52s and some B–58s) but it also had marked advantages in operational experience, in quality of aircraft, in refueling capabilities, and in a worldwide system of bases which made it possible to employ the full strength of SAC against the Soviet Union. The bulk of Soviet strength, on the other hand, lay in medium-range bombers, ill-suited for operations beyond the Eurasian periphery.

The dominant role of Europe in Soviet thinking probably accounted in some measure for Khrushchev's decision to invest substantial resources in BADGER procurement, while foregoing a larger effort in the heavy-bomber field. Medium-range strategic forces, for example, could demonstrably back up the Soviet policy of holding Europe hostage. Moreover, while such forces left much to be desired as a threat against the continental United States, they did promise to provide significant capabilities against US overseas bases,[78] upon which SAC at the time probably was thought to be greatly dependent. Since Soviet planners no doubt gave a very high priority to blunting a SAC strike, they may have been all the more inclined to concentrate on building BADGERS, which apparently could be made available in quantity earlier, and promised to be more reliable, than Soviet heavy-bomber designs.[79]

Khrushchev's compromise choice with respect to strategic bomber forces seems not to have aroused any particular misgivings within the Soviet military leadership, which on the whole had no strong historical or doctrinal commitment to strategic air power.[80] This is not to say that all military leaders

new Soviet medium jet bomber, the BLINDER, began as a replacement for the BADGER. See *Military Balance, 1960*, pp. 3, 7; Garthoff, *Soviet Strategy in the Nuclear Age*, p. 57; *Military Balance, 1963–1964*, p. 4; Bloomfield, *Khrushchev and the Arms Race*, pp. 36–41, 94.

[78] It may be recalled that the Soviet Union in the late fifties waged an incessant political campaign against US overseas bases around the Soviet periphery, which it regarded not only as the cement of the American alliance system but also as the springboard for alleged plans to launch a surprise attack against the USSR. The development of a military counter to the US overseas base network, therefore, doubtless carried considerable weight in Soviet thinking—first, when aircraft delivery systems offered the principal means to threaten the bases, and, later, when missile delivery systems entered the picture. See Cyril E. Black and Frederick T. Yeager, "The USSR and NATO," in Klaus Knorr, ed., *NATO and American Security* (Princton, N.J.: Princeton University Press, 1959), p. 43; Alvin J. Cottrell, "Soviet Views of U.S. Overseas Bases," *Orbis* (Spring 1963): 77–95.

[79] The technical and operational shortcomings of Soviet heavy-bomber designs may well have been an important factor bearing on the Soviet decision not to produce greater numbers of these aircraft. The BISON reportedly proved unsatisfactory on several counts, including the range needed for intercontinental operations. The turboprop BEAR, while possessing much better range, had a lower speed and ceiling than the BISON. A third heavy jet bomber, the delta-wing BOUNDER, was developed in the late fifties after the BISON and BEAR, but, although it was shown in Moscow air displays, it evidently was not put into production. See Kilmarx, *A History of Soviet Air Power*, pp. 253, 256; *Military Balance, 1960*, p. 3; Air Chief Marshal Sir Phillip Joubert, "Long Range Air Attack," in Asher Lee, ed., *The Soviet Air and Rocket Forces* (New York: Frederick A. Praeger, Inc., 1959), pp. 110–11.

[80] At various periods in Soviet history, including the mid-thirties and the years immediately after World War II, isolated voices among the Soviet military had urged the creation of "a power-

subscribed to Khrushchev's occasional views on the imminent obsolescence of manned bombers. Some argued that the use of air-to-surface missiles (ASM) could prolong the combat potential of strategic bombers.[81] Indeed, these arguments obviously carried weight, for even after the main emphasis of Soviet strategic force planning shifted to ballistic missiles, a program for equipping bombers with air-to-surface missiles was continued in the sixties.[82] If nothing else, this suggested that a concept of mixed offensive forces, incorporating both ASM-equipped bombers and strategic missiles, had gained acceptance.[83]

Although in a sense Khrushchev merely presided over a strategic bomber program which was already well underway before he took power, he played a more central role in the setting up of a strategic missile force,[84] the creation of which in 1960 was hailed as the product of his personal initiative.[85] In this case too, however, despite his obvious partiality toward the new strategic missile arm, Khrushchev was unable in practice to accomplish what he may have had in mind for this favored element of Soviet military power. The logic of his position called for exertions that would give *substance* to the *image* of preponderant Soviet missile power upon which he sought to trade politically. And yet, the Soviet Union under Khrushchev failed to convert its headstart in missile technology into an operational inventory of superior size. In part, this may have been due to technical and operational considerations, which merit a brief word here.

---

ful strategic air force," but in general Soviet military thinking was historically not oriented in this direction. Only from the latter forties on, and especially after the advent of nuclear weapons, did the role of strategic air power begin to enter significantly into Soviet military thinking. See Garder, *A History of the Soviet Army*, pp. 75–76, 89; Garthoff, *Soviet Strategy in the Nuclear Age*, pp. 171–89; Kilmarx, *A History of Soviet Air Power*, pp. 193–94, 250–56.

[81] For a discussion of Soviet views on the role of the long-range bomber and of arguments advanced by various military leaders on the worth of ASM-equipped bombers capable of "standoff" attacks from outside the opponent's air defense zone, see Wolfe, *Soviet Strategy at the Crossroads*, pp. 177–80.

[82] Development of air-to-surface missiles was under way in the Soviet Union in the late fifties. Public display of ASM-equipped bombers occurred regularly after 1961, when both BADGER medium jet bombers and long-range BEAR turboprop bombers thus equipped were flown in the July air show in Moscow. See Kilmarx, *A History of Soviet Air Power*, p. 256.

[83] Ibid. The mixed-force concept, as will be seen presently, also came to include submarine-launched missiles as part of the Soviet strategic delivery capabilities.

[84] One should distinguish here between creation of the strategic missile arm—the Soviet term for which is *raketnye voiska strategicheskogo naznacheniia* (Rocket Troops of Strategic Designation)—and the research and development program which preceded it. The ICBM research program itself evidently began as early as 1948, and was fairly well along before Khrushchev came to power. The important decisions to move from R&D programs to procurement and operational forces, however, were largely taken after Khrushchev was at the helm. See Kilmarx, *A History of Soviet Air Power*, p. 234. See also fn. 85.

[85] Among those who gave Khrushchev personal credit for creating the strategic missile forces, which were set up in May 1960 as a separate branch of the Soviet armed forces, was Marshal Malinovskii. See, for example, his speech in *Pravda*, October 25, 1961. Despite such public accolades for Khrushchev, there were signs that the Soviet decision to go ahead with a major effort in the field of ballistic missiles had met with some internal opposition. See Wolfe, *Soviet Strategy at the Crossroads*, pp. 157–58.

Normally, the development of any major new weapon system is attended by numerous difficulties and uncertainties. The first-generation Soviet ICBM, flight testing of which began in the fall of 1957, evidently had its share of these.[86] Moreover, this missile was very large and used nonstorable liquid fuel, posing ground-handling and readiness problems and requiring above-ground, or "soft," emplacement that would leave it highly vulnerable.[87] The shortcomings of this first ICBM, together with the prospect that follow-on missiles would be more suitable for operational deployment, may have helped to persuade Khrushchev not to invest heavily in the original system. Similarly, a second-generation ICBM that became available in the early sixties, though it had such improved characteristics as the use of storable liquid fuel,[88] may have had defects calling for further modification and testing. Other, more refined systems adaptable to emplacement in silos were still only in the process of de-velopment, thus again posing the question whether future technological and operational advantages did not argue against heavy investment in available early-generation ICBM systems.

To what extent such technical considerations prompted Khrushchev to hold back on a large-scale ICBM deployment program that would have been commensurate with the political load he chose to place upon these new "glamour weapons" is a matter of speculation. Certainly, many other factors were involved: economic pressures; bureaucratic opposition; belief in the deterrent effect of even second-best Soviet strategic forces; a preoccupation with Europe; and not least, perhaps, the evident determination of the United States not to relax its own efforts to stay ahead in the strategic power competi-tion.[89] Until after the Cuban episode of 1962, at any rate, Khrushchev seems to have believed that the Soviet Union stood a fair chance of deriving political profit from its missile image without paying the full cash price.

The ICBM deployment program under Khrushchev reflected this attitude rather closely. From the time of the first test launching in the autumn of 1957 to mid-1961, only a handful of ICBMs had been deployed, and it was another year or so before small numbers of the second-generation ICBM began to appear

[86] For example, according to information attributed by Colonel Penkovskiy to Marshal Varentsov and other officers connected with the Soviet missile program, the first Soviet strategic missiles proved to have many more shortcomings than the shorter-range tactical missiles, including elec-tronics difficulties. Penkovskiy also spoke of terrain problems encountered in siting strategic missiles at an unnamed location in northern Russia, indicating that the range of the first-generation missiles may have dictated their deployment in an unfavorable geographic environment. See Oleg Pen-kovskiy, *The Penkovskiy Papers* (Garden City, N.Y.: Doubleday & Company, Inc., 1965), pp. 339–43.

[87] *Military Balance, 1960,* p. 3, and *1963–1964,* p. 3. See also comment by Secretary of Defense McNamara on the soft configuration of Soviet missiles, *Hearings on Military Posture,* Committee on Armed Services, House of Representatives, Washington, D.C., 1963, p. 332.

[88] *Military Balance, 1963–1964,* p. 3.

[89] See our previous discussion of various constraints under which Khrushchev labored, and which led him, in effect, to settle for a second-best strategic position. (Chapter VI, pp. 101–6, and chapter VII, pp. 128–37, 140–48, 154–56.) See also Bloomfield, *Khrushchev and the Arms Race,* pp. 96–99; H. S. Dinerstein, *War and the Soviet Union,* rev. ed. (New York: Frederick A. Praeger, Inc., 1962), pp. xv–xviii.

in the operational inventory.[90] After Cuba, the pace of deployment picked up, bringing the total number of operational ICBM launchers to around 200 by the time of Khrushchev's ouster in 1964.[91] Most of this force was still in a "soft" configuration, although the emplacement of a few ICBMs, in hardened underground silos had begun toward the close of the Khrushchev period,[92] in apparent emulation of a practice already widely adopted by the United States.

Compared with the West, the Soviet ICBM posture in late 1964 remained numerically inferior on the order of four to one.[93] In the other major long-range delivery systems of this period—heavy bombers and submarine-launched ballistic missiles—the Soviet Union was also at a distinct disadvantage in numbers, according to informed Western estimates.[94] Soviet spokesmen, without exception, shunned specific numerical comparison of strategic forces, but frequently asserted that such factors as more powerful boosters and super-megaton warheads gave the Soviet Union a qualitative edge over the West.[95] As for solid-fuel missiles comparable to the US Minuteman and Polaris—a field of missile technology in which the USSR notably lagged behind the United States—no claims or demonstrations were to appear until after Khrushchev's departure from the scene.

In sum, then, Khrushchev's programs in the bomber and missile fields substantially improved the Soviet strategic posture, but left the Soviet Union still inferior to its major adversary in intercontinental delivery forces. In one respect, however, Khrushchev's missile programs did match the substance with the image of imposing preponderance. The case in point, upon which we have already dwelt,[96] concerned medium- and intermediate-range missiles (MRBM and IRBM), which were included in the Soviet strategic missile command along with the ICBM units.

Soviet MRBMs, already well along in development by the mid-fifties, went into series production sometime around 1955, and not long thereafter it became apparent that these weapons were meant to strengthen the Soviet military posture against Europe.[97] Throughout the late fifties and early sixties,

[90] *Military Balance, 1963–1964*, p. 3.

[91] *Military Balance, 1964–1965*, p. 5.

[92] Ibid. See also interview with Robert S. McNamara, "Is Russia Slowing Down in Arms Race?" *U.S. News and World Report*, April 12, 1965, pp. 52–61.

[93] US ICBM strength by late 1964 had grown to around 900, most of which were hardened MINUTEMAN solid-fuel types, compared with the estimated Soviet force of about 200 ICBM launchers, of which relatively few were hardened. See *Military Balance, 1964–1965*, pp. 5–6, 36.

[94] The Western advantage in heavy-bomber forces was about 3 to 1 (some 600 B-52s compared with an estimated 200 BEARS and BISONS), while in submarine-launched ballistic missiles the United States possessed 480 Polaris missiles compared with about 120 Soviet types of somewhat poorer performance. Ibid. See also fn. 133 below.

[95] For an examination of the Soviet treatment of this subject in the latter years of the Khrushchev period, see Wolfe, *Soviet Strategy at the Crossroads*, pp. 59–60, 162–63.

[96] See chapter VII, pp. 154–56.

[97] The first public display of a Soviet MRBM (the SHYSTER, by NATO designation) took place in Red Square on November 7, 1957, after the Soviet leadership had already claimed a missile capability. In an article on the Soviet missile forces written in 1967, the commander of these forces stated that "by 1955 the Soviet army already had several missile units equipped with

the size of the MRBM–IRBM force grew steadily, leveling off toward the end of the Khrushchev period at around 750 launchers, most of which were targeted against NATO Europe.[98]

Originally, this force possessed two types of missiles with respective ranges of 700 and 1,100 miles (like those sent to Cuba in 1962) and, like the early-generation ICBMs, was of soft configuration. Later, it reportedly received a new missile of 2,100-mile range,[99] but apparently little was done in Khrushchev's time to harden or otherwise improve the force. Having put a large share of the initial missile investment into the massive MRBM–IRBM force, Khrushchev may have been satisfied to amortize his investment, so to speak, by stretching out the life of the force as a cheap form of threat against Europe. It was left largely to his successors to decide how much further effort should go into modernization of the MRBM–IRBM force through such measures as extensive hardening or the introduction of mobile missile types that the Soviet R&D program had been developing.[100]

Strategic Defenses against Air and Missile Attack

The task of defending the Soviet Union against possible strategic attack, still far from solution at the close of the Stalinist period, was another question that demanded continuing attention in Khrushchev's time. In the first part of that decade, defense against bomber attack remained the central problem; later, with the advent of strategic missile systems, the development of anti-missile defenses (ABM) took on increasing importance.

Looking first at Soviet response to the bomber threat, one finds that the Soviet air defense system, or PVO,[101] entered its main period of growth in the wake of the Korean War, parallel in time both to the US strengthening of SAC and the build-up of the Soviet strategic air arm. Perhaps Khrushchev's principal concern, as he took over where the air defense program of Stalin's day had left off, was to improve the PVO's capabilities for coping with bomber attacks under all-weather conditions.[102] Toward this end, in a major reorganization of the air defense system undertaken in 1955, the PVO was set up as a separate major component of the armed forces under the command of

---

missiles of medium range." Marshal N. Krylov, "The Strategic Rocket Troops," *Voenno-istoricheskii zhurnal* (Military-Historical Journal), no. 7 (July 1967): 21. For a useful chronology of steps in the Soviet medium-range missile program, see Bloomfield, *Khrushchev and the Arms Race*, pp. 40–43.

[98] Small numbers of the MRBM–IRBM force also were deployed along the southern border areas of the USSR and in the Far East. *Military Balance, 1963–1964*, p. 3.

[99] Ibid.

[100] Evidence of continuing Soviet developmental work on mobile strategic missiles was to be provided later, under the Brezhnev–Kosygin regime, by the public display of such weapons in Moscow parades.

[101] As previously noted, "PVO" comes from the formal Soviet designation *Protivovzdushnaia Oborona Strany*, or Anti-air Defense of the Country. In addition to *PVO Strany*, the Soviet military establishment also includes *PVO Voisk*, or Anti-air Defense of Troops, which provides air defense for the armed forces in the field.

[102] See earlier discussion of the air defense program under Stalin, chapter III, pp. 47–49.

Marshal S. S. Biriuzov,[103] and two complementary lines of re-equipment for the PVO were begun.

The first of these was a program to provide the PVO with new and more advanced interceptor aircraft, along with refinement of warning and control facilities. Operational numbers of the new MIG–19 (FARMER) showed up in 1955,[104] and a year later, at the annual Moscow air show, to which various foreign observers were invited, the Soviets revealed a series of advanced supersonic fighter prototypes.[105] In the course of the next few years, several of these were introduced into the operational inventory of the PVO, which by the early sixties stood at around 4,000 aircraft.[106] The mainstay of this defensive fighter force had now become the MIG–19, some models of which possessed a restricted all-weather capability. Together with smaller numbers of the Yak–25 (FLASHLIGHT)—an earlier but not wholly satisfactory all-weather design—and such advanced supersonic fighters as the MIG–21 (FISHBED), the SU–7 (FITTER), and the SU–9 (FISHPOT),[107] the aircraft at the disposal of PVO were certainly better suited to the exacting requirements of a modern air defense system than those available when Khrushchev took office.

The second major line of approach to dealing with the bomber problem, and the one which represented the real innovation of the Khrushchev era, was the building of a surface-to-air missile (SAM) system for defense against strategic air attack under any weather conditions. Although the initial research-and-development phase of this program, like that for Soviet offensive missiles, went back to Stalin's time, it was under Khrushchev that the SAM system was actually deployed and put into operation as part of the PVO.

The first step in deployment, in the mid-fifties, was the installation of a ring of defensive missile sites around Moscow. This was a first-generation system (SAM–1, by the NATO designation), which presumably had basic shortcomings, for it was not duplicated elsewhere. Rather, a second-generation system (SAM–2, the type subsequently furnished to North Vietnam) was selected in the latter fifties for widespread deployment throughout the Soviet Union and in the East European countries.

Despite Soviet claims concerning the efficacy of the SAM system, which grew more pronounced after Gary Powers' U–2 plane was shot down by a surface-to-air missile in 1960, doubt remained whether the system in fact had settled the duel between modern offensive and defensive forces. As pointed out by some informed observers, the SAM system, which was designed to

---

[103] Asher Lee, "Strategic Air Defense," in Asher Lee, ed., *The Soviet Air and Rocket Forces* (New York: Frederick A. Praeger, Inc., 1959), pp. 124–25. Raymond L. Garthoff, "Soviet Air Power: Organization and Staff Work," ibid., p. 178.

[104] Kilmarx, *A History of Soviet Air Power*, p. 263.

[105] Among guests at this air show in the summer of 1956 were a number of foreign air force delegations, including an American contingent headed by General Nathan F. Twining. For General Twining's impression of the new Soviet aircraft, which included advanced fighter designs by Mikoyan and Sukhoi, see his "Report from Moscow," *Air Force* (August 1956): 61.

[106] Kilmarx, *A History of Soviet Air Power*, p. 266.

[107] Ibid. See also *Military Balance, 1963–1964*, p. 4.

counter high-altitude bomber attacks, was inadequate for defense against low-level tactics,[108] a vulnerability not likely to be overlooked by a resourceful opponent.[109] The relatively poor performance, later on, of Soviet SAM sites in North Vietnam against modern aircraft employing low-level and other evasive techniques seemed to bear out this point.[110] For that matter, Soviet strategic doctrine itself, while placing great emphasis on the continued value of active defense, had come to recognize explicitly in the early sixties that modern means of attack "are undoubtedly superior to the instrumentalities of defense against them."[111]

One may say that the Soviet air defense effort in Khrushchev's day never quite managed to catch up with the problems of defending the Soviet Union against bomber attack. But these difficulties were dwarfed by those involved in trying to protect the country against strategic missile attack. The Soviet leadership nevertheless embarked upon a program to develop an ABM system, impelled perhaps by the belief that a combination of strategic offensive forces with air and missile defense forces would provide greater military and political flexibility, and more promise of victory in case of war, than a deterrent posture based only on the threat of retaliation by offensive forces.[112]

According to Khrushchev, Soviet research efforts in the ABM field began at about the same time that serious work was started on offensive missiles.[113] The first specific claim of Soviet success was not heard, however, until Marshal Malinovskii reported at the Twenty-second Party Congress, in October 1961, that "the problem of destroying missiles in flight also has been successfully solved."[114] Khrushchev himself followed in July 1962 with the much-

---

[108] Lee, *The Soviet Air and Rocket Forces*, p. 128.

[109] Indeed, Soviet military literature of the early sixties recognized that low-level attacks, which would be difficult to deal with, had become standard operational practice as defense against high-level attacks improved. See, for example, Major General V. Bolotnikov, "Man, Altitude, Speed," *Krasnaia zvezda*, April 25, 1964.

[110] During the first year in which Soviet-supplied SAM sites were active in North Vietnam, for example, the number of US aircraft downed by surface-to-air missiles was 14 out of more than 300 attempts. In other words, only one out of every 22 missiles fired found its target—not an impressive record. Most US aircraft losses in North Vietnam were due to conventional AAA fire. See Hanson W. Baldwin, "Air Missiles in Vietnam," *New York Times*, July 15, 1966. The contention of some Communist commentators that deficiencies of SAM performance should be attributed to the relative inexperience of their launching crews in the earlier months of action were not borne out by the subsequent record. By February 1967, the SAM record has worsened to 31 aircraft out of about 1,500 missile firings, or a score of one kill for every 50 attempts. "Soviet SAMs Hit 1 Craft in 50," *Washington Post*, February 8, 1967.

[111] Sokolovskii, *Soviet Military Strategy*, p. 307. The second edition of this work, in 1963, made the same point. See Marshal V. D. Sokolovskii et al., *Voennaia strategiia* (Military Strategy), 2nd ed. (Moscow: Voenizdat, 1963), p. 252.

[112] For Soviet presentations of this viewpoint, see A. Golubev, "Some Problems of Military History in the Book 'Military Strategy,'" *Voenno-istoricheskii zhurnal*, no. 5 (May 1963): 94; Major General N. Talenskii, "Anti-Missile Systems and Disarmament," *International Affairs*, no. 10 (October 1964): 193–96. For useful Western analyses of factors conditioning the Soviet attitude toward ABM, see John R. Thomas, "The Role of Missile Defense in Soviet Strategy," *Military Review* (May 1964): 46–58; Walter F. Hahn and Alvin J. Cottrell, "Ballistic Missile Defense and Soviet Strategy," *Orbis* (Summer 1965): 316–37.

[113] See Khrushchev's interview with Arthur Sulzberger, *New York Times*, September 8, 1961.

[114] *Pravda*, October 25, 1961.

quoted statement that the Soviet Union had developed an anti-missile missile that "can hit a fly in outer space."[115] Thereafter, public allusions to Soviet progress in the ABM field multiplied rapidly.[116]

The first public display of a Soviet weapon for which an ABM role was claimed came at a Red Square parade on November 7, 1963. According to Western estimates, this missile, known in the West by the identifying nickname of GRIFFON, was a two-stage vehicle with an altitude of 25 to 30 miles, a slant range of about 100 miles, and a speed of Mach 3 to 5, and could probably be fitted with either a TNT or a nuclear warhead. Whether it was actually capable of intercepting ICBMs remained a matter of considerable doubt, however, and some experts have suggested that it may have been developed primarily as a counter to high-performance bombers armed with air-to-surface missiles (ASM), such as the B–58 or the then projected B–70.[117] A second and more likely candidate for the ABM role was first paraded by the Soviets a year later, in November 1964. This missile, nicknamed GALOSH, was described by Soviet commentators as capable of intercepting ballistic missiles at long distances from defended targets,[118] suggesting that it was an exoatmospheric weapon designed to take on incoming missiles several hundred miles above the earth.

The display of ABM-associated hardware such as the GRIFFON and GALOSH missiles in 1963–64 did not in itself go very far toward answering the prime question whether the Soviet Union had achieved an operationally satisfactory ABM system which it was prepared to deploy on a serious scale. Speculation in the Western press, and discussion in the US Senate in April 1963, dwelt on the possibility that the Soviets had already begun deployment of first-generation ABM defenses around Leningrad,[119] but the evidence relating to such deployment remained inconclusive. At the time of Khrushchev's ouster in the fall of 1964, despite occasional Soviet references to inclusion of anti-missile defense in the over-all "anti-air defense" system,[120] ambiguity as to the precise status of the ABM program persisted.

Apart from the standard barrier of secrecy in the Soviet Union, several factors helped to becloud the ABM situation while Khrushchev was still in office. The "state of the art" in 1963–64 was still such as to make deployment of ABM defenses a technologically uncertain course;[121] therefore, Khrushchev

---

[115] Statement by Khrushchev to a group of visiting US newspaper editors, *New York Times*, July 17, 1962.

[116] For an examination of such Soviet statements, see Wolfe, *Soviet Strategy at the Crossroads*, pp. 190–93.

[117] *The Soviet Military Technological Challenge*, Center for Strategic Studies, Georgetown University, Washington, D.C., September 1967, p. 88.

[118] *Pravda*, November 8, 1964. See also *Krasnaia zvezda*, November 10, 1965.

[119] See John R. Thomas, *The Role of Missile Defense in Soviet Strategy and Foreign Policy*, Research Analysis Corporation, McLean, Va., March 1965, p. 1.

[120] See Wolfe, *Soviet Strategy at the Crossroads*, p. 309, fn. 20.

[121] For commentary of the period on the technological uncertainties and cost involved in deployment of an ABM system, see Statement of Secretary of Defense Robert S. McNamara, *Hearings on Military Posture and H.R. 9637*, House Armed Services Committee, 88th Congress, 2nd Session, January 27, 1964, pp. 7010–11; Jack Raymond, "Soviet 'Missile Defense' Is Minimized by

may have hesitated to approve going ahead with large-scale investment in a first-generation system employing GRIFFON, especially if an improved second-generation system was already well along in development. Indeed, there is some indication that a GRIFFON defense complex may have been initiated around Leningrad in 1962 and then halted because of technical problems.[122] Furthermore, an ABM deployment program required very large resources and the constraints on resources had grown severe in the last years of Khrushchev's tenure, contributing to his desire for détente, and perhaps persuading him that major new expenditures in the ABM field had best be postponed. At any rate, it seems a reasonable conjecture that, for whatever reasons, Khrushchev left the final decisions on operational deployment of a Soviet ABM system to his successors, although he must have sanctioned most of the preparatory steps.[123]

Soviet Naval Preparations under Khrushchev

The Khrushchev period produced several notable changes in Soviet naval preparations. Soon after coming to power, Khrushchev, who on various occasions expressed his low esteem for surface ships and "backward-looking" admirals,[124] ordered a curtailment of the major surface-ship construction program which Stalin had launched in 1950. For opposing Khrushchev's policy, which aimed among other things at converting Soviet cruisers to missile armament rather than continuing to expand the conventional fleet,[125] the head of the Soviet navy was dismissed in 1955, and a more "forward-looking" admiral, S. G. Gorshkov, was installed in his place.[126] Khrushchev apparently enjoyed a fair amount of support from "modernizers" among the Soviet naval leadership, who voiced agreement that "to construct large vessels—battleships, heavy cruisers—is unprofitable."[127]

the U.S.," *New York Times*, November 10, 1963. The price tag put on a meaningful Soviet ABM deployment at that time, and subsequently by Secretary McNamara, was $20 to $25 billion. See *New York Times*, January 27, 1967.

[122] See Hedrick Smith, in *New York Times*, January 29, 1967.

[123] For further discussion of the Soviet ABM programs under the Brezhnev-Kosygin regime, see chapter XVI.

[124] On his trip to England in 1956, Khrushchev said that surface ships such as cruisers were good for little more than carrying political leaders on visits and firing salutes; on another occasion that year, he was quoted as saying that "admirals are always looking backward and living in the past." See Garthoff, *Soviet Strategy in the Nuclear Age*, p. 200. As late as June 1963, Khrushchev reiterated his views on the obsolescence of surface warships, although by that time—as in the case of his similar derogation of other traditional types of arms—he had obviously become reconciled to their continued existence. See Wolfe, *Soviet Strategy at the Crossroads*, p. 200.

[125] Garthoff, *Soviet Strategy in the Nuclear Age*, p. 200.

[126] Admiral N. G. Kuznetsov, whose career had its ups and downs under Stalin as well, was the man ousted by Khrushchev. Admiral Gorshkov, his successor, apparently served as "acting" head of the Soviet navy for about a year before being confirmed as the new commander-in-chief.

[127] Statement by Admiral L. Vladimirskii in *Komsomol'skaia pravda*, July 12, 1955, cited by Garthoff, *Soviet Strategy in the Nuclear Age*, p. 218. For a well-informed discussion of Khrushchev's views on sea power and of the changes in Soviet naval programs during his tenure, see Robert W. Herrick, *Soviet Naval Strategy: Fifty Years of Theory and Practice* (Annapolis, Md.: United States Naval Institute, 1968), pp. 67–91.

Although emphasis shifted away from quantitative naval construction, the surface ship program carried out under Khrushchev was by no means inconsequential. It included completion of most of the Sverdlov-class cruisers still on the ways when Khrushchev took over, and conversion of two of these to guided missile ships for air defense at sea. By 1964, with the addition of new units and retirement of some older Kirov and Chapayev-class cruisers, the Soviet navy had 19 cruisers afloat.[128] The destroyer force grew during the Khrushchev decade from 60 to more than 110, plus a number of destroyer-escort frigates. Modernization of this force included the introduction of several new classes, the last of which was the Kashin class, and provided for a number of destroyer and escort types equipped to fire surface-to-air missiles or anti-ship cruise missiles.[129] Another notable feature of the surface ship program was the building of a sizable force of some 400 patrol boats, many of which were armed with short-range surface-to-surface missiles.

The principal Soviet naval effort during Khrushchev's regime, however, lay in the submarine field. Here Khrushchev not only sanctioned continuation of the building program set in motion by Stalin but also presided over significant changes in the role of the submarine arm brought about by nuclear and missile technology. In terms of over-all size, the submarine fleet grew less rapidly than in the early fifties, leveling off at around 400 subs, but the number of modern oceangoing types within this total increased substantially, to well over 300 by the end of the Khrushchev period.[130] Of these, about 40 were nuclear-powered submarines, the first models of which entered service at the end of the fifties, and which thereafter were turned out at an estimated production rate of between five and ten per year.[131]

Along with the introduction of nuclear propulsion, the other major innovation with respect to the submarine fleet centered upon the build-up of a force of missile-launching submarines. This program, which gained impetus in the early sixties as the successful example of the US Polaris program impressed itself upon the Soviet leadership, had been foreshadowed in the mid-fifties by

---

[128] *Military Balance, 1963–1964,* p. 6; *Jane's Fighting Ships, 1964–1965,* pp. 424–26, and *1965–1966,* pp. 425–27. According to *Jane's,* fifteen of the original twenty-four Sverdlov-class cruisers were actually completed. At one point between 1955–60, before some of the older cruisers were either scrapped or put into "reserve" status, cruiser strength stood at an estimated twenty-five to twenty-seven units. See *Military Balance, 1960,* p. 5; Garthoff, *Soviet Strategy in the Nuclear Age,* p. 57.

[129] *Military Balance, 1963–1964,* p. 6, and *1965–1966,* p. 6; *Jane's Fighting Ships, 1964–1965,* pp. 424, 427–31, and *1965–1966,* pp. 425, 428–32. It should be noted that estimates of destroyer strength, as well as of most other categories of naval units, are somewhat higher in *Jane's* than in *Military Balance.* Figures used in the text are at the lower end of the bracket taken from the latter source. See also Herrick, *Soviet Naval Strategy,* pp. 76–79.

[130] *Military Balance, 1965–1966,* p. 5; *Jane's Fighting Ships, 1964–1965,* pp. 432–35. During the first years of the Khrushchev regime, as new oceangoing subs were added more rapidly than older coastal types were retired from service, the over-all strength of the submarine fleet went as high as 500, according to some Western estimates. How much of the apparent fluctuation was due to imprecision of the estimates or to the Soviet Union's lag in decommissioning old boats is difficult to say.

[131] *Military Balance, 1965–1966,* p. 5; Herrick, *Soviet Naval Strategy,* pp. 75–78.

expressions of Soviet interest in the potential of submarine-launched missiles.[132] The force built by the Soviets, however, was not modeled strictly on Polaris lines. It contained both nuclear and diesel powered submarines, and both cruise and ballistic missiles, with only some of the latter suitable for subsurface launching.[133] By 1964 the size of this force was estimated at about 40 submarines with a combined load of 120 ballistic missiles and approximately the same number of submarines equipped with cruise missiles.[134] According to Soviet naval doctrine enunciated concurrently with the build-up of this force, a strategic strike role would fall to its ballistic missile submarines, while those equipped with cruise missiles would be employed primarily against opposing naval forces, including aircraft carriers.[135]

Although the missile-launching submarine force brought into being in the Khrushchev period remained inferior in numbers as in many other respects to the US Polaris fleet,[136] its creation nevertheless marked a significant broadening of the role of naval power in Soviet strategy. Strategically, the introduction of submarines capable of delivering nuclear warheads against targets in North America meant that, in addition to its previous mission of interdicting sea communications between the United States and Europe, the Soviet submarine arm had acquired the new task of contributing to the intercontinental strike potential of the ICBM and long-range bomber forces.

Aside from emulating the example of the US Polaris in the effort to improve strategic delivery capabilities, the Soviet Union under Khrushchev also displayed growing awareness of the need to cope with the Polaris threat itself and to this end gave increased attention to anti-submarine warfare (ASW) measures. Indeed, the development of these ASW capabilities, which earlier in the

---

[132] For statements made by Soviet naval authorities in the 1955–57 period on the strategic utility of missile-launching (including submerged-launching) subs, see Garthoff, *Soviet Strategy in the Nuclear Age*, pp. 204–5.

[133] Soviet development of a submerged-launching capability evidently trailed somewhat behind the rest of the submarine-launched missile program. Soviet claims to such a capability did not appear until a visit by Khrushchev to fleet exercises in northern waters in July 1962. Later that year, a Soviet newspaper account identified naval missiles shown in the November Red Square parade as types that could be "launched from any position—on the surface or submerged." See *Krasnaia zvezda*, July 21, 1962; *Izvestiia*, November 8, 1962.

[134] *Military Balance, 1963–1964*, pp. 5–6, and *1964–1965*, pp. 5–6.

[135] The precise role which missile-launching submarines should play in Soviet plans proved to be a much-debated subject in the early sixties, as Soviet strategists weighed their relative contribution to strategic strikes against land targets on the one hand and to operations against enemy naval forces at sea on the other. For an examination of this question, see Wolfe, *Soviet Strategy at the Crossroads*, pp. 186–87. See also Herrick, *Soviet Naval Strategy*, pp. 87–99, passim.

[136] Apart from the ballistic missile-firing capacity of the Soviet force (about 120 in 1964 to 480 for the Polaris force), other comparative shortcomings of the Soviet force included its limited underwater-firing capability, the much shorter range of its missiles, its rather restricted access to the open seas, and its relatively small fund of experience in distant operations outside of home waters. In the last year or so of Khrushchev's regime, an effort was begun to repair this last deficiency by undertaking more extended blue-water operations in the Atlantic and Pacific, as well as in the Mediterranean. *Military Balance, 1963–1964*, p. 7; David Woodward, *The Russians at Sea: A History of the Russian Navy* (New York: Frederick A. Praeger, Inc., 1966), pp. 229–30.

Khrushchev period had apparently been overshadowed by the problem of countering US carrier forces, came to be described by 1963 as "the most important task of the Soviet navy."[137] The extent to which the ASW program prospered under Khrushchev was left somewhat obscure by conflicting commentary in the Soviet military literature;[138] however, there was evidently a substantial effort, involving air and naval forces as well as the reconnaissance potential of the large Soviet trawler fleet,[139] to extend the former coastal system of ASW to waters where Polaris operations might be expected.

As had been the case in Stalin's time, naval preparations under Khrushchev conspicuously failed to include any effort to develop attack carrier forces.[140] The alternative chosen lay in modifying the composition of the land-based naval air arm by introducing BADGER medium jet bombers and a few long-range BEAR turboprop bombers, thus converting what had been essentially a short-range naval air arm, suitable mainly for coastal operations, into a force with somewhat improved offensive and reconnaissance capabilities against NATO and US naval forces at sea.[141] Toward the end of Khrushchev's tenure, the Soviet naval air arm had an estimated strength of 750 to 800 aircraft, of

[137] See, for example, Sokolovskii, *Voennaia strategiia*, 2nd ed., p. 398. A pronounced shift in Soviet recognition of the need for vigorous measures to deal with the Polaris threat occurred between the first edition of this work in 1962 and the second, revised edition of 1963.

[138] Sanguine views of Soviet ASW progress by such spokesmen as Admiral S. G. Gorshkov, head of the Soviet navy, were balanced by more critical assessments of the difficulty of combating atomic-powered submarines, such as that by Admiral V. A. Alafuzov in January 1963. For an examination of these and other contradictory Soviet assessments, see Wolfe, *Soviet Strategy at the Crossroads*, pp. 184–85. See also Herrick, *Soviet Naval Strategy*, pp. 109–17.

[139] *Military Balance, 1963–1964*, p. 6.

[140] See our previous discussion (chapter III, pp. 44–47 and fn. 47) of Soviet failure to build aircraft carriers in the Stalinist period, which Admiral N. G. Kuznetsov, former head of the Soviet navy, considered in his memoirs to be a mistake. Kuznetsov's successor, Admiral S. G. Gorshkov, writing in 1967, also dealt with the carrier issue as it arose both in Stalin's and in Khrushchev's time. With respect to the Stalinist period, Gorshkov took a critical view, similar to that of Kuznetsov, of Soviet failure to acquire carriers, which he attributed to inadequate appreciation of the need at that time to provide air cover for naval operations distant from Soviet shores. With regard to the Khrushchev period, however, Gorshkov switched his stand, arguing that the advent of the nuclear age had made carriers vulnerable and marked their "inevitable decline" as the "main strike forces in naval warfare." This position would seem to justify the decision under Khrushchev, with which Gorshkov himself was associated, not to try to match US carrier forces, but it does not rule out Soviet interest in possible roles for carriers other than that of "main strike forces." See Admiral S. G. Gorshkov, "Development of Soviet Naval Art," *Morskoi sbornik* (Naval Collection), no. 2 (February 1967): 12–13, 18–19.

[141] In Stalin's time, most of the aircraft in the naval air arm were fighters with an air defense role in coastal regions, together with a miscellaneous inventory of torpedo bombers, mine-laying aircraft, and flying boats. IL-28 BEAGLE jet light bombers were introduced into the naval air arm in the last years of Stalin's rule, leading to a sizable expansion of the force to around 4,000 aircraft in the mid-fifties. Under Khrushchev, the introduction of the medium jet BADGERS was accompanied by a substantial reduction in the over-all size of the naval air arm, as large numbers of fighters and IL-28 BEAGLES were phased out. The net result was a smaller force with an extended operational perimeter. See Captain R. S. D. Armour, "The Soviet Naval Air Arm," in Commander M. G. Saunders, ed., *The Soviet Navy* (New York: Frederick A. Praeger, Inc., 1958), pp. 187–91; Kilmarx, *A History of Soviet Air Power*, pp. 268–70.

which about 500 were bombers, most of them BADGERS.[142] The larger part of this force continued to be deployed for operations over waters adjacent to Europe, although some of its aircraft were based in the Far East.[143]

Finally, the Khrushchev period produced evidence that the Soviet Union, traditionally a continental military power, was gradually moving toward acquisition of the basic elements of a maritime-air-logistical potential of the kind that would be needed should the USSR wish to project its military presence into distant conflicts in the Third World. Thus, the Soviet Union initiated military aid programs to a number of Third-World countries early in Khrushchev's regime, a subject we discussed previously.[144] The deployment of Soviet equipment and training personnel to recipient countries in diverse areas of the world meant, among other things, that potential logistical bases were being created against a time when political developments might permit their use.[145]

Other, more directly pertinent trends appeared later. In the early sixties, for example, the Soviet Union began improving its capabilities for amphibious landing operations, a field in which it lagged far behind the United States,[146] and in the summer of 1964 Soviet marine forces (naval infantry) were reactivated and put through special landing exercises with a good deal of attendant publicity.[147] Investment in a long-range airlift capacity, also a Soviet shortcoming, was suggested by programs to develop such large transport aircraft as the AN–22[148] and in the military literature of the early sixties it was pointed

[142] *Military Balance, 1963–1964*, p. 6.

[143] Ibid. It may be noted that deployment of the land-based naval air arm was such as to bring some of its aircraft within radius of each of the major operating areas of the four fleets—Baltic, Black, Northern Seas, and Pacific—of the Soviet navy. Kilmarx, *A History of Soviet Air Power*, p. 269.

[144] See chapter VII, pp. 137–39.

[145] The working out of arrangements with several countries for fishing fleet and trawler bases was a similar step with both current and future implications for the support of some kinds of Soviet naval activities, political conditions again permitting. Examples of such arrangements were the fishing agreements with the UAR of February 27, 1964, and June 1, 1965, and those with Cuba of April 3, 1963, and September 2, 1964.

[146] Expression of Soviet interest in amphibious landing operations increased notably around 1963, when some Soviet naval figures began to urge closer study of the wealth of US amphibious experience (both in World War II and since). For elaboration of these views, see Wolfe, *Soviet Strategy at the Crossroads*, pp. 187–88, and the same author's *Trends in Soviet Thinking on Theater Warfare, Conventional Operations, and Limited War*, The RAND Corporation, RM-4305-PR, December 1964, pp. 99–105. For the best description of a Soviet amphibious landing venture in World War II, see Raymond L. Garthoff, "Soviet Operations in the War with Japan: August 1945," *United States Naval Institute Proceedings* (May 1966): 50–63.

[147] The Soviet marines (*morskaia pekhota*, literally, naval infantry) had been employed in some World War II operations, but had dropped out of the picture by the mid-fifties, and may have been formally deactivated at that time. They were brought back to public attention in July 1964, when articles in the military press began to feature photographs of marine contingents engaging in special landing operations. See *Krasnaia zvezda*, July 24, August 22, 1964. Although much publicity was given the revival of the marines in connection with amphibious exercises, their numbers apparently remained small, somewhere on the order of 3,000 to 4,000 men, who were stationed with the various Soviet territorial fleets (*Military Balance, 1965–1966*, p. 6).

[148] The AN-22, an advanced heavy-transport aircraft roughly comparable to the Lockheed C-5A under development in the United States, was first displayed publicly by the Soviets at the

out that airborne landing operations in combination with amphibious operations would take on increasing significance.[149]

Meanwhile, the Khrushchev decade saw a steady rise in the tonnage of
Soviet merchant ships built both in the Soviet Union and in foreign shipyards.
This construction program brought Soviet merchant shipping up from about
1.5 million tons in 1959 to nearly 6 million by the end of 1964; if continued
at the rate of around a million tons annually which had been reached by the
time Khrushchev left the scene, it promised to make the Soviet Union one of
the world's leading maritime powers within the next decade.[150] From about
the middle fifties on, a substantial increase in oceanographic research and
deep-sea fishing fleets was also part of a general Soviet "turn toward the sea"
and away from a continental land-mass outlook.

The eventual consequences of this maritime growth in economic and political terms lie outside the scope of this chapter.[151] In a military sense, however, it can be said that the maritime program both improved the Soviet
Union's ability to take on global military responsibilities and posed new problems of no small dimension. On the one hand, for example, it certainly gave
the Soviet sea-lift capacity a much needed boost, whether for wartime transport purposes or for support of peacetime ventures of one sort or another. Inclusion in the merchant ship program of vessels especially configured for
carrying military equipment, such as the large-hatch ships used to supply
matériel to Cuba, attested to the fact that military as well as economic criteria
had been borne in mind.

On the other hand, a commensurate effort to provide naval means suitable
for protecting Soviet sea-lift in distant oceans was still lacking, perhaps be-

Paris air show in 1965. Development of this Soviet transport, an Antonov design, had begun, of
course, in the Khrushchev period. According to Soviet statements, the range of the AN-22 (named
the ANTAEUS) is more than 6,000 miles with a 45-ton cargo. Over shorter distances, the aircraft is
said to be capable of lifting 80 tons of cargo or 720 passengers. See Lt. Colonel E. Simakov,
"Antaeus Rises Above the Earth," *Soviet Military Review*, no. 7 (July 1966): 30–31.

[149] See, for example, Rear Admiral D. A. Tuz, "The Role of Amphibious Landing Operations
in Missile-Nuclear War," *Morskoi sbornik*, no. 6 (June 1964): 26–27. It should be noted, however, that this and other Soviet discussions of airborne landing and reinforcement operations were
generally set in the context of a major war rather than of distant local wars. This was also the
case with respect to airborne reinforcement of European theater operations, an activity which
became a prominent feature of joint Warsaw Pact exercises in the mid-sixties, after Khrushchev's
ouster. This will be discussed in detail in chapter XVII.

[150] See Noel Mostert, "Russia Bids for Ocean Supremacy," *Reporter*, February 10, 1966, p. 25;
Jane's Fighting Ships, 1964–1965, p. 424.

[151] The possible consequences of the steady growth of Soviet merchant shipping, together with
the web of associated activities and interests such growth entails, nevertheless raise some absorbing
questions. For example, does a widening maritime interest mean that the Soviet Union is likely
to evolve in the direction of greater economic interdependence with the rest of the world, giving
it a greater interest in fitting into the established international political order and in maintaining
world stability? Or is the Soviet Union more likely to employ its growing maritime capacity as
an economic weapon with which to undermine the established international order, and to buttress
such a policy by building up the naval elements of its power? Obviously, which of these alternative trends proves the stronger will be determined by many factors not susceptible to prediction.

cause Khrushchev felt that for the time being the task was beyond the Soviet Union's resources. For the future, therefore, the broad question, left essentially unresolved by Khrushchev, was whether the expenditure on a large merchant fleet now demanded a massive build-up of naval means to protect this investment—a *raison d'être* for naval power without precedent in Russian history.[152]

---

[152] For comment on this and other points relevant to the role of naval power in Soviet policy, see Thomas W. Wolfe's review of *The Russians at Sea: A History of the Russian Navy*, in *Russian Review* (October 1966): pp. 414–16.

IX

SOVIET THINKING ON THEATER
WARFARE IN EUROPE

The decade of Khrushchev's regime was not only a period in which Soviet military preparations and conceptions were greatly affected by the impact of the nuclear missile age, but one in which NATO's posture and strategy likewise went through a process of considerable change. The extent to which interaction between Soviet and NATO military preparations during this period of mutual change may have influenced Soviet thinking on theater warfare in Europe is important, but extremely difficult to gauge.

In the case of NATO, abandonment in the mid-fifties of the large Lisbon conventional force goals and adoption of a tactical nuclear posture and strategy were followed in the early sixties by another attempt to build up conventional strength and win acceptance of a strategy of graduated warfare, or flexible response. This fluctuation between conventional and tactical nuclear strategies, which remained essentially unresolved in NATO at the end of the Khrushchev period, had no parallel on the Soviet side.

Although, initially, the effort to nuclearize the Soviet theater forces undoubtedly had been stimulated in some degree by NATO's shift to a tactical nuclear posture in the mid-fifties, the Khrushchev program, once it was set in motion, tended to acquire a momentum of its own and did not appear to be very responsive to further fluctuations in NATO's position. To be sure, there were signs prior to Khrushchev's ouster that some Soviet military men thought nuclear dependence within the theater forces had been carried too far. Their expressed concern may have marked the start of a new but delayed cycle of Soviet reaction to NATO's revived interest in conventional forces and concepts of graduated response. However, until the end of the Khrushchev period, at least, Soviet theater-force planning and doctrine remained consistently oriented in a nuclear direction.

Relationship between Theater and Strategic Warfare

Much of the military theoretical debate which sprang to life in the Soviet Union during the Khrushchev period seemed to turn on the question of the kind of war for which the Soviet armed forces should be equipped and trained to fight—a war cast in the old mold of a European land-war strategy, or a new kind of war against a powerful transoceanic adversary. As the authors of the widely publicized Sokolovskii treatise, *Military Strategy*, put it in 1963:

In essence, the argument is over the basic ways in which a future war will be conducted. Will it on the one hand be a land war with the employment of nuclear weapons as a means of supporting the operations of the ground forces, or will it on the other hand be a fundamentally new kind of war in which the main means of solving strategic tasks will be missiles and nuclear weapons?[1]

In light of the great outpouring of assertions in Soviet military literature of the Khrushchev decade that a new war would be "fundamentally" different from any past war, and that strategic nuclear missile weapons would be the "decisive means" employed, it seems unlikely that any of the parties to this debate were arguing that the problems of global strategic warfare could simply be ignored.

Rather, the issue was probably less a matter of selecting one basic strategy versus the other—that is, a theater versus a global strategy—than one of debate over the ways in which theater campaigns on the Eurasian continent should be related in scope, timing, and order of importance to global strategic operations. Underlying the question of relative importance, of course, was the contention between those military interests who advocated priority allocation of resources to the traditional combined-arms theater forces and those who favored the newer strategic forces, both offensive and defensive.

What emerged from the debate over the relationship of theater and strategic operations was an essentially ambivalent doctrinal position, which elevated the "decisive" influence of strategic nuclear strikes to the status of a "new general law of warfare," while also reasserting the more traditional view that war can be won only through combined-arms operations, ending with seizure and occupation of the enemy's homeland by the ground forces. Both of these propositions were frequently to be found side by side in the same theoretical treatises,[2] with only occasional recognition that in a war against a powerful overseas adversary, and given the Soviet Union's inability to mount naval and amphibious operations of requisite scale, the Soviet ground forces would find it difficult to undertake their mission of invading and occupying the enemy's territory.[3]

The tendency to treat the problems of conducting a continental war in Europe in comparative isolation, as though the situation in the European theater would be somehow divorced from the effects of global strategic op-

[1] Marshal V. D. Sokolovskii et al., *Voennaia strategiia* (Military Strategy) (2nd ed.; Moscow: Voenizdat, 1963), p. 367. (Hereafter cited by its Russian title, as distinct from that of the earlier [1962] edition, for which we cite the English translation.)

[2] See, for example, *Voennaia strategiia*, 2nd ed., pp. 20, 246. See also Major Generals S. N. Kozlov and M. R. Smirnov, Colonels I. S. Baz and P. A. Sidorov, *O Sovetskoi voennoi nauke* (On Soviet Military Science) (rev. ed.; Moscow: Voenizdat, 1964), pp. 32, 298, 339.

[3] One Soviet critic, who pointed out that without requisite naval and amphibious capabilities the Soviet ground forces "would be in a terrible quandary, to say the least, in attempting invasion of enemy territory across the sea," was Admiral V. A. Alafuzov. See his review article, "On Publication of the Work 'Military Strategy,'" *Morskoi sbornik* (Naval Collection), no. 1 (January 1963): 92, 95. For further discussion, see Thomas W. Wolfe, *Soviet Strategy at the Crossroads* (Cambridge, Mass.: Harvard University Press, 1964), pp. 187, 229.

erations, was by no means unique with the Soviet Union, for a somewhat similar dichotomy characterized many of NATO's military policy and planning discussions. However, in the Soviet case, the tendency in question was no doubt fortified by a military tradition and body of experience in which preparation for land warfare in Europe had long been the dominant consideration. Thus, despite the increasing emphasis given under Khrushchev to the strategic missile forces and to the influence of strategic nuclear operations on the outcome of any future war, there was still a strong disposition to focus on the familiar problem of European theater warfare. One can hardly fail to note the parallel here to the fact that Soviet political attention also remained centered primarily upon the European arena, even though at the same time the Soviet Union's global interests and its competition with the United States on the world stage were growing.

Theater Doctrine in the Khrushchev Era

The central idea common to almost all Soviet professional discussion of theater warfare in Europe during the Khrushchev years was that a theater campaign would probably be fought within the framework of a general war opening with heavy nuclear exchanges. Exceptions to this image, which we shall come to later, were few and far between in the voluminous Soviet literature on theater warfare.

To judge from this literature, the major objectives of Soviet forces committed to theater operations in Europe would be three: the destruction of NATO forces, the rapid occupation of Europe, and its isolation from US support. To accomplish the latter objective, separate operations against sea and air lines of communication between Europe and America would be required.[4] For the most part, no distinction between NATO and non-NATO countries of Europe emerged from Soviet military discussion of European theater operations. However, there was occasional recognition that in the event of war some non-Communist countries might choose neutrality or even range themselves on the side of the Soviet bloc,[5] which suggested that the objective of over-running and occupying Europe might be less than all-inclusive.

With respect to how theater operations would be conducted, the governing concept of Soviet military theory in the Khrushchev period called for prompt seizure of the initiative and rapid offensive exploitation, in contrast with Stalin's improvised World War II formula of strategic defense followed by a deliberate counteroffensive build-up.[6] The principles adopted for the survival

---

[4] *Voennaia strategiia*, 2nd ed., pp. 382–90, 417.

[5] Ibid., p. 223; Sokolovskii et al., *Soviet Military Strategy* (Englewood Cliffs, N.J.: Prentice-Hall, 1963), p. 287.

[6] It should be noted that Stalin's doctrine of strategic defense, imposed by early reverses in World War II, was a departure from Soviet military theory developed in the thirties, which had extolled the value of offensive action and maneuver as a key principle of Soviet doctrine. The same axiom had been enshrined in the Russian military tradition built around the ideas of Peter the Great and Suvorov. In a sense, therefore, Soviet military theory in the Khrushchev period was

of Soviet theater forces under nuclear conditions were essentially the same as those prescribed for quick defeat of the enemy: surprise, a continuous offensive developing rapidly throughout the depth of the theater, and presentation of only dispersed, fast-moving targets by mobile tank, motorized rifle, and airborne units.[7]

The Image of Initial Theater Operations

The standard picture of the outbreak of war offered by Soviet doctrine was that of a massive surprise nuclear attack upon the Soviet Union, in response to which the opening Soviet moves would be retaliatory strategic nuclear strikes followed almost immediately by a full-scale theater offensive against Europe. If Soviet planners gave thought to circumstances in which the Soviet side would deliver the first blow, these were never mentioned directly in the open literature. Even the several variant scenarios of war outbreak occasionally recognized in the Soviet literature invariably ascribed war initiation to the adversary. One of these was a war starting under the cover of NATO field exercises, probably in a period of crisis.[8] Another was the possibility of third powers embarking on local hostilities into which the major powers would be drawn, with the presumption of West German intervention in East Germany apparently uppermost in the Soviet mind.[9] Wars beginning through miscalculation or accident, or through escalation of a local conflict outside Europe, also were among the Soviet scenarios.

No matter what the circumstances of war outbreak might be, however, Soviet theater operations, particularly in Europe, were customarily pictured as beginning in much the same fashion. The revised Sokolovskii volume, for example, described the initial phase of a theater offensive in these words: "Following the retaliatory nuclear strikes, airborne landings may be launched in great depth and—depending on the radiological conditions—the ground force formations which are still intact will initiate a rapid advance with the support of the air force, in order to complete the destruction of the surviving armed forces of the enemy."[10]

According to a somewhat more detailed account by another group of Soviet writers, the theater offensive

> will begin with powerful missile-nuclear strikes against the enemy's defenses throughout the whole of his operational-strategic depth. Ground forces, particularly tank and airborne forces, will quickly follow up the missile-nuclear strikes, operating customarily in open formation. Simultaneously with the beginning of the offensive by tanks and motorized

dipping back into the classical tradition of seizing the initiative and forcing one's plan on the adversary through offensive action. See Michel Garder, *A History of the Soviet Army* (New York: Frederick A. Praeger, Inc., 1966), pp. 17–18, 73, 81.

[7] For comment on the characteristics of these three types of divisions as they were developed during the Khrushchev period, see chapter VIII, pp. 165–75.

[8] *Soviet Military Strategy*, pp. 47–48, 356, 383–93, 396.

[9] See Wolfe, *Soviet Strategy at the Crossroads*, pp. 49, 128–29. See also pp. 214–16, below.

[10] *Soviet Military Strategy*, p. 374.

infantry, tactical and operational airborne landings will be conducted, both in the tactical and operational zones of the enemy's defenses.[11] Troops will penetrate the tactical zone at a rapid tempo, striving to break out into the operational-scale zone. For deep development of successes in the latter zone, powerful tank armies will be employed.[12]

The speedy follow-up of the initial nuclear strikes in these and other accounts was customarily described as imperative in order not only to seize the initiative from the enemy but also "to deny him the capability of bringing in fresh reserves and preparing himself for a renewal of organized resistance."[13] Both for the rapid exploitation of nuclear strikes against the enemy and to mitigate the effects of the enemy's own use of nuclear weapons, Soviet doctrine placed increasing emphasis on the importance of mobility and maneuver in theater operations. According to some accounts, "maneuver has become the basic feature" of such operations, especially from the standpoint of conducting offensive warfare.[14]

Stress on Offensive Operations

With regard to the question of the offensive, military theory during the Khrushchev period came to lay great stress on the point that, in both strategic and theater operations, "the offensive constitutes the basic method of warfare."[15] Room was left for such other methods as the "strategic defense," "holding operations," and "strategic withdrawal" under specified conditions,[16] but the main emphasis was on the idea that, "Only a decisive offensive with massive use of all forces, involving both mutual cooperation and the exploitation of their specific individual capabilities and taking into account the decisive role of missile-nuclear weapons, can bring victory."[17]

The notion of adopting the strategic defense during the first phases of a war, as was done under Stalin in the early part of World War II, no longer enjoyed acceptance in Soviet military theory of the nuclear age.[18] In fact, it was spe-

---

[11] In Soviet usage, a category called "operational" stands between the tactical and the strategic. An operation of this special scale might involve several fronts within a theater, but would be something less than a full theater campaign.

[12] Kozlov et al., *O Sovetskoi voennoi nauke*, p. 355.

[13] Ibid., p. 325.

[14] Colonel I. Vorob'ev, "Maneuver in Contemporary Combat of General Purpose Troops," *Krasnaia zvezda*, June 6, 1964; Colonel General I. S. Glebov, "Development of the Operational Art," ibid., April 2, 1964.

[15] Kozlov et al., *O Sovetskoi voennoi nauke*, p. 249.

[16] Ibid., pp. 261, 264, 326, 328. Major General V. Reznichenko and Colonel A. Sidorenko, "Tactics at the Present Stage," *Krasnaia zvezda, February* 12, 1964; Colonel General N. A. Lomov, "New Weapons and the Nature of War," ibid., January 7, 1964.

[17] Kozlov et al., *O Sovetskoi voennoi nauke*, p. 249.

[18] There is room for considerable semantic confusion over the term "strategic defense," depending on whether it is used, as here, in the sense of strategic defense as a mode of operations and a broad strategy, or in the sense of strategic defense forces to serve as an active counter to strategic air missile attack. Soviet doctrine stresses the virtues of taking the offensive over those of adopting the strategic defense as a mode of operations, and of an offensive as opposed to a defensive strategy. At the same time, it also attaches great value to strategic defense forces for protection against strategic air and missile attack.

cifically rejected by various military authorities such as Colonel General Shtemenko, who expressed strong opinions on the "unacceptability" of the strategic defense in a modern war, arguing that "orienting oneself on the strategic defense . . . means dooming oneself beforehand to irreparable losses and defeat."[19] Other Soviet military men, extolling the virtues of offensive-mindedness in theater operations, asserted that "history confirms that a defensive doctrine has never led to success."[20]

In speaking of the "offensive orientation of Soviet military doctrine," Soviet writers were careful to note that it has "nothing in common with the aggressive, predatory tendencies in the military doctrine of the USA and its allies." If the Soviet Union should be attacked, however, then Soviet forces would wage war at "maximum offensive intensity, in order to defeat the enemy in the shortest period of time."[21] One of "the laws governing the offensive," wrote the authors of On Soviet Military Science in 1964, is "to seize and hold the initiative," requiring, among other things, "that offensive formations be supplied with everything necessary, especially nuclear weapons."[22] In theater operations, they pointed out, new means of warfare had brought basic changes in the way offensive operations might be conducted; they had especially affected the once predominant role of the ground troops: "The essence of the new situation is that an offensive operation has ceased to be the prerogative of ground troops only. A modern offensive operation is least of all an inherently "ground-oriented" matter. It has become a general operation of various branches of the armed forces.[23]

Other Soviet military theorists likewise observed that the participation of ground troops in offensive operations had undergone a radical change of character: "An attack by foot soldiers will be a rare phenomenon," for the

---

A good deal of misunderstanding has in fact arisen around this semantically confusing point. It has often taken the form of Western observers' ascribing to Soviet military doctrine a deep-seated preference for defense over offense, or assuming that Soviet military men are "traditionally defense-minded." However, Soviet military spokesmen themselves offer the strongest testimony to the contrary as the statements quoted in the text make clear.

These statements relate, to be sure, to the Khrushchev period, with which the present chapter deals. However, Soviet military doctrine continues to insist, as an article on the subject put it in the spring of 1967, that "The decisive mode of military operations always has been and remains the offensive." See Lieutenant General I. Zav'ialov, "On Soviet Military Doctrine," Krasnaia zvezda, March 30, 1967. The same writer made the point that one should not confuse a "defensive strategy," which lacks the war-winning potential of an offensive one, with "active defenses" against nuclear attack, which do have "very great strategic significance."

The sentiment attributed to Lenin by another Soviet military writer probably sums up the attitude most characteristic of Soviet military thinking on the point in question. "Once war begins, it should be waged decisively, actively, until complete victory is attained . . . . As V. I. Lenin said: 'War must either be waged to the hilt, or not at all.' "

[19] Colonel General S. M. Shtemenko, "Scientific-Technical Progress and Its Influence on the Development of Military Affairs," Kommunist Vooruzhennykh Sil (Communist of the Armed Forces), no. 3 (February 1963): 27–28. See also Major D. Kazakov, "The Theoretical and Methodological Basis of Soviet Military Science," ibid., no. 10 (May 1963): 10–11; Colonel V. Konoplev, "On Scientific Foresight in Military Affairs," ibid., no. 24 (December 1963): 28.

[20] Lt. Colonel L. Korzun, "Defense in Modern Combat," Krasnaia zvezda, August 22, 1964.

[21] Kozlov et al., O Sovetskoi voennoi nauke, pp. 388, 389.

[22] Ibid., p. 319.

[23] Ibid., p. 261.

old infantry tactics "have given way to new tactics based on motorized troops in armored personnel carriers."[24] Such views as these represented a doctrinal accompaniment to the military reforms of the Khrushchev era, which had included the streamlining and motorization of theater force units.[25]

Vulnerability of Massed Troops to Nuclear Blows and Surprise Attack

Another change of great importance that was enforced upon Soviet doctrine by modern conditions of warfare concerned the "principle of mass employment of forces." The hallmark of Soviet field operations in World War II had been the deliberate massing of forces for a frontal breakthrough, followed by envelopment and thrusts into the enemy rear, with the pattern repeating itself after necessary intervals of build-up. Essentially a Russian version of the classical principle of the concentration of forces, this style of operation obviously was called into question by technological developments of the nuclear missile age, as Soviet military theorists came to recognize.

While concentration of forces "at the necessary place and time" for carrying out "the main, first-priority tasks" remained a valid principle, according to Soviet writers, it could no longer be applied routinely, for "it must be borne in mind, when conducting an offensive, that the enemy may employ nuclear weapons at any moment."[26] Therefore, "in order to avoid the destruction of large groupings with a single nuclear weapon," troops must operate in "dispersed formations," and "exceptional flexibility must be exercised in directing them so that they can be quickly concentrated for mass assaults in the necessary locale and just as quickly dispersed again."[27]

One effect of the requirement for dispersal and flexibility in theater operations, and one that received a good deal of attention in Soviet literature, was the high demands it placed on command and control, and on the instant readiness of forces to go into battle "from the march" without the lengthy preparation for launching an offensive customary in the past.[28] However, the difficulties of controlling widely dispersed, fast-moving forces were not readily surmounted; as indicated by Soviet professional commentary, they were compounded by continuing shortcomings with respect to both personnel and equipment.[29]

The vulnerability of troop concentrations would dictate new tactics of dis-

---

[24] Reznichenko and Sidorenko, *Krasnaia zvezda*, February 12, 1964.

[25] See chapter VIII, pp. 173–78.

[26] Kozlov et al., *O Sovetskoi voennoi nauke*, pp. 327, 329.

[27] Ibid., pp. 325, 355.

[28] Captain 3rd Rank V. Puzik, "The Commander's Thinking and Cybernetics," *Krasnaia zvezda*, May 27, 1964; Lieutenant General K. G. Kozhanov, "Discipline of a High Order," ibid., April 3, 1964; Reznichenko and Sidorenko, ibid., February 12, 1964.

[29] Puzik, *Krasnaia zvezda*, May 27, 1964; General of the Army P. A. Kurochkin, "Modern Warfare and One-Man Command," ibid., June 5, 1964. The latter article dealt not only with technical problems of control imposed by modern conditions of warfare but also with a long-standing issue having internal political overtones, that of "one-man" professional military command (*edinonachalie*) versus collegial command. Kurochkin argued that the collegial concept was deficient under conditions of nuclear warfare, where complex, fast-moving situations require quick and decisive action.

persal and maneuver not only when nuclear conditions actually prevailed on the battlefield; because of the ever-present nuclear threat, restrictions on massing troops in theater operations would apply also during any purely conventional operations that might occur. As put by the authors of *On Soviet Military Science*: "Even when conducting operations with conventional means, the principle of mass employment of forces must be applied with great care, since the chance of surprise missile-nuclear attack, even if with tactical nuclear weapons only, remains."[30]

Besides expressing the need for vigilance against surprise nuclear attacks on Soviet field forces by the enemy, Soviet theorists gave voice occasionally to the suggestion that their own side might profit from the same game. One such example was the statement that Soviet military theory considers important "the principle of secret preparation and surprise delivery of strikes in the course of a war on a strategic as well as operational and tactical scale."[31] Putting it still more bluntly, another Soviet officer wrote, in discussing the operations of general purpose forces in theater combat, that "secrecy" in maneuvering one's forces will "facilitate surprise strikes against the enemy; make it possible to take him unawares and inflict heavy losses on him."[32]

Size and Duration of Theater Campaigns

The size of the Soviet forces contemplated for campaigns in various theaters, including the European, is a subject not discussed in specific terms in the open Soviet literature. However, the general impression given in Soviet writing of the Khrushchev period, much of which reflected a doctrinal debate over troop cutbacks, was that combat forces of somewhat smaller size than formerly would be involved in theater operations.[33] For example, in discussing the combined-arms forces necessary to achieve major results in a theater of military operations, the authors of *On Soviet Military Science* observed that a "single front" could now perform the tasks carried out in the last war by "groups of fronts":

[30] Kozlov et al., *O Sovetskoi voennoi nauke*, p. 329.

[31] Ibid., p. 325.

[32] Vorob'ev, *Krasnaia zvezda*, June 6, 1964.

[33] The Soviet military policy debate concerning the size of the Soviet armed forces is discussed above on pp. 160–62. On the question of theater forces, the doctrinal position which tended to support Khrushchev's preference for smaller forces was expressed, among others, by the authors of the 1964 edition of *On Soviet Military Science*. They argued that such factors as the quantity of divisions, once a prominent feature of the Stalinist "permanently operating factors," no longer could be regarded as sacrosanct. "In the period when war was primarily a matter of military operations in land theaters," they wrote, "and when the military power of a state was based on ground troops, combat capability was defined in terms of the quantity and quality of tactical units—divisions. Nowadays, the new technical means of warfare, mainly missile-nuclear weapons, have emerged as the decisive factor in armed forces."

Moreover, they said, although "the numerical size of a division has been significantly reduced in comparison with the past, its combat capability has sharply increased." All this, they observed, "demonstrates that the 'quality and quantity of divisions' must not be considered in the abstract, apart from concrete historical conditions." See Kozlov et al., *O Sovetskoi voennoi nauke*, pp. 292–97, 389.

In contrast with the last war, when strategic operations [in a theater] usually unfolded in the form of operations by groups of fronts, they can be accomplished now in a theater of military operations by the forces of a single front, and in a maritime theater—by the forces of a single fleet.[34]

As our previous discussion indicated, the peacetime Group of Soviet Forces in Germany (GSFG) would in wartime be converted into a "front" for theater combat purposes.[35] While its peacetime strength of twenty divisions, organized into five field armies plus a tactical air army, would doubtless be augmented under war conditions,[36] the GSFG stands as a typical example of what the Soviet authors probably had in mind when speaking of a contemporary wartime front. Since the GSFG's deployment in East Germany would permit it to operate only on the main axis in Central Europe, other fronts presumably would be required on the flanks for a theater offensive involving the whole of Europe.[37]

The expected duration of a theater campaign in Europe, like the size of the forces involved, customarily has not been spelled out in the open military literature. Again, however, the general impression conveyed by Soviet discourse of the Khrushchev period was that theater operations would run their course much more rapidly than in the prenuclear age. The opinion expressed by some of the conservative wing of the Soviet military that a war, even one fought with nuclear weapons, might turn out to be a protracted affair was more than balanced by the frequently voiced belief that modern weaponry would "significantly shorten the duration of a war."[38] Although debate on the long-versus-short-war issue was never conclusively settled in Khrushchev's time, it certainly could be said that the short-war viewpoint emerged as the dominant one.[39]

Precisely how brief the European phase of a "quickly consummated" nuclear war might prove to be, however, was left vague. The extreme view sometimes offered was that individual countries might be knocked out in a nuclear exchange in a matter of hours or minutes before their field forces could even go into action,[40] but the fact that this assessment was not applied to either the NATO or the Warsaw bloc coalition as a whole implied that a theater engagement of some duration was expected to develop in Europe in any case.

---

[34] Ibid., p. 360.

[35] See chapter VIII, p. 175.

[36] For a discussion of the Soviet reinforcement capability, see chapter VIII, pp. 170–71, especially fn. 41.

[37] The Soviet forces deployed in Poland and Hungary would presumably provide the nucleus for additional Fronts; forces of various East European countries would probably also be incorporated in some of the wartime Fronts.

[38] Colonel General N. A. Lomov, *Sovetskaia voennaia doktrina* (Soviet Military Doctrine) (Moscow: Izdatel'stvo "Znanie," 1963), p. 26.

[39] See discussion of the long-versus-short-war issue in Wolfe, *Soviet Strategy at the Crossroads*, pp. 130–38.

[40] Marshal R. Ia. Malinovskii, "The Revolution in Military Affairs and the Tasks of the Military Press," *Kommunist Vooruzhennykh Sil*, no. 21 (November 1963): 9; Sokolovskii et al., *Voennaia strategiia*, p. 20. See also Wolfe, *Soviet Strategy at the Crossroads*, pp. 132, 225–26.

Perhaps the viewpoint most representative of Soviet thinking on the duration of an active theater offensive was that expressed by the authors of *On Soviet Military Science*. Speaking of the development of a typical offensive in a theater of war (Europe, though not specified, was implied) in which the stated objective would be "to destroy all the forces of the enemy in the theater, including his missile sites, airfields and rear bases," they said: "Such an offensive may take a varying amount of time. In the last war a strategic offensive continued without interruption for three to five months. In a missile-nuclear war, of course, it will be conducted at a much more rapid tempo, and will be of significantly shorter duration."[41]

Along with the vastly increased firepower of nuclear weapons, the rate of daily movement made possible in theater operations by modern mechanized warfare was often cited in Soviet military literature as a factor enhancing the prospect that the enemy could be overcome "in the shortest period of time."[42] Given the fact that Soviet theater doctrine in the latter part of the Khrushchev period called for rates of movement of 50 to 60 miles per day, compared with 10 to 15 under the conditions that existed at the close of the last war,[43] one might suppose that Soviet theater planners were hoping to advance across the 500 miles separating their forces from the English Channel in a matter of a few weeks.

Whether such an expectation could be regarded as realistic would depend, of course, on the extent and quality of the resistance encountered; judging from his reluctance to test it, Khrushchev seems not to have been convinced that Europe could be quickly over-run, especially without bringing down on the Soviet Union the strategic nuclear devastation against which Soviet theater doctrine itself apparently had no remedy to offer.[44]

Tanks and Airborne Forces in the Combined-Arms Concept

Soviet military thinking of the Khrushchev period continued to adhere to the formula of combined arms, holding that, despite the leading role of the strategic missile forces, one could not expect them to perform all the essential tasks of modern war or to ensure military victory without the combined action of other forces, especially when it came to seizing and consolidating territory in theater operations.[45] Although the combined-arms concept remained embedded in Soviet doctrine, however, there was a distinct shift in the relative weight assigned to the various elements of the combined-arms forces to be employed in theater warfare.

---

[41] Kozlov et al., *O Sovetskoi voennoi nauke*, p. 357.

[42] Vorob'ev, *Krasnaia zvezda*, June 6, 1964.

[43] Ibid.

[44] See Thomas W. Wolfe, *Soviet Military Power and European Security*, The RAND Corporation, P-3429, August 1966, p. 32.

[45] Sokolovskii et al., *Voennaia strategiia*, p. 246; Kozlov et al., *O Sovetskoi voennoi nauke*, p. 261; Colonel General S. M. Shtemenko, "The New Requirements Posed for the Combined-Arms Commander," *Krasnaia zvezda*, January 16, 1964; Major General N. Ia. Sushko, "The Laws Determining the Course and Outcome of Wars," ibid., February 7, 1964.

The traditional importance of infantry, for example, was frequently proclaimed to have diminished under modern conditions, as noted above in our discussion of offensive operations. At the same time, Soviet military theory put new stress on the value of tank forces in any future war, even though the views of such tank champions as Marshals Rotmistrov and Chuikov, who argued that the tank had taken on added significance for rapid battlefield exploitation in either a nuclear or a conventional environment,[46] apparently did not receive Khrushchev's wholehearted endorsement.[47] The military assessment of the role of tank forces was perhaps best summed up in the second edition of *On Soviet Military Science*, which states: "Modern tank forces represent a powerful means for conducting battlefield operations, either independently or in cooperation with other forces. They are also a most important means for exploitation of results following delivery of missile-nuclear strikes."[48]

The role of airborne operations likewise acquired greater weight in Soviet theater doctrine of the Khrushchev period. The second Sokolovskii volume, in 1963, for example, placed even more emphasis than the first edition on the contribution of airborne forces to theater warfare, observing that "air landing as well as paratroop operations have taken on a new significance."[49] Besides allotting airborne operations a major role in the quick follow-up of initial nuclear strikes, Soviet writers specified that such operations would be aimed particularly at seizure of enemy nuclear weapons, airfields, and naval bases.[50] Theoretical treatment of the enhanced value of airborne operations in Soviet planning was accompanied by suggestions that Soviet airborne forces now had at their disposal heavier weapons and equipment deliverable by airdrop than formerly.[51] Parallel to this interest in airborne operations went renewed attention to amphibious landing activities. As mentioned earlier,[52] the revived interest in amphibious landing capabilities may have been stimulated in part by the possibility of having to deal with local conflicts distant from the European arena, but in the main it seems to have been linked more closely with the problems of conducting operations on the flanks of the European theater in a general war.

Reappraisal of Tactical Aviation in Theater Warfare

The question of the relative contribution of tactical aviation and tactical missile units to theater operations was given a good deal of attention under

[46] Marshal P. Rotmistrov, "The Causes of Modern Wars and Their Characteristics," *Kommunist Vooruzhennykh Sil*, no. 2 (January 1963): 31; Marshal V. I. Chuikov, "Modern Ground Forces," *Izvestiia*, December 22, 1963.

[47] For previous comment on this point, see chapter VIII, pp. 174–75, and fn. 58.

[48] Kozlov et al., *O Sovetskoi voennoi nauke*, p. 340.

[49] Sokolovskii et al., *Voennaia strategiia*, p. 307.

[50] Ibid. See also Reznichenko and Sidorenko, *Krasnaia zvezda*, February 12, 1964; editorial, "Airborne Troops," ibid., August 24, 1964.

[51] Lieutenant General V. Margelov, "The Precepts of a Paratrooper," *Krasnaia zvezda*, January 31, 1963.

[52] See chapter VIII, pp. 191–92.

the Khrushchev regime, as Soviet theorists and planners evidently encountered some difficulty in making up their minds how to fit these two elements of the combined-arms team into theater doctrine. Throughout much of that decade it seemed that the theater role of aviation in Soviet thinking was on the decline. Writing as late as March 1963, for example, a Soviet air force general noted that the battlefield support tasks formerly given to tactical (*frontovaia*) aviation might be better performed by operational-tactical missiles.[53] Such signs of the doctrinal eclipse of tactical aviation, moreover, were underscored by the substantial reduction of tactical air strength in the early sixties, as previously discussed.[54]

Toward the end of the Khrushchev period, however, doctrinal sentiment began to swing the other way, with a tendency to upgrade the battlefield potential of tactical aviation once again, particularly with regard to its value for reconnaissance and for suppression of mobile targets. As stated in the revised Sokolovskii edition of 1963, for example: "There are many specific tasks, such as destruction of mobile targets, which can be more effectively carried out by bombers or fighter-bombers than by missiles. The future improvement of aircraft-missile technology may significantly increase the operational effectiveness of the bomber air forces on the battlefield."[55]

Interestingly enough, some of the staunchest advocates of tactical aviation appeared among military leaders not immediately associated with the air forces. One of these was Colonel General Shtemenko, then chief of staff of the ground forces, who in 1963 observed that there is "no substitute" for tactical aviation, "especially when independent searching out of targets is required."[56] Another powerful proponent turned up in the person of Marshal Rotmistrov, the tank expert, who singled out the role of aviation for special praise in a memorable article, in the spring of 1964, in which he also questioned the tendency to overemphasize missiles at the expense of other arms. Speaking of the use of air power in support of theater operations in a future war, Rotmistrov said:

> ... despite the employment of missiles, aviation also will play an important role, especially in the operations of tank forces and other strike groups separated from the remaining forces.
> In a war maneuver, aviation will become not only an irreplaceable means of reconnaissance, but also a reliable and adequately effective means for suppression of mobile targets, through use of both nuclear and conventional bombs.[57]

With regard to the problem of survival of aircraft operating in a battlefield environment where surface-to-air missile defenses might be a major threat, Rotmistrov expressed the view that aircraft would still be able to carry out

[53] Major General A. Kravchenko, "The Battlefield and Air Operations," *Aviatsiia i kosmonavtika* (Aviation and Cosmonautics), no. 3 (March 1963): 2–5.

[54] See chapter VIII, p. 169.

[55] Sokolovskii et al., *Voennaia strategiia*, p. 311.

[56] *Kommunist Vooruzhennykh Sil*, no. 3 (February 1963): 24.

[57] "Military Science and the Academies," *Krasnaia zvezda*, April 26, 1964.

their ground-support missions despite further developments in surface-to-air missiles. Along the same line, another military writer suggested that low-level operational techniques would enable aircraft to cope with the opponent's air defenses: "Military air operations at very low altitudes can yield precisely the most appreciable military effect; they are more suitable for overcoming the enemy's air defense system."[58]

Another point raised in connection with new thoughts on air support of theater operations was the need to reinstitute training in the use of unimproved airfields. A lead editorial in *Red Star* in 1964 dealing with this question criticized those who felt that unpaved airstrips were incompatible with modern high-performance jet aircraft, stating that "the rapid rate of advance by ground forces may require frequent redeployment of air units and make it necessary for them to get along essentially without airfields prepared in advance."[59] In addition to its function in theater operations, Soviet military discourse ascribed growing importance to the contributions of aviation to airborne operations, logistic support, and communications.[60]

Tactical Missiles and Theater Doctrine

While the theater role of aviation was thus undergoing re-evaluation, the process of working out a satisfactory place for tactical missile forces in Soviet theater doctrine presented a number of problems, despite the generally accepted proposition that tactical missiles with nuclear warheads[61] were to be regarded as the "main firepower" of the theater forces.[62]

One of these problems was related primarily to the appropriate distribution of effort between tactical missiles and tactical aviation. In the eyes of many Soviet military men, there was no longer any question by the early sixties about the superior value of tactical missiles over tactical aviation and artillery in theater operations. This view was strongly argued in late 1962 by such men as Marshal S. S. Varentsov,[63] who was in charge of tactical missile units before he fell into disgrace because of his connection with the Penkovskiy espionage case. The first Sokolovskii edition, published that year, also affirmed that tactical missile troops would "to a considerable degree replace artillery and aviation."[64] But the second edition, in 1963, toned down this appraisal,[65] and a year later the authors of *On Soviet Military Science* stated

---

[58] Major General V. Bolotnikov, "Man, Altitude, Speed," *Krasnaia zvezda*, April 25, 1964.

[59] Editorial, "Master Flying from Air Strips," *Krasnaia zvezda*, June 24, 1964.

[60] Sokolovskii et al., *Voennaia strategiia*, p. 312; Marshal K. A. Vershinin, "The Might of the Air Force Is Growing," *Krasnaia zvezda*, February 1, 1964.

[61] Soviet military as well as civil defense literature of the Khrushchev period referred occasionally to the use of chemical and bacteriological munitions as an alternative or supplement to nuclear warheads. But the open literature, at any rate, attributed plans for using such munitions to the West, leaving only the implication that the Soviet Union was prepared to do likewise. See *Soviet Military Strategy*, 1st ed., pp. 304, 337; Kozlov et al., *O Sovetskoi voennoi nauke*, p. 342.

[62] See chapter VIII, pp. 173–74.

[63] "Rockets: Formidable Weapons of the Ground Forces," *Izvestiia*, December 2, 1962.

[64] *Soviet Military Strategy*, p. 341.

[65] *Voennaia strategiia*, p. 304.

that tactics "for employment of various kinds of missiles" had only recently been worked out, implying that the views of the Varentsov school had been watered down to a more balanced formula under which the main firepower of the theater forces would be provided by tactical missiles with nuclear warheads "delivered both by the tactical missile troops and by aviation."[66]

A second problem associated with tactical missile doctrine evidently involved tendencies at lower levels of command to count on the prodigal use of these relatively costly weapons. It was brought to light in August 1964 in a series of articles by Marshal Sokolovskii and a colleague, who referred critically to the disposition of some ground-force officers to regard tactical missiles primarily as "a means of fire support for troops, like artillery." Artillery concepts should not be applied to the new tactical missile forces, according to Sokolovskii. Rather, tactical missile units should be regarded as a "special means of the command," to be used not indiscriminately against minor obstacles, but against major theater targets.[67]

A third doctrinal question was that of defining the relative contribution to be made by strategic and tactical missiles in theater operations. Up to about midway in the Khrushchev period, the tendency of some Soviet theorists had been to assume that the strategic missile forces would be used essentially to support the ground forces in theater campaigns. Criticized as an "incorrect concept" resulting from "over-valuing the experience of the last war and mechanically applying it to modern conditions,"[68] this view was gradually replaced by the formulation that strategic nuclear weapons should be properly understood to exercise "decisive" influence upon the outcome of war as a whole, as well as upon its component theater actions. By the end of the Khrushchev period, it was a generally accepted article of theater doctrine that the task of the tactical missile forces would be that of "destroying any important enemy targets and troop formations that may survive strikes by the strategic missile forces."[69]

A fourth set of considerations relating to the place of tactical missiles in Soviet theater doctrine took in such questions as whether employment of nuclear weapons might be *limited* to tactical types only, or whether theater warfare of significant scale might be conducted without recourse to nuclear weapons altogether. Since these questions turn on the broader issue of the Soviet attitude toward possible limitations upon military operations in Europe, we shall treat them below under this larger rubric.

Soviet Attitude toward Restraints upon Theater Operations

Neither Soviet theater doctrine as it evolved during the Khrushchev decade nor the changes in organization and weapons introduced into the theater

---

[66] Kozlov et al., *O Sovetskoi voennoi nauke*, pp. 264, 366.

[67] Marshal V. D. Sokolovskii and Major General M. Cherednichenko, "New Stage of Military Art," two-part article in *Krasnaia zvezda*, August 25 and 28, 1964.

[68] *Soviet Military Strategy*, p. 401.

[69] Ibid., p. 341; Sokolovskii et al., *Voennaia strategiia*, p. 304.

forces during that period tended to encourage the notion of imposing restraints of one kind or another upon the conduct of theater operations in
Europe. A doctrine assuming that military conflict in Europe would be in-
separably tied to general nuclear war and prescribing that Soviet forces must
promptly seize the initiative with an all-out theater offensive did not lend itself readily to the idea of limiting theater operations once they had been set
in motion. As for the theater forces themselves, their increasing nuclearization at the expense of conventional staying power, and the problems of command and control created by the more complex conditions of modern warfare, were among factors which, to some extent at least, raised questions as
to whether these forces possessed the requisite capabilities for conducting
carefully controlled and graduated operations. In addition to such doctrinal and technical considerations, there was also Khrushchev's own frequently stated position, adopted perhaps both out of conviction and for its
deterrent effect, that limitations on warfare in the European theater, where
vital interests of the great powers were closely enmeshed, would prove unfeasible.

Despite what would thus seem to be an outlook prejudiced against any form
of restraint upon military operations in Europe, Soviet thinking did not remain
wholly set in this direction, particularly toward the end of Khrushchev's
tenure. Rather, various shades of professional opinion emerged with respect
to such questions as the prospect of employing only conventional forces in
theater operations, the limitation of nuclear weapons to tactical types, and
the possibility of limiting third-power conflicts in Europe. Here let us trace
briefly the principal trends of Soviet thought on these matters up to the close
of the Khrushchev period.

Conventional Theater Warfare

Soviet military writing in the late fifties and early sixties gave little attention
to the use of conventional arms except within the framework of general nuclear war operations. In part, this may have reflected a frequently expressed
Soviet belief that any war "in the center of Europe, along the frontiers between the NATO powers and the members of the Warsaw Pact" would quickly
take on the dimensions of a general nuclear war.[70]

Even the attempts of Soviet military leaders to find doctrinal grounds for
resisting Khrushchev's inroads on the manpower of the theater forces rather
surprisingly failed to make much use of the argument that large ground
forces would be needed in case conventional theater campaigns had to be
fought. Almost invariably, the argument was that large forces were justified
precisely because the conduct of a nuclear war would entail heavy losses, and
substantial replacements would be required to ensure defeat of the surviving

---

[70] M. Vasil'ev commentary, Moscow broadcast to Germany, December 6, 1957. See also Khrushchev's comment on the danger that a local war in Europe could expand into global nuclear war,
Pravda, January 4, 1964.

enemy forces and occupation of enemy territory, in addition to handling internal security and the rear-area defense and rehabilitation tasks.[71]

Beginning around 1962, however, a shift seemed to be taking place in Soviet military opinion on the question of conventional operations, representing perhaps a professional reaction to NATO military planning and the strategy of "flexible response," as well as a more general recognition of the need to modify the rather rigid Soviet declaratory position on escalation.[72] Although the new tendency to take greater account of non-nuclear warfare was most often expressed in the specific context of local wars outside Europe, the employment of conventional forces was occasionally discussed in terms suggestive of a European theater situation.

One writer, for example, after speaking in early 1963 of the likelihood that the "imperialists" would launch any future war with a surprise nuclear attack, then turned to the possibility that they would not, and that the Soviet Union might thus be confronted with a different set of circumstances:

> One ought not to lose sight of the fact that the imperialists, fearing an inevitable retaliatory missile-nuclear blow, might launch against us one or another form of war without employing nuclear weapons. From this comes the practical conclusion—our armed forces must be prepared to deal with an appropriate rebuff with conventional means, while keeping missile-nuclear weapons in the highest state of readiness.[73]

Other Soviet military commentary likewise took up the conventional warfare theme from time to time. In 1963, Colonel General Shtemenko and Marshal Rotmistrov made a point of mentioning that the Soviet armed forces were being trained and equipped for either conventional or nuclear operations.[74] The following year Marshal Sokolovskii returned to the subject in a series of articles which, while devoted mainly to the idea that theater warfare and the over-all outcome of a war would be dominated by nuclear weapons, also noted that "in the course of operations there will frequently be occasions when combat tasks will have to be accomplished without use of nuclear weapons. Therefore, troops must be able to conduct such operations."[75] Another officer, Colonel General I. Glebov, writing in April 1964 on the current development of Soviet theater doctrine, said: "Finally, it must be pointed out that in addition to working out the theory and practice of employing operational-scale units in nuclear war, Soviet operational art also examines problems of operations and combat actions conducted without the employment of nuclear

---

[71] See, for example, Marshal R. Ia. Malinovskii, in *Pravda*, October 25, 1961, and *Kommunist*, no. 7 (May 1962); Major General V. Kruchinin, "Why Mass Armies?" *Krasnaia zvezda*, January 11, 1963; *Soviet Military Strategy*, pp. 338, 341.

[72] See chapter VII, pp. 138–39. See also Wolfe, *Soviet Strategy at the Crossroads*, p. 124.

[73] Major D. Kazakov, in *Kommunist Vooruzhennykh Sil*, no. 10 (May 1963): 11–12.

[74] Colonel General S. M. Shtemenko, "Ground Forces in Modern War and Their Combat Preparation," *Krasnaia zvezda*, January 3, 1963; Marshal P. Rotmistrov, "Historic Victory," *Moscow News*, no. 19, May 11, 1963. See also *Voennaia strategiia*, p. 374.

[75] *Krasnaia zvezda*, August 25, 28, 1964.

weapons, but under conditions in which they may possibly be employed at any time."[76]

Thus, by 1964, two somewhat divergent tendencies were apparent in Soviet thinking on conventional theater operations, especially with respect to a conflict in Europe. On the one hand was the new tendency to recognize that hostilities might begin at the conventional level and to conclude from this that Soviet forces should be prepared to "rebuff" a conventional attack with similar means, while keeping nuclear weapons ready for instant use. On the other hand, there was the persistent doctrinal view which emphasized the necessity of seizing the initiative immediately and neutralizing NATO's nuclear delivery capabilities, a view that would tend to put a premium on prompt nuclear strikes if hostilities should break out.

Which of these tendencies, freighted with such different implications for limiting a clash of arms in Europe to conventional forces, would actually prevail if the chips were down? No unambiguous answer to this critical question was to be found in Soviet military thought of the Khrushchev period. Perhaps the best that can be said is that Soviet military theory had again begun to entertain the possibility that warfare in Europe might under some circumstances be conducted in a conventional mode. There was little basis to suggest, however, that the priority concentration of Soviet theory on the problems of nuclear war had changed, or that a substantially higher expectation of conducting a non-nuclear war on a European scale had come to prevail.

Limitation of Nuclear Use to Tactical Weapons

If there was some shift of Soviet thinking in the Khrushchev period on the possibility of maintaining a "firebreak" between conventional and nuclear weapons, the same can hardly be said with regard to drawing the line between tactical and strategic nuclear weapons, particularly in the case of a European conflict. With very few exceptions, both military and political analyses of this period stuck to the view that no distinction was feasible between tactical and strategic nuclear arms, and that the use of nuclear weapons in any form would mean escalation to general world war, the kind of war in which neither side could be expected, in Khrushchev's words, "to concede defeat before resorting to the use of all weapons, even the most devastating ones."[77] Or, as Marshal Malinovskii put it in November 1962, when warning that an adversary should not count on being able to employ tactical weapons without courting massive retaliation, "No matter where a 'tactical' atomic weapon might be used against us, it would trigger a crushing counterblow."[78]

A few exceptions to this sort of cataclysmic linkage between tactical and strategic nuclear weapons did appear toward the end of the Khrushchev era, but they were nebulous at best. In 1963, for example, Soviet military writers

---

[76] Ibid., April 2, 1964.

[77] *Pravda*, March 8, 1961.

[78] Marshal R. Ia. Malinovskii, *Bditel'no stoiat' na strazhe mira* (Vigilantly Stand Guard Over the Peace) (Moscow: Voenizdat, 1962), p. 39.

began to express interest in the development of low-yield nuclear weapons,[79] suggesting perhaps that as supplies of nuclear material for tactical purposes became more plentiful somewhat more attention might be given to the possibility of nuclear warfare confined to the employment of tactical weapons. Also in 1963 a new note on the subject of nuclear escalation turned up in a brochure on military doctrine by Colonel General N. A. Lomov, who referred to the possible use of nuclear weapons in local war without adding the customary caveat that this would bring on "inevitable" escalation to general strategic warfare.[80]

Although there were thus scattered signs that at least some Soviet military theorists had begun to recognize a place for tactical nuclear weapons in local war situations,[81] and even to press subtly for development of the requisite means for conducting battlefield operations at the low end of the nuclear spectrum, it would be stretching things to infer that Soviet professional opinion was ready to embrace the idea of limiting the use of nuclear weapons in European warfare to tactical types. Even in a local war context, most Soviet writers continued to insist that tactical nuclear employment would soon lead to a strategic nuclear exchange. In 1963 the second Sokolovskii volume, for example, conceding that in a local war "it may happen that the belligerents will employ tactical nuclear weapons, without resort to strategic nuclear weapons," went on to say: "However, the war would hardly be waged very long with use of tactical nuclear weapons only. Once matters reach the point where nuclear weapons are used, then the belligerents will be forced to launch all of their nuclear power. Local war will be transformed into a global nuclear war."[82]

This tendency to single out the introduction of tactical nuclear weapons in local war as the point at which no further holds would be barred was matched by a consistently negative Soviet attitude toward concepts for the controlled use of strategic weapons and the observance of targeting restraints in a general war environment. Throughout the Khrushchev period, American advocacy of restraints in strategic warfare that would place limits on the level of civil destruction in the event of a major war met with disapproval from Soviet spokesmen, who branded damage-limiting concepts as an attempt to

[79] See, for example, Major General I. Anureev, "Physics and New Weapons," *Krasnaia zvezda*, November 21, 1963.

[80] Lomov, *Sovetskaia voennaia doktrina*, p. 15.

[81] Despite an occasional admission that tactical nuclear weapons might be used in local wars, Soviet doctrinal discussion rarely extended this possibility to that category of local wars described in the Soviet lexicon as "national liberation" wars. In fact, in order to exorcise the bogey of escalation from "national liberation" conflicts which the Soviet Union might wish to support, some Soviet writers avoided the tactical nuclear issue altogether, arguing simply that in such wars "the question of missiles and nuclear weapons being used will not arise." See, for example, Major General N. Ia. Sushko and Major T. Kondratkov, "War and Politics in the 'Nuclear Age,'" *Kommunist Vooruzhennykh Sil*, no. 2 (January 1964): 23. For a fuller discussion of these Soviet arguments, see Wolfe, *Trends in Soviet Thinking on Theater Warfare*, pp. 91–94.

[82] *Voennaia strategiia*, pp. 374–75. See also Kozlov et al., *O Sovetskoi voennoi nauke*, p. 6.

invent "rules of the game" that would merely "legalize" nuclear war, perpetuate the arms race, and help preserve the capitalist system.[83]

From the Soviet viewpoint, the rejection of nuclear limitation concepts in strategic warfare probably made some sense, for it helped to enhance the deterrent value of Soviet strategic forces, which by size and delivery capabilities were less suited to observing "city-sparing" ground rules than those of the United States. Moreover, acceptance of nuclear restraints in strategic warfare was hardly compatible with the Soviet disarmament line, which was intended to propagate the idea that the only measures to be considered were those aimed at averting war, rather than at limiting its destructiveness.

Much the same considerations doubtless discouraged the development in the Soviet Union of a publicly available professional literature and doctrine on the limited use of tactical nuclear weapons, however interested some military men may have been in not foreclosing professional exploration of the subject. In addition to these essentially political injunctions against embracing a doctrine of limited tactical nuclear warfare, another factor may also have been present, namely, uncertainty as to the operational prospects of implementing such a doctrine, particularly in the European theater.

In this regard, the efficacy of command and control arrangements for the Soviet theater forces in Europe was perhaps the central question. Throughout Khrushchev's time, efforts to develop a suitable command and control system for both the armed forces and the country as a whole engaged increasing attention, but the results often appeared to fall short of the requirements. With respect to the theater forces deployed against Europe, the system that emerged embodied a rather high degree of centralization in command and control functions, including those of nuclear custody, targeting, and firing authority. On the other hand, Soviet theater doctrine—with its emphasis on mobility, high rates of advance, and dispersal—underscored a need for greater independence and initiative of command at lower unit levels. How to reconcile tight central control with a tactical doctrine calling for greater flexibility was thus a complex problem for the system to meet.

The pros and cons of the arrangements adopted can hardly be weighed here, but several observations seem worth making. The tendency to exercise tight centralized control over the operations of lower echelons probably facilitated close supervision of the theater forces in peacetime crises or in hostilities among third parties, decreasing the chances of any unauthorized commitment of Soviet forces, especially nuclear weapons. Similarly, the prospect that the use of Soviet forces in minor clashes or incidents would be subject to close control probably posed no question. What would have happened had major

---

[83] See, for example, I. Glagolev and V. Larionov, "Soviet Defence Might and Peaceful Coexistence," *International Affairs*, no. 11 (November 1963): 30–31. For a fuller discussion of Soviet criticism of American damage-limiting concepts, including those given by Secretary of Defense Robert McNamara in his Ann Arbor speech of June 16, 1962, see Wolfe, *Soviet Strategy at the Crossroads*, pp. 163–65, 248–55.

operations been set in motion in the European theater, however, was another matter. In that event, the command and control system might neither have measured up to the task of conducting fast-moving operations on a maximum scale nor have permitted effective options for controlled limitation of the warfare already underway.

Limiting Third-Power Conflicts in Europe

The generally negative Soviet attitude of the Khrushchev period toward the prospect of applying limitations upon warfare in the European theater apparently rested on the professed view that the nuclear powers would find themselves immediately involved militarily in any local hostilities in the center of Europe and that such a conflict, therefore, would be extremely difficult to contain. However, as demonstrated by Soviet rhetoric and, more graphically, by Soviet crisis behavior, the Kremlin leadership was by no means insensitive to the problem of limiting third-power conflicts that might arise in Europe.

One such hypothetical case, which received a good deal of attention on the rhetorical level, was that of a conflict involving in some way the two rival German regimes. Whether they really considered it likely or not, the Soviets frequently asserted that West Germany might start a local war against East Germany on its own initiative, hoping thereby to draw in the major powers.[84]

Although Soviet propaganda, in its portrayal of West German "revanchism," emphasized the dire retaliation that any attack on a Soviet client in East Europe would call forth, and thus tended to obscure the Soviet Union's interest in crisis containment, there were occasional signs that some thought was being given to the possibility of isolating third-party conflicts so as to check the danger of their escalating to the level of a strategic nuclear exchange between the United States and the USSR. Among such indications were the remarks of four of the Sokolovskii authors in November 1963 in an article responding to US commentary on the first edition of their book.[85] The Soviet writers made a studied effort to explain that retaliatory nuclear attacks by the Soviet Union upon the United States would not follow automatically in the event of an attack by unnamed "imperialist forces" on a member of the Soviet bloc. Nuclear retaliation, they said, would be aimed at the United States only if the latter's forces had been used in the first instance. This suggested that, in the event of a local conflict in Europe, there were at least some situations in which the Soviet Union might hope to lower the possibility of automatic escalation by distinguishing between the actions of the United States and those of third powers.

[84] See, for example, A. Prokhorov, "The Possibility of Preventing and the Danger of Unleashing Wars," *Krasnaia zvezda*, December 26, 1962; "Dangerous Activity Threatening the Interests of Peace: Note of the Soviet Government to the Government of the USA," *Pravda*, July 13, 1964; Sokolovskii et al., *Voennaia strategiia*, p. 362.

[85] Major Generals I. Zav'ialov, V. Kolechitskii, and M. Cherednichenko, and Colonel V. Larionov, "Against Slanders and Falsifications: Concerning the U.S. Editions of the Book *Military Strategy*," *Krasnaia zvezda*, November 2, 1963. For fuller discussion of the Soviet riposte, see Wolfe, *Soviet Strategy at the Crossroads*, pp. 127–29.

The best gauge of the Soviet Union's interest in keeping the pot of local conflict situations in Europe and adjacent areas from boiling over and creating danger of a war between the superpowers was to be found, however, in its crisis behavior. Although the Soviet role in the various crises of the Khrushchev period differed in detail from one case to another, the Kremlin demonstrated that it was not prepared to allow its backing of a third-party disputant to embroil it in a major military showdown with the United States. Leaving aside the recurrent Berlin crises of 1958–62 and the challenge to Soviet authority from within the Warsaw bloc in the fall of 1956—instances in which the Soviet Union was acting less on behalf of the third parties than in its own immediate interests—perhaps the most pertinent examples of Soviet "crisis management" in serious third-party conflicts were those of Suez in 1956 and Cyprus in 1964. While peripheral in location to continental Europe itself, these crises were intimately interwoven with European political and security issues, and each posed the question of Soviet intervention at the risk of a great power clash.

In the 1956 Suez crisis, Khrushchev's rhetorical and material support of Egypt fell short of direct military intervention and thus foreshadowed in at least one key respect the steps taken by his successors during the crucial phase of the next Arab–Israeli clash, eleven years later. On the other hand, Khrushchev's contention that he had cooled down the "imperialists" and saved Egypt by threatening to bring his missiles into action against Britain was a feature of Soviet diplomacy in 1956 which his successors failed to emulate.[86]

In the Cyprus case, which grew to crisis dimensions in July and August 1964, toward the very end of Khrushchev's tenure, the Kremlin found itself in a position where the opportunity to fish in troubled waters and to enhance the divisive impact of that situation upon NATO had to be balanced against the danger of a widening war. The test of which element of Soviet policy would prevail—that of championing the Makarios government's campaign for "complete independence" at the risk of an escalating conflict or that of dampening a dangerous turn in the crisis—came when Turkish air strikes were carried out against northern Cyprus between August 7 and August 9. The result was a textbook case of Soviet crisis management under Khrushchev, marked by Soviet ambivalence at the peak of the crisis; vigorous expression of Soviet support and threats not to "remain on the sidelines" as the crisis entered the downslope; followed, as the crisis subsided, by assertions that Soviet policy had cut short "military gambles" and saved the peace.[87]

To sum up, one may say that, while Soviet military doctrine of the Khrushchev period was on the whole uncongenial to the idea of imposing effective limitations of one sort or another upon warfare in Europe, especially if the

[86] On Khrushchev's diplomacy in the Suez crisis, see chapter V, pp. 80–81.

[87] For a more detailed examination of Soviet crisis management in the Cyprus case, see Wolfe, *Trends in Soviet Thinking on Theater Warfare*, pp. 61–68. See also Dankwart A. Rustow, *The Cyprus Conflict and United States Security Interests*, The RAND Corporation, RM-5416-ISA, September 1967, FOUO.

armed forces of the nuclear powers had already come to grips, the same was not true of Soviet attitudes toward the containment of third-power conflicts. Here, in keeping with the long-standing Soviet practice of exercising tight political control over the use of Soviet military power, Khrushchev was evidently confident that crisis situations could be handled without posing the problem of unpremeditated commitment of Soviet forces. What the Soviet Union might do in a given situation to observe limitations on military involvement in third-party conflicts was therefore mainly a matter of weighing the political opportunities presented by the crisis against the danger of escalation which deliberate Soviet military intervention would entail. As the record shows, Khrushchev was not disposed to let an appetite for political profit becloud his judgment as to the risks of escalation.

X

THE END OF THE KHRUSHCHEV REGIME:
A SUMMING UP

Nikita Khrushchev's fall from power, in October 1964, underlined once more the uncertain historical fate to which Soviet political leaders are subject in a system that has found it necessary to disown or denounce virtually every leader of major stature save Lenin. In Khrushchev's case it is still not clear what place he will eventually occupy in the pantheon of aberrant Soviet leaders. Only upon rare occasions has Khrushchev's name appeared in Soviet accounts of the era in which he stood at the pinnacle of politics, and even criticism of his works has left him in the twilight status of an historical "unperson."[1]

This last phenomenon was particularly evident at the Twenty-third Party Congress, in April 1966, where not a single speaker pronounced Khrushchev's name, although his faults were freely criticized under the general label of "subjectivism."[2] Similarly, mention of Khrushchev was conspicuously absent

[1] Among the rare occasions upon which Khrushchev has emerged into public view since October 1964, apart from the few times he has come out to cast his ballot on election day in Moscow, was his appearance in 1967 in a televised film, ostensibly furnished to the West by "private" sources within the Soviet Union. The film, showing scenes of Khrushchev in retirement and including his reminiscences on some of the events in which he took part as leader of the Soviet Union, apparently was intended as a rebuttal to foreign criticism of the treatment of Khrushchev as a historical unperson. See "TV: A Study of Khrushchev Living in Retirement," *New York Times*, July 12, 1967.

Khrushchev's close associates in the upper levels of the Soviet hierarchy have studiously refrained from mentioning him by name, even when criticizing his leadership. For example, Leonid Brezhnev denounced Khrushchev's management of agriculture at a Central Committee Plenum in March 1965 at considerable length, without ever bringing his name into the discussion. See *Plenum Tsentral'nogo Komiteta Kommunisticheskoi Partii Sovetskogo Soiuza, 24–26 marta 1965 goda; stenograficheskii otchet* (Plenum of the Central Committee of the Communist Party of the Soviet Union, March 24–26, 1965: Stenographic Report) (Moscow, 1965). There has, however, been some slight easing of the ban on mention of Khrushchev's name in some Soviet media. Thus, a popularized account of Soviet foreign policy of the Khrushchev period published in both Russian and English in 1967 mentioned Khrushchev once in referring to President Kennedy's meeting at Vienna in 1961 with "Nikita Khrushchev, the then Chairman of the Council of Ministers of the USSR." V. Israelyan, chief editor, *Soviet Foreign Policy: A Brief Review, 1955–1965* (Moscow: Progress Publishers, 1967), p. 255. One of the few positive references to Khrushchev in Soviet media appeared in a 1966 party document, which approved his 1950 proposal to consolidate kolkhoz collective farms. A. A. Dobrodomov and A. N. Ponomarev, chief editors, *Ocherki istorii moskovskoi organizatsii KPSS, 1883–1965* (Outline History of the Moscow Party Organization, 1883–1965) (Moscow: Workers Publishing House, 1966), p. 624.

[2] In addition to "subjectivism," the mistakes generally charged to Khrushchev, at the Twenty-third Party Congress and earlier, without his being identified by name included "arbitrary decisions," resort to "administrative methods" as a cure-all for difficult problems, and "misinterpreta-

from the vast outpouring of articles and speeches devoted to looking back at a half-century of Soviet history in connection with the Soviet Union's anniversary celebration in November 1967.[3] All of this suggests that his successors have chosen to postpone the problem of assessing Khrushchev's theoretical and practical contributions to Soviet society by consigning him, at least temporarily, to what amounts to historical oblivion.

Needless to say, in summing up some features of the Khrushchev decade that are germane to this inquiry, we shall not be attempting to provide a definitive assessment of Khrushchev's career nor of the period in which he ruled. Apart from some observations on Khrushchev's as yet unsettled role in Soviet history and his contribution to processes of change in the Soviet system, we shall be mainly concerned with reviewing the consequences of his policies in the fields of foreign and military affairs, especially as these matters bear upon Soviet policy toward Europe.

Khrushchev as a Transitional Leader in a Period of Change

Pending an ultimate assessment of Khrushchev's place in his country's history,[4] many Western students of Soviet affairs have tended to regard him as an essentially transitional figure, who chanced to preside over a society in the process of change and who served as a bridge between the harsh autocracy of the Stalinist period and the less rigid oligarchic rule of the present collective leadership.[5] In this view, Khrushchev's salient contribution lay in recognizing that governance through coercion and ruthless goading from above had become more and more unsuitable as the Soviet Union evolved into a more mature and complex industrial society, a development that required a shift from the totalitarian "command system" of the age of Stalin to a system of rule somewhat more responsive to pluralistic pressures from below and employing more subtle methods of incentive and persuasion.

Although it is difficult to say whether Khrushchev will ever come to be con-

---

tion" of Communist theory. See, for example, speeches by L. I. Brezhnev, *Pravda*, March 30, 1966; and by N. G. Egorychev, V. S. Tolstikov, and D. A. Kunaev, *Pravda*, March 31, 1966. See also leading editorial, "The Ideological Weapon of the Party," *Kommunist*, no. 4 (March 1965): 7–11.

[3] Similarly, Khrushchev's presence was "edited out" of a series of documentary films inaugurated in the fall of 1967 to record the history of fifty years of Soviet rule. Reuters dispatch, "Soviets Put Nikita Out of Picture," *Washington Post*, January 7, 1968.

[4] Although a definitive assessment of Khrushchev's career and its impact on Soviet society probably awaits the longer perspective which only the passage of time can furnish, there is already a growing literature on the subject in the West. Among the more recent additions to this literature, see Martin Page, *The Day Khrushchev Fell* (New York: Hawthorn Books, 1965); Edward Crankshaw, *Khrushchev: A Career* (New York: Viking Press, 1966); Carl A. Linden, *Khrushchev and the Soviet Leadership, 1957–1964* (Baltimore, Md.: Johns Hopkins Press, 1966); Mark Frankland, *Khrushchev* (New York: Stein & Day, 1967); Michel Tatu, *Le Pouvoir en URSS: de Krouchtchev à la direction collective* (Paris: B. Grasset, 1967). See also review article by Richard T. Davies, "Lest He Be Forgotten," *Problems of Communism* (July–August 1967): 64–66.

[5] Merle Fainsod, "Khrushchevism," *Problems of Communism* (January–February 1965): 9; Richard Lowenthal, "The Revolution Withers Away," ibid., p. 14; Howard R. Swearer, "Cults, Coups and Collective Leaderships," *Current History* (October 1965): 243–44.

sidered a social architect of the stature of Lenin and Stalin, it is generally conceded that his rather flamboyant populism and his frequently impetuous search for effective leadership remedies helped to stimulate important forces of change within Soviet society after the death of Stalin, just as his de-Stalinization program and his promises of a better and more abundant life for the Soviet people lent impetus to a new revolution of rising expectations among the population.[6] Indeed, a substantial body of evidence can be summoned to document the process of internal change that marked the Khrushchev era. It includes: the emergence of what might be called "creeping pluralism" as various institutional and interest groups gradually found more elbow room within the system after Stalin's demise; greater attention at the top to popular attitudes and to feedback from the creative intelligentsia; reduction in the power of the secret police; recognition of the need to reform the Stalinist command economy by a somewhat more balanced allocation of resources and by contemplating, among other things, the introduction of techniques borrowed from Western market economies; a reorganization of the party *apparat* along production-oriented lines, accompanied by some blurring of distinctions between party and state functions; and tendencies toward the gradual *embourgeoisement* of Soviet society itself.

If few would question that Khrushchev left the Soviet Union a decidedly different place than he found it, there is less agreement on how to interpret the changes which took place during his regime. Were these changes, for example, indicative of a secular trend in the development of Soviet Communist society away from its earlier totalitarian forms and ideological drives, and can they therefore be interpreted to mean that a fundamental and at least potentially "benign" transformation of the Soviet system and the outlook of its ruling elite was set in motion under Khrushchev? Or should we wait until further returns are in with respect to changes at work within the Soviet Union, and the direction in which they may lead, before postulating a decisive erosion of the totalitarian syndrome which long characterized the Soviet system? Needless to say, there is no simple yardstick for determining which of these, or other, viewpoints answers to the reality of Soviet life.

It is worth noting, however, that the case for a far-reaching transformation of the Soviet system owes a good deal to the search among Western scholars for new models and methodologies for the study of Soviet society and politics in the post-Stalin period. The use of varied theoretical approaches to an understanding of Soviet reality is, of course, by no means a new phenomenon, as Daniel Bell made clear some years ago.[7] However, as the Khrushchev period unfolded, Western analysts of the Soviet system began increasingly to turn away from the model of self-perpetuating totalitarianism which has been

---

[6] Peter H. Juviler and Henry W. Morton, eds., *Soviet Policy-Making: Studies of Communism in Transition* (New York: Frederick A. Praeger, Inc., 1967), pp. v–xi; Linden, *Khrushchev and the Soviet Leadership*, p. 230.

[7] "Ten Theories in Search of Reality," in Daniel Bell, *The End of Ideology* (Glencoe, Ill.: Free Press, 1960), pp. 300–34.

generally employed to describe Stalin's Russia,[8] looking instead to the concepts of comparative systems analysis for new models better suited to the interpretation of the processes of change, diversification, and interest-group politics at work within the formal structure of Soviet institutions.[9]

Although some analysts still show a preference for what are essentially revised versions of the totalitarian model, such as Zbigniew Brzezinski's "voluntarist totalitarianism"[10] and Allen Kassof's "administered society,"[11] others offer a variety of new models, which suggest that the Soviet Union emerged during the Khrushchev period as a distinctly post-totalitarian society. Among the new approaches built around the concept of modernizing society is the "bureaucratic" model proposed by Alfred G. Meyer, who believes that one can best understand the Soviet system by comparing it with complex modern bureaucratic systems anywhere.[12] The "modernization" approach rests on the premise that Soviet development in essence is part of a general historical process through which various societies have sought to meet the challenge of industrialization and modernization, rather than the unique creation of a system whose primary aim it is to fulfill the millennial ideology of Marxism–Leninism or to keep a self-perpetuating party elite in power. In this view, the totalitarian model adequately described the Soviet system during its earlier stages of forced industrial growth and establishment of Communist authority and legitimacy, whereas the bureaucratic model applies more aptly to a well-established society in which modernization, rather than the maximizing of political power, is the driving force or chief aim of the system.[13]

[8] The totalitarian model found its fullest elaboration in the work of Hannah Arendt, *The Origins of Totalitarianism* (New York: Harcourt, Brace & Co., 1951), and Carl J. Friedrich and Zbigniew Brzezinski, *Totalitarian Dictatorship and Autocracy* (Cambridge, Mass.: Harvard University Press, 1956). Brzezinski anticipated a revision of the totalitarian model with his version of "rationalized totalitarianism," intended to take into account the reduction of overt coercion and terror in the Soviet Union after the death of Stalin (see his "Totalitarianism and Rationality," *American Political Science Review* [September 1956]: 751–63), and later offered a model of "voluntarist totalitarianism" as distinct from the earlier "terrorist totalitarianism" of the Stalinist period. For an exposition and critique of the "voluntarist" model, see Zbigniew Brzezinski, "The Nature of the Soviet System," and Robert C. Tucker, "The Question of Totalitarianism," in Donald W. Treadgold, ed., *The Development of the USSR: An Exchange of Views* (Seattle, Wash.: University of Washington Press, 1964), pp. 3–20 and 29–34, respectively.

[9] For an informative discussion of the model-building problem by several leading American scholars (Alfred G. Meyer, John A. Armstrong, John H. Kautsky, Dan N. Jacobs, and Robert S. Sharlet), see the symposium in *Slavic Review* (March 1967): 1–28. See also Arnold L. Horelick, *Fifty Years After October: Party and Society in the USSR*, The RAND Corporation, P-3630, September 1967, pp. 5–16.

[10] See fn. 8, above.

[11] Allen Kassof, "The Administered Society: Totalitarianism Without Terror," *World Politics* (July 1964): 558–74.

[12] See Meyer's article, "The Comparative Study of Communist Political Systems," in *Slavic Review* (March 1967): 3–12, and his "USSR, Incorporated," in Treadgold, *The Development of the USSR*, pp. 21–28. A more comprehensive presentation of Meyer's ideas on the inadequacy of the totalitarian model in depicting the Soviet system may be found in his book, *The Soviet Political System: An Interpretation* (New York: Random House, Inc., 1965), especially pp. 467–80. See also Robert C. Tucker, "The Dictator and Totalitarianism," *World Politics* (July 1965): 555–83.

[13] The interest attached to "model-building" by Western scholars raises the question of what

Differing Views on Internal Soviet Evolution

The once dominant totalitarian image of the Soviet system and the newer conceptual models are not necessarily mutually exclusive, but they do lead to somewhat different interpretations of the direction in which the internal development of post-Stalin Soviet may point. Analysts who favor the use of the modernization model or other variants derived from comparative social-political systems theory,[14] for example, often interpret trends of the post-Stalin period more or less optimistically, on the grounds that societal changes produced in the Soviet Union by the process of industrialization are helping to bring about an evolutionary transformation of the Soviet political system as well.

Only a minority is prepared to argue that the industrialization process is the great equalizer that is leading toward a "convergence" of the Soviet system and Western societies.[15] Indeed, some scholars of the modernization school are careful to point out that Soviet industrialization does not necessarily point toward democratization and may even lead Soviet society into some new form of totalitarianism.[16] The more common viewpoint, however, is one of guarded optimism about the prospects of the Soviet Union's advance along an evolutionary path of internal development, as contrasted with Stalin's coercive, revolutionary social engineering from above.[17] At the least, as some see it, industrial-technological change, by placing a premium on the USSR's

kind of model the Soviet leadership itself might entertain for the system. As Arnold Horelick observes (*Fifty Years After October*, pp. 11–15), if one were to postulate a model of the Soviet system as "officially" sanctioned by the Soviet leadership, it would probably prescribe at least three central aims for the system: to maximize the party leadership's political control and power; to promote industrial growth and modernization; and to reshape human behavior and social relations in accordance with the norms of an ideal future Communist society. Since these aims and the realities with which the Soviet leadership must deal are unlikely to fall harmoniously into line, the chances are that such a model approximates a working description of the system no better than many of those constructed by outside observers. It might be added that the "self-descriptive" Soviet model also fails to include external goals, such as increasing Soviet influence abroad.

[14] For an interesting demonstration of the way in which comparative social-political systems theory, as expounded by David Easton, Gabriel A. Almond, Karl W. Deutsch, Lucian W. Pye, and others, has been applied to analysis of the Soviet system, see Frederick C. Barghoorn, "Prospects for Soviet Political Development: Evolution, Decay or Revolution?" paper presented at the 6th International Conference on World Politics, Berlin, September 4–8, 1967. See also papers presented at the same conference by H. Gordon Skilling, "The Party, Opposition and Interest Groups: Fifty Years of Continuity and Change," and Dan N. Jacobs, "Politburo Actors in the First and Fifth Decades of the Soviet Power."

[15] For a discussion of the various grounds on which "convergence" theories rest, which comes to the conclusion that such factors as industrialization and economic rationality do not necessarily point toward erosion of the ideological and power monopoly of the ruling party in the Soviet Union, see Zbigniew Brzezinski and Samuel P. Huntington, *Political Power: USA/USSR* (New York: Viking Press, 1963), pp. 9–14, 419–29.

[16] See, for example, Alfred Meyer in Treadgold, *The Development of the USSR*, p. 25. Soviet leaders themselves have been antipathetic to convergence theories, terming them "silly" and "slanderous fabrications." See Adam B. Ulam, *Expansion and Coexistence: The History of Soviet Foreign Policy, 1917–67* (New York: Frederick A. Praeger, Inc., 1968), p. 722.

[17] Barghoorn, "Prospects for Soviet Political Development," pp. 2–3, 8. See also Frederick C. Barghoorn, *Politics in the USSR* (Boston, Mass.: Little, Brown & Co., 1966), pp. 375–85, 387.

scientists, engineers, and managers, is undermining the political monopoly of the party, which needs the professionally skilled more than these groups need the party.[18] In fact, the pressure of diverse professional and societal interests upon the party can be seen as opening an avenue toward development of some kind of constitutional order within the one-party Soviet system.[19] Khrushchev himself is sometimes credited with having created conditions, through such steps as de-Stalinization and restoration of party norms, which not only will make a return to one-man dictatorship difficult but also may lead to a more institutionalized pattern of restraints upon the arbitrary exercise of political power.[20] Even the fact that Khrushchev's removal from power, a bloodless one, did not precipitate an internal crisis can be regarded as a step toward normality in Soviet political life, an evolutionary triumph of sorts for Khrushchevism.[21]

On the other hand, analysts who still lean toward some version of the totalitarian model are apt to take a much less sanguine view of how deeply the process of change during the Khrushchev era may have affected the Soviet system, at least with respect to its evolutionary progress in a "benign" direction. At the extreme, for example, is the contention that the Khrushchev period was symptomatic of a grave inner crisis of a system which, unable in its totalitarian rigidity to cope with the increasingly complex problems confronting it, is headed for collapse in the not too distant future.[22] In short, what lies ahead, according to this view, is not evolutionary change but revolutionary breakdown. A more common variant of this belief, holding that crisis situations have been endemic to the Soviet system since its outset, sees crises in the post-Stalin period not in terms of outright collapse of the system but rather in terms of the degree to which the entrenched party elite can adapt its methods of rule to prevent the system from slowing down and losing its dynamism.[23] In this view, Khrushchev's leadership tended to provide an illusion of movement and political innovation which merely disguised the difficulties of transforming a doctrinaire party dictatorship into a more pluralistic and creative system of rule. Whether the party elite eventually will succeed in

[18] Albert Parry, "Will the Soviet Technocrats Take Over?" paper presented at research colloquium, Institute for Sino–Soviet Studies, The George Washington University, March 7, 1967, pp. 1–2.

[19] Barghoorn, *Politics in the USSR*, pp. 379–80.

[20] Jerome M. Gilison, "New Factors of Stability in Soviet Collective Leadership," *World Politics* (July 1967): 578–79.

[21] Ibid., p. 572. See also Frankland, *Khrushchev*, p. 206.

[22] For views of two outside observers on potential internal collapse of the Soviet regime, see Michel Garder, *L'Agonie du régime en Russie soviétique* (Paris: La Table Ronde, 1965); Michel Tatu, "The Beginning of the End?" *Problems of Communism* (March–April 1966): 44–47. For a biting analysis by a dissident Soviet historian who foresees collapse of the regime "sometime between 1980 and 1985," see Andrei Amalrik, *Will the Soviet Union Survive Until 1984?* (New York: Harper and Row, 1970), especially p. 64.

[23] Zbigniew Brzezinski, "The Soviet Political System: Transformation or Degeneration?" *Problems of Communism* (January–February 1966): 1–15. See also Seweryn Bialer, "Soviet Leadership: Some Problems of Continuity, Structure and Cohesion," paper delivered at the annual meeting of the American Political Science Association, New York, September 1966, pp. 2–3.

carrying out the institutional reforms necessary to preserve the vitality of the system, however, is left an open question.

Still different grounds may be found for reserving judgment on how far the trends of the post-Stalin period may go toward altering the Soviet political system. Rather than stress the crisis of transition from the old forms of totalitarian rule in a changing society, for example, some analysts place the emphasis on the political leadership's demonstrated ability to survive change without having either to curtail its power to initiate and veto or to open up Soviet society to broadly representative political forces in the Western sense.[24] Even though barriers may have been erected against autocratic dictatorship of the Stalinist type, oligarchic rule under the norms of "collective leadership" need not, in this view, presage a significantly wider sharing of political power. This rather cautious appraisal of the liberalizing potential of internal change in the Soviet Union derives from the presumed durability of the Soviet political leadership, a ruling elite of strongly authoritarian outlook inclined to impose upon Soviet society its own set of values, interests, and objectives, and apparently capable of doing so with some success. Although, during the Khrushchev period, the Soviet ruling elite was by no means immune to internal factionalism, including conservative-reformist cleavages in leadership politics,[25] it nevertheless had the cohesiveness and political skill to keep its internal policy conflicts from leading to any serious breakdown of established values and patterns of social-political action within the larger society. Thus it can be argued that the political leadership, rather than being carried along by the process of change, remained able to control it, and to apply the brakes should reformist ideas and expectations appear to threaten the integrity of the system itself.

As for Khrushchev's own innovatory activities, most of the measures he initiated in the field of internal policy, such as the Virgin Lands agricultural scheme, the reorganization of the party to delineate its role in economic supervision, and the various campaigns for grassroots social controls, may be seen as primarily improvisations responding to difficulties of the moment, rather than as steps informed by a consistent design for radical reform and transformation of the Soviet system.[26] Even if Khrushchev's reform policies

---

[24] For useful discussions setting out both the scope of changes in the Soviet system and the limits of such change in terms of evolution toward Western-style political values, see Henry W. Morton, "The Structure of Decision-Making in the USSR," in Juviler and Morton, *Soviet Policy-Making*, especially pp. 12–16; Adam B. Ulam, *The New Face of Soviet Totalitarianism* (New York: Frederick A. Praeger, Inc., 1965), pp. 111–16; Merle Fainsod, "Roads to the Future," *Problems of Communism* (July–August 1967): 21–23. See also T. H. Rigby and L. G. Churchward, *Policy-Making in the USSR, 1953–1961: Two Views* (Melbourne: Lansdowne Press, 1962), pp. 18–20, 40–42.

[25] Linden, *Khrushchev and the Soviet Leadership*, p. 7.

[26] The burden of Soviet criticism of Khrushchev's policies is, of course, that they were replete with hare-brained schemes and improvisations. Though it is probably unwise to judge Khrushchev's performance by the criticism of his successors, it would seem that consistency and a constant sense of direction were not among his virtues. So far as the issue of reform is concerned, it may well be that Khrushchev's associates were wary of his reforming zeal precisely because it

had a certain underlying consistency, or added up to an evolutionary pattern more or less by accident, there were obviously limits to the kinds of change he was prepared to tolerate. Thus, for example, his determination to combat ideological erosion, as shown in his insistence that a peaceful coexistence line did not mean "ideological coexistence." In short, while Khrushchev was no doubt a modernizer, he also remained a true believer in the Marxist–Leninist gospel.

Divergent Opinion on Changing Patterns of External Soviet Behavior

Just as there are divergent views of the extent to which the internal character of the Soviet system underwent evolutionary transformation during the Khrushchev decade, so there are differing opinions as to how deeply developments of this period may have altered Soviet conceptions of the USSR's role on the world stage and the operative behavior of its leaders. The compelling necessity to work out terms of nuclear coexistence with the United States, the disturbing discovery that world Communist unity had been fractured by the rise of a new center of Communist power in Peking, and the opening of opportunities for revolutionary progress in the underdeveloped countries of the former colonial world were among the developments of the Khrushchev era that undoubtedly had a strong influence on the Soviet leadership's view of the world, especially with regard to the prospects for further advance toward worldwide communism. However, the net effect of such factors upon the outlook of the Soviet ruling elite is subject to widely disparate interpretations.

According to one school of thought, the revolutionary dynamism of the Soviet ruling elite, already on the wane when Khrushchev came to power, slackened still further during the decade of his rule, even though he sought at times to furnish a fresh example of dynamic leadership.[27] A growing sense of the big powers' mutual interest in avoiding nuclear war, a desire to preserve the hard-won gains of a mature industrialized society, and an image of the Soviet state as the residuary legatee of Russian national interests were thought to account for a pattern of operative behavior by Khrushchev and his colleagues which could be construed as marking the abandonment of the Marxist–Leninist mission to remake the world, despite the ideological lip service that continued to be paid to this goal. Khrushchev's search for détente in Soviet relations with the United States and the West, following his series of spectacular but unsuccessful ventures in missile diplomacy, could be taken as the practical manifestation of this revisionist tendency, to which further testimony lay in charges from Peking that Khrushchev's fear of nuclear confrontation with the West was immobilizing the Soviet Union's support of the world revolu-

---

was directed erratically and unexpectedly in ways which offended vested interests within the regime. See Carl A. Linden, "No Room for Radicalism," *Problems of Communism* (May–June 1965): 39.

[27] Lowenthal, in *Problems of Communism* (January–February 1965): 15–16.

tionary movement and leading to its accommodation with the capitalist enemy.[28]

The inference sometimes drawn from this reading of tendencies in the leadership under Khrushchev is that an essentially pragmatic outlook had come to supplant the revolutionary ethos, leading perhaps toward a quiet shelving of the notion of a universal Communist order and the tacit acceptance of the traditional concept of the national state as the terminal form of the Soviet system. Such a state, in turn, might be expected to act more "conventionally" on the international stage, pursuing policies animated less by a revolutionary urge to reshape the world in the Communist image than by an evolutionary tendency toward accommodation with the world as it is.

Again, however, one can find expert opinion which for various reasons considers it premature to assume that the Soviet leadership in Khrushchev's day took on a frankly status quo mentality, even though it may have come to recognize that rival forms of sociopolitical and economic organization in the world were too hardy to succumb to the classical Marxist pattern of Communist revolution through capitalist breakdown.[29] Rather, as one school of thought would argue, the dual nature of Soviet foreign policy remained essentially unchanged, still combining revolutionary with traditional-national elements, though pursuing its aims in a more sophisticated fashion under the hazardous conditions of the nuclear age.[30] According to another view, ideological erosion within Soviet society need not necessarily lead to more reasonable international conduct, but may in fact cause the party leadership to seek ambitious foreign policy successes in order to revive flagging ideological expectations and enhance its authority.[31] Or, as a variant interpretation of the influence of Communist ideology upon Soviet foreign policy would have it, ideology has always served a primarily instrumental function of justifying moves taken for reasons of prudence or opportunity,[32] and the presumed erosion of ideological motives is thus largely irrelevant to Soviet conduct in the international arena.

The critical question left unsettled by the Khrushchev period, in any case, is the extent to which the Soviet leadership's new perception of the realities of world politics may have moved it toward acceptance of the prevailing system

---

[28] Crankshaw, *Khrushchev: A Career*, p. 280.

[29] For a perceptive analysis of the history of Communist revolutions, which points out that they have tended to be revolutions of underdevelopment and modernization rather than revolutions of capitalist breakdown in the classical Marxist sense, see Robert C. Tucker, "Paths of Communist Revolution: 1917–1967," paper presented at the Sixth Conference on World Politics, West Berlin, September 1967, especially pp. 8–11.

[30] Arguments supporting this viewpoint may be found in a paper by Kurt L. London, "Soviet Foreign Policy: Fifty Years of Dualism," delivered at the foregoing Conference. For a sage appraisal of the interacting role of ideology and *Realpolitik* in Soviet foreign policy, see James L. Richardson, *Germany and the Atlantic Alliance: The Interaction of Strategy and Politics* (Cambridge, Mass.: Harvard University Press, 1966), pp. 99–110.

[31] Ulam, *The New Face of Soviet Totalitarianism*, pp. 74–75, 87–90.

[32] See, for example, Robert V. Daniels, "Doctrine and Foreign Policy," *Survey* (October 1965): 5, 13.

of "conventional" power rivalry among national states, as distinct from a "double-standard" mode of competition aimed at scrapping that very system. Although there is a good deal to be said for the proposition that the hazards of the nuclear age and Soviet discord with China may have driven the Soviet Union closer toward genuine accommodation with the West, it is open to doubt whether Khrushchev and his colleagues had actually come around to the point of discarding their revolutionary heritage in order to embrace a truly revisionist doctrine of underwriting international stability and orderly change in concert with the Western world.

Only the future course of Soviet internal development and international conduct will tell us which of the alternative appraisals sketched above most accurately reflects the changes wrought in the Soviet system and the outlook of its ruling elite during the Khrushchev era. Should the repressive behavior to which Khrushchev's successors reverted in their efforts to enforce orthodox conformity at home and to stamp out Czechoslovak "reform communism" abroad continue to prevail, one would find it necessary to conclude that appraisals skeptical of mellowing changes in the Soviet system had come closest to the mark. On the other hand, should the more optimistic views of the evolutionary transformation of the system under Khrushchev turn out to stand the test of time better than other interpretations, then Khrushchev is indeed likely to go down in history as the Great Revisionist who, inadvertently perhaps helped to prepare the historical burial of the wrong party.

Khrushchev's Policy Record and Its European Implications

Whatever Khrushchev's claims to greatness as the leader of the world's foremost Communist state may ultimately be, his record in the foreign policy field seems unlikely to stand at the top of the list. From the Communist standpoint, perhaps the deepest disappointment of the decade in which Khrushchev served as the chief architect of Soviet foreign and military policy was the paradoxical fact that, even though he had at his disposal far more formidable instruments of power than Stalin, his policies yielded far less in the way of Communist expansion beyond the borders of the Soviet state than had been achieved under Stalin's rule.

Apart from the addition of North Vietnam and Cuba to the Communist camp—for which Khrushchev could scarcely take the credit—he could point to no new large-scale gains to sustain the notion of the continuing historical march of communism. Indeed, instead of improving the fortunes of the world Communist movement, his tenure left the Communist bloc in considerable disarray, its once-vaunted monolithic unity weakened by inner tensions and discord, of which the Sino–Soviet conflict was the most egregious example. Perhaps the most that could be said on Khrushchev's behalf with regard to improving the "world-historical" prospects of the Communist movement was that the divisive tendencies he helped to stir up within it might eventually stimulate the emergence of more supple doctrines of revolution, better suited to a world of diversity than the pseudo-monolithic precepts passed along from Stalin's day.

If Khrushchev's immediate contributions to the unity and the revolutionary momentum of world communism were unimpressive, his record as the promoter of the Soviet Union's great power interests in world politics was somewhat better, though still a bit untidy. He did preside over the Soviet Union's emergence as one of the two superpowers of the mid-twentieth century, wielding unprecedented influence over the affairs of the world. As the salesman of Soviet achievements in missile and space technology he left the Soviet Union's global prestige a good deal higher than he had found it, despite his inability to convert technological triumphs into concrete political gains. To the extent that persistent initiatives in foreign affairs helped to enhance his country's image as a great power, Khrushchev scored high with summit meetings, disarmament and peace-treaty proposals, and bids for Soviet influence among the new nations of the underdeveloped "Third World." He also managed to weather a series of conspicuous setbacks, from the unrest in Eastern Europe in 1956 to the Berlin and Cuba crises several years later, demonstrating, if nothing else, that he was a leader not easily discouraged by adversity.

And yet, though the impact of Khrushchev's policies and personality was widely and sometimes dramatically felt, there was curiously little to show, in terms of tangible gains, for the ten years in which his foreign policy maneuvers ran the gamut from intimidation to conciliation. On the plane of global rivalry with the United States, the Soviet Union under Khrushchev's aegis became a more versatile and powerful competitor, but still fell far short of closing the industrial-military gap, let alone the standard-of-living gap, between the two countries. In the Third World, where the "rules of engagement" between the United States and the Soviet Union remained much less distinct than those which evolved in Europe,[33] Khrushchev's policies met with mixed results. Although the Soviet Union improved its image as a new-found friend to emerging nations, the recipients of Soviet aid in many cases proved less eager to align themselves with the donor's interests than had been hoped. Moreover, the Kremlin's problem of exercising control over the new political forces in the Third World grew increasingly complicated as rivalry with Peking over the tactics and leadership of the "national-liberation" movement became more embittered.[34]

---

[33] As noted later, a tacit understanding emerged during the Khrushchev period that, in Europe, neither side could afford to encroach militarily upon the alliance system of the other. A similar set of clear-cut rules of engagement was lacking with regard to US–Soviet competition in the Third World. As pointed out by Herbert S. Dinerstein, one reason why US–Soviet differences over areas integral to each alliance system were often less intense in Europe than in the Third World was that, in the latter case, the *future* alignment of these countries was involved, and experience had shown that, if Third-World countries became communized, this was likely to be an irreversible process. See Dinerstein's "Fifty Years of Soviet Coexistence," paper delivered at the annual meeting of the American Political Science Association, Chicago, Ill., September 1967, p. 32.

[34] For discussion of various problems encountered by Soviet policy in the Third World, see Uri Ra'anan, "Tactics in the Third World: Contradictions and Dangers," *Survey* (October 1965):

As for Soviet policy toward Europe, the record of the Khrushchev decade
was hardly one to invite superlatives from Communist historians, although it
was by no means barren of useful results from other points of view. Perhaps
the chief illusion that Khrushchev was obliged to surrender after ten years of
restless European diplomacy was the hope that he could find a way to break
out of the stalemate in Europe which he had inherited from Stalin. That Khrushchev had hoped to bring about a major change in the European status quo
seemed amply demonstrated by the lengths to which he went in trying to dis-
lodge the Western powers from Berlin and to force a settlement of the German question. That he failed to do so was testimony not only to his inability
to bend history to his will—a limitation to which even the most resolute leaders are subject—but also to the obdurate character of the political and military realities that confronted him.

Among these, perhaps none was more fundamentally important than the
fact that Western Europe had recovered from its wartime exhaustion, attaining
an internal political stability and economic confidence that left it far less
vulnerable to many forms of Soviet pressure than it had been before Khrushchev's time. The healthy state of the advanced industrial countries of Western Europe, for example, virtually precluded the resumption of classical
revolutionary activities by the Communist parties in those nations, leaving it
largely up to Soviet *Realpolitik* to produce new gains in Europe for the
Soviet Union. Indeed, the rise of polycentric tendencies in some of the Communist parties of the West merely served to embarrass Khrushchev by lending further impetus to the centrifugal forces of "national communism" in the
countries of Eastern Europe.

But Soviet *Realpolitik* in Khrushchev's hands proved incapable of producing significant Soviet advances in Europe, not only because it was blunted by
the general European recovery but also because a variety of other factors
served to immobilize the Soviet military threat against Europe upon which,
in the last analysis, the efficacy of Khrushchev's power politics depended. The
physical dimensions of this threat, it may be recalled, grew appreciably during
Khrushchev's rule, and Soviet military theory also came up with a detailed
body of doctrine for conducting the European phase of any general war that
might occur. At the same time, however, even as the military-nuclear power
at Khrushchev's disposal was increasing, the prospect that it might be employed for a strategy of conquest in Europe, or even for lesser objectives in
Europe through military action, was declining, especially so after the Cuban
confrontation, the outcome of which went far toward dissipating any lingering
European fears of a Soviet military challenge in Europe.

Because, fortunately for all, Khrushchev's practice of *Realpolitik* at critical
junctures exposed him as a power politician whose bluff could be called, it
often has seemed only generous to credit him with basically peaceful inten-

26–37; Philip E. Mosely, "The Kremlin and the Third World," *Foreign Affairs* (October 1967):
64–77.

tions. Less widely recognized is the possibility that, if he had not been resisted, and if instead of rebuffs he had tasted important political and psychological victories over the Western powers, he might have been tempted to apply new and more dangerous pressures against Europe.[35] Whether Khrushchev's inhibitions against the active use of military forces to attain political ends in Europe grew primarily out of peaceful intentions or out of the conviction that military action in Europe was too dangerous to contemplate in the nuclear age is a matter of opinion which can hardly be settled here. But it does appear clear that, had Khrushchev wished to exert direct military pressure on Western Europe, he would have done so only if he had been confident that hostilities would not so spread as to endanger the Soviet Union itself and cause losses far outweighing anything he might hope to gain.

Here Khrushchev faced a basic dilemma which neither Soviet military policy nor political strategy could resolve. Only if convinced that the United States would not honor its commitment to employ its full war-making capacity in defense of the NATO countries could he calculate with assurance that hostilities, once started, would remain confined to Europe. As events suggested, the American deterrent in the service of European defense remained credible enough in Khrushchev's eyes to remove whatever temptation there might otherwise have been to exploit the local military advantages enjoyed by the Soviet Union in places like Berlin. Furthermore, the build-up of NATO itself, as manifested particularly in the rearming of West Germany and the growth of NATO's nuclear and conventional capabilities, also served to diminish the prospect of any easy or painless Soviet military moves, even though from the viewpoint of Western planners NATO's posture appeared less than satisfactory on various military and political grounds.

Other elements of the changing European situation with which Khrushchev was obliged to reckon also acted as constraints upon his ability to turn Soviet military power to political account in Europe. Though European recovery gradually reduced the sense of internal and external threat that had brought NATO into being, thus tending to loosen the unity of the Western alliance, Khrushchev was not in the best position to exploit this centrifugal trend. Not only was he obliged to contend with polycentric tendencies within the Eastern bloc that detracted from his efforts to manipulate differences among the NATO allies; his problem went further, for unless the Soviet Union could establish control over Europe in one swift move—a course virtually ruled out in his eyes by the danger of escalation to a major nuclear war—attempts to exploit Western disunity by missile diplomacy and other political-military pressures might, as in the past, merely stimulate European fears and bring about a new unity and resolve within the Western alliance.[36]

---

[35] Richardson, *Germany and the Atlantic Alliance*, pp. 296–98.

[36] Thornton Read, *Military Policy in a Changing Political Context* (Princeton, N.J.: Center of International Studies, Princeton University, December 1964), p. 25. It should be noted, however, that even though the nuclear balance in Europe ruled out hope of large-scale gains by direct Soviet military pressure, there was room for the Soviet Union to seek marginal gains from lower-level

That Khrushchev perceived the limitations of direct Soviet pressure upon Europe seems demonstrated by the search for alternatives that punctuated his policy toward Europe. For example, throughout the mid-fifties he employed a variety of diplomatic tactics to achieve such aims as preventing West German entry into NATO, creating dissension between the United States and its allies, winning recognition of the East German regime, securing arms limitations and a nuclear-free zone in Central Europe, and obstructing the consolidation of the Common Market. Unfortunately for Khrushchev, the payoff from these efforts was modest, save perhaps for the strain on NATO unity growing out of de Gaulle's later defiance of American leadership, for which Khrushchev himself could take little credit. Had the subtler forms of diplomacy which Krushchev called upon in the mid-fifties proved more successful, Khrushchev might never have embarked upon the riskier policy initiatives which began with his Berlin ultimatum of November 1958.

Even after the failure of the Berlin campaign, however, it apparently was not easy for Khrushchev to abandon the hope that he might wring significant concessions from the West through the renewed pressure of Soviet missile diplomacy. His last dramatic attempt to do so came in 1962, when, confronted with growing difficulties in the economic sphere at home and in party-state relationships within the Communist world itself, he undertook the secret deployment of missiles to Cuba. This was a move seemingly calculated to provide a stunning short-term improvement in the Soviet strategic posture vis-à-vis the United States, on the strength of which the Kremlin might then apply political pressure at trouble spots around the world, including Berlin.[37] With the failure of this bold improvisation, Khrushchev began to test the path of détente in relations with the United States and the West, coming to limited agreements in some fields—test ban, "hot line," nonorbiting of nuclear weapons—and to tacit acceptance of a kind of truce on such cold war issues as Berlin. While it provided a breathing spell during which Soviet policies in the interlocking areas of economics, defense, and foreign policy might be reexamined and perhaps repaired, his cultivation of even a modest atmosphere of détente with the West laid Khrushchev open to renewed charges from Peking that his fear of nuclear war was leading to accommodation with the capitalist enemy and a sellout of the interests of world communism.

In a sense it was true that Khrushchev's desire to minimize the danger of war with the United States had led him to recognize that the two superpowers shared certain mutual concerns, but this was hardly tantamount to a sell-out

pressures in ambiguous circumstances. As the author is indebted to Marshall Shulman for pointing out, such opportunities lay, for example, in encouraging center-left coalition groups in Western Europe to move in a neutralist direction, not under the pressure of palpable threats, but out of realistic awareness of the propinquity of Soviet power.

[37] There is, of course, room for argument that in addition to giving him a new fulcrum against Berlin, Khrushchev's Cuban missile deployment was intended to serve a variety of purposes: to provide reassurance to Castro, to stave off an expected US campaign against Cuba, to secure withdrawal of US missiles from Turkey, and so on. For previous discussion of this question, see chapter V, pp. 96–99.

as depicted by Peking. In terms of Soviet policy in Europe, the effect of détente in the last years of Khrushchev's rule was to make somewhat more explicit his distaste for further tampering with a delicate power balance under which the alliance systems on both sides had tended to become deterrent arrangements with no practicable potential for altering the status quo by direct attack of one on the other.[38] At best, therefore, it might be said that Soviet European policy under Khrushchev ended up in a continuing standoff with the West, based on the tacit understanding that a serious attempt by either side to press for major political gains at the expense of the other was unfeasible. Whether Khrushchev was resigned to living indefinitely with this situation, or whether he was on the verge of a new set of initiatives of some kind, as suggested, for example, by his overtures toward West Germany in the last months of his political life,[39] is a question which his removal from power left unanswered.

Khrushchev's Fall

It is scarcely warranted to lay the failures, any more than the successes, of Khrushchev's policies solely at his own door, for to do so would be to assume that he had acted upon history's stage wholly according to his own script, something no historical actor manages to do. Without going into the philosophical problem of the extent to which men in the seats of power control events or are controlled by them,[40] one may observe that Khrushchev's policies probably were seldom the product of deliberate choice among various alternative courses, the consequences of which had all been thought out beforehand in the search for the most "rational" optimum solution to the particular problem at hand. More likely, his policies were contrived under the influence of many factors over which he had imperfect control or of which he lacked cognizance, such as the organizational habits and preferences of the bureaucracy, the bargaining interplay among various groups within the Soviet power structure, and the external pressures exerted upon the Soviet Union by both allies and adversaries. Where his own responsibility for the policies pursued by the Soviet Union during his regime begins and ends is therefore a very elusive question.

Furthermore, what constitutes success and failure for "Khrushchev's" policies is itself a no less elusive question, the answer to which would depend on the criteria used in a given case. Among other things, Khrushchev operated under the necessity of adjusting Soviet foreign and military policy to the complex conditions of the nuclear age. That this process of adjustment may have required giving up opportunities for revolutionary advance and contributed

---

[38] Herbert S. Dinerstein, "The Transformation of Alliance Systems," *American Political Science Review*, (September 1965): 590–93.

[39] See previous discussion of this question, chapter VI, pp. 117–27.

[40] For an interesting effort to deal with this question, see Stanley Hoffman, *The State of War: Essays on the Theory and Practice of International Politics* (New York: Frederick A. Praeger, Inc., 1965), pp. 255–62.

to discord within the Communist camp can be read in one sense as failure of his policies, but in terms of having helped to avert the awesome possibility of nuclear war it can be chalked up on his record as a signal success. For that matter, even his having added to divisive trends within the Communist world may not necessarily remain a permanent black mark against Khrushchev in the eyes of Communist historians, if, as noted earlier, such trends were to lead to more flexible and nationally oriented Communist movements with greater popular appeal in many parts of the world.

Yet the fact that Khrushchev was repudiated by his peers in power permits one to assume that, from their viewpoint at least, his performance failed to meet the criteria of success. How much of the dissatisfaction which prompted Khrushchev's associates to oust him represented dissent against his policies as such or revolt against his personal power and style of leadership remains a matter of some disagreement among Western observers.[41]

On the one hand, it is not difficult to identify a copious list of policy grievances which may have culminated in the resolve of Khrushchev's colleagues to unseat him. Some of these were: the deterioration of Sino-Soviet relations and Khrushchev's evident resolve to read Peking out of the world Communist movement; his activist pursuit of détente with the West and his suspect flirtation with Bonn in the summer of 1964; and resource allocation disputes aggravated by the decline in rate of economic growth, by Khrushchev's overambitious scheme for chemical fertilizer expansion, and, in September 1964, by his railroading of guidelines for long-term economic planning which promised to downgrade heavy industry and defense requirements in favor of the more rapid development of consumer industry. To these issues might be added: strong opposition within the party apparatus to Khrushchev's reorganization move of 1962 which split the party into an industrial and an agricultural wing; concern among conservative party elements that Khrushchev's anti-Stalinist measures had gone too far and were undermining the party's prestige and authority; and resistance in military circles to Khrushchev's troop reduction proposals and to what some military leaders regarded as overemphasis on missile deterrence at the expense of well-balanced forces.

On the other hand, it can be argued that differences over major policy issues were less important in triggering the coup against Khrushchev than resentment over his increasingly personalistic style of leadership, which collided with a basically conservative tendency toward oligarchic solidarity within the ruling regime. This interpretation finds some support in the fact that those who deposed Khrushchev and took power in his stead, under the rubric of collective leadership, had themselves been ranged on different sides of the domestic and foreign policy issues of his day and, therefore, were unlikely to have united against him solely on grounds of policy. Furthermore, the argu-

---

[41] For both sides of this disputed question, see the exchange of opinions by Richard Lowenthal, Robert Conquest, Carl Linden, Adam Ulam, Leon Smolinski, and others in *Problems of Communism* (January–February 1965, May–June 1965, and July–August 1965).

ment runs, had policy differences alone accounted for the movement to displace him, a sweeping reversal of Khrushchev's policies and programs might have been expected once he had been brushed aside, whereas the policy course of his successors actually contained important elements of continuity as well as change.[42]

For the purposes of this inquiry, however, we need try no further to sort out the factors that lay behind Khrushchev's removal. Whatever the combination of causes may have been, when Khrushchev's colleagues, decided to make him the scapegoat for the difficulties and unresolved problems of the period of his premiership, they were left with a legacy of several broad policy choices: Should the Soviet Union seek to extend its influence in West European countries through renewed pressure tactics at the risk of reviving NATO unity, or was more to be gained by a subtler détente diplomacy? Should the problem of Germany be tackled by continuing efforts to portray the Federal Republic as a threat to peace and a hotbed of revanchism, or by a more conciliatory line aimed at encouraging West German neutralism? Should priority go to separating the United States from its NATO partners and fragmenting the Western alliance, or would Soviet interests be better served by collaboration with the United States toward maintaining some arrangement for stable spheres of influence in Europe? With regard to East Europe, the broad choice facing the new Soviet leaders seemed to be whether to risk an erosion of Soviet authority within the Warsaw bloc by continuing the more tolerant policies pursued under Khrushchev after the 1956 suppression of Hungary, or whether to seek the restoration of rigid Soviet control over the Eastern bloc at the sacrifice of opportunities for promoting closer economic and technical co-operation between East and West. How Khrushchev's successors addressed themselves to these and other questions affecting Soviet policy and purposes in Europe is the subject of Part Three of this study.

---

[42] Swearer, in *Current History* (October 1965): 194. See also the examination of Soviet policy under the Brezhnev-Kosygin regime in Part Three of this study.

Part Three

THE BREZHNEV–KOSYGIN PERIOD: ITS FIRST HALF-DECADE

XI

TRENDS IN SOVIET POLICY
UNDER KHRUSHCHEV'S SUCCESSORS

Although the main focus of our inquiry is upon the political and military aspects of Soviet policy toward Europe, the development of Soviet European policy under the Brezhnev–Kosygin regime can perhaps best be understood if viewed against the background of the regime's efforts to deal with the interrelated problems and priorities of Soviet domestic and foreign policy. In this chapter, therefore, we shall examine some of the general trends in Soviet policy after Khrushchev's ouster, before taking up specifically the present regime's approach to various European policy issues during its first five years in power.

When Khrushchev's successors took over the responsibility for the conduct of Soviet affairs, in the fall of 1964, they found important problems calling for their attention in three separate but interlocking areas of policy concern. The first of these centered on the delicate process of working out arrangements for collective rule in what was potentially, from past experience at least, an unstable period of succession. The second had to do with various tasks on the domestic front: finding realistic remedies for the perennially unsatisfactory agricultural situation; boosting declining rates of economic growth; and dealing with other cumulatively vexatious questions, such as the party's proper role in the management of a modern society, the restiveness of the intelligentsia, and pressure from the population for better living standards. The third major area of policy concern for the new collective leadership was that of foreign affairs and defense, where there was a manifest need to repair the Soviet Union's international position, not only in the power contest with the West but also in the increasingly bitter struggle with Peking for leadership within the Communist world itself.

Let us turn then to the manner in which the new Soviet regime under Leonid Brezhnev and Aleksei Kosygin sought to cope with the problems confronting it in each of these broad policy areas, beginning with that of keeping its collective leadership intact.

Status of the Collective Leadership

As the Brezhnev–Kosygin regime entered the 1970s, it was only fair to say that collective rule in the Soviet Union had weathered the half-decade since Khrushchev's ouster in better shape than many observers had thought likely in view of previous Soviet succession struggles. Whatever internal maneuvering for power may have taken place within the top leadership, no single leader had yet managed to thrust himself conspicuously forward in a bid for personal ascendancy over his fellow oligarchs. Nor did it appear that any of the leaders, with the possible exception of Brezhnev, were in a position from which such a bid for dictatorial power might be made.

Perhaps this meant that the recurrent pattern of one-man rule characteristic of most of the first half-century of the Soviet Union's existence had finally ended, marking another step in what some students of Soviet affairs regard as the post-totalitarian evolution of the Soviet system toward some sort of constitutional political order.[1] On the other hand, perhaps only a temporary equilibrium had been struck among the handful of collective oligarchs making up the interlocking directorate of party and government leaders. A major crisis, or the Soviet system's cumulative failure to cope with basic issues and dilemmas, could conceivably destroy this equilibrium, thereby reviving the prospect that a strong and resourceful leader with dictatorial ambitions might come to power. As only time can test the ultimate stability of the collective leadership arrangements of the post-Khrushchev period, suffice it to note here some of the principal features of collective rule thus far.

One of these has been a studied effort to work out a division of labor within the collective leadership, designed to achieve both efficiency and harmony while keeping any individual from gathering too many strands of power into his own hands. With Brezhnev heading the party chain of command and Kosygin the machinery of government and industry, other leading posts in the top party and government organs have been parceled out among a small inner circle of perhaps some twenty oligarchs,[2] including such figures as N. V. Podgornyi, M. A. Suslov, A. P. Kirilenko, D. S. Polianskii, K. T. Mazurov, P. N. Demichev, and A. N. Shelepin. Although previous collective leadership arrangements—notably the sharing of dual command over the party and government by Khrushchev and Malenkov, respectively, in 1953–54—did not endure for long, it would appear that the distribution of responsibilities in the Brezhnev–Kosygin regime has held up somewhat better. Certainly, there has been little indication of any open party-government rivalry that would pit Brezhnev and Kosygin directly against each other.

A second noteworthy feature of the present collective rule has been the rather marked continuity of leadership at both the top echelon of the system and at broader, intermediate levels. As Seweryn Bialer has pointed out,

---

[1] See discussion in chapter X, especially pp. 218–22. See also David T. Cattell, "The Fiftieth Anniversary: A Soviet Watershed?" *Current History* (October 1967): 224–26.

[2] Precisely what may be the size of the inner oligarchy which comprises the collective leadership, and what relative ranking should be ascribed to its members, are matters upon which Kremlinologists in the West do not wholly agree. The nominal figure of "some twenty," cited here, is based on the combined membership of the party Politburo and Secretariat after the Twenty-third Party Congress, in April 1966. Counting overlapping assignments, twenty-three men occupied the nineteen places in the Politburo and the ten in the Secretariat. Some of these men also held top posts in the Council of Ministers, so that it seems appropriate to identify this group of twenty-three as an "interlocking directorate" controlling both party and government. For a useful set of charts which brings out the interlocking character of the top leadership, see Frederick C. Barghoorn, *Politics in the USSR* (Boston, Mass.: Little, Brown and Company, 1966), pp. 397–410.

Khrushchev's successors not only managed to prevent open conflict among themselves but they also avoided a large-scale turnover of personnel in the ranks of party and state officialdom that might have created confusion and uncertainty during the succession period.[3] Reflecting a "don't rock the boat" attitude, this stabilization of leadership cadres was enhanced at the Twenty-third Party Congress, in April 1966, by the repeal of provisions in the party statutes requiring periodic turnover of officials and by the tightening of party membership requirements.[4] Although, in the aggregate, no wholesale changes have occurred in the composition of the leadership—a factor which has had the important incidental effect of closing the top political echelon to younger men and thus creating a generation gap of sorts—there has been considerable movement up and down the official ladder.[5] An attempt to trace the shifting fortunes of various individual leaders would take us beyond the scope of the present narrative; however, at least two cases merit mention in terms of a potential threat to the stability of collective rule.

The first case in point is that of Brezhnev, who, while apparently possessing few of the attributes of a contender for one-man charismatic rule, has had the advantage of operating as head of the party apparatus, the traditional springboard to power used by both Stalin and Khrushchev.[6] Brezhnev's stature has grown gradually, beginning with his assumption of the initiative for major new agricultural programs in March 1965 and his emergence as the regime's chief spokesman on such matters as defense. After the Twenty-third Party Congress, where Brezhnev became the second man in Soviet history to be accorded the title of "General Secretary" of the party,[7] his star rose still further.

Toward the end of 1966 there were even a few small signs that a Brezhnev "cult" might be forming, as his sixtieth birthday, in December, was celebrated with accolades beyond those tendered to any other member of the collective oligarchy, and his wartime record was the object of fulsome praise by a Politburo colleague.[8] Brezhnev's standing as *primus inter pares* within the collective leadership seemed once again to be publicly affirmed by the deference with which he was treated at the celebration of the Soviet Union's fiftieth anniversary, in November 1967.[9]

---

[3] Seweryn Bialer, "Soviet Leadership: Some Problems of Continuity, Structure and Cohesion," presented at the Annual Meeting of the American Political Science Association, September 6–10, 1966, pp. 4–11, 22.

[4] Report of L. I. Brezhnev to the Twenty-third Party Congress, *Pravda*, March 30, 1966; and "Resolution of the Twenty-third Congress of the Communist Party of the Soviet Union on Partial Revisions of the Statutes of the CPSU," *Pravda*, April 9, 1966.

[5] See Bialer, "Soviet Leadership," p. 9.

[6] Barghoorn, *Politics in the USSR*, p. 198.

[7] Stalin was the other holder of the title of General Secretary, which was changed after his death to First Secretary. Restoration of the Stalinist title for the top party office at the Twenty-third Congress was accompanied by a change of the name of the party Presidium back to Politburo. See speech of N. G. Egorychev, First Secretary of the Moscow City Committee CPSU, proposing the title change to the Twenty-third Party Congress, *Pravda*, March 31, 1966; "Resolution . . . on Partial Revisions of the Statutes of the CPSU," *Pravda*, April 9, 1966.

[8] A. P. Kirilenko's speech at Novorossiisk, *Krasnaia zvezda* (Red Star), December 2, 1966.

[9] Brezhnev, for example, made all of the principal speeches during the several days of jubilee ceremonies in Moscow and Leningrad leading up to the November 7th celebration. Occupying

Despite the fact, however, that Brezhnev has gradually come to overshadow Kosygin, the next most prominent oligarch, he has evidently not sought to encroach upon Kosygin's area of responsibility or to step far ahead of the rest of the collective leadership. Rather, he has seemed to prefer the relatively self-effacing role of a consensus leader. Whether he may yet seek to aggrandize his own power at the expense of his colleagues thus remains a question for the future.

The second individual whose case might point to a possible threat to stability is Aleksandr Shelepin, a former head of the Committee for State Security (KGB) and one of the youngest members of the collective oligarchy. Because of his association with the secret police, his later experience in other control activities, and his alleged "hardline" leanings, Shelepin was looked upon by some Western analysts as the potential focal point of a "neo-Stalinist" faction within the regime. Rumors emanating from Soviet sources, in the fall of 1965, that Shelepin was maneuvering to replace Brezhnev as head of the party apparatus gained some substance in December 1965, when the Party-State Control Committee of which he was chairman was abolished and Shelepin was also deprived of his post as Deputy Chairman of the Council of Ministers.[10] Subsequent demotions of several men considered to be Shelepin's protégés, including V. S. Tikunov, V. E. Semichastnyi, and N. G. Egorychev,[11] further pointed to the possibility that action was being taken to suppress an internal resistance originating in a coterie sympathetic to Shelepin's hard line.

By early 1970, Shelepin had achieved a partial comeback as the party leader in charge of labor union activities. Although his political destiny remained uncertain, there was cumulative evidence of factional rivalries within the leadership from which Shelepin might hope to profit. While by no means such as to suggest that a breakdown of collective rule was imminent, the situation did serve as a reminder that Soviet elite politics were perhaps less tranquil than the outward stability of the collective leadership would indicate.

Finally, perhaps the most distinctive characteristic of collective rule as exer-

---

the center of the stage with Brezhnev were Kosygin and Podgornyi, but neither shared the symbolic honor of delivering commemorative speeches, not even in Leningrad, which is Kosygin's home territory. See Anatole Shub, "Brezhnev Looms Above All in 50th Anniversary Fetes," *Washington Post*, November 6, 1967; Henry Kamm, "Three Soviet Leaders Honor Leningrad," *New York Times*, November 6, 1967.

[10] See Barghoorn, *Politics in the USSR*, p. 368.

[11] The first of this trio of Shelepin's associates to be demoted was Tikunov, who was relieved from a high post in the police hierarchy in September 1966. On May 18, 1967, Semichastnyi was replaced as head of the KGB by Iu. V. Andropov, and on June 27, 1967, after an intervention at a Central Committee plenum where he reportedly criticized the Soviet handling of the Arab–Israeli crisis, Egorychev was removed from his post as First Secretary of the Moscow City Committee of the CPSU. A few months later, in October 1967, Egorychev was dropped from the Presidium of the USSR Supreme Soviet. See "Chronicle" and "Decree of the Presidium of the Supreme Soviet USSR on the Appointment of N. A. Shchelokov as Minister of Protection of Public Order USSR," *Izvestiia*, September 18, 1966; "Decree of the Presidium of the Supreme Soviet USSR," *Pravda*, May 19, 1967; "Plenum of the Moscow City Committee USSR," *Pravda*, June 28, 1967; "Resolution of the Supreme Soviet USSR on the Release of Deputy N. G. Egorychev from the Duties of Membership in the Presidium of the Supreme Soviet USSR," *Pravda*, October 13, 1967.

cised by the Brezhnev–Kosygin regime during its first five years in office was a gradual drift toward deepening conservatism and orthodoxy. At the beginning, the post-Khrushchev oligarchy appeared merely to be given to the cautious and colorless pursuit of what might be called consensus politics, both as a device for reducing friction within the leadership and as a pragmatic way of dealing with policy problems. In contrast to Khrushchev and his bold style of "assaultism" and innovation from above, his successors deliberately stressed *delovitost'*—business-like behavior—as the hallmark of their approach.[12] Initially, this expressed itself in realistic stocktaking and the setting of feasible short-term goals, especially in the economic realm.

As time went on, however, the collective leadership revealed itself increasingly as an oligarchy of conservative bureaucrats, who were not only distrustful of arbitrary innovation from above, as under Khrushchev, but fearful also of pressure for liberal reform from Soviet intellectuals below. Although the shift toward a rigidly defensive orthodoxy did not necessarily lead to immobilism and policy paralysis, it did produce an ample quota of unimaginative measures and ambivalent policy positions which might not answer to the dynamic requirements of long-term development. Indeed, as events at home and abroad tested the quality of Soviet collective rule, perhaps the salient question which emerged was whether the bureaucratic oligarchs in the Kremlin would prove capable of finding fresh and constructive solutions to the problems facing the Soviet Union in an age of pervasive change, or whether they would simply seek to maintain themselves in power by reverting to the orthodox habits and sterile methods of the past.[13]

Domestic Policy: Economic Developments

On the home front, the Brezhnev–Kosygin regime found it necessary initially to devote a large share of its energies to improving the performance of the economy and redefining the party's role in the supervision of economic activity. Among the regime's first significant measures affecting the Soviet economy was the elimination, in November 1964, of Khrushchev's bifurcated party

[12] The speeches of various leaders and editorials in the party press abounded with exhortations to avoid such things as "voluntarism," "subjectivism," "administrative methods," and "bragging," and to approach problems instead in a "business-like," "painstaking," and "disciplined" way. Among examples, see A. N. Kosygin's speech, "Feat of Arms and Valiant Labor," *Izvestiia*, July 13, 1965; N. V. Shelepin's speech in Sevastopol', *Krasnaia zvezda*, July 25, 1965; editorial, "The Policy of the Party Expresses the Living Interests of the People," *Pravda*, September 26, 1965; L. I. Brezhnev's speech to the Plenum of the CPSU, *Pravda*, September 30, 1965.

[13] The ability of the present collective leadership to adapt to change is a moot question among students of Soviet affairs. Some, like Robert Conquest, feel that the Soviet leaders are "third-rate men" whose mediocrity rules out prospects of constructive change. Others, like Michel Tatu, believe that major transformations of both the system and the men who run it must take place, even though the present leaders seem to be conducting a "rearguard action" on behalf of narrow conservatism. My own view is that much will depend on the still unknown qualities of the upcoming leadership generation that will begin to replace the present leaders within the next decade. See Testimony of Robert Conquest in Hearings Before the Subcommittee on National Security and International Operations, Ninety-first Congress, Washington, D.C., December 15, 1969; Michel Tatu, *Power in the Kremlin* (New York: Viking Press, 1969), pp. 525–31.

organization which had put party *apparatchiki* directly into industrial and agricultural operations.[14] Besides removing a source of internal friction between the industrial and the agricultural wings of the party apparatus, this decision seemed to be aimed at restoring party officials to their former role of overseeing and checking the technical-economic experts instead of engaging directly in economic tasks.[15]

Other early moves in the economic field, such as the cutback of the more grandiose parts of Khrushchev's chemical industry expansion plan,[16] suggested an awareness by the new regime that resources had been spread too thin in Khrushchev's time and that a more realistic approach was called for that would match available resources with the most pressing requirements. The chief development reflecting this need for a shift of resources was the new agricultural program announced by Brezhnev in March 1965.[17] It involved, among other things, a planned investment of 71 billion rubles in agriculture over the next five years, plus greater incentives to peasants and the reduction of state quotas upon collective farms. At about the same time, the regime initiated administrative steps toward better centralized control over resources by doing away with the State Committees, set up under Khrushchev's 1957 economic decentralization scheme, and returning to the system of centralized ministries for industrial management, especially within the cluster of defense industries.[18]

The Economic Reform Program

The task of revitalizing the Soviet economy demanded a good deal more, however, than merely improving control over the use of resources. From about 1958 on, there had been both a marked slowdown in the rate of economic growth and a sharp rise in the capital-output ratio.[19] Together, these were disturbing signs of an unhealthy trend, which minor administrative tinkering with the economy was unlikely to correct. Rather, the situation called for

[14] "Resolution of the Plenum of the CC/CPSU on the Unification of the Industrial and Agricultural Oblast' and Krai Party Organizations," *Pravda*, November 17, 1964.

[15] Interestingly enough, this reform did not settle the problem of party supervision of the economy. Within a year, exhortations to avoid excessive economic intervention by party representatives were dropped, and the new line taken was that party officials must not stand aside when difficulties arise and the economic managers require outside advice and assistance. See, for example, editorial, "The Cause of the Entire Party and the Entire People," *Pravda*, October 1, 1965.

[16] See Theodore Shabad, "Soviet Reducing Stress on Chemical Output," *New York Times*, February 2, 1965; I. Barskov, "To Be Completed, Not Carried Over—Commission Chemical Projects More Rapidly," *Ekonomicheskaia gazeta*, no. 1, January 6, 1965, p. 30.

[17] Report by L. I. Brezhnev to the Plenum of the CPSU, "On Urgent Measures for the Further Development of Agriculture in the USSR," *Pravda*, March 27, 1965.

[18] See "In the Presidium of the USSR Supreme Soviet," *Pravda*, March 4, 1965.

[19] For useful discussion of these questions, see Marshall I. Goldman, "Soviet Economic Growth Since the Revolution," *Current History* (October 1967): 234–35; Stanley H. Cohn, "Soviet Growth Retardation: Trends in Resource Availability and Efficiency," *New Directions in the Soviet Economy*, Part II-A, *Economic Performance*, pp. 102–9 ff., study prepared for the Joint Economic Committee, US Congress, Government Printing Office, Washington, D.C., 1966; John P. Hardt, *Soviet Economic Development and Policy Alternatives*, Reprint Series no. 15 (Washington, D.C.: Institute for Sino-Soviet Studies, The George Washington University, November 1967), pp. 16–23. See also chapter VI, pp. 101–2.

major reforms that would boost productivity and efficiency, stimulate the introduction of new technology, and provide for the orderly growth of all sectors
of the economy.

Against this background the Brezhnev-Kosygin regime, in September and
October 1965, came up with a series of corrective measures and reforms that
represented, potentially at least, a significant departure from past "command
economy" practice.[20] These reforms, which completed the dismantling of
Khrushchev's industrial-administrative structure, were designed to place more
authority in the hands of centralized ministries in Moscow and at the same
time to provide for greater exercise of initiative and independence at local
management levels—aims seemingly difficult to reconcile with each other. The
new program proposed in the fall of 1965 also envisaged the use of profitability,
market demand, interest, and other devices adapted from capitalist economics
to improve Soviet economic performance. Initially, these "rationalizing" innovations, many growing out of suggestions first broached in the latter part of the
Khrushchev period by such economic reformers as Evsei Liberman and A. M.
Birman, were to be tried out in the consumer industry sector before being
extended to other areas of the Soviet economy.[21] Toward the end of 1968, the
shift of enterprises to the new system of planning, management, and incentives
had affected about 25,000 enterprises, accounting for about 70 per cent of the
country's output, according to the Soviet Union's chief economic planner.[22]

How successful the Soviet economic reforms may ultimately prove to be in
speeding up economic growth and promoting greater resilience in the traditionally heavy-industry-oriented Soviet economy remains to be seen. Numerous
difficulties, including those of working out the kind of realistic pricing system
on which meaningful profit criteria must rest, have attended the reform program, which on the whole has been less impressive in practice than on paper.[23]

[20] See "On Improving the Management of Industry, Perfecting Planning and Strengthening
Economic Incentives in Industrial Production: Resolution of the Plenary Session of the CPSU
Central Committee Adopted September 29, 1965," *Pravda*, October 1, 1965; "Law of the Union
of Socialist Republics on Changing the System of Agencies for the Management of Industry and
Transforming Certain Other Agencies of State Management," *Pravda*, October 3, 1965.

[21] The first tentative experiment based on the Liberman proposals actually began during the
Khrushchev period, when two clothing factories were placed on the system of "direct links"
between producer and user in July 1964. Kosygin, in April 1966, announced the beginning of the
new system of planning and management under the successor regime. Report of A. N. Kosygin to
the Twenty-third Party Congress, *Pravda*, April 6, 1966.

[22] N. K. Baibakov, "Plan and Production Under the New Conditions," *Pravda*, October 1, 1968.
Baibakov's figures covered mainly industrial and construction enterprises. Transfer of other
enterprises in communications and agriculture is not scheduled for completion until 1970. See
"Results of Fulfillment of the 1967 State Plan for Economic Development," Report of USSR
Central Statistical Board, *Pravda*, January 25, 1968.

[23] For assessments of progress and difficulties encountered in the first years of the economic
reform program, see Theodore Frankel, "Economic Reform: A Tentative Appraisal," *Problems of
Communism* (May–June 1967): 29–41; Keith Bush, "The Reforms: A Balance Sheet," ibid. (July–
August 1967): 30–41; Konstantin A. Krylov, "Soviet Economic Reformers Still Await Expected
Breakthroughs," *Analysis of Current Developments in the Soviet Union*, no. 514, September 10,
1968, Institute for the Study of the USSR, Munich. For a Soviet account of reform difficulties, see
Baibakov, *Pravda*, October 1, 1968.

Most Western observers tend to agree that the present reforms must be carried a good deal further if they are to produce a real economic revolution in the Soviet Union, but opinions differ on how likely this is to happen. Some observers, for example, have emphasized the dilemma created for Soviet economic planning by the attempt to combine market mechanisms with arbitrary centralized control;[24] others have pointed out that Soviet economics has shown a considerable ability to make pragmatic adjustments to the needs of the times and that the Soviet Union is also in a position to learn from reform schemes pioneered in East Europe.[25] At any rate, no matter where the economic reforms may ultimately lead, the uneven performance of the Soviet economy during the first five years of the Brezhnev–Kosygin regime suggests that the reform program has fallen short of the hopes originally held for it.

Uneven Economic Performance

Up to 1968 the Soviet economy appeared to be recovering from the sluggishness which had overtaken it toward the end of the Khrushchev regime. Thanks in part to good harvests in all but one year of the 1964–68 period, including an all-time record grain harvest of 170 million metric tons in 1966,[26] the new regime was able to take credit for an upturn in the over-all performance of the economy. According to figures released at a Supreme Soviet session in Moscow just prior to the Soviet Union's fiftieth anniversary celebration, in the fall of 1967, the annual rates of growth for several key economic categories had risen somewhat above the levels recorded during the latter years of Khrushchev's rule. The average annual growth rate of "national income," for example, reached 7.2 per cent in 1966–67, as against 5.7 per cent for the period 1961–65; industrial output growth rates for the same periods were 9.4 per cent compared with 8.6 per cent; while agricultural growth rates were 4.2 per cent compared with 2.4 per cent in the earlier period.[27]

Western analyses of Soviet economic performance, incidentally, show that the growth record in the three-year period 1965–67 did not surpass that of Khrushchev's latter years to the extent suggested by the Soviet-released figures. For example, in terms of gross national product (a method of measurement different from the Soviet concept of "national income"), the Western estimates show an average growth rate of about 5.8 per cent for 1965–67, com-

[24] See Leon Smolinski, "Planning Without Theory, 1917–1967," *Survey* (July 1967): 125–27; John P. Hardt, *Choices Facing the Soviet Planner*, Reprint Series no. 7 (Washington, D.C.: Institute for Sino–Soviet Studies, The George Washington University, January 1967), pp. 23, 36–43; and Frankel, in *Problems of Communism*, p. 41.

[25] See Alfred Zauberman, "Changes in Economic Thought," *Survey* (July 1967): 168; Cattell, *Current History* (October 1967): 227.

[26] Soviet grain harvests for other years under the Brezhnev–Kosygin regime, in million metric tons, were: 1964—152; 1965—120.5; 1967—147.6; 1968—169.2; 1969—160.5. See *Pravda*, February 3, 1966; January 29, 1967; January 25, 1968; December 17, 1969; *Ekonomicheskaia gazeta*, no. 5 (January 1969): 8.

[27] Report by N. K. Baibakov, Chairman of the USSR State Planning Committee, *Pravda*, October 11, 1967.

pared with 4.9 per cent for the last three years of the Khrushchev period.[28] Nevertheless, even though the average growth rate may have flattened out more than Soviet authorities cared to admit, the upturn was sufficient to enable the Brezhnev–Kosygin regime to view with some optimism the prospect of meeting planned performance goals for 1970. This was the terminal year of the eighth Five-Year-Plan,[29] whose goals had been considerably scaled down by the new rulers from those projected earlier by Khrushchev.[30]

Despite some improvement on the economic front during the early years of the Brezhnev–Kosygin regime, however, the Soviet leadership was to find by 1968 that its economic problems were far from over. Not only had the economy's growth rate begun to decline again as measures to increase labor productivity and the introduction of new technology fell short of expectations, but the perennial problem of competition for resources remained as intractable as ever. Basically, three pressing sets of requirements competed for priority: (1) consumer needs; (2) military and defense industry claims; (3) over-all economic growth. In making trade-offs among these competing categories, the regime apparently chose to put priority upon responding to long-neglected consumer demands and upon strengthening the Soviet military posture, but at the expense of hoped-for high rates of growth-oriented investment.

A shift in priority with regard to consumer goods was first announced at the Supreme Soviet session in October 1967, when it was made known that the percentage increase of consumer goods for 1968 would be slightly greater than that of producer goods—8.6 per cent compared with 7.9 per cent. Even though in absolute terms producer-goods production remained favored by a large margin (for example, planned goals for 1970 still came to 250 billion rubles of output for producer goods compared with 100 billion for consumer goods), this was the first time in Soviet history that the growth rate for consumer goods exceeded that for producer goods. This notable reversal of a traditional priority was attributed by Western observers in part to inflationary

---

[28] See the chapter "Comparative Growth of the Soviet Economy," in *Soviet Economic Performance: 1966–1967*, Materials prepared for the Subcommittee on Foreign Economic Policy of the Joint Economic Committee, Congress of the United States, Government Printing Office, Washington, D.C., May 1968, pp. 11–18. The annual figures from which the three-year averages were derived for comparative purposes were: 1962—4.2; 1963—2.8; 1964—7.9; 1965—6.2; 1966—7.1; 1967—4.3 per cent.

[29] The eighth Five-Year-Plan had a curious history. Set forth initially in tentative draft outline in February 1966, and later in more detail at the Twenty-third Party Congress in April 1966 and at the Supreme Soviet session of October 1967, its formal adoption and ratification by the Supreme Soviet was periodically postponed, presumably because of differences of view over resource allocations and other difficulties. Only successive annual plans for the years 1966–70 were approved, leaving a "final version" of the entire plan formally unratified.

[30] At the Twenty-second Party Congress, in October 1961, Khrushchev had laid out a set of ambitious goals for 1970 as part of a longer-range twenty-year program of economic development which was supposed to leave the US economy far behind. Key targets for 1970 were scaled back on the order of 13 to 17 per cent (and some by as much as 68 per cent) by his successors in early 1966, at the time draft directives for the eighth Five-Year-Plan were promulgated. For an examination of these cutbacks, see Keith Bush, "The New Five-Year-Plan," *Problems of Communism* (July–August 1966): 1–7.

pressure created by the fact that incomes were rising at a faster rate than was the supply of consumer goods.[31] Again in the economic plan for 1969, the consumer category was given a slight edge in growth rate of 7.5 per cent over 7.2 per cent for producer goods.[32]

These concessions to consumer expectations, meanwhile, were accompanied by a continuing upward trend in military allocations, a subject we shall take up more fully in a subsequent chapter. As for investment designed to promote long-term economic growth, there was consistent slippage in the planned rates. This first came to light in October 1967, when the projected over-all investment growth for the 1966–70 period was lowered from 47 to 43 per cent.[33] In agriculture, investment also slipped, lagging in 1968 about 10 per cent behind the planned rate; paradoxically, this may have been due in part to the bumper harvest of 1966, which, according to Dmitri Polianskii, the party leader in charge of agriculture, had "gone to the heads of some comrades" who were "beginning to argue" in 1967 that agricultural investment could be cut back to permit diverting resources to other claimants.[34] These comrades evidently had their way, as indicated by the fact that agricultural investment for the first three years of the 1966–70 Five-Year-Plan fell 4.4 billion rubles short of the 21.2 billion which Brezhnev in 1965 had said was intended for the period.

Investment shortfalls, combined with such factors as a sluggish rate of growth in labor productivity, lagging retirement of obsolete plant equipment, and diversion of capital resources from major national projects, evidently contributed to a slight downturn in the industrial output growth rate for 1968, which declined to 8.1 per cent from a claimed rate of almost 10 per cent for the preceding year.[35] If this was an unwelcome trend from the Kremlin's viewpoint, the performance of the Soviet economy in 1969 must have seemed even more disappointing. The industrial growth rate fell off to 7 per cent; labor productivity dropped from a growth rate of 5.2 per cent in 1968 to 4.4 per cent; and agricultural output was 3 per cent less than the 1968 figure.[36] Moreover, these developments came at a time when the American edge in

[31] See Keith Bush, "The Supreme Soviet Session of October 1967," Research Bulletin, no. 42, Radio Liberty, Munich, October 18, 1967, p. 7; Henry Kamm, "Soviet Consumers Are Coming into Style," New York Times, January 15, 1968.

[32] Report by N. K. Baibakov, Chairman of the USSR State Planning Committee, Pravda, December 11, 1968.

[33] See reports of N. K. Baibakov and V. F. Garbuzov, Pravda, October 11, 1967. See also Bush, "The Supreme Soviet Session of October 1967," pp. 6, 12.

[34] See electoral speech in Pavlovsk by D. S. Polianskii, Pravda, March 3, 1967, and his article "On the Role of the Alliance of Workers and Peasants in Reconstruction of the Present-Day Village," Kommunist, no. 15 (October 1967): no. 24. Subsequent appeals for restoring higher resource priorities to agriculture were made in 1969 by less well-known figures, including A. Drygin in Kommunist, no. 13 (September 1969), and L. Bulochnikova in Voprosy ekonomiki (Problems of Economics), no. 9 (September 1969). .

[35] The industrial output growth rate for 1968 was first given as 8.3 per cent (in Baibakov's report, Pravda, December 11, 1968), but was later amended downward to 8.1 per cent. See Report on Results of State Plan for Development of the USSR Economy in 1968, Pravda, January 26, 1969.

[36] Report by N. K. Baibakov, Chairman of the USSR State Planning Committee, Pravda, December 17, 1969. See also Harry Schwartz, "Moscow Has a Nagging Pain in the Economy," New York Times, February 8, 1970.

advanced technical and economic resources had been underscored by the Apollo 11 and 12 moon landings—events which apparently had a sobering effect upon a Soviet leadership already concerned over lagging nondefense technology in the USSR.

Signs that the loss of economic momentum was disturbing to the Soviet leadership were numerous, ranging from repeated delay in publishing the outlines of the ninth Five-Year-Plan[37] to an unusually frank report on economic difficulties by Brezhnev, part of which was made public in early 1970.[38] Although further tinkering with the economy could be expected, it still remained unclear—as the decade of the seventies opened—whether the Soviet Union would manage to reform its economic system to meet the increasingly complex demands placed upon it in the era of modern technology. Needless to say, failure to do so might have far-reaching implications for the Brezhnev–Kosygin regime, possibly weakening its political position at home and abroad.

Domestic Policy: Control of Social and Cultural Change

Coming to power at a time of quickening social and cultural change in Soviet society, the Brezhnev–Kosygin regime inherited the problem—already grown serious in Khrushchev's time—of keeping such change under control. Essentially, this was for the ruling Communist elite the dual problem of how to insure discipline and conformity, on the one hand, while at the same time encouraging the kind of initiative and creativity needed to make a modern society tick. In the economic realm, as we have seen, the regime sought to deal with this dilemma by adopting reforms intended to combine centralized ministerial authority with greater independence and initiative at local management levels. With respect to the social and intellectual sectors of Soviet society, a somewhat analogous attempt to find a workable blend of imposed conformity and constructive participation also characterized the initial approach of the post-Khrushchev regime. Unfortunately, as time went on the emphasis tended to shift to the first element of this combination.

Social Problems and Control Measures

Soviet life has produced a variety of social problems that, theoretically, should never have arisen in a Communist society or should at least be on the decline at this stage of its development. However, as Soviet authorities themselves

[37] As early as May 1968, Gosplan Chairman Baibakov had said that the main outlines and targets of the ninth Five-Year-Plan (1971–75) would be published by August 1968. See *Ekonomicheskaia gazeta*, no. 21 (May 1968): 5. However, up to early 1970 no projection was forthcoming, evidently because of inability to resolve economic priorities in the face of competing claims on resources and the uncertainties of the international situation.

[38] "Toward New Accomplishments," *Pravda*, January 13, 1970. This editorial gave a condensed account of what Soviet sources described as "an unusually frank report" by Brezhnev at a Central Committee session on December 15, 1969. Brezhnev's remarks on unsatisfactory economic performance had been foreshadowed by similar complaints in a November 7, 1969, anniversary speech by N. V. Podgornyi, *Pravda*, November 7, 1969. See also Bernard Gwertzman, "Brezhnev Reports Wide Economic Ills, Asks Tight Control," *New York Times*, January 16, 1970.

complain, many of these troublesome problems seem to be on the rise. One category includes the dodging of "socially useful labor," widespread alcoholism, and the growth of crime and "hooliganism," the last ranging from theft of state property to crimes of sex and violence, often involving gangs of wayward youths.[39]

Particular concern also has been expressed by representatives of the Soviet "establishment" over a second category of problems, perhaps best described as tendencies among the younger generation that reflect its alienation, in one form or another, from present-day Soviet society. These tendencies, some of which seem akin to the questioning of established values by youth elsewhere, include indifference to Marxism–Leninism as a repository of answers to the main problems of life,[40] aversion to military service,[41] growing resistance to the appeal of Komsomol membership,[42] and the incursion of "bourgeois values and ideology" into the thinking of Soviet youth.[43]

The official response to these problems has taken various forms, which can perhaps be roughly divided into coercive and constructive efforts to improve social control. In the first category, one of the Brezhnev–Kosygin regime's early measures was the revision, in September 1965, of the "antiparasite law" of 1961. The revised law provided that persons who "avoid socially useful labor and have an anti-social, parasitic way of life" could be assigned to mandatory labor in their home locality, but it eliminated the feature of the previous law that rendered such people subject to deportation.[44] This was followed in July 1966 by stiffer decrees, which strengthened the power and authority of the police (militia) and included the replacement of the Ministry of Internal Affairs (MVD) by a new central body called the Ministry for Protection of Public Order, or MOOP.[45]

---

[39] For some typical Soviet commentary on manifestations of "hooliganism," "banditry," and "crude disregard for ... the rules of Communist morality and behavior," see I. Shatunovskii, "Forbidden Place," *Pravda*, June 19, 1966; Ed. Polianovskii, "Sweep!" *Izvestiia*, August 7, 1966; B. Kulikov, "The Soviets and Social Order," ibid., August 25, 1966. For a useful examination of Soviet literature on this subject, see Valeri M. Albert, "Efforts Redoubled To Stem the Crime Wave in the USSR," *Analysis of Current Developments in the Soviet Union*, no. 424, Institute for the Study of the USSR, Munich, October 11, 1966.

[40] For discussion of the new Soviet regime's concern over the ideological estrangement of Soviet youth, see Boris P. Regal, "Party Criticizes Ideological Neutralism of Soviet Youth," *Analysis of Current Developments in the Soviet Union*, no. 404, Institute for the Study of the USSR, Munich, April 12, 1966; Andrei V. Babich, "Resurgence of the 'Fathers and Sons' Polemic and Party Dissatisfaction with Youth," ibid., no. 392, January 18, 1966.

[41] For an appraisal of the changing outlook of Soviet youth toward military life, see Thomas W. Wolfe, *The Soviet Military Scene: Institutional and Defense Policy Considerations,* The RAND Corporation, RM-4913-PR, June 1966, pp. 47–53.

[42] Brezhnev at the Twenty-third Party Congress cited the flagging hold of the Komsomol upon Soviet youth, and urged measures to repair "serious deficiencies" in this youth organization (*Pravda*, March 30, 1966). In June 1968, the top Komsomol leadership was replaced in an effort to make the organization more effective in inculcating a correct ideological approach to life among its members.

[43] See Regal, "Party Criticizes Ideological Neutralism . . . ," pp. 3–6.

[44] *Vedomosti verkhovnogo soveta RSFSR* (Records of the Supreme Soviet of the RSFSR), no. 38, September 23, 1965, pp. 737–39.

[45] "Decree of the Presidium of the Supreme Soviet USSR, On Formation of a Union–Republican Ministry for the Protection of Public Order USSR," *Pravda*, July 28, 1966. In November 1968,

These moves toward more rigorous law enforcement seemed to down-grade the role of voluntary social organs, like the "comrades' courts," which had been encouraged in Khrushchev's time. The new laws did not, however, impinge on the functions of the secret police. The powers of the latter, as during Khrushchev's administration, continued to be under close party control, although a campaign to restore the public image of the KGB as the defender of Soviet security against foreign intelligence operations was launched soon after the new regime took over. Later, with the growing official concern over intellectual protest at home and potential infection from the reform ferment in East Europe, the KGB gradually was given greater freedom of action against domestic dissent.

Parallel with more stringent laws and disciplinary measures, the Brezhnev–Kosygin regime launched an extensive effort toward better social control, especially over youth, through educational reforms and indoctrination. These measures included an overhaul of the educational system and creation of a new, centralized USSR Ministry of Education,[46] the revision of propaganda and recreation programs aimed at Soviet youth,[47] and appeals to military veterans to take a more active part "in the indoctrination of young people in the revolutionary, militant and working traditions of the Soviet people."[48] A new military service law, introduced in 1967, also apparently sought to expose a larger slice of the country's youth to the virtues of "patriotic education" within the armed forces.

Another development in the social sector that received at least some encouragement under the Brezhnev–Kosygin regime was recognition of the need for greater use of sociological research in dealing with social problems that had not yielded to standard Marxist–Leninist remedies. The founding, in February 1965, of the Institute of Concrete Social Research in Leningrad was an example of new interest in developing empirical sociological research techniques. However, the reluctance of party officialdom to allow the social sciences to compete with Marxism–Leninism, "the only scientific teaching" about society, was also evident from the outset.[49] Later, as the party's concern over ideological erosion

MOOP in turn was renamed the Ministry of the Interior, and the police forces under its jurisdiction were again strengthened.

[46] In the fall of 1966, for the first time in Soviet history, the new regime created a centralized USSR Ministry of Education, and upgraded the RSFSR Academy of Pedagogical Sciences to all-union level. This centralizing measure, intended to give better control over educational policy, was accompanied, however, by provisions to allow more flexibility in dealing with local problems. See *Pravda*, August 4, 1966, September 9, 1966. For discussion of these educational reforms, see Jeremy R. Azrael, "Fifty Years of Soviet Education," *Survey* (July 1967): especially 58–60.

[47] A joint party-state decree in August 1966, for example, outlined a sweeping new recreation and physical education program designed, apparently, to counteract the malaise among Soviet youth over which the authorities showed growing concern. *Pravda*, August 25, 1966.

[48] Slogan no. 102, *Pravda*, October 23, 1965. See also Marshal N. Krylov, "Army, Patriotism, and Youth," *Sovetskaia Rossiia* (Soviet Russia), October 8, 1965.

[49] See, for example, S. P. Trapeznikov, "Marxism-Leninism Is the Firm Foundation of the Development of Social Science," *Pravda*, October 8, 1965. For a useful discussion of the emergence of Soviet sociology, along with the limitations imposed upon it in many important areas of inquiry, including crime, see Paul Hollander, "The Dilemmas of Soviet Sociology," *Problems of Communism* (November–December 1965): 34–46. See also George Fischer, *Science and Politics: The New Sociology in the Soviet Union* (Ithaca, N.Y.: Cornell University Press, 1964).

in the Soviet Union increased, the question of making better use of Soviet social science became one of the issues in the struggle of the liberal intelligentsia for greater freedom of expression and reform from within the Soviet system.

The New Regime and Soviet Intellectual Dissent

The new regime's need to make more effective use of the creative intelligentsia has come into recurrent conflict with its demands for conformity from Soviet intellectuals. The situation here has been complicated by the regime's differing attitudes toward the scientific-technical and the cultural-artistic intel- ligentsia. In general, the regime has seemed to feel that the first group should be encouraged to play a more vigorous role in Soviet affairs and to explore new paths, especially in the fields of science and technology, for the sake of promoting efficiency and innovation. Yet, at the same time, the leadership apparently has not allowed similar latitude to the second group, preferring that it be constrained to avoid the kind of intellectual inquiry and artistic expression that might challenge the party's authority and monopoly of power or run counter to Marxist–Leninist concepts of society. A scattering of "liberal-minded" intellectuals from both groups appears to have taken up the case for greater freedom of expression and reform from within, thus posing for the governing establishment the delicate problem of how to deal with dissenters whose professed aim is to make the Soviet system work better.

After the new regime took office in 1964, there were several periods when the liberal intelligentsia enjoyed relative freedom to air its viewpoint, but each permissive phase was followed by a fresh effort to enforce conformity. One of the periods of tolerance lasted from the spring to the fall of 1965, when Soviet intellectuals drew encouragement from such developments as the repudiation of Lysenkoism; the demotion of L. E. Il'ichev, a strongly orthodox supervisor of ideological affairs; and the publication of two notable articles by *Pravda's* newly appointed editor, A. M. Rumiantsev, which stressed the formula of "freedom of creativity."[50] During this half-year, the liberal intelligentsia pressed its case for a more realistic portrayal of Soviet society and its short- comings, and there was an outburst of experimental literary and dramatic production, with avant-garde journals such as *Novyi mir* taking the lead in publishing the works of young or previously banned writers.[51] In the fall of

[50] Rumiantsev's *Pravda* articles in February and September 1965 were widely regarded as a new charter for the intelligentsia, whose members were assured that, while their works would still be subject to socialist values, arbitrary attacks on individual writers would no longer be tolerated. See "The Party and the Intelligentsia," *Pravda*, February 21, 1965; "The Party Spirit of the Soviet Intelligentsia's Creative Labor," ibid., September 9, 1965.

[51] Aleksandr Tvardovskii, the editor of *Novyi mir* (New World), was among the more articulate spokesmen for the liberal intelligentsia. See, for example, his article, "On the Occasion of the Jubilee," *Novyi mir*, no. 1 (January 1965): 3–18. Among the writers of liberal bent whose works appeared in *Novyi mir*, *Iunost'* (Youth), and other journals during the 1965 period of "creative freedom," were V. P. Aksenov, V. Semin, Boris Kulikov, and F. Abramov. For a fuller discussion of activity on the Soviet literary front during this period, see Timothy McClure. "The Politics of Soviet Culture, 1964–1967," *Problems of Communism* (March–April 1967): 26–43; A. Gayev, "Socialist Realism Begins a New Offensive," *Bulletin*, Institute for the Study of the USSR (June 1966): 21–26.

1965, however, the pendulum began to swing the other way. The liberal-minded Rumiantsev was removed from the editorship of *Pravda* in early October, about the same time that conservative proponents of a hard cultural policy, including S. P. Trapeznikov, launched a strong attack on liberal tendencies.[52] Another ominous note for the liberal intelligentsia was the arrest, in late September, of authors A. D. Siniavskii and Yuli Daniel, whose conviction, in February 1966, for having published abroad a fictional satire on Stalinism was to stand as a warning against attempts to evade literary censorship.[53]

Throughout 1966, as the harsh disciplinary action against Siniavskii and Daniel cast a pall over the cultural scene and the liberals became the targets of dogmatist broadsides in the magazine *Oktiabr'*,[54] most of the liberal intellectuals remained silent.[55] By the spring of 1967, however, spokesmen for the liberal viewpoint again began to make their voices heard,[56] apparently encouraged by the demotion of several orthodox hardliners in the party hierarchy, including V. E. Semichastnyi, the head of the KGB. The liberal argument was also sounded by social scientists and journalists, and in at least one case by a distinguished natural scientist.

In June and July 1967, a number of articles called for better use of Soviet social science, attributing its backwardness to intellectual stagnation of the "not too distant past," and urging that Soviet sociologists be allowed to address themselves to "real social problems" and to play a greater role "in changing the very structure of society" instead of merely helping the regime to impose social controls.[57] A recurrent theme was that the interests of communism would

[52] The Trapeznikov article is cited in footnote 49.

[53] Siniavskii and Daniel were sentenced on February 14, 1966, to seven and five years, respectively, in a forced labor camp for having published abroad (under pseudonyms) writings judged harmful to the Soviet regime. The trial drew bitter criticism in the West. See "Trial in Moscow Scored in West," *New York Times*, February 15, 1966. For a description of the trial resting on a transcript which found its way to the West, see *On Trial: The State versus "Abram Tertz" and "Nikolai Arzhak,"* translated, edited, and with an Introduction by Max Hayward (New York: Harper and Row, 1966).

[54] See, for example, the extravagant attack upon liberal tendencies in Soviet intellectual and artistic life by V. A. Kochetov, "A Nasty Profession," in the conservative journal *Oktiabr'*, no. 3 (March 1966): 211–18. In early 1967, as became known later, the suppression of liberal tendencies took on an uglier turn with the arrest of professors and students at Leningrad University. See "4 in Leningrad Reported Jailed as Plotters Against the Regime," *New York Times*, December 22, 1967. See also Patricia Blake, "This Is the Winter of Moscow's Dissent," *New York Times Magazine*, March 24, 1968, pp. 122, 124.

[55] The chief exception perhaps was a letter of protest sent to the Kremlin by twenty-five scientists and writers on the eve of the Twenty-third Party Congress, warning that any attempt to rehabilitate Stalin's reputation might provoke "serious dissension within Soviet society." See chapter IV, pp. 63–69.

[56] One well-known figure was the novelist Aleksandr Solzhenitsyn, who at the Fourth USSR Writers' Congress, in May 1967, circulated a petition against censorship and criticized the KGB for confiscating some of his unpublished manuscripts. Another was Andrei Voznesenskii, who in early July drew applause from a Moscow theater audience for a poem on the adverse effect of censorship on creative contributions to society, and who later that month sent a letter to *Pravda* denouncing officials who prevented his appearance at a poetry reading in New York. See pertinent accounts in *New York Times*, June 5, August 11, October 24, 1967.

[57] A. M. Rumiantsev, "To Those Entering the World of Science," *Komsomol'skaia pravda*,

best be served by frank analysis of difficulties encountered by the Soviet system, and that attempts to curb the creative work of artists and other intellectuals by narrow fiat raised the danger of "subjective" decisions.[58] But perhaps the most eloquent plea for intellectual freedom came from a leading Soviet physicist, Professor Andrei D. Sakharov, whose privately circulated essay calling for enlightened reform of the Soviet system appeared in print only in the West.[59]

Official reaction to the round of liberal argument in the summer of 1967 was not long in coming. On July 8, an unsigned editorial in *Komsomol'skaia pravda* repudiated the more liberal articles published in that newspaper during June and called for stricter party control over intellectual expression.[60] In August the Party Central Committee issued a decree condemning departures from Marxist–Leninist orthodoxy, especially in the social sciences.[61] Soon thereafter, it became apparent that a new and harsher crackdown on liberal dissent was underway, as events stemming from the earlier Daniel–Siniavskii affair came to a head in Moscow. There, in January 1968, a thirty-year-old poet, Aleksandr Ginsburg, and three young codefendants[62] were tried and convicted after

---

June 8, 1967. See also subsequent article by Rumiantsev and two co-authors, F. Burlatskii and I. Bestuzhev, "Soviet Society and Social Prognosis," *Pravda*, June 17, 1967; and article by A. Ianov, "Time To Grow Up," *Komsomol'skaia pravda*, June 2, 1967.

[58] See, for example, F. Burlatskii and L. Karpinskii, "En Route to a Premiere," *Komsomol'skaia pravda*, June 30, 1967.

[59] The Sakharov "manifesto," a lengthy essay originally entitled "Thoughts on Progress, Peaceful Coexistence and Intellectual Freedom," had been privately circulated among Soviet scientists before a text that had reached the West appeared in *New York Times*, July 22, 1968. A far-ranging document written, as Marshall Shulman has put it, "in the great tradition of the moral conscience and sense of social responsibility of the Russian intellectual," the Sakharov essay argued that intellectual freedom is essential to human society and that the division of mankind into opposing political-ideological systems threatens it with destruction. In what amounted to a version of the convergency theory, Sakharov foresaw the prospect that the capitalist and Communist systems would draw closer to each other in a number of essential respects, leading, he hoped, by the end of the century to a situation in which the Soviet Union and the United States would address themselves co-operatively to solving global problems of poverty, health, overpopulation, and the like, for the benefit of mankind, and perhaps making possible progress toward creation of a world government.

Existence of the Sakharov manuscript was not directly acknowledged in the Soviet Union, although, following its publication in the West, its theses were indirectly attacked in references to proponents of "futurology" who "deny the need for a revolutionary transformation of the world." (Viktor A. Cherpakov, "Problems of the Last Third of the Century," *Izvestiia*, August 11, 1968.) Sakharov himself, presumably because of his stature as a scientist, was spared personal abuse from Soviet media, although little is actually known about what pressures may have been brought to bear upon him. At forty-seven, Sakharov had been the recipient of high Soviet honors for his work in physics, including important theoretical contributions to the Soviet thermonuclear bomb and development of controlled thermonuclear fusion. One can assume that his views on intellectual freedom and enlightened reform of the Soviet system are sympathetically regarded by many of his colleagues, though few have been as bold as he in committing them to paper. For a perceptive discussion of the Sakharov case, see Marshall D. Shulman, "The Sakharov Manifesto," *Saturday Review*, November 23, 1968, pp. 51–53 ff. See also the Sakharov essay in book form with an Introduction and notes by Harrison Salisbury, *Progress, Coexistence and Intellectual Freedom* (New York: W. W. Norton & Company, Inc., 1968).

[60] Editorial, "Party Spirit of the Artist," *Komsomol'skaia pravda*, July 8, 1967.

[61] "On Measures for the Further Development of the Social Sciences and for Raising Their Role in Communist Construction," *Pravda*, August 22, 1967.

[62] The other defendants in the Ginsburg case were Iurii Galanskov, Aleksei Dobrovol'skii, and

almost a year of imprisonment on charges of "agitation aimed at subverting or weakening the Soviet regime," charges based on their having compiled a "white book" on the Daniel–Siniavskii case and having helped to edit an underground literary journal, *Phoenix 1966.*

The trial, conducted under circumstances which showed the crude hand of the KGB,[63] aroused a measure of protest in the Soviet Union that the regime doubtless found disquieting. The first critical voice to be heard was that of Pavel M. Litvinov, a thirty-year-old physicist and grandson of the late Foreign Minister Maksim Litvinov. He not only spoke out on behalf of fair play for the Ginsburg defendants but also braved the KGB by making an unauthorized disclosure of closed-door proceedings that had taken place in September 1967 against three youths sentenced for leading a street demonstration against the detention of Siniavskii and Daniel.[64] On the heels of Litvinov's action, which cost him his job and may have placed his future in jeopardy, several hundred persons representing a broad segment of the Soviet intelligentsia signed petitions of protest against the Ginsburg trial,[65] including a public appeal addressed to the Budapest conference of Communist parties in late February 1968.[66] Although indicating a widespread disposition among Soviet intellectuals to reject the official version of the Ginsburg affair, even at considerable risk to themselves, these protests did not bring a relaxation of pressure against the liberal intelligentsia.[67]

Vera Lashkova, all young and relatively obscure members of the literary "underground." Ginsburg and Galanskov were sentenced to five and seven years, respectively; the other two received lighter sentences.

[63] In addition to questioning the charges against the defendants, critics of the trial condemned its arbitrary judicial conduct, the packing of the courtroom with a hostile audience, and the harsh sentences meted out to Ginsburg and Galanskov, who apparently based their defense on the right to free expression nominally guaranteed by the Soviet constitution. For pertinent pretrial accounts, see Henry Kamm, "Four Dissidents Face Trial in Moscow on Anti-Soviet Propaganda Charge," *New York Times*, December 10, 1967; Raymond H. Anderson, "Trial of Four Young Dissidents Opens in Moscow," ibid., January 9, 1968. For accounts of the trial itself, which were relayed to Western news sources by friends and relatives of the accused, see *New York Times* and *Washington Post* for January 9 through 15, 1968. See also Blake, in *New York Times Magazine*, March 24, 1968, pp. 126, 129.

[64] See "A Litvinov Sends Account of Secret Trial to West," *New York Times*, December 27, 1967; Richard C. Longworth, "Litvinov Urges Younger Generation of Russians To Speak Out Frankly," *Washington Post*, January 16, 1968. The secret trial in September 1967, which Litvinov disclosed despite KGB warnings not to do so, involved Vladimir Bukovskii, a twenty-five-year-old writer, and two companions, E. Kushchev and V. Delone.

[65] More than 400 Soviet intellectuals signed the several protest documents against the Ginsburg trial and the arrest of Aleksandr Esenin-Volpin, a mathematician and son of a famous Soviet poet, in connection with it. That this many Soviet citizens were willing to commit themselves suggested a much broader base of sympathy with their views. For a breakdown of the occupations of the signers, and for a generally excellent analysis of the significance of the protest movement, see Paul A. Smith, Jr., "Protest in Moscow," *Foreign Affairs* (October 1968): 151–63.

[66] See Richard Reston, "Party Gets Plea for Soviet Writers," *Washington Post*, February 29, 1968. The appeal, which was not acknowledged by the Budapest conference, said in part: "We appeal to the participants in the consultative conference to fully consider the peril caused by the trampling on man in our country." The conference itself is discussed in chapter XIV.

[67] In addition to the Ginsburg affair, which drew the greatest attention, it also became known that the regime's crackdown on dissent had wider ramifications. In late 1967 and again in March 1968, for example, small groups of intellectuals in Leningrad were brought to trial on conspiracy

On the contrary, the regime's concern about nonconformity at home apparently began to merge with fear that the reform ferment from developments then unfolding in Czechoslovakia might spill over into the Soviet Union.[68] The result was a series of sterner steps to enforce discipline upon the Soviet intellectual community. Some of the Soviet scientists who had signed protests against the Ginsburg trial were expelled from the party, and others were told to toe the line or lose their privileged status.[69] "Last warnings" were issued to a number of persons to cease talking with foreign correspondents, part of a general curtailment of contacts between Soviet citizens and the foreign colony in Moscow.[70] The press also took a hard line toward the dissent evoked by the January trial; its position was typified by a *Pravda* article in March which compared the defendants with "Trotskyite" and other "renegade" elements purged in the 1930's, and charged that "bourgeois propaganda" was trying to use the trial to discredit the Soviet system.[71]

In late March the regime's new efforts to combat dissidence among Soviet intellectuals received an authoritative stamp when Brezhnev made a speech calling for "iron discipline" in party ranks and indicating that writers and scientists who failed to shun "the praise of our ideological opponents" and were not "ready to work for the well-being of their homeland" could not "expect immunity." This speech, and a resolution adopted at a Central Committee plenum in early April, set the stage for a new tightening of ideological controls

charges growing out of the previous arrest of some 150 to 300 persons, some of whom were students and professors at Leningrad University. In the Ukraine, students and professors were also among the victims of a wave of arrests beginning in 1966, which came to light in February 1968 in letters of protest written by a Ukrainian newsman and smuggled to the West. See "4 in Leningrad Jailed as Plotters Against the Regime," *New York Times*, December 22, 1967; Peter Grose, "15 in Soviet Tried Secretly in 1966," ibid., February 9, 1968; "7 on Trial in Leningrad as Subversives," *Washington Post*, March 15, 1968; Blake, in *New York Times Magazine*, March 24, 1968, pp. 122, 124.

[68] The Czechoslovak developments are taken up in chapters XIV and XV. Signs that liberal influences from Czechoslovakia were particularly disturbing in the Ukraine, where aspirations for intellectual freedom had joined with Ukrainian nationalism to cause continuing restiveness, were to be seen in strictures laid down against reformist sentiment there in mid-1968 by party officials. See Raymond H. Anderson, "Czech Ferment Spreads to the Ukraine," *New York Times*, July 14, 1968. In Soviet intellectual circles, despite the regime's tightening of controls on expression of sympathy for the Czechoslovak reform movement, an occasional approving voice was heard. One was that of Professor Andrei Sakharov, who, in his previously mentioned manuscript, circulated privately in Moscow, said that the Soviet Union should "support the bold initiative" of the Czech reformers, rather than try to suppress them.

[69] In addition to scientists, members of the Soviet Writers' Union who signed protest documents were warned to recant or face expulsion from the union. See "Soviet Party Is Said To Expel Scientists Who Joined Protest," *New York Times*, April 24, 1968; "Writers' Dissent Scored in Soviet," ibid., April 29, 1968; "Soviet Scientists Told To Back Party," *Washington Post*, April 28, 1968.

[70] Among those so warned were Pavel Iakir, scientist and son of a Red Army leader purged by Stalin; retired Major General Petr Grigorenko; and relatives and friends of defendants at the Ginsburg trial. See Anatole Shub, "Soviet Police Crack Down on Authors," *Washington Post*, February 18, 1968. For a general description of various security measures invoked in 1968 to isolate resident foreigners in the Soviet Union from the population, see Shub's article, "Alien Is Lonely in Today's Moscow," ibid., July 7, 1968.

[71] See D. Kraminov, "Crocodile Tears," *Pravda*, March 3, 1968.

in the Soviet Union and a massive propaganda campaign against what Soviet authorities chose to describe as "subversive" efforts by the West aimed at "undermining socialist society from within."[72]

In October 1966 the arrest and conviction of Pavel Litvinov and four other intellectuals for having staged a public protest against the Czechoslovak invasion added another dreary chapter to the mounting campaign for orthodox conformity,[73] while during the following year there were further reported arrests of dissident Soviet citizens, including several naval officers accused of urging liberalization of Soviet society.[74] Among the regime's least savory methods of silencing its critics was the occasional practice of committing them to mental institutions, a measure taken in December 1969 against retired Major General P. G. Grigorenko.[75] On the other hand, however, such an articulate critic as the young historian Andrei A. Amalrik continued to remain at liberty, deprived only of the opportunity—at least up to early 1970—of publishing his works in the Soviet Union.[76]

Although the issues that lay beneath the restiveness of an articulate segment of the Soviet intellectual community were not likely to be resolved by either fiat or propaganda, the outlook for reform through critical protest was not bright at the beginning of 1970, for the repressive campaign against intellectuals had become part of a more pervasive trend toward what might be described as neo-Stalinism.[77] At best, this seemed to suggest that the liberal

[72] See "Speech of Comrade L. I. Brezhnev at XIX Conference of Moscow City Organization CPSU," *Pravda*, March 30, 1968, and "Resolution of the Plenum of CPSU Central Committee, adopted 10 April 1968: On Current Problems of the International Situation and the Struggle of the CPSU for Unity of the World Communist Movement," *Pravda*, April 11, 1968. Like Brezhnev's speech a few days before, the Plenum resolution emphasized that a sharp aggravation of the ideological struggle between communism and the capitalist West had taken place.

[73] In addition to Litvinov, the wife of Yuli M. Daniel was among those sentenced for protesting the Czech invasion. Her statement at the trial in October, together with remarks by retired Major General P. G. Grigorenko at the funeral of a comrade in November, stood out as brave indictments of Soviet totalitarianism. See Henry Kamm, "3 Soviet Dissidents Exiled and 2 Jailed," *New York Times*, October 12, 1968; "Excerpts from the Proceedings of Trial in Moscow," ibid., October 16, 1968; "Soviet Is Denounced at Dissident's Rites," ibid., November 15, 1968.

[74] See Bernard Gwertzman, "3 Soviet Officers Reported Seized," *New York Times*, October 24, 1969. The naval officers in this case were the first military men on active duty known to have taken part in protest activities; an army officer arrested for shooting at either a Soviet cosmonaut or Brezhnev during a Kremlin ceremony in January 1969 was supposedly not linked to any dissident group. See Theodore Shabad, "Soviet Doubts Political Plot in Kremlin Shooting," *New York Times*, February 5, 1969.

[75] James F. Clarity, "Soviet Dissident Reported 'Insane'," *New York Times*, December 13, 1969.

[76] Amalrik is the author of an openly critical book, *Will the Soviet Union Survive Until 1984?*, published in the United States in early 1970. (See chapter X, fn. 22.) Despite rumors that Amalrik may be a KGB collaborator because he has escaped jail, the contents of his work strongly suggest that this is not the case. See James F. Clarity, "Soviet Dissident Publishes Abroad Without Police Interference," *New York Times*, December 24, 1969.

[77] As discussed previously (chapter IV, pp. 63–69), a cautious rehabilitation of Stalin had begun as early as 1965, seemingly to counter the notion that the period of his rule was a sorry aberration in Soviet history. This trend grew more pronounced as the Brezhnev–Kosygin regime "regressed" toward dogmatic defense of orthodoxy, capped by the Czechoslovak suppression. In effect, the leadership increasingly leaned toward neo-Stalinism without some of the more overt features of Stalinist terror. As men like S. Trapeznikov maneuvered to clamp conformity upon Soviet intellectuals, word apparently went out to stop writing about Stalin's mistakes. Military memoirists,

wing of the intelligentsia faced further intimidation before its protests against
narrow conformity could again be countenanced. At the worst, it meant that
official sanctions and lack of general public support were gradually forcing the
protesting intellectuals to resign themselves to the futility of trying to improve
the system from within.[78]

Trends in Foreign Policy

In keeping with its general style of eschewing flamboyant personal initiatives, the collective leadership team under Brezhnev and Kosygin apparently
set out to conduct Soviet foreign policy in a more restrained fashion than had
been the case under Khrushchev. If the new leaders were dissatisfied with the
Soviet Union's position in foreign affairs as they found it in the fall of 1964,
they did not immediately advertise the fact by criticizing either Khrushchev's
general line of "peaceful coexistence" or specific policies initiated by him.
Rather, their approach seemed to be based on a resolve to work patiently for
improvement of the Soviet Union's economic potential and its military position
vis-à-vis the United States, while avoiding unsettling initiatives like those that
Khrushchev had undertaken in Berlin and Cuba.

Paradoxically, however, though the new leaders may have taken office hoping
to concentrate their energies on economic and other tasks at home rather than
raise fresh issues abroad, they soon found that foreign policy problems had
sought them out. Of the more immediate issues thrust upon the new leadership, the first was an impending showdown in the Sino–Soviet conflict, posed
by Khrushchev's timetable for a conference of Communist parties in Moscow
at the end of 1964, which presumably he had called in preparation for reading
Peking out of the world Communist movement.[79] The second issue, or, more
accurately, a whole series of issues, grew out of the increased American commitment to the war in Vietnam, beginning in mid-February 1965 on the heels
of Kosygin's visit to Hanoi. Among other things, the extension of American
air attacks to North Vietnam ended the sanctuary customarily enjoyed by
established Communist regimes, thus bringing the Soviet leaders face to face
with the uncomfortable question of having to honor obligations for the defense

---

among them Marshal Zhukov, came forward to give more sympathetic portrayals of Stalin's wartime
role, and the party's leading theoretical journal explicitly appraised Stalin as "an outstanding
military leader." See E. Boltin, "Stirring Pages from Chronicles of the Great Fatherland War,"
Kommunist, no. 2 (January 1969): 127.

[78] For a perceptive account of the alienation of Soviet intellectuals and the general apathy of
the Soviet public toward their plight, see the series of three anonymous articles, beginning with
"Neo-Stalinism: An Inside Report of the New Reign of Fear," in *Sunday Times,* London, January
12, 19, 26, 1969. For the most comprehensive treatment to date of dissent in the Soviet Union, see
the collection of essays and original documents in Abraham Brumberg, ed., *In Quest of Justice:
Protest and Dissent in the Soviet Union Today* (New York: Praeger Publishers, 1970).

[79] Khrushchev in July 1964 had scheduled a twenty-six party conference to make preparations
for a new world conference strenuously opposed by Peking. For a detailed examination of the
conference issue, see William E. Griffith, *Sino–Soviet Relations, 1964–1965* (Cambridge, Mass.:
Center for International Studies, M.I.T., 1965), pp. 9–71. See also Thomas W. Wolfe, *The Soviet
Union and the Sino–Soviet Dispute,* The RAND Corporation, P-3203, August 1965, pp. 5–8.

of a client Communist state far from the continental base of Soviet military power.

The Soviet response in each of these instances suggested that, while the Brezhnev–Kosygin regime was eager to steer clear of any sharp new crisis in its relations with China and the United States, it was not prepared to make fundamental concessions involving the Soviet Union's political interest and prestige for the sake of reaching a compromise with either its Communist or its capitalist adversary.

Moscow's Handling of the Sino–Soviet Dispute

In the Sino–Soviet case, the new regime initially sought to get off a collision course with Peking by deferring the December 1964 preparatory meeting of Communist parties to March 1965 and changing it to a "consultative" session.[80] This and other gestures aimed at moderating the Sino–Soviet polemics failed, however, to mollify Peking, which made clear that its price for harmony was a basic reversal of Soviet policies.[81] Although the Soviet leadership may have been tempted to repay Chinese intransigence in kind, and in fact did occasionally relax its self-imposed ban on polemics,[82] it was careful on the whole not to allow itself to be drawn into untimely or ill-considered moves against Peking. By sticking to tactics of minimum retaliatory invective and appealing for "unity" within the Communist camp in support of North Vietnam, the Soviet regime gained ground steadily at Peking's expense throughout 1965 and 1966, as underscored by the virtual isolation of the Chinese at the Twenty-third Party Congress in Moscow, in April 1966.[83]

The Soviet position was strengthened further with the onset of Mao's "cultural revolution" in China, the excesses of which added lustre to the "moderate" Soviet posture. By the autumn of 1966 the Soviet leaders had contained Peking's influence to the point that they felt it profitable to revive the

[80] Postponement of the scheduled conference came after Chou En-lai's visit to Moscow in November 1964 had failed to resolve differences between Moscow and Peking. When eventually held, in March 1965, the conference was whittled down from twenty-six to nineteen parties, for the Chinese and their client parties refused to attend. As a result of the meeting, the idea of a world conference was buried for the time being.

[81] As early as November 1964, in a twelve-point editorial on Khrushchev's fall, the Chinese emphasized that they wanted nothing less than repudiation of the whole of Khrushchev's "revisionist" foreign and domestic policies. In March 1965 Soviet overtures for an end to open polemics were flatly rejected in an editorial in which the Chinese again demanded Soviet capitulation on all major issues. See editorial, "Why Khrushchev Fell," *Red Flag*, November 21, 1964, in *Peking Review*, no. 48, November 27, 1964; joint *People's Daily* and *Red Flag* editorial, March 23, 1965, in *Peking Review*, no. 13, March 26, 1965.

[82] See, for example, "The Supreme International Duty of the Countries of Socialism," *Pravda*, October 27, 1965.

[83] The success of Soviet maneuvers in isolating the Chinese was pointed up by Brezhnev's announcement at the Twenty-third Party Congress that all foreign party representatives present endorsed the Soviet "unity" line for the world Communist movement. The isolation of China was marked similarly at the celebration of the fiftieth anniversary of the Bolshevik revolution in November 1967. See Report of L. I. Brezhnev to the Twenty-third Party Congress in *Pravda*, March 30, 1966; Report of Brezhnev to the Central Committee of the CPSU, the Supreme Soviet USSR, and the Supreme Soviet RSFSR, *Pravda*, November 4, 1967; and "Red China Ignores Bid to Soviet Fete," *New York Times*, October 29, 1967.

idea of a conference of Communist parties.[84] Thereafter, Moscow's lobbying
for such a world conference was coupled, in 1967 and early 1968, with increasingly open attacks on "Mao Tse-tung and his clique,"[85] which suggested that
the Kremlin leaders had finally given up hope of reconciliation with Mao's
regime and were now willing to encourage any dissident party factions in
China that might seek his overthrow. Indeed, one of the "theses" issued by
the CPSU in 1967 to commemorate the fiftieth anniversary of the Soviet
Union included what amounted to an open invitation to the Chinese Communist party to break with Mao's "ruinous policy."[86]

As political attacks on Maoist rule sharpened in 1967, Sino–Soviet trade
declined to an all-time low,[87] and a series of further irritants led to mutual
reduction of embassy staffs just short of a formal diplomatic break.[88] Throughout 1968 the dispute between Moscow and Peking continued to simmer, with
both sides scoring a few points. For its part, the Soviet leadership again managed to demonstrate Mao's isolation from the rest of the world Communist
movement by convening a "consultative" session of some sixty parties at Budapest in February, without the Chinese.[89] Moscow also sought, with some
success, to rally Communist opinion behind its position by asserting that there
was danger of a breakdown of party rule under Mao which might imperil the
very existence of the Communist system in China.[90] On the other hand, thanks

[84] The idea of a conference was first reopened in Sofia on November 14, 1966, by Bulgarian
party leader Todor Zhivkov, who said that conditions for such a meeting were "ripening." The
following day Brezhnev approved the idea, although making no specific commitments to a conference. See "Report of Todor Zhivkov, First Secretary of the Central Committee of the Bulgarian
Communist Party, to the Ninth Bulgarian Communist Party Congress," *Pravda*, November 15, 1966,
and L. I. Brezhnev's speech to the Ninth Bulgarian Party Congress, *Pravda*, November 16, 1966.

[85] The opening of Soviet attacks on Mao and his "false leadership" began with a major *Pravda*
editorial of November 27, 1966, entitled "Apropos of Events in China." The anti-Mao campaign
gathered momentum thereafter, with charges, among other things, that Mao was imperiling
world Communist unity by his "chauvinist" policy, that he was violating Marxist principles by
establishing a "military-bureaucratic state," and that he was guilty of "advancing territorial claims"
against the USSR. See particularly, *Pravda* articles of February 16 and August 16, 1967; and two
special articles, "On the Nature of the 'Cultural Revolution' in China" and "On the Political
Course of Mao Tse-tung in the International Arena," published in *Kommunist*, no. 7 and no. 8
(May 1968): 103–14 and 95–108, respectively.

[86] See "50 Years of the Great October Socialist Revolution; Theses of the CPSU Central Committee," *Pravda*, June 25, 1967.

[87] See *Soviet Economic Performance: 1966–1967*, p. 103. Interestingly enough, Peking acted to
discharge its financial obligations to the USSR early in the Brezhnev–Kosygin regime, paying off
its full indebtedness to the Soviet Union by the end of 1965, two years ahead of schedule.

[88] Among the irritants in Sino–Soviet relations which preceded the recall of diplomatic personnel
were demonstrations against the Soviet embassy in Peking in the summer of 1967 and retaliatory
"protest marches" against the Chinese embassy in Moscow. Other signs of friction included recurrent allegations of border incidents from both sides, the detention by the Chinese of a Soviet ship
at Dairen in August 1967, and of another, bound for Vietnam, in April 1968.

[89] At the Budapest "consultative" meeting in February 1968, the Soviets had to contend with
a Rumanian walkout. Nevertheless, they managed to score points against Peking, not by threatening
to excommunicate China, but by emphasizing the need for unity against alleged "imperialist
aggression," and by letting Peking's refusal to have any part of an ecumenical Communist gathering speak for itself.

[90] According to a typical Soviet assertion, "the activity of Mao Tse-tung and his group shows
that the cult of personality and the obliteration of inner-Party democracy undermine the leading

to the Soviet intervention in Czechoslovakia in August, Peking acquired a ready-made argument that Moscow was no respecter of the rights of other Communist countries.

Then, in 1969, Sino–Soviet relations deteriorated dramatically, as border clashes erupted along the Ussuri River in March[91] and again along the Sinkiang frontier in August, accompanied in the latter instance by veiled hints from Moscow that nuclear strikes against China's atomic installations were a possibility.[92] Although this threat may have been intended mainly to coerce Peking into border talks, it helped to stimulate widespread speculation that Russia and China were heading toward a military showdown.[93] Should war occur, of course, it would shatter one of the fundamental tenets of Marxist–Leninist theory, namely, that war is a product of the capitalist order, unthinkable between "fraternal" Communist states. Aware perhaps of the damage that this concept would suffer, not to mention the material costs of settling their dispute by war, both sides agreed in October 1969 to another effort to negotiate their differences.[94]

---

role of the Party and jeopardize its very existence." *Kommunist*, no. 8 (May 1968): 107. Another Soviet statement, circulated prior to the Budapest "consultative" conference, said: "What is now taking place in China arouses growing concern and anxiety among Marxist–Leninists throughout the world. This is understandable, for the very existence of the Communist Party of China as one of the largest units of the international Communist movement is being jeopardized." See Moscow dispatch, " 'Wave of Discontent' Threatens Communism in China, Soviets Say," *Washington Post*, April 24, 1968.

[91] Although the Soviet Union described the series of Ussuri incidents as a "bloody provocation" which testified to Mao's war-like readiness to "sacrifice half the population of China and even of the world," and indicated that it was prepared to deal appropriately with "any attempts to talk to the Soviet Union...in the language of weapons," interestingly enough it was Moscow which first struck a reasonable stance by proposing to cool off the Ussuri crisis through border negotiations. See "The Policy of the Mao Tse-tung Group in the International Arena," *Kommunist*, no. 5 (March 1969): 107; "Statement of the Government of the USSR," *Pravda*, March 30, 1969.

[92] These hints took two forms. A *Pravda* editorial of August 28, 1969, criticizing "the adventurist course of Peking," warned in general terms that any war with China would involve nuclear weapons and modern delivery means. More specific reference to possible nuclear attack against China's atomic installations at Lop Nor came in mid-September from Victor Louis, a Soviet journalist, who, in a dispatch to the *London Evening News*, wrote that such an attack was being discussed by "Marxist theoreticians" and that, if it took place, "the world would only learn about it afterwards." See "Controversial Russian Newsman Hints Russians Might Launch Attack on China," *New York Times*, September 18, 1969.

[93] Western speculation on the rising danger of war was matched in late 1969 and early 1970 by statements from both Moscow and Peking blaming each other for stepping up military preparations and fanning a war psychosis. See Stanley Karnow, "Soviet Attack Coming, Peking Tells Its People," and "China Warns of Nuclear War, Urges World Revolution," *Washington Post*, September 11 and 17, 1969; "Documents on Chinese Military Provocations on the Soviet–Chinese Border," *Izvestiia*, September 11, 1969; Anthony Astrachan, "Moscow Alleges Peking Fans Arms 'Psychosis'," *Washington Post*, January 9, 1970; Iu. Andreev, "Militaristic Fumes in Peking," *Krasnaia zvezda*, January 21, 1970. For a reflective work dealing with the likelihood of a Sino–Soviet war, see Harrison Salisbury, *War Between Russia and China* (New York: W. W. Norton & Company, 1969).

[94] "Text of Chinese Statement Agreeing to Discuss Border Issue with Soviet Union," *New York Times*, October 8, 1969. This statement noted that China would never be intimidated by "nuclear war threats" or the possibility that "a handful of war maniacs" might "dare to raid China's strategic sites," but the fact that China agreed to negotiate suggested that the threats had served their purpose. The talks were suspended in mid-December 1969, and resumed again in January 1970.

By early 1970 the negotiations had yielded no visible results, leaving the Sino–Soviet feud as far from resolution as ever. From the standpoint of Soviet policy, however, it appeared that the Brezhnev–Kosygin regime now faced a whole series of problems more complicated than those on the Soviet agenda at the time of Khrushchev's ouster. The first, no doubt, was that of averting an outright war with China. Another was to prevent China from moving toward a rapprochement with the United States, while a third was to explore the prospects of creating a new "collective security" system in Asia that might help to hem in the Chinese.[95] Finally, there was the question of priority between Europe and Asia. Should the Soviet Union continue to give top priority to its foreign policy concerns in the West, or should it shift its primary attention to dealing with the "China problem"? This, too, was a question which the Kremlin leadership, accustomed to looking upon Europe as the central arena of world politics, would probably find it difficult to resolve.

The New Regime's Involvement in the Vietnam War

During most of the Brezhnev–Kosygin regime's first five years in office, issues growing out of the war in Vietnam made themselves felt increasingly in the conduct of Soviet foreign policy. Besides calling for enlarged commitment of Soviet resources to the support of Hanoi and sharpening debate within the Soviet leadership over hardline versus moderate policies abroad, the Vietnam conflict also created propaganda and political opportunities of which the Soviet Union sought to take advantage in its relations with Europe, largely to the detriment of the détente with the United States that had been achieved under Khrushchev.

The new Soviet regime's first manifest step toward reasserting an interest in the Vietnam situation was Kosygin's trip to Hanoi with a military aid delegation which was announced in *Pravda* on January 31, 1965. The reasons for this trip, which seemed to betoken a definite departure from Khrushchev's policy of de facto disengagement from the Vietnam problem, are still open to speculation. At least two explanations are consistent with the assumption that the new Soviet leadership believed at the time that it was embarking on an approach that carried a relatively low risk, even though it reversed Khrushchev's hands-off attitude toward the Southeast Asia area. One theory is that the Soviet leaders were persuaded that the United States was about to write off its commitments in South Vietnam, where the political and military situation had greatly deteriorated in late 1964 and early 1965, and that therefore Soviet entry upon the scene could be accomplished without much risk of a US–Soviet confrontation and without serious detriment to their relations elsewhere. A second explanation, perhaps overlapping the first, is that the Kosygin mission

---

[95] A Soviet proposal for an Asian collective security system was first broached by Brezhnev in June 1969 and again by Gromyko the following month. Later in the year, the Soviets were reported to be taking diplomatic soundings among China's Asian neighbors on the prospects for such a system. See *Pravda*, June 8, 1969; *Izvestiia*, July 11, 1969; Richard Halloran, "Soviet May Propose Asian Security Talks," *New York Times*, October 25, 1969.

was meant to re-establish Soviet influence in Hanoi both to counter Chinese influence and to exert moderating leverage upon the North Vietnamese, lest the Hanoi regime be inclined to provoke the United States into an unnecessarily vigorous reaction.

If the new regime thought that the United States was on the verge of abandoning South Vietnam and that a display of Soviet support for Hanoi would entail little risk of a strong US response, events proved otherwise. The Viet Cong attacks on Pleiku while Kosygin was in Hanoi provoked precisely such a response; with the extension of US bombing to North Vietnam and the increasing commitment of American forces to South Vietnam, the Soviet leadership discovered that the United States was in fact prepared to employ its military power to thwart a Communist takeover in South Vietnam.

The precise steps by which the Soviet Union moved toward a deeper involvement in Vietnam after February 1965 need not be traced here. Suffice it to say that having made some unsuccessful private efforts to induce Hanoi and Peking to consider negotiation of the crisis,[96] Moscow took up an uncompromising diplomatic stance in the spring of 1965 and thereafter moved toward progressively larger commitment of its political and military resources in support of the Communist side in Vietnam.[97] At the same time, despite the increased scale of military aid and a coy reluctance to help bring about a negotiated solution, the Soviet leadership abstained from a formal commitment of its own military forces, remaining consistently unwilling to intervene in the Vietnam hostilities in a fashion that could involve the Soviet Union in a major confrontation with the United States.

Soviet hesitancy to play a conspicuous role as a peacemaker in the Vietnam conflict has sometimes been attributed to the fear of driving Hanoi into the arms of Peking. (Kosygin, in his celebrated talks with Prime Minister Wilson in London in February 1967, may have stepped briefly into the peacemaker's role, but he quickly backed out of it.[98]) Other factors doubtless entered the picture also, such as the temptation to exploit the political and propaganda

[96] Some of the evidence concerning the Soviet Union's initial peace-making efforts derives from a secret exchange of letters between Moscow and Peking in which the latter accused Moscow of advocating "peace negotiations" as part of "the line of Soviet–U.S. collaboration for domination of the world." The contents of these letters was made public several months later by the British journalist Edward Crankshaw. See "Peking Pushes Moscow to the Brink: Letters Tell of Vietnam Clash," *Observer*, November 14, 1965. See also Chinese reference to Moscow's advice on negotiating the February 1965 crisis in *Peking Review*, no. 46, November 12, 1965, pp. 15–16.

[97] The Soviet Union has never released figures on the total military and economic aid extended to North Vietnam, but according to Western estimates it came to more than $1 billion in the 1965–67 period, reaching an annual peak of about $500 million in military aid and $200 million in economic help in 1967. After the US bombing halt in 1968 military aid declined to an annual rate of about $300 million, while economic aid rose to about $250 million. The bulk of military aid has consisted of surface-to-air missiles, AAA guns, fighter aircraft, and electronics equipment for the air defense system of the DRV, together with standard logistics items. See Thomas W. Wolfe, *The Soviet Military Scene: Institutional and Defense Policy Considerations*, pp. 110–21; Hedrick Smith, "Hanoi Found Dependent on Outside Aid but Master of Own Strategy," *New York Times*, November 5, 1967; Lewis Gulick, "Soviets Trim Arms Aid to N. Vietnam," *Washington Post*, October 20, 1969.

[98] This matter is treated in chapter XIII, fn. 80.

value of a war whose prolongation was so obviously discomfiting to the American government at home and abroad. In any event, whatever the reasons that persuaded the Soviet leadership to eschew a peacemaker's role, when the diplomatic breakthrough that led to preliminary talks between the United States and North Vietnam in Paris did come, in the spring of 1968, it was apparently a US presidential initiative, not a helping hand from Moscow, that got the process of negotiation started.[99]

Although it endorsed the agreement to begin talks,[100] the USSR showed little disposition to mediate seriously for their success. Asserting that the United States had never expected Hanoi to agree to President Johnson's suggestion of March 31 that talks be held,[101] Soviet spokesmen maintained a generally skeptical attitude toward the outcome of the Paris negotiations, taking the position that "pre-election propaganda considerations" had motivated the American offer and that the United States was still hopeful of attaining a "military solution" in Vietnam rather than prepared to "embark upon the road of political settlement."[102] Besides passing up the opportunity to interpose a moderating voice during the early months of the Paris talks, the Soviet Union continued to promise the "utmost assistance" to Hanoi's war effort, and underlined this pledge by signing a new military aid agreement with North Vietnam in July.[103]

Subsequently, the Soviet stance shifted slightly; in the bargaining which led to President Johnson's October 31 announcement of a bombing halt and the widening of the Paris talks, Soviet diplomacy played a discreet though apparently still minor role.[104] After the change of administration in Washington in early 1969, Moscow's wait-and-see attitude toward the policies of the new Nixon administration extended also to the Paris talks. What contribution the Soviet Union might be prepared to make to help break the continuing deadlock in Paris remained, for the time being, an open question.

Let us return now to some of the effects that the Vietnam war had upon the general development of Soviet foreign policy after the Brezhnev–Kosygin

[99] There was nothing in the public record at the time to indicate that behind-the-scenes activity by the Soviet Union helped prepare the way for President Johnson's March 31, 1968, announcement of a bombing reduction and his accompanying offer to begin talks with Hanoi. Throughout the period of haggling over a site for the talks, the Soviet Union's public role was that not of an intermediary but of an uncompromising partisan censuring the United States for not accepting the DRV's choice of Phnom Penh or Warsaw. What part, if any, Soviet diplomacy played in reaching the agreement of May 3, which was followed by the opening of talks in Paris on May 13, 1968, also remains to be divulged.

[100] See "Wide Support for the DRV Position," *Pravda*, April 5, 1968.

[101] See, for example, Aleksei Vasil'ev, "The Good Will of the DRV," *Pravda*, May 5, 1968.

[102] See Iurii Zhukov, "The Aggressors Will Have to Leave," *Pravda*, May 19, 1968; and V. Kudriavtsev, "Where Is Harriman Leading the Situation?" *Izvestiia*, May 21, 1968. See also Kosygin's April 17 speech in Rawalpindi, *Pravda*, April 18, 1968; and Podgornyi's remarks at a state dinner, ibid., May 21, 1968.

[103] See "Collaboration Between USSR and DRV Is Strengthened," *Izvestiia*, July 6, 1968.

[104] See "Behind the Bombing Halt: An Account of Bargaining," *New York Times*, November 11, 1968.

regime's decision, in early 1965, to commit itself to increasing support of Hanoi.

Impact of Vietnam on Soviet Foreign Policy

The conflict in Vietnam was accompanied by a gradual hardening of Soviet foreign policy pronouncements, manifested in a tendency to soft-pedal the theme of peaceful coexistence and to dwell more than before on the danger of war posed by the "aggressive forces of imperialism." The down-grading of "peaceful coexistence," which began in *Pravda* editorials in the fall of 1965,[105] was given formal cognizance at the Twenty-third Party Congress in 1966 by Brezhnev, who placed it fourth on a list of six foreign policy priorities, below such goals as strengthening the unity of the Communist camp and supporting "national liberation" movements in the developing countries.[106] The increasing attention to the danger of war ran parallel to this lessening of emphasis on peaceful coexistence with the "imperialists." Beginning in the summer of 1965, both military and political commentary in the Soviet press took up the theme that "the aggressive character of imperialism" was growing, making it "the most important duty" of the Soviet party and other Marxist–Leninist parties "not to permit an underevaluation of the danger of war."[107] Thereafter, most of the top Soviet leaders periodically found it expedient to express some degree of concern about the possibility of a major new war, linking this possibility sometimes to the general worsening of the international situation and sometimes specifically to the danger of escalation by "American imperialism" in Vietnam.[108]

As suggested in an earlier chapter, it has often been important to distinguish between Soviet declaratory utterances on the likelihood of war—which serve various purposes of internal argument and external propaganda—and the private convictions of the leadership.[109] What the latter may be in the present regime is, of course, a speculative matter. This writer is inclined to suppose that Khrushchev's successors still consider a major war between the rival systems unlikely—if not thanks to benign US intentions then because of a combination of Soviet nuclear deterrent power and the political forces generally described as the "world peace movement."[110] At the same time, however, it is

[105] See, for example, "The Policy of the Party Expresses the Living Interests of the People," *Pravda*, September 27, 1965; and "The Highest International Duty of the Countries of Socialism," ibid., October 27, 1965.

[106] Report of L. I. Brezhnev, *Pravda*, March 30, 1966.

[107] See, for example, Fedor Burlatskii, "Lessons of the Struggle for Unity," *Pravda*, June 24, 1965, and General P. Kurochkin, "Strengthening of Aggressiveness—A Characteristic Trait of Contemporary Imperialism," *Krasnaia zvezda*, July 9, 1965.

[108] Among such expressions, see speeches by Brezhnev, *Pravda*, September 11, 1965, and *Izvestiia*, October 24, 1965; by M. A. Suslov, *Pravda*, October 31, 1965; Kosygin interview with James Reston, *New York Times*, December 8, 1965; Garbuzov, *Pravda*, December 8, 1965; Brezhnev speech at the Twenty-third Party Congress, *Pravda*, March 30, 1966; and Brezhnev fiftieth anniversary keynote speech, *Pravda*, November 4, 1967.

[109] See chapter VII, pp. 156–59.

[110] For an elaborate Soviet analysis of how the combination of Soviet military power and "peace

best not to dismiss the possibility that the present leaders differ from their predecessors in their private views on the danger-of-war issue. They may indeed have come to believe, as their propaganda has so tirelessly asserted, that American military intervention in Vietnam and the Dominican Republic, together with such other matters as the alleged American backing of the "Israeli aggressors" and the military junta in Greece, betokened a shift of US policy in a direction that could involve the major powers in a larger war.[111]

Certainly, Soviet military preparations under the Brezhnev–Kosygin regime seem to reflect a gradually rising estimate of the possibility that tensions in the international arena might cause the Soviet Union to become involved in armed conflict of one sort or another. Although these preparations have not been in the form of "crash" programs that would suggest concern over an imminent outbreak of a major war, they have nevertheless required increased military budget outlays with each successive year[112]—indicating, among other things, that the leadership has deemed it prudent to seek a higher level of military preparedness despite domestic economic demands on Soviet resources.

As we shall see later, the arms build-up carried out by the Brezhnev–Kosygin regime probably derived its initial momentum less from the war in Vietnam than from the regime's resolve to alter the image of a Soviet Union strategically inferior to its principal Western adversary. At the same time, of course, Vietnam underscored what to Moscow probably looked like hostile and dangerous American policies, thereby convincing the leadership of the wisdom of taking measures to strengthen the Soviet military posture.

The potential effect of these measures on the military power balance, together with the implications that might flow from any substantial shift in the balance favorable to the Soviet Union, will be discussed later.[113] As to the Vietnam war and its influence on Soviet foreign policy, perhaps one of its principal effects was to sharpen the regime's problem of deciding between the virtue of a hard and militant line abroad and that of a policy of restraint and moderation.[114]

---

forces" abroad acts to prevent a world war, see Major General N. Ia. Sushko and Colonel S. A. Tiushkevich, eds., *Marksizm–Leninizm o voine i armii* (Marxism–Leninism on War and the Army) (4th edition; Moscow: Voenizdat, 1965), pp. 83–91.

[111] For a perceptive discussion of the Soviet reading of American policy, see Marshall D. Shulman, "Reds Really Think U.S. Is Militant," *Washington Post*, p. E–1, November 27, 1966. For some characteristic Soviet propaganda pieces portraying US foreign policy as a threat to peace and as a persistent effort to suppress "national-liberation" movements and establish US world domination, see Y. Melnikov, "U.S. Foreign Policy—A Threat to Peace," *International Affairs* (Moscow), no. 1 (January 1967): 64–70; I. Mikuson, "Imperialist Conceptions of Preventing Revolution," ibid., no. 2 (February 1967): 78–84; B. Teplinsky, "U.S. Military Programme," ibid., no. 8 (August 1967): 46–51.

[112] For figures on Soviet military budgets and more detailed discussion of this subject, see chapter XVI, pp. 428–29.

[113] See, in particular, chapter XVIII.

[114] For an interesting analysis of this Soviet policy dilemma, see Marshall D. Shulman, "The Critical Decision for Moscow," *New Leader*, July 3, 1967, pp. 3–6. See also John C. Campbell, "Soviet-American Relations: Conflict and Cooperation," *Current History* (October 1967): 241.

From the beginning of its tenure, the new collective leadership was marked by a controversy between advocates of what could loosely be described as the "hard-line" and the "moderate" policy course. The hard-line approach implied not only a larger and possibly more dangerous level of support for Hanoi's war effort but also the adoption of a tougher attitude on Germany and other European questions, a more vigorous attempt to extend Soviet influence in the Middle East and elsewhere in the Third World, and a further build-up of military forces that probably would quicken the tempo of the arms race. The moderate line, on the other hand, implied a willingness to work seriously for a negotiated solution of Vietnam, and a readiness to seek an easing of international tensions by helping to promote greater stability in Europe and the Middle East, by mending Soviet relations with the United States, and by exploring new approaches to bringing the arms race under control.

The Vietnam war, of course, was only one of many factors bearing on the Soviet Union's choice between these two broad lines of policy. However, to the extent that Soviet policy decisions under the collective rule of the Brezhnev–Kosygin regime have been the product of "committee compromise" between hard-line and moderate factions within the leadership,[115] the war in Vietnam probably tended to weaken the case of those leadership elements favoring priority for economic improvement at home and a tension-easing policy of moderation abroad. Even so, it can be argued that the greater part of the Brezhnev–Kosygin regime's foreign policy record testifies to an inability to pursue a clear-cut policy line in either direction, at least in dealing with countries outside the Soviet bloc.[116] In this view, rule by "committee compromise" has tended to produce a policy deadlock of sorts, with hard and soft factions often canceling each other out, leaving the regime to steer a middle, and frequently ambivalent, policy course.[117]

Whatever effect the internal interplay of collective leadership politics may have had upon the foreign policy decisions of the Brezhnev–Kosygin regime, however, it would appear that the Kremlin has found it particularly difficult to settle upon an unequivocal policy line toward the United States, a problem that perhaps reflects the tangle of conflicting and interdependent interests characteristic of the relationship between these two global rivals.

[115] It is hardly necessary to point out that classification of the Soviet leadership in terms of hard-soft, hawk-dove, conservative-liberal, dogmatist-pragmatist, or similarly polarized groupings vastly oversimplifies the situation, where in practice alignments along many other axes of interest, institutional position and outlook undoubtedly exist. However, even though precise identification of various interest-group alignments and syndromes cannot be readily made, it may still be assumed that important Soviet foreign policy decisions under the Brezhnev–Kosygin regime have tended to reflect a kind of "committee compromise" among contending preferences and views within the ruling oligarchy.

[116] In the matter of intrabloc relations, on the other hand, it can be argued that hardline advocates within the collective leadership gradually managed to get their way, as attested to by the crackdown on Czechoslovakia in 1968 and promulgation of the Brezhnev doctrine of "limited sovereignty."

[117] For commentary reflecting this view, see Anatole Shub, "Politburo Tug-of-War Suspected in Conservative Soviet Policies," *Washington Post*, December 3, 1967.

Soviet–American Relations

As noted previously, a perceptible cooling in Soviet–US relations first became evident in early 1965, after a brief interlude during which the Brezhnev–Kosygin regime had adhered officially to Khrushchev's priority on "peaceful coexistence" and the United States, in turn, had expressed the hope of fostering mutual understanding and co-operative relations with the Soviet Union and East Europe. Such hopes were expressed, for example, in President Johnson's State of the Union message of January 4, 1965,[118] the first of a number of overtures he was to make to the new Soviet regime on the theme of East–West "bridge-building." One may observe, incidentally, that the beginning of an overtly hostile Soviet stance toward the United States by the Brezhnev–Kosygin regime came in the Soviet reaction to this speech—and not after the initiation of US bombing attacks against North Vietnam more than a month later, as is often assumed.[119]

By mid-1965 there was no mistaking that little was left of the détente in Soviet–US relations which had carried over from the Khrushchev period. In addition to reviving old charges that the United States was encouraging the "revanchist" aspirations of West Germany by sponsoring the multilateral force (MLF) project which allegedly would enable Bonn to acquire nuclear weapons, the Soviet leadership began to lay new stress on other aspects of American policy that it considered inimical to Soviet interests, especially the growing American military commitment in Vietnam. From then on, Soviet attacks on American policy became increasingly sharp, as one spokesman after another sought to pin upon "American imperialism" the full responsibility for "threats to peace" throughout the world and asserted that only American withdrawal from Vietnam could halt the deterioration of Soviet–US relations.[120]

In the face of this campaign of anti-American invective, there was little response to Washington's periodic overtures for better East–West understanding, as illustrated by the reaction to President Johnson's major speech of October 7, 1966, in favor of a "bridge-building" policy. This speech, in which the President called for a return to the spirit of détente and suggested various steps toward reconciliation with the Soviet Union and the East European countries,[121] met with a chilly reception in Moscow, where a week later Brezhnev delivered a public rebuff, stating that American officials labored under a "strange and persistent delusion" if they thought it possible to improve relations with the USSR and Eastern Europe despite the conflict in Vietnam.[122]

118 For text of this speech, see *New York Times*, January 5, 1965.

119 See, for example, "Observer" commentary on the President's message, *Izvestiia*, January 6, 1965, which signaled the first of a series of negative responses to Johnson's proposal of an exchange of visits with the Soviet leaders.

120 See Campbell, in *Current History*, pp. 198–99.

121 Besides calling for bridge-building steps such as removal of trade barriers, improvement of communication, and possible mutual troop cutbacks in Europe, President Johnson's speech was notable for avoiding stress on questions likely to raise Soviet hackles, such as German reunification or NATO nuclear-sharing proposals. For text of the speech, see *New York Times*, October 8, 1966.

122 Speech of L. I. Brezhnev to visiting Polish party-state delegation, *Pravda*, October 16, 1966.

Negotiations on Nuclear Nonproliferation and Other Matters

Although such dramatic American diplomatic initiatives as the bridge-building speech of October 1966 and President Johnson's tête-à-tête with Premier Kosygin at Glassboro in June 1967, during the Arab–Israeli crisis, failed to produce any notable shift in the Soviet Union's public criticism of American policy, the Kremlin leadership tacitly demonstrated in a number of other instances that it was prepared to deal with the United States on certain specific questions without making resolution of the Vietnam crisis a precondition for negotiations.

Thus, for example, the Soviet Union responded to an American initiative of May 1966 for negotiation of an outer-space treaty designed to amplify and formalize earlier understandings on the regulation of space activities, including the 1963 UN resolution against placing weapons of mass destruction in orbit. The treaty, negotiations on which proceeded simultaneously with angry Soviet denunciations of US policy in Europe and Asia, was signed in almost record time on January 27, 1967, the first multilateral agreement with arms control provisions since the partial test ban of 1963.[123] The renewal of a cultural exchange agreement between the two countries in March 1966, a Soviet decision in September 1966 to exchange weather satellite photos with the United States, and resumption of talks which in November 1966 led to the signing of an agreement to set up direct commercial flights between the United States and the USSR,[124] were other examples of matters on which Moscow chose to deal with Washington in this period.[125]

But perhaps the most notable manifestation of this willingness to overlook Vietnam as a barrier to participation in negotiations with the United States came in connection with the nuclear nonproliferation treaty, a matter which had been under intermittent discussion in arms control conferences since 1960. After having insisted, at the recess of the Eighteen Nation Disarmament Committee (ENDC) in the fall of 1965, that the Vietnam situation barred the way to fruitful negotiation on nonproliferation and other arms control matters, Soviet spokesmen adopted a different attitude when the Geneva talks recon-

[123] The space treaty signed on January 27, 1967, besides incorporating a ban on orbiting of mass destructive weapons, established rules for aid to astronauts and recovery of space vehicles and prohibited claims for sovereignty over other planets or the moon. For text of the treaty, see *Department of State Bulletin*, December 26, 1966, p. 953. Subsequently, a sequel to the space treaty dealing with aid to astronauts was worked out and endorsed by the UN General Assembly in December 1967.

[124] See Murrey Marder, "U.S., Russia Finally Sign Culture Pact," *Washington Post*, March 20, 1966; Harold M. Schmeck, "U.S. and Moscow Trade Space Data," *New York Times*, September 27, 1966; Richard Eder, "U.S. and Soviet Sign Air Service Accord," ibid., November 5, 1966. A delay of almost two years over "technical" questions ensued before the first flights under the air agreement took place in July 1968.

[125] One issue of peripheral importance upon which Moscow declined to act during this period was that of reciprocal consular arrangements. The US Senate on March 16, 1967, after heated debate, ratified the consular treaty which had been negotiated in June 1964 in Moscow. Despite this move from the American side, which was widely represented as a sign of goodwill, ratification by the Soviet Union was held up for another year. It was eventually announced on May 4, 1968, as one of the first of a new series of Soviet gestures signaling a warmer phase of co-operation.

vened, in January 1966, placing new emphasis on the need for a nonproliferation agreement.[126] The prospect of using a nonproliferation treaty as a means
of blocking German access to nuclear weapons doubtless counted heavily with
the Soviet leaders, outweighing any risk that their readiness to explore the
subject anew would be construed as unseemly "collusion" with the United
States while the Vietnam war was in progress.[127] At any rate, the ensuing
negotiations yielded their first fruit in August 1967 with the joint US–Soviet
acceptance of a draft nonproliferation treaty, complete except for Article III
on inspection, which was left blank.[128]

Although the nonproliferation talks bogged down for several months because
of unresolved differences over inspection and the dissatisfaction of various
non-nuclear countries with some aspects of the proposed treaty,[129] a joint US–
Soviet draft of a completed treaty was presented at Geneva on January 18,
1968, marking yet another significant step in collaboration despite the constraints of the war in Vietnam. Amendment of this draft followed, and a later
version was submitted to the UN General Assembly in March 1968.[130] On
July 1, 1968, the effort culminated in the signing of the treaty by the Soviet
Union, the United States, Britain, and fifty-eight other countries.[131]

[126] See Thomas W. Wolfe, *The Soviet Union and Arms Control*, The RAND Corporation,
P-3337, April 1966, pp. 18–19.

[127] Not surprisingly, the Chinese made precisely this accusation in connection with Soviet interest
in nonproliferation negotiations. See, for example, the text of Peking's letter of refusal to attend the
Twenty-third Party Congress of the CPSU, *New York Times*, March 24, 1966.

[128] On August 24, 1967, after having reached agreement on a proposed nonproliferation treaty
several weeks before, the Soviet Union and the United States presented identical texts of
the treaty, minus the unresolved article on inspection, to the Eighteen Nation Disarmament Committee (ENDC). For the text, see *New York Times*, August 25, 1967.

[129] Soviet–US differences on inspection to prevent diversion of peaceful atomic activity to military
purposes did not hinge on problems of inspecting each other, since inspection was to be applied
only to states not possessing nuclear weapons. The USSR insisted that the International Atomic
Energy Agency (IAEA) should inspect atomic activities in West Germany and other countries
belonging to the European Economic Community from the outset. The United States, on the other
hand, in deference to the wishes of Germany and other members of the EEC (except France, which
spurned the treaty altogether) to be inspected by Euratom, supported the idea of a gradual transfer
of inspection from Euratom to the IAEA. For discussion of these inspection differences, as well as
reservations expressed by various non-nuclear states toward the treaty, see statements by various
participants in the ENDC negotiations, in *Documents on Disarmament, 1967*, United States Arms
Control and Disarmament Agency, Washington, D.C., July 1968, pp. 135–688 passim. See also
Thomas B. Larson, *Disarmament and Soviet Policy, 1964–1968* (Englewood Cliffs, N.J.: Prentice-
Hall, Inc., 1969), pp. 151–56.

[130] The first complete draft of January 18, 1968, was revised after the objections raised by some
of the allies of both the US and the USSR, as well as nonaligned countries. (For Soviet–Rumanian
differences over the treaty, see chapter XIV, pp. 477–78.) The amended joint draft was presented
at Geneva on March 11, and submitted to the UN General Assembly on March 14. There it met
further criticism, which led to Soviet–US acceptance of changes designed to provide stronger
security guarantees to non-nuclear powers and to enjoin the big powers to make more urgent
efforts to end the arms race. This final amended version was endorsed by an Assembly vote of
92 to 4, with 22 abstentions, on June 10, 1968.

[131] For text of the final treaty document signed on July 1, 1968, see *Department of State Bulletin*, July 1, 1968, pp. 8–11. On the same day the treaty was signed, the Soviet government issued
a memorandum proposing nine disarmament measures upon which it was prepared to begin
negotiation. These were: a ban on use of nuclear weapons; a proposal to end manufacture of
nuclear weapons and reduce stockpiles; limitation and reduction of strategic delivery means; a ban

Thus, although some important nations held out against signing,[132] the nonproliferation negotiations established a new landmark in the effort to control nuclear weapons. As regarded the relationship between the two nuclear superpowers, they demonstrated that neither US–Soviet rivalry nor the tensions of the Vietnam conflict precluded agreement in a case where both sides presumably perceived a treaty as serving important interests, albeit for somewhat different reasons. The Soviet Union's view of the treaty as a way to forestall any NATO nuclear-sharing arrangements with Germany, and its desire to profit from the political embarrassment that this might introduce into relations between the United States and its allies,[133] were obviously not shared by the United States. However, the latter's primary interest in the treaty as a device for inhibiting the uncontrolled spread of nuclear weapons so as to reduce their destabilizing influence upon the international environment may have been shared to some extent by the Soviet Union. Perhaps an additional reason why the Soviet Union and the United States could join in supporting the treaty was that, for the time being at least, it left each free to pursue unilaterally the military programs by which it could hope to weight the strategic balance in its favor.

Soviet Reluctance to Hold ABM Talks

By contrast with their readiness to pursue uninterrupted negotiations on the nonproliferation treaty even when Soviet–American relations were at their most frigid over the Vietnam war, Soviet authorities displayed a marked reluctance to enter talks on another major arms control issue raised by the United States, namely, a moratorium on deployment of missile defenses, linked later with limitations on strategic offensive systems. This issue came to the fore in early 1967, after US Defense Secretary Robert S. McNamara had disclosed officially in November 1966 that the Soviet Union had embarked on the deployment of anti-ballistic missile (ABM) defenses.[134] American hopes of persuading the Soviet Union to reconsider this step and agree to a mutual freeze on ABM deployment in order to head off a new and expensive round in the strategic arms race were voiced by President Johnson in his State of the Union message of January 10, 1967, along with an invitation to enter negotiations on the subject.[135]

---

on nuclear-armed bomber flights beyond national borders and limitation of nuclear-armed submarine patrols; prohibition of underground nuclear tests; ban on chemical and biological weapons; liquidation of foreign military bases; establishment of nuclear-free zones and regional arms reduction, including the Middle East; and a proposal for peaceful use of the ocean floor. See *Pravda*, July 2, 1968.

[132] The initial holdouts included West Germany, India, Japan, Israel, Sweden, Switzerland, and Canada. Half of the thirty-four non-nuclear countries possessing atomic reactors were not among the initial signatories. Two of the world's five countries possessing nuclear weapons—China and France—also were conspicuously missing from the list of adherents to the treaty.

[133] For further discussion of some of the treaty's political implications, see chapter XIII, pp. 323–24.

[134] Transcript of McNamara news conference, *New York Times*, November 11, 1966. More detailed discussion of the Soviet ABM program will be found in chapter XVI, pp. 437–41.

[135] In his State of the Union message (text in *New York Times*, January 11, 1967), President

Reaction from the Soviet side was both cool and equivocal, as typified by Kosygin's comments in February, and again in June 1967, in which he showed no enthusiasm for an ABM moratorium, but did not slam the door shut on possible negotiations.[136] There were a few signs at the time to suggest that the US initiative may have touched off an ABM policy debate within the Soviet leadership,[137] which might explain why the Soviet government was slow to respond formally to the American offer. When, in September 1967, Secretary McNamara announced with obvious regret that the United States had decided to go ahead with deployment of a "relatively light" and "Chinese-oriented" ABM system, later named the "Sentinel" system,[138] it was felt in some quarters that this initiative might end the Soviet Union's footdragging.[139]

For the next ten months, however, neither this move nor other promptings from the American side had any perceptible effect in eliciting a formal reply from Moscow. Not until mid-June 1968, almost a year-and-a-half after President Johnson's initial bid, did the Soviet leadership finally indicate that it was prepared to discuss ABM deployment and the related question of strategic offensive forces. By then, looming troubles within the Communist world, and other factors, evidently had persuaded the Soviet leaders that it was time to seek a new breathing spell in relations with the United States. Their assent to mis-

---

Johnson noted, as an added inducement for Soviet agreement to an ABM moratorium, that the United States was still deferring deployment of an anti-missile defense system of its own. To give further weight to American interest in the subject, Llewellyn Thompson, the distinguished American diplomat returning in January for his second tour as US ambassador in Moscow, took with him a personal letter from the President intended to help in getting diplomatic soundings on ABM talks underway.

[136] For accounts of Kosygin's remarks during an interview in London on February 10, 1967, see "Kosygin Is Cool to Missile Curb," *New York Times*, February 10, 1967; "Soviet ABM Shift Denied," *Washington Post*, February 18, 1967. A Soviet rendering of Kosygin's comments, in which he stressed that deployment of ABM should not be regarded as a new step in the arms race, was given by Radio Moscow on February 10, 1967. For Kosygin's remarks on the subject during his visit to the United States in June 1967, see "Transcript of Kosygin News Conference at the UN," *New York Times*, June 26, 1967.

[137] Among signs that internal policy differences in Moscow may have arisen over the question of ABM negotiations was the publication of a *Pravda* article on February 15, 1967, in which Kosygin was made out to be more receptive to the idea of an ABM moratorium than his actual remarks in London a few days before warranted. Two days after the *Pravda* article, written by F. Burlatskii, Western news agencies in Moscow reported that the article had been privately repudiated by Soviet sources, who claimed that the regime's position on ABM negotiations was negative, as would be made clear in a new article. However, a corrective article did not appear, suggesting that the issue was at that point too contentious to handle. On March 31, a strong statement by a military spokesman of the case for continuing with an ABM deployment program appeared in a *Red Star* article stressing the importance of strategic defense measures along with the value of a powerful offensive posture. (This article is discussed in chapter XVI.) Both the article and its timing again suggested that an internal ABM policy controversy might be going on, with various parties seeking to influence the debate. For further comment on this subject, see Thomas W. Wolfe, prepared statement furnished to the Subcommittee on Military Applications, Joint Committee on Atomic Energy, US Congress, 90:1, and published in *Hearings on the Scope, Magnitude, and Implications of the United States Antiballistic Missile Program*, November 6 and 7, 1967 (Washington, D.C.: Government Printing Office, 1968), pp. 63–75.

[138] See Secretary McNamara's speech in San Francisco, *New York Times*, September 18, 1967. See also McNamara's subsequent elucidation of the rationale behind the "light" or "thin" ABM system in an interview with *Life* magazine, September 29, 1967, pp. 28a, b, and c.

[139] See, for example, Stephen S. Rosenfeld, "Russia Cautious on U.S. ABM Move," *Washington Post*, October 15, 1967.

sile talks was a signal to this effect. Before we discuss this and other signals that seemed to herald the opening of a new diplomatic dialogue between Moscow and Washington, let us turn briefly to another aspect of limited "co-operation" in Soviet relations with the United States that remained relatively unchanged under Khrushchev's successors, even during the most virulent season of anti-American utterance from Moscow.

Soviet–American "Crisis Collaboration" to Avoid War

If at least one constant feature could be found in the Brezhnev–Kosygin regime's approach to Soviet–American relations, it was the recognition that the two powers had a common interest in avoiding a direct military collision that could lead to nuclear war—a danger manifestly enhanced wherever their respective great-power commitments might be invoked in a local conflict. Thus, in the various "hot" crises that developed after they came to power, the new Soviet leaders, like Khrushchev before them, in a sense collaborated with the United States to steer clear of this hazard.

Perhaps the principal example was the case of Vietnam itself, where both powers sought to sidestep an open confrontation despite their deepening stakes in the struggle. The India–Pakistan war in the autumn of 1965, brought to a halt after Kosygin's mediation at Tashkent in early 1966, provided another occasion for a momentary conjunction of Soviet and US crisis diplomacy, although the two countries' parallel interest in dampening this crisis probably stemmed less from fear of being drawn into military conflict with each other than from a common desire to contain China.[140] The Middle East crisis of May 1967, climaxed by the six-day Arab–Israeli war in June, once more demonstrated that Moscow and Washington saw eye to eye on the necessity of not allowing local hostilities to develop into a military showdown between themselves. Doubtless, the very brevity of the war helped to prevent a direct Soviet–US confrontation, but it is nevertheless significant that at the height of the fighting both Soviet and American diplomacy sought to contain the conflict, making the first use of the "hot line," among other things, as a means of crisis communication.[141]

Once the immediate danger of a Soviet–US military entanglement subsided, however, the limits of this mutual interest in crisis control soon became apparent. Indeed, Soviet propaganda found it expedient to charge that the United States had been itching all along to intervene on the side of the Israeli "militarists" with the "big stick" of the US Sixth Fleet.[142] Bent upon recouping its prestige in the Arab world and improving its position in the Middle East, the

[140] See Adam Bromke, "Two Alliances: Conflict and Independence," in Adam Bromke and Philip E. Uren, eds., *The Communist States and the West* (New York: Frederick A. Praeger, Inc., 1967), p. 227.

[141] The Washington–Moscow "hot line," established by agreement in 1963, was put to use by the Soviet leadership during the early hours of June 5, 1967, ostensibly to insure that Washington would understand that no direct Soviet military intervention in the war was contemplated. See Chalmers M. Roberts, "U.S.–Russian Efforts Told," *Washington Post*, June 9, 1967; Murrey Marder and Carroll Kilpatrick, " 'Hot Line' Helps Keep Big Powers Cool," ibid.

[142] See, for example, A. Kafman, "U.S. Big Stick to the Mediterranean," *International Affairs* (Moscow), no. 8 (August 1967): 75.

Soviet Union showed little interest in responding to American appeals for restoration of stability in the area and the curbing of another arms build-up. Although it joined in the November 1967 resolution of the Security Council to restrict a "ruinous arms race" in the Middle East,[143] the Soviet Union went ahead with large-scale arms shipments to put the defeated Arab armies back on their feet.[144]

The Soviet leadership doubtless found it difficult to pass up the opportunity to strengthen the USSR's political-strategic foothold in the Middle East because it came at a time when British withdrawal from the region and American preoccupation with Vietnam combined to reduce the chances that such a Soviet effort would encounter concerted Western opposition, except in an acute crisis like that of the six-day war. Somewhat similarly, with respect to the larger question of Europe itself, the Soviet leadership apparently also was tempted to take advantage of a situation which saw the day-to-day attention of US policy-makers increasingly distracted from the European scene by the war in Vietnam. In any event, as will be brought out in more detail later, the Soviet Union in 1966–67 gradually shifted to a more active European diplomacy, perhaps hopefully calculated to channel the anti-American line of Charles de Gaulle and other European discontents into a political force effective enough to bring about a significant decline in the presence and influence of the United States in Europe.

The prospects of making progress in this direction may have looked promising to the Kremlin leaders until the ground began to heave under their own feet in East Europe. After the early months of 1968, as the reformist heresy in Czechoslovakia generated a crisis that threatened to split the Warsaw bloc itself, much of the momentum went out of the Soviet campaign to detach the United States from its NATO allies. Now the need to patch up relations with the United States and to free Moscow for whatever measures might be required in East Europe apparently assumed new importance for the Soviet leaders. It was at this point that they began to explore anew the possibilities of rapprochement with the United States, although the strongly hostile notes that could still be heard suggested that internal differences were making it difficult for the Kremlin leaders to orchestrate a less palpably anti-American policy line.

Tentative Emergence of a New Soviet Stance toward the United States

Signs of a Soviet disposition to encourage a thaw in Soviet–American relations appeared in the spring of 1968, at a time when the imminent conclusion

---

[143] For text of resolution, see *New York Times*, November 23, 1967.

[144] A massive Soviet airlift to resupply Nasser's forces and to ferry in replacement aircraft for his badly battered air force was one of the first Soviet measures taken in the days immediately following the Israeli victory. (See chapter XVI.) Subsequently, further steps to rebuild the various Arab forces were undertaken, including a large increase in the number of Soviet military advisers and technicians. Among accounts of Soviet support to the Arab countries in the post-hostilities phase of the Arab–Israeli conflict, see Peter Grose, "Russians at U.N. Say Arabs Must Be Re-equipped," *New York Times*, June 21, 1967; Hedrick Smith, "Rebuilding of Egyptian Army Seen as 2-Year Task," ibid., August 21, 1967; idem, "U.S. Sees No Peril in New Shipments," ibid., October 12, 1967; idem, "Soviet Comeback as Power in Middle East Causes Rising Concern in West," ibid., January 15, 1968; William Beecher, "Role of Egypt's Russian Advisers Is Worrying U.S.," ibid., October 22, 1968.

of the nuclear nonproliferation treaty, the opening of the Paris talks on Vietnam, and Washington's scrupulous observance of a hands-off attitude toward developments in East Europe had combined to produce a momentary slackening of Soviet-American political tensions. Among the first conciliatory gestures from Moscow were the announcement, on May 4, that the Supreme Soviet had finally got around to ratifying the consular treaty,[145] and the Soviet Union's agreement later that month to resume negotiations on a new cultural exchange pact.[146] But the principal move suggestive of a shift in Moscow's approach was the decision to enter talks on limiting missiles and the ABM, which had been delayed for almost eighteen months. It was made known not in a direct reply to the American invitation but in this passage of a speech by Foreign Minister Gromyko to the Supreme Soviet on June 27:

> One of the unprobed areas of disarmament is the search for an understanding on mutual restriction and subsequent reduction of strategic vehicles for the delivery of nuclear weapons—offensive and defensive—including anti-missile. The Soviet Government is ready for an exchange of opinion on this subject.[147]

Although readiness for an exchange of opinion gave no grounds for supposing that agreement was just around the corner on what promised to be the most complex technical and political negotiations yet undertaken between Moscow and Washington in the nuclear age, Gromyko's statement nevertheless prompted far-reaching speculation that an historic turning point in Soviet–American relations was at hand, if the two superpowers could indeed find a formula to impose limits on the dynamics of the strategic arms race.[148] Why the Soviet Union had finally chosen to embark on the talks was likewise a question of widespread interest, the more so because the decision apparently had been contested right up to the end by groups within the Soviet leadership who were skeptical of its wisdom.[149]

[145] See fn. 125 above. The Soviet announcement by TASS on May 4, 1968, one day after opening of the Paris peace talks, stated that the ratification action on the consular treaty had been taken on April 26, 1968.

[146] The Soviet decision to reopen negotiations for a new two-year cultural agreement reportedly was communicated to Washington around May 26, 1968. See Richard Reston, "Cultural Exchange Talks Set by Soviets," *Washington Post*, May 29, 1968.

[147] See Report by USSR Foreign Minister A. A. Gromyko, "On the International Situation and the Foreign Policy of the Soviet Union," *Pravda*, June 28, 1968. Hints that the Soviet decision to enter missile talks may have been taken a month or two before Gromyko's announcement were reportedly dropped by Soviet diplomats. See Robert H. Estabrook, "Soviets May Be Willing To Discuss ABM Limit," *Washington Post*, May 23, 1968; Peter Grose, "Deal in Kremlin Seen Behind Stance Toward U.S.," *New York Times*, July 8, 1968.

[148] For some representative samples of such speculation, see Roscoe Drummond, "Unlimited Potential for Peace Seen in Disarmament Talks," *Washington Post*, July 3, 1968; Peter Grose, "U.S. Encouraged by Soviet Stand," *New York Times*, June 28, 1968; Robert Kleiman, "Hope for Calling Off the 'Mad' Missile Race," ibid., June 30, 1968.

[149] The view that the missile-talk decision met with continuing internal opposition rests on several rather indirect bits of evidence. One appeared in Gromyko's June 27 speech, when he said: "To the good-for-nothing theoreticians who try to tell us . . . that disarmament is an illusion, we reply: By taking such a stand you fall into step with the most dyed-in-the-wool imperialist reaction, weaken the front of struggle against it." Although leaving unnamed the theoreticians whose advice he was rejecting, Gromyko apparently was attempting here to rebut internal objectors

In a later chapter we shall examine some of the strategic considerations which may have influenced the Soviet decision to engage in missile talks.[150] Here, let it suffice to say that—in the immediate context of troubles brewing within the Warsaw bloc in mid-1968—a desire to clear the decks for dealing with these problems may have helped to account for Moscow's changed attitude toward the talks. If the United States could be encouraged to believe that the talks held promise of improving relations with the USSR, Washington might be hesitant to jeopardize their progress by making difficulties over any steps the Soviet Union found necessary to keep the Czech reformist movement in line. Internal Kremlin politics also may have entered the picture, with the missile-talk offer and other Soviet gestures of accommodation toward the United States representing, as some observers saw it, the product of bargaining between hard and moderate factions within the Politburo. In this view, the "hard-line ideologues" may have given in to the "moderate pragmatists" by agreeing to ease relations with the United States in return for a tougher campaign for conformity at home and in East Europe.[151] How Soviet policy would straddle the contradiction between a more amicable approach to the US government and an ideological conformity drive based on the theme that the Soviet Union had to combat a massive "subversive campaign" directed against it by that very same government was not entirely clear.

Indeed, such contradictions remained characteristic of Moscow's stance toward the United States, as gestures of accommodation were interspersed with abusive attacks on American policy. In May 1968, for example, only a few days before Moscow's propitiatory announcement that the consular treaty had been ratified, speakers at May Day ceremonies on Red Square accused the United States of "embarking ever more openly upon the path of aggression" and of "stepping up ideological subversion against the socialist states."[152] In early June, after President Johnson had made at least one private plea for better Soviet–American co-operation and issued three more public appeals to

to the missile talks. Another sign of opposition was the disparity between statements by such leaders as Gromyko, Brezhnev, and Kosygin indicating that the military might of the Soviet Union had successfully "contained" imperialism and thereby forced the latter to seek mutually acceptable means to limit the arms race, and views advanced in a military periodical to the effect that "aggressive imperialist quarters" were still "taking desperate steps" to prepare their armed forces for a "surprise nuclear strike against the Soviet Union," from which it was argued that "there might be no time to build up forces" after war started, making it necessary for the Soviet Union "even in peacetime to have a stable superiority over the probable adversary." See Col. I. Grudinin, "Qualitative and Quantitative Determination of Forces," Kommunist Vooruzhennykh Sil (Communist of the Armed Forces), no. 11 (June 1968): 15–22. This line of argument, though not unfamiliar, carried the suggestion that at least some Soviet military opinion was questioning the wisdom of entering talks which might cut off further Soviet efforts to achieve superiority. For some thoughtful but speculative Western analysis of these indications of internal opposition, see Victor Zorza, "Russian Military Contests Civilian Decision to Shift Priority from Armament Buildup," Washington Post, July 5, 1968; Stephen S. Rosenfeld, "Brezhnev Makes Reply to Missile-Talk Foes," ibid., July 9, 1968. See also fn. 137 above.

[150] See chapter XVIII. Eighteen more months were to pass, of course, before the strategic arms limitation talks (SALT) began on November 17, 1969.

[151] See Peter Grose, in New York Times, July 8, 1968.

[152] See, for example, speech by Marshal A. A. Grechko, Pravda, May 2, 1968.

the Soviet Union to put aside "old antagonisms,"[153] Soviet spokesmen responded coldly, declaring once again that relations between the two countries would not improve so long as the United States continued to wage its "barbarous war" in Vietnam, to plot against the "progressive" Arab states, and to support "revanchist forces" in West Germany.[154] In early July, at a moment when Soviet–American relations seemed to be newly infused with a spirit of co-operation, as demonstrated by Gromyko's acceptance of missile talks, the signing of the nonproliferation treaty, and the Soviet Union's release of a Vietnam-bound American airliner that had been forced down by MIGs near the Kurile Islands, Brezhnev chose to deliver a vitriolic indictment of the United States as a land "of political gangsterism that causes contempt and disgust throughout the world."[155]

The tendency for Moscow to speak with two voices on Soviet–American co-operation was perhaps least evident in the Soviet Union's treatment of the US position on the situation in East Europe. On this question, the hard voice held sway. Despite the fact that the American government leaned over backward to avoid involving itself in the events of Czechoslovakia,[156] Moscow repeatedly accused the United States of being behind the Czech liberalization movement and of trying to restore "the capitalist order" there.[157] Morover, in a transparently crude effort to buttress its case, Moscow sought to plant "evidence" that American arms were being smuggled to subversive forces in Czechoslovakia,[158] thus concocting a plot that it might then use either as an instrument in the war of nerves against the Dubcek reform government or as an excuse for military intervention in Czechoslovakia.

There was more than a touch of irony in the fact that the harsher the Soviet accusations against the United States and the West for alleged meddling in the Czech situation, the more Western officials sought to stand aside from the crisis. Following the American lead, NATO adopted a "correct" hands-off

---

[153] President Johnson's private plea for co-operation was reportedly contained in a letter sent to Premier Kosygin in April 1968. His public overtures came in a commencement speech at Glassboro, N.J., on June 4, in an address before the UN General Assembly on June 12, and in remarks at a White House ceremony on June 13, 1968. See Max Frankel, "Johnson Letter Sent to Kosygin," *New York Times*, May 9, 1968; idem, "President Makes Another Appeal to the Russians," ibid., June 14, 1968.

[154] See, for example, V. Matveev, "Where Is the Obstacle?" *Izvestiia*, June 13, 1968; Viktor Maevskii, "Necessary Reminders," *Pravda*, June 19, 1968.

[155] See "Speech of Comrade L. I. Brezhnev," *Pravda*, July 4, 1968.

[156] US officials, reportedly on President Johnson's orders, declined to comment publicly on the Czechoslovak–Soviet tension, and there was no attempt to mount a propaganda campaign either in support of the Czechs or to exploit Soviet attempts to dictate to Prague—a rather glaring contrast to Soviet readiness to condemn US "intervention" anywhere around the globe at the drop of a hat. On July 22, 1968, Secretary Rusk protested to Soviet Ambassador Dobrynin over Soviet accusations against the United States in the Czechoslovak case. See Benjamin Welles, "U.S. Terms Charges by Moscow False," *New York Times*, July 20, 1968; "U.S. Denies Czech Meddling," *Washington Post*, July 23, 1968.

[157] See, for example, "The Defense of Socialism Is Our Common Task," *Krasnaia zvezda*, July 19, 1968; speech by Podgornyi to RSFSR Supreme Soviet, ibid., July 20, 1968; S. Seliuk, "The Party's Strength Is in Leninist Unity," *Pravda*, July 25, 1968.

[158] For further discussion of this "evidence," see chapter XIV, pp. 369–70 and 382–83.

attitude, and in July, to avoid any suggestion of provocation, a field exercise of West German, American, and French troops previously scheduled to take place near the Czech border was moved to another location in West Germany.[159] It was almost as if the West, by adopting a posture of restraint and trying to remove any excuse for Soviet intervention, had been cast in the role of looking out for the enlightened self-interest of the Soviet Union as well as its own—a role that unfortunately awakened in the West a sense of frustration and even shame not unlike that produced by the abandonment of Czechoslovakia at Munich, thirty years before.[160]

It would perhaps be unwarranted to assume that a peaceful and enlightened solution of the Soviet Union's dilemma in East Europe was beyond the capacity of any Soviet leadership group. But the Brezhnev–Kosygin regime, for one, demonstrated that it could do no better than revert to the pattern of military suppression employed against Hungary in 1956. Despite a widespread belief that the Soviet Union was merely bluffing and would not risk the political cost of invading another Communist country, its leaders did precisely that when, in August 1968, they called upon Soviet arms to snuff out the reform experiment in Czechoslovakia.

In regard to Soviet–American relations, the invasion of Czechoslovakia brought to a momentary halt the tentative exploration of specific steps toward accommodation such as the strategic arms limitation talks; in a broader sense, it seemed to suggest that East–West bridge-building looked more dangerous to the orthodox oligarchs in the Kremlin than did a return to the frowning hostility of a Cold War environment. However, if the past imprint of Hungary and Vietnam on the attitudes of the Soviet Union and the United States toward each other was a reliable guide, one could expect that, even though the Czechoslovak intervention threw up a formidable obstacle to genuine improvement of relations, the two nuclear superpowers would sooner or later resume their groping search for some basis of accommodation.

Indeed, after a period of "mourning" in the West over Czechoslovakia, developments in 1969 and early 1970 suggested that the superpowers were once more seeking ways to extend their tacit "survival pact" and to keep open lines of negotiation with each other. This became most evident, perhaps, when

---

[159] Because the maneuvers in West Germany, involving 30,000 West German troops and only small French and US supporting elements, were not under formal NATO auspices, the decision on July 24, 1968, to relocate them was made by Bonn. However, US and NATO interest in the matter was obvious. See Philip Shabecoff, "Bonn Shifts Maneuvers Away From Czech Line," *New York Times*, July 25, 1968. It was significant that precisely as the controversial West German maneuvers were being rescheduled to take place in September at a different location, the Soviet Union announced that large-scale maneuvers of its own forces were in progress along Czechoslovakia's eastern borders. The Soviet maneuvers will be discussed later.

[160] An eloquent expression of this sense of frustration over the West's self-imposed restraint in the Czech crisis was voiced in July 1968 by Sir Fitzroy Maclean, a Member of Parliament, in a letter to *The Times* of London, in which, recalling Munich, he said: "Today Czechoslovakia is once more threatened with armed aggression. It seems scarcely conceivable that, in such a situation, no word of warning should be uttered by any Western statesman, that the matter should be referred neither to the Security Council nor to the General Assembly of the United Nations." See Anthony Lewis, "Echoes of Munich," *New York Times*, July 26, 1968.

the two sides finally managed to get together for the initial round of the long-delayed SALT talks in Helsinki. As the head of the American delegation noted afterward, the Soviets adopted "a business-like approach" which made the prospect of progress "a little brighter than it has appeared in the past."[161] A somewhat similar cautious appraisal from Moscow described the talks as a "positive step" which would provide a "useful" basis for further discussion of "major problems" upon resumption of the talks in Vienna in April 1970.[162]

Although the talks at Helsinki seemed to indicate a Soviet readiness to respond affirmatively to the Nixon administration's expressed hope of entering an "era of negotiation" with the Soviet Union, the Soviet–American dialogue on a number of other issues tended to produce fewer optimistic notes. For example, conversations aimed at finding some formula for mediating the Middle East crisis bogged down in December 1969, when the Soviet Union rejected US suggestions as "one-sided" in favor of Israel and later unveiled its own patently pro-Arab proposals.[163] With regard to assuming a peacemaker's role in Vietnam, the Soviet Union likewise declined to budge from its previous position. Thus, when President Nixon, in a lengthy foreign policy message of February 18, 1970, observed that the Soviet Union had "failed to exert a helpful influence on the North Vietnamese,"[164] Soviet sources let it be known that American diplomacy could expect no help from Moscow in bringing the war to a close.[165]

As for Europe, where lay, perhaps, the real test of Soviet readiness to cooperate with the United States in moving from an era of confrontation to one of negotiation, the outlook by early 1970 remained at best indeterminate. On the one hand, doubtless in part because of its difficulties with China in the Far East, the Brezhnev–Kosygin regime showed an interest in promoting negotiations which might help to restore an atmosphere of détente in Europe.[166]

[161] Transcript of White House Press Conference of Ambassador Gerard C. Smith, Office of the White House Press Secretary, December 29, 1969.

[162] TASS dispatch, "Preliminary Talks Have Ended," *Pravda*, December 23, 1969; Gennadii Vasil'ev, "Positive Step," *Pravda*, December 24, 1969.

[163] The conversations in question were conducted over a period of several months in 1969 between Soviet Ambassador A. F. Dobrynin and Assistant Secretary of State Joseph J. Sisco. American proposals for a Middle East settlement, advanced on October 28, were rejected in a Soviet response delivered in Washington on December 23, 1969. According to press reports, the Soviet Union reneged on a number of points to which Dobrynin had previously agreed. The Soviet Union's own counter-proposals were made public on January 27, 1970. See "Text of Speech by Secretary Rogers on U.S. Policy in Middle East," *New York Times*, December 11, 1969; A. D. Horne, "Russians Reject U.S. Formula for Mideast Talks," *Washington Post*, December 24, 1969; "Text of Soviet Note to U.S. on Mideast Settlement," *New York Times*, January 13, 1970; E. Maksimov, "The Road to a Just Peace," *Pravda*, January 27, 1970.

[164] See "United States Foreign Policy for the 1970's: A New Strategy for Peace," text of President Nixon's foreign-affairs message, as published in *New York Times*, February 19, 1970, p. 24 M.

[165] Bernard Gwertzman, "Soviet Officials, in Interview, Score Nixon on Middle East and Vietnam, but Look to Improved U.S. Ties," *New York Times*, February 26, 1970.

[166] Several sets of talks to which the Soviet Union gave its blessings, mostly in response to initiatives from the Brandt government in Bonn, were either underway or scheduled in early 1970. These included bilateral Soviet–West German talks on a renunciation-of-force treaty which began in Moscow in December 1969; Polish–West German political discussions, which opened in Warsaw

On the other hand, however, it was still by no means clear upon what terms the Soviet leadership was prepared to address such intractable issues as Berlin, the problem of a divided Germany, mutual troop reductions, and European collective security. Time alone, therefore, would tell whether Moscow was in fact ready for a fresh start on negotiation of these and other long-unresolved issues in Europe. Upon this note, let us now turn to the evolution of Soviet policy toward Europe in the five years following the Brezhnev–Kosygin regime's assumption of power.

in February 1970; and talks between leaders of the two German governments set for late March. In addition, the Soviet Union indicated in February that it would participate in four-power talks on Berlin proposed by the Western powers as one of several issues which should be taken up in advance of any agreement to hold a general conference on European collective security. Another issue thus specified was that of mutual troop reductions. The information publicly available on these various negotiating moves in early 1970 indicated that the Soviet Union, despite a change of tone, was still sticking to its past positions on contested European questions.

XII

SOVIET EUROPEAN POLICY UNDER
BREZHNEV–KOSYGIN: 1964–1966

It may be useful to begin this discussion of Soviet policy toward Europe under Khrushchev's successors by recalling briefly the general state of affairs which obtained in Europe at the time the Brezhnev–Kosygin regime came to power. Although a divided Europe in which both the Soviet Union and the United States maintained a strong presence was still doubtless the dominant feature of the political landscape, by the autumn of 1964 this once rigid division of postwar Europe was clearly giving way to a more fluid situation. The loosening of internal ties within both alliance systems and some broadening of relations between the two halves of Europe seemed to have set the stage for unpredictable changes which might eventually lead Europe far from the division of the Cold War and at the same time alter the roles of the two external superpowers in European affairs.

In Western Europe the process of economic and political recovery, along with a belief that the threat of military attack from the East had virtually vanished, contributed to a more relaxed atmosphere than at any time in the past two decades. Deterrence, based essentially on the high risks of a nuclear war growing out of military action in Europe, had come to be taken for granted as the source of European security. In most Western opinion there was little likelihood, after the lesson of Cuba, that the Soviet Union would soon again try to upset the power balance under which a continuing political stand-off and a reassuring measure of East–West détente in Europe had come into being.

In this atmosphere, the erosion of NATO under the acid of de Gaulle's attitudes caused no great concern in Europe; indeed, most members of the Western alliance, displaying pale reflections of the Gaullist outlook, seemed to be moving in one degree or another away from their close dependence upon American leadership. Incidental to the feeling that the countries of Western Europe could and should begin to play more active and autonomous roles on the European stage was the onset of disillusionment with some of the grander designs for the integration of Europe that had originally been conceived at American urging.

A somewhat analogous situation existed in the autumn of 1964 in Eastern Europe, where members of the Warsaw bloc were showing varying shades of a nationalist self-assertiveness that sometimes ran counter to Soviet interests and perspectives. Although the challenge to Soviet hegemony here remained more or less muted, except in the case of Rumania, the Soviet Union could no longer count on unquestioning obedience from its East European partners; rather, the problems of maintaining discipline and unity within the bloc now called for the exercise of something more closely akin to traditional coalition politics. At the same time, however, nationalist trends in East Europe were not wholly adverse to Soviet interests, for they tended to fragment any concerted regional opposition to the Russians. Moreover, if some decline of the Soviet Union's authority within its alliance system had set in, the East European Communist regimes were still keenly aware that their ultimate security rested on Soviet arms, especially in the sense that Soviet military power served as the final guarantee against the rise of revisionist aspirations in Germany.

The problem of Germany and her future doubtless remained the focal issue of East–West relationships in Europe in the fall of 1964. A divided Germany, denied the infinitely difficult goal of reunification, or even the less elusive prospect of "reassociation," would continue to be the source of tension and discord in the heart of Europe. A Germany rejoined, and thereby transformed once more into the most potent European state, not only would become a prize that neither East nor West could afford to lose, but might, if she should seek to go her own way, prove equally disturbing to both. The only satisfactory way to resolve the German problem, it seemed, would be to integrate a reunified Germany into an economically and politically unified European system. But, at best, such a system lay clearly at the end of a long process of evolution, and not within the realm of near-term possibilities. Thus, despite a generally welcome improvement in the Cold War climate, and notwithstanding even some signs, such as Khrushchev's overtures to Bonn in 1964, that Moscow might be considering new initiatives with respect to Germany,[1] there still appeared to be little immediate prospect for the solution of the profound dilemma posed by the German problem throughout the postwar period.

This, then, in barest outline, was the background against which the new Kremlin leadership took up the task of forging its own policies toward West and East Europe. In this and subsequent chapters we shall consider the nature of the policies which have emerged since the autumn of 1964, beginning with an examination of the trends in Soviet policy toward Western Europe.

General Pattern of Policy toward Western Europe

Soviet policy toward Western Europe under the Brezhnev–Kosygin regime went through several distinct phases in the period between October 1964 and early 1970. In the first, which lasted about a year-and-a-half, Soviet European policy remained relatively subdued, in keeping with the general tendency of the new regime to eschew foreign policy initiatives while it was still consolidating its domestic position.

The second phase began in the summer of 1966, roughly between the Twenty-third Party Congress, which was held in Moscow in April, and the

[1] See chapter VI, pp. 117–27.

Bucharest conference of Warsaw Pact states in July. The outlines of a new European policy bearing the impress of the successor regime had gradually taken shape. Characterized by a firm effort to improve Soviet relations with Western Europe, with the notable exception of the Federal Republic of Germany, the new policy line also was marked by more active exploitation of the vulnerability of the United States on the issue of the Vietnam war, in an attempt to weaken European–American ties, and by renewed advocacy of an all-European security conference for a European settlement that would aim to exclude the United States from any substantial influence in European affairs.

A third phase of Soviet European policy under the Brezhnev–Kosygin regime can be most conveniently dated from the invasion of Czechoslovakia, which had the effect, among other things, of placing the Soviet Union at least temporarily on the political defensive in Europe, while it sought to repair its badly tarnished image. A good argument can be made, however, that well before the events of August 1968 the Soviet leaders had become so preoccupied with arresting the erosion of their authority in East Europe that they were no longer in a position to make the most of the opportunities afforded by a flexible Soviet diplomacy in the western half of Europe.

In any event, within a year or so after the Czechoslovak "interruption" had definitely slowed its momentum, Soviet policy toward Western Europe entered a fourth phase as the Brezhnev–Kosygin regime began to search anew for ways to regain the initiative in European affairs which it had let slip from its grasp.

We are concerned here with the first of the several policy phases denoted above, that is, the period from Khrushchev's ouster in the autumn of 1964 to the Bucharest conference in mid-1966. At the outset, despite trends in Western Europe toward a further loosening of the ties between the United States and its NATO allies, the new Soviet leaders showed little disposition to plunge headlong into a diplomacy designed to take advantage of the situation. Indeed, they made an almost studied effort not to disturb the delicate balance in Europe, as though they wished to preserve a détente atmosphere in this part of the world while the tension was rising in Southeast Asia and Soviet relations with China were passing through a new phase of uncertainty.

To be sure, an insistent propaganda campaign was carried on in the early months of the new regime against the MLF and other proposed forms of NATO nuclear organization, capped by a demonstrative Warsaw Pact meeting in Poland in January 1965 to consider countermeasures to the MLF, if it should come into being.[2] This campaign, however, was essentially a continua-

---

[2] This seventh meeting of the Warsaw Pact, held, according to Kosygin, at the initiative of the GDR (see Leipzig speech by Kosygin, in *Pravda*, March 2, 1965), went on record as opposing a NATO nuclear-sharing arrangement "in any form whatsoever"; should such plans be implemented, the Warsaw Treaty states would be "compelled to take the defense measures necessary to ensure their security." See "Communiqué on the Meeting of the Political Consultative Committee of the Member States of the Warsaw Treaty," *Krasnaia zvezda* (Red Star), January 22, 1965.

tion of the one previously pursued under Khrushchev. While it showed that Soviet opposition to any form of German participation in nuclear affairs remained adamant,[3] it represented no new initiative that would threaten to upset the quiescent state of the East–West confrontation in Europe, such as any serious effort to reopen the question of a German settlement and the status of Berlin.

Initial Soviet Policy toward West Germany

With respect to Germany, the new Soviet regime promptly dropped Khrushchev's project for warming up relations with the Federal Republic, and turned a deaf ear to suggestions from Bonn that the invitation for a high-level Soviet visit was still open. On the basic questions of a German peace treaty and of Berlin, however, the new Soviet leaders gave no hint of wishing to press for alteration of the situation registered by the Soviet–GDR friendship treaty of June 1964, which had served to mollify the Ulbricht regime to some extent, while avoiding any real hardening of fundamental East–West positions.[4] In fact, early pronouncements of the new regime even suggested some slight softening of the Soviet stand on Germany. Brezhnev's anniversary speech of November 6, 1964, and a major foreign policy editorial in *Pravda* shortly thereafter, exhibited a modification of the standing demand for a peace treaty covering the two Germanys and dropped the rider calling for a change in the status of Berlin that had been a customary part of the peace treaty formula.[5] Soviet Foreign Minister Andrei Gromyko, speaking at the United Nations on December 7, 1964, also gave an indication that the new Soviet regime was disposed to shelve the matter of a German peace treaty for the time being. Although Gromyko mentioned the need for a German peace settlement in general terms, he did not call for conclusion of a peace treaty, nor did he revive the demand regarding the status of West Berlin.[6]

These signs of willingness to keep the Berlin and German issues on the shelf were the more notable in light of the pall which Khrushchev's rumored toying with a "sellout" of East Germany had cast over relations between Moscow and the Ulbricht regime. Brezhnev and Suslov, it may be recalled, had taken special pains to allay East German fears of a sellout just prior to Khrushchev's overthrow.[7] Once having disposed of Khrushchev, however, the new collective

[3] In addition to reiterating long-standing Soviet opposition to any NATO nuclear-sharing plans that would allegedly put nuclear weapons in Bonn's hands, the new Soviet regime also expressed a negative attitude toward creation of a special NATO committee for nuclear planning and consultation, as proposed by Secretary of Defense McNamara at a meeting of NATO defense ministers in June 1965, and later (in November 1965) brought into being. In July 1965, the McNamara committee proposal was characterized by one Soviet source as "perhaps even more dangerous than the MLF." See Observer, "Undermining European Security," *Pravda*, July 20, 1965.

[4] See chapter VI, pp. 121–23.

[5] L. I. Brezhnev speech in *Pravda*, November 7, 1964; editorial, "Unshakeable Loyalty to the Interests of Peoples," *Pravda*, November 13, 1964.

[6] Thomas J. Hamilton, "Gromyko, in U.N., Says Soviet Aims for Bonn Amity," *New York Times*, December 8, 1964; "Excerpts from Gromyko's Speech Before the U.N.," ibid.

[7] See chapter VI, pp. 169–71.

leaders not only made no further reference to his alleged flirtation with Bonn at East Germany's expense, but by softening their attitude on Berlin and a peace treaty they seemed to be showing little deference to East German sensibilities.

All of this might be taken to mean that, while the new Soviet regime had seen fit to cut off the overtures to Bonn launched in the latter days of Khrushchev's tenure, it did not care to be hurried into a position that might make impossible the eventual working out of some improvement in the Moscow–Bonn relationship. Little tangible effort was forthcoming on Moscow's part, however, to encourage Bonn's hopes for better relations. Although Kosygin tossed out a kind word or two for the new generation of West Germans during a VE-Day celebration speech in East Germany on May 7, 1965,[8] this was but a faint note in the barrage of anti-Bonn propaganda called forth by the occasion;[9] moreover, it came in the midst of what many thought was the development of a new Berlin crisis.

Temporary Berlin Harassment

Beginning in April 1965, coincident with a Bundestag session in West Berlin, and continuing through about June, Soviet and GDR agencies carried out a series of harassments of Western land and air communications with Berlin, which included the buzzing of West Berlin's Congress Hall by Soviet jets, the occasional closing of the Helmstedt–Berlin autobahn for joint Soviet–GDR troop maneuvers, and other interference with air and barge traffic.[10] Whether the initiative for this "retaliatory" campaign against the Bundestag meeting[11] came primarily from the Ulbricht regime or from Moscow was open to question, but there was no doubt that Moscow had given its approval, for Soviet forces took an active part in some of the harassment measures.

From the Soviet viewpoint, a demonstration of "toughness" at this time may

---

[8] In his East Berlin speech, Kosygin noted that "it would be unfair to place the responsibility for the crimes of Nazism on the present-day youth of West Germany," but nevertheless he attacked Bonn's "ruling circles" for wanting to "absorb the German Democratic Republic." See *Pravda*, May 8, 1965. See also "East Berlin Revisited: Kosygin Reassuring," *Christian Science Monitor*, May 10, 1965.

[9] See Arthur J. Olsen, "Reds' Propaganda Trained on Bonn," *New York Times*, April 28, 1965; Report of Comrade L. I. Brezhnev, "Great Victory of the Soviet People," *Pravda*, May 9, 1965.

[10] For some contemporary accounts of these activities, see Arthur J. Olsen, "Soviet Jets Harass Berlin as Bundestag Meets There," *New York Times*, April 8, 1965; Katherine Clark, "Reds Twice Close Autobahn to Berlin, Detain U.S. Convoys," *Washington Post*, April 9, 1965; Harry B. Ellis, "Red Overflight in Berlin Weighed as Precedent," *Christian Science Monitor*, April 26, 1965; Philip Shabecoff, "German Reds Insist that West Negotiate Air Access to Berlin, *New York Times*, June 26, 1965.

[11] Meetings of the Bundestag in Berlin had been regarded by Bonn as a symbolic means for strengthening the Federal Republic's ties with West Berlin, and for the same reason, no doubt, had been bitterly protested by the GDR. Such meetings were convened annually from 1955 to 1958, when Khrushchev's campaign against Berlin led to their suspension. The meeting of April 7, 1965, marked the resumption of this practice, against which "retaliatory" East German–Soviet measures were taken. Prior to the April 1965 Bundestag session, the Soviet Union on March 23, 1965, officially protested to the Western Big Three against plans for the meeting. See "In the USSR Ministry of Foreign Affairs," *Izvestiia*, March 27, 1965.

have been calculated to offset the image of Soviet hesitancy toward the Vietnam situation, and also to remind the United States that the Soviet Union held cards in Europe that could be played to the discomfiture of the West if US policy in Southeast Asia were not altered. In any case, the campaign against Berlin's communications with the West was allowed to cool off before it took on the dimensions of another major crisis,[12] but not without having achieved the objective of discouraging further meetings of West German parliamentary bodies in Berlin for the time being. As we shall see later, the revival of Soviet opposition to the maintenance of this particular kind of symbolic bond between the Federal Republic and West Berlin was to become a factor of some consequence in the development of Soviet policy toward Bonn.

Once the harassment of Berlin had subsided, the summer of 1965 brought no evidence of new Soviet initiatives against West Germany. However, the Soviet Union displayed some interest in resuming a quiet diplomatic dialogue with Bonn when Dr. Karl Carstens, the West German deputy foreign minister, was received in Moscow in September 1965. The Carstens visit, reflecting another step in Bonn's attempt to improve the climate of its relations with Moscow and selected East European countries,[13] may have been regarded by the Soviet leaders as a gesture by which West Germany sought to isolate the East German regime from its Warsaw Pact neighbors; if so, they were careful to sidestep any such maneuver, as suggested by the coincidence that an East German delegation headed by Ulbricht was ostentatiously welcomed in the Soviet Union while Carstens was present.[14] Nevertheless, although the Carstens visit may have accomplished little more than to help stimulate Soviet–West German trade, which in 1965 was running at about a half-billion dollars annually,[15] the fact that the visit took place at all testified to a slight warming of relations between the two capitals.

Any hopes, however, that a new corner had been turned in Soviet–West German relations receded toward the end of 1965 as various Soviet leaders again began to belabor the foreign policies of the Erhard government. Besides questioning the Federal Republic's right to be treated as an equal and accusing

[12] Soviet treatment of the situation had generally sought to minimize the idea that a genuine crisis was in the making, as illustrated by the comment that the "retaliatory measures ... to Bonn's revanchist move affect only the participants of the unlawful Bundestag meeting" (*Pravda*, April 7, 1965). On the other hand, Brezhnev in a speech on April 8 in Poland denounced the meeting in strong terms as a move blessed by the Western powers in order to reassert Bonn's claim to "something that does not belong to West Germany" and to "produce new tension" in Europe. See "Speech of Comrade L. I. Brezhnev," *Pravda*, April 9, 1965.

[13] The Federal Republic's effort to improve its image in the East had been underway, of course, before the Brezhnev–Kosygin regime came to power. This effort of the Erhard government was particularly associated with Foreign Minister Gerhard Schroeder. Aimed mainly at various East European countries, but also with an eye to reducing Soviet hostility toward Bonn, it had led, among other things, to establishing West German trade missions in Rumania, Poland, Hungary, and Bulgaria prior to Carstens' visit to Moscow.

[14] For a discussion of the Ulbricht visit, see "The East German Visit to the Soviet Union," *Radio Free Europe*, September 29, 1965.

[15] See Harry B. Ellis, "Bonn Pushes for Soviet Trade," *Christian Science Monitor*, September 27, 1965.

Bonn of cynically abusing its membership in NATO for its own "revanchist" purposes, Soviet spokesmen also took up the charge, which was to be heard more and more frequently, that US support of the FRG was leading to the emergence of a special Washington–Bonn military axis within NATO.[16] In the early months of 1966, the Soviet line toward Bonn grew progressively harder, especially after the Erhard government sought to press its policy of "reconciliation" toward Germany's eastern neighbors one step further with its Peace Note of March 25, 1966.[17]

Reaction to Bonn's Peace Note

This note, in which Bonn offered to conclude agreements with the Soviet Union, Poland, Czechoslovakia, and "any other East European state" to renounce the use of force for the settling of international disputes, contained nothing that implied abandonment of West Germany's position on such central issues as Germany's future frontiers[18] and reunification; but it did recognize that reunification could come only at the end of a long process of détente and reconciliation that would dispel "distrust with regard to alleged German aggressive intentions." As the note did not concede the existence of separate German states, it obviously was unpalatable to the GDR, and the Soviet Union was thus, in effect, presented with a choice between treating the note as a friendly gesture from Bonn or spurning it in order to back up the Ulbricht regime's resistance to West German conciliatory moves. It chose the latter alternative.

Formal Soviet rejection of Bonn's Peace Note was delayed about two months, but the treatment accorded it in Brezhnev's opening speech at the Twenty-third Party Congress on March 29 foreshadowed what was to come. Brezhnev brushed aside Bonn's proposals with the cryptic comment that they only

[16] These and other criticisms of West German policy, linked in part with Soviet efforts in late 1965 to make it clear that Moscow would not tolerate any arrangements in connection with a nonproliferation treaty that would leave room for West German nuclear access, also were directed toward rebutting a major policy statement by Erhard in December 1965. See particularly, Gromyko's Supreme Soviet speech of December 9, 1965, *Pravda*, December 10, 1965, and Kosygin's interview of December 6 with James Reston, *New York Times*, December 8, 1965. In talks with various Western visitors, including Danish Prime Minister Jens Otto Krag in October and British Foreign Secretary Michael Stewart in November 1965, the Soviet leaders evidently also gave private emphasis to the hardened tone of their public criticisms of West German policy.

[17] Bonn's note was sent to some one hundred governments, including all the East European countries with the exception of the GDR. See Thomas J. Hamilton, "Bonn Urges Pacts with East Europe Renouncing Force," *New York Times*, March 25, 1966. A "White Book" containing the Peace Note and related materials, *Die Bemühungen der deutschen Regierung und ihrer Verbündeten um die Einheit Deutschlands 1955–1966* (Efforts of the German Government and Its Allies toward the Unification of Germany, 1955–1966), was published at Bonn in April 1966.

[18] On the question of frontiers, the Peace Note reiterated Bonn's position that Germany's 1937 frontiers remained valid under international law "until such time as a freely elected all-German government recognized different frontiers." This formula left open the question whether Germany would ever get back the territory east of the Oder–Neisse line held by Poland, as well as the question of the FRG–GDR boundary, but it naturally drew no approval from the Soviet Union, which remained adamant in its position that no settlement of the German question is possible which does not recognize the present status of European boundaries.

showed that "the FRG intends to continue its aggressive and revenge-seeking policy."[19] Like other speakers at the Congress,[20] he included in his denunciation of West German revanchism the warning that a bilateral military partnership was "taking shape between the ruling circles of the USA and the FRG," with each partner "seeking to aggravate tension in Europe—each for his own purpose." According to Brezhnev, the US purpose in aggravating European tensions was to create a pretext for "keeping its troops and war bases in Europe, and thereby to have a means for directly influencing the economy and policy of the West European countries." Bonn's purpose, he charged, was "to involve the USA and its other NATO partners more deeply in its revanchist plans in order to secure a revision of the results of World War II in its favor."

Having pictured a growing Washington–Bonn axis as the main threat to European security, Brezhnev later in his speech returned to the European security theme by proposing "an appropriate international conference" on that subject. Although his suggestion was vague as to participants and agenda for such a conference, it provided a preview of what would shortly become one of the main features of the new regime's European policy approach. In a sense, the notion of an all-European security conference, which had lain more or less dormant for a decade,[21] was also the Soviet answer to Bonn's Peace Note of March 1966. Incidentally, whereas Brezhnev tended to attribute the Peace Note initiative to encouragement from the United States, some Soviet interpretations of Bonn's "Eastern Policy" took a different tack, asserting that the note was Bonn's own reply to the failure of the United States and other NATO members to respond to West Germany's desire for a new "Western initiative on the German question."[22]

When the formal Soviet answer to the Peace Note came, on May 18, amidst signs that Bonn's initiative had scored at least a minor success in Eastern Europe,[23] the counter-conditions laid down for improvement of Soviet

[19] Report of 1st Secretary L. I. Brezhnev to the Twenty-third Congress of the CPSU, *Pravda*, March 30, 1966.

[20] See, for example, Gromyko's speech of April 2 at the Twenty-third Congress, *Pravda*, April 3, 1966.

[21] See chapter V, pp. 74–78, for discussion of the various Soviet proposals for a European security conference put forth in 1954 and early 1955. The gradual revival of the idea of a European security conference after Khrushchev's ouster began, not with the Soviet leadership but with Poland's Foreign Minister Adam Rapacki, who broached the subject in a UN General Assembly speech on December 14, 1964. (See "Conference on European Security Urged by Poland in U.N.," *New York Times*, December 15, 1964.) The Rapacki suggestion was endorsed in the January 20, 1965, communiqué of the Warsaw Pact meeting in Poland, but the first high-level Soviet leader to take up the theme was Brezhnev, who on April 8, 1965, during a visit to Poland included the idea of a conference of European states in a "program of measures" for guaranteeing European security in the face of West German policy, described by him as "the mine which threatens to blow up Europe's security." See *Pravda*, April 9, 1965. Brezhnev's return to the European security conference theme in his March 29, 1966, speech at the Twenty-third Party Congress was soon followed by other Soviet suggestions on the subject, culminating in the Bucharest declaration of July 1966.

[22] Such an interpretation may be found in M. S. Voslenskii, *"Vostochnaia" politika FRG, 1949–1966* (The "Eastern" Policy of the FRG, 1949–1966) (Moscow: Izdatel'stvo "Nauka," 1967), pp. 289–91.

[23] Although Poland (on April 29, 1966) and Czechoslovakia (on May 7, 1966) gave negative replies to Bonn's note, arguing as did the Soviet Union that it was a misleading document which

relations with the Federal Republic conspicuously included the holding of a European conference to take up "the proposals of the Socialist and other states of Europe on questions of European security," linked with other measures to bring about a German peace settlement, "reflecting the real situation in Europe."[24] The range of measures stipulated by the Soviet Union called for settlement of virtually all outstanding European problems as the prerequisite for improved Moscow–Bonn relations, making it evident that the Soviet Union was primarily interested in preparing the way for a new diplomatic offensive in Europe—one of the objects of which was to blunt the edge of the West German government's policy of reconciliation.

Indeed, from mid-1966 on, when the Bucharest conference served as the platform from which to launch this offensive in earnest, the Soviet leadership displayed little interest in feeling out the prospects for better relations with either the Erhard government or the coalition under Kiesinger that succeeded it later in 1966.[25] Rather, the Soviet Union chose to step up its attacks on West German "militarism and revanchism," accusing Bonn in more and more strident terms of pursuing an aggressive foreign policy with the support and blessing of the United States. It seemed as though the Brezhnev–Kosygin regime had come to consider the Federal Republic beyond redemption, and instead of entertaining the possibility of dealing bilaterally with Bonn, had in effect resigned itself to backing up Ulbricht's resistance to a conciliatory Eastern policy on the part of West Germany.

Yet, despite the strident attacks on rampant revanchism in Bonn, there was an occasional suggestion that the Soviet Union might be allowing itself elbow room for an alternative policy approach. One Soviet writer, for example, in a particularly damning attack on FRG policy in June 1966, still took pains to point out that "exposing Bonn's aggressive foreign policy" did not mean looking upon the Federal Republic "as an outcast among states." West Germany, he said, was not "inhabited solely by militarists and revenge-seekers. There are also healthy forces in the country who realize the need for a radical

---

marked no change in the FRG's "revanchist policy," some of the other East European addressees, notably Rumania and Hungary, avoided making polemical answers, suggesting something less than bloc unanimity behind the position taken by the Soviet Union. At this time, of course, Rumania was engaged in exploratory dialogue with Bonn which was to lead to establishment of diplomatic relations between the two governments in early 1967.

24 Among other steps set out in the eight-point Soviet counterproposal were: conclusion of a nonproliferation treaty; elimination of foreign military bases; liquidation of military blocs, including NATO and the Warsaw Pact organization; renunciation of nuclear weapons by both German states and creation of a nuclear-free zone in Central Europe; development of closer political, economic, and scientific relations among European states; and the admission of both German states to the United Nations. See "To Make the European Situation Healthier, to Strengthen the Peace and Security of Peoples," *Pravda*, May 19, 1966.

25 During the German governmental crisis in the autumn of 1966 which culminated in the fall of the Erhard government and the formation in November of the CDU–SPD "Grand Coalition" headed by Kurt Georg Kiesinger, the Soviet Union maintained a relatively restrained "wait-and-see" attitude. Not long after installation of the Kiesinger government, however, Soviet attacks on FRG revanchism and neo-Nazism were resumed, spearheaded by a particularly sharp outburst from Kosygin during his visit to Paris in December 1966. See, for example, Waverly Root, "Kosygin Assails Bonn at Reception in Paris," *Washington Post*, December 3, 1966; Henry Tanner, "Kosygin Asserts Fascism Is on the Rise in Germany," *New York Times*, December 3, 1966.

revision of the foreign and home policy."[26] This, together with the notation that differences as well as coinciding interests existed between Bonn and Washington,[27] was typical of the hints slipped now and then into Moscow's anti-German propaganda, suggesting that under appropriate conditions the Soviet Union might be prepared to play a different policy card of some sort.

Growth of Soviet–French Cordiality

By contrast with its increasingly hard line toward West Germany between October 1964 and mid-1966, the Soviet Union displayed a growing interest in closer bilateral relations with France. At the outset, be it said, the new regime's inclination to pick up the cultivation of de Gaulle where Khrushchev had left off apparently was tempered by some of the same considerations that had kept Khrushchev wary of staking Soviet policy in Europe exclusively upon a Moscow–Paris axis: the limitations of de Gaulle's power; the long-standing Soviet disposition to deal directly with the real source of power in the West; and perhaps an ambivalent attitude toward the prospect of having US influence —with its potential restraint upon German ambitions—removed from the scene. Whatever may have been the weight of such considerations in the councils of the new Soviet regime, however, factors suggesting that it would be useful to continue moving toward the Soviet–French rapprochement initiated under Khrushchev soon proved persuasive. As it happened, a reciprocal interest in rapprochement existed in Paris.

For the Soviet Union, the possibilities of turning de Gaulle's anti-Americanism to good account were to be seen largely in terms of further weakening NATO unity and undermining American influence in Europe without the liability of having to exert direct Soviet pressure upon the Western alliance—a course which had often proved unproductive in the past. Improved relations with France also provided an instrument for exerting subtle leverage on Germany; at the same time, they offered Moscow a way to defuse France's potential for attracting the countries of East Europe away from the Soviet orbit, for Paris could not encourage greater East European independence without risk of rupturing the rapprochement with the Soviet Union itself.

To de Gaulle, convinced that there was no longer any military danger in a Europe secure under the umbrella of a nuclear stalemate, the situation promised the great prestige of playing the prophet of détente with the Soviet Union and the satisfaction of leading the European disengagement from the United States. De Gaulle's growing belief that the Federal Republic of Germany could no longer be counted on to support his idea of an independent Europe based on a Franco–German axis centered in Paris also apparently sharpened his interest in forging closer links with the Soviet Union.[28]

In any event, out of these partially convergent, if not always basically com-

---

[26] P. Kryukov, "Bonn's Aggressive Foreign Policy," *International Affairs*, no. 6 (June 1966): 19.
[27] Ibid., p. 17.
[28] For a discerning account of factors underlying the development of French–Soviet relations, see Alfred Grosser, *Franco–Soviet Relations Today*, The RAND Corporation, RM-5382-PR, August 1967.

patible, interests grew an increasing number of Soviet–French contacts. Beginning early in 1965, the Soviet Union made a series of gestures suggesting that development of closer Soviet–French relations would "open interesting prospects" for both.[29] These steps included the renewal in January 1965 of the standing Soviet invitation to de Gaulle to visit Moscow, the appointment in March of a new and more prestigious Soviet ambassador to Paris,[30] and the conclusion later the same month of a television agreement committing the Soviet Union to adopting the French system of color television—a flattering bow to the value of French technology.[31] In late April, Soviet Foreign Minister Gromyko paid a five-day visit to de Gaulle, and by the summer of 1965 it had become apparent that, while Soviet–French differences remained on a number of questions,[32] the two countries were moving toward a collaborative relationship from which both might hope to profit.

Soviet approval of the course of French policy in Europe became perceptibly warmer in early 1966, as de Gaulle's dissatisfaction with NATO grew sharper. Thus, when the French leader, in an exchange of letters with President Johnson in March 1966, made it known that he had decided to withdraw French forces from NATO integrated military commands and that US military facilities in France would have to be renegotiated,[33] the Soviet Union promptly commended de Gaulle on the "realism" of this initiative to restore "French sovereignty." At the same time Soviet commentary charged that the United States, together with Britain and West Germany (its only "loyal partners" in NATO), was trying "to frighten the French government by threatening it with isolation if it should not rescind its intention to remove its troops from NATO control."[34]

De Gaulle's Soviet Visit

The development of closer ties between the Soviet Union and France in the first year-and-a-half after the fall of Khrushchev came to its most conspicuous

[29] See, for example, "Observer" commentary on de Gaulle's February 4, 1965, press conference, *Pravda*, February 14, 1965.

[30] The new Soviet ambassador to France was Deputy Foreign Minister Valerian A. Zorin, whose high standing in Soviet officialdom compared to that of his predecessor, Sergei A. Vinogradov, was widely interpreted as evidence of Moscow's desire to promote closer Soviet–French contacts.

[31] One implication of the television agreement, like subsequent agreements to co-operate in the field of space research, was that French technology, and thus of course, France itself, was taken more seriously in Moscow than in Washington. See Grosser, *Franco–Soviet Relations Today*, p. 46.

[32] Among such differences were the respective Soviet and French attitudes on the German issue. Gromyko, for example, at a press conference in Paris on April 30, 1965, gave the impression that France had accorded de facto recognition to East Germany. Shortly thereafter, a French spokesman carefully pointed out that while France took into account the existing division of Germany, this should not be considered the diplomatic recognition of the GDR. See "Talks With French Hailed by Gromyko," *New York Times*, May 1, 1965.

[33] See "De Gaulle Writes to Johnson on Control of Bases," *New York Times*, March 8, 1966; "Plan To Run U.S. Bases Is Rejected," *Washington Post*, March 8, 1966; "De Gaulle Confronts NATO," *Christian Science Monitor*, March 10, 1966.

[34] See, for example, Iakov Viktorov commentary, Moscow radio broadcast, March 9, 1966; S. Zykov, "Jupiter Is Angry," *Izvestiia*, March 11, 1966; S. Vishnevskii, "Pressure Campaign Misfired," *Pravda*, April 23, 1966.

juncture with de Gaulle's much-heralded journey to the USSR in June 1966. The French President's two-week state visit, during which he was accorded unprecedented honors[35] and held long talks with the Soviet leaders, produced neither a dramatic "reversal of alliances" nor specific political commitments with respect to such hard-core issues as a German settlement or the Soviet proposal for a conference on European security.[36] It did, however, in addition to a variety of agreements on mutual consultation and scientific-economic co-operation, produce a significant affirmation on both sides "that the problems of Europe should be considered first of all in a European framework."[37] Although de Gaulle qualified this formula as not "denying in any way the vital role which the United States must play in the pacification and transformation of the world,"[38] he left little doubt as to his preference for a greatly circumscribed American role in Europe.

One is tempted to assume that for de Gaulle and his Soviet hosts the chief effect of their talks was to confirm a mutual readiness to minimize American influence in Europe, yet it may be that neither party came away from the visit without certain reservations on this account. De Gaulle, though his emotional preference was doubtless to see the United States excluded from Europe, may also have realized that a Europe without some form of American support probably would not be strong enough politically and strategically to balance Soviet influence. Moreover, any purely European combination, in order to be strong enough to do so, would almost surely have to provide a greatly expanded role for Germany, which de Gaulle's policy was hardly meant to encourage. As for the Soviet leaders, despite their presumable interest in co-operating with Paris as a means of promoting the political isolation of the United States (and of Bonn) in Europe, they had reasons for not embracing de Gaulle too warmly. The Kremlin, at the time, was trying hard to hammer out a co-ordinated European policy within the Warsaw Pact, and concentration on a détente with de Gaulle before Pact unity was achieved might only undermine the quest for the latter. There was also the possibility that the Soviet leaders regarded their flirtation with de Gaulle essentially as a useful way of marking time until termination of the war in Vietnam and other developments made it propitious once more to take up seriously with the United States the matter of reaching a settlement in Europe.

[35] In addition to the high ceremony with which de Gaulle was received in Moscow and during a six-day tour to other Soviet cities, he became the first Western leader to be taken to the Soviet Union's space-launching center at Tyura Tam (or Baikonur) in Central Asia. See Henry Tanner, "De Gaulle Visits Soviet Space Site: Sees a Launching," New York Times, June 26, 1966.

[36] Among contemporary accounts of the de Gaulle visit, see Peter Grose, "De Gaulle Opens Visit to Russians: Deplores Blocs," New York Times, June 21, 1966; Henry Tanner, "Paris and Moscow Plan To Consult on Regular Basis," and "De Gaulle and Brezhnev Deadlocked on Germany," ibid., June 29 and 30, 1966, respectively; Waverley Root, "Franco–Soviet Text Lacks Surprises," Washington Post, July 1, 1966.

[37] See "Text of Soviet–French Declaration on Intent to Collaborate on Leaders in Europe," New York Times, July 1, 1966.

[38] See De Gaulle's Kremlin toast of June 20, 1966, cited by Grosser, Franco–Soviet Relations Today, pp. 44–45.

Other Elements of Emerging Soviet Policy in Europe

If the Soviet regime in its private councils did in fact believe that the time might come when it would be more profitable to turn from de Gaulle to a diplomatic dialogue with the United States about terms for a European settlement, this was not evident in 1966, as the outlines of a new Soviet policy toward Europe gradually took shape. In addition to dwelling upon the familiar theme of the dangers posed by West German revanchism and siding with de Gaulle as exponents of a Europe that should assert its own identity, the Soviet leaders sought in a variety of ways to persuade Western Europe that improved relations with the Soviet Union would serve its political, economic, and security interests better than continued "subservience" to an American government which, according to Soviet propaganda, added to the international tension both by its own "aggressive" behavior in Vietnam and by its support of West German "revenge-seekers" in Europe.

One expression of these Soviet efforts to encourage organized opposition to US policies was the revival of the "Popular Front" idea of the mid-thirties. In October 1965, at the time of the thirtieth anniversary of the Seventh Congress of the Comintern, at which the original Popular Front had been launched, Soviet spokesmen such as B. N. Ponomarev began to urge that Western Communist parties seek a "broad coalition" of "anti-imperialist, democratic forces," including even "right-wing Social Democrats," in order to oppose "American imperialism."[39] As various Soviet accounts put it, a basis for the collaborative struggle of Communist and non-Communist groups against "American imperialism allied with West German revanchism" was to be found in a "new element" in world capitalism, namely—"the striving of West European states to defend their national interests."[40] Although the renewed emphasis on Popular Front tactics in late 1965 and 1966 brought no results in terms of formal alliance between Communist and non-Communist parties in Europe, with the possible exception of Finland,[41] it did serve to give West European Communists somewhat greater flexibility in trying to influence popular and official sentiment in their countries.[42]

[39] Ponomarev was head of the CPSU's international department. See his speech to the anniversary meeting of the Seventh Congress of the Comintern, held in Prague, October 21–23, 1965. The speech, entitled "The Historic Significance of the Seventh Congress of the Comintern and Our Time," may be found in *World Marxist Review* (December 1965): 5–12.

[40] See "Unity of All Revolutionary Forces in the Command of the Epoch," *Kommunist*, no. 11 (July 1965): 83–94; "Soviet Foreign Policy and Social Progress," ibid., no. 12 (August 1965): 3–12.

[41] In Finland, the Communist party was formally admitted in May 1966 into a four-party government coalition headed by Social Democrats. Marking the inclusion of Communists in a Finnish government for the first time in eighteen years, this move was praised by Kosygin during his visit to Finland in June 1966. See UP International dispatch, "Finnish Coalition to Include Reds 1st Time Since '48," *New York Times*, May 22, 1966; Peter Grose, "Kosygin Praises Finnish Coalition," ibid., June 15, 1966.

[42] For discussion of some of the limitations of a Popular Front approach for the Communist parties of Western Europe, see William McLaughlin, "Return of the Popular Front," *Radio Free Europe*, February 10, 1966.

Soviet Talks with Western Leaders

Another aspect of the Soviet effort to persuade West Europeans that their interest lay in siding with the Soviet Union against the alleged threat of a Washington–Bonn axis was to be seen in the growing number of visits which Soviet leaders exchanged with their European counterparts in 1966. Besides de Gaulle's journey to Moscow in mid-summer, which Kosygin repaid later in the year with a nine-day state visit to France, the flow of visits in both directions included two trips to Moscow by British Prime Minister Wilson, a call upon the Pope and the Italian government by Gromyko, and visits to Finland and Austria by Kosygin and Podgornyi, respectively.

Wilson's talks with the Soviet leaders brought out the interesting but hardly surprising point that Britain could expect little improvement in relations with the Soviet Union so long as she continued her traditionally close relationship with the United States. Whatever the private tenor of the conversations, the Soviet government let it be known publicly that such things as Britain's backing of US-sponsored nuclear consultative arrangements in NATO and her failure to denounce US policy in Vietnam stood in the way of better Soviet–British relations.[43] During Wilson's first Moscow trip, in February 1966, Kosygin took pains to point out that the visit had been at British initiative, and both then and on the second visit, in July 1966, it was apparent that Wilson could not expect to enlist Soviet co-operation in efforts toward a negotiated settlement in Vietnam unless he was prepared to put pressure on the United States to reverse its stand.[44] Although the talks in Moscow produced no visible progress on outstanding issues, both sides chose to regard them as useful in keeping open the dialogue between East and West, and Kosygin agreed to pay a return visit to London,[45] which took place early the following year.

Perhaps the most unexpected object of Soviet diplomatic attention, as various Soviet leaders shuttled about Europe, was Pope Paul VI, upon whom Gromyko paid a call in the course of a visit to Italy in April 1966. Marking a historic first meeting between a high Soviet official and a Roman pontiff,[46] Gromyko's visit underscored Moscow's interest, not only in paving the way for more amicable relations between the Catholic Church and the Soviet Union

---

[43] See V. Matveev, "England and the War in Vietnam," *Izvestiia*, February 17, 1966; O. Orestov, "In London and 'East of Suez'," *Pravda*, February 17, 1966; B. Dmitriev, "To Deal With the Facts," *Izvestiia*, March 3, 1966.

[44] "Wilson and Kosygin Open Moscow Talks With Impasse on Vietnam," *New York Times*, February 23, 1966; Peter Grose, "Moscow Rebuffs Appeal by Wilson on Hanoi POW's," ibid., July 19, 1966; William H. Stringer, "Wilson Reports Moscow Leaders Deeply Committed to Hanoi," *Christian Science Monitor*, July 20, 1966.

[45] Kosygin's acceptance of an invitation to visit London reversed an earlier cancellation of a projected visit in April 1965.

[46] Khrushchev's son-in-law, Aleksei I. Adzhubei, had called on Pope John XXIII in 1963, when Soviet attitudes toward the Vatican first began to thaw slightly, but Adzhubei's official standing, whatever his family ties with Khrushchev, was a good many rungs below that of Foreign Minister. Gromyko's papal visit in 1966 was followed the next year by Podgornyi's visit. The latter, of course, stood even higher in the Soviet hierarchy than Gromyko.

but also in courting broader support for the notion of a pan-European conference on European security problems. The recurrent theme of "Europe for the
Europeans," to which Gromyko reportedly alluded in his talks both with the
Pope and with Italian government officials, was coupled with the suggestion
at his press conference that all people should join with the Soviet Union in
"the search for relaxation of international tensions and peace regardless of
differences in ideology and religion."[47]

Meanwhile, on May 4, 1966, on the heels of Gromyko's visit to Italy, the
Soviet Union took a much-publicized practical step in another direction with
the signing of an agreement under which Italy's Fiat Company was to build
a major automobile plant in the USSR. This move in the economic sphere
served notice that the Soviet Union was interested in developing not only
better political relations with co-operative countries in Western Europe but
closer industrial-technical ties as well.[48] If this were to encourage Europeans
to believe that co-operation with the Soviet Union would pay economic dividends and offset the so-called "technological gap" and "brain drain" that were
disturbing European–American relations,[49] so much the better, although it was
not clear that the export of Western auto manufacturing techniques and other
advanced technology to the Soviet Union would necessarily prompt a reverse
flow of Soviet technology from which Western Europe might expect to profit.[50]

Soviet Reluctance to Enter a Dialogue with the United States on European Security

Just as it was increasingly evident in the summer of 1966 that such overtures
from Moscow as the bid for closer political-economic co-operation with Western
Europe and for a pan-European security conference heralded a new and more
active phase in the Soviet Union's European policy, so it had become equally
obvious that Moscow at this juncture did not wish to enter into a direct dia-

[47] See Robert C. Doty, "Gromyko Sees Pope: They Talk of Peace," *New York Times*, April 28,
1966; Leo J. Wollemborg, "Gromyko Asks Europe Summit Talks," *Washington Post*, April 28,
1966.

[48] AP dispatch, "Fiat To Build Plant in Soviet To Produce 2,000 Autos a Day," *New York
Times*, May 5, 1966. The $400 million agreement with Italy's Fiat Company was the largest single
Soviet order placed in the West, accounting for almost half of the $900 million in Soviet orders
for Western industrial equipment in 1966. The following year, Soviet machinery orders came to
about $600 million. See *Soviet Economic Performance: 1966–1967*, Materials Prepared for the
Subcommittee on Foreign Economic Policy, Joint Economic Committee, US Congress (Washington,
D.C.: Government Printing Office, May 1968), p. 105.

[49] Although it was a fairly common attitude among West Europeans in the mid-sixties to look
upon the technological gap as another of the many irritants in US–European relations, by 1967
there was a growing tendency in West Europe to recognize that the lag in technology was more
a product of management shortcomings and other factors in European society than a reflection of
American attempts at domination. See, for example, Clyde N. Farnsworth, "West Europeans
Attribute Continuing Technology Lag Behind the U.S. to Inferior Management," *New York Times*,
December 13, 1967.

[50] See Zbigniew Brzezinski, "The Framework of East-West Reconciliation," *Foreign Affairs*
(January 1968): 262. For a later Soviet argument on Europe's ability to get along without US
technology, especially if close European–Soviet collaboration were encouraged, see Iurii Zhukov,
"Possibilities of a Greater Europe," *Pravda*, March 21, 1968.

logue with the United States on European problems in general or European security issues in particular. Virtually all Soviet pronouncements on the need for a European security conference implied the exclusion of the United States from at least the preparatory stages of such a gathering and stressed that there should be a "European settlement" of issues involving the security of the Continent.[51] Moreover, it almost seemed as though the Soviet leaders were afraid that their own access to West European audiences would suffer if they lent an attentive ear to American suggestions bearing on the subject of East–West relations.

Throughout the spring and summer of 1966 there had been growing public discussion in the United States, fed by a series of hearings on Capitol Hill, on the future role of NATO and on the need for initiatives to reopen an East–West dialogue on European questions, despite the strain on US–Soviet relations caused by the Vietnam war.[52] In the course of one of these hearings, in June 1966, Secretary of Defense McNamara made the significant point that the time might be ripe to consider a reciprocal reduction of forces in the rival organizations of NATO and the Warsaw Pact,[53] a suggestion repeated in a slightly different context several months later in President Johnson's "bridge-building" speech of October 7, 1966.[54]

However, just as Moscow was showing no interest in the general US initiative for bridge-building discussion,[55] so it declined to pick up the specific suggestion that mutual troop reductions might become part of an East–West accommodation in Europe. Rumors of possible Soviet troop withdrawals from East Germany circulated freely on the eve of de Gaulle's visit to Moscow, but

[51] The stress on a "European settlement" was, for example, a feature of the Bucharest declaration of mid-1966, which we shall take up later in this chapter.

[52] See, for example, Benjamin Welles, "U.S. Seeking Shift in NATO Emphasis," *New York Times*, May 18, 1966; Robert Kleiman, "Can NATO Shift Gears From War to Peace?" ibid., May 23, 1966; Max Frankel, "U.S. European Policy," ibid., June 22, 1966; Chalmers M. Roberts, "NATO: 'Give' or Give Up," *Washington Post*, June 5, 1966. See also *The Crisis in NATO*, Hearings Before the Subcommittee on Europe of the Committee on Foreign Affairs, House of Representatives, 89th Congress, 2nd Session, March 17 ... June 13, 1966 (Washington, D.C.: Government Printing Office, 1966). Hearings on NATO and the Atlantic Alliance were also held in the summer of 1966 in the Senate. See *The Atlantic Alliance*, Hearings Before the Subcommittee on National Security and International Operations, Committee on Government Operations, United States Senate, 89th Congress, 2nd Session (Washington, D.C.: Government Printing Office, 1966).

[53] Secretary McNamara's views on a reciprocal reduction of forces were given while he was testifying before the Subcommittee on National Security and International Operations on June 21, 1966 (*The Atlantic Alliance*). See also Chalmers M. Roberts, "U.S. Would Match Red Troop Cuts," *Washington Post*, June 22, 1966. The question of mutual troop reductions also emerged from the hearings in the House of Representatives on NATO. The report on these hearings recommended, among other things, that "new initiatives [be] undertaken to pave the way for a possible reciprocal reduction in land forces between NATO and the Warsaw Pact." See *The Crisis in NATO*, p. 9.

[54] President Johnson in his October 7, 1966, speech suggested that, "If changing circumstances should lead to a gradual and balanced revision in force levels on both sides, the revision could—together with the other steps that I have mentioned—help gradually to shape a new political environment." See text of the President's speech in *New York Times*, October 8, 1966.

[55] See previous discussion of the Soviet response to US "bridge-building" overtures, chapter XI, p. 266.

no actual moves of this sort took place.[56] Moreover, even though the question of troop reductions remained before the public in the summer of 1966 as a result of senatorial urging in Washington that US forces in Europe be cut back,[57] the Soviet Union refrained from exploring the subject with the United States.[58]

This reluctance to be drawn into discussions with the United States on troop withdrawals from Europe doubtless stemmed to some extent from the situation in Vietnam. Throughout 1966, Moscow increasingly found itself the target of allegations from Peking that it was "colluding" with the United States to ease the European situation and thereby permit the transfer of American troops to Southeast Asia.[59] Direct response to suggestions emanating from Washington on the touchy question of troop reductions would not only have seemed to lend substance to the Chinese criticism but it would have tended to embarrass the Soviet Union's own diplomacy, aimed at taking advantage of the growing isolation of the United States on the Vietnam war issue. Hoping to keep the United States on the defensive in Europe, the Soviet leaders were of no mind to let the initiative slip from their own hands on the matter of European security arrangements, including the question of troop reductions. Indeed, when the Bucharest conference of July 1966 provided the occasion for publicizing a new Soviet initiative on European security, the package of proposals put forward on this subject included reference to mutual troop withdrawals, but, at the same time, was notably ambiguous as to what voice the United States should have in the proposed process of settling European security problems.

The Bucharest conference not only served as a platform for inviting the

[56] See Murrey Marder, "U.S. Wary of Soviet Troop Cutback Rumor," *Washington Post*, June 16, 1966; Berlin dispatch, "A Moscow Review of Strategy Seen," *New York Times*, October 24, 1966. Further discussion of the troop reduction issue will be found in chapter XVII.

[57] In July 1966, Senator Mike Mansfield called for a 10 per cent reduction of US troops in Europe, plus return of troops stationed in France, without specifying reciprocal reduction of Soviet forces in Europe. A temporary reduction of US troops in West Germany from 225,000 to 210,000 had already been announced in April 1966, in connection with training needs for Vietnam. See Benjamin Welles, "Mansfield Urges Cutback of U.S. Forces in Europe," *New York Times*, July 28, 1966.

[58] Apart from commentary in the United States on the matter of troop reductions, which might have been expected to stimulate Soviet interest in the subject, there were various exploratory suggestions from political figures in Europe. Among the potentially most interesting of these from the Soviet viewpoint was the trial balloon sent up by Dr. Rainer Barzel of West Germany, who, in a June 15, 1966, speech proposing fresh inducements to the Soviet Union to enhance the prospect of reunification, included the suggestion that Moscow might be ceded the right to maintain Soviet troops in a reunited Germany. However, Barzel's proposals fell flat, neither eliciting much support in his own country nor arousing any show of interest in Moscow. See Max Frankel, "West German Proposes Offers To Speed Reunification," *New York Times*, June 16, 1966; Thomas J. Hamilton, "Reunification Debate," ibid., July 5, 1966.

[59] For a sample of such Chinese allegations, see Commentator, "Confessions Concerning the Line of Soviet–U.S. Collaboration Pursued by the New Leaders of the C.P.S.U.," *Red Flag*, no. 2, February 11, 1966, as reprinted in *Peking Review*, no. 8, February 18, 1966, p. 10. See also Observer, "Confession of Worldwide U.S.–Soviet Collusion on a Big Scale," *People's Daily*, October 16, 1966, as reprinted in *Peking Review*, no. 43, October 21, 1966, p. 20.

countries of West Europe to give thought, as it were, to bypassing the United States in a move toward a general European settlement; it also was significant in providing the occasion for Soviet efforts to promote united action by the Warsaw states on Vietnam and to counter tendencies of some individual bloc members, particularly Rumania, to stray from a common policy on Warsaw Pact matters. Before examining the transactions of the Bucharest conference itself, therefore, let us retrace briefly the development of Soviet relations with East Europe in the period from Khrushchev's ouster to mid-1966.

Relations with East Europe Prior to the Bucharest Conference

A few words on some of the underlying trends that shaped the system of Soviet–East European relationships to which Khrushchev's successors fell heir may usefully precede our discussion of specific policy issues in the period leading up to the Bucharest conference of July 1966. It is difficult to find a label that properly describes the evolving alliance system in East Europe, which, at the time the Brezhnev–Kosygin regime came to power, was held together by a web of ideological, economic, political, and military ties.[60] The East European states clearly were no longer completely subordinated to Soviet power, yet limits were set upon independent national action both by the control and influence the Soviet Union was capable of exercising and by the interaction of the East European regimes upon one another.[61] Each of these states was obliged in a sense to work out an adjustment between its own national aspirations and the requirements of bloc solidarity, just as domestically each tended to develop its own brand of "nationalized" communism.[62]

From the Soviet viewpoint, ever since the green light had been given under Khrushchev for greater autonomy in East Europe, Moscow had found itself alternating between bilateral dealings with the individual East European regimes and attempts to exercise its leadership through some multilateral form of "institutionalized unity." Even though the multilateral approach to economic

[60] H. Gordon Skilling, *The Governments of Communist East Europe* (New York: Thomas Y. Crowell, 1966), p. 226; Melvin Croan, "Moscow and Eastern Europe," *Problems of Communism* (September–October 1966): 63; Andrew Gyorgy, "Diversity in Eastern Europe: Cohesion and Disunity," *Canadian Slavic Studies* (Spring 1967): 24–43.

[61] In some cases, this interaction took the form of dependence, an example being the dependence of the Ulbricht regime upon the other Warsaw bloc countries to support the GDR's international position on the existence of two sovereign German states. In other cases it took the form of revival of old rivalries, such as Hungary's resentment over Bucharest's attempts to assimilate the Magyar minority in Rumania, and the reciprocal mistrust of the Rumanians concerning Hungarian intentions toward Transylvania. See J. F. Brown, *The New Eastern Europe* (New York: Frederick A. Praeger, Inc., 1966), pp. 190–91; Skilling, *The Governments of Communist East Europe*, p. 229.

[62] Although the domestic variants of communism in East Europe had not worked out precisely the same in any of these countries, there was a broad pattern characteristic of the region. Internal development in the East European countries, as in the Soviet Union itself, reflected a process of change, with the rise of competing interest groups and trends toward "market" versions of socialist economies, but with neither a visible decline in the political monopoly of the ruling parties nor the emergence of anything resembling a genuinely constitutional system. In some cases, a struggle between two internal elements—the party-state apparatus on the one hand and the economic-technical intelligentsia on the other—seemed to be underway. See Skilling, ibid., p. 231.

integration through CEMA had fallen rather flat in 1962–63,[63] the Warsaw Pact continued to be upgraded as a multilateral instrument through which both military and political integration could be promoted.[64] The Pact had proved to be a means through which intrabloc conflict and friction could be resolved or at least contained,[65] but at the same time it remained, like CEMA, something less than an ideal instrument for carrying out common policies emanating from Moscow. In fact, though both CEMA and the Warsaw Pact were joint multilateral bodies, the system still lacked a set of organs for policy-making and centralized enforcement of decisions. Authoritative policy formulation rested mainly with Communist party leaders from the member states, meeting together as circumstances demanded in what has sometimes been described as a system of "mutual concessions, conference and discussion."[66] Even then, the policy decisions they reached were not binding and were implemented largely by the national states and parties rather than through the international machinery of the bloc.[67]

If past experience indicated that neither bilateral nor multilateral principles for the management of Soviet relations with the other Warsaw Pact members were altogether satisfactory, a third alternative presented itself to the Brezhnev-Kosygin regime. This was to cultivate further the trend toward regional differentiation which had developed in Khrushchev's day between the Northern Tier of states—Poland, East Germany, Czechoslovakia—and the southern, or Balkan, grouping. The Northern Tier countries, which together with the Soviet Union itself formed a quartet sometimes referred to as the "first strategic echelon" of the Warsaw Pact,[68] were obviously of prime strategic and political importance to Soviet European policy, for not only did their territory lie astride what in wartime would be the main axis of a Central European campaign but they were the countries sharing the most immediate geopolitical interests against West Germany.

According to one East European witness, the idea for a northern regional grouping with a preferential relationship with Moscow originated with Gomulka between 1959 and 1963 and was inspired by his concern that a bilateral Soviet–East German axis might be formed at Poland's expense.[69]

---

[63] See Michael Kaser, COMECON: Integration Problems of the Planned Economies (London: Oxford University Press, 1965), pp. 83–107; John Michael Montias, "Communist Rule in Eastern Europe," Foreign Affairs (January 1965): 332–33; Egon Neuberger, Soviet Bloc Economic Integration: Some Suggested Explanations for Slow Progress, The RAND Corporation, RM-3629-PR, July 1963.

[64] See Robin Alison Remington, The Changing Soviet Perception of the Warsaw Pact (Cambridge, Mass.: Center for International Studies, M.I.T., November 1967), p. 5. See also Thomas W. Wolfe, "The Warsaw Pact in Evolution," in Kurt London, ed., Eastern Europe in Transition (Baltimore, Md.: The Johns Hopkins Press, 1966), pp. 213–17.

[65] See Remington, The Changing Soviet Perception, p. 6.

[66] Kazimierz Grzybowski, The Socialist Commonwealth of Nations: Organization and Institutions (New Haven, Conn.: Yale University Press, 1964), p. 2.

[67] See Skilling, The Governments of Communist East Europe, p. 227.

[68] See Wolfe, "The Warsaw Pact in Evolution," p. 220. See also Brown, The New Eastern Europe, p. 187.

[69] This version of Gomulka's sponsorship of the Northern Tier grouping was given by Wladyslaw

Whether or not this fear was justified, the Soviet Union evidently found it advantageous to confer a privileged status upon Northern Tier countries, which received a more important regional role in Soviet military and economic planning than did countries of the Southern Tier.[70] Discrimination in favor of the Northern Tier was heightened in Khrushchev's time by the erosion of Soviet influence in the Southern Tier, where in 1961 Albania had broken away from the Pact,[71] and where by early 1964 Rumania was beginning to balk against Warsaw Pact military arrangements in much the same fashion in which she had taken the lead in resisting Soviet proposals for economic integration and division of labor through CEMA.

These, then, were some of the trends at work in Soviet relations with East Europe when the Brezhnev–Kosygin regime took office. Basically, the decline in the Soviet Union's once unquestioned dominance in East Europe during the past decade had left Khrushchev's successors with the broad choice of either making the best of an unsatisfactory situation or trying to reimpose the Soviet writ throughout the region. On the whole, they apparently accepted the former alternative in the first years of the new regime,[72] when the Soviet Union followed a largely conciliatory and fence-mending line in East Europe, partly perhaps to ease fears and uncertainties that had arisen there after the change of leadership in Moscow. Eventually, of course, the Brezhnev–Kosygin regime reversed itself when it called upon troops to restore Soviet authority in Czechoslovakia.

The German Democratic Republic

The new Soviet leaders hastened to reassure Ulbricht that no Soviet deal with Bonn at Pankow's expense was in the works, although, as noted earlier, they left themselves some room for maneuver toward a possible rapprochement with West Germany.[73] On several occasions prior to the Bucharest conference, the Soviet leadership showed that it was responsive to East German concerns about the possibility that a solid Warsaw Pact front might not be maintained against Bonn.

One such occasion was the convening of the Pact's Political Consultative Committee in Warsaw in January 1965. This meeting, the first since July 1963,

---

Tykocinski, for many years chief of the Polish Mission in Berlin, who sought political asylum in the West in May 1965. See "Poland's Plan for the 'Northern Tier': An Interview with Wladyslaw Tykocinski," *East Europe* (November 1966): 14–15.

[70] Ibid., p. 15. One should note, however, that the Soviet Union did not institutionalize the separate status of the Northern Tier, which would have tended to formalize yet another division in the Warsaw bloc.

[71] Although no formal expulsion of Albania from the Warsaw Pact took place, Albania's departure was for all practical purposes complete after the Twenty-second CPSU Congress in October 1961, where the Soviet Union "lost a 'satellite'" and China "gained a bridgehead in Europe." Cf. Brown, *The New Eastern Europe*, pp. 201–2. Yugoslavia had also been "lost" to the Soviet Union, of course, in 1948, before the Warsaw Pact was formed.

[72] See, for example, Brown, *The New Eastern Europe*, pp. 189–90.

[73] See pp. 282–83. Ulbricht himself, of course, was adept at allowing himself room for maneuver, not only vis-à-vis the Soviet Union but in East German leadership politics between hardline and moderate factions.

was called at Ulbricht's insistence, according to Kosygin,[74] suggesting that
Ulbricht had put in a special claim for placing GDR interests high on the
policy agenda of the Warsaw Pact. The principal professed object of the
meeting was to put the Warsaw Pact states jointly on record as opposed to any
NATO nuclear-sharing arrangement that might "give West Germany access
to atomic weapons."[75] As subsequent commentary indicated, the meeting also
was intended to demonstrate "the complete emptiness of the imperialists' hopes
of disuniting the socialist countries."[76] Another display of Soviet willingness
to stand behind Ulbricht against the potentially disruptive effects of economic
and other overtures from Bonn came with the cold reception tendered the
Federal Republic's Peace Note of March 1966. Three months later, the Soviet
Union likewise quickly deflated the conciliatory trial balloon launched by West
Germany's Rainer Barzel.[77]

Meanwhile, however, the Soviet leaders made plain that their political
support of Ulbricht carried a price tag in the form of economic concessions,
such as those embodied in a Soviet–GDR economic agreement signed on
December 3, 1965, after an apparently arm-twisting trip to Berlin by Brezhnev
a few days before. The suicide, on December 3, of Dr. Erich Apel, chairman of
East Germany's State Planning Commission, was reportedly in protest over the
disadvantageous terms of this agreement.[78] Among these terms, according to
some critics, was Moscow's insistence on charging artificially high prices for
Soviet products exported to East Germany, as well as its demand that payment
be partly in hard currency. The five-year agreement covering an exchange of
some $15 billion worth of goods also was said to peg GDR exports to the
USSR below world market prices. The Soviets later reportedly justified these
price differentials as necessary to offset the large armament burden borne by
the USSR on behalf of the Warsaw bloc.[79]

Poland

With respect to Poland, the Soviet leaders lost no time in letting Gomulka
know that, like Khrushchev, they regarded Poland as a key member of the
Northern Tier of Warsaw bloc states, so situated that if she should begin to

[74] Kosygin's speech in Leipzig, reported in *Pravda*, March 2, 1965.

[75] Communiqué on the Meeting of the Political Consultative Committee of the Member States
of the Warsaw Treaty, *Pravda*, January 22, 1965. For possible implications of this meeting with
regard to the question of nuclear-sharing within the Warsaw bloc, see discussion in chapter XVII.

[76] See, for example, "Unrealizable Designs," *Izvestiia*, February 11, 1965.

[77] See "The Old in a New Package," *Izvestiia*, June 18, 1966. See also Harry B. Ellis, "Moscow
Slams Door on Barzel Détente Hopes," *Christian Science Monitor*, June 22, 1966. For previous
comment on the Barzel proposal, see fn. 58 above.

[78] For commentary on the Apel suicide, see Paul Wohl, "East Germany Rocked by Loss of Key
Planner," *Christian Science Monitor*, December 9, 1965; Anatole Shub, "W. German Says Apel
Left Notebook, Bonn Links Suicide to Russian Pact," *Washington Post*, December 11, 1965.
Communist sources dismissed as "impudent inventions" Western reports that Apel's suicide was in
protest against the trade pact. See editorial, "Lowest Level," *Neues Deutschland*, December 8, 1965;
commentary, ibid., December 9, 1965; TASS broadcast, December 8, 1965.

[79] See Berlin dispatch, "Ulbricht Visited Soviet on Trade," *New York Times*, September 11,
1966.

assert independent tendencies in the fashion of Rumania, this could have
adverse effects on the Soviet position in Central Europe and even on the
existence of the German Democratic Republic.[80] Gomulka, in turn, was not
unmindful of his own dependence on the Soviet Union, economically and as
the guarantor of Poland's western frontier.

Several times during the first year of their tenure, both Brezhnev and
Kosygin visited Poland to confer with Gomulka.[81] These meetings were
cited as illustrations of the Soviet Union's "proper and friendly relations"
with its bloc neighbors, demonstrating, as Brezhnev put it during his visit
to Poland in April 1965, the "correct combination of individual and common
interests" which countries of the Communist world should seek in their relations with one another.[82] But coming, as they did, shortly after the March
1965 "preparatory" meeting of Communist parties in Moscow had conspicuously failed to conciliate Peking or produce a formula for worldwide Communist unity,[83] Brezhnev's remarks only accentuated the limitations of the
Soviet–Polish example as a model for intra-Communist relations. Indeed, on
one issue on which the Soviet Union made a strong plea for joint "practical
action"—that of bloc support for Vietnam—Poland itself was slow to heed the
summons, as were most of the other East European countries.[84] Down to the
time of the Bucharest conference, for example, only Bulgaria and Hungary
had followed the Soviet lead in offering volunteers.

Bulgaria

With Bulgaria, long considered the most conformist of the Soviet Union's
Warsaw Pact partners, the new Soviet leadership presumably expected to carry
on business as usual. Any complacency, however, that Moscow may have felt
at the outset with respect to Soviet–Bulgarian relations was punctured in April
1965, when an abortive plot against the regime of Todor Zhivkov was disclosed
in Sofia. Although details of this internal conspiracy, involving General
Tsvetko Anev and several other Bulgarian army and party officials, are obscure,
it had a decidedly anti-Soviet tinge, having apparently been inspired by a
nationalist faction that hoped to reorient Bulgarian policy in a more independent direction, perhaps on the Rumanian model.[85]

[80] Brown, *The New Eastern Europe*, pp. 186–87.

[81] Kosygin paid the first call on Gomulka less than two weeks after Khrushchev's ouster. Both
Kosygin and Brezhnev conferred privately with the Polish leader immediately after the Pact meeting
in Warsaw in January 1965, while in April 1965 they headed another Soviet delegation to Warsaw to renew the Soviet–Polish treaty of friendship and mutual assistance.

[82] For text of Brezhnev speech see *Pravda*, April 9, 1965.

[83] See Henry Tanner, "Red Parties Hint Failure of Talks," *New York Times*, March 10, 1965.
See also chapter XI, p. 257.

[84] Brown, *The New Eastern Europe*, p. 185. It should be noted, however, that by February 1966
Poland did come around to heeding this summons, taking the initiative in calling for a conference
of Communist countries to co-ordinate aid to Vietnam. The conference, incidentally, failed to
materialize. See Henry Kamm, "Satellites Look Inward," *New York Times*, March 6, 1966. See
also Remington, *The Changing Soviet Perception*, p. 126.

[85] See dispatches in *New York Times*, April 18 and 21, 1965; David Binder, "Bulgarians Find
9 Guilty of Plot," ibid., June 20, 1965. See also J. F. Brown, "The Bulgarian Plot," *World Today*
(June 1965): 261–68; "The Mystery in Sofia," *East Europe* (June 1965): 14–16; Raymond L.

To prevent further erosion of Soviet authority in the already shaky Southern Tier, Moscow quickly dispatched a high-level troubleshooter in the person of Mikhail Suslov to make an on-the-spot investigation in Bulgaria.[86] Suslov's conclusion seems to have been that the Zhivkov regime had the situation under control; but the Soviet Union thereafter could not take the steadfast loyalty of its Bulgarian partner wholly for granted.

Hungary

In the case of Hungary, a country that both geographically and politically hovered between the Northern and the Southern Tier of the Warsaw bloc, the new Soviet leaders evidently recognized from the outset that they had a fence-mending job on their hands, for Janos Kadar had proved to be the most outspoken of all East European leaders in defending Khrushchev's record and voicing concern that his ouster might presage regression to heavy-handed Soviet tactics in East Europe.[87] A soft approach to Kadar, which Mikoyan was shrewdly chosen to spell out in person, helped to improve Soviet–Hungarian relations considerably,[88] but Hungary's posture within the Pact suggested nevertheless that she might not be altogether immune to the Rumanian brand of independent behavior.

Perhaps the strongest hint that interest in expanded trade and credits from West Germany might lead Hungary to break ranks on a common political line despite the displeasure of Moscow and Pankow came on June 3, 1966, after Kadar had conferred with Marshal Tito of Yugoslavia, when Hungary published a generally favorable appreciation of Bonn's March 1966 Peace Note.[89] From time to time, there were other signs of Hungary's toying with potentially heretical foreign policy ideas, such as a Danubian confederation of some sort.[90] But Kadar remained careful not to step out of the role of a loyal, though by

---

Garthoff, "The Military Establishment," *East Europe* (September 1965): 7–8, 15. The Bulgarian military figures involved in the plot along with General Anev, commandant of the Sofia garrison, are said to have been members of the wartime Bulgarian partisan group which co-operated with Tito's partisan movement.

[86] See "M. A. Suslov Leaves Moscow for Bulgaria," *New York Times*, May 30, 1965; "Soviet–Bulgarian Friendship Will Live Forever," *Pravda*, June 5, 1965 (this includes Suslov's speech in Sofia on June 2).

[87] Brown, *The New Eastern Europe*, p. 186; John Beaufort, "Red Amity Chafed by Soviet Shake-Up," *Christian Science Monitor*, October 23, 1964; George Mueller and Herman Singer, "Hungary: Can the New Course Survive," *Problems of Communism* (January–February 1965): 38.

[88] Ibid. The aptness of sending Anastas Mikoyan to Budapest in April 1965 as an envoy to soothe Kadar lay in the fact that Mikoyan had been closely associated with Khrushchev's de-Stalinization policy, widely regarded in East Europe as the charter for greater East European autonomy.

[89] The Hungarian comment on Bonn's Peace Note recited a list of "compelling facts" which had led Bonn "to open a diplomatic conversation with the socialist countries of East Europe." It then stated, however, that the West German initiative "is nonetheless significant as it is indicative of Europe's changing conditions whose influence even Bonn cannot evade." See "Communiqué on the Note of the German Federal Republic to the Government of the Hungarian People's Republic," Budapest international broadcast, June 3, 1966.

[90] For example, Hungarian Foreign Minister Janos Peter in April 1965 broached the idea that the countries of Central Europe and the Danubian basin might move to enlarge their contacts in the interest of common action to improve the international situation—a suggestion implying emergence of a grouping within the Warsaw bloc that would not necessarily draw its inspiration from Moscow. For discussion of this and other similar expressions by Hungarian leaders, see "An Alternate Foreign Policy for Hungary?" *Radio Free Europe*, March 29, 1966.

no means obsequious, ally of the Soviet Union, and Moscow responded by giving Hungary something like the preferential treatment accorded the Northern Tier members of the Pact.[91]

Czechoslovakia

Czechoslovakia's relations with the Soviet Union suffered an initial set-back in the fall of 1964, for the Czech leader Antonin Novotny, like Kadar in Hungary, showed some resentment of Khrushchev's dismissal.[92] The old-guard party leadership under Novotny was not in a good position, however, to contemplate any basic reorientation of Czechoslovak policy, and its attitude toward Moscow returned to one of official warmth, interspersed with discreet chafing at what it considered inequities in the relations between the two countries, especially in the economic field.

The economic difficulties that came to light after negotiation of a five-year trade agreement in October 1965 were apparently related to the Soviet Union's reluctance to commit itself to adequate supply of agricultural and industrial raw materials upon which the Czech economy, like the economies of most of the East European countries, had grown heavily dependent.[93] The Soviet Union, for its part, was not happy either about the raw materials situation, for the traditional pattern had become reversed, so that the USSR now found itself exporting more raw materials to East Europe than it imported and, moreover, upon an unfavorable basis in terms of investment costs.[94] Politically, from the Soviet viewpoint, these economic difficulties could have undesirable side-effects if, as had happened in some other East European capitals, they were to increase Prague's receptivity to Western initiatives, particularly from Bonn.

Despite such strains in Soviet–Czechoslovak relations, Moscow could take satisfaction in the general support which the Novotny leadership gave to a common front of bloc countries against West Germany,[95] as well as to the

[91] An example of this treatment occurred in the fall of 1966 when the "Vltava" joint Warsaw Pact military exercise was held in Czechoslovakia, a Northern Tier country. Hungarian military elements were invited to participate, a symbolic welcome marking the first time that Hungary had been associated with a joint exercise of the northern grouping. Further discussion of the various joint Warsaw Pact exercises will be found in chapter XVII.

[92] Novotny showed his pique at being taken by surprise by Khrushchev's ouster when he declined to attend the 1964 anniversary celebration of the October Revolution in Moscow, sending Jiri Hendrych in his place. Brown, *The New Eastern Europe*, p. 172.

[93] For an analysis of incipient Soviet–Czechoslovak difficulties brought to light by negotiation of the October 5, 1965, trade treaty, see Victor Meier in *Neue Zuercher Zeitung*, October 11, 1965. See also Eric Bourne, "Czech Issue: Food," *Christian Science Monitor*, November 24, 1965; "Czech Criticism Is More Audible," *New York Times*, November 14, 1965.

[94] Soviet dissatisfaction with the raw materials situation was illustrated by statements that it costs the Soviet Union three or four times as much in investments to produce a given value of raw materials for export to East Europe as it would to produce machinery of equal value for export to the region. See Michael Kaser and John Michael Montias, "Policy Factors in East-West Trade," in *The Atlantic Community and Eastern Europe: Perspectives and Policy* (Paris: The Atlantic Institute, July 1967), p. 61. See also "Soviet Aid to Bloc Foreseen," *New York Times*, July 4, 1966.

[95] Czechoslovakia, for example, adhered to the line taken by Poland and the Soviet Union in giving a negative response to Bonn's March 1966 "Peace Note." It should be noted that the Novotny regime also sided with the Soviet Union to lecture the Rumanians for over-accentuating "irregularities and distortions" in the relations of national parties with the Comintern.

Soviet "unity" line against Peking. In the latter connection, beginning with Novotny's speech at a Kremlin reception in September 1965, the Czechoslovaks became the most vocal backers in East Europe of Soviet lobbying for a new world conference of Communist parties "at an appropriate time."[96] Given the generally co-operative attitude of the Novotny regime, together with Czechoslovakia's key position as a member of the Northern Tier within the Warsaw Pact, the new direction taken by the Dubcek reform government in 1968 was all the more discomfiting to the Kremlin leadership, as its efforts to stamp out the Czech experiment were so graphically to illustrate.

Rumania

Toward Rumania, the maverick of the Warsaw bloc, the new Soviet leaders initially adopted a conciliatory attitude tantamount to "turning the other cheek," but they were to find that this approach did little to narrow the breach which had begun to open between Moscow and Bucharest in Khrushchev's day.[97] Rumania's gradual emancipation from Soviet dominance, which originally had been facilitated by the withdrawal of Soviet troops from Rumania in 1958 and later was symbolized by a memorable Rumanian "declaration of Marxist independence" of April 27, 1964,[98] continued to manifest itself along three principal lines: Rumania's resistance to the process of military integration and centralization within the Warsaw Pact, her opposition to supranational economic planning under CEMA,[99] and her insistence on

[96] On September 14, 1965, during a visit to Moscow, Novotny said that "all must strive" toward a world party conference "at an appropriate time" in order to discuss "a number of urgent problems" of the world Communist movement, *Pravda*, September 15, 1965. Again in late 1965 and early 1966, the Czechs took it upon themselves to endorse a world conclave which many parties were still opposing. See "An Important Step in the Building of Socialism," *Pravda*, January 8, 1966; Communiqué on Novotny talks with Spanish CP Representatives, *Rude Pravo*, January 20, 1966. Later in the autumn of 1966, the Bulgarians joined the Czechs in carrying the ball for the Soviet Union on the world conference issue.

[97] The initial Soviet tactics included not only conciliatory gestures and friendly speeches but also attempts to lay the blame for past deterioration of Soviet–Rumanian relations on Khrushchev, one of the few instances in which the new Soviet leaders sounded this note in East Europe, where Khrushchev's ouster was generally regretted. See Brown, *The New Eastern Europe*, pp. 187–88; Remington, *The Changing Soviet Perception*, pp. 74–81.

[98] This declaration, which anticipated many of the points made two years later in a strongly nationalistic speech by Nicolae Ceausescu, was issued by the Rumanian Central Committee to signal rejection of CEMA's plans for multilateral economic integration as "incompatible with national sovereignty." For the text of the declaration, entitled "Statement on the Stand of the Rumanian Workers' Party Concerning the Problems of the International Communist Movement," see William E. Griffith, *Sino–Soviet Relations, 1964–1965* (Cambridge, Mass.: The M.I.T. Press, 1967), pp. 269–96.

[99] After Rumania's sharp rejection, in April 1964, of Khrushchev's proposals for bloc-wide economic integration, the new Soviet leadership did not press as hard for integration and, in fact, began in 1965 to work on a bilateral basis to co-ordinate the national economic plans of various East European countries with the Soviet Union. Nevertheless, on a range of matters, including joint industrial planning, the raising of investment capital, and currency adjustments, efforts continued within CEMA to draft co-operative measures which the Rumanians considered restrictive of free national choice in their own economic development. See David Binder, "Soviet Bloc Easing Comecon's Control of Trade Planning," *New York Times*, January 2, 1965; "Rumania Upholds Economic Policy," ibid., March 21, 1965; Theodore Shabad, "Soviet Bloc Split on Eco-

"equality" and "independence" in interparty and interstate relations. The last, translated into foreign policy terms, meant among other things that Rumania reserved the right to deal as she saw fit with the West, particularly West Germany, and to play a neutral role as the "honest broker" in the dispute between Moscow and Peking.

Rumanian dissatisfaction with Warsaw Pact military arrangements was expressed in several ways soon after Khrushchev's ouster. In November 1964 Rumania reduced compulsory military service from 24 to 16 months;[100] at about the same time, in interviews with Western correspondents, Rumanian officials spoke of "the need for new ways" of reaching decisions within the Pact and recalled earlier Rumanian statements favoring the "abolition of all military blocs."[101] In June 1965 Nicolae Ceausescu, who had but recently taken over the post of party secretary left vacant by the death of Gheorghiu-Dej in March, made a speech before a group of Rumanian officers in which he stressed "national" requirements for defense of the "fatherland" and pointedly omitted all reference to the Warsaw Pact.[102] That same month, a new Rumanian constitution was published; it contained a proviso on declaration of war which was aimed both at preventing Rumania from being drawn into extraneous conflicts by her Warsaw Pact commitments and at keeping any war decision in Rumanian hands.[103] Meanwhile, the reported reduction of the Rumanian army from 240,000 to 200,000 men, together with indications that Rumania was balking at sending her troops out of the country for participation in joint Warsaw Pact exercises in the summer of 1965,[104] suggested that recalcitrance in the military sphere had come to parallel Bucharest's determination not to follow the Soviet Union blindly in foreign policy and economic matters.

Faced with an obstructionist Rumanian attitude whose possible spread to other members of the bloc was doubtless disquieting, the Soviet leaders evidently decided in the fall of 1965 that the time had come to counter Rumanian

nomic Ties," ibid., September 16, 1965. For informative analyses of Rumanian conflicts with Soviet ideas of bloc economic co-operation, see John Michael Montias, "Economic Nationalism in Eastern Europe: Forty Years of Continuity and Change," *Journal of International Affairs*, vol. 20, no. 1 (1966): 45–71; Stephen Fischer-Galati, "Rumania: A Dissenting Voice in the Balkans," in Andrew Gyorgy, ed., *Issues of World Communism* (Princeton, N.J.: Van Nostrand Co., Inc., 1965), pp. 128–29.

[100] Decree of the Rumanian National Assembly, November 14, 1964.

[101] See David Binder, "Rumania Stresses Independent Role in Red Fight," *New York Times*, November 20, 1964; Max Frankel, "Rumania Widens Independence Lines," ibid., December 19, 1964. Rumanian interest in abolishing military blocs had been expressed as early as April 8, 1958, in a joint statement with Peking, while the April 14, 1964, "declaration of Marxist independence" had also come out for "abolition of all military blocs," on the heels of published remarks by Khrushchev advocating improvement of the organizational forms of both the Warsaw Pact and CEMA. See Remington, *The Changing Soviet Perception*, pp. 46, 67–68.

[102] For a Soviet account of this speech, which was cautiously noncommittal on its negative implications with respect to the Warsaw Pact, see "Unity Is a Dependable Shield," *Izvestiia*, June 17, 1965. For a concise general account of Ceausescu's tactics in challenging Soviet domination, see David Binder, "Ceausescu of Rumania: Man Battering at the Kremlin Wall," *New York Times Magazine*, May 29, 1966, pp. 10, 45 ff.

[103] *Scientia*, June 29, 1965, cited by Brown, *The New Eastern Europe*, p. 185.

[104] See Wolfe, "The Warsaw Pact in Evolution," in *Eastern Europe in Transition*, p. 219.

efforts to water down the Warsaw Pact. The grounds on which the Soviets chose to grapple with the Rumanian deviation concerned the question of Pact reorganization, a matter which the Rumanians themselves had already brought up. The first open Soviet initiative took the form of a proposal by Brezhnev for tightening the organization, ostensibly in order to strengthen bloc "unity" in the field of defense. Speaking at a Soviet–Czechoslovak friendship rally in Moscow in September 1965, Brezhnev said: "The current situation places on the agenda the further perfection of the Warsaw Pact organization. ... We are all prepared to work diligently to find the best solution."[105] Two weeks later, in a speech to the party plenum, Brezhnev again took up the question of Pact reorganization, as he described a series of talks recently held in Moscow with various East European leaders:[106]

> Great attention [was] paid to the coordination of the foreign policy of the socialist countries, particularly to coordinating our actions in the United Nations.[107] We discussed the question of improving the activity of the Warsaw Treaty Organization, the need to set up within the framework of the Treaty a permanent and prompt mechanism for considering pressing problems.

From the evidence available, it is difficult to determine just how the Soviet Union's allies lined up on the need for organizational reform of the Pact, or the extent to which they themselves may quietly have lobbied for change.[108] However, it may be surmised that competing suggestions for reform were offered by at least the Soviet and Rumanian sides, each for its own reasons. Two kinds of organizational change seem to have been at issue: first, changes in the Pact's political mechanism for co-ordination and enforcement of a common foreign policy line; second, reform of the military command arrangements within the Pact.

For their part, the Soviets apparently were interested primarily in organiza-

---

[105] *Pravda*, September 16, 1965.

[106] Brezhnev speech at September Party Plenum, *Pravda*, September 30, 1965. The talks to which Brezhnev referred had occurred throughout September, when leaders of virtually all the East European countries trekked to Moscow in quick succession, including Ceausescu, who brought with him the first top-level Rumanian party-government delegation to visit Moscow since 1961. The meeting with Ceausescu was described as "sincere and frank," and the resultant communiqué avoided any reference to Soviet–Rumanian differences over Warsaw Pact matters. See "Communiqué on the Visit to the USSR of the Party-Government Delegation of the Socialist Republic of Rumania," *Pravda*, September 12, 1965.

[107] The reference to policy co-ordination at the United Nations was doubtless aimed at Rumania, which had shown a growing tendency to vote independently of the Warsaw bloc.

[108] It has generally been assumed, since Soviet and Rumanian spokesmen did most of the talking about reorganization, that the issue was drawn between their two countries. However, the fact that other East European leaders failed to register public enthusiasm for the Soviet proposals could be interpreted as a sign that there may have been quiet opposition to the Soviet case and perhaps even some sympathy for the Rumanian position. For views of two well-informed Western analysts on this question, see Remington, *The Changing Soviet Perception*, pp. 83 ff; Fritz Ermarth, *Internationalism, Security, and Legitimacy: The Challenge to Soviet Interests in East Europe, 1964–1968*, The RAND Corporation, RM-5909-PR, March 1969, pp. 33–40. See also chapter XVII, pp. 459–60, 472–73.

tional reform in the first category, designed to put teeth into such organs as the Political Consultative Committee, or perhaps to create new ones,[109] as a way of bringing pressure on independently inclined Pact members like Rumania to conform to joint foreign policy positions. With regard to the Pact's military command structure, which was already thoroughly Soviet-dominated, Moscow at the time presumably was satisfied with the existing situation, although, as we shall see, there was later to be a shift of Soviet thinking in this area of Pact reform as well.[110]

Rumania seems to have approached the issue of organizational reform the other way around. On the one hand, the Rumanians were interested essentially in preserving the Pact's existing political machinery, which gave the individual bloc members considerable latitude for an independent stand on foreign policy matters, or even in loosening this machinery still more. With regard to the military command structure, on the other hand, it was apparently the Rumanians who were then pressing for Pact reforms intended to lessen the Soviet Union's military control. From the Rumanian viewpoint, no doubt, there was tactical logic in this order of approach, for, if Rumania could weaken the Soviet grip on the Pact's military structure, it might thereby hope to reduce the chances of Moscow's acquiring a tighter hold over foreign policy decisions.

Following Brezhnev's talks with various East European leaders in the fall of 1965, the Soviet Union evidently continued to work behind the scenes to promote its version of organizational reform within the Warsaw Pact. The public record again is skimpy as to alignments within the Pact on the reorganization issue, although, as later reported by a Western journalist who cites "informed sources," a private and unproductive session of Pact leaders was believed to have been held in East Berlin in February 1966 to thrash out Rumanian demands for Pact reform.[111] At the end of March 1966, Brezhnev once more returned publicly to the theme of "improving the mechanism of the Warsaw Pact" in a speech at the Twenty-third Party Congress.[112]

About a month later, Ceausescu in turn took a position which seemed to indicate that Rumania remained as unsympathetic as ever to any proposals drawn up by Moscow for organizational reform of the Warsaw Pact. In a strongly nationalistic speech on May 7, 1966, the forty-fifth anniversary of the Rumanian Communist party, he not only denounced "military blocs ... and

[109] The Political Consultative Committee, which met only periodically, the Permanent Commission, which nominally was supposed to make general foreign policy recommendations, and the Joint Secretariat were the principal Warsaw Pact organs with which Soviet reorganization recommendations may have been intended to deal, although the Soviets did not spell out publicly what changes they had in mind. As noted earlier in this chapter (see pp. 296–97), the several existing policy organs of the Pact provided no effective means for systematic policy-making and centralized enforcement of decisions; presumably, it was this situation which the Soviet Union hoped to remedy by its proposals.

[110] See chapter XVII, pp. 489–92.

[111] Stephen S. Rosenfeld, "Warsaw Pact Nations Called to Pact Summit," *Washington Post*, May 3, 1966.

[112] *Pravda*, March 29, 1966.

the sending of troops to other countries" as an "anachronism incompatible with independence and national sovereignty" but he also lashed out at a variety of historical and contemporary examples of Soviet meddling in Rumanian affairs.[113] Although Brezhnev made a hurried trip to Bucharest a few days later, presumably to persuade Ceausescu to desist from tactics destructive of bloc unity, the Rumanians apparently retracted nothing.[114] On the contrary, a series of press leaks suggested not only that Rumania had not budged from its position on matters of issue[115] but that she was not prepared to reveal her own proposals for Warsaw Pact reform designed to reduce Soviet control and influence within the Pact.

One of the leaks from Rumanian sources in May 1966 concerned a proposal on Warsaw Pact reform said to have been circulated to other Pact members. An official denial was issued in Bucharest on May 18, but excerpts from the alleged document were published by the French Communist newspaper *L'Humanité,* suggesting that the Rumanians had used this channel to make their views known. Among the points included, most of which were consistent with Rumanian positions expressed on other occasions, were: (1) There should be prior consultation before any use of nuclear weapons; (2) the practice of having a Soviet officer in the post of supreme commander of the Warsaw Pact forces should be changed to allow rotation of the post; (3) Rumania objected to pro rata sharing of overhead costs of the Pact; (4) the presence of Soviet troops in East Europe, with the exception of East Germany, was no longer necessary, and any country that wanted such troops should bear the cost itself.[116] Another Rumanian leak at this time revealed that a meeting of the Pact's Political Consultative Committee would be held in July in Bucharest, where it could be expected that the contending Soviet and Rumanian ideas on the organization and functions of the Pact would be thrashed out.

Meanwhile, in late May and early June 1966, while visiting Czechoslovakia, Brezhnev anticipated further attacks on the Rumanian position in two speeches in which he argued for strengthening the Warsaw Pact and indirectly chided

---

[113] Ceausescu's speech linked the nationalist theme of the right of the Rumanian people "to decide their own fate" with the right of each Communist party to determine its own policies without pressure from outside influence. Soviet manipulation of relations with the Rumanian and other parties through the Comintern in the past was assailed, and irredentist grievances against the Soviet Union were again aired with regard to the "lost" provinces of Bessarabia and Northern Bukovina. These provinces had been taken over by the USSR in 1940 after the Nazi–Soviet Pact of 1939, which Ceausescu also criticized for its adverse effect on Rumania's national interests. For portions of the Ceausescu speech, see "Rumania Is Silent on Brezhnev Trip," *New York Times*, and "Rumania Jabs at Soviet Role," *Washington Post*, May 12, 1966.

[114] See "Traveler Brezhnev," *New York Times*, May 15, 1966; "Rumania Is Silent on Brezhnev Trip," ibid., May 12, 1966.

[115] These leaks to both the Western and the Communist press had the apparent function of keeping Rumania's skirts officially clean while permitting rumors to suggest Rumanian opposition to Soviet policies. See "Rumanian Rebuff to Soviet on Cost of Pact Reported," *New York Times*, May 17, 1966; "Bucharest Silent on Note," ibid., May 18, 1966; "Rumania—Moscow's France," ibid., May 22, 1966.

[116] See "Rumania Opposes Soviet on Control of Armies," *New York Times*, May 18, 1966; "Rumania Seen Asking Greater Defense Voice," *Washington Post*, May 17, 1966.

those who might be "naive" enough to call for a loosening of the Warsaw military alliance while the military bloc of the North Atlantic alliance still existed to serve "the policy of the revanchists and militarists."[117]

While advance preparations for the Bucharest conference were underway, including a twelve-day meeting of Warsaw Pact foreign ministers in Moscow in the middle of June and a gathering of Pact defense authorities in Berlin the same month,[118] the Rumanians maintained an officially correct, if somewhat cool, attitude toward Moscow. During a visit of Chou En-lai to Bucharest in June, for example, they took pains to stress their neutral stance as "honest brokers" in the Sino–Soviet quarrel, and refrained from publishing some of the more outspoken anti-Soviet thrusts in speeches by the Chinese delegation. So far as the impending Bucharest conference was concerned, Rumania apparently was not thinking seriously of trying to dissociate herself from the Warsaw military alliance whose protection she enjoyed; rather, she seemed bent upon finding out what price the Soviet Union would be willing to pay for the appearance of bloc unity.

The Soviet leaders, for their part, seemed eager to avoid a public display of annoyance toward Rumania, but occasionally their vexation showed through, as when Brezhnev, during his visit to Prague in May, indirectly scolded the Rumanians for their divisive attitudes, or when Kosygin, in a speech in Cairo that same month, pointedly omitted mention of Rumania while listing "friends and allies" of the Soviet Union who had extended help to the UAR.[119] On the whole, however, the Soviet leaders managed to "keep their cool," as it were, in the face of what must have appeared to them as a provocative challenge from their Balkan ally. As the Bucharest conference approached, the Kremlin leadership, if not quite sure how best to handle the recalcitrant Rumanians, was probably counting on fraternal pressure from other bloc members to help bring Rumania into line.

The Bucharest Conference Line on European Issues

Perhaps the first thing to be said about the Bucharest conference itself is that proposals for internal reform of the Warsaw alliance apparently got nowhere. Notwithstanding the standard assurances that the conference had pro-

[117] See David Binder, "Brezhnev, in Prague, Urges Stronger Warsaw Pact," *New York Times*, June 1, 1966; idem, "Brezhnev Warns Again on Divisions in Red Bloc," ibid., June 3, 1966.

[118] The meeting of foreign ministers in Moscow produced a heated clash between the East German and Rumanian ministers over the question of Rumania's independent policy toward West Germany, with the Rumanian official, Corneliu Manescu, threatening to pull out of the meeting. At the concurrent meeting of Pact military officials in East Berlin, the fact that Northern Tier countries and a large Soviet contingent provided the representation to the exclusion of Southern Tier officials led to speculation that reorganization plans to lend formal substance to the Northern Tier grouping may have been discussed. If so, however, nothing concrete emerged from this meeting or the subsequent Bucharest conference. See Peter Grose, "East Bloc Aides Meet in Moscow," *New York Times*, June 7, 1966; David Binder, "East-Bloc Clash on Bonn Reported," ibid., June 16, 1966; "Pact Arms Chiefs Meet in East Berlin," *Washington Post*, June 13, 1966; "East Bloc Generals Meet with Ulbricht," *New York Times*, June 13, 1966.

[119] For text of Kosygin's speech see *Pravda*, May 18, 1966.

duced a "full identity of views" and further improvement in "the working of the Warsaw Treaty Organization,"[120] the conferees, so far as specific disclosure of the meeting's transactions permits one to judge, endorsed neither Soviet advocacy of institutional improvements to provide a "permanent and prompt mechanism" for co-ordination of Pact policy nor Rumanian suggestions for the further loosening of Soviet control over the alliance machinery. From the Soviet standpoint, therefore, the net effect was failure to tie the hands of Rumanian or any other Pact members who might wish to follow Rumania's example in pursuing independent policies toward West Europe, and especially on the German question. Similarly, the CEMA session tacked on at the end of the Bucharest conference failed to come to grips with such divisive economic issues as price differences, intrabloc sharing of investment in raw materials development, and currency convertibility; indeed, its joint resolution merely stated that the organization would carry on its work in accordance with previous principles.[121]

Although the Bucharest conference may have contributed little to Soviet hopes of ironing out the many internal differences over political, military, and economic relationships within the Warsaw bloc, it did achieve at least surface unanimity among the member states on a common approach to the war in Vietnam and to the issues of European security. The conference "Statement in Connection with U.S. Aggression in Vietnam," which contained a blanket condemnation of alleged American misdeeds in Southeast Asia and endorsement of Hanoi's terms for settlement of the Vietnam conflict, marked no basic change in the Soviet position on Vietnam, but it was noteworthy to the extent that it included some points to which not all of Moscow's Warsaw Pact allies had previously subscribed.[122] Our interest here, however, lies primarily in the joint "Declaration on Strengthening Peace and Security in Europe,"[123] a document described by *Izvestiia* as the most comprehensive and realistic plan for European security ever offered the people of Europe,[124] and one to which

[120] See, for example, N. Polianov, "The Course Dictated by Reason," *Izvestiia*, July 7, 1966; editorial, "Unanimity and Solidarity," *Pravda*, July 10, 1966; V. Smolianskii, "Bucharest Conference of the Political Consultative Committee of Member States of the Warsaw Pact," *Sovetskaia Rossiia* (Soviet Russia), September 1, 1966.

[121] See Paul Wohl, "Communist Bloc's Economic Talks Scuttled by Price Differences," *Christian Science Monitor*, July 13, 1966; "Comecon Clouds Hint of a Storm," *New York Times*, August 7, 1966.

[122] One of these points was the joint offer to send volunteers to Vietnam if Hanoi should request them, an offer which had not previously been made by Poland, Czechoslovakia, and the GDR, although the Soviet Union had publicly voiced its willingness to allow Soviet citizens to "volunteer" as early as March 1965 (*Pravda*, March 24, 1965). The declaration also put all the Warsaw Pact members on record for the first time as being prepared to furnish aid to Vietnam proportional to any escalation of the conflict by the United States, a position previously taken by Brezhnev at the Twenty-third Party Congress and in a speech to Soviet military academy graduates just before the Bucharest meeting. For the full Bucharest communiqué, see *Pravda*, July 8, 1966.

[123] Of the two joint statements issued in the communiqué on the Bucharest conference, that on European security has generally come to be referred to in Soviet bloc circles as the "Bucharest declaration." See Stephen S. Anderson, "Soviet Russia and the Two Europes," *Current History* (October 1967): 205.

[124] Editorial, "The Mighty Strength of Unity," *Izvestiia*, July 12, 1966.

Kosygin later referred as having enabled the Soviet Union and its allies to "hold the initiative in raising the urgent problems of European security."[125]

The declaration, which offered a further modification of the series of Soviet-sponsored programs for European security that had begun with Brezhnev's brief proposal in April 1965, most nearly resembled the eight-point program set forth in the Soviet reply of May 1966 to Bonn's Peace Note.[126] Like the May 1966 document, the Bucharest declaration called for settlement of a broad range of European issues, noting that "two decades after the end of World War II, its consequences in Europe have not yet been eliminated; there is no German peace treaty, and centers of tension, abnormal situations in the relations between states, continue to exist." Much of the declaration was given over to denunciation of US policy in Europe, which was pictured as "all the more dangerous for the European peoples because of being increasingly based on collusion with the militarist and revanchist forces of West Germany."[127] The specific proposals were listed under a seven-point program at the end of the declaration.

The first point on this program was a generalized plea for good-neighbor relations among European countries and the development of closer economic, technical, and cultural contacts. Next came a proposal to liquidate military alliances in Europe, with the added proviso that, if the West was not prepared for this step, the military organizations of NATO and the Warsaw Pact might be abolished, with the alliances themselves temporarily remaining. The third point catalogued a list of partial disarmament measures "toward a military détente in Europe," to include dismantling of foreign bases, withdrawal of all foreign troops within their national frontiers, phased reduction of the armed forces of the two German states, creation of nuclear-free zones, and cessation of flights over European territory by nuclear-armed foreign aircraft. The fourth point dealt with the need to rule out West German access to nuclear weapons "in any form whatsoever"; the fifth called for recognition of the immutability of Europe's postwar boundaries as the basis of a durable peace. A solution to the problem of a German peace settlement stood sixth on the list, with the stipulation that the starting point must be acceptance of the "reality" of the existence of two German states. The final point of the Bucharest program was a proposal for "an all-European conference to discuss security and promote European co-operation."

What the agenda for such a conference should be was again left open, the only new element being the suggestion that the conference might formulate a "general European declaration on co-operating in maintaining and consoli-

[125] Kosygin's speech of October 13, 1966, Pravda, October 14, 1966.
[126] See fn. 24 above.
[127] The declaration did note "as a positive phenomenon" that there were some circles in West Germany opposed to "revanchism and militarism" in favor of "normal relations between the two German states." It also stressed the "growing influence" of other forces in West Europe aware of the need to work toward "mutually advantageous relations among all the states of Europe" and toward "the complete independence of their countries and the preservation of their national identities."

dating European security," which presumably would serve as a substitute for a collective security treaty to replace the existing NATO and Warsaw treaties. The question whether the United States would be invited to participate in the proposed "all-European conference" also was left vague. An assertion in the Bucharest declaration that American policy aims in Europe "have nothing in common with the vital interests of the European peoples and the tasks of European security," together with a pointed observation that "the European states are capable of solving problems of relations among themselves without outside interference," tended to stamp the United States as an outsider without a valid claim to admission. On the other hand, the declaration also said that in addition to the Warsaw Pact countries, the proposed conference was expected to bring together "other interested states, both members of NATO and neutrals," thereby leaving the door open to the United States as a NATO member. Notwithstanding the ambiguity of the declaration on this question— an ambiguity with perhaps the subtle intent of accenting a West European sense of separateness from the United States—the Soviet leadership probably entertained no serious expectations that any meaningful conference could be arranged without American participation.

To sum up, the central significance of the Bucharest proposals for Soviet policy in Europe seemed to hinge on two points: first, that the existing military alliances were to be dissolved in favor of new, all-European security arrangements; and, second, that under these arrangements the participating states were to guarantee a new European order recognizing the permanent division of Germany. In turn, the sleeper in this design for a European settlement appeared to be its studied silence on the Soviet Union's bilateral treaties with the Communist states of East Europe. Renewal of these treaties, which we shall take up in a subsequent chapter,[128] provided a backstop for dissolution of the Warsaw Pact; under the bilateral treaty network, Soviet military access to East Europe would remain unimpeded after an American withdrawal from Europe, and the Soviet Union would thus remain alone as the dominant military power on the European continent.[129]

[128] See chapter XIV, p. 350.
[129] The author is indebted to Richard Lowenthal for offering this insight into the implications of the Bucharest proposals for Soviet European policy.

XIII

SOVIET INITIATIVES IN EUROPE AFTER THE
BUCHAREST CONFERENCE

With the promulgation of the Bucharest declaration in mid-1966, the forging of a new Soviet European policy line under the Brezhnev–Kosygin regime was for all practical purposes complete. In regard to Western Europe, this policy seemed pointed primarily toward the familiar aim of breaking up NATO and loosening Europe's links with the United States, although a secondary element, reflected in negotiations with the United States on a nuclear nonproliferation treaty, also kept alive the notion of Soviet–American collaboration on matters affecting Europe's future. In both instances, an important Soviet objective appeared to be the isolation of Bonn and the underwriting of the permanent partition of Germany.

What gave the policy toward Western Europe a fresh cast was mainly its emphasis upon proposals intended to elicit closer political-economic-technical ties between the West and the Soviet Union and to encourage the idea of new collective security arrangements as a timely alternative to a NATO that had allegedly outlived its usefulness. Looking two or three years ahead, a Soviet line attuned to the Gaullist theme of "Europe for Europeans" might lend itself nicely to the suggestion that West European members of NATO would be well advised to exercise their option to leave the alliance after its twentieth anniversary, in 1969. In the context of such a strategy for separating Western Europe from American influence, however, the problem of Germany remained troublesome. Continuation of a tough line toward Bonn would tend to drive West Germany closer to the United States, while receptivity to a West German policy of reconciliation would threaten the stability of the East German regime and perhaps reduce the common fear of German "revanchism" which had helped to cement the Soviet hold on East Europe. There was a further impediment to a Soviet line aimed at encouraging West European relaxation and the fragmenting of Western alliance arrangements; this grew out of the sharp contrast between gestures of rapprochement from Moscow and the steady strengthening of the Soviet military machine under Khrushchev's successors—a process that was becoming increasingly visible by late 1966, and one we shall take up in detail later.

Although the present chapter deals mainly with the evolution of Soviet policy toward Western Europe, it would be observed that the Soviet Union's interests in the eastern half of Europe were closely linked with the new policy line staked out toward the western half of the Continent. In a broad sense, perhaps the basic Soviet problem was how to maintain the cohesion of the Warsaw bloc while at the same time encouraging closer co-operation and more relaxed relations with Western Europe. In particular, there was the knotty matter of keeping various East European regimes from breaking ranks on a common line toward West Germany, so as not to compromise the position of the German Democratic Republic. This problem was further complicated by the Soviet Union's own interest in the potential advantages of better bilateral relations with Bonn.

Beyond these questions stood that of the Soviet attitude toward the Warsaw Pact itself. Besides its purely military potential and its function as an instrument through which Soviet political control and influence could be exercised in East Europe, the Pact had also become a useful vehicle of sorts for "conflict resolution" among its member states. Therefore, how far and how fast to move in the direction of scrapping the Warsaw Pact for some broader European security scheme was a problem of by no means negligible proportions for the Soviet leadership.

The Soviet Diplomatic Offensive in Western Europe

Following the Bucharest conference, it became more apparent than ever that Soviet diplomacy had taken the initiative in Europe, in part perhaps because the Vietnam war had increasingly drawn American attention from the European scene and provided tempting opportunities for Moscow to play upon strains between the United States and its West European allies. During the latter months of 1966 and in 1967, top Soviet leaders continued an unprecedented round of visits to various European capitals,[1] tirelessly preaching the advantages of co-operation with the Soviet Union and the dangers of subjection to American political and economic hegemony. As previously discussed, the suggestions for "bridge-building" in President Johnson's speech of October 7, 1966, received a chilly reception in Moscow, where Brezhnev declared that the United States was laboring under a "persistent delusion" if it thought relations with the Soviet bloc could be improved despite the war in Vietnam.[2]

Interestingly enough, although the Soviet message to Western Europe depended in part on persuading Europeans that their interests were being damaged by the US involvement in Southeast Asia, there was no suggestion from Moscow that Europe had ceased to be the decisive arena of world politics. On the contrary, as Gromyko put it in a speech at the United Nations in September 1966, Europe was still to be considered "the barometer of the world's political weather."[3] Or, as another Soviet spokesman argued, the main focus of US strategic attention had not shifted from Europe to Asia despite the war in Vietnam, and therefore it would be a mistake to accept the notion that "the

[1] This round of visits included a trip by Kosygin to Paris in December 1966 and another to Ankara later that month; Kosygin's visit to London in February 1967; and a trip to Rome, in January 1967, by Podgornyi, who, like Gromyko the summer before, called on the Pope. In November 1966 Podgornyi had also visited Austria.

[2] See chapter XI, p. 266.

[3] Andrei Gromyko's speech at the UN General Assembly on September 23, 1966, *Soviet News*, Soviet Embassy, London, September 26, 1966, p. 125.

situation in Europe has stabilized and there is no threat to world peace."[4] Like-wise, in the mounting volume of Soviet propaganda centering on the dangers of a new Bonn–Washington axis, and on the need for a European security pro-gram like that advanced in the Bucharest declaration, this point was con-sistently made in late 1966 and early 1967:

> In spite of the menacing events unfolding on other continents, Europe is the world focus of political contradictions. It is in Europe that the two systems directly confront each other and that enormous political and mili-tary forces are concentrated, and it is also in Europe that unsolved prob-lems are pregnant with the threat of dangerous conflicts.[5]

This picture of a Europe pregnant with the danger of new conflicts doubtless was meant to reinforce the Soviet contention that European tranquillity was still threatened by West Germany, against which a new system of European security must therefore be built. But the picture was so overdrawn that it served, in a sense, to bring out certain elements of contradiction in the Soviet position. To begin with, the image of a conflict-prone Europe was curiously out of keeping with the prevailing impression in the West that Europe in the mid-sixties was a fairly secure place, thanks to a stabilized military environment "governed by tacit common interest in preventing war";[6] but, if one did con-cede that European stability was illusory, then Soviet arguments that NATO had become a useless anachronism would tend to fall flat. For it would then appear unwise to many West Europeans to start scrapping a security system of their own for an unknown alternative, especially as NATO's functions already included the implicit one of "containing" West Germany within the NATO framework.

Moreover, even though the re-emergence of an aggressively nationalistic Germany was an objectionable thought to most West Europeans, their latent fears on this score were unlikely to be seriously aroused by a Soviet propaganda that chose to intensify its familiar attacks on German revanchism and mili-tarism, along with new warnings about the "rise of neo-Nazism" in West Germany,[7] at the very time that a new coalition government in Bonn was

---

[4] Mikhail Stepanov commentary, Moscow radio broadcast, September 6, 1966.

[5] I. Orlik and V. Razmerov, "European Security and Relations Between the Two Systems," *International Affairs* (Moscow), no. 5 (May 1967): 3. For other examples of this propaganda campaign, see M. Voslenskii, "Union for the Sake of Aggression," *Krasnaia zvezda* (Red Star), September 13, 1966; Anatolii Antonov's commentary, Moscow radio broadcast, September 26, 1966; M. Kazakov, "Fraternal Alliance," *Pravda*, May 14, 1967. In April 1967 at Karlovy Vary, in a speech to be discussed later in this chapter, Brezhnev, too, added his voice on "the question of military danger in Europe today." "Is the threat so serious?" he asked. "Yes, comrades, there are grounds for this. While we do not want to exaggerate the danger of war, neither do we wish to underestimate it."

[6] See Pierre Hassner, *Change and Security in Europe, Part I: The Background* (London: Adelphi Papers, no. 45, The Institute for Strategic Studies, February 1968), p. 6.

[7] Kosygin was the first prominent Soviet leader to introduce the theme that the rise of neo-Nazism in West Germany posed a new threat to peace. He did so in a speech on December 2, 1966, during his visit to Paris, citing electoral gains of the German National Democratic party (NPD) as evidence of neo-Nazi trends over which "even the most heedless should be alarmed."

displaying an obvious readiness to move toward reconciliation. Suffice it for the moment to note that these inconsistencies served to weaken the Soviet diplomatic offensive in Europe, as we now look briefly at the development of Soviet policy toward West Germany following the Bucharest conference.

Soviet Policy toward West Germany

Internal political developments in West Germany in the fall of 1966, which led to the formation, early in December, of a "Grand Coalition" government of the Christian Democratic Union (CDU) and the Social Democratic party (SPD), presented Moscow with a choice between continuing an uncompromising line toward Bonn or responding more affirmatively to the new Eastern policy advanced by the Kiesinger–Brandt coalition. This policy, the essence of which was to seek reconciliation with the Soviet Union and East Europe and "regulated coexistence" (*geregeltes Nebeneinander*) with East Germany,[8] reflected the leaning of the Social Democrats toward a more liberal and active Eastern policy. It involved, among other things, a partial abandonment of the so-called Hallstein Doctrine,[9] as indicated by Kiesinger in a Bundestag speech on December 13, 1966, in which he made known that Bonn was prepared to establish diplomatic ties with the countries of East Europe.[10]

Soviet treatment of this newest conciliatory overture from Bonn was at first restrained, but did not suggest any readiness to enter into more amicable relations with West Germany. Although a few Soviet commentators initially viewed Kiesinger's statement as a "step in the right direction,"[11] most Soviet appraisals, like one offered by Brezhnev in mid-January of 1967, professed to find it "ample evidence that the goals of West German imperialism unfortunately remain unchanged."[12] On January 28, just as Bonn's new policy was about to bear its first fruit with the establishment of diplomatic relations between the Federal Republic and Rumania,[13] the Soviet Union delivered a particularly harsh attack against Bonn in the form of a note to the American, British, and French governments, pointedly observing that these powers, along with the Soviet Union, were "responsible under the Potsdam Agreement for

---

See Henry Tanner, "Kosygin Asserts Fascism Is on the Rise in Germany," *New York Times*, December 3, 1966; Waverley Root, "Kosygin Assails Bonn at Reception in Paris," *Washington Post*, December 3, 1966.

[8] Herbert Wehner, West Germany's Minister of All-German Affairs and one of the chief architects of Bonn's *Ostpolitik*, is also credited with having fathered the idea of "regulated coexistence" with East Germany.

[9] See chapter XIV, fn. 3.

[10] See *New York Times*, December 14, 1966. In this speech Kiesinger not only made a bid for better relations with the Soviet Union and the countries of East Europe; he also gave high priority to repairing Bonn's ties with France, toward which end he met with de Gaulle about a month later. With respect to America, Kiesinger reaffirmed that the Federal Republic's bonds with the United States in NATO were of "vital importance," but at the same time he took up a stance more independent of Washington than that of either Adenauer or Erhard before him.

[11] Viktor Glazunov commentary, Moscow radio broadcast, December 14, 1966; V. Mikhailov, "Words and Reality," *Pravda*, December 16, 1966.

[12] Brezhnev's speech in Gor'kii, January 13, 1967, *Pravda*, January 14, 1967.

[13] See chapter XIV.

preventing the resurgence of German militarism and Nazism."[14] In this note, which stressed that neo-Nazi trends in West Germany could produce "a new Hitler...armed with nuclear weapons," Bonn's desire to improve relations with the USSR and East Europe was acknowledged. However, the note concluded, Bonn had not given up the "revanchist aims" of former German governments, such as "territorial claims to other states, a striving for nuclear weapons, provocative designs against Berlin and the like."

It is unlikely that the Soviet government expected this denunciation to prevent Bonn and Bucharest from establishing diplomatic relations, but, once they had done so, Moscow again faced the question whether to go along gracefully with Bonn's efforts to normalize relations with the Soviet bloc, or to lend its support to Ulbricht, who had immediately dug in his heels to resist any further East European movement toward the Federal Republic. After what may have been momentary reservations about letting Ulbricht's fears dictate Soviet policy,[15] the Soviet leaders evidently, for reasons of their own, chose to back him up. Two reasons may be supposed to have been particularly persuasive: First, the Federal Republic's pursuit of détente with the East not only might stimulate divisive forces within the Soviet bloc but also promised to alleviate a source of discord between Bonn and the Western allies, and thus threatened to work against the Soviet goal of keeping West Germany isolated; second, there was the plain fact that, with her advanced industrial-technical resources, West Germany, if given access to East Europe, could be expected to make important economic inroads in the region, thus paving the way for greater political influence.[16]

The Soviet Approach to Countering Bonn's Eastern Policy

In opposing Bonn's new Eastern policy, the Soviet Union pursued a dual approach. On the one hand, it took various steps in concert with East Germany and Poland to erect a common bloc front against Bonn's efforts to establish further diplomatic ties in East Europe. These steps will be discussed in the next chapter. Concurrently, the Soviet Union also moved quietly toward a series of bilateral conversations with Bonn, designed, apparently, to turn West German hopes for détente to Soviet advantage. Characteristic of this element of Soviet policy was the proposal that West Germany—as the precondition for improved relations—abandon various positions: on borders, Berlin, nuclear equality, the role of the Federal Republic as spokesman for all Germans, and so on. If

[14] "Soviet Government Issues Warning Against Neo-Nazi and Militarist Activities in West Germany," Soviet News, January 31, 1967.

[15] Such reservations were suggested by Kosygin at his press conference in London on February 9, 1967, where he tempered critical remarks on West German "revanchism" with refusal to echo the GDR's condemnation of Rumania, stating that it was up to the Rumanians themselves to decide whether establishment of diplomatic relations with Bonn was a step in the right direction. See New York Times and Pravda, February 10, 1967.

[16] For a discerning discussion of possible Soviet reasons for opposing the Kiesinger–Brandt–Wehner Eastern policy, see William E. Griffith, The United States and the Soviet Union in Europe: The Impact of the Arms Race, Technology and the German Question (Cambridge, Mass.: Center for International Studies, M.I.T., October 1967), pp. 18–21.

these conditions were met, the net effect would be to change the status quo on the West European side while confirming it in East Europe.

This second line of Soviet policy took shape between July and October 1967. In July, as subsequently disclosed, private talks were held in Bonn between Foreign Minister Willy Brandt and Soviet Ambassador Semyon Tsarapkin, at which, along with several German suggestions for improving relations, the possibility of working out a renunciation-of-force agreement was broached.[17] This idea, recalling Bonn's March 1966 Peace Note,[18] was taken under consideration by the Soviet Union. After about three months, during which other efforts by Bonn to improve the climate of relations with both Moscow and East Germany had made little progress,[19] Tsarapkin again met with Brandt on October 12, this time to convey Soviet readiness to discuss an agreement renouncing the use of force. However, Tsarapkin reportedly said, such a step toward improving relations would only be possible if East Germany were also included in an exchange of declarations on the same basis as other East European states.[20] Thus, the price for Bonn was willingness to move toward recognition of the GDR, a price it declined to pay.

Two months later, after further conversations between Brandt and Tsarapkin had produced no easing of Soviet terms for a renunciation-of-force agreement, the price was steeply raised on December 8 in a Soviet government statement to the three Western powers and Bonn.[21] Besides denouncing "neo-Nazism and

[17] See "On Renouncing Force: Moscow Offers Bonn Talks," *Washington Post*, October 15, 1967. In a radio interview on July 2, 1967, Brandt also publicly stated Bonn's willingness to renounce the use of force and give up all claims to nuclear weapons, along with a proposal for troop cuts by each side. See "West Germany Plans a Sizable Cut in Its Defense Budget," *New York Times*, July 7, 1967.

[18] See discussion of this Peace Note, chapter XII, pp. 285–88.

[19] Among these efforts was a West German appeal for improving relations between the two parts of Germany through high-level contacts between leaders. This proposal and the lengthy exchange of unfruitful responses which followed it are taken up in the next chapter. From its position on the sidelines during the Bonn–GDR exchanges, the Soviet Union occasionally assailed "the stubborn unwillingness" of the Kiesinger government to accept the GDR's terms for "normalization" of relations. See, for example, remarks by Kosygin at Kishinev, September 30, 1967, *Sovetskaia Moldaviia* (Soviet Moldavia), October 1, 1967.

[20] David Binder, "Soviet Reported Taking Initiative on German Split," *New York Times*, October 14, 1967. See also first article cited in fn. 17 above. Many of the details of Soviet demands on this occasion and in subsequent confidential Soviet–West German talks on a renunciation-of-force agreement came to light later in July 1968. In *Izvestiia* of July 11, 1968, the Soviet government revealed parts of its exchanges with Bonn, including a hitherto unpublished note of October 12, 1967. Brandt in turn held a press conference on July 12, 1968, in which he expressed regret that Moscow had chosen to resort to further polemical attacks on West Germany instead of "quiet and factual discussion of problems." At the same time, Brandt's remarks underlined the steady escalation of Soviet demands. See Philip Shabecoff, "Bonn Discloses Russian Demands," *New York Times*, July 13, 1968. Even this airing of Soviet–West German differences did not result in burying the idea of a force-renunciation agreement, however. Gromyko returned to the subject in a major foreign policy speech on June 27, 1968, noting that the Soviet Union was still interested in an exchange of views on an agreement, but adding that progress would require "recognition of the fact of the existence of the GDR—our friend and ally whose security is inseparable from our own." This was the speech, incidentally, in which Gromyko also gave notice that the Soviet Union was prepared to begin talks on ABM and missile limitation with the United States. See *Pravda*, June 28, 1968.

[21] "Statement of the Soviet Government to the Government of the FRG," *Pravda*, December 9, 1967.

militarism" in West Germany in terms similar to those of the Soviet note of January 28, 1967, the new statement stipulated that a renunciation-of-force agreement could now be had only if Bonn met East Germany's maximum conditions for "normalizing" relations; these included the familiar demands for the recognition of existing frontiers, abandonment of Bonn's claim to represent all Germans, and renunciation of nuclear arms, as well as a disavowal of the claim that West Berlin is a part of the Federal Republic.[22]

The addition of the last item to the price tag for improvement of Bonn's relations with the Eastern bloc immediately suggested that Soviet diplomacy had now set its sights on loosening the Federal Republic's ties with Berlin— an objective which had been more or less quietly shelved since the brief harassment of Berlin's communications not long after the Brezhnev–Kosygin regime came to power.[23] This supposition was strengthened a few days after the December 8 statement, when a joint Soviet–East German declaration, again assailing West German "aggressiveness," included the pointed warning that "illegal encroachment on West Berlin by the FRG will meet a firm rebuff."[24] Coupled with ominous statements issued later in December by various East German spokesmen to the effect that institutions and activities of the Federal Republic should be driven out of West Berlin,[25] this warning seemed to imply that a new Berlin crisis might be brewing as the year 1968 began.

Efforts to Loosen Bonn's Ties with Berlin

At this point, the Soviet leadership had to make up its collective mind whether to permit the Ulbricht regime to launch a campaign of harassment that might indeed bring on a full-blown crisis or whether to try more subtle tactics by which to turn Bonn's reconciliation policy to Soviet advantage. Although there was speculation that the Soviet leaders may have differed among themselves over this choice,[26] the second alternative apparently won out. In an aide-mémoire presented to Bonn on January 6, the Soviet Union set out a long list of complaints on activities of the Federal Republic in West Berlin that allegedly contravened the city's four-power status, but at the same time

[22] Besides officially demanding for the first time a disavowal of the FRG's constitutional position that West Berlin is an integral part of the Federal Republic, the statement also called for recognition that the Munich Treaty of 1938 on the dismemberment of Czechoslovakia was void *ab initio*.

[23] See chapter XII, pp. 283–85.

[24] See "Communiqué on the Visit to the USSR by the GDR Party-Government Delegation," *Pravda*, December 13, 1967.

[25] See remarks by Foreign Minister Otto Winzer in an interview with Finnish TV, December 12, East Berlin radio broadcast, December 13, 1967; Politburo member Albert Norden's press conference in Berlin, December 16, 1967; East Berlin radio broadcast, December 18, 1967; Wolfram Neubert, "Current German Realities," *Neues Deutschland*, December 28, 1967; Albert Norden's speech at international press conference in Berlin, December 18, *Neues Deutschland*, December 19, 1967.

[26] As some speculation had it, Brezhnev was for a very hard line on Berlin, backing Ulbricht's position, while Kosygin was inclined toward a softer and more subtle approach. See, for example, David Binder, "Red Bloc Upset by German Issue," *New York Times*, December 21, 1967.

suggested that Bonn's policy of seeking better relations with East Europe might receive more generous consideration if the Federal Republic were to reduce its political presence in West Berlin.[27] This would include giving up the practice of holding Bundestag committee meetings in West Berlin and forgoing other public shows of unity with the city.[28]

In February 1966 a fresh Soviet protest against Bonn's "unlawful activities" in West Berlin alleged that these were being carried on with the "connivance" of the Western occupation authorities.[29] This was soon followed by another formal denunciation of "neo-Nazism" in West Germany.[30] The latter statement declared that Bonn had "pronounced a death sentence on its so-called 'new Eastern policy'" by refusing to clamp down on neo-Nazi trends; but it also held out a sprig of reassurance by noting that the Soviet Union was willing "to grant full support to the Federal Republic" provided the latter would pursue "a peaceful foreign policy."

Bonn's replies to the barrage of protests from Moscow disputed Soviet charges of fostering neo-Nazism, and also declared that West Germany was only following long-existing practices in West Berlin, which in no way could be construed as tampering with the city's four-power status.[31] The Federal Republic also sought to regain some initiative for its normalization policy by once more proposing to negotiate renunciation-of-force agreements with the Warsaw Pact countries, sweetening the proposal on this occasion with an offer to con-

[27] For accounts of the Soviet proposal, as partly disclosed by Western sources, see David Binder, "Moscow Offers New Berlin Deal," *New York Times*, January 16, 1968; Dan Morgan, "Soviet Envoy Tells Bonn To Halt Displays of Unity with West Berlin," *Washington Post*, January 17, 1968; "The Russians Change Their Tune," *New York Times*, January 21, 1968. Much the same ground as that in the aide-mémoire was apparently covered again in a meeting on January 18 between the Soviet Ambassador to East Germany, Petr Abrasimov, and West Berlin's Mayor, Klaus Schütz. This aide-mémoire, incidentally, marked the first time the Soviets had addressed a major communication to Bonn on Berlin matters without also addressing the Western occupation powers.

[28] The most recent meeting of a Bundestag committee in West Berlin prior to this Soviet note had been in October 1967. The "work week" meeting of the committee provoked a Soviet protest at the time, but in much milder form than had greeted the last plenary session of the Bundestag in Berlin, in April 1965.

[29] This protest took the form of a letter from the Soviet Ambassador in the GDR to the American, British, and French ambassadors in West Germany. See "Unlawful Activity of the FRG in Western Europe," *Pravda*, February 15, 1968.

[30] This statement, critical of Bonn for having chosen to regard earlier Soviet protests on neo-Nazism as "interference in the domestic affairs of the FRG," was released at a Foreign Ministry press conference in Moscow on February 24. An interesting·point, in connection with the notion that the Soviet Union was prepared to apply a combination of pressure and persuasion in its relations with Bonn, was that the statement drew a clear distinction between "Nazi elements" and "the majority of citizens of the Federal Republic who hold other views." See "To Stop the Activity of Neo-Nazists," *Izvestiia*, February 25, 1968.

[31] Bonn's reply of December 22 to the Soviet statement of December 8, 1967, received the backing of the three Western powers, who on December 29 informed the Soviet Union that "there is no evidence whatsoever that the government of the Federal Republic of Germany has supported or now supports totalitarian ideas in any way." Bonn's March 1, 1968, reply to the Soviet aide-mémoire of January 6 reportedly was delayed in order to avoid heating up an exchange of polemics. See Osgood Caruthers, "Bonn Regrets Soviet Charge It Fosters Militarism, Nazism," *Washington Post*, December 2, 1967; "Bonn Is No 'Threat,' U.S. Assures Moscow," ibid., December 30, 1967; "Kiesinger Rejects Soviet Complaint that Bonn Changes Status of Berlin," ibid., March 2, 1968.

sider some understanding on nonaggression with East Germany after bilateral negotiations with the Soviet Union.[32]

Nevertheless, the Soviet protest tactics of early 1968 had placed Bonn in an awkward predicament, for they amounted to saying that the Federal Republic could now expect to advance its normalization policy only at the cost of severing its ties with West Berlin. In the eyes of the Soviet leadership, the situation in West Berlin—given a growing malaise among the city's population and its increasingly precarious economic position—may have appeared shaky enough to justify the hope that a combination of pressure and persuasion would prompt Bonn voluntarily to relinquish its influence in the city.

Further developments in the spring and summer of 1968 bore out the point that the Soviet Union—in what appeared to be close collaboration with the Ulbricht regime—was prepared to continue a probing campaign designed to weaken the Federal Republic's ties with West Berlin. In this phase of the campaign against Berlin, however, the Soviet Union remained in the background, allowing East Germany to apply a graduated series of restrictions upon West German access to Berlin[33] but avoiding a direct challenge to the access rights of the Western powers—a tactical ploy presumably meant to keep a major crisis from erupting, and one with the added potential of creating friction between the Federal Republic and its Western allies.

The initial GDR move came on March 11, 1968, with an order prohibiting travel to Berlin and to points in the German Democratic Republic by West German citizens who were members of the right-wing National Democratic party (NPD) or who "engaged in activities of a neo-Nazi nature."[34] The next restriction, applied on April 13, was a "temporary" ban on travel by West German officials to West Berlin through GDR territory.[35] This was followed on June 11 by an East German announcement that transit visas would be required of all citizens of the Federal Republic, and that special transport taxes would be applied after July 1, 1968, to passengers and freight moving to Berlin.[36] Hints from Pankow suggested that additional restrictions, possibly extending to air travel, might be in store.

[32] See David Binder, "Bonn Asks Talks with Moscow for a Pact Renouncing Force," *New York Times*, April 10, 1968; Dan Morgan, "Bonn Tells Soviet of Aim for Pacts," *Washington Post*, April 10, 1968.

[33] As usual, it was not possible to determine whether the Ulbricht regime had itself taken the initiative with Soviet assent, or whether the GDR was simply acting upon instructions laid down in Moscow. The author tends to the view that the GDR probably urged the access curbs upon Moscow in the first instance, but that the latter retained control of the harassment campaign.

[34] See "Neo-Nazis Warned of Red Travel Ban," *Washington Post*, March 12, 1968. This East German move came a few days after a Bundestag committee had met again in West Berlin, from March 4 to 8, 1968. The Soviets on March 4 publicly condemned the committee "work week."

[35] "German Reds Cut Access to Berlin," *New York Times*, April 14, 1968. The first high official barred from driving to Berlin from West Germany was the city's mayor, Klaus Schütz, who was stopped by GDR border guards on April 26. Schütz was president of the West German Bundesrat as well as mayor of Berlin. Soviet propaganda treated his trip as a "deliberate provocation," and defended the measures taken by the GDR as "legal and necessary" actions in light of the allegedly "intolerable nature of Bonn's encroachments on West Berlin." See N. Polianov, "What the Fuss Is About," *Izvestiia*, May 2, 1968; E. Grigor'ev, "Illegal Claims," *Pravda*, May 3, 1968.

[36] "East Germans Set New Berlin Curbs," *New York Times*, June 12, 1968. The reason given

Despite protests from the Western allies, labeling the East German curbs on travel invalid and "inconsistent with the goal of a relaxation of tension in Europe,"[37] neither the tripartite powers nor the West German government seemed disposed to take any counteraction that might precipitate a new Berlin crisis of major dimensions, thus conveying to Moscow and Pankow the message that "salami tactics" judiciously applied might succeed in slicing away still further the rights of free access to Berlin. How far this process might be carried would depend largely on the restraint which the Soviets chose to exercise over Ulbricht's appetite for more slices. This, in turn, depended at least in part on what use the Soviet Union saw in maintaining a sense of tension over the Berlin question.

From one viewpoint, the tensions caused by the squeeze on traffic between West Germany and Berlin could be regarded as useful in justifying increased Warsaw Pact vigilance and a tightening of co-operative military activity among Pact members in the Northern Tier, where Czechoslovakia's reform course had introduced an unexpected challenge to Soviet power in the early months of 1968.[38] To the extent that the Soviet leaders shared with Ulbricht an interest in checking unwelcome changes in Czechoslovakia's orientation, a heating up of the Berlin situation probably was a convenient device for attempting to restore discipline and unity in the Warsaw Pact.

At the same time, however, there was a case to be made against allowing the Ulbricht regime too much leeway. Not only might the East Germans manage to whip up a full-blown Berlin crisis to which the Western powers would find it imperative to react but the prospects for development of a more flexible Soviet policy toward West Germany—an alternative not without some potential appeal to Moscow—might also be set back. In this connection, the Soviet Union's interest in obtaining Bonn's signature on the nuclear nonproliferation treaty provided a further incentive for not letting Ulbricht go too far and too fast in applying a squeeze on Berlin; as Bonn let it be known, its price for signing the treaty might include as a *quid pro quo* the relaxation of "massive Soviet political pressure" against the Federal Republic and a letup on GDR harassment of traffic to Berlin.[39]

---

by the GDR for these measures was the passage by the West German Bundestag, a short time previously, of the so-called "emergency laws" for dealing with crises.

[37] Western protests were strung out in a series of statements and notes following the June curbs. See, for example, Dan Morgan, "3 Allies Call Curbs on Berlin Invalid," *Washington Post*, June 13, 1968; Morton Mintz, "Rusk Protests to Soviet over E. German Curbs," ibid., June 16, 1968; Benjamin Welles, "Western Allies Denounce East German Travel Curb," *New York Times*, June 13, 1968; "West Protests on Berlin Curbs," ibid., July 4, 1968. At virtually the same time that identical three-power notes were delivered in Moscow on July 3 calling upon the Soviet Union to fulfill its obligations for insuring normal traffic to Berlin, Brezhnev made a speech in which he declared that the West would have to accept the measures instituted by the GDR. See *Pravda*, July 4, 1968.

[38] For discussion of developments in Czechoslovakia and their impact on Soviet policy, see chapters XIV, XV, and XVII.

[39] The first hint from Bonn that the squeeze on access to Berlin might be countered by refusal to sign the nonproliferation treaty came in April 1968. On July 1, 1968, when West Germany abstained from joining the original signatories of the treaty, Bonn made it still more explicit that signing the treaty would be contingent upon Communist restraint in Berlin and cessation of

That the Soviet Union was indeed wary of permitting Ulbricht to overreach himself was suggested by the invitation extended to Foreign Minister Willy Brandt to confer in East Berlin with Petr A. Abrasimov, the Soviet ambassador to East Germany.[40] The eight-hour session, on June 18, between the chairman of West Germany's Social Democratic party and the Soviet plenipotentiary in East Germany seemed to serve several purposes: It was a reminder to Ulbricht that management of the Berlin situation remained in Soviet hands; it gave the Soviets the opportunity to play upon internal differences between the West German coalition partners—CDU and SPD—over the handling of the Berlin question; and it allowed the Soviet Union to convey the impression that no major crisis was brewing, a point which Brandt was also happy to make.[41]

A further interesting aspect of the Brandt–Abrasimov meeting was that it marked one more move toward direct bilateral dealings between Moscow and Bonn.[42] A short time earlier, it may be recalled, a step in the same direction had been Bonn's suggestion, in April, that progress might be made toward renunciation-of-force agreements with the Warsaw Pact countries if the subject were first tackled bilaterally between Moscow and Bonn. In mid-1968, after Moscow's disclosure of previously unpublished aspects of its confidential talks with Bonn on a force-renunciation agreement had drawn a riposte from Brandt, the rather one-sided nature of Moscow's terms for an agreement became more clear. In particular, as Brandt revealed, a Soviet memorandum of July 5, 1968, had specified that the Soviet Union would reserve the unilateral right to use force against West Germany under some circumstances even if it signed a mutual declaration renouncing force. Despite this evidence of the abrasive character of bilateral dealings between Moscow and Bonn, however, the possibility that bilateralism might enter into future Soviet policy toward West Germany was not necessarily to be ruled out.

Implications of Bilateralism for Soviet Policy toward Bonn

Venturing here onto rather speculative terrain, one might suppose that even though Soviet attitudes toward West Germany hardened perceptibly in 1967 and the early months of 1968, the Soviet leadership had not closed its mind completely to the potential advantages of a more flexible policy aimed at bilateral settlement of the Berlin question and other issues with Bonn. Such an

---

"massive political pressure" from the Soviet Union. Several days later, Chancellor Kiesinger told a news conference that Bonn also would seek a US guarantee against nuclear aggression, over and above existing NATO commitments, before signing the nonproliferation treaty. See Dan Morgan, "Some Bonn Officials Link Support of A-Treaty to Berlin Access Rights," *Washington Post*, April 26, 1968; "West Germans Tie Signing of A-Pact to Red Pressures," ibid., July 2, 1968; Philip Shabecoff, "Bonn Won't Sign Nuclear Pact Until 'Problems' Are Resolved," *New York Times*, July 2, 1968; "Bonn Seeks U.S. Guarantee Against Soviet Atom War," ibid., July 6, 1968.

[40] "Brandt Crosses to East Berlin To See Soviet Envoy on Curbs," *New York Times*, June 19, 1968.

[41] Philip Shabecoff, "No Berlin Crisis, Brandt Declares," *New York Times*, June 20, 1968.

[42] See James Reston, "Washington: The Conflict of Policy and Personality," *New York Times*, June 30, 1968.

alternative policy, though departing from the customary, intransigent Soviet line toward West Germany, would not necessarily be incompatible with the Soviet goal of keeping Germany divided, nor with that of weakening the Federal Republic's attachment to NATO; indeed, it might hold more promise of prying Bonn away from its Western partners, especially the United States, than an unmitigated hard line.

Several circumstances might have persuaded Moscow that it would pay to pursue a serious bilateral game with Bonn. Despite Soviet insistence that revanchism remained rampant in West Germany and that nothing had really changed behind the façade of a conciliatory *Ostpolitik,* there were some grounds for supposing that the Soviets perceived a qualitative change in Germany and her leadership,[43] a change that created a more fluid situation with possibilities for policy reorientation. One of its aspects was the emergence under the Grand Coalition of a more independent German diplomacy, which, though still in a formative stage, seemed inclined to abandon its old fixations in favor of "recognizing realities."[44] Bonn's uncertainty as to how much Western backing it could count upon was another factor that, in Soviet eyes,

[43] See fn. 30 above. Among factors contributing to a possible shift in Moscow's evaluation of the Bonn leadership was the entry of Social Democrats into the German government via the Grand Coalition of 1966 for the first time since the days of the Weimar Republic. Although, historically, the thesis that Social Democracy was the "main enemy" and "greatest danger" to communism had long dominated the Soviet outlook—and indeed had lain behind Stalin's policy of supporting the Nazis against the Weimar Republic in the early 1930's—the situation three decades later had changed significantly. In particular, following formation of the Grand Coalition government, the West European Communist parties sought to persuade Moscow to disown the theory of "social fascism" under which Social Democrats were branded the "main enemy," and to adopt a co-operative policy toward the new coalition in Bonn. These urgings had no palpable effect on Soviet policy in 1966, but a revision of the underlying attitude toward Social Democracy may have begun to take shape at this time—to emerge somewhat more clearly in early 1969, when such Soviet leaders as Suslov and Ponomarev criticized the "main enemy" thesis in what then appeared to be a possible prelude to a major reorientation of Moscow–Bonn relations. For speculation on this matter, see Anatole Shub, "Soviet Shift on Bonn Breaks with Party Policy Dating to 1928," and "E. German, Soviet Ties Show Strain," *Washington Post*, March 27 and 28, 1969.

[44] See Hassner, *Change and Security in Europe*, p. 13. The West German tendency toward a more independent foreign policy stance was illustrated by Chancellor Kiesinger in a speech on March 11, 1968, in which he said that as much as Germany values its membership in NATO, the Western alliance should not stand in the way of a détente toward East Europe that could help to end the division of Germany. Likewise, while acknowledging the US contribution to Europe's security, he pointed out that the US–Soviet arms race tended to cement the status of a divided Germany, making it important to seek a policy course toward a European peace system that would eliminate a permanent East–West demarcation line through the middle of Germany.

Other shifts in long-standing West German attitudes also were apparent, although they did not necessarily indicate agreement on what direction the recognition of "realities" should take. One example of such a shift was Brandt's statement of March 18, 1968, to an SPD conference, in which he violated a nineteen-year-old taboo of West German politics by suggesting that it was time to recognize the permanence of the Oder–Neisse boundary between Germany and Poland. Speaking for the other half of Bonn's coalition government three days later, Chancellor Kiesinger of the CDU expressed reservations on the subject, but, as noted by some observers, reaction in West Germany to Brandt's initiative was "surprisingly mild." (See David Binder in *New York Times*, March 24, 1968.) In the same connection, Heinrich Albertz, former mayor of West Berlin, speaking on behalf of an independent citizens committee on July 11, 1968, not only urged acceptance of the Oder–Neisse line but also advocated full-scale recognition of East Germany as a step which might help to create conditions favorable to the survival of West Berlin.

might make the West Germans more amenable to abandoning some of their old positions in the light of new "realities." In part, this uncertainty grew out of circumstances such as the distraction of the United States by the war in Vietnam, American concern over the balance of payments, pressures for troop reduction, and other problems that tended to create doubt about the durability of American commitments in Europe. But perhaps the most specific, and in some sense unwitting, source of West German disquiet was the nuclear nonproliferation treaty.

As noted by a number of European observers, nothing except Vietnam and de Gaulle had done more to drive a wedge between the United States and Europe in the mid-sixties than the negotiations on a nonproliferation treaty.[45] Politically, the treaty in essence would have seemed to convey to the Soviets that the United States was willing to negotiate, against German interests, for an agreement which, though less offensive to the Federal Republic than in its original form, nevertheless promised to place a non-nuclear Germany at a permanent disadvantage vis-à-vis the Soviet Union and France. Given this apparent demonstration of US reluctance to advance German interests against the Soviet Union, Moscow may well have counted on new opportunities to arise that would enable it to press for the settlement of other issues with Bonn without encountering significant opposition from the United States. Furthermore, if the Federal Republic were ultimately to sign the nonproliferation treaty and thereby formalize the attainment of Moscow's long-sought goal of barring the nuclear door to Bonn, the Soviet leaders also might come to feel more confident than before that they could handle West Germany alone without the restraining benefit of an American presence in Europe, thus resolving their old ambivalence on this score.

Bonn, in turn, if persuaded that American support of German interests vis-à-vis the Soviet Union could no longer be taken for granted, would have a further incentive to seek a rapprochement with Moscow. This need not necessarily take the form of a new Rapallo, but it might result in Germany's accepting some new European security arrangement that would be tantamount to her giving up the NATO path to German security, and that would perhaps be accompanied by Soviet-dictated changes in the GDR regime calculated to make East Germany a more palatable neighbor, or even a confederate partner, for the Federal Republic.

Although the prospect of a bilateral Moscow–Bonn rapprochement in the direction speculatively outlined here was obviously set back in 1968 by the Czech invasion, it was still not to be dismissed out of hand as a possible alternative pattern for the future development of Soviet–West German relations.[46]

[45] Hassner, *Change and Security in Europe*, p. 20. See also Anatole Shub, "Nuclear Treaty Spawns Diplomatic Paradoxes," *Washington Post*, February 26, 1967; David Binder, "Bonn Less Eager To Rely on NATO," *New York Times*, February 19, 1967; *Strategic Survey, 1967* (London: The Institute for Strategic Studies, 1968), pp. 2, 12.

[46] For discussion of the sharp deterioration of Soviet relations with West Germany which ensued in the immediate wake of the Czech invasion, see chapter XV, pp. 414–18. It is worth noting, incidentally, that even before the Soviet Union in the beginning of 1969 evinced some interest in

Soviet Diplomacy's Intensified Drive against NATO

At the same time that Soviet diplomacy was seeking ways of dealing with Bonn's new Grand Coalition government in late 1966 and 1967, it also busied itself with other matters on Moscow's European policy agenda. These included drumming up support for the European security proposals advanced at the Bucharest conference, appealing for increased technical co-operation between Western Europe and the Soviet bloc, agitating against the American military and economic presence in Europe, and campaigning for the dissolution of NATO. All of these themes, which various Soviet leaders had dwelt upon in their recent travels to European capitals[47] and which Soviet propaganda organs had taken up with new vigor,[48] were brought together by Brezhnev at a meeting of European Communist parties held at Karlovy Vary, Czechoslovakia, in April 1967.[49]

Here Brezhnev, playing upon European resentment toward the United States over such problems as the technological gap, declared that a new and "promising trend" toward pan-European co-operation in the economic and technical fields had set in and would help ensure Europe's "liberation from the dollar."[50] Belaboring the American military presence in Europe as a factor which "encourages West German militarism and increases the threat to peace in Europe," Brezhnev prescribed adoption of the Bucharest collective security proposals as a general answer to this threat. In a more specific tack directed against American naval deployment in the Mediterranean area, he asserted

---

reopening a post-Czechoslovakia dialogue with Bonn, talk of a second Rapallo as a possible alternative for West German policy was heard in some German circles. See Chalmers M. Roberts, "Bonn Has Stake in Nov. 5," *Washington Post*, September 22, 1968.

[47] Kosygin, for example, on his trips to London and Ankara in December 1966, as well as during his Paris visit in February 1967, had lobbied for the Bucharest European security formula and for pan-European technical co-operation, through which he claimed Europeans could close the "technological gap" and end the "brain drain." He also alluded to the desirability of abolishing NATO. Podgornyi, during his Austrian visit in November 1966, solicited support for a European security conference and praised Austrian neutrality, but he also warned his hosts against making any "arrangement with the Common Market." He again plugged the virtues of a security conference on his visit to Italy in January 1967. See " 'Active Coexistence' Upheld in Podgorny's Talks in Rome," *Washington Post*, January 27, 1967.

[48] For a representative Soviet treatment of the themes that the Bucharest call for a security conference had received a favorable response in the West and that it had stimulated a "West European movement in favor of withdrawal from NATO," see S. Beglov, "European Security Problems: Dialogue Goes Ahead," *International Affairs*, no. 3 (March 1967): 44–49.

[49] See "Speech by Head of CPSU Delegation Comrade L. I. Brezhnev," *Izvestiia*, April 26, 1967. The implications of the Karlovy Vary meeting for internal Soviet bloc affairs are discussed in the next chapter.

[50] Other Soviet representatives also pushed Brezhnev's theme that technical and scientific co-operation with the Soviet Union would enable Europeans to liberate themselves from dependence on the United States. One of these was Vladimir Kirillin, the Soviet Minister of Technology, who pressed for an all-European agreement on scientific-technical co-operation at a meeting of the ECE (United Nations Economic Commission for Europe) in April 1967. Another was A. Yakovlev, the Soviet aircraft designer, who argued in June 1967 that European countries were capable of solving the most complex technological problems without US help. See "Economic Cooperation Needed Among All European States," *Soviet News*, April 18, 1967, p. 28; A. Yakovlev, "1967 Aviation: Achievements and Perspectives," *Pravda*, June 26, 1967.

that "the time has come to demand the complete withdrawal of the US Sixth Fleet from the Mediterranean."[51] Curiously, Brezhnev also found it expedient to claim that it was important "to tie down the forces of imperialism in Europe" as a "real help to the liberation struggle ... on other continents," which would suggest that he saw some virtue in a contained military stalemate in Europe.

Perhaps the most notable aspect of Brezhnev's Karlovy Vary speech, however, was its call for a broad program of political action aimed at bringing about the demise of NATO. After paying note to Western discussions on the future of NATO,[52] and dismissing as "absurd" the idea that "NATO is capable of playing a positive role in developing contacts between West and East,"[53] Brezhnev gave the signal for concerted agitation against NATO with the following words:

> In weighing the possibilities opened up by evolving events in Europe, we cannot ignore the fact that in two years the governments of the NATO countries will have to decide whether or not NATO is to be extended.[54] In our opinion, it is quite correct that Communists and all progressive forces should try to use this circumstance to develop still more widely the struggle against the preservation of this aggressive bloc.

In subsequent months, this call for an intensified campaign against NATO was followed by a series of opportunistic propaganda attacks against various

---

[51] Brezhnev's demand for withdrawal of the Sixth Fleet came at a time when the Soviet Union was in the process of gradually increasing its own naval presence in the Mediterranean, a development which was shortly to capture a wide public notice in connection with the Arab–Israeli war of June 1967. Although Soviet agitation against US naval movements in the Eastern Mediterranean, Turkish Straits, and Black Sea areas had been carried on long before Brezhnev spoke at Karlovy Vary (cf. "Soviet Note to the United States on Nuclear-Free Zone in Mediterranean, May 20, 1963," *Documents on Disarmament, 1963*, [Washington, D.C.: United States Arms Control and Disarmament Agency, 1964], pp. 187–93), his statement heralded a new round of Soviet propaganda on the subject. See, for example, Vladimir Nikolaev, "Polaris Diplomacy," *Pravda*, May 8, 1967; A. Kafman, "U.S. Big Stick in the Mediterranean," *International Affairs*, no. 8 (August 1967): 71–75.

[52] The question of NATO's future role and its interest in moves to help bridge the East-West division of Europe had been under wide discussion in the West from the fall of 1966, paralleling the reconciliation policy of the new Bonn coalition government. The NATO Council of Ministers meeting in Paris in December 1966 adopted a proposal by Belgium's Foreign Minister, Paul Harmel, to study and evaluate the alliance in terms of changed European conditions, which subsequently led to the Harmel Report. It was these developments upon which Brezhnev sought to dash cold water in his Karlovy Vary speech. See Anthony Lewis, "NATO Vows Moves To Increase Ties with Soviet Bloc," *New York Times*, December 17, 1966; Clyde H. Farnsworth, "Belgium Seeking Disarmed Europe," ibid., January 25, 1967.

[53] Earlier Soviet commentary had also taken a negative attitude toward Western attempts to transform NATO "from a purely military instrument into one for settling political relations with members of the Warsaw Pact" but not in such strong terms as did Brezhnev. See, for example, Beglov, in *International Affairs* (March 1967): 49.

[54] Brezhnev was incorrect in stating that NATO's members would have to decide on extension of the alliance at the time its twentieth anniversary came due (April 1969). Article 13 of the treaty permits members to withdraw upon one year's notice after the treaty has been in force twenty years (it was signed on April 4, 1949, and entered into force on August 24, 1949), but the treaty contains no provision requiring a decision to extend its life. Later Soviet commentary in 1968 dwelt on differences within NATO over interpretation of Article 13, suggesting that the French view permitting withdrawal without waiting for one year was the correct interpretation. See Iurii Zhukov, "NATO: To Be or Not To Be?" *Pravda*, March 12, 1968.

NATO activities, real or alleged. Among the targets were a proposal to create a NATO standing destroyer force; a tentative idea for establishing a nuclear mine belt along the Turkish frontier; NATO's alleged "provocations" against "independent Arab countries" in the Middle East conflict; and its similarly alleged backing of "Greek reactionary circles" in the Greek coup of April 1967 and again in the November 1967 Cyprus crisis.[55] Following the first meeting of the NATO Ministerial Council outside France, in mid-June 1967, Soviet propaganda focused on alleged attempts of the United States to make its NATO partners give "direct support to the aggressive expansionist designs of Israel," and harped on the growing "fear" among NATO countries of "being involved in policies alien to their national interests."[56]

The anti-NATO campaign touched off by Brezhnev at Karlovy Vary reached a crescendo after the next meeting of the NATO Ministerial Council in Brussels, in mid-December 1967. At this meeting, the NATO members, including France, agreed to a political report on the future tasks of the alliance which stressed, among other things, that "the way to peace and stability in Europe rests in particular on the use of the alliance constructively in the interest of détente."[57] On military questions, and without French participation, the members adopted a new strategic concept, formally replacing the outmoded one of "massive retaliation" with a strategy of "flexible response"; approved the creation of a standing naval force in the Atlantic; and set up a five-year military planning cycle. They also agreed on reduced force levels for ground troops, and called on the Warsaw Pact countries to join in a phased reduction of opposing armies in Europe.[58]

For those hoping that Soviet hostility toward NATO might be softened by the accent on détente sounded at the Brussels session, the Soviet response was hardly encouraging. With one voice, Soviet propaganda organs asserted that NATO's "aggressive" nature remained unchanged, despite attempts to put on a "new face" at Brussels with the adoption of the "so-called Harmel Plan." Thus, deriding "talk about plans to modernize the Atlantic alliance" so as to make it "a practical instrument for co-operation with the East," a Moscow commentator declared that "the Brussels session shows plainly enough that NATO will continue as an instrument of war."[59] The main line taken in Soviet commentary on the Brussels meeting depicted NATO as "torn by serious

[55] See, for example, Evgenii Grigor'ev, "The Bustle of Provocation," *Pravda*, April 9, 1967; Vladimir Nikolaev, "Polaris Diplomacy," *Pravda*, May 8, 1967; "Conspiracy Against Cyprus," *Izvestiia*, July 6, 1967; Moscow broadcast on NATO Nuclear Planning Group meeting in Ankara, September 29, 1967; "Soviet Government Statement" (on Cyprus), *Pravda*, November 23, 1967; Igor' Beliaev, "Arsonists in the Role of Firemen," *Pravda*, December 14, 1967.

[56] Anatolii Potopov commentary, Moscow radio broadcast, June 15, 1967.

[57] "Text of Final Communiqué," Ministerial Meeting of the North Atlantic Council, December 12–14, 1967, *Department of State Bulletin*, January 8, 1968, p. 51.

[58] Ibid., pp. 49–50. See also Donald H. Louchheim, "NATO Asks Warsaw Pact To Join in Troop Reduction" and "New NATO Is Stressing Harmony," *Washington Post*, December 15 and 17, 1967; John Allan May, "NATO Asks Itself: What Is My Role?" *Christian Science Monitor*, December 15, 1967.

[59] Viktor Glazunov commentary, Moscow radio broadcast, December 14, 1967. See also editorial, "NATO Is NATO," *Krasnaia zvezda*, December 15, 1967; V. Pustov, "Bonn's Nuclear Variants," ibid., December 15, 1967.

contradictions," with its members increasingly unhappy over being tied to US policy, especially over "the growing risk of being drawn into dangerous military ventures, alien to their interests."[60] Under the "cover of talks about 'reform'," the United States was said to be trying to get a firmer grip on the other NATO members, to make them shoulder a greater share of military expenditure, and to bind them to long-term commitments.

The creation of a standing Atlantic destroyer force was viewed in this light by some Soviet observers, as a commitment intended to forestall "the disintegration of the bloc in 1969 in connection with expiration of the North Atlantic Treaty."[61] Other commentary described the destroyer force as a "substitute for the abortive MLF project."[62] NATO's adoption of the "flexible response" doctrine drew criticism on the grounds that it was even "more dangerous" than the concept of "massive retaliation," because it "may raise false hopes that a military conflict in Europe can be kept within local bounds and not allowed to develop into a big war with use of all means of extermination."[63] One military matter raised at the Brussels meeting, however, was virtually ignored; namely, the call for mutual troop reductions, which was dismissed by a Soviet radio panelist as "only a gesture."[64]

Soviet Relations with France and Britain

In Soviet attacks on NATO, both before and after the Brussels meeting, France fared better than the other alliance members, generally being commended for not truckling to the United States.[65] The co-operative tenor of Soviet–French relations, which had been set by de Gaulle's trip to Moscow in mid-1966 and Kosygin's return visit at the end of the year, continued throughout the early months of 1967. There was, for example, an increased exchange of various economic and technical delegations, as working ties between the two countries were expanded in aviation, electronics, food processing, and other industries.[66] Toward the end of April, about a month after the departure of US and other NATO forces from France, a symbolic gesture of closer Soviet–French rapport in the military field took place when France's top military man was invited to Moscow for the annual May Day parade in Red Square. He was General Charles Ailleret, French chief-of-staff and

[60] Editorial, "NATO Readjusts," *Izvestiia*, December 16, 1967.

[61] Iurii Glukhov, "Under a Pirate Flag," *Pravda*, December 22, 1967.

[62] Editorial, *Krasnaia zvezda*, December 15, 1967.

[63] Viktor Glazunov radio commentary, December 14, 1967. See also Iu. Kharlanov, "NATO Remains an Instrument of War," *Pravda*, December 14, 1967; Viktor Levin's commentary, Moscow radio broadcast, December 15, 1967; Boris Stolpovskii's commentary in *Trud* (Labor), December 17, 1967.

[64] Moscow radio broadcast, December 17, 1967.

[65] Potopov radio commentary, June 15, 1967; Glazunov radio commentary, December 14, 1967. See also Iurii Zhukov, "In the Interests of Peoples," *Pravda*, July 12, 1967; S. Zykov, "Atlantic Hysterics," *Izvestiia*, August 24, 1967; E. Grigor'ev, "Warsaw Dialogue," *Pravda*, September 14, 1967.

[66] Waverley Root, "French, Russians Forge Multiple Economic Ties," *Washington Post*, April 26, 1967. See also "Cooperation With France," *Soviet News*, May 2, 1967, p. 68; "On a Good Road," *Izvestiia* interview with V. A. Kirillin on Soviet–French economic and technical relations, July 2, 1967.

expositor of France's "all-azimuths" nuclear strategy, who was later to perish in an airplane crash.[67] Several months after his trip to Moscow, his visit was returned by Marshal M. V. Zakharov, chief of the Soviet General Staff.[68] In June, in another demonstration of Soviet–French collaboration, Kosygin twice stopped off in Paris on short notice to confer with de Gaulle during a trip to the United Nations in connection with the Arab–Israeli crisis.[69]

Yet, along with these manifestations of continuing cordiality, signs of a subtle change in Soviet–French relations appeared in 1967. Suggestions of a slight cooling-off in the political sphere first arose when projected spring visits to Paris by Brezhnev and Podgornyi failed to materialize.[70] As some Western observers saw it, the French national elections in March, which showed de Gaulle slipping and brought gains to the French Communist party, may have reduced Moscow's previous ardent interest in courting the French leader.[71] De Gaulle's trip to Poland in September 1967, during which he suggested to Gomulka that Poland might profit from France's example by steering a more independent course between the world's two "colossi,"[72] probably irritated the Russians no less than some of his other utterances irked the West Germans.[73] Even at the Brussels meeting in December 1967, where French abstention from the military discussions was applauded by the Soviet Union, France's adherence to a declaration that "the pursuit of détente must not be allowed to split the alliance"[74] served notice that de Gaulle was not necessarily Moscow's man. So, too, did the French leader's public approval of President Johnson's Vietnam peace initiative of March 1968.

What probably gave Moscow the clearest notice that the time had come to hedge its bets on de Gaulle, however, was the latter's handling of the domestic crisis that arose in May 1968 out of the protest movement of students and workers. De Gaulle's resort to the theme that "totalitarian communism" was attempting "to take over the country," and his harsh strictures against the French Communist party,[75] must have placed a serious strain on the for-

[67] See "France's Chief of Staff Visits Moscow," *Soviet News*, May 9, 1967, p. 71. Ailleret was killed on March 9, 1968 (see "Plane Crash Kills French Military Boss," *Washington Post*, March 10, 1968).

[68] Marshal Zakharov's visit to France in October 1967, hailed in a Soviet broadcast of October 15 as a contribution to "strengthening Soviet-French ties and the cause of peace in Europe," was the first visit by a head of the Soviet General Staff to a Western country. Marshal Malinovskii, as Defense Minister, had of course visited France in 1960 with Khrushchev.

[69] Henry Tanner, "Kosygin Stops in Paris," *New York Times*, June 17, 1967; "Kosygin Says Paris Favors Soviet View," ibid., July 5, 1967.

[70] Reuters Moscow dispatch, "Brezhnev Visit Off?" *Christian Science Monitor*, April 3, 1967.

[71] Editorial, "Moscow Reassesses de Gaulle," *Christian Science Monitor*, April 13, 1967.

[72] See Donald H. Louchheim, "De Gaulle Overtures Rejected by Warsaw," *Washington Post*, September 12, 1967; editorial, "De Gaulle's Polish Voyage," *New York Times*, September 14, 1967.

[73] For example, de Gaulle's repeated references to the permanence of the Oder–Neisse boundary and his description of the former German town of Hindenburg as "the most Polish of all cities" apparently served as an irritant in Paris–Bonn relations.

[74] See "Text of Final Communiqué," *Department of State Bulletin*, January 8, 1968, p. 51.

[75] See, for example, de Gaulle's speech of May 30, 1968, in which he declared his intention to remain in power, and his televised election appeal of June 7. "From General Strike to General Elections," *Economist*, June 8, 1968; Henry Tanner, "De Gaulle Offers a Changed Society," *New York Times*, June 8, 1968.

bearance of the Soviet leadership, the more so as Moscow had sought to throw the influence of the French Communist organization behind de Gaulle against what it described as "politically adventurist" student radicals.[76] De Gaulle's resounding electoral success in June, which he owed in part to evoking the threat of a Communist takeover, added a further element of doubt as to the future of Soviet–French collaboration. Although the public Soviet response to the French crisis avoided a direct censure of de Gaulle, it came close to the target by charging that the Gaullist party had chosen to present itself to the electorate as "the savior of the country against 'The Red Menace'."[77]

Perhaps none of this added up to the conclusion that the Soviet leadership was prepared to write off de Gaulle's further potential as an alliance-splitter and a rallying point for anti-American sentiment in Europe. It did suggest, however, that the Soviet–French rapprochement had passed its peak by mid-1968 and entered a stage in which its usefulness to Soviet policy would tend to decline—an impression strengthened, as we shall see, by de Gaulle's own evident disenchantment with the Soviet Union after the invasion of Czechoslovakia, in August 1968.

Soviet relations with Britain warmed up several degrees after Kosygin's London visit, in February 1967, as a result of pledges by both sides to develop trade and technical co-operation,[78] but Soviet policy achieved no visible success in inducing the Wilson government to veer away from its close association with the United States or to lessen its support of NATO. Moscow's hopes of exploiting Anglo–German differences over troop costs and other issues to drive a wedge between London and Bonn likewise were blunted,[79] partly perhaps because of Britain's need to win West German backing for British membership in the European Economic Community.

From the point of view of the Soviet Union, the Wilson government's reluctance to repudiate US policy in Southeast Asia despite its strong desire to help bring the Vietnam war to the conference table[80] remained a distinct

---

[76] See, for example, L. Volodin, "Why the Sorbonne Is Closed," *Izvestiia*, May 6, 1968; Iurii Zhukov, "The Background Story of the False Prophet Marcuse and His Noisy Students," *Pravda*, May 30, 1968. The latter article, among other things, contained a harsh criticism of the ideas of Herbert Marcuse and the "New Left" in the West, which it linked with the philosophy of "the Mao Tse-tung group" as the source of inspiration for the "politically adventurist" and "ultra-revolutionary" French student radicals.

[77] S. Zykov, "Before the Elections in France," *Izvestiia*, June 6, 1968. See also B. Kotov, "France: The Results of Parliamentary Elections," *Pravda*, July 2, 1968. The first public statement by a high-level Soviet official on French–Soviet relations after the French crisis came in Gromyko's speech of June 27, 1968, in which he avoided reference to de Gaulle and the future prospects for Soviet–French co-operation, merely noting that there had been some "positive shifts" in the two countries' relations in the past few years. See *Pravda*, June 28, 1968.

[78] See "Text of the British–Soviet Communiqué," *New York Times*, February 14, 1967.

[79] See, for example, "More Complicated Than a Tunnel under La Manche," *Izvestiia*, March 10, 1967; Viktor Maevskii, "The Little Europe of Big Dissents," *Pravda*, May 6, 1967; Oleg Orestov, "Smoke Without Fire?" ibid., October 31, 1967; Kosygin's remarks to Harold Wilson during the latter's visit to the USSR, *Pravda*, January 24, 1968.

[80] A notable example was Prime Minister Wilson's hope that the Kosygin visit to London in February 1967 might be a vehicle for arranging peace talks, a hope which proved abortive. See Anthony Lewis, "Wilson Says Misunderstanding Arose on Talks," *New York Times*, February 8,

impediment to the improvement of Anglo–Soviet relations. Thus, even though the Soviet leadership continued the dialogue with Britain on various major issues, the Soviet press in 1967 and early 1968 remained sharply critical of what it chose to describe as British subservience to American policy; later in the year, Gromyko noted publicly that Soviet–British relations would be improving somewhat more rapidly "if British foreign policy overcame its one-sided orientation on a number of major international issues."[81]

The rather slow pace of efforts to establish closer Soviet–British ties, despite some increase in economic contacts,[82] was illustrated by the cautious sparring over terms for a treaty of friendship and peaceful co-operation, which Kosygin had proposed during his London visit. Discussions on the subject in 1967, during which British Foreign Secretary George Brown visited Moscow, and again in January 1968, when Wilson paid a brief visit to the Kremlin,[83] yielded no apparent progress on the treaty. Another project for which Kosygin had sought British backing in February 1967, the proposal for a European security conference, was discussed again during Wilson's Moscow visit of January 1968. Soviet unwillingness to make clear whether such a conference would include the United States apparently left the British wary of giving it unqualified endorsement, although the joint communiqué covering Wilson's visit noted that a security conference "could be valuable, subject to the necessary preparation."[84]

In talks with other European leaders, as with the British, Soviet efforts to promote a European security conference along the lines of the Bucharest proposal continued to meet with a mixed response, owing in part to the question of American participation. In March 1968, for example, Austria agreed "in principle" to the idea of an all-European security conference, but reportedly balked in private at the exclusion of the United States.[85] Similar reservations

---

1967; "No Gain on Vietnam Seen in Wilson–Kosygin Talks," ibid., February 13, 1967. For an examination of the Wilson–Kosygin search for a Vietnam peace formula, see David Kraslow and Stuart Loory, "The Wilson–Kosygin Talks—A Lost Opportunity?" *Washington Post*, April 25, 1968. This article is drawn from the book, *The Secret Search for Peace* (New York: Random House, 1968).

[81] *Pravda*, June 28, 1968. See also V. Matveev, "Maneuvers without Laurels," *Izvestiia*, January 21, 1968; M. Sturua, "The Criterion—Business," *Izvestiia*, January 28, 1968.

[82] In September 1967, for example, the Soviets signed two large contracts with British companies for the purchase of machine tools and instruments. The same month a British aviation delegation toured Soviet aircraft plants. See "British Minister Meets Soviet Aircraft Designers," *Soviet News*, September 19, 1967, p. 131.

[83] Brown visited Moscow in May–June 1967, where, in addition to private conversations with Soviet officials, he gave a public lecture on foreign policy questions that was notable for its frank refutation of Soviet "revanchist" charges against the West German government. Wilson had been invited in February to visit Moscow in July 1967, but the Soviet government later found this time "inconvenient" and his trip was postponed until January 1968. See "Visit of Mr. George Brown to Moscow," *Soviet News*, May 30, 1967, p. 116; "Wilson, Soviet Chief, Confer on 'Problems'," *Washington Post*, January 23, 1968.

[84] "Joint Soviet–English Communiqué," *Pravda*, January 25, 1968.

[85] See "Soviet–Austrian Communiqué," on the visit of Austria's Foreign Minister, Kurt Waldheim, to the USSR, March 18–23, 1968, *Pravda*, March 24, 1968. For comment on Austria's attitude toward exclusion of the United States, see Benjamin Welles, "Moscow Opposes Vienna Proposal, Seeks To Exclude U.S. from European Security Talks," *New York Times*, April 11, 1968.

were shared by a number of other European governments whose endorsement had been sought, including that of Italy. Another obstacle that made it difficult for Soviet diplomacy to sell its version of a European security conference was the question of GDR participation. Insistence that East Germany be included was logical enough from the Soviet viewpoint as a way of enhancing the Ulbricht regime's international stature, but at the same time it raised for several West European countries the complicated issue of diplomatic recognition of the German Democratic Republic.

Nonetheless, whether or not Soviet diplomacy could take the credit, the idea of a European security conference gained some headway. In February 1968, for example, at a Dutch parliamentary discussion it was urged that more active steps be taken in this direction,[86] giving impetus to the notion that some of the smaller countries in both West and East Europe might explore ways of removing the various hindrances to a security conference. Meanwhile, paradoxically, the Soviet Union itself—perhaps because of increasing distraction by troublesome developments in East Europe—began to show less interest in the idea of an all-European security conference. However, there were occasional signs that the project had by no means been dropped from the Soviet agenda. In his *tour d'horizon* of June 27, 1968, for example, Gromyko once more devoted major attention to the need for a European security conference, stating that the Soviet Union was ready to enter preparatory discussions "with those governments of European states which understand the need and urgency of co-ordinating and pooling efforts for this purpose." Interestingly enough, however, he no longer linked the conference proposal with the subject of mutual dissolution of NATO and the Warsaw Pact.[87]

Soviet Policy toward Countries on NATO's Northern and Southern Flanks

Along with the developments discussed above, Soviet European policy in the period following the Bucharest conference was notable for the increased attention given to improving relations with countries on the northern and southern flanks of NATO. With regard to the Scandinavian countries, which Soviet commentary occasionally singled out as recognizing "more clearly than any other region of West Europe" the need to normalize relations with the Soviet bloc,[88] Moscow's principal aim seemed to be to encourage the Nordic members of NATO—Norway and Denmark—to quit the Western alliance in favor of a neutral grouping of northern states, along with Sweden and Finland.

Although the Soviet Union sought to promote the idea of Scandinavian

[86] See questioning of Dutch Foreign Minister Joseph M. Luns at a February 7, 1968, parliamentary session at The Hague, reported in *Tweede Kamer, Vaststelling hoofdstuk V, Buitenlandse Zaken 26ste vergadering, 7 februari '68* (Minutes of the Second Chamber, chapter V, Foreign Affairs 26th Session, February 7, 1968), The Hague, p. 1144.

[87] From mid-1967 on, as Soviet concern over developments in East Europe grew, references to dissolving the opposing alliances had disappeared from Soviet propaganda.

[88] Lev Andreev commentary, Moscow radio broadcast, September 6, 1967.

neutrality, its attitudes toward this question varied from time to time, largely perhaps because of uncertainty as to whether a Scandinavian defense alliance unassociated with NATO would represent a form of neutrality acceptable to Moscow. In the fall of 1966, for example, following NATO maneuvers in the north of Norway designed to meet a simulated threat to NATO's northern flank via the Arctic, the Soviet Union launched a press campaign to warn Norway that her security would be better assured through a policy of Nordic neutrality than through association with NATO. The idea that a defense alliance of Scandinavian states might serve as a substitute for NATO membership was specifically attacked by *Izvestiia* in September 1966, at which time it was also suggested that Great Power guarantees of Scandinavian neutrality might be a useful alternative to NATO.[89] A month later, however, the Soviet Union tentatively recognized that a Scandinavian defense alliance was a "possible alternative," provided it stayed outside existing military blocs.[90] Subsequently, this idea disappeared from Soviet commentary, which focused once more on the straightforward theme that, since there was no Soviet threat to Scandinavian security, there was no longer any need for Norway to look to NATO for protection.

In its approach to Norway and Denmark, the Soviet Union applauded groups in the two countries that were demanding the "liquidation of NATO" and advancing "positive programs" for a "neutral, atom-free North," as well as pushing for a popular referendum on withdrawal from NATO.[91] There were both soft and hard elements in the Soviet attitude toward Norway. On the one hand, Soviet propaganda expressed sympathy for Norway, pictured as having been "drawn into NATO against her will" and having found NATO membership "a heavy yoke on her foreign policy."[92] A brief interlude of hostility toward the Norwegian coalition government that had taken office in 1966 was followed by efforts to establish cordial relations with the new government,[93] which led to the signing of a trade agreement in September 1967 and a visit to Moscow by the Norwegian Defense Minister, Otto G. Tidemand, a month later.[94] On the other hand, however, the Soviet Union complained that Norway was lending herself to the purposes of NATO's "northern strategy," aimed at making Scandinavia "an anti-Soviet jumping-off point," and warned

---

[89] "Scandinavian Alternatives," *Izvestiia*, September 10, 1966.

[90] "Futile Attempts of the Former Minister," *Izvestiia*, October 20, 1966.

[91] Iu. Goloshubov, "Why Do They Come?" *Izvestiia*, September 16, 1967; G. Deinichenko, "Letter from Norway: At the Turning Point," *Izvestiia*, December 22, 1967; Iu. Iakhontov, "NATO Has Outlived Its Time," *Pravda*, February 7, 1968.

[92] Deinichenko, in *Izvestiia*, December 22, 1967.

[93] Initial Soviet attacks on the new Norwegian government's NATO policies abated somewhat after the visit of Norwegian Foreign Minister John Lyng to Moscow in November 1966. Although Norway's NATO affiliations, and especially the presence of West German officers on NATO staffs in the northern area, continued to be criticized, Soviet–Norwegian relations took on a warmer tone in 1967.

[94] The communiqués marking the Tidemand visit in October 1967 noted that he had talked with Kosygin as well as with Soviet defense officials, but they were noncommittal on the matters discussed. It was announced that Marshal Grechko, the Soviet Defense Minister, would pay a return visit to Norway at an unspecified date.

that leaders "who countenance such strivings subject their countries to great risk."[95] Soviet spokesmen also asserted that the USSR had been falsely accused of having a "particular interest in ice-free harbors in Norwegian territory."[96] Similarly, while treating anti-NATO trends in Denmark as an encouraging sign of "political maturity," the Soviet Union found fault with Denmark's failure to recognize certain political realities, as in her refusal to establish diplomatic relations with the German Democratic Republic.[97]

Toward Sweden, the Soviet Union pursued a cordial line, marked in 1967 by an increasing exchange of military visits,[98] a trip to Stockholm by a Supreme Soviet delegation, and a visit to Moscow by Swedish Foreign Minister Torsten Nilsson. Soviet commentary took particular satisfaction in the growth of anti-American sentiment in Sweden, noting that the United States was "becoming alarmed" at Sweden's friendly relations with the USSR,[99] and applauding the Swedes for dismissing charges by a visiting US congressional delegation that anti-American demonstrations were compromising Swedish neutrality.[100] In July 1968, during a visit to Stockholm that was cut short by the need for his presence at a Warsaw Pact meeting on the Czech situation, Kosygin sounded the standard Soviet line that Norway and Denmark should emulate Sweden's neutral stance by abandoning NATO. He also on this occasion expressed opposition to the idea of a Nordic defense alliance.

With respect to Finland, Soviet policy continued to promote the warmer relations which had developed since the Finland Communist party had been taken into Finland's coalition government, in the summer of 1966, providing an example of the kind of Popular Front government that the Soviet Union was interested in seeing set up in the West.[101] In May 1967 Moscow greeted with approval measures adopted by a new permanent commission for "expanding the economic foundation of neighborly relations between the two coun-

---

[95] Goloshubov, in *Izvestiia*, September 16, 1967.

[96] Andreev commentary, Moscow radio broadcast, August 27, 1967. Among items denied by Soviet spokesmen were periodic reports in the Western press in 1966–67 that unidentified submarines, suspected to be Soviet, were appearing in Norwegian waters and fjords. Soviet propaganda later seized on the crash of a nuclear-armed US bomber in Greenland to emphasize the risks that Scandinavian countries were running by being tied to NATO. See Iu. Goloshubov, "Scandinavian Alarms," *Izvestiia*, February 8, 1968.

[97] Andreev commentary, September 6, 1967.

[98] These included the visit to Sweden in August 1967 of a group of Soviet MIG-21 fighters, the first time a Soviet military air unit had flown to a Western country. There also were several exchange calls of naval vessels at Leningrad and Stockholm, and a visit in September 1967 to Sweden by the head of the Soviet Navy, Admiral S. G. Gorshkov. *Pravda*, June 3, 1967, June 21, 1967; "Aviators' Visit Ends," *Pravda*, September 1, 1967; Admiral Gorshkov leads delegation to Stockholm, Moscow radio broadcast, September 11, 1967.

[99] Iu. Kuznetsov, " 'Washington Post' on the Job," *Pravda*, October 7, 1967.

[100] G. Deinichenko, "Congressmen's Mistake," *Izvestiia*, November 18, 1967. Only occasionally did Soviet commentary express displeasure over Swedish relations with the United States, as when Swedish universities were criticized for doing research allegedly helpful to US military programs. See, for example, Iu. Iakhontov, "And What about Neutrality?" *Pravda*, February 15, 1968.

[101] See chapter XII, p. 291.

tries";[102] in December, on the occasion of the fiftieth anniversay of Finnish independence, Podgornyi visited Helsinki, where new pledges were made to strengthen trade, cultural, and other ties between Finland and the Soviet Union. Soviet commentary on this anniversary paid particular tribute to Finland's support of the idea of convening a European security conference and to the Finnish "suggestion for creating an atom-free zone in Scandinavia."[103]

The Soviet desire to see Finland remain as a show window for Popular Front governments was underscored in the spring of 1968, after the Finnish Communist party lost ground in the March elections and changes in the Cabinet had the effect of reducing Communist influence in the government. Despite these changes, Moscow accepted the situation without notable protest, presumably in order not to jeopardize Communist participation in a continuing, though somewhat diluted, Popular Front arrangement in Finland.[104]

On NATO's southeastern flank, meanwhile, the Soviet Union devoted further attention to the improvement of relations with Turkey, which had shown signs of warming ever since early 1965, when Turkey evidently began to feel that her interests in the Cyprus question had been slighted by her NATO partners.[105] Agreements reached in 1966 and 1967 for Soviet economic and technical aid helped to melt at least some of Turkey's traditional coolness toward her powerful neighbor to the north,[106] and although Turkish officials presumably continued to regard Moscow's overtures with a wary eye, the two countries moved gradually toward a détente of sorts. From Moscow's viewpoint the problem of balancing carefully between Turkey and Greece on the Cyprus issue was eased considerably by the military junta's coup in Greece, in April 1967, after which Soviet diplomacy aligned itself squarely with Turkey,

---

[102] A permanent Soviet–Finnish Economic Co-operation Commission was agreed to in Moscow in February 1967 and held its first session in May 1967. See "USSR–Finnish Co-operation Pact Ratified," Moscow radio broadcast, May 30, 1967; "Soviet–Finnish Commission Ends Session," Moscow radio broadcast, June 3, 1967.

[103] K. Danilov, "Portentous Anniversary," Izvestiia, December 5, 1967. See also Takashi Oka, "Finns Toe Neutral Line with Soviet Neighbor," Christian Science Monitor, December 7, 1967.

[104] See Roland Huntford, "Finland's Communists Relinquish Some Power," Washington Post, April 28, 1968.

[105] One of the first signs of a warming up of Turkish attitudes toward the Soviet Union following the Cyprus conflict in the fall of 1964 had been the visit of a Soviet parliamentary delegation to Turkey in early 1965, at which time the Russians reportedly pledged to support the Turkish position on a settlement of the Cyprus issue. See " 'Soviet–Turkish Frontier Should Be Made a Frontier of Growing Friendship.' Delegation of Soviet MPs in Ankara," Soviet News, January 5, 1965, p. 6. For a general assessment of these and prior Soviet efforts in the sixties to improve relations with Turkey, see Geoffrey Wheeler, "Soviet and Chinese Policies in the Middle East," World Today (February 1966): 64–78.

[106] Besides agreements in 1966–67 for a substantial increase in Soviet–Turkish trade and the signing of a protocol on redemarcation of the Soviet–Turkish border, the Soviet Union in March 1967 extended $200 million in aid to Turkey for a number of industrial construction projects, including an aluminum plant, an oil refinery, and a glass factory. See Bertram B. Johnson, "Turks Warm Up Toward Soviets," Christian Science Monitor, December 11, 1967; James Feron, "Soviet Increasing Ties with Turkey," New York Times, June 15, 1968.

although not without some impediment to Soviet relations with the Cypriot regime of Archbishop Makarios.[107]

In September 1967, when Turkish Premier Suleiman Demirel visited Moscow in return for Kosygin's visit to Turkey the previous December, the Soviet press noted that both sides had reached "close or identical" views on various international questions and that there were no longer any territorial disputes to obstruct Soviet–Turkish relations.[108] Along with such assurances of amity toward Turkey, a querulous note occasionally crept into Soviet commentary over such matters as the proposal for a nuclear mine belt at the Soviet–Turkish frontier, an idea which the Turks themselves had suggested to their NATO partners. For the record, the Soviet press sought to gloss over this last point in its attacks upon the mine-belt proposal, picturing it as "a barefaced US propaganda provocation aimed at poisoning the favorable development of Soviet–Turkish relations";[109] on a clandestine level, however, Soviet-inspired propaganda took on a harsher tone to the effect that Turkey risked being turned into a graveyard if the mine belt were installed.[110]

Despite the probability that doubts about the other party were not resolved in either Moscow or Ankara, the Soviet Union could at least feel that its policy of "practical collaboration" with Turkey was paying off in undermining the position of the United States in Turkey and loosening to some degree the latter's affiliation with NATO.[111] These doubtless appeared as no small gains, given the strategic importance of Turkey as the Soviet Union's door to the Eastern Mediterranean and the growing significance which this region assumed in Soviet plans in the aftermath of the Arab–Israeli war of June 1967.

Soviet Policy in the Middle East and Its Impact on Europe

At the Brussels meeting of the NATO Council in December 1967, note was taken of "a marked expansion in Soviet forces in the Mediterranean" and of the need to give particular attention to the "defense problems of the exposed areas," such as NATO's "South-Eastern flank"; at the next meeting of the Council, in Iceland, six months later, the same question again received close attention.[112] This sensitivity in NATO to problems of safeguarding the south-

---

[107] As pointed out by the London *Economist* on December 2, 1967, the Soviet Union sought to play the Cyprus crisis of November 1967 both ways, assuring the Turks of full Soviet backing while advising Makarios that "Turkish threats are bluff and that as a genuine neutralist he must do everything in his power to resist the pressures of the Anglo-Americans."

[108] See A. Sharifov commentary in *Izvestiia*, September 30, 1967, as well as Moscow radio broadcast of the same day. See also "Joint Soviet–Turkish Communiqué," *Pravda*, September 30, 1967.

[109] "The Bustle of Provocation," *Pravda*, April 9, 1967; "NATO Forced To Concentrate Strength on Flanks; Turkish 'Nuclear Belt'," Moscow radio broadcast, October 3, 1967.

[110] As stated, for example, by an "Our Radio" (clandestine) broadcast in Turkish to Turkey, September 29, 1967.

[111] In March 1968, for example, Soviet commentators noted with satisfaction that Turkey was among the NATO countries "seeking revision of the Atlantic Treaty." See Iurii Zhukov, "NATO: To Be or Not To Be?" *Pravda*, March 12, 1968.

[112] See texts of Final Communiqué, *Department of State Bulletin*, January 8, 1968, pp. 50–51,

ern flank of Europe grew not only out of immediate concern over possible repetition of such regional conflicts as the Arab–Israeli war of 1967 and the Cyprus crisis but also out of a more deep-seated apprehension that the Soviet Union might see in the turbulent Middle East an opportunity to expedite the removal of Western influence from the area and to establish itself as the dominant power at the strategic crossroads of the European, Asian, and African continents. NATO's disquiet over the creeping growth of Soviet military and political influence in the Mediterranean increased still more after the invasion of Czechoslovakia.

Behind such Western concern lay the long-time ambition of Russian leaders, from the Czars to Stalin, to obtain a strategic–political foothold in the Middle East.[113] Should the incumbent Soviet leadership be bent upon an energetic pursuit of this traditional aspiration, the potential consequences could indeed be felt in Europe. Among other things, the Soviet Union might manage to acquire a position from which it would be possible to outflank Turkey and Greece, to raise the political and economic costs of European access to Mid-East oil, and to interpose Soviet military power across lines of communication through the area. Moreover, the very threat to European interests implicit in any Soviet attempt to establish a dominant sphere of influence in the Middle East[114] could spill over into Europe in the form of revived Cold War animos-

---

and July 15, 1968, pp. 75–77; "NATO Sees Red Effort To Stall Détente," *Washington Post*, June 26, 1968.

[113] Russian aspirations in North Africa and the Middle East, which go back at least to the end of the seventeenth century, probably first took on meaningful form under Catherine the Great in the eighteenth century. Her policy included military aid to Egypt in order to threaten the Turkish empire from the rear, and in 1784 she reportedly agreed to support Egypt's independence in return for the right to station Russian troops in Alexandria and other Egyptian cities. Under the last of the Czars, Russia's long-time ambition to obtain access to the Mediterranean was re-emphasized in diplomatic maneuvering in 1914 aimed at Russian annexation of Constantinople and the Turkish Straits. Like his Czarist predecessors, Stalin cast his eyes toward the Middle East. In 1940, dickering through Molotov with Germany for spheres of influence, he specified that the area "in the general direction of the Persian Gulf should be recognized as the main area of Soviet aspirations." After World War II, Stalin sought to establish a Soviet foothold from Iran to the southern shores of the Mediterranean. Besides attempts to detach parts of Iranian and Turkish territory, his moves included: a 1945 proposal for "combined defense" of the Turkish Straits; a request for bases in the former Italian possessions of Libya, Eritrea, and the Dodecanese Islands; and a demand in 1946 for revision of the Montreux Convention.

In 1955, with Khrushchev in power and the Egyptian revolution having opened more favorable prospects for Soviet penetration in the Middle East, the USSR began a large-scale program of arms aid to the anti-Baghdad Pact countries, which was to alter the local military balance in the area. The Soviet role in the Suez crisis of 1956 helped to consolidate Soviet relations with Egypt, and shortly thereafter Syria became the next client state which the Soviet Union undertook to shield from alleged "imperialist" aggression, in this case, from Turkey. Again in 1958, the Soviet Union played the role of self-proclaimed "protector" during the Lebanon crisis, asserting that Soviet warnings to the West and military maneuvers in the Caucasus had saved the new revolutionary government in Iraq from being crushed. By the end of Khrushchev's tenure the policy of supporting Arab aspirations against Israel and outside "neocolonialist" powers had gone a long way toward strengthening the Soviet position in the Middle East. This, in brief, was the background against which the Brezhnev–Kosygin regime took up the task of advancing Soviet interests in the area.

[114] For analyses of historical and contemporary Russian interests in the Middle East, see Sergius Yakobson, "Russia and Africa," and Firuz Kazemzadeh, "Russia and the Middle East," in

ities and perhaps even lead to a Great Power confrontation in the Mediterranean. For all these reasons, even though Soviet involvement in the Middle
East is a subject which lies largely outside our study, it seems appropriate here
to examine briefly the links between the evolving situation in the Middle East
and Soviet European policy.

The June War and Its Aftermath

The pivotal event that brought fundamental changes in established political
and power relationships in the Middle East during the tenure of the Brezhnev–
Kosygin regime was, of course, the six-day Arab–Israeli war in June 1967. The
extent to which prior Soviet policies contributed to the outbreak of the June
war need not be debated here. Suffice it to say that despite Russia's role as arms
supplier to the Arab states and her somewhat dubious part in exacerbating the
crisis in May 1967, which immediately preceded the Israeli attack,[115] the war
itself probably came as an unwelcome surprise to the Soviet leadership.
Attempts in concert with the United States to contain the conflict, which we
have already discussed, suggest that avoidance of a Great Power confrontation
was uppermost in the Soviet leaders' minds during the period of active
hostilities, although at the very close of the war they issued an ambiguous
threat to take unspecified measures against Israel.[116]

The aftermath of the war, however, presented a new and fluid situation, full

---

Ivo J. Lederer, ed., *Russian Foreign Policy* (New Haven, Conn.: Yale University Press, 1962),
pp. 453–530; Walter Laqueur, *The Soviet Union and the Middle East* (New York: Frederick A.
Praeger, Inc., 1959); Benjamin Shwadran, "The Soviet Union and the Middle East," *Current
History* (February 1967): 72–77; John A. Armstrong, "Soviet Policy in the Middle East," paper
presented at the Sixth International Conference on World Politics, Berlin, September 4–8, 1967;
Süleyman Takiner, "Soviet Policy Toward the Arab East," *Bulletin* (Munich: Institute for the
Study of the USSR, March 1968), pp. 29–37; *Sources of Conflict in the Middle East*, Adelphi
Papers, no. 26 (London: The Institute for Strategic Studies, March 1966), especially pp. 2–6.

[115] At the beginning of May 1967, the Soviet Union warned Syria and Egypt of an alleged
large-scale Israeli military build-up on the Syrian border which had not in fact occurred. The
warning, however, apparently helped to inflame the spiral of mutual Arab–Israeli suspicions which
culminated in the June war. For discussion of this question, see Walter Laqueur, "The Hand of
Russia," *Reporter*, June 29, 1967, pp. 18–19; Michael Howard and Robert Hunter, *Israel and the
Arab World: The Crisis of 1967*, Adelphi Papers, no. 41 (London: The Institute for Strategic
Studies, October 1967), pp. 15–27; Joseph G. Whalen, *The Soviet Union and the Middle East:
A Survey and Analysis*, Legislative Reference Service, Library of Congress (November 1967):
54–69; George Heitmann, "Soviet Policy and the Middle East Crisis," *Survey* (October 1968):
136–37.

[116] See chapter XI, p. 271. An ambiguous Soviet threat of measures against Israel came
after the Israelis had halted their advance into Egypt and turned their attention to Syria, possibly
heading for Damascus. On June 10, a note handed to the Israeli Ambassador in Moscow warned
that "unless Israel ceases military operations immediately, the Soviet Union jointly with other peace-
loving states, will impose sanctions against Israel, with all the consequences arising therefrom."
(See *Pravda*, June 11, 1967.) The broad term "sanctions" left the Soviet Union a good deal of
elbow room, but it was given to understand that this might mean participation of Soviet forces in
defense of Syria unless the Israeli advance was halted. A discussion of this episode may be found in
John A. Baker, Jr., "Soviet Policy in the Middle East and Eastern Mediterranean," paper presented
at Center for International Affairs, Harvard University, Cambridge, Mass., April 19, 1968,
pp. 68–69.

of both pitfalls and opportunities for Soviet policy. While it is still far from clear what course this policy eventually may take, some of the choices made by the Soviet leaders—who apparently differed on occasion among themselves[117]—can be identified. One choice, obviously made promptly after the fighting ceased, was a decision to put the shattered Arab armies back on their feet, toward which end large arms shipments were dispatched, along with additional military advisers.[118] Initially, this move may have been dictated by a desire to recoup Soviet prestige in the Arab world and, as Soviet sources put it, to "restore the military balance" between the Arab states and Israel.[119] However, it had several other effects: It reduced the prospects for avoiding another expensive round of the Middle East arms race; it increased Arab dependence on the Soviet Union; and it raised the possibility that the rearmed Arab countries might precipitate another war in the Middle East by attempting to avenge their latest military setback at the hands of Israel.

In connection with repairing the military posture of the Arab states, particularly Egypt, the Soviet Union faced the decision whether or not to make its help contingent upon internal political reforms that would give "progressive" Soviet-oriented elements more influence and would help prepare the way for revolutionary changes in the sociopolitical order. Two schools of Soviet opinion seem to have been involved. One, taking an essentially ideological

---

[117] The demotion of Nikolai G. Egorychev, a high Soviet party official, in June 1967, was widely interpreted in the West as the result of an internal Kremlin split over policy toward the Middle East crisis, with Egorychev pictured as spokesman for a "hawkish" faction which urged more forceful Soviet intervention. Reports of internal Soviet policy differences rested in part on an interview given to the French left-wing weekly, *Le Nouvel Observateur*, by an unnamed Soviet official. See Paul Wohl, "Desert War Surprised Kremlin, Press Reports," *Christian Science Monitor*, June 24, 1967. See also Victor Zorza, "Kremlin Split Over Mideast," *Washington Post*, July 2, 1967; James Reston, "Washington: Diplomatic Reports from Moscow," *New York Times*, July 7, 1967. The present writer is indebted to a colleague, Fritz Ermarth, for a somewhat different interpretation, which argues that Egorychev was probably speaking not for Kremlin "hawks" but for a faction critical of the Brezhnev–Kosygin leadership for squandering Soviet arms and prestige in support of the Arab states.

[118] See chapter XI, pp. 271–72. In addition to closer supervision of training activities in Egypt by Soviet advisory personnel, estimated to number about 3,000 officers, it was also reported in 1968 that some 300 Egyptian pilots had been sent to the Soviet Union for a rigorous training course in MIG-21 operations. Other reports indicated that 70 to 100 Soviet pilots were posted to flight duties with Egyptian units. See "Soviet Training 300 Egyptians To Pilot Supersonic Aircraft," *New York Times*, June 18, 1968; Drew Middleton, "The Arab World: Soviet Role Widens," ibid., July 16, 1968.

[119] See "Soviet–Syrian Communiqué," *Pravda*, December 3, 1967. The extent of Soviet replacement of matériel losses suffered by the Arab states was a matter of some dispute in the first months after the June war, but by November 1967 the re-equipment figure was placed at 80 to 100 per cent, except for Jordan, which continued to rely on the West as a source of arms. See "Soviet Replacement of Arab Weapons Confirmed by U.S.," *Washington Post*, July 8, 1967; Hedrick Smith, "Soviet Comeback as Power in Middle East Causes Rising Concern in West," *New York Times*, January 15, 1968; *Strategic Survey, 1967* (London: The Institute for Strategic Studies, 1968), p. 37; "Into the Middle East with Smiles and Missiles," *Life*, November 29, 1968, pp. 22–31. One of the purposes of Nasser's visit to Moscow in July 1968 reportedly was to seek a higher level of arms build-up. See Anatole Shub, "Nasser in Moscow: He'll Regain Lands," *Washington Post*, July 6, 1968.

position, favored a line aimed at "breaking up the old government machine" and weeding out bourgeois elements, especially in the armed forces.[120] The other, more pragmatic, apparently felt it prudent to go slow in pressing for a revolutionary transformation which Nasser might regard as unwarranted interference in Egyptian affairs. The counsel of the second school of thought evidently prevailed, although some pressure undoubtedly was put on Nasser to let local Communists out of jail and to purge the "military bourgeoisie" in his officer corps.[121]

Another Soviet decision of considerable consequence was to keep on station in the Mediterranean the bulk of the augmented naval force which had made its presence highly visible during and immediately after the six-day war. This force, details of which we shall take up in a later chapter, was credited by Soviet spokesmen with having played a "decisive role in frustrating the adventurous plans of the Israeli aggressors."[122] Some of its units put in at Egyptian and Syrian ports during the tense period following the sinking, in October 1967, of the Israeli destroyer *Eilat* by an Egyptian missile patrol boat, ostensibly to warn Israel of the risks of retaliatory action.[123] Publicized flights of Soviet strategic bombers on "friendly visits" to "fraternal Arab countries," in December 1967 and subsequently, seem to have had a similar function.[124]

Besides these displays of its military presence in the immediate theater of the Arab–Israeli conflict, the Soviet Union also chose to show the flag in a widening area beyond the Eastern Mediterranean. To the westward, its naval units called at ports in Algeria, where the possibility arose that the Soviet Union might seek to arrange with the Boumédienne government for the use of the former French naval facility at Mers-el-Kébir.[125] At the same time, the Soviet Union

---

[120] This position was reflected in an article by Evgenii Primakov and Igor' Beliaev, "When War Stands at the Threshold," in the weekly *Za rubezhom* (Life Abroad), no. 27, June 30–July 6, 1967, pp. 7–8. Even prior to the Arab defeat of June 1967, Soviet proponents of "the breaking up . . . and purge of the state machine" in countries with "national democratic regimes" (the category in which Egypt and Syria were placed) had made their voices heard. See, for example, R. Ul'ianovskii, "Some Problems of Non-Capitalist Development in Countries Undergoing Liberation," *Kommunist*, no. 1 (January 1966): 115.

[121] Soviet commentary on Nasser's release of political prisoners noted that this would help to put his regime "on a more progressive basis." See I. Beliaev, "UAR: People and Revolution," *Pravda*, July 23, 1967. The authors of the *Za rubezhom* article cited in fn. 120 above observed with satisfaction that a purge under way in late June 1967 in the Egyptian armed forces had already brought dismissal of "34 generals and more than 650 officers." Reports from Cairo in July 1968 suggested that the purge had been carried further, with obligatory retirements of some 200 officers in the early months of 1968. See "200 Officers Retired," *New York Times*, July 5, 1968.

[122] Admiral S. G. Gorshkov, "Our Powerful Oceanic Fleet," *Pravda*, July 30, 1967.

[123] Israel did retaliate a few days later by shelling an Egyptian oil refinery at Suez, where there was no Soviet military presence to act as a deterrent.

[124] The arrival of visiting Soviet bombers in Egypt was first publicized by a Moscow radio broadcast on December 3, 1967. Ceremonies welcoming the aviators were mentioned in a Moscow radio broadcast on December 9, 1967; in a Cairo radio broadcast on December 6, 1967; and by L. Chuiko, "Stars Over the Nile," *Krasnaia zvezda*, December 14, 1967.

[125] The friendly reception tendered Soviet naval units in Algeria was described in a Moscow radio broadcast, September 26, 1967. In February 1968, following French evacuation of the naval facility at Mers-el-Kebir in Algeria, the Soviet Union denied that it was seeking base rights at this facility or other "privileges in Algeria." However, in July 1968, while Soviet Defense Minister

turned its attention toward the southern part of the Arabian peninsula, where British power was in the process of vacating the strategic rimlands governing access to the Indian Ocean from the Red Sea and the Persian Gulf. In November 1967 Moscow decided to intervene in the Yemeni civil war, sending air support, including both transport and combat aircraft flown by Soviet pilots, to aid the republican regime in Yemen against the royalists.[126] This step was taken just as the last of Nasser's troops were being withdrawn from Yemen and the British had pulled out of Aden in neighboring South Arabia.[127] It was followed about a year later by the signing of a Soviet military and technical aid agreement with the new South Yemen government in Aden.

Although only time will tell whether Soviet military aid activity in the two Yemeni states was a passing episode or the prelude to a larger plan for extension of Soviet political and military influence into adjacent Arabian areas,[128] the fact remains that tentative first steps were taken toward establishing a Soviet presence at the gateway to the Indian Ocean. Incidentally, it was a matter of some interest that in the spring of 1968, following a trip to India earlier in the year by Admiral Sergei Gorshkov, head of the Soviet navy, a group of Soviet naval vessels for the first time made an extended "goodwill" cruise through the northern Indian Ocean and the Persian Gulf.[129] Soviet military aid programs in the Sudan and Somalia were also pertinent to the extension of Soviet military influence along the western rim of the Indian Ocean in 1968.

Throughout the period after the June war, while the Soviet Union was helping to rebuild the armed forces of the Arab states and making its own military presence felt in the Middle East, Soviet spokesmen stoutly denied that the USSR had any intention of setting up military bases on NATO's southern flank. As one commentator put it, "the Soviet Union never has had, nor is it

---

Marshal Grechko was in Algeria to discuss military co-operation with the Boumédienne regime, sources in neighboring Morocco—also a recipient of Soviet military aid—said that arrangements had been made to send Soviet technicians to Mers-el-Kebir. Reports persisted later in 1968 that Soviet personnel were in the process of rehabilitating the former French base. See Drew Middleton, in *New York Times*, July 16, 1968; "Algeria Improves Ties with Soviet," ibid., November 17, 1968.

[126] Hedrick Smith, "Soviet Airlift Said To Aid Yemen's Republicans," *New York Times*, December 15, 1967.

[127] Withdrawal of British forces from Aden began in late August 1967 and was completed in November. On November 30, with the British departure, the National Liberation Front in South Arabia proclaimed the newly independent People's Republic of South Yemen. Some British forces remained in the Persian Gulf area, from which they are scheduled for withdrawal in 1971–72.

[128] It should be noted that Soviet activity in Yemen was not new. As early as 1928, the USSR had recognized the then new state of Yemen, and had made several trade agreements with Yemen's royalist government. Yemen also received some Soviet military aid prior to the republican revolution in 1962.

[129] The group of five Soviet warships cruised in the Indian Ocean and adjacent waters from March through July 1968, calling at various ports in the Indian subcontinent, the Middle East, and northeast Africa. See Nicholas Herbert, "Visit to Gulf by Soviet Navy," *Times*, London, May 13, 1968; Rowland Evans and Robert Novak, "Soviet Naval Forces in Persian Gulf Pose Threat to Western Interests," *Washington Post*, May 15, 1968. For an account of Admiral Gorshkov's visit to India, see "Russia: Power Play on the Oceans," *Time*, February 23, 1968. See also chapter XVI, fn. 78.

working toward the acquisition of bases, spheres of influence, or oil concessions" in the Mediterranean basin.[130] In a formal sense, it was true that the
Soviet Union did not move to acquire its own bases; however, by making use
of local facilities in the Arab countries and seeking access to Yugoslav naval
installations,[131] the USSR was hardly displaying indifference toward the utility
of supporting bases in the area. At the same time that it was denying interest
in acquiring bases of its own, Moscow continued to press for the elimination
of Western bases in the Mediterranean area, making those in Libya and Cyprus
the particular targets of its propaganda. The presence of foreign bases was
singled out as a major cause of the November 1967 Cyprus crisis.[132] After the
June war, the Soviet Union also stepped up its propaganda against NATO
naval activities in the Mediterranean, labeling naval maneuvers in August 1967
as an attempt by NATO to offset its "seriously weakened political position in
this area."[133]

The Soviet Military and Political Commitment in the Middle East

One result of the June war, as suggested by these various steps of the Soviet
Union, was a gradual increase in its military commitment in the Middle East.
How much more deeply the USSR might choose to commit itself militarily
remained to be seen, but the Soviet leaders clearly had made up their minds
to demonstrate that the Mediterranean could no longer be regarded as an
exclusively Western preserve.[134] At a minimum, the maintenance of a military
presence in the area seemed designed to restore damaged Soviet prestige in the
Arab world by a visible show of support that would deter Israel from any
serious military moves against the Arab states. Another function of the Soviet
military presence may have been to retain some local control over possible
provocative actions by client Arab states. Also, the maintenance of a Soviet
military foothold in the Middle East, together with military aid programs to
selected states in the region, may have been counted upon to reduce hostile
access to the southern border areas of the Soviet Union itself in the event of
a major crisis in either Europe or the Far East.[135]

Beyond this, however, one could not say with assurance that the Soviet
Union had more ambitious military undertakings in mind, such as a major
build-up of forces and supporting bases in the Mediterranean capable of out-

[130] Rafael Arutiunov commentary, Moscow radio broadcast, November 28, 1967.

[131] See "Soviet Warships at Yugoslav Port," New York Times, June 21, 1967. In October 1967
Yugoslavia announced that a Soviet naval detachment had arrived at Split on an "informal visit."
"Soviet Black Sea Fleet Sails into Split," Belgrade TANYUG International Service announcement,
October 18, 1967. More extensive Soviet use of Yugoslav naval facilities took place in 1968.

[132] See "Soviet Government Statement" on Cyprus, Pravda, November 23, 1967.

[133] Lev Andreev commentary, Moscow radio broadcast, August 27, 1967.

[134] Besides Soviet assertions to this effect, others also recognized that the Soviet naval build-up
in the Mediterranean had changed things. Tunisia's President Habib Bourguiba, for example, noted
in May 1968 that deployment of Soviet naval forces to the area, as well as Soviet arms aid to
neighboring countries like Algeria, had undermined the old balance of power in the Mediterranean.
See "Bourguiba Says Soviet Navy Is Upsetting Mideast Balance," Washington Post, May 20, 1968.

[135] See Baker, "Soviet Policy in the Middle East," pp. 13, 63, 75.

flanking Europe strategically from the south. The character of the Soviet forces rotated into the Mediterranean and the problems of reinforcing and logistically supporting them under hostile conditions were such as to suggest that the Soviet Union was far from being in a position to confront NATO power in the area directly.[136] Rather, while asserting that as a Black Sea and Mediterranean power it had an "irrefutable right" to send its warships into Mediterranean waters,[137] the Soviet Union seemed prepared for the time being to go no further than to employ its forces for surveillance and occasional harassment of NATO naval operations in those waters. With regard to committing naval forces to the Indian Ocean as a routine matter, the Soviet Union's capacity to sustain a permanent offshore presence of significant size likewise seemed somewhat limited, unless arrangements were made with suitably located countries for support facilities ashore. In this connection, Soviet aid programs for the construction of port facilities in such countries as India and Somalia opened the possibility of bargaining for use privileges.

In the political sphere, Moscow's efforts in the aftermath of the June war to rally international support for the Arab cause, including attempts to bring the various Warsaw Pact countries together on a common line toward the Arab states and Israel,[138] testified to the Soviet Union's continuing intention to play a major political role in the affairs of the Middle East. Perhaps the most pressing immediate issue before the Soviet leadership was whether to pursue a policy of uncompromising support of the Arab position, which was likely to keep Middle East tensions dangerously high, or to advise the Arab states to offer mutual concessions that might lead to a settlement and reduce the danger of a new war.[139]

---

[136] The size of the Soviet Mediterranean naval force—averaging around forty to fifty combatant and auxiliary units, including perhaps a dozen submarines—left it no match for NATO naval forces in the Mediterranean. Peacetime resupply of the Soviet force in anchorages at sea or from Egyptian and Syrian ports was inadequate to sustain it under combat conditions except against local forces possessing limited air and naval power. Lack of unhindered access to the Mediterranean from home waters of the several Soviet fleets was another major liability confronting the Soviet Union should it become involved in a direct confrontation with NATO forces in the Mediterranean. See chapter XVI, pp. 443–44, 449.

[137] Explicit Soviet assertions to the effect that Soviet naval power had come to the Mediterranean to stay "in accordance with the interests" of the Arab states and "to insure the security" of the southern borders of the USSR itself were advanced in late 1968 after NATO, on November 16, had warned against any new Soviet intervention "affecting the situation in Europe or the Mediterranean." See V. Ermakov, "American Billyclub in the Mediterranean Sea," *Pravda*, November 27, 1968. See also chapter XVI, fn. 79.

[138] Soviet attempts to forge a common Warsaw Pact line toward the Arab states and Israel are discussed in chapter XIV.

[139] During the first half of 1968, the closest that Moscow had come to publicly reminding the Arab states of the need for concessions was reference in February to a possible two-stage approach to a settlement, whereby in the first stage the Arabs would be prepared to end the "state of war prevailing since 1948" in return for Israel's withdrawal from all territory occupied after June 5, 1967, while in the second stage the Arabs would be prepared "to reconsider the question of Israeli ship transit through the Suez Canal" provided the Palestine refugee problem were satisfactorily solved. See Igor' Beliaev, "Dirty Work," *Pravda*, February 18, 1968; V. Kudriavtsev, "The Aggressor Must Leave," *Izvestiia*, February 24, 1968. For the most part, however, public Soviet commentary took the position, as had Kosygin in a January 1968 interview with *Life* magazine, that any possi-

According to some observers, Soviet spokesmen, in private discussions with Arab leaders in 1968, tended to counsel the latter course.[140] But their public utterances often conveyed the impression that the Soviet Union was interested in keeping the Middle East situation just below the boiling point,[141] perhaps on the calculation that an incomplete settlement and continuing tension would keep the Arab world conscious of its dependence on the Soviet Union and firmly aligned against the West.

Only after a spiraling cycle of incidents in late 1968 and in 1969 posed the danger of open renewal of warfare did the Soviet Union begin to take what looked like serious diplomatic initiatives to break the Arab–Israeli impasse.[142] The first of these came with a *Pravda* editorial, on December 3, 1968, voicing support of the Jarring UN mediation mission in order to head off "a new dangerous flareup" in the Middle East. This was followed on December 30 by a Soviet note to France, Britain, and the United States proposing terms for a settlement which reflected a somewhat more flexible attitude than Moscow had previously displayed on such questions as border adjustments and which raised the possibility of "guarantees by the four permanent Security Council members."[143]

Although the Soviet proposal connoted having the Great Powers bring pressure to bear, especially upon the Israeli side, and reportedly was unacceptable to the United States on a number of points,[144] it did lead to the start of informal four-power talks in New York as well as bilateral Soviet–US conversations to explore the prospects for a political settlement. Unfortunately, these efforts, throughout 1969, to find a formula for mediating the Middle East

---

bility of settlement was contingent upon prior Israeli troop withdrawal from "territory seized by the aggressor." See *Life*, February 2, 1968, p. 29. A similar stipulation accompanied the Soviet memorandum on disarmament measures of July 1, 1968, in which "reduction of armaments in various regions, including the Middle East" was proposed. *Pravda*, July 2, 1968.

[140] See, for example, Robert H. Estabrook, "Soviets Said To Press Arabs for Peace," *Washington Post*, April 9, 1968, and Eric Pace, "Moscow Pressing for Suez Opening," *New York Times*, July 13, 1968.

[141] See Kosygin's speech in Rawalpindi, *Izvestiia*, April 19, 1968; Bernard D. Nossiter, "Kosygin Warns Israel: Return to Border," *Washington Post*, April 19, 1968; Robert Estabrook, "Soviets Urge the UN To Act Against Israel," ibid., May 2, 1968; Alfred Friendly, "Israelis Say Soviets Tread Close to Brink," ibid., May 9, 1968.

[142] In 1968 these incidents included attacks on Israeli airlines abroad and stepped-up activities by Arab guerrillas on the one hand and Israeli actions such as a commando foray in the vicinity of the Aswan Dam and a raid on Beirut airport on the other. The level of violence escalated still further in 1969, as heightened Arab guerrilla sabotage and infiltration was matched by Israeli air raids into Egypt, along with recurrent artillery duels and armored assaults across the Suez Canal. By early 1970 the inability of Egypt to protect its airspace against the Israeli air force had begun to create pressure upon the Soviet Union to help strengthen Egyptian air defenses.

[143] The contents of the Soviet note of December 30, 1968, which was not made public at the time, first appeared in a Lebanese newspaper on January 10, 1969. An editorial article in *Pravda* fifteen days later gave the first published Soviet version of the proposal, which Andrei Gromyko evidently had worked out with Nasser during a hasty visit to Cairo in December 1968. See E. Vasil'ev, "A Just and Stable Peace in the Near East Is an Urgent Necessity," *Pravda*, January 25, 1969.

[144] See, for example, Alfred Friendly, "U.S. Challenges Soviet Mideast Points," *Washington Post*, January 20, 1969.

crisis proved unsuccessful, as noted previously,[145] so that by early 1970 a settlement seemed as far away as ever.

Meanwhile, the Soviet leadership faced decisions which could have a critical bearing on the course of events in the Middle East. One immediate question was whether to send Soviet "volunteers" into action against the Israelis; this applied particularly to pilots, of which the Egyptians had an admitted shortage.[146] An intensified propaganda campaign against Israel, both within the Soviet Union and abroad, suggested that preparations for such a step might be in the making.[147] But beyond a decision on this matter lay larger and still unresolved questions as to the Soviet Union's objectives in the Middle East and the extent to which its leadership was prepared to adopt high-risk policies in their pursuit.

On the one hand, it could be argued that the Soviet leaders, having suffered political setbacks and loss of momentum in Europe, might find themselves the more tempted to seek compensating gains by pursuing a radical policy course in the Middle East. In this view, they might hope to pull off a political end run through the Middle East, putting themselves in a position to threaten Europe by cutting off her oil supply, by bringing pressure on less stable states on the southeast rim of Europe, and so on. Within the Middle East itself, a companion feature of this essentially high-risk policy might be for the Soviet Union to use its increased political leverage to install "progressive" revolutionary regimes in the Arab countries,[148] hoping thereby both to consolidate its influence and to demonstrate that Soviet political strategy is capable of achieving dynamic ideological successes, which would help offset the rival claims of Peking's Third World strategy.

On the other hand, however, there was no reason to suppose that the merits of a more moderate and patient policy course in the Middle East were lost upon the Soviet leaders. Doubtless, the principal factor favoring a conservative approach was to avoid an escalation of Arab–Israeli hostilities that might embroil the Soviet Union with the United States. Another consideration was

---

[145] See chapter XI, p. 277.

[146] In a speech in February 1970, Nasser acknowledged that the Israelis possessed air superiority and said: "The problem we feel here in the Arab countries—notably here in Egypt—is the problem of pilots." See Peter Grose, "Nasser Concedes Israeli Air Power," New York Times, February, 8, 1970.

[147] In a note to the heads of government of the United States, Britain, and France, Kosygin in early February alluded to Israeli air attacks and said that the Soviet Union would "see to it that the Arab states have means at their disposal" to deal with them. This and other Soviet statements were widely interpreted as foreshadowing additional aid, including "volunteer" pilots. Another purpose of the Soviet propaganda against Israeli air attacks may have been to bring about the diplomatic isolation of Israel and to generate international pressure for a political settlement favorable to Moscow's clients. See "Text of Kosygin, Nixon Exchange of Mideast Notes Made Public," Washington Post, February 26, 1970; Joseph Alsop, "Kosygin Hints of Aid to Egypt Could Involve 'Volunteer' Pilots," ibid., February 6, 1970; L. Koriavin, "The Middle East: Tel-Aviv and Its Patrons," Izvestiia, February 5, 1970.

[148] The overthrow of the conservative monarchy in Libya in 1969 by a military cabal, though greeted with approval by Moscow, apparently was not the result of a Soviet-fostered revolutionary movement; rather, it appeared to have its roots in Arab nationalism.

that denial of oil resources to traditional Western consumers could cut both ways, increasing the economic demands of Middle East countries upon the Soviet Union to make up for lost revenue. Similarly, continued closure of the Suez Canal, while damaging to Western interests, would also be hard on Egypt and the Soviet Union, the more so as transit of the Suez Canal has been of declining value to the West with the development of supertankers, while becoming more important to the USSR for routing supplies to North Vietnam and for establishing a strategic link with the Indian subcontinent. Finally, there was the possibility that, even though "progressive" Arab regimes could perhaps be launched on the "socialist path" with generous Soviet aid, such regimes might prove jealous of their independence and defy Soviet control in the manner of Castro's Cuba.[149]

In light of such considerations, it might well be argued that the Soviet leaders would prefer to work toward such objectives as reducing Western influence and improving the Soviet Union's own position in the Middle East by using such relatively conventional foreign policy methods as economic projects, military aid, and diplomatic support to strengthen the pro-Soviet orientation of existing Middle East governments. A parallel feature of this approach, which might also recommend itself to the Soviet leadership, would be an attempt to seek larger economic gains from the Soviet Union's improved position in the Middle East. Soviet activity has already been pointed toward such aims as acquiring a major role in the development and marketing of Persian Gulf oil resources and Iranian natural gas[150]—partly to regain a payoff on the considerable credits the USSR had extended in the area,[151] and partly perhaps to use Middle East oil (which costs less to produce than Soviet oil)—in an effort to channel more of the Soviet Union's own investment resources into other sectors of the Soviet economy.[152]

Whether Soviet policy in the Middle East will tend to move along the extreme or the moderate lines sketched above remains to be seen. To a considerable extent, the answer may turn on the opportunities which present

---

[149] On this point, see Arnold L. Horelick, *Soviet Policy Dilemmas in the Middle East*, The RAND Corporation, P-3774, February 1968.

[150] This activity took on significance with offers to Iran and Iraq in 1967 to assist them in the development of their oil resources. In the case of Iraq, an "initial agreement" was reached on December 24, 1967, for Soviet help in developing a nationalized oil industry and marketing its products. In 1966 an agreement with Algeria had brought the Soviet Union into collaboration with that country's national oil industry as well. See "Oil Deal Aids Soviet in Mideast," *Washington Post*, December 27, 1967; "Economic Cooperation With Algeria," *Soviet News*, August 9, 1966, p. 68.

[151] From 1955 to 1968, Soviet economic aid to countries in North Africa and the Middle East, including Turkey and Iran, came to more than $2.5 billion, while military aid to the same countries approached $3 billion.

[152] The cost in the Soviet Union of producing a ton of crude oil was about twice that in the Persian Gulf area. As pointed out by Baker, "Soviet Policy in the Middle East," pp. 22–23, indirect evidence that the Soviet Union was interested in the use of Middle East oil both to conserve its own reserves and to permit investment in other areas of the Soviet economy was forthcoming in 1967, when Soviet crude-oil production targets for the future were scaled down substantially.

themselves, together with the risks and costs of pursuing them. The Soviet leaders may find that Arab nationalism, a force that worked for them as long as the common object was to expel dominant Western influence from the area, will begin to work against them if it becomes plain that Western influence is simply to be replaced by Soviet domination. At the same time, the attitudes of the Western powers are likely to represent a factor of no little consequence in shaping the opportunities perceived by the Soviet leadership in the Middle East. Should the policies of the Western powers, for any of a variety of reasons, seem to signal a declining interest in the area, Moscow may come to the conclusion that the way is open for further Soviet penetration, with reduced risk of encountering serious outside resistance.

XIV

SOVIET RELATIONS WITH EAST EUROPE: 1966–1968

In the two years after the Bucharest conference of July 1966, the Soviet Union was obliged to cope with progressively troublesome threats to its control over East Europe and to the unity of the Warsaw bloc. These challenges began early in this period with Rumania's breaking of ranks on a common line toward West Germany, which made more difficult the problem of maintaining bloc cohesiveness in the face of Bonn's diplomatic drive in East Europe. However, it was the subsequent, and perhaps largely unforeseen, train of events in Czechoslovakia which posed the most severe problems for the Soviet leadership.

Regarded in Moscow as the gravest challenge to Soviet interests in East Europe since the Hungarian rebellion of 1956, Czechoslovakia's new course under the Dubcek regime not only raised disturbing questions as to the steadfastness of the military and foreign policy position of a key member in the Warsaw Pact's Northern Tier, but in the eyes of the Soviet leaders it also threatened to weaken the internal structure of Communist power in that pivotal country—perhaps an even more disturbing prospect.

In this chapter we shall deal with the efforts of the Brezhnev–Kosygin regime to stem the gradual erosion of Soviet authority in East Europe, including the developments that culminated in the invasion of Czechoslovakia in August 1968. The management of military affairs within the Warsaw bloc, as well as the impact of the Czechoslovak intervention upon Soviet European policy, will be taken up in later chapters.

Efforts to Counter Bonn's Bridge-building Diplomacy

The most notable sign that neither the Bucharest conference nor another gathering of Warsaw Pact leaders later in 1966[1] had produced a workable formula for a united policy front came on January 31, 1967, when Rumania took the independent step of establishing diplomatic relations with the Federal Republic,[2] thus openly breaking the common line on West Germany. This

---

[1] From October 17 to 22, 1966, party and government leaders of the Warsaw Pact states and their defense ministers (plus representatives from Cuba and Mongolia) met in the Soviet Union, but no report on issues discussed was forthcoming. In the course of this gathering, one purpose of which was to familiarize the high-level guests with "the achievements of Soviet science and technology," a demonstration launching of missiles and space vehicles took place, similar to that staged several months earlier for de Gaulle. See TASS communiqué, "In an Atmosphere of Friendship and Cordiality," *Pravda*, October 22, 1966; Radio Prague broadcast, "Party Delegates in Moscow Review Defenses," October 23, 1966.

[2] The agreement to establish full diplomatic relations was reached in Bonn on January 31 between German Foreign Minister Willy Brandt and Rumanian Foreign Minister Corneliu Manescu, but the exchange of ambassadors came only several months later, in July. See Philip Shabecoff,

move, which at the same time signaled Bonn's abandonment, at long last, of the so-called Hallstein Doctrine,[3] was made in the face of strenuous opposition from Ulbricht's regime, backed by Poland and the Soviet Union.[4] In fact, only three days previously the Soviet Union had delivered a particularly harsh attack on the reconciliation policy enunciated in December 1966 by the new Kiesinger–Brandt coalition government in Bonn.[5]

Once Rumania had broken the ice, the possibility arose that other East European countries might be tempted to follow suit, with Hungary and Czechoslovakia among the more likely candidates.[6] Although the Soviet leaders may have had some reservations about letting Ulbricht define the terms for a bloc response to the Federal Republic's overtures, on balance they apparently decided to stand behind his efforts to slow down any precipitous East European movement toward Bonn. These efforts began in early February with sharp East German criticism of Rumania, which the latter promptly rejected as unwarranted "interference" in her affairs;[7] this was followed by a hastily arranged

"Bonn and Bucharest Agree To Establish Full Diplomatic Tie," *New York Times*, February 1, 1967; Dan Morgan, "Rumania's New Envoy Is in Bonn," *Washington Post*, July 11, 1967.

[3] The 1955 Hallstein Doctrine had ruled out diplomatic relations with any state recognizing the East German regime (except the USSR), and was in effect an instrument to uphold the Federal Republic's contention that it is the sole democratically elected government representing the German people. Although Bonn issued a statement noting that this position was not altered by establishment of diplomatic relations with Rumania, it was clear that the Hallstein Doctrine itself was no longer operative with respect to other East European countries.

[4] As previously noted (chapter XIII, p. 315), the new Grand Coalition government in Bonn had made it known, through a Bundestag speech by Kiesinger in December 1966 and other statements, that it was prepared to seek diplomatic ties with various East European countries. The GDR and Poland promptly assailed this initiative, declaring that Bonn must meet such prior conditions as recognition of East Germany and acceptance of the Oder–Neisse boundary. Soviet commentary was initially more restrained, but subsequently hardened into denunciation of Bonn's overtures as "the same old policy of nonrecognition of the results of the last war." On the other hand, both Czechoslovakia and Hungary reportedly expressed readiness to consider diplomatic ties without insisting on prior conditions, until pressure from Pankow and Moscow subsequently brought them into line. Among pertinent accounts, see Anatole Shub, "Bonn Is Optimistic on Improving Ties with East Europe," *Washington Post*, January 18, 1967; editorial, "Revanchists' Rights," *Neues Deutschland*, January 28, 1967; David Binder, "Stand Stiffened by East Germany," *New York Times*, January 8, 1967; Harry B. Ellis, "Ulbricht Protests Bonn Ties with East," *Christian Science Monitor*, January 26, 1967; David Binder, "Two Red Nations Respond to Bonn," *New York Times*, January 26, 1967; Henry Tanner, "Rapacki Adamant in Stand on Bonn," ibid., January 28, 1967; Eric Bourne, "East Bloc Differs over Bonn Ties," *Christian Science Monitor*, January 31, 1967.

[5] See previous discussion of the Soviet note of January 28, 1967, chapter XIII, pp. 315–16. This statement, timed to coincide with Rumanian Foreign Minister Manescu's arrival in Bonn, was probably not expected to dissuade him from accomplishing his mission.

[6] See fn. 4 above. Bulgaria too may have fitted into this category, for prior to the establishment of diplomatic relations between West Germany and Rumania, Bonn had carried on talks with the Bulgarian as well as the Hungarian and Czech governments on the same question.

[7] Criticism of Rumania for establishing relations without having repudiated Bonn's "presumptuous claim to sole representation" of the German people was voiced in East Germany's *Neues Deutschland*, February 3, 1967. In a *Scinteia* editorial the following day, the Rumanians retorted that the GDR had "disregarded the principles of Marxism–Leninism" in setting itself up as a "foreign policy adviser" to another socialist state. In addition to questioning Rumania's actions, the Ulbricht regime also pressed ahead with a series of new measures it had instituted in January to curtail contacts between East and West Germany, as if to set an example for others to follow. Whether the Soviet Union was in sympathy with these steps was not clear, just as it had been

meeting of Warsaw bloc foreign ministers, reportedly called at Ulbricht's insistence to set conditions for further contacts with West Germany.[8] Several weeks later, the Soviet Union came out openly in support of Ulbricht's line when Brezhnev, speaking in Moscow on March 10, asserted that West Germany remained the prime obstacle to peace and security in Europe, and that it would be "extremely naive to accept the current manifestations of Bonn's policy as signs of a change in its foreign policy course."[9]

Other steps taken in the spring of 1967 to blunt Bonn's bridge-building diplomacy toward East Europe included a drive to enact, or in some cases to renew ahead of schedule, a series of bilateral defense treaties between countries of the Warsaw Pact, with initial emphasis on the Northern Tier states. The first of these steps was the renewal on March 1, 1967, of the Polish–Czechoslovak Treaty of Friendship, Co-operation and Mutual Assistance, followed later in March by new treaties between East Germany and Poland, and East Germany and Czechoslovakia.[10] By the fall of the year, all the Warsaw Pact allies, with the conspicuous exception of Rumania, had signed bilateral mutual assistance treaties with Pankow, at the same time that the Soviet Union had updated its bilateral treaties with each Pact member, again with the exception of Rumania. As noted earlier, one significant effect of this widening network of bilateral treaties was to provide back-up arrangements in the event that Soviet proposals for the dissolution of the opposing military alliances were accepted.[11] Another effect was to demonstrate solidarity with the Ulbricht regime, and thus to take the edge off Bonn's bid for further diplomatic ties in East Europe.

Thanks to the countermaneuvering of the German Democratic Republic,

---

uncertain whether Ulbricht himself or his Soviet mentors had taken the initiative in breaking off an incipient set of SPD–SED public debates in June 1966, immediately before the Bucharest conference. See, for example, Berlin dispatch, "Soviet Said To Bar German Debates," *New York Times,* June 20, 1966.

[8] Henry Kamm, "Ministers Meet in Warsaw," *New York Times,* February 9, 1967. The Rumanian Foreign Minister, Manescu, rather pointedly stayed away from this meeting, sending a subordinate official in his stead. In a speech on February 13, Ulbricht denied foreign "speculation" that the site of the meeting had been shifted from East Berlin to Warsaw because of Rumanian objections. What agreement, if any, was reached at this meeting on how to respond to Bonn's new Eastern diplomacy was not divulged.

[9] *Pravda,* March 11, 1967.

[10] The East German treaties with Poland and Czechoslovakia were signed, respectively, on March 15 and 17, 1967. See Paul Wohl, "Soviet Bloc Trio Shapes Entente," *Christian Science Monitor,* March 20, 1967. The text of the GDR–Polish treaty was broadcast by East Berlin radio on March 15, 1967, that of the GDR–Czech treaty on March 17, 1967; and the Czech–Polish treaty articles were broadcast by Prague radio March 1, 1967. For Soviet comment, see "Brotherly Solidarity," *Izvestiia,* March 19, 1967.

[11] See chapter XII, pp. 310–11. The Soviet bilateral treaty with Rumania, due for renewal on February 4, 1968, came up for consideration during the rash of treaty renewals in 1967, but nothing was done about it. Subsequently, the twentieth anniversary of the Soviet–Rumanian treaty on February 4, 1968, passed without its formal renewal, although its provisions allowed for an automatic five-year extension. Among reasons for this failure to reconfirm the old treaty were presumably its clauses calling for automatic consultation on all international issues and its stringent condemnation of West Germany, both of which Rumanian policy at the time would doubtless have found objectionable.

with assistance from Poland and the Soviet Union, much of the initial momentum of Bonn's diplomatic offensive had been checked by April 1967. Outwardly at least, the Warsaw bloc leaders, including upon occasion even Rumania's Ceausescu,[12] adopted a uniform line toward West Germany's striving for "normalization" of relations with East Europe, specifying that Bonn must meet such prerequisites as recognition of existing European frontiers, acceptance of the existence of two German states, and renunciation of nuclear weapons. However, this posture was not wholly resistant to continued feelers from Bonn, as illustrated by the response to a new West German appeal on April 12 for improving relations between the two parts of Germany.[13] This initiative not only gave encouragement to Southern Tier countries wishing to broaden their contacts with West Germany but it even set off a series of alternately hard and soft replies from Pankow, suggesting that Ulbricht himself saw some advantage in the opening of a new dialogue with Bonn.[14] Moreover, despite the outward adherence of the East European states, save Rumania, to a policy of keeping Bonn politically at arm's length, this did not prevent most of these countries from continuing to expand their economic relations with the West generally and the Federal Republic in particular.[15]

That the East European regimes were in one degree or another determined to retain their freedom of maneuver vis-à-vis the Soviet Union, no matter what

[12] See, for example, Ceausescu's Bucharest speech of February 20, 1967, in which he not only defended his country's establishment of diplomatic ties with the Federal Republic as a positive contribution "to developing European interstate co-operation" but also declared that "Rumania proceeds from the principle that the existence of the two German states ... is the prerequisite for improving the atmosphere in Europe." The speech was broadcast by TASS International Service, Moscow, February 20, 1967.

[13] The appeal took the form of a declaration addressed to the East German Socialist Unity party (SED), transmitted under cover of a letter from SPD party Chairman Willy Brandt. It proposed a variety of measures to strengthen co-operation in economic, technical, and cultural fields, as well as to ease conditions of daily intercourse between the divided German territories. See "Bonn Socialists' Letter Asks Reds for Dialogue," New York Times, April 14, 1967.

[14] An initial negative response from Ulbricht on April 13 was followed a few days later by an expression of interest in direct negotiations between Chancellor Kiesinger and GDR Premier Willi Stoph. An exchange of alternative proposals continued for several months thereafter. See Norman Crossland, "E. Germany Rejects Bonn Overtures," Washington Post, April 14, 1967; "Bonn Plan Backed by East Germans," New York Times, April 24, 1967; "East German Bid Sent to Kiesinger," ibid., May 12, 1967; "Reds Interested in Bonn Overture," ibid., May 15, 1967; Dan Morgan, "East Germans Balk Bonn's Move," Washington Post, June 17, 1967; GDR Government memorandum, Neues Deutschland, July 22, 1967; "Bonn Policy Unchanged Despite Stoph Proposal," ibid., September 28, 1967; "Bonn Continues To Follow Policy of Revanchism; Chancellor Kiesinger's Reply to GDR Proposal," Soviet News, October 10, 1967, p. 28.

[15] Besides a general rise in the volume of East European trade with West Europe (imports rose about 4 per cent and exports about 5 per cent in 1967), various "industrial co-operation" ventures between Western firms and East European countries continued to grow during 1967, and such steps were taken as the entry of Poland and Yugoslavia into GATT, of which Czechoslovakia was already a member. Czechoslovakia, in particular, moved closer in the spring of 1967 toward an exchange of commercial missions and conclusion of a trade agreement with West Germany, and an agreement was signed in early August. Economic relations between West Germany and Rumania also broadened during this period in the wake of their establishment of diplomatic ties. See David Binder, "Bonn and Prague Sign Trade Pact," New York Times, August 4, 1967; idem, "Brandt Carries Vow of Support from Bucharest," ibid., August 8, 1967; "Rumanian–West German Agreement Implemented," Bucharest radio broadcast, October 25, 1967.

they thought individually about relations with Germany, was demonstrated during the Karlovy Vary conference of European Communist parties, in April 1967. As noted in the preceding chapter, Brezhnev used this occasion to decry the presence of US naval forces in the Mediterranean and to call for a program of political action built around the idea of European security and aimed specifically at casting doubt on the utility of NATO as a medium for promoting East–West understanding.[16] However, Soviet hopes of turning this "historic" meeting of twenty-four Communist parties from both East and West Europe[17] into a unified front against Peking did not materialize,[18] nor, for that matter, was Moscow able to muster unanimous endorsement for its European policy line, inasmuch as two European Communist parties—the Yugoslav and the Rumanian—refused to attend the conference.

In declining to appear at Karlovy Vary, the Yugoslavs and the Rumanians not only showed themselves wary of being drawn into an anti-Chinese front but also maintained that the pursuit of European security arrangements was properly a matter for governments rather than for a party conclave. In the months prior to the Karlovy Vary meeting, Yugoslav differences with Moscow had sharpened over these and other issues, including Soviet criticism of the more liberal political trends in Yugoslavia that followed Tito's moves in 1966 against the conservative Rankovic wing of the Yugoslav party.[19] If the Karlovy Vary meeting left Soviet–Yugoslav relations unimproved,[20] this was even more true in the case of Rumania.

Continuing Tensions in Soviet–Rumanian Relations

Soviet displeasure at Rumania's boycotting of the Karlovy Vary meeting, expressed in references to the "unfortunate" absence of certain parties from the conference, evidently irritated the independent-minded Rumanians. On May 7, 1967, eleven days after the close of the Karlovy Vary gathering and exactly one

[16] See chapter XIII, pp. 325–26.

[17] Soviet commentary on the Karlovy Vary conference emphasized its "historic" character as the first gathering to bring together Communist parties from all of Europe, apart from worldwide conclaves like that in Moscow in 1960. See, for example, editorial, "In the Interests of Peace and Progress," *Pravda*, April 30, 1967.

[18] See Stephen S. Anderson, "Soviet Russia and the Two Europes," *Current History* (October 1967): 207.

[19] See Richard Eder, "Soviet–Yugoslav Rift Is Growing over Red Talks and Reforms," *New York Times*, March 12, 1967. For an analysis of the Rankovic dismissal and its significance for political reform in Yugoslavia, see R. V. Burks, *The Removal of Rankovic: An Early Interpretation of the July Yugoslav Party Plenum*, The RAND Corporation, RM-5132-PR, August 1966.

[20] A meeting between Tito and Brezhnev in January 1967, prior to Karlovy Vary, also had conspicuously failed to mend relations between the two countries. However, when Tito took up a pro-Nasser position during and after the Arab–Israeli war, Moscow and Belgrade found themselves close together on at least this issue. Practical expression of support of the Soviet line in the Middle East was to be seen in Yugoslavia's granting the rights of transit to Soviet aircraft during the air resupply effort to Egypt after the June war, and in her extending the use of her naval facilities to warships of the Soviet navy's augmented Mediterranean force. On the other hand, despite such co-operation, Yugoslavia remained opposed to Soviet policy in other matters, Tito's subsequent backing of the Czech reform government being a case in point.

year after his strongly nationalistic forty-fifth-anniversary speech,[21] Ceausescu published an article which again denounced meddling in Rumanian party affairs and defended the "legitimate right" of a given Communist party not to participate in international conferences if it saw fit.[22] This indication that Soviet–Rumanian relations were again wearing thin came on the heels of rumors that Rumania was still taking an obstreperous stand on military arrangements within the Warsaw Pact.

In early May, Western news agencies reported that Rumania was resisting the appointment of a Soviet officer to the post of Warsaw Pact commander, left vacant when Marshal Andrei Grechko was reassigned to the position of Soviet Defense Minister after the death of Marshal Malinovskii, in late March. One version of these reports had it that Bucharest was asking that the Warsaw Pact post be rotated and given to a non-Soviet officer, in line with its rumored demands a year earlier;[23] another version reported a proposal to create new subordinate commands for the Northern and Southern Tiers, under an over-all Soviet commander.[24] Subsequently, Marshal Ivan Iakubovskii, a Russian, took over the top job of Warsaw Pact commander without there being a reorganization into subordinate commands, but the delay of almost three months in making known his assignment lent some substance to speculation that Rumania had made a contentious issue of the matter.[25]

New difficulties in keeping Rumania aligned with the rest of the Warsaw bloc arose for the Soviet Union in 1967, in connection with the Arab–Israeli conflict. Even before the actual outbreak of hostilities on June 5, Bucharest had declined to fall in with Soviet efforts for a co-ordinated bloc stand in support of the Arab states, indicating instead that both sides ought to contribute to a settlement of the crisis.[26] After the war broke out, a hastily summoned conference of Warsaw Pact representatives in Moscow issued a statement condemning alleged Israeli–American aggression and pledging support to the Arab countries.[27] Rumania, although represented at the conference, refused to sign the statement and subsequently urged the Arab states and Israel to negotiate a settlement. Moreover, she was alone among the Warsaw Pact countries repre-

---

[21] See chapter XII, pp. 306–7.

[22] *Scinteia*, May 7, 1967.

[23] See chapter XII, p. 307.

[24] These versions, emanating from unnamed but presumably Rumanian diplomatic sources, were reported by UPI and Agence France Presse, respectively, on May 3, 1967. A further discussion of questions relating to Warsaw Pact reorganization will be found in chapter XVII.

[25] Marshal Iakubovskii's assumption of the post vacated by Grechko became known on July 7. "E. Europe Post Kept by Soviets," *Washington Post*, July 8, 1967.

[26] Poland, too, displayed some reluctance to join wholeheartedly in the Soviet position during the May crisis. See Victor Zorza, "Not All Satellites Echo Russia's Mideast Views," *Washington Post*, June 2, 1967. For expressions of the Soviet position, see "For the Unification of All Progressive Revolutionary Forces in Arab Countries," *Pravda*, June 2, 1967; Iu. Popov, "The Test of Sincerity," *Izvestiia*, June 3, 1967.

[27] "Statement of the Central Committees of Communist and Workers Parties and Governments of the People's Republic of Bulgaria, Hungarian People's Republic, German Democratic Republic, Polish People's Republic, USSR, Socialist Republic of Czechoslovakia, Socialist Federal Republic of Yugoslavia," *Pravda*, June 10, 1967.

sented in Moscow in declining to sever diplomatic relations with Israel. A month later, Rumania stayed away from a similar gathering in Budapest.[28] Although she subsequently attended two further meetings on the Middle East situation (at Belgrade in September and Warsaw in December 1967),[29] she apparently succeeded on both occasions in causing the communiqué to be watered down,[30] and found other ways of demonstrating her independent policy line.[31]

If Soviet tactics in this series of meetings were aimed at achieving a unified position on the Middle East with which even Rumania could agree, they can be judged reasonably successful. However, Moscow's problem of forging co-ordinated bloc policies did not end with the question of the Middle East. Another issue, which gradually came to a head in 1967 and early 1968, was that of winning solid support for a new world conference of Communist parties. Here again, the Soviet Union was to find Rumania a stubborn holdout and a potentially dangerous example for other parties seeking to retain their freedom of maneuver in the contest for Communist leadership between Moscow and Peking.

The Budapest "Consultative" Meeting and Rumania's Walkout

From the autumn of 1966, there had been a perceptible increase in Soviet-encouraged lobbying for a new international Communist conference of the kind that had last met in Moscow in December 1960.[32] In October 1967 a rising volume of statements from various Soviet supporters was capped by a declaration from the head of the French Communist party that conditions were finally "ripe" for a "consultative meeting" to make "practical preparations" for such a world conclave.[33] One month later, after further behind-the-scenes maneu-

[28] "Information Statement on Budapest Meeting of the Leaders of Fraternal Parties and Governments of Socialist Countries," *Pravda*, July 13, 1967. At the meeting in Budapest of July 11–12, 1967, which Rumania refused to attend, a number of the other East European leaders present reportedly were "less than enthusiastic" about furnishing economic and military aid to help make up for Arab losses in the June war, although they did pledge some assistance. See AP dispatch, "Soviet Satellites Reportedly Agree to Help Foot Bill for Arab Recovery," *Washington Post*, July 18, 1967; Robert Evans, "Rumania's Israel Stand Irks Soviet," ibid., July 16, 1967.

[29] "Conference in Belgrade," *Pravda*, September 7, 1967; "Communiqué of Conference of Foreign Ministers of European Socialist Countries," ibid., December 23, 1967.

[30] The communiqué issued by the December 1967 meeting in Warsaw, for example, was the first joint bloc statement to call upon all UN member states in the Middle East to recognize that "each of them has a right to exist as an independent national state," an evident concession to the Rumanian position, although Kosygin had broached the same idea in his speech at the UN General Assembly on June 19, 1967. On the other hand, Rumania also gave some ground by joining the communiqué's stipulation that Israeli withdrawal from occupied territory was the main condition "for restoring and maintaining peace." See "Communiqué of Conference . . . ," *Pravda*, December 23, 1967; "Red Bloc Unites on Mideast," *Washington Post*, December 23, 1967. For Kosygin's UN speech, see *New York Times*, June 20, 1967.

[31] For example, at the very time that the Pact foreign ministers were meeting in Warsaw in December 1967 to work out co-ordinated backing for the Arab states, Bucharest sent off a high-level delegation to Tel Aviv to negotiate a trade agreement with Israel, one result of which was a doubling of Rumanian–Israeli trade in 1967. See Peter Grose, "Rumania and Israel Are Expanding Economic and Cultural Ties," *New York Times*, March 19, 1968.

[32] See chapter XI, pp. 257–58, and chapter XII, p. 302.

[33] The statement that conditions for a conference had finally ripened was made at a plenum of

vering, invitations were issued for a "consultative" meeting to take place in Budapest in February 1968.[34] Thus the stage was set for what a *Pravda* editorial hopefully foresaw as a major step toward restoration of "Communist unity," with no intent to "excommunicate" any party from the world Communist movement.[35]

The Budapest meeting, which opened on February 26 with some sixty parties represented but a number of important dissenters missing,[36] proved to be less than a resounding display of unity. On February 29 the Rumanians, whose misgivings had been voiced in advance,[37] pulled out of the consultative talks, charging that the Soviet Union had violated its assurances that there would be no criticism of China, and asserting that to hold a world conference under existing conditions of discord would "only flagrantly illustrate on a world scale the lack of unity between Communist parties."[38] Prior to the Rumanian walkout, the chief Soviet delegate, Mikhail Suslov, seconded by hard-line speeches from the Polish and East German delegates,[39] had warned against

the French Communist party by its General Secretary, Waldeck Rochet, on October 19, 1967. Soviet media promptly gave it wide circulation. See "For Peace and Socialism," *Pravda*, October 20, 1967.

[34] The invitation was issued on November 24, 1967, in the name of eighteen of the nineteen Communist parties which had taken part in the fruitless March 1965 "consultative" meeting in Moscow. See chapter XI, p. 257. Cuba was the missing party among these nineteen, reflecting no doubt the deterioration of Castro's relations with the Kremlin. See "On the Convocation of a Consultative Meeting of Communist and Workers Parties," *Pravda*, November 25, 1967.

[35] Editorial, "For Solidarity of the International Communist Movement," *Pravda*, November 28, 1967. Subsequent Soviet comment on the upcoming consultative meeting stressed that it would seek unity of action against "imperialism" without specifically mentioning the problem of China's opposition to the Soviet "unity line." Assurances were also given that the "independence" of all parties would be respected, that no single "guiding center" for all parties was contemplated, and that a "broad democratic approach" would be followed in preparing for the world conference. See, for example, Brezhnev's Leningrad speech, February 16, 1968, *Leningradskaia pravda*, February 17, 1968; editorial, "Before the Consultative Meeting," *Pravda*, February 22, 1968.

[36] Among the notable absentees were six of the fourteen ruling Communist parties: China, Cuba, and Albania refused to accept invitations; Yugoslavia was not invited; and North Korea and North Vietnam found it expedient to stay away. Several other, nonruling parties did not put in an appearance for one reason or another, including those of Japan, Indonesia, Thailand, and Burma.

[37] During January and early February, while making up their minds whether to attend the Budapest meeting, the Rumanians held a series of consultations with twenty other Communist parties, designed to set limits on the agenda. When the Rumanian decision to attend was announced on February 14, 1967, it was made clear that Rumania intended to defend its independent position and to lobby against convocation of a world conference on any terms that might suggest condemnation of China or other "absent" parties. In addition to the Rumanians, the Hungarian, Czech, and Italian parties also expressed varying degrees of concern about guidelines for the meeting, as did the Yugoslavs, who had not been invited. The statement of the Rumanian Communist party's Central Committee Plenum on plans to attend the Budapest conference was announced in a Bucharest radio broadcast, February 14, 1968. See also Peter Grose, "World's Reds Open Parley in Budapest in Disunity Monday," *New York Times*, February 23, 1968; Anatole Shub, "Rumanians Set Terms at Red Parley," *Washington Post*, February 27, 1968; Paul Wohl, "Parley Seeks Red Consensus," *Christian Science Monitor*, February 28, 1968.

[38] AP dispatch, "Rumania Quits Red Talks Over Criticism of Peking," *New York Times*, March 1, 1968. Rumania's dramatic walkout was preceded by demands of the Rumanian delegate, Paul Niculescu-Mizil, for a joint apology for Syrian charges that Rumania displayed a "destructive" and pro-Israel attitude.

[39] Poland's Zenon Kliszko and East Germany's Erich Honecker both took tough positions, arguing for a new "basic document," such as that issued by the 1960 Moscow world conference, to lay down a "common general line" and "joint strategy and tactics" for the world Communist movement. Honecker's speech, reminiscent of the Stalinist period, defined loyalty to Moscow as

"dangerous nationalistic tendencies" and declared that Peking's attempts to discredit "the very idea" of a new world conference could "in no way serve as an argument for the further postponement of the conference."[40] When the Budapest session came to a close, on March 5, it issued a communiqué ignoring Rumania's walkout and stating that the conferees had agreed to set up a preparatory committee that would go ahead the following month with arrangements for a formal world party conference, tentatively scheduled to be held in Moscow in November–December 1968.[41]

Thus, by virtue of what were described as "steamroller tactics,"[42] the Soviet delegation under Suslov—himself generally identified as one of the hard-line figures in the Soviet leadership—managed at Budapest to win formal backing for the long-deferred world conference. Although the endorsement given by some of those present, especially the Czechs,[43] may have been only lukewarm, the Soviet Union had succeeded in isolating Rumania without precipitating a revolt against its authority among other Warsaw bloc parties, or for that matter, among the West European Communist parties.[44] The prospect of facing another showdown with the Rumanians, however, was just around the corner, for on the day after the Budapest meeting, a session of the Warsaw Pact Political Consultative Committee—reportedly called at Rumania's request to discuss her objections to the draft treaty on nuclear nonproliferation as well as certain Warsaw Pact military matters[45]—opened in Sofia.

---

the "binding yardstick" to govern the actions of all Communist parties. Honecker's speech was broadcast by East Berlin radio on February 28, 1968. See also Anatole Shub, "Most Submit to Soviet Bloc at Conference," *Washington Post*, February 29, 1968; Henry Kamm, "A Cold Wind From Moscow," *New York Times*, March 3, 1968.

[40] "Speech of the Head of the CPSU Delegation, Comrade M. A. Suslov," *Pravda*, February 29, 1968.

[41] "Communiqué of the Consultative Meeting of Communist and Workers Parties," *Pravda*, March 7, 1968. See also Osgood Caruthers, "Pro-Soviet Parties Plan Moscow Summit Parley," *Washington Post*, March 6, 1968.

[42] See Henry Kamm, in *New York Times*, March 3, 1968.

[43] The Czechoslovakian delegate, Vladimir Koucky, unlike the East German and Polish delegates, opposed adoption of a single, binding general line and told journalists that "we agree with the Rumanian comrades on most basic questions." He also spoke approvingly of "positive tendencies" in West German policy toward East Europe, in contrast to his colleagues' bitter attacks on Bonn. The Czechs, feeling their way under a new regime which had but recently ousted the Novotny Old-Guard faction, were doubtless interested in preserving their freedom of maneuver without a head-on clash. It was also reported that the Czech and Hungarian parties would both seek to mediate the Rumanian differences with the other Budapest conferees. See Jonathan Randal, "Anti-Bonn Policy Is Eased Further by Prague," *New York Times*, March 3, 1968; Anatole Shub, "New Problems Rise for Soviet at Red Parley," *Washington Post*, March 3, 1968; AP dispatch, "2 Soviet Bloc Nations To Coax Rumania," ibid., March 5, 1968.

[44] One of the minor surprises of the Budapest conference was that the Italian Communist party, which had long opposed the idea of a world conference for somewhat the same reasons as the Rumanians, fell quietly into line. See Henry Kamm, *New York Times*, March 3, 1968.

[45] See, for example, "Rumania Hints at a New Showdown," *Washington Post*, March 2, 1968. In light of subsequent disclosures by Ceausescu, it would appear that the Soviets anticipated trouble with the Rumanians over the nonproliferation treaty and managed to outmaneuver them on this issue. In a statement on April 26, 1968, citing examples of Soviet disregard for Rumania's views, Ceausescu charged that the Soviets had presented a joint declaration at the Sofia meeting endorsing the treaty without having given Rumania a chance to register its objections. See reference to Ceausescu's speech in chapter XVII, fn. 98.

Contrary to expectations that the meeting in Sofia might boil up into an open row, possibly including a Rumanian threat to bolt the Warsaw Pact, the two-day session ended with both Soviet and Rumanian leaders apparently having decided merely to let their differences simmer. With respect to Rumania's complaints about the joint Soviet–US draft of a nonproliferation treaty,[46] a final amended version of which was to be presented at Geneva just a few days later, on March 11,[47] the Sofia meeting registered no concession to the Rumanian viewpoint. Rather, it issued a separate statement on this subject on behalf of all the delegations except Rumania's, endorsing the draft treaty and leaving Bucharest again standing alone.[48] The Rumanians did, however, join in a declaration condemning US "aggression" in Vietnam.[49] On the matter of Warsaw Pact military arrangements, nothing was disclosed at the time about any discussion that may have taken place,[50] although one hint that Czechoslovakia, too, might be sliding toward the Rumanian position was given by a Czech commentator who said on March 6 that perhaps the time had come when "the Warsaw Pact member countries might ask some questions similar to those which some time ago caused de Gaulle to quit NATO."[51]

Unresolved Soviet Dilemma: How to Handle the Recalcitrant Rumanians

Following the Budapest and Sofia gatherings in the early months of 1968, Soviet–Rumanian relations appeared likely to deteriorate still further, especially as Rumania showed no disposition to aid the Soviet Union in efforts to bring

[46] Soviet–Rumanian differences over the nonproliferation treaty (NPT) had become increasingly apparent after a joint US–Soviet draft of a complete treaty was presented on January 18, 1968. The Rumanian delegate at the seventeen-nation disarmament talks in Geneva attacked this draft, on February 6, as "profoundly discriminatory" against non-nuclear powers for several reasons, including its exclusion of the nuclear powers from inspection of peaceful nuclear activities and its failure to provide a security guarantee to non-nuclear powers. *Pravda* on March 2 rejected various arguments against the NPT, but did not single out Rumania as an objector, following the usual practice of focusing on Bonn as the chief obstacle to the treaty. On March 7, at Geneva, proposals for a security guarantee outside the NPT framework were offered by the USSR, United States, and Britain, but Rumania later found them inadequate. When the final, amended joint draft of the NPT was presented at Geneva on March 11, prior to submission to the UN General Assembly, the Soviet Union rejected last-minute proposed changes by Rumania. But in a *Pravda* editorial of the same day on the Sofia Warsaw Pact meeting, the Soviets again soft-pedaled Rumanian resistance to the treaty and asserted that Bonn's nuclear ambitions were the main reason for seeking the NPT. Reuters dispatch, "Rumania Calls Treaty To Check Spread of A-Arms Discriminatory," *Washington Post*, February 8, 1968; editorial, "In the Interests of All People," *Pravda*, March 2, 1968; "Nonatomic States Get Big 3 Pledge of Defense Moves," *New York Times*, March 8, 1968; editorial, "Curb the Forces of War and Aggression," *Pravda*, March 11, 1968; editorial, "In the Interest of International Détente and Peace," *Scinteia*, March 13, 1968.

[47] For previous discussion of the sequence of negotiations on the nonproliferation treaty, see chapter XI, pp. 267–69.

[48] See "Communiqué of Meeting of Political Consultative Committee of Warsaw Pact Governments," *Pravda*, March 9, 1968.

[49] The declaration on Vietnam was much like that issued at the Warsaw Pact's summit meeting of July 1966 in Bucharest.

[50] Subsequently, it was disclosed that the question of changes in the Warsaw Pact command structure had been debated at Sofia. See further treatment of this question in chapter XVII, pp. 490–91.

[51] See further discussion of this matter in chapter XVII, p. 489.

Warsaw Pact pressure to bear on the new reform government in Czechoslovakia. At a meeting in Dresden on March 23, which witnessed the first joint attempt of Warsaw bloc leaders to call the Dubcek regime to account, Rumania's chair remained vacant,[52] and, as we shall see, the Rumanians continued to support Prague's refusal to bow to Moscow's dictate.

When the preparatory meeting of Communist parties convened in Budapest in April to discuss arrangements for the formal world conference in Moscow, Rumania was again missing, along with a number of other ruling parties.[53] Meanwhile, Moscow and Bucharest continued to give signs of discord over other matters, with occasionally a few polite words for each other. For example, at the same session of the Rumanian Central Committee in April, at which Ceausescu criticized Soviet disregard at Sofia and Dresden for Rumania's interests as a co-equal in the Warsaw Pact, his regime also undertook some internal house cleaning with strong anti-Soviet overtones,[54] while the Soviet Union responded with propaganda attacks questioning the ideological rectitude of the Rumanians.[55] On the other hand, when de Gaulle arrived in Bucharest in May for his long-announced visit to Rumania, his invitation for "combined political action" by France and Rumania met with a cautious response from Ceausescu, who made clear that bilateral co-operation between their two countries would not be at the expense of Rumania's Warsaw Pact ties, and who used the occasion to offer some unaccustomed words of praise for the Soviet Union's wartime "heroism and sacrifice."[56]

For the Soviet leaders, however, such rhetorical gestures from Ceausescu were scarcely enough to gloss over the stubborn fact that Rumania remained

[52] Rumania was not invited to attend the Dresden meeting, as Ceausescu disclosed in his April 26, 1968, speech (see fn. 45 above). However, it was obviously clear to those who arranged the meeting that Rumania—a staunch defender of the principle that no Communist party has the right to interfere in the affairs of another—would not take part in chastisement of the Czechs.

[53] Seven of the fourteen ruling parties did not show up at the preparatory meeting in Budapest, to which fifty-four parties sent representatives. At the close of the five-day Budapest meeting it was announced that November 25 had been set as the opening date for the world conference in Moscow. Subsequently, because of the Czech invasion, the conference was again postponed. See "Communiqué of the Preparatory Commission for an International Meeting of Communist and Workers Parties," *Pravda*, April 30, 1968.

[54] Foreshadowed by a Ceausescu speech on March 22, 1968, promising some internal liberalization in Rumania, the April session of the Central Committee took some steps to put a more liberal face on Rumania's regime by reducing the powers of the secret police and endorsing a number of modest internal reforms. At the same session, Stalinist practices under Rumania's former ruler, Georghe Gheorghiu-Dej, were denounced, while the reputations of several other Rumanian leaders, purged during the Stalinist period under presumed Soviet orders, were restored. It was this aspect of the Rumanian housecleaning that served as a reproach to past Soviet influence within the country. See Peter Grose, "A Liberalization in Rumania Seen," *New York Times*, April 29, 1968.

[55] Immediately after the Rumanian Central Committee session, the Soviet Union opened a new barrage of anti-Rumanian propaganda, centering on an incident which occurred in early April during a visit of Rumanian Premier Maurer and Foreign Minister Manescu to Finland, when they laid a wreath on Marshal Mannerheim's grave. Soviet propaganda zeroed in on this honoring of "the memory of a White General" by a delegation from a socialist country as evidence of Rumanian indifference to the imperatives of "the ideological struggle." See Anatole Shub, "Rumanians Criticized by Russians," *Washington Post*, May 1, 1968.

[56] See Donald Louchheim, "Ceausescu Cautious on Bloc Ties," *Washington Post*, May 17, 1968.

bent on an independent and even defiant course in her policies toward the Soviet Union. Taking stock of their relations with Rumania as the situation in East Europe grew more trying, they doubtless asked themselves once more how best to deal with the defiance of this troublesome ally. Should they take the path of persuasion through appeals to Communist unity, or should they turn more vigorously to such political, economic, and military pressures as could be brought to bear on Bucharest?

Politically—to judge by Moscow's tendency to strengthen its ties with the bloc members most disposed to follow its cue, such as East Germany and Poland—the Soviet leadership no doubt saw some virtue in a tougher course, designed to isolate Rumania still further. However, the damage that such an approach might do to the image of bloc unity was likely to counsel against carrying it too far, which would seem to leave the situation just about where it had been.

The prospects of forcing Rumania back into line through economic sanctions were not much better. During 1967, according to Rumanian charges,[57] some economic pressure had been applied, and a still more massive squeeze was possible, but only at the risk of driving Rumania closer to the West and Yugoslavia.

Direct military pressure was hardly feasible for the Soviet Union, except in the case of extreme provocation, which the wily Rumanians were likely to avoid. Yielding some ground to Bucharest's demands for greater equality and reform within the Pact promised perhaps to ease differences in the military domain,[58] but any such relaxation of Soviet control would run counter to moves already underway toward an organizational tightening of the Pact machinery[59]—the need for which is likely to have taken on added urgency for the Soviet leaders in mid-1968.

New Ferment in East Europe and the Czechoslovak Challenge

If Rumania posed a perplexing problem for the Soviet Union, developments elsewhere in East Europe in the early months of 1968 doubtless gave the Soviet leadership still greater cause for concern over how to restore respect for

[57] Rumanian complaints of economic pressure, such as alleged Soviet footdragging in the delivery of goods and materials promised under bilateral trade agreements, had led to talks between Brezhnev and Ceausescu in Moscow in December 1967, without announcement of results other than that the two sides had exchanged opinions. See "Communiqué on the Visit to the Soviet Union of the Party-Government Delegation of the Socialist Republic of Rumania," *Izvestiia*, December 17, 1968. See also Anatole Shub, "Rumanian, Soviet Ties Near Crisis," *Washington Post*, December 17, 1967.

[58] A possible precedent for the tendering of concessions to the Rumanians had occurred in August 1967. At that time, Podgornyi reportedly made a secret visit to Bucharest to smooth out Soviet–Rumanian differences. His visit was followed by Rumania's participation, for the first time in three years, in a joint Warsaw Pact exercise, suggesting that some mutual understanding on military questions had been reached to reduce tension between Moscow and Bucharest. See Anatole Shub, in *Washington Post*, December 17, 1967.

[59] These efforts to tighten up the organizational machinery of the Pact are discussed in chapter XVII, pp. 490–91.

its authority and to maintain the cohesion of the Warsaw bloc. Beginning in January 1968, a new ferment of reform, with disturbing implications for the Soviet hold upon East Europe, arose in Czechoslovakia after the ouster of the Novotny regime, at the same time that Poland also was briefly and to a lesser degree subjected to an upsurge of internal protest. This new restiveness in East Europe, which must have evoked memories of the difficulties of 1956, was no doubt especially perturbing to the Soviet leaders, coming as it did at a time when they were having to cope at home with a mood of disquiet among Soviet intellectuals over cultural controls and the trials of dissident writers.

Ouster of Novotny and Launching of the Czech Reform Movement

The Novotny regime in Czechoslovakia, though not always an unquestioning servant of Soviet policies in East Europe, had nevertheless been among the Kremlin's more docile and orthodox Warsaw Pact partners. It was probably with some anxiety, therefore, that the Soviet leadership looked on during the fall and winter of 1967 as an increasingly severe internal political struggle in Prague threatened the position of the fifteen-year-old Novotny regime. The discontents that lay behind this power struggle in Prague are matters with which we cannot deal at length here, but they apparently included dissatisfaction with the halting progress of new economic programs, unresolved political and economic grievances of the Slovak half of the country, and Novotny's failure to heal a growing friction between the regime and the country's students and intellectuals.[60]

In mid-December 1967, a few days after Brezhnev had made a surprise visit to Prague in an apparent effort to save Novotny's position,[61] the revolt against Novotny's Old-Guard leadership came into the open at a Czech Central Committee plenum.[62] Shortly thereafter, at the plenum of January 3–5, 1968,

[60] For an informative examination of the origins of the Czechoslovak ferment, including such factors as the decline of the highly industrialized economy, the re-evaluation in Prague of the German danger, and the resurgence of Slovak nationalism, see Richard V. Burks, *The Decline of Communism in Czechoslovakia*, The RAND Corporation, P-3939, September 1968. See also Deryck Viney, "Cutting the Moorings in Czechoslovakia," *Communist Affairs* (January–February 1968): 3–10; "The Change of Political Direction," *Radio Free Europe*, January 9, 1968; H. Gordon Skilling, "Crisis and Change in Czechoslovakia," *International Journal*, Toronto (Summer 1968): 456–65; Stanley Riveles, "Slovakia: Catalyst of Crisis," *Problems of Communism* (May–June 1968): 1–9. For commentary by various Czechoslovak writers and reformers on what went wrong under the Novotny regime, see material published in *East Europe*, March through July 1968.

[61] Novotny reportedly arranged Brezhnev's surprise visit to Prague on December 8, 1967, without consulting the Czech Central Committee. See Hanus J. Hajek, "What Next in Czechoslovakia?" *East Europe* (March 1968): 3. There is a strong presumption that Brezhnev threw his weight behind Novotny, although lack of specific charges to this effect by Prague after Novotny's ouster leaves room for assuming that Brezhnev may have tried to mediate as a neutral between the opposing Czech factions. For an interpretation along this line, see Fritz Ermarth, *Internationalism, Security, and Legitimacy: The Challenge to Soviet Interests in East Europe, 1964–1968*, The RAND Corporation, RM-5909-PR, March 1969, pp. 63–64.

[62] This plenum, one of three in the period from October 1967 to January 1968 in which the struggle to unseat Novotny was fought out, was held December 19–21, 1967. See Neal Ascherson, "Czechs Are Waiting Word on Novotny's Fate as Leader," *Washington Post*, December 22, 1967; "Stalinist at Bay; Central Committee Discusses Novotny's Future," *Newsweek*, January 1, 1968, pp. 34–35.

Novotny was replaced as party secretary by Alexander Dubcek,[63] a relatively obscure forty-six-year-old Slovak party functionary, who was soon to find himself a national hero. At the end of March, Novotny's fall was made complete when he also lost the purely titular post of president.[64]

Concurrently with the unseating of Novotny, a broad process of internal reform, described by some Czech intellectuals as a "bloodless revolution," was tentatively set in motion by the new Dubcek regime.[65] Besides ousting numerous officials of the Old Guard, a task made easier by the embarrassing defection of one general and the suicide of another who allegedly had conspired to use the armed forces to put Novotny back in power,[66] the Dubcek regime promised liberalizing reforms in many aspects of the country's economic, political, and cultural life. Among symbolic signs of change, perhaps none was more dramatic than the public homage paid to the memory of Jan Masaryk on the twentieth anniversary of his death, the first such observance since the Communist coup in Czechoslovakia in February 1948.[67]

For the new leadership in Prague the reform movement presented multiple problems, among the most critical of which was how to keep the pressures for change from upsetting the internal structure of Communist authority and from creating a demand for a reorientation of Czech foreign policy that could call down the wrath of the Soviet Union. During what can be regarded as the unfolding of the Czech experiment—the period from January 1968 until the issuance of the regime's new "action program" in early April—the new leadership in Prague showed itself aware of the need to control the reform movement so as to keep it from provoking either an internal attempt at a comeback by conservative party elements or outside intervention.

Illustrative of the new regime's careful tightrope walking were major

[63] "Czechs Turn Out Novotny," *Washington Post*, January 6, 1968; "Novotny Deposed as Party Leader; Slovak Gets Post," *New York Times*, January 6, 1968.

[64] See Richard Eder, "Novotny Resigns Czech Presidency on Party Demand," *New York Times*, March 23, 1968.

[65] Dan Morgan, "Zeal of Reform Stirs Czechs," *Washington Post*, February 25, 1968; "Reforms Pushed in Czechoslovakia under Dubcek," *New York Times*, March 3, 1968.

[66] The close relationship of Novotny to Major General Jan Sejna, who defected to the United States in February 1968 after an apparent attempt to rally the army on Novotny's side, strengthened the hand of the new, anti-Novotny leadership in carrying out a housecleaning of both military and civilian officials. Colonel General Vladimir Janko, who committed suicide in March, also was apparently implicated in the military coup plans, details of which remain obscure. The position of General Bohumir Lomsky, the Czech Minister of Defense and a deputy commander of the Warsaw Pact, also was left shaky by these events. In April 1968, he was replaced by General Martin Dzur.

[67] Large crowds turned out in Prague to commemorate the twentieth anniversay of the death of Jan Masaryk, who either jumped to his death or was thrown from a window on March 1, 1948, two weeks after the Communist takeover in Czechoslovakia. Rehabilitated along with his name was that of his father, Thomas G. Masaryk, first President of the Czechoslovakian Republic. Subsequent Czech moves to investigate the circumstances of Jan Masaryk's death, which raised the question of Soviet security police complicity, became one of many heated issues between Prague and Moscow in 1968. See Henry Kamm, "Masaryk's Grave Is a Shrine Again," *New York Times*, March 18, 1968; Richard Eder, "Czech Party Paper Links Death of Masaryk to Beria 'Gorillas'," ibid., April 17, 1968; Raymond H. Anderson, "Role on Masaryk Denied by Soviet," ibid., May 8, 1968.

speeches by Dubcek in February and March, in which he sought to strike a balance between the demands of intellectuals, students, and other reform-minded groups on the one hand and the misgivings of conservative elements in the party and state bureaucracy, the army, and the police on the other.[68] With regard to the internal scene, Dubcek promised that there would be no return to "administrative methods" of governing—a Communist euphemism for arbitrary rule. At the same time he reassured those who had expressed "fears that a more or less widely tolerated democratism . . . might weaken the foundations of power and . . . the principles of socialism" by telling them that the new regime itself was aware of the danger of "going too far in the process of democratization." As for external relations, Dubcek hinted on the one hand at greater independence in foreign policy by saying that Czechoslovakia would formulate "standpoints of her own on basic international questions" and that she would also make better use of her position as an industrialized nation "in the center of Europe" to seek the "extension of co-operation between states—irrespective of their social system." In effect, this meant that Prague would seek better relations with West Germany, a move sure to raise Soviet hackles. On the other hand, Dubcek also reaffirmed Czechoslovakia's fidelity to the Soviet Union, declaring that the Czech Communist party "stands firmly and unshakably" linked to the USSR by its "fraternal bonds with the CPSU" and that "our future plans and prospects cannot be imagined without Czechoslovakia's membership in the community of socialist countries."[69]

At a meeting of the Czechoslovak Party Presidium on March 21, where Novotny's full retirement from the political scene was announced, the new Czech leadership reiterated that it would "not allow itself to be taken in" by attempts to legalize "nonsocialist moods" under "the guise of democracy or rehabilitation."[70] Two days later at Dresden, where an emergency meeting of Warsaw Pact members, without Rumania, had been convened to elicit an accounting from Dubcek and his associates, the Czech leaders once more sought to quiet the fears of their allies that Czechoslovakia's liberalization program might endanger Communist rule in the country and her adherence to the common policies of the Warsaw bloc.

What went on at the Dresden meeting was only partly disclosed in its communiqué, which stressed the danger of "militaristic and neo-Nazi activity" in West Germany and the need "to carry out practical measures in the immediate future to consolidate the Warsaw Treaty and its armed forces."[71] An apparent warning to Czechoslovakia not to stray from the fold was contained

---

[68] The first of these was a speech in Prague on February 22, 1968, marking the twentieth anniversary of the Communist takeover, with Brezhnev and other Soviet leaders present. The second was a speech at Brno on March 16. *Rude Pravo*, February 23 and March 17, 1968. See also Anatole Shub, "New Czech Chief States Aims," *Washington Post*, March 17, 1968.

[69] *Rude Pravo*, February 23, March 17, 1968.

[70] Statement on March 21 Central Committee Presidium meeting, Prague radio broadcast, March 22, 1968.

[71] See TASS, "Information Communiqué," *Pravda*, March 25, 1968. See also Henry Kamm, "Dubcek Has Talks with Bloc Chiefs," *New York Times*, March 24, 1968.

in a passage stating that the conference members expected the new Czech leadership to "insure the further progress of socialist construction" in that country; it also was reported that they had pressed Dubcek to look to the Warsaw Pact countries for temporary financial aid, so as to discourage Czechoslovakia from seeking credits and other economic assistance from Bonn.[72]

So far as outside onlookers could determine, however, this first employment of collective pressure against the Dubcek regime apparently involved only a mild form of political and economic arm-twisting. Perhaps the one foretaste of things to come was furnished by rumored Soviet–East German troop maneuvers hastily mounted in the German Democratic Republic near the Czechoslovak border while the Dresden meeting was being held.[73] But on the whole, apart from the Dresden court of inquiry, the initial Soviet response to events in Czechoslovakia was studiously circumspect, whatever may have been the private misgivings in the Kremlin about the course upon which the Dubcek regime had embarked.

Thus, during most of the first three months of 1968, the Soviet press remained discreetly silent on what was going on in East Europe. Only after the launching of a domestic propaganda campaign, on March 14, to stress the need for vigilance against "bourgeois" and other unhealthy outside influences,[74] was the press permitted a fragmentary coverage of the new political crisis that was taking shape in East Europe. A cryptic report of Novotny's resignation from the presidency on March 22,[75] the communiqué of the Dresden meeting, and an interview with the new political chief of the Czechoslovak armed forces in which he pledged his country's continued co-operation with the Soviet Union[76] were among the few items to emerge toward the end of March from the virtual blackout in the Soviet press on Czechoslovak developments.

By contrast with the Soviet Union, most of the other Warsaw Pact members in East Europe were somewhat more outspoken. Predictably, the Ulbricht regime in East Germany took the most vocal and hostile stand on the Czechoslovak situation, asserting that "counterrevolutionary" and "imperialist" forces

---

[72] See Richard Eder, "Dresden Parley Disturbs Czechs," *New York Times*, March 25, 1968; David Binder, "Bloc Considering Credit to Czechs," ibid., March 26, 1968.

[73] Rumors of the use of joint military exercises to bring collective pressure on Dubcek ran along two lines. One version was that joint Soviet–East German formations were dispatched to exercise north of the Czech border during the Dresden meeting, a rumor given some substance by closure of various GDR areas to foreign travel. Another was that Moscow advised Prague that it had decided to schedule joint spring maneuvers in which Soviet and East German troops would move into Czechoslovakia to join in exercises with Czech units. As it subsequently turned out, maneuvers were held in Czechoslovakia in June, becoming by then an obvious instrument of pressure on the Czechs. See Henry Kamm, in *New York Times*, March 24, 1968; Dan Morgan, in *Washington Post*, March 26, 1968.

[74] Editorial, "The Education of Patriotism," *Pravda*, March 14, 1968. For subsequent examples of this campaign, see L. I. Brezhnev's speech at nineteenth conference of the Moscow Party Organization, *Izvestiia*, March 30, 1968; A. N. Kosygin's speech honoring the one hundredth anniversary of the birth of Gor'kii, ibid., March 31, 1968; editorial, "Powerful Propaganda Resources," *Pravda*, March 22, 1968; Georgii Mariagin, "Together with the Party, the People," *Krasnaia zvezda* (Red Star), April 24, 1968.

[75] "A. Novotny's Resignation," *Pravda*, March 23, 1968.

[76] See "Leaving for Home," *Krasnaia zvezda*, March 22, 1968.

were at work in Prague,[77] and moving to restrict travel between the two countries.[78] Rumania, as previously noted, took no part in the Dresden inquiry, and on March 23 Ceausescu suggested that he was not averse to emulating the Czech example in a modest way, when he said that every Rumanian should be permitted "to express his views freely on the policies of the Communist party."[79] Poland, busy with its own crisis,[80] initially frowned on expressions of solidarity between Polish and Czech students, while the regimes of Hungary and Bulgaria refrained from open disapproval of developments in Czechoslovakia. Of the two, the Hungarians took a somewhat more pliable tack; a leading party official wrote in mid-March that a democratization process was planned in Hungary also, though he cautioned that it could not be carried out in a hurry.[81] Bulgarian officials were less sympathetic to the idea of internal reform, hinting publicly that the Sofia regime was prepared to deal with any "trouble-makers."[82]

Why the Soviet Union maintained a cautious, even temporizing, attitude toward the Czechoslovak situation during the first months of 1968 is not altogether clear. Differences within the Soviet leadership over whether to take a hard or a soft approach may have led to hesitation, but this explanation alone does not fully account for the early months of the year, when Moscow seemed prepared to go along with Dubcek.[83] The careful silence of the Soviet press during this period may have reflected both an effort to isolate the Soviet people from the unrest in East Europe and a prudent decision not to exacerbate that unrest by critical public comment from Moscow. The Soviet leaders may even have hoped to be able to stem the reform movement in Czechoslovakia by bringing about a relatively quiet accommodation between the opposing factions within the Prague leadership, perhaps counting on Dubcek to restrain "extremist" liberal elements and perhaps overestimating the influence retained by the conservative wing of the Czech Communist party. But if the Soviet leaders did begin by hoping that delaying tactics would resolve the Czech problem,

[77] See comments on Czechoslovak development, Neues Deutschland, March 12, 1968; David Binder, "Events in Prague Vex German Reds," New York Times, March 14, 1968.

[78] It was reported at this time that East Germany had confiscated Czechoslovak newspapers and imposed travel restrictions to prevent news of developments under the Dubcek regime from circulating freely in the GDR. AP dispatch, "Acts by East Germany," New York Times, March 24, 1968.

[79] Ceausescu's speech before the party Central Committee, Bucharest radio broadcast, March 23, 1968. See also fn. 54 above.

[80] The Polish crisis is discussed later in this chapter, pp. 366–69.

[81] See Rezso Nyers comments on the impact of economic reforms in Tarsadalmi Szelme, March 1968. See also AP dispatch, "Hungarian Sees 'New Democracy'," Washington Post, March 15, 1968.

[82] See T. Zhivkov's speech on domestic and international developments, Sofia radio broadcast, March 13, 1968.

[83] When Dubcek was elected to succeed Novotny as First Secretary on January 5, for example, Moscow immediately sent him a congratulatory telegram, and various laudatory accounts of the new Czechoslovak leader appeared in the Soviet press, indicating that Moscow then regarded Dubcek as a satisfactory compromise choice with whom they could get along. Although the Soviet leaders later revised their opinion of Dubcek, he was not personally attacked in the violent Soviet press campaign waged against Czechoslovakia in mid-1968 prior to the invasion.

they evidently were disabused of this idea in early April, when the Dubcek regime's new "action program" was adopted.

This program, which was approved in Prague on April 5 at a week-long Central Committee meeting that also ordered sweeping changes in the leadership of both party and government,[84] provided new guarantees of freedom of speech, broader electoral laws, more powers for parliament and the government vis-à-vis the party apparatus, somewhat greater scope for non-Communist groups in Czech political life, and other political and economic reforms.[85] If given more than lip service, these changes would add up to an experiment in the "democratization" of a Communist country more far-reaching than anything on record. While the reforms embodied in the action program clearly made it, in Communist terms, a "revisionist" program, from the viewpoint of the Czech moderates associated with Dubcek its aim could be considered conservative, for it was intended to preserve the rule of the party by tackling creatively the various problems in Czechoslovak life which under Novotny had threatened to undermine the party's leading role. The Soviet leaders, or most of them, evidently did not see it this way, but tended to regard the Czechoslovak experiment as a dangerous departure from orthodoxy that ultimately might threaten the basis of party legitimacy everywhere, the Soviet Union included.[86]

Little wonder, given the orthodox outlook of most of the ruling group in Moscow, that alarm over the liberal reform movement in Czechoslovakia should gradually have persuaded the Soviet leaders of the need for more serious measures to bring it under control—a task most of them evidently felt could no longer be entrusted wholly to the moderate Dubcek leadership itself. Before turning to the active and often contradictory efforts of the Soviet Union to

[84] Among the important appointments to high offices, taking their places alongside Dubcek and President Ludvik Svoboda, were two outspoken reform leaders—Oldrich Cernik as Premier and Josef Smrkovsky as President of the National Assembly. For a full list of the top government appointees, see "Czechoslovaks List New Cabinet; Young Intellectuals in Key Posts," *New York Times*, April 9, 1968.

[85] The action program, contained in a sixty-page document entitled "Czechoslovakia's Road to Socialism," was released in summary form on April 9, although approved five days earlier. For a condensed version of the program, see "Excerpts from Reform Program of the Czech Communist Party," *New York Times*, April 11, 1968. The foreign affairs portion of the program called for encouragement to "realistic forces" in West Germany, reflecting Prague's revised view of the German danger and its hopes for better relations with Bonn—tendencies which doubtless were disturbing to the Soviet Union. This section of the program also called for more Czech influence in developing the "military doctrine of the Warsaw Pact," and adoption by Czechoslovakia of her own position "on fundamental questions of international policy."

Besides the freedoms of press and assembly, a crucial part of the domestic section of the action program concerned the scope to be given the various non-Communist parties and mass organizations grouped together in the National Front. Liberal reformers presumably hoped that the several token non-Communist political parties in the National Front would be allowed to form the basis for a political opposition outside the Communist party, but this was clearly not the intention of Dubcek and his associates. In an interview on April 5 Dubcek made this plain, saying he saw "no reasons" for the existence of opposition parties in the country (Prague radio broadcast, April 6, 1968).

[86] For a perceptive discussion of this question, see Ermarth, *Internationalism, Security, and Legitimacy*, especially pp. 60–61.

stamp out the liberal contagion in Czechoslovakia, let us go back for a moment to the internal crisis which flared up in Poland in the spring of 1968 and which, for a time at least, seemed as though it might serve to channel Polish nationalism in an anti-Soviet direction and perhaps bring about an upheaval parallel to that in Czechoslovakia.

Student Unrest and the Party Power Struggle in Poland

To Poland, a country which twelve years earlier, upon Gomulka's accession to power, had undergone its own briefly euphoric reform experience but then had lapsed back into another restrictive phase under the same leader, the early months of 1968 also brought a new wave of internal ferment, stimulated in part perhaps by events in neighboring Czechoslovakia. Among its first signs was a protest resolution on March 1 by the Polish Writers Union against the government's cultural and censorship policies.[87] This was followed a few days later by an outbreak of student riots at Warsaw University which soon spread to other university cities. Although the immediate incident out of which these protests grew was the closing of a classical Polish play containing certain anti-Russian lines that audiences applauded vigorously,[88] behind them lay the long-smoldering resentment of Polish intellectuals toward the increasingly repressive practices encouraged by a dogmatic faction within the Polish Communist leadership.[89]

The government's response to the student rioting and strikes included vigorous repressive measures by the police and a propaganda campaign blaming the disorders on Zionists, intellectuals, and former Stalinists; a number of officials of Jewish background who were the parents of alleged student ringleaders were dismissed from their jobs.[90] Gomulka, in a speech to the nation about two weeks after the student demonstrations had begun, sought to moderate the anti-Zionist tone of the propaganda campaign to which some of his own subordinates had presumably given official blessing, but he held out no specific promise of reform measures to alleviate the unrest that was abroad in the country.[91]

By the end of March the protesting student groups and liberal intellectuals

[87] See Stephen S. Rosenfeld, "Polish Writers Attack Regime's Cultural Policy," *Washington Post*, March 2, 1968.

[88] The play was *Dziady* (The Forefathers), a work by the nineteenth-century poet Adam Mickiewicz depicting Polish suffering under czarist Russian rule. See Jonathan Randal, "Polish Students in 2d Day of Riots" and "Thousands in Poland Fight Police as Protest Mounts," *New York Times*, March 10 and 12, 1968.

[89] For useful background on the origins of intellectual unrest in Poland, see Jerzy Ptakowski, "Behind the Unrest in Poland," *East Europe* (April 1968): 5–11; Joseph Helder, "Poland: A Realm of Frustration," *Interplay* (January 1968): 16–18; A. Ross Johnson, "Poland: The End of the Post-October Era," *Survey* (July 1968): 87–98; "Documents: Poland," ibid., pp. 99–117.

[90] See, for example, commentary in *Zycie Warszawy, Trybuna Mazowiecka*, and "In Our Opinion," *Kurier Polski*, March 16, 1968. See also "4th Official Ousted in Unrest in Poland; Gomulka To Speak," *New York Times*, March 19, 1968.

[91] Gomulka's address to the Warsaw Party *Aktiv*, Warsaw radio broadcast, March 19, 1968. See also Jonathan Randal, "Gomulka Seeks To Quiet Drive Against 'Zionists'," *New York Times*, March 20, 1968.

opposing the policies of the Gomulka regime appeared to have been fairly well isolated,[92] with a good deal less support from working-class elements of the population and less access to the corridors of power than in the parallel case of Czechoslovakia. The Soviet leadership, which had kept studiously silent toward the Polish unrest, perhaps on the theory that a "low profile" was the best insurance against the release of any latent anti-Soviet element in the situation as well as to protect its own people from the infection of rebellion, apparently began to breathe a little easier. On March 22 the Soviet public finally learned of Poland's student disorders, along with the explanation provided by Gomulka's speech several days earlier that they had been stirred up by "anti-Soviet agitators."[93]

From the Soviet viewpoint, the fact that the student revolt had collapsed without arousing wide popular support for reform reduced any immediate concern that a second Czechoslovakia was in the making. Although there was always the possibility—given a Polish populace in which strong anti-Russian sentiments slumbered—that a crisis stemming from the suppression of nationalist feelings offensive to the Soviet Union might take a turn unwelcome to Moscow, this danger, too, seemed to have been alleviated by the Gomulka regime's handling of the situation. In addition to Gomulka's own strong reassertion of Poland's close ties with the Soviet Union, attention had been diverted from potential Soviet–Polish discord during the March unrest by a Polish propaganda line which stressed that demands for reform could weaken Poland's stand against the revanchist aims of a West Germany still bent upon robbing Poland of the Oder–Neisse territories.[94]

From Gomulka's own standpoint, however, the March disorders represented something more than an abortive protest against his regime from frustrated intellectuals and students. They also served as the cover, and in part the pretext, for a challenge to his leadership from within party ranks.[95] Whether this was merely a power struggle among potential contenders for his post, if and when he should choose to step down, or an active effort to unseat him was not at first altogether clear, although charges were aired during the factional in-

[92] After some two weeks of turmoil, student sit-ins in Warsaw were at least temporarily abandoned before a show of militia force on March 23. See "Warsaw Students End Sit-in Protests," *Washington Post*, March 24, 1968.

[93] "Comrade Gomulka's Speech at Warsaw *Aktiv* Meeting," *Pravda*, March 22, 1968.

[94] See, for example, commentary in the Polish army daily, *Zolnierz Wolnosci*, Warsaw radio broadcast, March 16, 1968; speech by Jan Szydlak, First Secretary of the Poznan Voivodship Party Committee, Warsaw radio broadcast, March 16, 1968; "Unruffled by Being Alert," *Zolnierz Wolnosci*, March 17, 1968. Incidentally, some of the steam was taken out of the Polish contention by Brandt's curiously well-timed statement at Nuremberg on March 18 calling for West German recognition of the Oder–Neisse boundary. Although Brandt's words did not amount to an official shift of Bonn's position, they opened the possibility that a traditional obstacle to improvement of Polish–West German relations might be coming down.

[95] Jonathan Randal, "Polish Unrest Is Seen as Pretext for an Intensified Power Struggle for Dominance in Party" and "Poland's Troubles," *New York Times*, March 19 and 24, 1968. For background on factionalism within the Polish Communist leadership, see A. Ross Johnson, in *Survey* (July 1968): 91–98; Hansjakob Stelle, "Polish Communism," in William E. Griffith, ed., *Communism in Europe* (Cambridge, Mass.: M.I.T. Press, 1965), vol. 1, pp. 85–176.

fighting in March that a coup d'état against his leadership had been in preparation.[96]

At least three factions within the party leadership seem to have been involved in the triangular struggle for power which came to the surface during the spring ferment in Poland. The first was the older group of men around Gomulka himself. The second, led by General Mieczyslaw Moczar, Minister of the Interior and head of the secret police, was the so-called "Partisan" faction, a hard-line group with an ultranationalist, anti-Zionist tinge. The third group consisted of younger, potentially reformist elements advocating technological progress, whose most influential spokesman was Edward Gierek, provincial party boss in industrial Silesia. We cannot here go into the details of the internal struggle among these groups. Suffice it to say that in the purge of middle-echelon officials and in other personnel shifts that went on in the summer of 1968[97] Gomulka managed to retain his authority, although Moczar gained some ground in a party reshuffle in July.[98] Subsequently, at the Fifth Party Congress, in November 1968, Gomulka's leadership again won at least temporary endorsement.[99]

As seen from Moscow, the party struggle in Poland was probably somewhat disturbing, for neither of the factions maneuvering against Gomulka seemed likely to prove as reliable in support of Soviet interests as that veteran sixty-four-year-old leader had been.[100] Moreover, Moscow could hardly have wel-

[96] This charge was made in the March 24, 1968, issue of *Prawo i Zycie* by Kazimierz Kakol, a journalist generally regarded as the mouthpiece of General Mieczyslaw Moczar, Minister of the Interior and himself a contender for Gomulka's mantle. Kakol attributed the alleged coup attempt to "a conspiratorial group connected with the Zionist center," although some observers have interpreted the Kakol piece as part of a devious maneuver by Moczar to divert attention from his own plans. See Jan Nowak, "The Struggle for Party Control in Poland," *East Europe* (June 1968): 2–3.

[97] Among shifts of important officials close to Gomulka was the resignation of Edward Ochab as Chairman of the Council of State and his replacement by Marshal Marian Spychalski in April 1968. Spychalski's post of Minister of Defense was taken in turn by General Wojciech Jaruzelski, a professional soldier apparently not involved in the domestic political in-fighting. By putting the military establishment in his hands, Gomulka presumably kept it out of the hands of a Moczar supporter, thus thwarting the latter's effort to extend his own control.

[98] At a two-day Central Committee plenum in July 1968, Moczar was elected to the party Secretariat and made a candidate member of the Politburo, marking a double-step up the ladder for this fifty-four-year-old rival of Gomulka. See Reuters dispatch, "Moczar Gets 2 Posts in Polish Party Shift," *Washington Post*, July 10, 1968.

[99] It had been expected that General Moczar might be moved up to full Politburo membership at the November Party Congress, and that other leadership changes might bring a dilution of Gomulka's authority. However, Moczar was denied further promotion and Gomulka's position as party chief was reaffirmed at the Congress, which was attended by a Soviet delegation headed by Brezhnev. Among Polish leaders demoted at the Congress was Adam Rapacki, the onetime prominent foreign minister, who was dropped from the Politburo. See Jonathan Randal, "Power Struggle in Poland Remains Inconclusive," *New York Times*, October 31, 1968; idem, "Gomulka Retains Party Leadership," ibid., November 17, 1968.

[100] The Partisan factional group organized around Moczar had its origins among World War II partisan members who stayed behind in Poland, as distinct from the Polish Communist elements who sat out most of the war in the Soviet Union and became known as "Muscovites." Besides some historical tension between the Partisan and Muscovite factions, the ultranationalist bent of the Partisans—sometimes regarded as a crypto-Fascist outlook—might well produce an anti-Soviet orientation were they to come to power. The younger technocrats and progressives grouped behind

comed any instability in Poland's leadership that stemmed from an inner party fight at a time when East Europe was in the throes of uncertainty created by the upheaval in Czechoslovakia. So long as Gomulka kept his hold on power, however, these concerns were not overriding. In the mid-months of 1968, as the problem of dealing with the Czechoslovak heresy rose to the top of Moscow's agenda, Gomulka's Poland proved a co-operative partner by lining up with the Soviet Union's effort to use the Warsaw Pact as an instrument of collective pressure upon the Dubcek regime.

New Pressures on Prague and the July Crisis

In early April, after a brief relaxation of tensions following the Dresden meeting, the Soviet Union displayed its first open disapproval of Prague's new course. On April 12, a few days after a CPSU plenum in Moscow had sounded the alarm about new threats of "subversion" from the West,[101] *Pravda* for the first time condemned "rightist excesses" that allegedly were showing up in Prague.[102] A hasty trip to Moscow in early May by Dubcek (who among other things sought, unsuccessfully, to obtain a hard-currency loan from the Soviet Union[103]) apparently failed to reassure the Soviet leadership that the process of democratization in Czechoslovakia was fully under control, for on May 6, upon his return to Prague, Dubcek disclosed that the Soviet leaders had "expressed anxiety" on this score.[104] At this point, as if to underline the Soviet Union's growing impatience with liberalizing trends in Czechoslovakia, a meeting of hard-core Warsaw Pact allies was convened in Moscow to discuss the Czech situation.[105] At the same time, Soviet propaganda stepped up its

Gierek, while not notable advocates of "democratization" in the Czech sense, were mostly interested in pragmatic solutions to Poland's economic problems. Their less doctrinaire outlook might lead them to seek wider contacts with the West, away from Poland's close ties with the Soviet Union. For background on the history of these factional groupings, see J. F. Brown, *The New Eastern Europe* (New York: Frederick A. Praeger, Inc., 1966), pp. 50–64.

[101] See chapter XI, pp. 254–55.

[102] "The March–April Plenum of CC Czech CP," *Pravda*, April 12, 1968. This account of the Czech Central Committee plenum which adopted the new "action program" withheld criticism of the program itself, but cast doubt on the ability of the Czech leadership to keep the reform movement under control. Perhaps the first harsh critique of developments in Czechoslovakia to appear publicly in the Soviet Union was an article in *Sovetskaia Rossiia* (Soviet Russia) on April 4, 1968, in which it was asserted that "nationalism" and "revisionism" in Prague posed a threat to the unity of the Communist camp.

[103] See Anatole Shub, "Czech–Russian Sessions End Coolly," *Washington Post*, May 6, 1968. See also fn. 109 below.

[104] See Dubcek interview on May 6, *Rude Pravo*, May 7, 1968. On May 8, *Pravda* quoted Dubcek to convey to the Soviet public that official concern over Czechoslovak developments was now felt at the highest level in Moscow.

[105] Party leaders from the GDR, Poland, Bulgaria, and Hungary met in Moscow on May 8 in what was evidently a new phase of the Soviet effort to mount collective pressures upon Prague. See "Arrival in Moscow of Leaders of Fraternal Parties," *Pravda*, May 9, 1968. It was reported at this time that the Hungarian leadership sought to moderate the stand toward Prague urged by such hard-line Pact leaders as Ulbricht and Gomulka, a report made credible by the generally sympathetic attitude of Kadar, as displayed publicly during Dubcek's visit to Budapest in June. Later in the summer, as the collective squeeze on Prague tightened, the Hungarian leadership also shifted, though perhaps with some reluctance, to a tougher stance. See "Prague Warned," *Washington Post*, July 4, 1968; speeches of L. I. Brezhnev and Janos Kadar, in *Pravda*, July 4, 1968.

attacks around the general theme that activities by "antisocialist" elements in Czechoslovakia were being exploited by the West to sow discord within the Warsaw bloc.[106]

Despite the increasing severity of Soviet propaganda assaults upon Prague in mid-May, there was some indication that the Soviet leadership was not of a single mind on shifting to an undiluted hard-line approach to the Czech problem. This was perhaps best brought out by Kosygin's surprise arrival in Czechoslovakia on May 17 for a ten-day "work-and-cure" sojourn at Karlovy Vary, concurrent with the appearance in Prague of a Soviet military delegation under Marshal Grechko for a six-day round of conversations with Czech defense officials. The seemingly conciliatory nature of Kosygin's visit, which the Czechs said had been arranged at short notice on his initiative,[107] suggested that at least some elements of the Soviet leadership were still hopeful that Dubcek could be prevailed upon to assert stricter party control over the reform movement, and thus spare the Soviet Union the onus of having to crack the whip itself.[108]

While Kosygin was still taking the waters at Karlovy Vary, and presumably trying through personal diplomacy to persuade Dubcek to muzzle the increasingly outspoken Czech press and otherwise to set his house in order,[109] it was announced simultaneously in Moscow and Prague in late May that Warsaw Pact maneuvers would take place on Czechoslovak territory in June under the

[106] See, for example, Mikhail Alekseev commentary in *Literaturnaia gazeta,* May 15, 1968; editorial, "Charters of Brotherhood," *Izvestiia,* May 18, 1968. Similarly, in an article on the Warsaw Pact, Marshal Iakubovskii warned of Western "subversive" activities and "bridge-building" efforts aimed at driving a wedge into "the combat alliance" of the Warsaw Pact countries. (*Krasnaia zvezda,* May 14, 1968.) Other issues over which a sharp increase in polemics arose at this time included the Czech investigation into Jan Masaryk's death and a Soviet article by M. Shirianov in *Sovetskaia Rossiia* of May 14, attacking the alleged crimes of Thomas Masaryk which aroused indignation in Prague.

[107] Prague radio broadcast, May 17, 1968. Kosygin apparently decided to pick up an invitation which had been extended to him earlier by Dubcek. The possibility that a dogmatist faction in the Soviet Union may have attempted to prejudice the climate for Kosygin's visit by publication of the Shirianov article attacking Thomas Masaryk has been suggested by some analysts. See "USSR Attitudes to Czechoslovakia, May 13th–19th," *Radio Free Europe,* May 22, 1968.

[108] In this connection, although the Moscow propaganda apparatus toned down its attacks on Prague during the Kosygin visit, it pursued one line suggesting that the Soviets were still hopeful of encouraging "healthy forces" in Czechoslovakia to take a hand in restoring Communist authority if Dubcek should falter. Specifically, on May 22 a Moscow radio broadcast cited approvingly a resolution adopted by a Prague People's Militia group to the effect that "we will not allow a disruption of our socialist system." The People's Militia, commonly regarded as a stronghold of support for the orthodox party outlook in Czechoslovakia, subsequently became the object of more direct Soviet appeals to take up battle against "counterrevolutionary forces" in Czechoslovakia. See p. 373.

[109] The Kosygin visit took place at a time when Prague was increasingly troubled by Soviet foot-dragging on the Czech request for a hard currency loan of 400–500 million gold rubles, as indicated by a Prague radio broadcast of May 16, 1968. It may be surmised that Kosygin expected the Czech need for a loan to serve as bargaining leverage for curbs on the reform movement, but that the terms he set were too steep for Dubcek's taste. For the Czechs, there was doubtless bitter irony in the fact that Moscow refused to help out with a hard currency loan, despite Czechoslovakia's having previously granted the Soviet Union credits worth a half billion dollars for development of extractive industry in the USSR. See Burks, *The Decline of Communism in Czechoslovakia,* p. 4.

command of Marshal Iakubovskii.[110] Czech agreement to these maneuvers, apparently extracted during the Grechko delegation's Prague visit,[111] proved later to have been a tactical error, for the maneuvers permitted the introduction of Soviet troops into Czechoslovakia and gave the Soviet Union a major instrument of pressure for the climactic phase of the war of nerves against the Dubcek regime which was to unfold in July.

Before we come to the July crisis, however, a few intervening developments in the contest of wills between the Dubcek regime and the Soviet leadership deserve mention. At the end of May, immediately after Kosygin's return to Moscow, a three-day Central Committee plenum was held in Prague, evidently to weigh whatever propositions the Soviet leader had advanced for settling the conflict. The results were a setback for Moscow and a victory for the Czech progressives, who won endorsement for convoking an extraordinary party congress in September 1968, two years ahead of schedule—a move which Moscow had opposed for fear that it would result in the removal of the remaining "orthodox" members from the top echelons of the party in Prague.[112] The plenum also made known that implementation of the action program would proceed without delay, although it again gave notice that no opposition parties would be tolerated.[113]

In Moscow a two-week period of hesitation ensued, during which the Soviet leadership apparently reached a consensus to tighten the screws on Prague a few more turns, for on June 14 a new barrage of anti-reform propaganda opened with a *Pravda* article in which Academician F. Konstantinov attacked Cestmir Cisar, a secretary of the Czech Central Committee, as a revisionist.[114] Although the German Democratic Republic, in its own heated polemics with Prague, had already launched personal diatribes against a number of prominent

110 See "Mutual Maneuvers," *Krasnaia zvezda*, May 25, 1968.

111 In a May 21 interview on Prague radio and television, the new Czech defense minister, General Martin Dzur, stated that the question of maneuvers in Czechoslovakia on a "reduced scale" had been discussed during the Grechko visit. A day later, Dzur denied that there was any basis for Western press reports that the Soviet Union also raised the question of stationing 11–12,000 Warsaw Pact troops as a permanent garrison in Czechoslovakia. Despite Dzur's denial, it seems plausible that at some point during this period the Soviets may have proposed the permanent stationing of Soviet troops in Bohemia, ostensibly to stiffen Warsaw Pact defenses along the Czechoslovak–West German border, but also to gain greater political leverage against Prague. A similar Soviet desire to put Soviet troops in Czechoslovakia had, according to long-standing rumor, previously been rebuffed by the Novotny regime, and therefore was hardly likely to be palatable to the Dubcek regime.

112 Although alignments within the Czech party leadership could hardly be specified with precision, it was generally felt that about one-third of the 169 Central Committee members consisted of firm Dubcek supporters, about one-third of orthodox conservatives, and the remainder of waverers. The decision to convoke the Fourteenth Party Congress on September 9, 1968, seemed to augur a cleaning out of the conservative faction before it could muster enough strength for a comeback, hence the Soviet disapproval.

113 The text of the proclamation to party members and all the people, issued by the Czechoslovak Communist Party Central Committee on June 1, was broadcast by Prague Domestic Service, June 1, 1968. See also "Czech Reds Promise Safeguards, Plan Congress," *Washington Post*, June 2, 1968; report of Alexander Dubcek to Brno *Aktiv*, Prague Domestic Service, June 3, 1968.

114 F. Konstantinov, "Marxism–Leninism—The Only International Doctrine," *Pravda*, June 14, 1968.

Czechoslovak figures,[115] the Konstantinov article was the first from Moscow to single out a high Czech official for criticism. It was followed, in the latter part of June, by even more vituperative attacks on Czech reformers,[116] while mass meetings of factory workers were organized throughout the Soviet Union to pledge support to the People's Militia and other "healthy forces" in Czechoslovakia.[117]

At this juncture, two developments bearing upon the Czech democratization process occurred in Prague. On June 27, the National Assembly voted to abolish censorship, formalizing one of the key promises of the party's action program. That same day a manifesto entitled "2000 Words," written by Ludvik Vaculik and signed by seventy prominent scientists, artists, athletes, and other public figures, was published in several Prague papers.[118] This document, which called for a radical speed-up of the reform program by grass-roots action, was deplored by some Prague party leaders, including Dubcek,[119] but it seemed to confirm Soviet forebodings about what could be expected once the Czech censorship apparatus had been dismantled.

If any single turning point in the Soviet response to the Czechoslovak challenge during the first six months of 1968 can be identified, it probably came at this time, for from the early days of July throughout the remainder of the month Moscow mounted a steadily intensified war of nerves against the Dubcek regime, against the backdrop of military moves which first implied that the Soviet Union was preparing for armed intervention should the Czechs persist on their democratization course. As the first step in this heavy-handed phase of pressure against Prague, Moscow delayed the departure of its troops from Czechoslovakia upon completion of the joint Warsaw Pact exercises on

[115] Among prominent Czech supporters of the reform movement attacked by the East German press were Professors Antonin Snejdarek and Jindrich Filipec. For typical GDR diatribes against Czech reformers, to which Prague made strong ripostes, see Kurt Hager's speech to a philosophy congress on Marx, in *Neues Deutschland*, March 27, 1968; H. H. Angermueller, G. Kroeber, and J. Streisand, "Prof. Snejdarek and the European Concept of F. J. Strauss," ibid., May 11, 1968; Helmut Baierl addressing "Some Authors in the Czechoslovak Socialist Republic," ibid., May 12, 1968; Dr. Hajo Herbell, "Bonn Between Fear and Hope," ibid., May 24, 1968.

[116] On June 21, for example, two well-known Czech liberals, Alexander Kramer and Ivan Svitak, were attacked for advocating reforms which would "allow full freedom for political demagogy" and undermine the party's leading role. Gr. Ognev, "What Does 'The Student' Teach?" *Komsomol'skaia pravda*, June 21, 1968. See also V. Platkovskii, "The Major Force in the Struggle for Communism," *Izvestiia*, June 25, 1968.

[117] "Strengthen Fraternal Unity," *Izvestiia*, June 27, 1968.

[118] For text of the "2000 Words" manifesto by Ludvik Vaculik, a popular Czech novelist, see *East Europe* (August 1968): 25–28. In addition to being widely published in the Czech daily press, the manifesto also appeared in *Literarni Listy*, weekly organ of the Czech writers' union and a vocal supporter of the reform movement. See also "Czech Aide Urges Tougher Stand on Those Opposing Reforms," *Washington Post*, July 6, 1968; Anatole Shub, "Soviet Journal Decries Liberal Czech Appeal," ibid., July 11, 1968.

[119] Dubcek on June 27 referred to a Czech party Presidium statement issued immediately after the appearance of "2000 Words," censuring the document for trying to push the pace of democratization too rapidly. Some other Czech officials, however, including Premier Oldrich Cernik and National Front chairman Frantisek Kriegel, expressed a more moderate view of the document. Henry Kamm, "Prague Spurns Plea for a Drastic Purge," *New York Times*, June 29, 1968.

June 30. Using a variety of flimsy pretexts, including a reported finding by Marshal Iakubovskii that the exercises showed Czech troops to be incapable of manning their defenses against West Germany without the presence of outside help,[120] the Soviet Union kept a sizable force in the Czech countryside, much to the embarrassment of Czechoslovak authorities, who repeatedly announced that the Soviet troops were to be withdrawn "without delay."[121]

On July 11, following Dubcek's rejection of a peremptory summons to attend a Warsaw bloc summit meeting in Poland on the Czechoslovak situation,[122] Moscow sounded another stern warning to Prague with the publication of a *Pravda* article by I. Aleksandrov which not only attacked the "2000 Words" manifesto as evidence of "the activation of right wing and counterrevolutionary forces in Czechoslovakia" but, more ominous still, laid down essentially the same rationale for intervention as that used in Hungary in 1956.[123] Then, on July 15, the Soviet Union and its four most orthodox Warsaw bloc partners, in a joint letter couched in almost brutal language, delivered what amounted to an ultimatum to the Dubcek leadership to mend its ways or face the conse-

---

[120] Warsaw dispatch, "Poor Showing Held Cause," *New York Times*, July 17, 1968. According to Professor John Erickson of the University of Manchester, England, the Soviet general staff had already concluded, after previous joint exercises, that Czechoslovak forces would be unable to contain a conventional NATO attack, and had therefore raised the question of introducing Soviet forces permanently along the Bavarian border. See statement of Erickson's views in R. T. Rockingham Gill, "Europe's Military Balance After Czechoslovakia," *East Europe* (October 1968): 19. See also fn. 111 above.

[121] On July 10, Czech Defense Minister Martin Dzur said that 35 per cent of the Warsaw Pact forces engaged in the June maneuvers had left Czech soil, and that the remainder—which apparently included all of the Soviet forces involved—would be withdrawn without delay. How many Soviet troops were present was never accurately established. "Authoritative" Czech sources were reported to have named a figure of 16,000, while other estimates ranged from 6,000 to 24,000. The first of these Soviet troops began to leave Czechoslovakia on July 13, according to Prague, but their departure was halted the next day. Thereafter, throughout July, despite several announcements by Czech spokesmen giving deadlines for their withdrawal, most of the Soviet troops apparently stayed on. See "Prague Uncertain on Soviet Troops," *New York Times*, July 11, 1968; "Soviet Troops Start Leaving Czech Soil," *Washington Post*, July 14, 1968; Henry Kamm, "Soviet Troop Withdrawal Halted in Czechoslovakia," *New York Times*, July 15, 1968; idem, "Russian Forces Seem To Put Off Leaving Slovakia," ibid., July 22, 1968. See also fn. 130 below.

[122] Separate letters were sent to Prague during the first week in July by the Central committees of the Soviet, Polish, East German, Bulgarian, and Hungarian parties, demanding that the Czechoslovak leaders attend a joint meeting in Warsaw to explain why they had not dealt more firmly with "counterrevolutionary" elements. The Czechs declined this summons, but offered to hold bilateral meetings with each of the other parties. See Henry Kamm, "Prague Bars Call for Bloc Parley" and "Prague To Offer Bilateral Talks on Reform Steps," *New York Times*, July 10 and 12, 1968.

[123] I. Aleksandrov, "The Attack Against the Socialist Foundations of Czechoslovakia," *Pravda*, July 11, 1968. In 1956 the rationale advanced for Soviet intervention in Hungary had been that "counterrevolutionary" elements supported by the West were threatening the "foundations of the socialist order" in a fraternal country, whose "true patriots" had rallied to face this "mortal danger" and called upon the Soviet Union for assistance. (See, for example, *Pravda*, October 28, November 4, 1956.) The Aleksandrov article not only pictured Czechoslovakia as similarly threatened, but made the parallel explicit by charging that the tactics of those plotting to overthrow socialism in Czechoslovakia were the same as those previously used by "counterrevolutionary" elements in Hungary who attempted to undermine the Hungarian people's socialist achievements in 1956."

quences.[124] Spelling out the dangers to Communist rule posed by the Czech reform movement, the letter enjoined the party leadership in Prague to reimpose control over mass media, to suppress all "anti-socialist" forces and organizations, and to observe the principles of Marxism–Leninism and "democratic centralism." It also invoked an appeal to "healthy forces" in the country, such as the People's Militia, to "mobilize" for "battle against the counter-revolutionary forces in order to preserve and consolidate socialism in Czecho-slovakia." But the letter's central message seemed to be that the Soviet Union, with the assent of at least its hard-core Warsaw allies,[125] would no longer hesitate to intervene as it saw fit in the internal affairs of Czechoslovakia, for by fiat these affairs had now become the business of Prague's Communist neighbors. Said the letter:

> This is no longer your affair alone.... We shall never agree to having imperialism, by peaceful and non-peaceful methods, making a breach in the socialist systems, from inside or outside, and transforming power relations in Europe to its own advantage.

Upon the heels of this letter, which was followed by a demand from Moscow for an immediate meeting of the full Soviet Politburo and the Czecho-slovak Presidium on Soviet soil,[126] several menacing new moves set the stage for intervention. One of these, discussed in a previous chapter, was the "revelation" on July 19 of the alleged discovery of arms caches and secret documents "proving" that American and West German agencies were conspiring to aid subversive and counterrevolutionary elements in organizing uprisings in Czechoslovakia.[127] Another was the announcement on July 23 that Soviet forces were engaged in extensive maneuvers all along the western frontiers of the USSR, including the border with Czechoslovakia.[128] Shortly thereafter it was

[124] The July 15 joint letter by the Soviet, East German, Polish, Bulgarian, and Hungarian Communist parties was delivered to Prague on July 16, 1968. It was published in Moscow on July 18. For the texts of this letter and the Czechoslovak reply of July 18 disputing its charges, see *New York Times*, July 19, 1968.

[125] It was generally believed that Hungary, though a cosigner of the five-party letter of July 15, was not altogether enthusiastic about the squeeze being applied to the Dubcek regime. See, for example, "Current Developments," *East Europe* (August 1968): 35.

[126] On July 18 the Soviet Union made public a message to the Communist Party Presidium of Czechoslovakia demanding that the top ruling bodies of both Communist parties meet on July 22 or 23 in Moscow, or alternatively in Kiev or Lvov. This summons for a gathering of the full membership of the Politburo and Presidium was unprecedented. See "To the Central Committee of the Communist Party of Czechoslovakia," *Pravda*, July 18, 1968.

[127] In the opinion of many Western observers, including this writer, the turning point indicating that the Soviet Union might in fact be on the verge of repeating its military intervention of 1956 in Hungary came with Soviet disclosure of alleged "evidence" purported to reveal "the perfidious plans of American imperialism and West German revanchism" to assist "insurgent elements" in East Europe and Czechoslovakia. See "The Defense of Socialism Is Our Common Task," *Krasnaia zvezda*, July 19, 1968; "Documents of Great Urgency" and "Arms Caches on Czech Territory," ibid., July 21, 1968; V. Ragulin and I. Chushkov, "Adventurist Plans of the Pentagon and CIA," *Pravda*, July 19, 1968.

[128] "Rear Services Exercises," *Izvestiia*, July 24, 1968. These maneuvers, nicknamed "Nemen" and originally said to involve personnel of regular army units and reservists in logistics exercises

made known that East German and Polish troops also were co-operating in the exercises;[129] at the same time there were reports that Soviet forces stationed in these countries and in Hungary were moving closer to Czechoslovakia, within whose borders other Soviet troops were still encamped.[130] Finally, to ensure that Prague would get the message, *Pravda* published letters from two groups of Czech factory workers asserting that the presence of Soviet troops in Czechoslovakia would make "every honest man feel more secure in his work," while an article in the Soviet press recalled the welcome extended to the Soviet forces that liberated Czechoslovakia from German occupation in 1945.[131]

Presumably, as the last days of July approached and the world became uncomfortably aware that a momentous new crisis had arrived, Moscow counted upon the Czech leadership's nerves to crack under the strain. They did not. Apart from what appeared to be a minor concession or two, such as the "demotion" of a defense official who had openly criticized Soviet domination of the Warsaw Pact military setup,[132] the Dubcek regime held firm, winning

---

along the USSR's western borders, were scheduled to last until August 10. An unusual amount of publicity was given the "Nemen" maneuvers, including several interviews with General Sergei S. Mariakhin, logistics chief of the Soviet armed forces and commander of the exercises, who described them on one occasion as the "largest" of their kind ever held in the Soviet Union. On another occasion he stated that simulated nuclear attacks were a part of the maneuvers, and it was also announced that major air exercises, named "Sky Shield," were carried out in conjunction with the war games. All of this tended to draw attention to the flexing of Soviet military muscle at a time when a showdown meeting with the Czechs was approaching. See Lt. Col. V. Andrianov, "They Inspect the Field," and "Kilometers of Courage," *Krasnaia zvezda*, July 25 and 31, 1968, respectively; Col. P. Kniazev and Lt. Col. V. Zaivorodinskii, "The Duty of Those Who Go in First," ibid., July 28, 1968; V. Gol'tsev, "On the Military Skill of the Expert," *Izvestiia*, July 30, 1968. For a later Soviet account of the "Nemen" and "Sky Shield" exercises, see *Soviet Military Review*, no. 9 (September 1968): 22.

[129] On July 29, the day when the confrontation at Cierna began, the Soviet Union disclosed that East German and Polish troops had joined in the border maneuvers. TASS International Service, Moscow radio broadcast, July 29, 1968; "At the Rear Services Exercises," *Krasnaia zvezda*, July 31, 1968.

[130] The number of Soviet troops still within Czechoslovakia was uncertain; some accounts gave a figure of around 8,000 out of the original force which had entered the country in June. See Raymond H. Anderson, "Moscow Continues Prague Pressure," *New York Times*, July 28, 1968; Richard Eder, "A Tense Test of Will," ibid.; "Soviet Troops in Germany Are Reported on Alert," ibid., July 30, 1968; "Prague Reported Tense: Soviet Troops on Move," *Washington Post*, July 30, 1968; "Red Bloc Forces Near Czech Border," ibid., July 31, 1968; Richard B. Stolley, "The Tense Watch on the Red Army," *Life*, August 2, 1968, pp. 24–27; James H. Billington, "Czech Stand: Beaver Against Rhinoceros," ibid., pp. 28–28C. See also fn. 121 above.

[131] Letter of Czechoslovak Workers, "We Look to Our Friends," *Pravda*, July 30, 1968; Lt. Col. A. Dudko, "Greetings, Friends," *Krasnaia zvezda*, July 30, 1968.

[132] The official was Lt. Gen. Vaclav Prchlik, head of the military department of the Central Committee, whose call for a basic revision of the Warsaw Pact in a July 15 interview, sharply criticized by the Soviet Union, led to the abolishment of his post and his assignment to "other duties" on July 25. Subsequently, Czech liberals rallied to Prchlik's defense, and, following the Cierna–Bratislava meetings, a partial step toward clearing his name was taken when on August 9 a previous government statement rebuking him was repudiated. However, conservatives in the Czech Defense Ministry's Military Council struck back on August 15, reaffirming the previous rebuke to Prchlik and criticizing him for allegedly having disclosed secret information about the Warsaw Pact military structure. It thus appeared that the Prchlik case had become one of several focal points of controversy between conservative and reform-minded groups. See Henry Kamm, "Czechs Demand a Basic Revision of Warsaw Pact," *New York Times*, July 16, 1968; "Whom Does General V. Prchlik Satisfy?" *Krasnaia zvezda*, July 23, 1968.

the first round of the July crisis by successfully insisting that a showdown meeting with the Soviet Politburo be held at Cierna, on Czechoslovak soil.[133]

What is more, as the crisis entered its second round at Cierna on July 29, it became apparent that Moscow's heavy-handed methods had backfired, causing the party in Czechoslovakia to close ranks behind Dubcek and unifying the country as a whole in solid support of his regime.[134] This national rallying around the beleagured party leadership, which the Soviet leaders must have regarded with a mixture of chagrin, envy, and respect, was probably a key factor in the showdown at Cierna, together with warnings to Moscow by Ceausescu, Tito, and a number of West European Communist leaders against trying to bludgeon the Czechs into submission.[135]

The display of internal Czechoslovak solidarity upset any Soviet hopes of splitting the Prague leadership and finding within its ranks a group of men more amenable to Moscow's bidding than Dubcek and his close associates.[136] The warnings from other Communist parties, on the other hand, served notice on the Soviet Union that an attempt to force the Czechs to submit to its dictate might tear the Communist movement wide open and torpedo the world conference of parties scheduled for the following November. Temporarily, at least, the Soviet effort to bring the Czechs to heel faltered before these obstacles. After a tense four-day confrontation at Cierna, the Soviet leaders backed down, ordering withdrawal of their troops from Czechoslovakia and dropping for the time being the more blatant demands of the July 15 letter.[137]

[133] Soviet agreement to meet the Czechoslovak leaders on the latter's territory was disclosed on July 22. At the time, it was indicated that the entire eleven-member Politburo would attend the meeting, which would have marked the first simultaneous absence of the top ruling oligarchs from the USSR. As it turned out, two Politburo members stayed behind, D. S. Polianskii and A. P. Kirilenko. See "The Forthcoming Soviet–Czechoslovak Meeting," *Pravda*, July 23, 1968. See also Raymond H. Anderson, "Soviet Politburo Yields to Prague on a Parley Site," *New York Times*, July 23, 1968.

[134] Typical of the backing given the party leadership was a manifesto published by *Literarni Listy* on July 26, which was widely circulated among Czech citizens as a petition pledging the country's support for a firm stand in the Cierna talks. For its text, see *New York Times*, July 27, 1968.

[135] While the rallying of Rumania's Ceausescu and Yugoslavia's Tito behind Prague may have given the Soviet leaders momentary pause, it also may have strengthened Soviet suspicions that a new version of the Little Entente was rapidly coming into being, with potentially disruptive implications for Soviet hegemony in East Europe. A revival of Czech–Rumanian–Yugoslav ties also would have had unpleasant connotations for Hungary, against which the original Little Entente historically was aimed, thus perhaps persuading Kadar to look somewhat less benevolently upon developments in Czechoslovakia.

[136] The Soviet press later asserted that there had been a split in the Czech leadership at Cierna between a minority of "right-wing revisionists" led by Dubcek and a majority favoring a "principled line" against "anti-socialist forces" in Czechoslovakia, but this apparently was largely an attempt to uphold the Soviet contention that "healthy" forces within the country had finally found it necessary to call for Soviet help. See "Defense of Socialism Is the Highest International Duty," *Pravda*, August 22, 1968.

[137] The brief and uninformative communiqué issued at the close of the Cierna meeting on August 1 gave no indication of what agreements were reached, but it was generally regarded as an armistice document, signifying a Soviet backdown from the demands of the five-party letter of July 15 in exchange for exercise of "self-restraint" by the Czech reformers. For the full text of the communiqué, see *Washington Post*, August 2, 1968.

Thus, the July crisis ended, as was confirmed on August 3 at Bratislava, where the leaders of the Soviet Union and of its four orthodox Warsaw Pact partners met with the Czechs to endorse the truce agreed on at Cierna. The Bratislava communiqué, while somewhat more wordy than the cryptic Cierna announcement, was couched in broad platitudes which told little about any specific understandings reached.[138] It was a document which the Czechs could interpret as a license to continue their reform program on a circumspect basis, while the other parties could regard it as a Czech commitment to restrain the reform movement and as a reaffirmation of Warsaw bloc solidarity. On the face of things, however, the outcome of the Cierna and Bratislava meetings seemed to signify that Prague had successfully defied the power and authority of the Soviet Union.

A Short-Lived Truce

Soviet spokesmen sought to salvage something from the collapse of the effort to intimidate Prague by asserting that the Cierna–Bratislava compromise was proof that the members of the Warsaw alliance were able to settle their differences in a "fraternal" manner.[139] But throughout the world it was generally felt that the July confrontation had produced a serious setback for the Soviet Union. True, some observers cautioned that the Soviet leaders had driven a hard bargain with Dubcek without giving up the continuing threat of intervention if he should let things get out of hand;[140] however, the prevailing impression was that the world had witnessed another David-over-Goliath victory. If we thought this was the last chapter in the contest of wills between Prague and Moscow, many deemed it likely that the Dubcek regime had at least won a breathing spell, for the Soviet leaders—having brandished the threat of military intervention and then backed away—presumably were not prepared to repeat this crisis scenario immediately.

From the Soviet viewpoint there were certainly good arguments for honoring the Cierna–Bratislava truce until at least after the scheduled world party conference in Moscow, the success of which would depend in large measure on the Soviet Union's display of readiness to accept "mutual accommodation" of conflicting positions within the Communist camp. Given this circumstance and the characteristic vacillation of the Brezhnev–Kosygin regime toward the Czechoslovak problem during the preceding seven months, one might have

---

138 For the full text of the Bratislava communiqué, see *Pravda*, August 4, 1968. There was, however, one prophetic point in the Bratislava declaration: it substituted for the traditional phrase "non-interference in each other's internal affairs" the words "fraternal mutual assistance."

139 Editorial, "The Call of the Times," *Izvestiia*, August 6, 1968; editorial, "Strength in Unity," *Pravda*, August 5, 1968.

140 For a challenge to the generally held view that the outcome of the July crisis represented a Soviet setback and demonstrated that the Kremlin leadership lacked the stomach to use military force against Czechoslovakia, see Crosby S. Noyes, "Czechs Will Find Terms of Soviet Accord Stiff," *Washington Star*, August 15, 1968. For a presentation of the various arguments, prior to the July–August crisis situation, that the Soviet leadership was unlikely to use armed force to impose its will upon Czechoslovakia, see R. T. Rockingham Gill, "Czechoslovakia: Will the Soviet Army Intervene?" *East Europe* (July 1968): 2–6.

expected Moscow to adopt an interim policy of watchful waiting to see what changes would be registered at the Fourteenth Czechoslovak Party Congress in September, as well as to ascertain whether the Czechs would actually adhere to their side of the Bratislava agreement with regard to Warsaw Pact co-operation, a common line on Germany, the exercise of discipline in the press, and other restraints upon the reform movement.[141]

Even a modest period of grace, however, apparently was more than Moscow could abide, for within less than two weeks after the Bratislava armistice it became evident that a new round of political-military pressures had been launched against the Dubcek regime. Soviet polemics against Prague reopened on August 14 with an article attacking reform-minded elements of the Czech press,[142] followed the next day by a lurid account of the details of an alleged West German plot for a two-pronged military offensive against East Germany and Czechoslovakia, intended "to confront the Warsaw Pact countries with a fait accompli."[143] The "slanderous" anti-Soviet activities of the Czech press again became the target of a *Pravda* diatribe on August 16,[144] the same day that Dubcek—on the occasion of a visit by Ceausescu to Prague—appealed to the Czech people not to move too fast toward reform, so that the country might still enjoy freedom of action to go ahead with the "democratization process."[145] During the next four days the Soviet press charged in mounting crescendo that the Dubcek leadership was not acting vigorously enough to suppress "subversive activities by anti-socialist forces" within the country.[146]

The military aspect of this renewed Soviet pressure upon Prague first became manifest on August 11, when it was announced that still another Warsaw

---

[141] That the Dubcek regime's side of the compromise at Cierna and Bratislava had called for demonstrating self-restraint was rather soon made evident by the Czech Party Presidium's warning on August 14 against political activity which violated "law and order," and by other efforts to keep free discussion in line, such as the dismissal of liberals on the editorial staff of *Rude Pravo*, the party daily, for alleged "lack of discipline." See Henry Kamm, "A Discussion Curb Asked in Prague," *New York Times*, August 15, 1968.

[142] The article marking the renewal of the pressure campaign against Prague, signed by "Zhurnalist," appeared in *Literaturnaia gazeta*, August 14, 1968. Entitled "The Political Milk of *Literarni Listy*," it directed its fire against editors of the liberal Czech weekly for having allegedly urged the West to send "rescue divisions" into Czechoslovakia "if something should happen."

[143] Ernest Henry, "What Kind of New Policy Has Bonn Devised?" *Izvestiia*, August 15, 1968.

[144] Iurii Zhukov, "Instigators," *Pravda*, August 16, 1968.

[145] Prague radio broadcast, August 16, 1968.

[146] The keynote article in this last-minute pre-invasion propaganda campaign came on August 18; it was by I. Aleksandrov, whose byline (believed to be a pseudonym) had appeared over an article on July 11 containing a rationale for intervention similar to that used in Hungary. (See fn. 123 above.) The new article charged the Dubcek regime with failure to curb "rightist reactionary" forces and warned that the "fraternal" countries which signed the Bratislava agreement were "fully resolved to rebuff the schemes of internal and external reaction." Soviet propaganda at this time also raised the threat posed to Czechoslovakia by the Sudeten Germans and zeroed in on the case of the Prague factory workers who had written a sympathetic letter to Moscow on July 30 (see fn. 131 above), with Moscow charging that these workers were being "persecuted" by subversive elements seeking to damage Czech–Soviet relations. See I. Aleksandrov, "Brazen Thrust of Reaction," *Pravda*, August 18, 1968; Viktor Maevskii and Vasilii Zhuravskii, "Once Again on the Letter of the Czechoslovak Workers" and "A Volcano That Is Not Extinct," *Pravda*, August 19 and 20, 1968.

Pact exercise along Czechoslovakia's borders had begun immediately after the conclusion, on August 10, of the large-scale "Nemen" logistics exercises carried out during the July crisis.[147] Visits by several of the Soviet Union's highest-ranking military leaders to Poland and East Germany within the next few days in connection with the new maneuvers gave further evidence that Moscow was again flexing its military muscle.[148] As it later became known, the maneuvers inspected by Marshals Grechko, Iakubovskii, and others had in effect served as a dress rehearsal for the impending invasion,[149] but at the time there was no public hint that the Soviet leadership had made up its mind to take the fateful step from which it had drawn back in July.

There remains considerable uncertainty as to the sequence of the Soviet leaders' decisions on military intervention both before and after the Cierna–Bratislava meetings. According to anonymous East German sources cited in the Western press, plans had been made to intervene before the Cierna meeting; the July pressures and troop maneuvers were said to be the prelude to this intervention, which was to take place after a "cry for help" from the Novotny wing of the Czech leadership. Soviet failure to find anyone to call for help allegedly caused this move to be canceled "at the eleventh hour," just before the Cierna gathering.[150] In the opinion of Ota Sik, the Czech economic leader who took temporary refuge in Yugoslavia after the invasion, the intervention had been decided on before Cierna and Bratislava, and these meetings were merely a "smoke screen" while final preparations were being made.[151] The Soviet version, of course, is that the intervention decision came with great reluctance only *after* the Czechs had failed to live up to the Bratislava agreement of August 4, but the brief interval of truce, hardly enough to allow a fair test of Czech performance, tends to cast doubt on this contention. Whether the intervention decision was made well in advance or was reached only on the eve of the invasion,[152] it does seem plain that preparatory steps for such a

[147] The new maneuvers, described as "joint exercises of communication troops," began on August 10 along Czechoslovakia's northern and eastern borders with participation by Soviet, Polish, and East German forces. On August 16 the maneuvers were extended to Czechoslovakia's southern border, and Hungarian troops joined Soviet forces there. Among the participants in the subsequent invasion, only Bulgaria, which has no common frontier with Czechoslovakia, was not publicly included in the exercises. See "At the Headquarters of the Joint Forces of the Warsaw Pact Countries," *Krasnaia zvezda*, August 11, 1968; "Communication of the Hungarian Telegraphic Agency—MTI," *Krasnaia zvezda*, August 17, 1968.

[148] The Soviet visitors included Marshal A. A. Grechko, Minister of Defense; Marshal I. I. Iakubovskii, commander-in-chief of the joint Warsaw Pact forces; General A. A. Epishev, chief of the main political administration of the Soviet armed forces; General S. M. Shtemenko, chief of staff of the joint Warsaw Pact forces; and Marshal P. K. Koshevoi, commander of the Group of Soviet Forces in Germany (GSFG). See "A. A. Grechko Meets with H. Hoffman," *Pravda*, August 17, 1968; "In an Atmosphere of Friendship," ibid., August 18, 1968.

[149] See, for example, David Lawrence, "U.S. Knew of Buildup for Invasion," *Washington Star*, September 4, 1968.

[150] David Binder, "July Plan To Oust Dubcek Reported," *New York Times*, August 9, 1968.

[151] "Brezhnev a Bureaucrat, Ota Sik Says," translation of Sik interview with Italian writer Alberto Moravia, *Radio Free Europe*, September 12, 1968, p. 4.

[152] It might be surmised that the final invasion decision was taken on August 17. This was the day of a Politburo meeting in Moscow, following the return to the Soviet capital on August 16

contingency had begun as early as the July border maneuvers and rear-area mobilization, and that by August 10 (the start of the "communications troop" exercises that proved to be the dress rehearsal) the military phase of preparation was well in hand.

The Invasion of Czechoslovakia

On the night of August 20–21, the blow fell. Striking with virtually complete surprise, Soviet-led invasion forces rolled across Czechoslovakia's borders from their several maneuver areas,[153] while Soviet airborne troops began landing at Prague's main airport, whence they penetrated eight miles to the heart of the city to invest such key points as radio, parliament, and other government buildings.[154] Dubcek and other leaders of the stunned nation, after appealing to the population to remain calm and offer no resistance, were taken into custody in their offices. Meanwhile, the Czech armed forces, which in the words of the Prague radio had "not received a command to defend the country," stood by as the occupation of Czechoslovakia was quickly consummated.[155]

---

of most of the senior leaders who had been "officially" on vacation in the Crimea. There does not seem to be any basis, however, for rumors to the effect that the senior leaders had been summoned back to Moscow to be presented with a decision arrived at by subordinates during their absence. What the triggering factor in the invasion decision may have been remains entirely a matter of speculation. According to one view, the critical circumstance may have been the setting of a new date by Prague for holding the Congress of the Slovak wing of the party at the end of August, prior to the September Congress of the entire Czechoslovak party. The August meeting would have threatened to unseat such Slovak conservatives as Vasil Bilak, who was in constant touch with Soviet Ambassador Chervonenko in Prague. In this view, Bilak and other conservative party figures had managed to persuade Chervonenko that internal dissatisfaction with Dubcek was mounting, and that once Soviet troops arrived they would be "welcomed" by a reversed majority (i.e., of conservatives) within the Prague leadership. For a presentation of this argument, see Richard Lowenthal, "The Sparrow in the Cage," *Problems of Communism* (November–December 1968): 21–22. With respect to the question of when military intervention first may have been seriously contemplated, some observers have traced the likely date back to April 1968, when General A. A. Epishev, chief of the main political administration of the Soviet armed forces, reportedly declared at a Moscow party meeting that the Soviet army was ready to "do its duty" whenever "loyal Communists" in Czechoslovakia might appeal for help. See Michel Tatu, "The Soviet Union," *Interplay* (November 1968): 5.

[153] In addition to Soviet troops, which comprised the bulk of the invasion forces, the GDR, Poland, Hungary, and Bulgaria also furnished contingents to the invading forces. For more detailed discussion of the forces involved, see chapter XVII, pp. 466–71.

[154] The seizure of Prague's Ruzyne International Airport to provide an airhead for the troops who invested the capital's key points and took the Dubcek leadership into custody was illustrative of the meticulous planning which went into the military phase of the operation against Czechoslovakia. For an account of the airport's capture, which involved co-ordination with Soviet Embassy personnel in Prague, see Kenneth Ames, "Coup at Airport Led Invasion," *Washington Post*, August 31, 1968. For other accounts of the invasion itself see Tad Szulc, "Broadcast Appeals to Officials to Remain at Their Jobs," *New York Times*, August 21, 1968; Dan Morgan, "Prague Is More Confident," *Washington Post*, August 25, 1968; Paul Wohl, "One of the Stealthiest Operations in Modern History," *Christian Science Monitor*, August 26, 1968; Stanislav Budin, "Czech Editor Tells of Events Leading to Invasion," *New York Times*, August 28, 1968; Harold Jackson, "A Czech History of the Occupation," *Washington Post*, August 29, 1968.

[155] Details of how the Czech armed forces were immobilized have not been forthcoming. Presumably, the decision not to make a fight of it against hopeless odds grew out of the general belief of the Czech leadership that no provocation should be offered the invaders, thus depriving them of an ex post facto justification for the intervention. Although the Czech forces put up no organized military resistance, and in a sense may have "co-operated" to keep the population

If the military phase of the intervention gave every sign of having been carefully planned and decisively conducted, the same could not be said for the political aspects of the operation. Nothing pointed up more vividly the contrast between the chilling efficiency of the military seizure of Czechoslovakia and the poor political preparation for its occupation than the collapse of the Soviet Union's original alibi that it acted with other "fraternal socialist countries" to satisfy a "request by party and state leaders of the Czechoslovak Socialist Republic for immediate assistance, including assistance with armed forces."[156] Despite denials from all responsible Czechoslovak authorities that any request for assistance had been made,[157] the Soviet Union sought for several days to present the invasion as a legitimate response to a call for help from loyal Communists in Prague, stressing that Communist rule in Czechoslovakia was in dire peril from "counterrevolutionary forces" within the country, which had "entered into collusion with external forces hostile to socialism."[158]

It became apparent almost immediately, however, that Moscow had again failed to reckon with the uncompromising solidarity of the Czechs and Slovaks. Not only were the Russians unable to produce a single Czechoslovak leader to authenticate the alleged call for help, but, more embarrassing still, no one could be found in Prague to form a puppet government—even among the most orthodox party conservatives who were considered to be in Moscow's pocket.[159] In those first days of the occupation, Ludvik Svoboda, the old soldier and

---

from engaging in more than sporadic clashes with the invaders, the Czech military establishment apparently did make a notable contribution to the operation of a clandestine radio network, which helped to sustain the unity of the country during the early days of the occupation. See Constantine Menges, *Prague Resistance, 1968: The Ingenuity of Conviction*, The RAND Corporation, P-3930, September 1968.

[156] The first Soviet announcement of the invasion—a TASS statement over Moscow radio in the early morning hours of August 21, which appeared later the same day in *Pravda* and *Izvestiia*—began with reference to the alleged request for armed assistance.

[157] Beginning with an initial announcement over Prague radio, shortly after midnight of August 21, that the Pact forces had entered Czechoslovakia around 11 P.M. on August 20, Czechoslovak authorities issued a series of statements during the following hours. These included declarations by the party Presidium and the National Assembly denouncing the invasion as an "aggression" which was taking place without the knowledge of the Czechoslovak leadership, personal appeals from Dubcek and Svoboda for calm, and a request to the governments of the invading Warsaw Pact countries to withdraw their troops.

[158] Soviet attempts to portray the invasion as a response to a call for assistance included publication of an unsigned appeal, which was then repeatedly referred to as having "fully substantiated" the "historic decision to request assistance from the Soviet Union and other fraternal socialist countries"—a fine example of circular logic. See "Appeal by Group of Members of the CCP Central Committee and C.S.R. Government and National Assembly," *Pravda* and *Izvestiia*, August 22, 1968. See also Iurii Zhukov, "What Did They Strive For? The Calculations and Miscalculations of the Enemies of the Czechoslovak People," *Pravda*, August 21, 1968; editorial, "Defense of Socialism Is the Highest International Duty," ibid., August 22, 1968.

[159] Among the orthodox stalwarts within the Czechoslovak Communist leadership who were considered likely collaborators with the Russians but who nevertheless held back from trying to form a government were Vasil Bilak, Alois Indra, Drahomir Kolder, and Antonin Kapek. One reason for Soviet reticence in naming potential collaborators immediately after the invasion may have been to avoid isolating them until their ranks grew and an alternative pro-Soviet government was formed. But when the potential collaborators found that they had in fact been isolated, they proved unwilling to form a government which could get no stamp of legitimacy from the Czechoslovak party, the National Assembly, or President Svoboda. See Lowenthal, in *Problems of Communism* (November–December 1968): 22.

President of Czechoslovakia who flew to Moscow, was virtually the sole link between the occupied nation and its occupiers—the party channel of communication and the intergovernment relationship between Prague and Moscow having been severed. Faced with the incongruous situation of having a military pro-consul ensconced in Prague without a government to give orders to, the Soviet leaders tried to prevail upon Svoboda to put together a makeshift regime. Failing in this, they were obliged to turn again to Dubcek, whom only a few days before they had imprisoned and denounced as a traitor.[160]

Surely, there is no more bizarre chapter in the whole sorry invasion episode than the abduction of Dubcek and his close associates, who, after being taken to Moscow in manacles, were freed so that they might "negotiate" with their captors, because no one could be induced to form a puppet government. Svoboda's insistence that the Soviets deal with Dubcek and Cernik was an act of high courage, but in the end it also spared the Russians the political embarrassment of having to set up their own, alien military regime to rule the Czechoslovak people directly. As one perceptive observer has put it, the Soviet leaders evidently came to the belated realization that their best bet was to return Dubcek and his colleagues to Prague to serve, temporarily at least, as a "protective political cushion" between Soviet power and the Czechoslovak people.[161]

Once the Moscow agreement of August 26 was concluded and the Dubcek regime reinstalled in Prague,[162] the Soviet Union's diplomatic and propaganda effort to justify the invasion took a new turn. Around the end of August, the line shifted toward laying the blame at the door of NATO in general and West Germany in particular.[163] Preinvasion allegations that NATO and Bonn had drafted plans for subversive intrigues and military operations against Czechoslovakia were revived, and emphasis was placed on the right and the duty of the Soviet Union and its hardcore Warsaw allies to intervene in Czechoslovakia to keep it from being "torn away" from the bloc and thereby upsetting the power balance between the West and the Communist camp.[164] The theme that the danger of war had been averted by the preventive occupa-

[160] Svoboda arrived in Moscow on August 23 for talks with the Soviet leaders, heading a small delegation which did not include Dubcek, Oldrich Cernik, Josef Smrkovsky, Frantisek Kriegel, and other Czechoslovak leaders who had been arrested in Prague and taken to Moscow. Cryptic Soviet statements on Svoboda's arrival and on the August 23–26 talks did not mention that the incarcerated Czech leaders had been released to join the talks until after the talks were over. *Pravda*, August 24, 25, 26, 1968; editorial, "The Svoboda Mission," *New York Times*, August 24, 1968; Anatole Shub "Czech Talks Are Shrouded in Secrecy," *Washington Post*, August 27, 1968. For an account of the treatment of Dubcek, see Vincent Buist, "Soviets Flew Dubcek Out in Manacles," ibid., August 29, 1968.

[161] James H. Billington, "Cost to the Soviets: Loss of Their Dazzling Myth of Infallibility," *Life*, September 6, 1968, pp. 60–61.

[162] See "Communiqué on Soviet-Czechoslovak Talks," *Pravda*, August 28, 1968; "Text of Speeches by Svoboda and Dubcek on Moscow Talks," *New York Times*, August 28, 1968.

[163] Michael Hornsby, "Moscow Decided To Put the Blame on West Germany," *Times*, London, August 31, 1968.

[164] See chapter XV, pp. 409–10. See also the White Book, *K sobytiiam v Chekhoslovakii* (On Events in Czechoslovakia), issued by "Press Group of Soviet Journalists," Moscow, 1968.

tion of the country, which had been briefly sounded at the outset, also reappeared in the statements of Soviet spokesmen.[165]

Perhaps the principal fruit of the Soviet effort to justify the invasion, however, was the emergence of what came to be labeled the "Brezhnev doctrine."[166] In it, the Soviet Union claimed the right, in the name of the "class struggle" and "proletarian internationalism," to intervene forcibly in the affairs of any member of the "socialist commonwealth," despite such "abstract" notions as national sovereignty and self-determination. Although this doctrine struck many observers abroad as something new, its antecedents in Soviet history go back quite far;[167] its reformulation in the aftermath of the Czechoslovak invasion, therefore, was more a reversion to orthodoxy than the enunciation of a novel concept. Either way, however, its implications were disturbing.

The outlines of the Brezhnev doctrine were laid down in September 1968 by several Soviet writers, one of whom, Sergei Kovalev, dismissed the "formal-legal arguments" of "those who speak about the 'illegality' of the actions of the socialist countries in Czechoslovakia" and declared that the socialist states

[165] The original TASS statement of August 31 on the entry of Warsaw Pact troops had implied that in meeting a "threat to the socialist system in Czechoslovakia" the Soviet Union was averting a "threat to the foundations of peace in Europe." The coupling of the intervention with the preservation of peace was later reintroduced by various Soviet spokesmen, including Gromyko at the United Nations on October 3, 1968. The critical point that was skirted in these allusions to preservation of peace was: who was likely to break the peace? Since the West had shown unmistakably that it did not intend to go to war over Czechoslovakia, the only implication left was that the Soviet Union was prepared to start a war to prevent Czechoslovakia—or any other country within the Soviet bloc—from moving out of the Soviet orbit. See M. Mikhailov, "Don't Be Confused, Gentlemen," *Izvestiia*, September 4, 1968; editorial, "To Strengthen the Peace in Europe," *Pravda*, September 20, 1968; "Excerpts from Gromyko's Address Before the United Nations General Assembly," *New York Times*, October 4, 1968.

[166] Brezhnev's name came to be associated with the postinvasion doctrine of intervention after he expounded some of its features at the Polish party Congress in Warsaw on November 12, 1968, although by that time both Soviet theoreticians and other Kremlin leaders had already begun to spell out the doctrine.

[167] Perhaps the origins of the intervention doctrine go back to the concept of "proletarian internationalism" as it was understood in Lenin's latter days and in most of the Stalinist period, when all Communist parties abroad were obedient instruments of Kremlin policy, recognizing loyalty to only one "workers' homeland," the Soviet Union. Versions of the doctrine were later advanced under Khrushchev to legitimize the Soviet Union's "obligation" to intervene in Hungary in 1956, and to serve notice that once Communist regimes came to power they were to be regarded as irreversible. In a speech on August 14, 1958, for example, Khrushchev had said: "We are faithful to our obligations and our international duties . . . in the event of any new outside effort to change the order in a socialist country . . . we will not be mere bystanders and will not leave our friends in the lurch." Again, the document issued by the 1960 world meeting of eighty-one Communist parties in Moscow had stated that every ruling Communist party was "accountable" not only to the "working people of its country" but to "the Communist movement as a whole," and that under the reciprocal obligations of proletarian internationalism it was the responsibility of the combined forces of the socialist camp to "safeguard every socialist country against encroachments by imperialist reaction." Similar doctrinal assertions that the individual sovereignty of Communist states is subordinate to the security of the "socialist commonwealth"—a term which came into use around 1955—were to be found in abundance before the intervention doctrine was elaborated to fit the Czechoslovak case. For a Soviet treatise in May 1968 which expounded the notion of limits on national sovereignty within the "socialist commonwealth" and foreshadowed the use of the principle of "mutual friendly assistance" to justify Czechoslovak intervention, see I. Dudinskii, "V. I. Lenin's Ideas on the Socialist Commonwealth," *Kommunist*, no. 8 (May 1968): 26–37.

could not "remain inactive in the name of some abstract idea of sovereignty when they saw how the country was exposed to the danger of anti-socialist degeneration."[168]

The keystone of the intervention doctrine as elaborated after the invasion was the assertion that "counterrevolution" with Czechoslovakia, abetted from without by "world imperialism," had threatened to open the gates of the "indivisible" socialist system. This, it was alleged, would have resulted in Czechoslovakia's becoming a corridor through which NATO troops could approach the Soviet frontier, as well as in carving up the commonwealth of European socialist countries and in violating the right of these countries to "socialist self-determination."[169] Obviously, this theoretical edifice would collapse if it were to be established that no real counterrevolutionary danger ever existed in Czechoslovakia. Hence the Soviet Union's attempt to wring from the Czechoslovaks themselves a confession that counterrevolution was rampant in their country prior to the invasion.[170]

Although the Brezhnev doctrine justified the invasion as fulfilling an international "class" duty to suppress anti-socialist elements who had "step by step prepared a counterrevolutionary coup" in Czechoslovakia, it did not stop there. Its expositors also suggested that socialist countries which toyed with "new brands" of socialism that "play on the national sentiments of the people,"[171] and even socialist countries "seeking to adopt a 'non-aligned' position," should be aware that they, too, were subject to the doctrine of preventing "a weakening of any link of the world socialist system."[172] The suggestion that there was to be no middle ground in the struggle between "two opposing social systems" was accompanied by a reminder that nonaligned socialist states owed their "national independence" to "the might of the socialist commonwealth and primarily of its main power—the Soviet Union and its armed forces."[173]

Needless to say, the implications of this argument were not lost on such countries as Yugoslavia, whose long adherence to the principle of multiple roads to communism was clearly put in jeopardy by the Soviet Union's asser-

---

[168] Sergei Kovalev, "The Sovereignty and International Obligations of the Socialist Countries," *Pravda*, September 26, 1968. For other contributions to the new theoretical rationale for intervention, see Kovalev's earlier article, "On 'Peaceful' and Nonpeaceful Counterrevolution," *Pravda*, September 11, 1968; Professor N. Farberov, "General Laws Governing the Building of Socialism," *Izvestiia*, September 28, 1968.

[169] Kovalev, in *Pravda*, September 26, 1968.

[170] The Soviet Union's attempt to beat down the Czechoslovak leadership's argument that there had been no counterrevolution tended to center on the question of putting counterrevolutionaries on trial. Prague resisted the staging of political trials, while the Russians reportedly pressed for them to demonstrate that the invasion was justified. See Clyde H. Farnsworth, "Russian at Justice Ministry," *New York Times*, October 8, 1968.

[171] Farberov, in *Izvestiia*, September 28, 1968.

[172] Kovalev, in *Pravda*, September 26, 1968. A similar point aimed at "nonaligned" Yugoslavia appeared in the CPSU's theoretical journal in October 1968, in an article warning that no state can be "absolutely independent of the system of states in which it exists" and that "proletarian internationalism . . . considers it necessary to guarantee the defense of any socialist state's sovereignty when it is threatened by the machinations of the imperialists," Iu. Georgiev, "Yugoslavia: 'New Variant of Socialism'?" *Kommunist*, no. 15 (October 1968): 96–97.

[173] Kovalev, in *Pravda*, September 26, 1968.

tion that it had the right to set itself up as the final arbiter of Communist development in another socialist state and to intervene whenever it deemed communism to be "threatened" there. This was tantamount to saying that the Soviet Union refused to recognize the sovereignty of any Communist state within the reach of Soviet military power.[174] Edward Kardelj, Yugoslavia's leading theoretician, promptly sounded his country's concern that the Soviet Union was promulgating "a very dangerous doctrine."[175] But misgivings about the pernicious character of the Brezhnev doctrine were voiced in the non-Communist West as well. Secretary of State Dean Rusk, for example, warned the Soviet Union that it would damage any chance of a renewed détente if this doctrine meant that such principles of the United Nations Charter as the sovereign equality of nations and the prohibition against use of force did not apply to Soviet relations with the countries of East Europe.[176]

The Soviet Union for its part did not concede one inch to its critics. Having covered up Soviet self-interest in maintaining control over East Europe with an ideological cloak that elevated the principle of class struggle above any forms of bourgeois "legality," the Soviet leaders took the position that no one had grounds to reproach them "in connection with the events surrounding Czechoslovakia."[177] Nevertheless, it was clear that the invasion of Czechoslovakia, whatever the reasons that prompted Moscow to launch it, had created as many new problems for the Soviet Union in Europe as it may have solved.

[174] As expounded in the fall of 1968, the Soviet intervention doctrine was understood to apply to states in which communism had already established itself as the ruling order. This left ambiguous the question of the doctrine's application to any previously non-Communist country in which the Communist party might in the future come to power, by parliamentary means or otherwise. Obviously, if the doctrine were construed to apply in such cases, even a "temporary" Communist electoral victory in a European country accessible to Soviet military power would have to be regarded as irreversible. Needless to say, under the shadow of this logic the West European Communist parties could hardly expect to find themselves welcome in the domestic political arena.

[175] Speech commemorating the twenty-fifth anniversary of the people's uprising in the Slovene Primorje, Ljubljana radio broadcast, September 15, 1968.

[176] See Robert H. Estabrook, "Russians Lectured by Rusk," *Washington Post*, October 3, 1968; Bernard Gwertzman, "Rusk Says Soviet Hinders Détente," *New York Times*, October 11, 1968.

[177] See speech by Soviet Foreign Minister Andrei A. Gromyko at the United Nations, *New York Times*, October 4, 1968.

XV

IMPACT OF THE CZECHOSLOVAK INVASION ON
SOVIET EUROPEAN POLICY

The conduct of Soviet policy toward Europe during the Brezhnev–Kosygin regime's first few years in power provided little indication, except perhaps in retrospect, that by the autumn of 1968 the Soviet Union would find itself once more branded an aggressor for having repeated in Czechoslovakia the sort of ruthless military intervention it had perpetrated twelve years earlier in Hungary.[1] Yet, within eight or nine months after the beginning of the Czech reform experiment in early 1968, the Soviet leadership managed, through its treatment of Czechoslovakia, to tarnish its prestige and to undo many of the gains that Soviet policy had achieved in Europe since Khrushchev's ouster. In their attempt to turn back the clock of history in East Europe the Soviet leaders accomplished their immediate aim of crushing Czechoslovakia's democratization program, but in the process they squandered a good deal of their political capital in Europe and elsewhere, and the divisive effect of their clumsy intervention in Czechoslovakia threatened to have unsettling repercussions in other parts of the Communist world, including perhaps the Soviet Union itself.

The ultimate consequences of the Soviet Union's attempt to reimpose on East Europe by force of arms the authority it originally acquired there through military victory in World War II are, of course, unforeseeable. Here, we shall be concerned mainly with three aspects of Soviet European policy in light of the Czechoslovak episode: the factors which lay behind the intervention; its immediate effects upon Soviet relations with both halves of Europe; and the ensuing efforts of the Soviet Union to repair the damage dealt to its interests by the invasion of August 1968.

Factors behind the Intervention

Among the problems growing out of relations between the Soviet Union and its East European allies, perhaps none was more fundamental and perplexing

[1] On the whole, the predictive record of Western analyses is rather poor with respect to the likelihood that the Brezhnev–Kosygin regime would repeat the Soviet experience of military intervention in East Europe regardless of political cost. One of the few serious analyses before the event which foresaw tendencies within the Soviet leadership that might precipitate a move in this direction was the work of Robert Conquest. See his "The Limits of Détente," *Foreign Affairs* (July 1968): especially 736–37. Other retrospective studies have brought out the point that the Czechoslovak intervention represented the logical culmination of trends in the foreign and domestic policies of the Soviet collective leadership which had been visibly gathering strength for a couple of years before the event. See, for example, Richard Lowenthal, "The Sparrow in the Cage," *Problems of Communism* (November–December 1968): 3–10; Fritz Ermarth, *Internationalism, Security, and Legitimacy: The Challenge to Soviet Interests in East Europe*, The RAND Corporation, RM-5909-PR, March 1969.

than that of deciding where to set the limits of Moscow's tolerance for diversity and change in East Europe. During its first four years in power, the Brezhnev–Kosygin regime had learned to live with a considerable range of restiveness in East Europe, including challenges to Soviet authority from a frequently unco-operative Rumanian ally. Presumably, it could have done the same with respect to Czechoslovakia. Why, then, did the Soviet leaders in August 1968 choose to put down the Czechoslovak reform experiment by force—a step they had backed away from at the height of the July crisis a few weeks before?

A full accounting of the reasons for this fateful decision in Moscow may be long in coming, for it will probably require another candid "secret" speech by some new Soviet leader of the future to help explain what prompted the present generation of leaders to act as they did. Some of the considerations behind the move against Czechoslovakia, however, are evident even from today's perspec-tive, though it is difficult to determine their relative weight in the pattern of Soviet motivation.

Apart from the immediate circumstances previously discussed that triggered the invasion,[2] at least five broadly related motivating factors seem to have been important: the suspicion that "reform Communism" in Czechoslovakia was tending toward some form of social democracy that would undermine the orthodox basis of monopoly party rule; the belief that toleration of creeping reform would jeopardize the Soviet Union's control in East Europe; the fear of feedback from the liberal experiment in Prague upon the interlocking legiti-macies of the other Communist regimes in East Europe and the Soviet Union itself; the worrisome prospect that a Czechoslovak reorientation toward West Germany would undermine the East German regime and set an example likely to open the rest of East Europe to economic-political penetration by Bonn; and concern that all of these developments would weaken the military and strategic position of the Soviet Union and its Warsaw coalition vis-à-vis the West.

With respect to the issue of orthodoxy versus reform and the various dangers which the Soviet leadership apparently perceived in the developments in Czech-oslovakia in 1968, it should perhaps first be noted that there had been for some time a growing difference within the leadership elites of most of the East European countries—and to some extent within the Soviet ruling elite as well—between defenders of Marxist–Leninist orthodoxy and advocates of what might be called reform communism. No simple formula will describe reform commu-nism, which took varying forms in East Europe, depending on the particular political culture in which it arose. Nationalism was one of its chief ingredients, blended with recognition of the need for economic modernization and, in some cases, toleration of more liberal political values than were condoned under ortho-dox communism. Some of the East European proponents of reform may have been tending toward what William Griffith has labeled "covert social fascism"—an authoritarian mobilization of society intended to achieve modernization on an essentially nationalist basis while still using the internationalist vocabulary of

[2] See chapter XIV, pp. 369–80.

Marxism–Leninism.[3] Others—and this would seem to have been true of the Czechoslovak reform Communists—apparently believed that they could best serve the party's leading role in society, not by clinging to old modes of rule based on orthodox conformity but by liberal or "humanizing" reforms intended to promote modernization by establishing closer rapport with the people and the restless intellectuals.[4]

To the Soviet leadership the issue of orthodox versus reform communism in East Europe posed a peculiarly difficult problem, for in these countries reform communism—whether bearing an authoritarian or a liberal tinge—was closely linked with the assertion of national consciousness and independence, which almost by definition tended to be directed against the Soviet Union as the obvious dominant outside power. Therefore, even the pragmatist elements among the Soviet leadership, who may have been in some degree sympathetic to reform communism in the abstract, could scarcely afford to sanction it in practice; indeed, they were probably obliged to dig in their heels for orthodoxy alongside the most diehard Soviet dogmatists. Here, then, was a problem that fed on itself: Whatever the potential merits of reform communism might be in making Communist regimes in East Europe more effective and popular, the more they succeeded the greater the threat they were likely to present to Soviet control and influence in the area.

Partly as a consequence of this situation, the Soviet leaders found themselves, as the Czech experiment progressed, increasingly committed to the defense of orthodoxy in East Europe, even though this ran counter to their professed doctrine of "different roads" to communism and, instead, set up the Soviet Union as the only model for the Communist regimes of East Europe. On the homefront, meanwhile, this commitment to orthodoxy tended to rigidify the Kremlin leadership against pressures for reform within the Soviet Union itself, and to heighten its concern over the example that was being set by Czechoslovakia. Thus, among the first internal preventive reflexes after the July crisis was a series of warnings by the Soviet Central Committee against expecting a liberalization of centralized party rule or the introduction of "so-called bourgeois freedoms" into Soviet society.[5] ·

[3] Griffith traces the emergence of "covert social fascism" as a brand of reform communism in East Europe to the interaction, after 1953, between de-Stalinization and rising nationalism and popular pressures for economic modernization. See William E. Griffith, *Eastern Europe After the Soviet Invasion of Czechoslovakia*, The RAND Corporation, P-3983, October 1968, especially pp. 2–10. Ceausescu in Rumania and Moczar in Poland seem to be representatives of this trend, which, while disagreeable to the Soviet Union, probably appeared to Moscow as a less serious threat to Soviet-style orthodoxy than the kind of liberalization in politics which manifested itself in Czechoslovakia and to some extent in Yugoslavia.

[4] It should be pointed out that the Czechoslovak leadership intended to keep reform within the context of a Communist system in which party rule would remain dominant. However, intellectuals and professionals outside the party apparatus, with perhaps some allies within it, apparently hoped for an embodiment of the liberal ethos in the new model of humanized Marxism which went beyond what Moscow felt were safe limits. See Richard V. Burks, *The Decline of Communism in Czechoslovakia*, The RAND Corporation, P-3939, September 1968, pp. 18–20.

[5] Resolution of the Central Committee of the CPSU, "On Preparations for the 100th Birthday of Vladimir Il'ich Lenin," *Pravda*, August 10, 1968. See also P. Rodionov, "The Firm Principles of the Marxist–Leninist Party," ibid., August 9, 1968.

Not surprisingly, the more a fear of feedback from the ferment in Czechoslovakia prompted the Soviet leaders to insist upon strict conformity at home, the less leeway was left them to tolerate the experiment in Prague. How many more deviations could they afford to accept, if each new apostasy were to increase the difficulty of holding the line against reform at home? In a sense, they were confronted with a Communist version of the domino theory, and the problem was the more acute because the ultimate domino to topple might well be the legitimacy of their own claim to a monopoly of political power.

One way for the Soviet leaders to resolve this problem might have been to adjust themselves gracefully to diversity and experimentation in Czechoslovakia and wherever else in East Europe the reform trend might manage to take hold, allowing some features of reform communism to seep back into the Soviet Union itself. But precisely because the Soviet leadership saw party rule imperiled by such liberalizing reforms and its grip upon East Europe threatened, this path was exceedingly difficult to contemplate. Indeed, it would perhaps become possible only after a long process of internal change in the outlook and composition of the Soviet party leadership itself.[6] Another way to tackle the problem was to be found in dogmatic reassertion of the old verities and willingness to reimpose them by force. Although this alternative was none too attractive either, since it could well boomerang by arousing more fervid national sentiment in East Europe and fresh resentment against the Soviet Union, it was the course embraced by Moscow.

In choosing to resort to repression rather than bow to reform, the Soviet leadership probably found its dilemma somewhat eased by the co-operation it received from orthodox party leaders in some of the East European countries. The Ulbricht regime in East Germany and the Gomulka regime in Poland, their own concerns aroused both by the infectious example of Prague's internal reforms and by the possibility that the Dubcek leadership might adopt a more lenient policy toward West Germany, apparently proved willing accomplices in the suppression of Czechoslovakia, although the extent to which they may have urged military intervention upon Moscow is less clear.[7] Bulgarian and Hungarian party leaders also went along, the latter perhaps with some reluctance.[8] But even though joined by subservient partners within the Warsaw

---

[6] For an interesting exposition of some of the problems making it difficult for the present Soviet ruling group to accommodate its outlook to reform communism, see Robert Conquest, "Communism Has To Democratize or Perish," *New York Times Magazine,* August 18, 1968, pp. 22–23, 81–83. See also Andrei Amalrik, *Will the Soviet Union Survive Until 1984?* (New York: Harper & Row, 1970), pp. 21–44.

[7] There was speculation that Ulbricht in particular, after receiving a cool reception from the Czech leaders during a brief visit to Karlovy Vary on August 12, 1968, had concluded that the Dubcek regime was beyond redemption and urged Moscow to intervene militarily. While he may have done so, the decision was certainly Moscow's. See Henry Kamm, "Ulbricht Setback in Dubcek's Policy Is Seen by Czechs," *New York Times,* August 14, 1968; idem, "Why Did Moscow Switch?" ibid., August 25, 1968; Dorothy Miller, "Military Intervention After Ulbricht's Visit to Karlovy Vary?" *Radio Free Europe,* August 26, 1968; idem, "East Germany Urges Thorough Cleaning," ibid., September 2, 1968.

[8] The failure of Kadar and other top Hungarian leaders to comment publicly on the invasion, even though lesser officials in Budapest did so, was interpreted as an indication that they had not been enthusiastic about being associated with the undertaking. See Alvin Shuster, "Hungary Uneasy

bloc, the Soviet Union had not necessarily resolved its problems in East Europe, as we shall see presently. Not only had the traditional friendliness of the Czechoslovak people toward the Soviet Union been replaced by smoldering enmity, but strongly ambivalent and contradictory emotions were doubtless generated in the other Warsaw bloc countries which had lent themselves to the cold-blooded invasion of a sister East European state.[9]

According to some interpretations, the Soviet decision to intervene militarily in Czechoslovakia was dictated less by an urge to snuff out a threat to ideological and political orthodoxy than to forestall a more concrete threat to the strategic security of the Soviet Union.[10] However, in Moscow's concept of security in Europe, the need to preserve the ideological and political basis of the Soviet Union's hold upon East Europe is so intimately linked with its interest in maintaining a forward military position in this half of a divided Europe that it would be difficult to say where the one leaves off and the other begins.

If a threat to Soviet security were to be defined in the narrow sense of military activities in the West against which the Soviet Union felt compelled to protect itself, there would seem to have been no grounds whatever for ascribing the invasion of Czechoslovakia to "genuine" security concerns. Despite Soviet claims that West Germany was engaged in menacing NATO-backed military machinations against Czechoslovakia, the Western powers had leaned over backward to avoid any semblance of military provocation during the Czech crisis.[11] As for the long-term trends in NATO prior to the invasion, their general direction had been toward a slackening of effort and withdrawal of forces rather than toward a build-up which might have looked threatening to the Soviet Union. It is difficult to believe that the Soviet charges, so patently

---

on Invasion Role," *New York Times*, September 20, 1968; William F. Robinson, "Hungary—What Now?" *Radio Free Europe*, October 28, 1968.

[9] There was little direct evidence on how the people of the other East European countries which participated in the invasion felt about it, but reports that there had been spontaneous student demonstrations in East Germany and that the Polish regime had reinstituted compulsory two-year courses on Marxism–Leninism in Polish universities suggested that, among youth at least, there was questioning of official explanations on the need for military intervention. See David Binder, "Many in East Germany Show Disapproval of Moscow Action," *New York Times*, August 24, 1968; Ralph Blumenthal, "Protest Staged, East Germans Say," ibid., September 10, 1968; Jonathan Randal, "Insistence on Marxist Orthodoxy Strong in Poland," ibid., September 30, 1968; dispatch from *Observer*, London, "E. Germans Show Sympathy for Czechoslovakia in Subtle Ways," *Washington Post*, October 3, 1968; "Situation Report, Poland," *Radio Free Europe*, September 4, 1968; Francis Miko, "GDR Reaction 23–26 August: East German Public Opposing Czechoslovakia's Occupation," *Radio Free Europe*, August 26, 1968; "Current Developments: Hungary," *East Europe* (October 1968): 60; Slobodan Stankovic, "Polish Citizens Visiting Yugoslavia Against Occupation, Belgrade Paper Says," *Radio Free Europe*, September 30, 1968 (translation from Belgrade newspaper *Vecernje*, September 27, 1968).

[10] Dubcek's statement, after his return from the grueling Moscow talks of August 23–26, to the effect that the Czechs had "underestimated" the Soviet "strategic interest" in Czechoslovakia was among the factors cited to support this view. See, for example, Dan Morgan, "Strategic Concern Held Motive: The Whys of Soviet Invasion," *Washington Post*, September 15, 1968; Paul Hoffman, "Moscow Concern on Security Seen," *New York Times*, September 23, 1968.

[11] The relocation away from eastern Bavaria of previously scheduled West German maneuvers was illustrative of Western efforts during the July crisis to avoid what might be interpreted as provocative moves. Likewise, during the August invasion itself, the West refrained from conspicuous announcement of the military alerts, maneuvers, and other "warning" signals customary in past crisis situations.

linked with Moscow's desperate effort to concoct a rationale for the invasion, had been taken seriously by the Soviet leaders themselves.[12]

On the other hand, so far as the trends in Czechoslovakia may have seemed to point toward a loosening of Prague's adherence to the Warsaw Pact, there was doubtless real concern in Moscow—shared by at least East Germany and Poland—that in the important Northern Tier the military structure of the Pact was endangered. But, despite Czechoslovakia's more outspoken attitude on the need for military reforms within the Pact,[13] there was no indication that the Dubcek regime had proposed to renounce its military obligations to the Warsaw alliance. Had it done so, the Soviet Union would hardly have failed to produce concrete corroborating evidence, on a point so central to its argument, that Czechoslovakia intended to quit the Pact.[14] Therefore, one might suppose that what carried weight in Soviet councils was not any demonstrable evidence of Czech military malfeasance but the possibility that Czechoslovakia's political evolution might be leading toward a military reorientation.

The Soviet military security system in East Europe was built both on a substantial forward deployment of its forces in the area which were reinforceable from the Soviet Union and on the contributions of its East European allies. Presumably, the Soviet Union was prepared to tolerate some reduction of East European contributions to the collective military posture of the Pact—as it had done in the case of Rumania—but not a threat to its own military access to East European territory, particularly territory as strategically important as that of Czechoslovakia.[15] The possibility that was perhaps particularly disturbing to Soviet military authorities in the period between Bratislava and the invasion was that Prague—having rid itself once of the Soviet troops which overstayed their leave during the July crisis—might renege on granting them access to Czech territory in the future. That this problematical contingency would have tipped the scales toward intervention seems unlikely, however, had the Soviet leadership not been seized, rightly or wrongly, with the larger concern that the Czechoslovak example was placing the basis of Soviet authority and control in East Europe in jeopardy.

Apart from the various political, ideological, and security factors that had

---

[12] See discussion of the Soviet attempt to justify the invasion, chapter XIV, pp. 382–84, and pp. 414–16 below. If in the process of fabricating this invasion rationale the Soviet leaders managed to convince themselves that it was genuine, one must conclude that they were capable of putting themselves out of touch with reality to a truly alarming degree.

[13] See chapter XVII, pp. 491–92.

[14] Neither the remarks of General Prchlik at his July 15 press conference nor those of General Dzur, the defense minister, contained a threat to leave the Pact. See discussion of Prchlik's remarks, chapter XVII, pp. 491–92. The only Czech official upon whom the Soviets could pin the charge of having called "for 'neutralization' of Czechoslovakia, involving withdrawal from the Warsaw Treaty Organization" was Venta Silhan, who took part in the emergency Fourteenth Party Congress of the CCP in a Prague factory on August 22. Since the alleged statements by Silhan were made at the Fourteenth Party Congress *after* the invasion, they could hardly be presented as having been a factor in the decision to invade. See V. Kudriavtsev, "Counterrevolution Masked as 'Rebirth'," *Izvestiia*, August 25, 1968; V. Zhuravskii and V. Maevskii, "A Rebuff to the Enemies," *Pravda*, August 27, 1968.

[15] For comment on the strategic importance of Czechoslovakia within the Northern Tier, see chapter XVII, pp. 493–94.

helped to create a crisis of Soviet authority in East Europe, persuading Moscow that it must intervene in Czechoslovakia, another element in the intervention decision was the attitude of the Western powers, particularly the United States, toward the situation. According to a view widely voiced in the West by both critics and friends of American diplomacy,[16] a hands-off American attitude encouraged interventionist elements within the Soviet leadership to believe that they could move into Czechoslovakia without risk. Some maintain, though apparently without foundation, that Moscow received the green light in the form of specific American assurances against interference in any action the Soviet Union might take;[17] others believe that the impression grew simply out of America's failure to keep the Russians guessing. By either argument, the Soviet decision to invade might not have been taken had explicit warnings against such a move been delivered.[18] It may well be, of course, that the Soviet Union would have gone ahead with the operation against Czechoslovakia, warning or no warning.[19] A final judgment on the extent to which Soviet decision-makers were swayed by their advance reading of the probable Western reaction to an invasion awaits better information as to what went on in the minds of the Soviet leaders; in the meantime, one can hardly overlook the sad irony that US hopes of eliminating an excuse for Soviet intervention by not "meddling" in the Czechoslovak situation may in fact have contributed to the Kremlin's decision to go ahead.[20]

[16] See discussion of this point later in this chapter, pp. 418–19.

[17] See, for example, Drew Pearson, "LBJ's Czech Assurances Backfired," *Washington Post*, September 17, 1968. See also denial by the State Department that any assurances had been given. ("U.S. Go-Ahead to Russia on Czechs Is Denied," *Washington Post*, September 18, 1968.) The Soviet Union, incidentally, also made an indignant denial of Western press reports that it had informed Washington of the invasion in advance and had received assurances that the United States would not react. See Iurii Zhukov, "About One Political Diversion," *Pravda*, September 4, 1968.

[18] Sometimes cited in this connection was the Rumanian case. In late August, immediately after the invasion of Czechoslovakia, when the Soviet press opened a campaign against Rumania, rumors abounded that Rumania was to be the next target, with maneuvers in Bulgaria serving as the cover for invasion preparations. Although it was subsequently indicated that there was no evidence of invasion preparations, the possibility was taken seriously enough to prompt President Johnson's warning of August 30 to Moscow against any new military adventures in East Europe. Some believe that this warning may in fact have cut short incipient preparations for a move against Rumania. See V. Kudriavtsev, "Counterrevolution Masked as 'Rebirth'," *Izvestiia*, August 25, 1968; Commentator, "A Strange Position," ibid., August 27, 1968; Eric Wentworth, "Russian Envoy Calls on Ceausescu," *Washington Post*, August 26, 1968; Hans Benedict, "Rumanian Citizens in Drills," ibid., September 1, 1968; "U.S. Doubts that Invasion of Rumania Is Imminent," *New York Times*, September 2, 1968.

[19] How large a risk the Soviet leaders were prepared to run is, of course, a salient question, but the answer must remain speculative. For what it may be worth, I have heard it said by Soviet citizens who probably had no part in the decision that the Soviet leaders would have gone ahead with the invasion even if they had thought it meant World War III. In my opinion, the Soviet leaders probably were convinced before they acted that the West was not prepared to go to war over Czechoslovakia.

[20] Another irony worth noting is that the intervention in Czechoslovakia coincided with publication of a book in the Soviet Union arguing that the USSR was a proponent of genuine diversity within the socialist bloc and that military pressure against another socialist state was unthinkable. Witness the following passage: "Socialist states are advocates of non-intervention in each other's internal affairs; they respect the laws and traditions of the fraternal countries, and consider it impermissible to utilize any means of economic, political, and military pressure in

Effects of the Intervention on Soviet Interests in East Europe

For whatever reasons, the intervention did take place. What can be said then as to its effects, favorable and adverse, upon the Soviet position in East Europe? There seems to be little question that one significant result of the invasion was to re-establish the credibility of Soviet military power as the ultimate instrument of Soviet control in East Europe. This credibility had been steadily diminishing in the twelve years since Khrushchev had demonstrated his willingness to employ raw force against Hungary. Perhaps from the Soviet viewpoint, the final swift erosion of respect in East Europe for the authority of Soviet arms appeared to have set in after the backdown at Cierna and Bratislava, which may have helped to persuade even noninterventionists within the Kremlin leadership that the time had come to act forcibly.

Evidence that the action against Czechoslovakia had made East Europeans far more cautious and had restored their respect for Soviet military power and the Kremlin's will to use it was to be seen in the case of Rumania, in particular. Although continuing to express disapproval of Soviet interference in the affairs of a fraternal Communist country, the Rumanians became notably more guarded in their criticism of Soviet policy and let it be known in September that they were amenable to offering various concessions (such as renewal of the Soviet–Rumanian friendship treaty, which had run out early in 1968) in return for a Soviet guarantee of nonintervention.[21] A further co-operative gesture toward Moscow was Rumania's agreement to participate in a joint Warsaw Pact staff exercise in neighboring Bulgaria in March 1969, though Ceausescu still managed to stave off Soviet insistence on holding joint maneuvers on Rumanian soil.[22] If Rumania, the notorious maverick of the Warsaw bloc, found it expedient to toe the line more carefully, other members of the bloc were even less likely to give Moscow offense by showing signs of policy independence.

Although some East European leaders may have been left uncomfortable by the thought that the crude treatment meted out to Czechoslovakia might be turned against their own countries should Moscow find itself crossed, they no longer had much room for maneuver. Unlike the leaders of the West European Communist parties, who were beyond the reach of Soviet military power (in a sense, one might even say that they enjoyed the "protection" of NATO) and therefore could exert at least some political leverage on the Kremlin by threaten-

---

their mutual relations; they fight against any acts in inter-state relations designed to discredit or replace the composition of the party and state organs which the people have entrusted with the administration of the country." A. P. Butenko, ed., *Mirovaia sotsialisticheskaia sistema i antikommunizm* (The World Socialist System and Anticommunism) (Moscow: Izdatel'stvo "Nauka," 1968), p. 148.

[21] A toning down of Rumania's initial outspoken criticism of the invasion began after opening of harsh Soviet press attacks and a meeting on August 24 between Ceausescu and Tito, where the latter may have cautioned the Rumanian leader against carrying defiance too far. See Eric Wentworth, "Rumania Eases Its Criticism of Soviet Invasion," *Washington Post*, August 27, 1968; Anthony Astrachan, "Rumania Seeks Ways of Deflecting Future Soviet Threat," ibid., September 4, 1968; Hans Benedict, "Rumania Seen Ready To Sign Soviet Pact," ibid., September 7, 1968; J. Arthur Johnson, "Speculations About Rumania," *Radio Free Europe*, November 6, 1968.

[22] See chapter XVII, fn. 68.

ing to boycott the scheduled November world party conference in Moscow,[23] the East European leaders found that they were more tightly than ever in Moscow's embrace. If a further reminder of their lot were needed, the so-called Brezhnev doctrine of intervention provided it, for among other things this doctrine had the effect of limiting the sovereignty of states belonging to the "socialist commonwealth."[24]

While the assault against Czechoslovakia thus served to restrict the freedom of action of the participating East European members of the Warsaw bloc, it also had the somewhat paradoxical effect of making the Soviet Union more dependent than ever upon the Pact as an instrument through which to assert its control and bring collective pressure to bear on heretics within the fold. The pains taken by the Soviet Union to drape the mantle of collective Warsaw Pact sanction over the chastisement of Czechoslovakia attested to this dependence, which was heightened by the awkward miscarriage of Soviet expectations that a quisling government could be speedily found in Prague to welcome the occupying forces. Similarly, the Soviet Union's attempt to depict the invasion as a "family affair" of no concern to the rest of the world also depended on seconding motions from the Warsaw bloc satellites, just as the demand for continued stationing of Soviet forces on Czechoslovak territory pending "normalization" of the country was advanced in the name of collective defense of the Warsaw camp.

Even the Brezhnev doctrine implied a somewhat symbiotic need for the Warsaw Pact, since the ambiguously defined "socialist commonwealth" to which the doctrine applied had no institutional form of its own apart from the Warsaw Pact organization and CEMA. Pending some new institutional formula for the socialist commonwealth,[25] any future intervention presumably would again involve use of the Warsaw Pact machinery.

If in a political sense the Soviet Union's need for the collective façade of the Warsaw Pact may have tended to offer the East European members of the Pact a bit of leverage on Soviet policy, this was hardly true in a strictly military sense. Indeed, the invasion had underscored the reality of the USSR's dominant military role in the Warsaw alliance, and may even have prompted some elements of the Soviet leadership to believe that the Soviet Union should place less

[23] See Victor Zorza, "Western Reds Blackmailing Kremlin," *Washington Post*, September 18, 1968. See also pp. 420–21 below.

[24] See previous discussion of the Brezhnev doctrine, chapter XIV, pp. 383–85. Though it could be argued that the doctrine was essentially an ex post facto justification for intervention in the particular case of Czechoslovakia, where Moscow felt its vital interests were in jeopardy, and therefore not necessarily a policy blueprint in general, few of the states affected were likely to care to test the doctrine by asserting their untrammeled sovereignty. Rumania was obviously a ripe target, for it lay within direct reach of Soviet military power. Yugoslavia and Albania, whose status within the "socialist commonwealth" was left rather ambiguous by the Soviet Union, were less threatened by the intervention doctrine, if only because they were not immediately accessible to Soviet power.

[25] For discussion of signs that the Soviet Union may have considered but discarded the creation of a new organizational grouping to distinguish between "loyal" members of the socialist commonwealth (supporters of the invasion) and "second-class" members with tarnished credentials like Czechoslovakia and Rumania, see chapter XVII, pp. 495–96.

military reliance generally upon its Warsaw Pact allies than had been the case before the crisis in Czechoslovakia threatened to open a gap in the important Northern Tier area of the bloc's defenses.[26]

So far as the over-all military posture of the Warsaw alliance was concerned, the Czechoslovak crisis would seem to have yielded both advantages and disadvantages from the Soviet viewpoint. On the one hand, it settled the question of Soviet access to Czech territory and left a somewhat larger net deployment of Soviet forces in the Northern Tier area than before. Moreover, thanks to the successive maneuvers and mobilization which preceded the invasion, as well as the co-ordinated conduct of the operation itself, the Soviet theater forces involved were brought to a high level of combat readiness, and their mobility and logistical support were tested with rather impressive results.[27]

On the other hand, however, the Czechoslovak armed forces, the second largest in East Europe, had for all practical purposes been deleted from the Pact's order of battle for the time being,[28] and the necessity of keeping a watchful eye on them was tying up most of the Soviet occupation troops, not to mention the uncertainties that the situation was bound to pose for Soviet planners in the event of military hostilities across the East–West dividing line in Europe. Apart from raising questions as to Czechoslovakia's contribution to the Pact's posture in the critical Northern Tier triangle, the invasion also seemed to have shifted a still larger share of the joint security burden to the Soviet Union itself. In the short term, this meant extra expenditure to cover the immediate costs of the invasion and occupation;[29] in the long run, it could also mean a greater demand on Soviet resources to maintain the theater forces at a higher level than previously planned. Finally, the Czechoslovak events had aroused new concern in the West about Soviet intentions and about the USSR's demonstrated ability to alter the conventional military balance in Central Europe on short notice. As a result, NATO was again prompted to take a close look at its own defense; this interaction, to which we shall return later, might well offset any momentary military margin that the Soviet Union had gained from the operation in Czechoslovakia.

In another sense, the spiral of interacting suspicion and mistrust touched off by the invasion spelled an end, for the moment, to the idea that the opposing military alliances in Europe had become little more than "relics of a fading confrontation." For the Soviet Union, this meant among other things that shoring

[26] See chapter XVII, pp. 492–98.

[27] See chapter XVII, pp. 473–77.

[28] Despite assurances of military officials in Prague that the Czechoslovak forces were still capable of meeting their Pact commitments, these forces were likely to be regarded by Moscow as potentially unreliable and not to be entrusted with manning a vital sector of the bloc's defenses until the outcome of the "normalization" process in Czechoslovakia became somewhat clearer. See Kenneth Ames, "Czech Army Called 'Fully Capable'," *Washington Post*, September 18, 1968.

[29] According to some Western estimates, for example, the extra expenditures connected with the build-up of Soviet theater forces in East Europe for the invasion and occupation could be expected to add at least a billion rubles, or about 6 per cent, to the Soviet military budget for 1968 alone. See William Beecher, "U.S. Aides Expect Soviet Union To Cut Force in Czechoslovakia," *New York Times*, October 4, 1968.

up the Soviet political and military position in Europe remained high on the priority list, reducing the prospect of pursuing more active policies against China in the Far East. Although Peking professed to see in the action against Czechoslovakia a portent of more aggressive Soviet behavior toward China,[30] the Soviet leaders now had their hands full in Europe, making it unlikely that they would find much time or energy for new initiatives against China, at least for the time being.[31]

Indeed, the central Soviet preoccupation with Europe was made strikingly clear by Soviet Foreign Minister Andrei Gromyko, speaking before the UN General Assembly on October 3, 1968. In the course of his speech—the first by a high-level Soviet official other than the USSR's representative to the United Nations to defend publicly the Soviet Union's invasion role—Gromyko said: "When the question of the arms race or of hotbeds of international tension, and especially of the entanglement of interests and counterinterests of states is raised, one's mind involuntarily turns to Europe. History takes revenge for forgetfulness, if someone deliberately forgets the significance of European affairs, or neglects them."[32]

Even the November world party conclave in Moscow, originally aimed primarily at unifying the Communist movement against Maoist influence, fell victim temporarily to the Soviet Union's intervention in Czechoslovakia. Faced with the prospect of a protest boycott by many Communist parties previously aligned on the Soviet side, not to mention such confirmed protégés of China as the Albanians,[33] the Soviet Union found it expedient to postpone once more

---

[30] In a protest note of September 16, 1968, Peking charged that the Soviet Union in August had stepped up aircraft intrusions over northeast China in support of its "aggression against Czechoslovakia," implying concern in Peking that increased Soviet military pressure might be applied against China. The Czech invasion also prompted a great outpouring of anti-Soviet propaganda from Peking, much of it aimed at undercutting Soviet influence in East Europe, and seeking to portray the invasion as an example of "U.S.–Soviet collaboration for world domination." Somewhat illogically, the Chinese at the same time blamed the invasion on "sharpening contradictions" between the United States and the Soviet Union in their "scramble for spheres of influence." Peking's attempts to exploit the intervention in Czechoslovakia at Soviet expense were somewhat hampered by the fact that China's strongly orthodox ideological position and Czech reform communism had very little in common. See "Soviet Military Aircraft Intrusion Into China's Air Space Protested," *Peking Review*, no. 38, September 20, 1968, p. 41. See also Chou En-lai speech of August 23, "Chinese Government and People Strongly Condemn Soviet Revisionist Clique's Armed Occupation of Czechoslovakia," in Supplement to *Peking Review*, no. 34, August 23, 1968, pp. III–IV; Stanley Karnow, "Old China-Russia Feud Erupts," *Washington Post*, September 18, 1968.

[31] As noted previously (chapter XI, p. 260), the matter of priority between Europe and Asia has come to be one of the central issues on the Soviet foreign policy agenda. How far the shifting of Soviet attention to the "China problem" had proceeded prior to the Czech invasion is a moot question; there seems to be little doubt, however, that the Czech affair again brought European policy concerns to the forefront in Moscow.

[32] See "Excerpts from Gromyko's Address," *New York Times*, October 4, 1968.

[33] Albania, long tied closely to China, had not, of course, been expected to attend the conference. The Albanians, incidentally, made known their disapproval of the Czech invasion by formally withdrawing from the Warsaw Pact on September 12, 1968. For all practical purposes, Albania had not been an active member of the Pact since 1961. Another effect of the invasion was to prompt Albania and Yugoslavia to start thinking about mending their relations. See

the conference it had so long labored to bring about.[34] Not only did this postponement reflect a loss of political ground in the old struggle with Peking but it also deprived the Soviet Union for the time being of a compliant forum in which it may have hoped to fortify its hand for dealing with a new set of problems in East Europe.

Soviet Search for a Settlement in Czechoslovakia

By all odds, the Soviet Union's most troublesome problem in East Europe was how to bring about a stable settlement of the postinvasion situation in Czechoslovakia. On a short-term basis, the Soviet Union certainly had achieved many of its presumed objectives: the restoration of censorship; the banning of free assembly and of non-Communist organizations; the weeding out of officials particularly objectionable to the Kremlin; and the spiking of any possibility that Czechoslovakia might waver in her adherence to the Warsaw bloc or seek closer relations with West Germany. Under the guns of the occupation forces the Soviet writ ran large again, even to the point of preventing the Czechoslovak people from referring to their uninvited guardians as occupiers.[35] What is more, the intervention had laid to rest, for the time being, Soviet fears that the élan of reform and independence manifested during the Prague Spring might spread to other parts of the Soviet Union's East European domain.

But, despite all this, the Soviet Union found itself in an uneasy position, caught in a political quagmire of its own making. In the world at large, the invasion had earned for it an obloquy which even Soviet self-righteousness and doctrines of Marxist–Leninist necessity could hardly cover, while in Czechoslovakia it was apparent from the early days of the occupation that the Soviet Union was hard put to it to persuade the people and their leaders to co-operate amiably in their own resubjugation. Thanks to the solidarity between the Dubcek regime and the people during the immediate postinvasion days, when Moscow botched the political phase of its intervention, the installation of a subservient puppet regime had been thwarted, making it necessary to leave the

---

"Albania Acts To Pull Out of Reds' Military Pact," *Washington Post*, September 13, 1968; Paul Hoffman, "Soviet Action Spurs New Alignments in Balkans," *New York Times*, September 30, 1968.

[34] In announcing on November 25, 1968, that the world party conference was to take place in May 1969, the Soviet Union avoided any reference to the fact that disunity in the Communist movement stemming from the Czech invasion had required postponement of the conclave. The "preparatory" meeting at which a new time for the conference was apparently reached took place in Budapest, November 17–21, 1968. Subsequently, another preparatory meeting was substituted for the world conference in May, and the date for the main event was put off until June 5, 1969. See editorial, "To Strengthen the Unity of Communist Ranks," *Pravda*, November 25, 1968; Reuters dispatch, "58 Communist Parties Postpone Moscow Summit Conference," *Washington Post*, October 2, 1968; UPI dispatch, "Soviet Overrides Dissent and Wins Red Parley in May," *New York Times*, November 22, 1968; Henry Kamm, "World Red Talks Planned To Open in Moscow June 5," ibid., March 23, 1969.

[35] This crowning indignity was visited upon the Czechs and Slovaks by new censorship regulations first disclosed on September 3, 1968, under which any criticism of the Warsaw Pact or the five Pact armies which had invaded the country was forbidden, and the terms "occupation armies" or "occupiers" were proscribed. See Tad Szulc, "New Czech Censorship Rules Bar Use of Word 'Occupation'," *New York Times*, September 5, 1968.

Dubcek–Cernik–Svoboda leadership in office.[36] Seemingly, the Soviet design was to divide and conquer: to let Dubcek and his associates discredit themselves by serving as the dismantlers of their own reforms in the name of "normalization,"[37] and to count upon time to disillusion the people and undermine their unity.

Yet the occupied nation showed a surprising talent for observing the letter of the normalization process while continuing to circumvent it in spirit, calling forth repeated complaints and warnings from Moscow. A particular source of Soviet frustration was the apparent disposition of the Czechoslovak people to go on giving the occupiers the cold shoulder when, instead, they should have been displaying gratitude for having been spared the horrors of "counterrevolution" by the Russian intervention.[38] Other criticism from Moscow included recurrent charges that anti-socialist forces were obstructing the normalization process by "trying to inspire in the population a false understanding of normalization" and by encouraging the people not to co-operate with the occupation forces. Failure to purge undesirable officials was a frequent complaint. It was reported, for example, that the Soviets had presented a list of 20,000 party and government officials they wanted removed from their posts, a sacrificial offering far larger than Prague apparently was willing to make. Czech news media were repeatedly attacked for violating their "obligation" not to criticize the occupying powers. It was also charged that anti-socialist forces were exploiting calls for national unity in attempts "to poison the minds of the people" and to carry out "overt and covert sabotage of the Moscow agreement."[39]

Gradually, however, it became apparent that Dubcek and his associates were being forced into one concession after another, powerless, it seemed, to fulfill

---

[36] See chapter XIV, pp. 381–82.

[37] Precisely what was to constitute "normalization" remained a contentious issue. The August 23–26 meeting in Moscow produced a fourteen-point agreement, not published in the official communiqué but made available to the Western press from notes kept by the Czechs. The conditions set out in this agreement apparently were interpreted differently by each side. For text of the fourteen points, see *New York Times*, September 8, 1968.

[38] The Soviet allegation that a bloody counterrevolution had been averted by the intervention fell flat in the face of the fact that the Dubcek regime had the solid support of the people. To account for the absence of any violent threats against the Czech Communist leadership, the Soviets invented the theory of "quiet counterrevolution," claiming that it was only the first stage of what would have turned out to be a *violent* counterrevolution. As put by a *Pravda* writer, the Soviets were right not to wait for "the shooting and hanging of Communists" before coming to the aid of "the champions of socialism" in Czechoslovakia. Just who these champions were, however, was not specified. See Sergei Kovalev, "On 'Peaceful' and Non-Peaceful Counterrevolution," *Pravda*, September 11, 1968.

[39] For a small sampling of Soviet sources which aired such complaints in the early months of the occupation, see Iurii Zhukov, "The Truth Will Be Victorious!" *Pravda,* August 28, 1968; V. Matveev, "In the Name of Protecting and Strengthening Socialism," *Izvestiia*, August 28, 1968; V. Zhuravskii and V. Maevskii, "On the Streets of Prague," *Pravda*, August 30, 1968; E. Grigor'ev, B. Dubrovin, and V. Zhuravskii, "Prague: Everyday Life and Contrasts" and "Overcoming Difficulties," ibid., September 6 and 9, 1968; Iu. Filonovich, "Prague Dialogues," *Izvestiia*, September 10, 1968; E. Grigor'ev and V. Zhuravskii, "Solidarity. But on What Basis?" *Pravda*, September 22, 1968; Lt. Colonel A. Sgibnev, "The Great Brotherhood," *Krasnaia zvezda* (Red Star), September 22, 1968; V. Zhuravskii and T. Kolesnichenko, "The Demands of Life," *Pravda,* October 3, 1968; "On the Situation in Czechoslovakia," *Izvestiia*, October 3, 1968.

the hopes of the Czechoslovak people that somehow the occupation might be softened or reversed. A second "negotiating" session between the Czech and Soviet leaders in Moscow in early October,[40] six weeks after the invasion, produced what appeared to be an even more humiliating submission to the Soviet dictate than the Moscow agreement of August 26. Besides acceding to demands that the internal life of Czechoslovakia and its foreign policy be more speedily brought into line with the Soviet formula for normalization, the Czech leaders pledged themselves to sign a treaty providing for the stationing of occupation troops in their country.[41] This pledge was coupled with a declaration that both sides viewed "as their prime task the implementation of measures to create a reliable barrier in the way of mounting revanchist strivings of West German militaristic forces." In other words, the occupation was to be legitimatized in the name of defense against an alleged military threat from West Germany.

For two or three months after the signing of the harsh October treaty,[42] the complex tug-of-war between the Czechoslovaks and their occupiers yielded conflicting evidence as to which side might be gaining the advantage. To the outsider taking a hardheaded, "realistic" look at the situation, it seemed only a matter of time until the Kremlin would succeed in bending the Czechs and Slovaks to its will. Having accepted the political liability of stamping out the Prague Spring by force, the Soviet Union, in this view, would hardly prove squeamish about strangling any residual Czechoslovak efforts to salvage some measure of freedom. For that matter, was it not also clear in Prague that the Soviet Union possessed both the might and the determination to brook no further nonsense from its dependency?

As evidence that this lesson had sunk in, it could be observed that the Soviet tactics of fomenting division within the Prague leadership already had seriously eroded the position of Dubcek and his more loyal associates. New men, sensing the futility of hatred against Soviet power, were coming forward to help by quietly reimposing party and police controls over their countrymen and adopt-

[40] The October 3–4 meeting in Moscow, first scheduled for September 20, came after several postponements reportedly caused by disagreement over the agenda and the composition of the Czech delegation. When Dubcek finally went to Moscow, he was accompanied by Premier Oldrich Cernik and Gustav Husak, first secretary of the Slovak Communist organization, who later replaced him. See Dan Morgan, "Delay Reported on Czech-Soviet Summit," *Washington Post*, September 24, 1968; Tad Szulc, "Visit to Moscow by Dubcek Is Off," *New York Times*, September 25, 1968; Henry Kamm, "Dubcek in Soviet for Crucial Talk," ibid., October 4, 1968.

[41] The communiqué of the October 3–4 meeting stated that the treaty would cover "the temporary stationing of allied troops in Czechoslovakia," and that the withdrawal of "other troops" would be "carried out by stages." No timetable was given for either the troops to be "temporarily stationed" in Czechoslovakia or the "other troops" to be withdrawn. See "Communiqué," *Pravda*, October 5, 1968. Text of the Soviet–Czech Communiqué may also be found in *New York Times*, October 5, 1968.

[42] The treaty was signed in Prague on October 16, 1968, and published three days later. Like the earlier announcement, it called for the stationing of an unspecified number of Soviet troops in Czechoslovakia for an indefinite period of time. There was no provision to compensate Prague for damage caused by the invasion. See "Treaty Between the Government of the Union of Soviet Socialist Republics and the Czechoslovak Socialist Republic on Conditions for the Temporary Stationing of Soviet Troops on Territory of the Czechoslovak Socialist Republic," *Pravda*, October 19, 1968.

ing a "sensible" stance of co-operation with the Soviet Union. The new "compromise-seekers,"[43] not tainted as pro-Moscow agents and holdovers from the Novotny past, could be expected eventually to engineer a settlement under which Moscow's interpretation of "normalization" would prevail.

On the other hand, there were some grounds for questioning how successful the Soviet Union was in rooting out subtle resistance to its occupation rule. Despite the Czechosolvak leadership's formal compliance with Soviet demands, the Soviet Union had not managed to break the country's morale. There was, for example, the phoenix-like quality of Czechoslovak nationalism, which arose to inspire quiet defiance among students and workers in the latter months of 1968, just about the time the exasperated Russians seemed to be making progress in splitting the Prague leadership,[44] while shortly after the turn of the year the immolation of Jan Palach testified to the depth of the feeling against the occupation among the country's youth.[45] From the Soviet viewpoint, the surprising spirit of resistance manifested by the Czechoslovak working class was likely to be even more discomfiting than the anti-Soviet student sentiment, especially since both groups seemed to be pooling their support for continuation of the reform program.[46]

If for a time it seemed possible that an emerging alliance of students and workers might rally behind Dubcek and help to prevent Moscow and its potential collaborators from unseating him, this prospect ebbed rapidly in the early months of 1969. Finding himself obliged to threaten resort to "undemocratic" methods to quell protest against the occupation,[47] but temperamentally unequipped to play the role of stern disciplinarian, Dubcek was able to satisfy neither his supporters nor his critics; consequently, his leadership suffered a steady decline. The pressures on him came to a head in April 1969—following an outbreak in Prague of anti-Soviet demonstrations to celebrate a Czechoslovak ice-hockey victory over a Soviet team. The Soviet Union promptly condemned the Dubcek regime for failing to control "anti-socialist" elements and dispatched its Defense Minister and a Deputy Foreign Minister to Czechoslovakia to bring word that its patience was at an end.

[43] The so-called "compromise seekers" represented a centrist group among Czech and Slovak Communists. At first, they did not challenge Dubcek's leadership directly, but in the inner politics of the party they moved to isolate him gradually by setting up a new "Executive Committee" of the party Presidium as the top policy steering group. They included Premier Oldrich Cernik, who previously had been close to Dubcek, and Deputy Premiers Gustav Husak and Lubomir Strougal, who were key party figures as well as holders of government posts. See Tad Szulc, "Dubcek Struggles for Survival," New York Times, November 17, 1968.

[44] Anti-Soviet student demonstrations occurred in October and November, while in December 1968 workers at major factories and the country's largest labor union, the metal workers, threatened to strike if leading "progressives" were ousted from the Prague leadership. See Karl E. Meyer, "Invasion Turned Czech Workers into Revolutionaries," Washington Post, December 20, 1968.

[45] Jan Palach, a philosophy student, set fire to himself on January 16, 1969, to dramatize the protest of youth against the occupation. Several other young people followed his example of self-immolation.

[46] See Alois Rozehnal, "The Revival of the Czechoslovak Trade Unions," East Europe (April 1969): 2–7; Anita Dasbach, "Czechoslovakia's Youth," Problems of Communism (March-April 1969): 24–31.

[47] See Karl E. Meyer, "Dubcek Warns Protesters of Sterner Measures," Washington Post, December 22, 1968.

Precisely what these emissaries said is not a matter of record, but they are reported to have demanded an immediate housecleaning of the Prague leadership, and to have backed up their demand by threats of new military measures against the country.[48] At any rate, they made their point. On April 17 Dubcek was replaced as First Secretary of the Czechoslovak Communist party by Gustav Husak, while other changes in the party's Presidium resulted in the return to power of several orthodox pro-Soviet leaders and the dropping of a number of "progressive" members, including Josef Smrkovsky.[49] Significantly, there were no public protests over the demotion of Dubcek and his more liberal lieutenants from student-worker groups, whose heady but brief protest alliance appeared to be dissolving in the face of blunt warnings from Husak that anti-Soviet attitudes would not be tolerated.

Along what path Husak might lead the country, no one could say. He himself was a Slovak nationalist, and no novice in the in-fighting of Communist politics. Under his leadership might emerge, not a one-sided settlement on strictly Soviet terms, but rather a precarious *modus vivendi* with Moscow, subject to continuing negotiation and adjustment.[50] For the Soviets, guarantees of orthodox party rule in Czechoslovakia and a foreign policy dictated from Moscow would doubtless be among the minimum conditions of any such living arrangement, while for the Czechoslovaks it might include the assurance that there would be no return to open punitive terror. Conceivably, the uneven struggle between the Czechoslovak people and their occupiers could be terminated on far bleaker terms for the occupied country. In either case, the Soviet rulers might find that in imposing their will upon Czechoslovakia they had lost a friendly ally and gained a grudging subject whose allegiance henceforth would remain uncertain.

Postinvasion Policy Alternatives in East Europe

Beyond the immediate outcome of the Kremlin's effort to bring Czechoslovakia to heel lay more lasting problems of Soviet policy in East Europe. Even though the Czechoslovak reform experiment had been smashed, the question still remained whether it had really been extinguished once and for all. Having tasted a measure of freedom under a reformist Communist regime, the Czechoslovak people might bide their time until conditions made possible a new start

---

[48] Marshal A. A. Grechko and Deputy Foreign Minister V. S. Semenov were the Soviet officials sent to Czechoslovakia, at the same time that it was indicated that additional occupation troops might follow them. See Alvin Shuster, "Anti-Soviet Riot of Czechs Brings New Press Curbs" and "Prague Retracts Word that Soviet Is Sending Troops," *New York Times*, April 3 and 13, 1969.

[49] Idem, "Dubcek Is Ousted as Prague Yields to the Russians," ibid., April 18, 1969.

[50] This appeared to be the pattern emerging in the latter months of 1969, as Husak found himself not only bargaining with the Russians but also locked in an internal power struggle with an ultraconservative faction quietly backed by Moscow. At a Central Committee meeting in September, at which Prague hardliners like Vasil Bilak apparently pressed for political trials of former Dubcek supporters, Husak warned against turning the party into a "slaughterhouse" by a return to terror tactics. See Husak's Central Committee speech, published in *Rude Pravo*, October 11, 1969. See also Paul Hoffman, "Power Struggle Looms in Prague," *New York Times*, September 30, 1969; Eric Bourne, "Czech Committee writes 'Finis' to Dubcek Era," *Christian Science Monitor*, September 30, 1969.

in the direction that was closed off in August 1968. A critical question, therefore, and one applicable not only to Czechoslovakia, was whether the Soviet Union could prevent such conditions from arising again within its East European domain. In 1956 it had crushed Hungary's defiance, only to find twelve years later that the process of change in East Europe had brought new challenges to its authority—first from Rumania and then from Czechoslovakia. Might not a similar pattern be expected to recur?

In the cold afterlight of the Czechoslovak experience, "yes" might seem too facile an answer. By demonstrating anew in Czechoslovakia that the Soviet Union would not shrink from armed suppression of challenges to its control in East Europe, the Soviet leaders undoubtedly had dealt a severe blow to those elements within the East European party elites whose sights had been set on modifying the Soviet-style Communist system to fit their particular national conditions. By the same token, the orthodox hard-line factions in these countries, unsympathetic to reform and dependent to a considerable extent on Soviet backing for their own political foothold, were probably strengthened by the Czechoslovak reminder of the grim reality of Soviet power. The circumstances were not apt to encourage renewed agitation for change and reform in East Europe among party elites at the top, where effective action in these societies necessarily rests, whatever the pressures from below.

On the other hand, there was no warrant that the clock could be made to stand still. The very fact that the Soviet Union again had been obliged to invoke naked military power to sustain its authority testified to the vitality of the forces of change at work in the political, social, and economic life of East European society. Though raw power might intimidate the countries of East Europe and compel their servile obedience to the Soviet dictate, it could not prevent new internal tensions from arising in these countries, widening the gap between the regimes and their people, especially youth and the intellectuals. For that matter, the Soviet leadership itself sat somewhat uneasily upon the lid which it had clamped over its restive intelligentsia at home; there was always the possibility that something like national remorse seeping up from below, and dissension developing within its own ranks at the top, might cause the Soviet leadership to question the wisdom of repressive measures in East Europe and, as had been the case under Khrushchev after Hungary, lead gradually to more flexible policies in that region. Thus it might be argued that, once the immediate impact of Czechoslovakia subsided, something like the pattern of the past could again emerge—with the Soviet Union finding it expedient to give some ground to diversity and change in East Europe while seeking also to reopen the interrupted effort toward an East-West détente.

But, even if this were to happen, another critical question would still remain. The earlier cycle ended, not with Moscow's relaxation of strict control following forcible intervention, but with the fear that Soviet authority had been dangerously eroded and had to be reimposed by force. If history were to repeat itself, therefore, would it again go the full cycle, producing the armed suppression of another Hungary or Czechoslovakia, or would the Soviet Union manage to break this fateful sequence by peaceful accommodation to evolutionary change in East Europe?

Obviously, there was no ready answer to this question in the aftermath of the Czechoslovak crisis. But at least three policy choices, each with a salient bearing on the nature of the Soviet Union's future relations with East Europe, appeared to stand before the Soviet rulers. The most radical of these, and hence perhaps the least likely, was outright acceptance of fundamental reforms of the Communist order in East Europe. Before the Soviet Union could accept any sort of systemic reform in the East European political order, involving a lessening of Soviet control and abandonment of the principle of strict political conformity, it seemed fairly certain that there would have to be basic changes in the outlook of the Soviet leadership and its guiding political ethic at home. Unfortunately, given the marked regression of the incumbent leadership to ultraconservatism and the defense of orthodoxy, its tolerance of systemic reform and liberalization either in the Soviet Union or in East Europe promised to remain rather low. Indeed, barring a collapse of the incumbent collective leadership under the weight of cumulative policy failures and frustration and its replacement by men of greatly different vision, one could hardly suppose that the ruling elite would willingly set out on a path of liberalization that would jeopardize its own claim to a monopoly of political power.

If the reform road thus seemed one the Soviet leadership was unlikely to take, at least in the near future, there was a second, and perhaps less remote, alternative bearing on the Soviet Union's relationship with the countries of East Europe. This was the doleful prospect that the Soviet leadership might increasingly dedicate itself to a kind of neo-Stalinist restoration, demanding more rigid conformity at home and stamping out revisionist and reformist trends elsewhere in the Soviet camp by reimposing physical control wherever Soviet military and police power could be brought to bear. Although the so-called Brezhnev doctrine of intervention within a hazily defined socialist commonwealth was not necessarily an action blueprint for such a course, as we have noted, it was available as the ideological rationale for any attempt to keep East Europe under rigid Soviet control and to insulate it from the dangers of Western influence.

Depending on the resilience and political imagination of the Soviet rulers, there was a third and somewhat less heavy-handed approach to managing Soviet relations with East Europe. It amounted essentially to dealing with pressures against the Soviet position in East Europe opportunistically, seeking to manipulate and divide the forces of political change and modernization rather than attempting to stifle them by resort to a neo-Stalinist despotism. Though this course, too, would doubtless rest in the last analysis on the reminder that Soviet military power stood ready to ensure Soviet hegemony in East Europe, it could allow more room for any internal differences that might arise within the collective Kremlin leadership over how best to cope with challenges to Soviet interests in that region.

Whether the governing opinion within the Soviet leadership were to favor strict defense of orthodoxy or more subtle techniques of control in East Europe, however, one thing which seemed likely was that Soviet policy in this half of Europe could not be divorced from Soviet policy toward the other half of the divided continent. A basic problem for the Soviet Union, as Fritz Ermarth has noted, remained that of how to preserve its hegemony in East Europe while keeping open the prospects for extending its influence in West Europe.[51] On the one hand, disciplinary measures to keep dissent down in the East could prompt NATO to keep its guard up in the West. On the other hand, a relaxation of Soviet policy in East Europe for the sake of improving opportunities for political advance in Western Europe carried the risk of new erosion of Soviet authority and the repetition of experiences like that of Czechoslovakia.

Almost two years after the invasion of Czechoslovakia, it was still by no means clear whether the Soviet leaders, in order not to prejudice their chances for exploiting favorable political opportunities in the West, would manage to rise above the anxious authoritarianism they had come to display toward East Europe. But, as we shall see later, there were indications that the Kremlin leadership had at least begun to move again in the direction of a more active diplomacy in the West, aimed especially perhaps at exploiting Bonn's insecurities and hopes of reunification. Before we come to these indications, however, let us look at some of the consequences of the invasion for the Soviet Union's policy toward Western Europe, where the Czechoslovak affair also proved to be a major political watershed in relations between the Soviet world and the West.

Soviet Preinvasion Prospects in the Western Half of Europe

There is no easy way to reckon the damage done to Soviet interests in Western Europe by the brutal resubjugation of Czechoslovakia. Prior to that crisis, things had seemed to be going rather well there for the Soviet Union under the Brezhnev–Kosygin regime. Keeping their eye on the decisive weight of industrial Europe in the world power balance, while the United States was increasingly distracted from European affairs by the Vietnam war, the Soviet leaders had sought through active diplomacy and political maneuver to establish closer technical, economic, and political ties with West European countries and to foster the idea that new collective security arrangements would provide a timely alternative to NATO. By playing upon West European desires for a role more independent of the United States, and especially upon de Gaulle's anti-Americanism, the Soviet Union seemed to have found a convenient formula for weakening NATO unity and undermining US influence in Europe without having to exert blatant pressures on the Western alliance, a course which had often proved unproductive in the past.

The tendency of America's European allies to move in one degree or another

---

[51] See Ermarth, *Internationalism, Security, and Legitimacy: The Challenge to Soviet Interests in East Europe, 1964–1968*, pp. 131–43. The present author is indebted to this analysis for perceptive insight into the policy alternatives confronting the Soviet Union in East Europe.

away from their former close dependence on American leadership was not the only factor favoring the new European diplomacy of the Brezhnev–Kosygin regime. There was also the feeling in the West that disunity within the Communist world had weakened any threats from that quarter and thus partly offset the lack of unity in NATO, besides perhaps increasing the chances for East–West reconciliation. Above all, there was the widespread belief in the West that the naked use of Soviet military power anywhere in Europe could virtually be ruled out, both because of the strategic nuclear standoff and because of presumed evolutionary changes in the Soviet system itself, which were thought to point toward more temperate, nonideological foreign policy decisions.[52]

In this general atmosphere, the European diplomacy conducted by the Brezhnev–Kosygin regime prior to the Czechoslovak crisis seemed to offer reasonable prospects for progress toward some of the principal objectives of Soviet policy in Western Europe. Although, as in the Khrushchev era, it could be doubted whether the Soviet Union counted any longer upon bringing about revolutionary social and political transformations in Western Europe, Soviet policy appeared still to be aimed at such long-standing objectives as the break-up of NATO, the weakening of West European ties with the United States, and the isolation and demoralization of West Germany—objectives which, if attained, would leave the Soviet Union dominant on the European continent and enhance its global power position relative to the United States.

In a sense, Soviet aims could be described as seeking to upset the status quo in the West of Europe while preserving it in the East. Just as there had been an inherent contradiction in Soviet policy in Khrushchev's time between the idea of bilateral Soviet–US collaboration for particular ends and the exclusion of the United States from Europe, so there was some ambivalence on this point under the Brezhnev–Kosygin regime, though the latter seemed somewhat less equivocal than Khrushchev about making removal of American power from Europe an explicit aim of its diplomacy. In the Mediterranean basin on Europe's southern flank as well, the Soviet Union under the Brezhnev–Kosygin regime sought to improve its military-political position in the wake of the Arab–Israeli war at the expense of American and other Western influence in the area.

Although the situation in Europe as it evolved between 1966 and 1968 was scarcely one in which the fragmentation of the Western alliance had advanced far enough to satisfy maximum Soviet aims, the Soviet Union nevertheless had seemed to be gaining influence in Western Europe at the expense of its superpower rival. By the time of the Bucharest conference of July 1966, the initiative in Europe had increasingly shifted to the Soviet Union; if nothing else, following de Gaulle's military withdrawal from NATO and pressures within the United States itself for reduction of American forces in Europe, the Western alliance appeared to be coming apart at the seams more rapidly than the Soviet Union's own Warsaw bloc, which was not without troubles of its

---

[52] For an excellent discussion of these points, see Marshall D. Shulman, " 'Europe' Versus 'Détente'," *Foreign Affairs* (April 1967): especially 391–98.

own. Provided the Soviet Union managed to maintain reasonable discipline within the Warsaw bloc while continuing to hold the initiative for solution of outstanding European problems, the chances looked fairly good for important gains, perhaps including a few defections from NATO after its twentieth birthday, in 1969, and a continuing American disengagement from Europe without the need for substantial political concessions from the Soviet bloc in return. In effect, the very fluidity of European political life which many in the West hoped would help to soften the old Cold War divisions in Europe provided an environment in which the Soviet Union could hope to change the status quo in Western Europe to its advantage.

There were still many problems for Soviet policy in Western Europe, to be sure. Britain continued to resist Soviet efforts to pry her loose from her traditional association with the United States. In France, where de Gaulle had revived the image of a Communist menace in order to cope with domestic disorder in the spring of 1968, Soviet-French cordiality was beginning to cool. The situation in West Germany also remained in many ways not to the Soviet Union's liking, as German bonds with the United States continued to withstand the diverse strains placed upon them, and Bonn's *Ostpolitik* seemed likely to make further inroads in East Europe. But things were looking up a bit: The CDU–SPD coalition was showing serious signs of wear, West Berlin's morale was sinking, and there had been only half-hearted opposition to the slicing away of access rights to Berlin in the spring of 1968. Moreover, the nonproliferation negotiations had helped to advance the dual objective of barring the nuclear door to Bonn and introducing a troublesome issue into German–American relations,[53] while within West Germany itself the stirring of small but vocal nationalist elements, such as the National Democratic party (NPD), had given the Soviet Union a fresh target for its tired warnings to both Warsaw allies and West Europeans that their security was threatened by German revanchism and neo-Nazism.

Perhaps the general picture sketched above suggests a somewhat more purposeful and successful exploitation of the policy openings available to the USSR in Western Europe prior to the invasion of Czechoslovakia than the record of Soviet accomplishments actually warrants. Despite a situation "objectively" ripe for important Soviet gains, it might be argued, Soviet diplomacy had not in fact made substantial progress toward such major objectives as neutralizing Western Europe and weaning it away from the United States. Moreover, it might also be said that, well in advance of the Czechoslovak crisis, the Soviet leaders had become so preoccupied with defending their position in East Europe against the undermining effects of freer East–West intercourse in general and Bonn's *Ostpolitik* in particular that they had virtually surrendered the initiative in European affairs which circumstances seemed to have bestowed upon them in 1966 and early 1967.

[53] See chapter XIII, pp. 323–24.

Effects of the Invasion on Soviet Interests in Western Europe

Seen in retrospect, there is much to be said for the view that an inadequate Soviet response to the opportunities at hand in Western Europe preceded the turning point reached in Czechoslovakia, and that therefore the invasion itself was more an event that suddenly illuminated the ineptitudes of Soviet policy than one which marked a wholly unexpected reversal of form.[54] Nevertheless, it is hardly to be denied that the invasion created new difficulties for the Soviet Union in its relations with the Western half of Europe, and that a number of Soviet policy interests which might otherwise have remained undamaged were at least temporarily set back by the action against Czechoslovakia.

NATO's Reaction to the Czechoslovak Episode

One of the immediate repercussions in Western Europe, where in the after-math of the invasion Soviet popularity sank to probably an all-time low, was the reawakening of old anxieties about the Soviet military threat to Europe. This, in turn, promised to pump new life into NATO, whose members now found themselves disabused of the comfortable notion that the naked use of Soviet military power in the heart of Europe need no longer be taken seriously. To be sure, Soviet armies had not crossed the dividing line in Europe, but if the Soviet leaders were capable, in cold blood, of a massive military invasion of an ally professing basic loyalty to the Warsaw bloc and the Communist political order, what compunction would they feel about taking military action against the non-Communist Western half of Europe if it should ever let its defenses lapse? In such an event, how inviolable, after all, might the military dividing line through the middle of Europe prove to be?

From Moscow's viewpoint, the revival in Europe of fear and respect for Soviet arms may have appeared to be a not unwelcome by-product of the opera-tion against Czechoslovakia, so long as it did not shock NATO into closing its ranks once more and embarking upon a new build-up of its defenses. Whether NATO's reaction would go this far was by no means clear, however, either to its own members or the Soviet Union. In general, the invasion of Czechoslo-vakia could be said to have resolved NATO's doubts about the need for its existence and to have given it collectively a fresh sense of its relevance to Euro-pean security; but beyond this, views as to what measures NATO should take and how urgently it should pursue them varied from country to country during the initial period of reaction to the invasion.

---

[54] An emphatic presentation of the thesis that the Brezhnev–Kosygin leadership consistently failed to exploit a fluid political situation in Western Europe long before its own Eastern bloc troubles came to a head in Czechoslovakia may be found in Ermarth, *Internationalism, Security, and Legitimacy*, pp. 52–59. For a somewhat divergent but not wholly dissimilar appraisal, which argues that the Soviet Union's successful seizure of the political initiative in Europe gave way, around the beginning of 1967, to retreat from a flexible diplomacy, as priority shifted to preserv-ing the cohesion of the Soviet power sphere in East Europe, see Richard Lowenthal, in *Problems of Communism* (November–December 1968): 5–9.

On the one hand, France—the least enthusiastic supporter of the alliance—
remained as reluctant as ever to restore her formal military ties with NATO,
and de Gaulle seemed little disposed to do anything in response to the invasion
of Czechoslovakia except to call it "reprehensible."[55] In several other countries,
such as Norway, Denmark, Greece, and Turkey, where sentiment in support
of NATO had been flagging, there were varied expressions of revived interest
in the value of the alliance, but no initiatives for strengthening it were forthcoming.[56] In Germany, on the other hand, where anxiety over the new influx
of Soviet troops into Central Europe was coupled with concern that the United
States might not adopt a firm enough stance against Soviet pressure, the Bonn
government stressed how seriously it viewed the postinvasion situation, and
Kiesinger urged a prompt conference of heads of government of the NATO
countries to consider measures for strengthening West European security.[57]

Britain, though among the countries that reportedly were initially cool to
the idea of convening either a special summit or a ministerial meeting to discuss
the security implications of the Soviet intervention—one of the objections being
that no major decisions were likely to be reached until a new administration
took office in the United States—subsequently indicated that she would go along

[55] De Gaulle expressed his views on the invasion in a statement on August 21 and at a press
conference on September 9, in which he castigated the Soviet Union, but declared that the invasion
had dealt only a "momentary setback" to France's policy of seeking détente with Moscow. On
both occasions he also charged that part of the blame for the invasion could be traced to the
Yalta agreement between the United States and Russia to carve up Europe into "spheres of influence." See Charles Hargrove, "France To Pursue Détente Policy Despite Invasion," *Times*, London,
August 30, 1968; Henry Tanner, "De Gaulle Assails Soviet But Backs Policy of Détente," *New
York Times*, September 10, 1968; Donald H. Louchheim, "France Still for Détente, de Gaulle
Says," *Washington Post*, September 10, 1968.

[56] In Norway, leaders of the local movement for withdrawal from NATO renounced their
former views, while Foreign Minister John Lyng declared that the invasion "shows the importance
of our membership in NATO." Similarly, in Denmark the invasion brought at least a momentary
end to debate over Denmark's continued membership in the alliance. The Greek government
condemned the invasion, but was rather guarded in speculating on what changes in Greece's
relationship might be expected. In Turkey, Prime Minister Demirel noted that events in
Czechoslovakia had thrown politicians who questioned Turkey's participation in NATO into "a
terrible contradiction." Some public figures stated that "the importance of Turkey's membership in
NATO has increased." Others, however, notably the Republican People's party leader, Ismet Inonu,
treated the invasion as an internal Warsaw bloc affair and cautioned Turkey to "refrain from
assuming a leading position in connection with the proposed increase of NATO forces." See
"Crisis Strengthens Norway's NATO Ties," *New York Times*, August 29, 1968; Greek government communiqué, August 22, 1968, Greek Embassy Press and Information Service, Information
Bulletin no. 22, August 24, 1968; Demirel press conference, Ankara radio broadcast, September
14, 1968; speech by Turhan Feyzioglu, Ankara radio broadcast, September 23, 1968; editorial,
"Hasty Judgments and Actions Must Be Avoided," *Ulus*, Ankara daily, September 12, 1968.

[57] Chancellor Kiesinger's call on August 23 for a NATO summit meeting met with little
response, partly because it would have involved an invitation to de Gaulle, who presumably would
have turned it down. See "Bonn Asks Study of NATO Defenses," *New York Times*, August 24,
1968; Warren Unna, "W. Germans Seeking NATO Move for Czechs," *Washington Post*, September 10, 1968. Perhaps the closest thing to a favorable echo from Kiesinger's appeal was word that
the political commission of the Consultative Assembly of the Council of Europe, meeting in Rome
on September 4, would propose a summit meeting of the Council's eighteen member-nations to
discuss closer collaboration in the wake of the invasion, which that body regarded as "a menace
to peace on the continent." See *Times*, London, September 5, 1968.

with a ministerial meeting in advance of the regular December session of the NATO Council.[58] In the United States, meanwhile, advocates of unilateral American troop reduction in Europe conceded that their case was dead for the time being,[59] while the Johnson administration, after drawing criticism from European capitals for having hesitated at first to take up a position that might close the door to strategic arms talks with the Soviet Union,[60] moved to declare itself on August 30 with a presidential warning to Moscow not to "unleash the dogs of war" by further military actions in East Europe.[61] The following day, the United States announced that, in view of the "changed East–West military situation" brought about by the massive influx of Soviet forces into Czechoslovakia, it had begun a review with its European allies of their common defense arrangements in NATO.[62]

Out of this initial flurry of somewhat disjointed responses by NATO's members, during which the question of possible NATO intervention in Czechoslovakia was never raised,[63] perhaps the main point which emerged was that NATO intended to take a fresh look at its own defenses in light of the circumstance that the Soviet Union had upset the long-standing military balance in Europe by introducing into Central Europe larger forces than had been present there "at any time since the early postwar period." From the Soviet side, there were immediate protestations that the occupation of Czechoslovakia had not disturbed the power balance in Europe, but had saved it by preventing the "neutralization" and ultimate Western takeover of a Communist bloc country.[64]

[58] Karl E. Meyer, "British Back NATO Meeting," *Washington Post*, September 12, 1968. See also Henry Tanner, "France Rules Out Special NATO Talk," *New York Times*, September 11, 1968. The regular December ministerial meeting was subsequently changed to mid-November 1968.

[59] Carroll Kilpatrick and George Lardner, Jr., "Sen. Mansfield Abandons Drive for U.S. Troop Cuts in Europe," *Washington Post*, August 23, 1968.

[60] For discussion of European criticism of the initial US response in the invasion, see pp. 418–19 below.

[61] President Johnson's August 30 warning to the Soviet Union came at a time when there were widespread rumors that Soviet forces might be preparing for an invasion of Rumania, although he did not specifically name Rumania. See Carroll Kilpatrick, "LBJ Warns Russia on 2nd Invasion," *Washington Post*, August 31, 1968.

[62] Stephen S. Rosenfeld, "NATO Reviews Defenses," *Washington Post*, September 1, 1968; Peter Grose, "U.S. Says Russians Changed Balance in Middle Europe," *New York Times*, September 1, 1968.

[63] As described by a high official at NATO, the first collective decision after the invasion was to "lie low"—that is, to avoid demonstrative measures like mobilization or implied threats of intervention in Czechoslovakia in order not to detract from efforts to condemn the Soviet intervention at the UN Security Council. See Harlan Cleveland, "NATO After the Invasion," *Foreign Affairs* (January 1969): 257–58.

[64] According to Soviet propagandists, it was actually the West which had hoped to revise the existing balance by snatching Czechoslovakia from "the central zone of the defense system of the socialist countries"; when the intervention foiled the "far-reaching plans" of the NATO leaders and the West German "revanchists," they resorted to the "theory" of a changed status as a propaganda "smokescreen." See M. Mikhailov, "Don't Be Confused, Gentlemen!" *Izvestiia*, September 4, 1968. Subsequently, as the Soviet Union sought to construct a convincing alibi for the invasion, the argument that it was prompted by the need to keep Czechoslovakia from leaving the Warsaw camp and thus upsetting the "delicate balance" in Europe assumed increasing prominence. See, for example, "No Excuse for Propaganda About 'Threat from East'," *Soviet News*,

Coupled with this rebuttal from Moscow were Soviet warnings against what were labeled West German attempts to stampede NATO into building up its defenses.[65]

As we shall see in a later chapter, the issue of a shift in the conventional arms balance in Central Europe subsided when the Soviet Union, at the approach of winter, withdrew the bulk of its forces from occupied Czechoslovakia.[66] During the early postinvasion period, however, it was the presence of these additional forces at NATO's doorstep, along with fresh uncertainty about Soviet behavior, which helped the Western alliance partners to arrive at what has been described as a "stopgap policy" to suspend any further consideration of troop withdrawals from West Germany or other economy measures until the effects of the Czechoslovak invasion had been fully evaluated.[67] This stopgap position, made known at a meeting of NATO's Defense Planning Committee on September 4, 1968, still left unclear what was to be done to strengthen NATO's security and who should take the initiative in doing it.[68]

The process of working out a collective NATO response went forward during the next couple of months, yielding its first formal product in mid-November at the NATO ministerial meeting in Brussels, where the Western allies outlined a new military program for NATO based on their studies of the postinvasion situation. The military measures announced at Brussels amounted largely to pledges that the NATO members would try to meet previously agreed standards of manning, equipment, and training, and would take several other

---

September 10, 1968; V. Matveev, "Once More About Those Spreading Confusion," *Izvestiia*, September 11, 1968; K. Petrov, "When Illusions Are Shattered," ibid., September 22, 1968. See also the explanation given by a Polish official, Jozef Winiewicz in an interview with Drew Pearson, "Poland Explains," *Washington Post*, September 22, 1968.

[65] See Mikhailov, *Izvestiia*, September 4, 1968. See also V. Kuznetsov, "Web of Intrigue," *Pravda*, September 11 1968; editorial, "To Strengthen the Peace in Europe," ibid., September 20, 1968; Iurii Kharlanov, "Status Quo According to Bonn," ibid., September 26, 1968; Col. M. Ponomarev, "NATO Increases Tension," *Krasnaia zvezda*, September 20, 1968.

[66] See chapter XVII, pp. 476–77.

[67] The governments of Canada, Belgium, and Britain, as well as the United States, had been under pressure to withdraw more of their troops prior to the invasion. Assurances that such moves would be held in abeyance were given at a September 4 meeting of NATO's Defense Planning Committee, in which France was not a participant. See "Soviet Move Bars Cuts in NATO Now," *New York Times*, September 6, 1968; "NATO To Redeploy Its Defences," *Times*, London, September 5, 1968; Harlan Cleveland, in *Foreign Affairs* (January 1969): 258.

[68] The United States, through statements by the President and other administration officials, suggested that the initiative should come primarily from the European side of the Atlantic. Washington expressed its willingness to bolster US combat capabilities in Europe by such actions as sending previously withdrawn fighterbomber units and mechanized infantry to Germany for maneuvers, provided the other alliance members also made extra efforts to do their share. Among the steps urged were bringing up to full strength the allied divisions currently assigned to NATO, speeding a program to improve the conventional capabilities of the West German Air Force, and improving procedures for rapid mobilization of reserves in the European countries. None of these measures fell in the category of a build-up beyond previously planned NATO levels. See Anthony Lewis, "NATO Build-Up Doubted Despite the Prague Crisis," *New York Times,* September 8, 1968; Peter Grose, "U.S. To Ask Moves by NATO in Wake of Prague Crisis," ibid., September 9, 1968; Carroll Kilpatrick, "Europe's Unity Is Up to Europe: Johnson Urges Local Initiative Despite Czech Invasion," *Washington Post*, September 15, 1968; William Beecher, "U.S. Maps an Interim Rise in Force in West Germany." *New York Times*, September 17, 1968.

steps toward modest improvements in NATO's posture and its alert procedures.[69] Although these measures were directed more toward improving the quality of NATO's forces than their size, a notable feature of the November program was that, for the first time, the European members of NATO (France excepted) had pledged a larger contribution to the collective effort than the United States.[70] Even France exhibited a readiness to move closer once more to practical military collaboration with her NATO allies. Thus, the French were willing to co-operate with a new NATO command, Maritime Air Forces Mediterranean, which was activated a few days after the Brussels ministerial meeting with the mission of keeping an eye on Soviet naval activities in the Mediterranean.[71]

If, on the whole, the November program offered as NATO's first concrete response to the Czech invasion seemed unlikely to pose any formidable new military problems for the Soviet Union in Europe, it served at least to confirm NATO's resolve to halt the gradual erosion of its military posture which had been taking place over the previous few years, and which the Soviet Union doubtless would have liked to see continue. Beyond the somewhat limited commitments undertaken at Brussels to repair NATO's defenses, the November ministerial meeting also produced several rather noteworthy policy statements bearing on NATO's future.

One of these was the declaration that recent events had demonstrated that NATO's "continued existence is more than ever necessary"; this was a formal way of saying that the invasion of Czechoslovakia had put an end to debate over the possibility of withdrawals from NATO after its twentieth birthday in 1969. A second significant declaratory element of the Brussels communiqué

[69] Among the military measures pledged were British increases of an RAF squadron and infantry battalion in West Germany, together with transfer of an aircraft carrier to the Mediterranean; additional Canadian, Greek, and Italian naval contributions; West German improvement of conventional air capabilities and measures to keep more army noncommissioned officers in service; an increase in the size of Belgium's standing army; and maintenance of larger ammunition stocks by Norway. Further US contributions pledged to NATO included assignment of more advanced F-4 Phantom aircraft to interceptor units in Europe; a program to build shelters for American combat aircraft in Europe; an accelerated program to improve NATO's electronic warfare capabilities; and reinforcement of three strategic reserve divisions kept in the United States for rapid deployment to Europe if necessary. An inquiry into the warning problem and development of new alert procedures also constituted part of the new NATO program. Deferred until January 1969, however, were decisions on the commitment of additional budgetary resources to cover new measures to be incorporated in the five-year NATO planning cycle up to 1973. See "Text of Communiqué Issued by NATO Ministers," *New York Times*, November 17, 1968; Drew Middleton, "NATO Flexes Its Muscles," ibid.; Donald H. Louchheim, "NATO Shifts Policy," *Washington Post*, November 13, 1968; Charles Douglas-Home, "Lord Wigg Calls NATO Czech Alert a Fiasco," *Times*, London, November 16, 1968; Harlan Cleveland, in *Foreign Affairs* (January 1969): 253, 258–61.

[70] According to Harlan Cleveland, 80 to 90 per cent of the new defense effort called for by the November program was pledged by the European members of NATO. See *Foreign Affairs* (January 1969): 261.

[71] See Drew Middleton, "France Moving to Cooperation with NATO Again," *New York Times*, November 21, 1968. For further comment on the establishment of the Maritime Air Forces Mediterranean and on Soviet reaction, see chapter XVI, fn. 84. DeGaulle's resignation in April 1969 also brought promise of somewhat closer French military co-operation with NATO, though not formal renewal of previous ties.

was a warning that any further Soviet intervention by force in Europe or the Mediterranean would "provoke an international crisis of grave consequences." Although presumably voiced for its deterrent effect on Moscow, whose enunciation of the Brezhnev doctrine had seemed to make such countries as Rumania, Yugoslavia, and Albania potential targets of Soviet intervention, this warning prompted some critics in the West to observe that NATO appeared to be extending its protection to countries beyond the alliance's traditional area of responsibility.[72] A third important declaration at Brussels reaffirmed that the pursuit of European reconciliation remained a major policy goal of the Atlantic alliance. The NATO allies also noted, however, that the Soviet action in Czechoslovakia had dealt a severe setback to hopes of progress in this direction.

Taken together, the military program and the policy statements that made up NATO's collective response at Brussels suggested that the invasion of Czechoslovakia would have not only the short-run effect of interrupting such détente-oriented measures as "balanced mutual force reductions," aimed at easing tensions between the opposing military alliances in Europe, but also, in the longer run, the effect of postponing indefinitely any prospects for dismantling of these alliances in favor of a new European security system. Few West European members of NATO seemed disposed to gamble upon replacing their common defense arrangements with some untested scheme of pan-European collective security, as the Soviets had proposed in years past; and the Soviet Union for its part now appeared to have a greater need than ever for the institutional framework of the Warsaw Pact as a device for keeping its military forces deployed in East Europe.

The Shattered Image of a Moderate Soviet Leadership

The image of a Soviet Union progressing toward moderation, stability, and traditional norms of international behavior under an essentially prudent and pragmatic collective leadership had come to be widely accepted in the West during the tenure of the Brezhnev–Kosygin regime. This image, together with many of the assumptions about Soviet conduct upon which it rested, was a conspicuous casualty of the adventure in Czechoslovakia, from which the Soviet leaders emerged with a new reputation for unpredictable and irresponsible behavior.

Perhaps the chief factor in stamping the Soviet leaders as men capable of unpredictable, ruthless, and even desperate actions was their surprising resort to military intervention after the Czech crisis had passed its climax at Cierna and Bratislava in early August. As several observers have noted, massive invasion coming on the heels of a negotiated agreement was bound to give the Soviet action an aura of irrationality and to call into question the predictability of Soviet decision-making.[73] Even if one conceded that the Soviet leaders had

---

[72] See, for example, Charles Douglas-Home, "NATO Is Developing a New Ambiguity," *Times*, London, November 19, 1968.

[73] See Anatole Shub, and his reference to the comment of Professor Leo Mates of Yugoslavia, in "Lessons of Czechoslovakia," *Foreign Affairs* (January 1969): 267.

inched hesitantly and indecisively toward the use of force, and that in terms of their own premises and the values they felt to be at stake they had acted logically and "rationally" in finally deciding to invade Czechoslovakia, the fact remained that in most Western eyes men prone to make abrupt and unpredictable moves, like that against Czechoslovakia, were capable of unleashing equally unpleasant surprises in some future crisis. Moreover, the flagrant disregard for the "decent opinion of mankind" shown by the Soviet leadership in the assault upon Czechoslovakia, together with signs that the Kremlin was still not rid of an almost neurotic fear of deviations from Marxist–Leninist orthodoxy, helped to dispel the widespread image of the Soviet collective leadership as an inherently cautious group of bureaucratic oligarchs with little propensity for rash action. Rather curiously, despite all this, no alarm was raised during the Czech invasion that the Soviet leaders were recklessly courting the danger of nuclear war. Perhaps it was thanks to Western restraint and the "lie low" policy of NATO during the crisis that the charge of risking nuclear disaster was not laid at the Soviet door.

From the Soviet viewpoint, the reputation for unpredictability and ruthless assertion of power acquired from the Czechoslovak invasion was not necessarily to be deplored, for it could serve to breed fear and paralysis among opponents. But even though helpful in this sense to Soviet diplomacy, such a reputation could become a questionable asset if it should end by persuading the West that the mellowing of Soviet power was but a pious hope and that no reasonable basis for getting along with the Soviet Union could be found. Indeed, one of the most regrettable effects of the Czechoslovak episode might prove to be its having undermined those assumptions of rationality and predictability of Soviet conduct upon which the stability of co-existence of the opposing systems in the nuclear age had been greatly dependent.

Besides casting doubt on the behavior of the Soviet leadership in general, the Czechoslovak affair strengthened the impression in the West that dogmatic hard-line elements had gained the ascendancy in the Kremlin, a development which also seemed to portend that Europe would have to gird itself for a renewed period of harsher East–West confrontation. Whether, in fact, the Czech crisis left the Soviet leadership internally torn between orthodox hard-liners and pragmatic moderates was, however, difficult for outsiders to determine. Perhaps no aspect of the crisis prompted more speculation based on flimsier evidence than the question of differences between contending factions within the Soviet leadership. That there was a split in the Politburo between those who felt that the Czech reform experiment must be stamped out by force and those who wanted to kill it by slow attrition seemed highly plausible, but how deeply this cleavage ran and who lined up on either side were matters on which little could be said with certainty.[74]

74 For an interesting analysis, which finds evidence of Soviet leadership disagreement over Czechoslovakia in the Politburo's reluctance to parade its differences before the Central Committee, see Victor Zorza, "Soviet Leadership Still Unable To Agree on Czech Position," *Washington Post*, September 25, 1968. For other commentary on the internal Soviet debate over handling of the

While it may be supposed that the issue of how to deal with Czechoslovakia aggravated the political problems within the Kremlin, and may even have placed some members of the collective leadership in a vulnerable position, the Brezhnev–Kosygin regime did manage to contain any sharp differences within its ranks. Eventually, the sensitive issue of Soviet policy toward Czechoslovakia might prove divisive enough to bring about a shake-up in the ruling group, especially if dissatisfaction with the outcome of the intervention should mount, but for the time being, at least, the regime had weathered what was probably the most severe test of its stability since it took power in October 1964.

Whatever the balance between hard-line and moderate factions within the Kremlin, however, hope in the West of being able to deal on reasonable terms with temperate elements among the Soviet leadership was badly shaken by the Czechoslovak repression. Not only had supposed moderates of the Kosygin and Podgornyi stripe apparently turned up among the hawks on the intervention issue,[75] but the moderate position seemed likely to suffer in any event. If the West were to swallow Czechoslovakia's subjugation with little more than a gulp of moral indignation and offer to go back to business as usual, the policy of the Soviet hard-liners would be vindicated and the position of the moderates further undermined. If, on the other hand, the West refused to treat the situation as a mere "family affair" within the Warsaw camp and put some sting into its disapproval, the Soviet hard-liners could be expected to claim that they were right all along about meddling interference from the West, while the moderates would find themselves either obliged to agree or placed in the compromising position of siding with the meddlesome adversary. In short, the currency of moderation in East–West diplomacy seemed to have been debased by the Soviet handling of the Czechoslovak situation.

Impact of the Invasion on Soviet–German Relations

Another consequence of the assault on Czechoslovakia was a further deterioration in Soviet relations with West Germany. While the invasion might have

---

Czechoslovak problem, see Anatole Shub, "Whose Turn Is It After the Czechs?" ibid., August 11, 1968; editorial, "Who Rules Russia?" *New York Times*, August 14, 1968; Harry Schwartz, "Kremlin's Hawks Won Debate," ibid., August 22, 1968; David Binder, "Soviet Split Over Invasion Described," ibid., August 25, 1968; Richard Wilson, "Czech Affair Could Bring Upheaval in Kremlin," *Washington Star*, September 16, 1968.

[75] One of the curious details to emerge from the Czech crisis was the apparent shift in roles customarily ascribed to some of the top Soviet leaders. According to several accounts, derived from Czechoslovak exposure to the Russian leaders in negotiations at various stages of the crisis, Kosygin and Podgornyi turned out to be among the toughest of the Kremlin group rather than the doves they had usually been pictured as being. On the other hand, Suslov, reportedly a leader of the orthodox hard-line faction, was said to have taken up a conciliatory position, presumably in the hope of salvaging the November world party conference for which he was responsible. The crisis image of Brezhnev was that of a vacillator trying to straddle the hard-line and moderate positions, more or less in keeping with the posture customarily attributed to him. It should be emphasized, of course, that these vignettes rest on rather uncertain evidence. See, for example, Rowland Evans and Robert Novak, "Czech Invasion Viewed as Move To Block U.S.-Russian Summit," *Washington Post*, September 11, 1968; Drew Pearson, "Soviet Invasion Poses Vital Questions," ibid., September 18, 1968.

been expected to aggravate long-standing Soviet–German differences in any event, it was probably the Soviet Union's attempt to concoct a rationale for its armed intervention which first led it to turn up the heat against Bonn. After the collapse of its initial pretext that Soviet troops had been "requested" by unidentified members of the Prague leadership to put down internal "counterrevolutionary" elements, the Soviet Union fell back on allegations that it intervened just in the nick of time to forestall "a major politico-military operation" against Czechoslovakia which the West had been preparing under cover of a policy of building "bridges" to the East.[76] According to Soviet claims, the "timely" and "decisive" intervention in Czechoslovakia "shattered" Bonn's plans for "tearing the country away from the Warsaw Pact and turning it into a 'corridor' for the Bundeswehr on the road to the Soviet frontier."[77]

Despite its patent absurdity,[78] this fictional justification was accompanied by the very real presence of numerous Soviet combat divisions and air units in Czechoslovakia, where at least some of them seemed likely to remain for some time.[79] These forces, in addition to providing leverage against the stubborn Czechoslovak population and its leaders, were postured in depth against the West to sustain the fiction of a newly arisen military threat from that quarter. Thus, impaled in effect on a fantasy of its own making, the Soviet Union itself had created a new military threat in the heart of Europe which NATO could scarcely afford to ignore.

However, the mischievous effects of Moscow's insistence that Germany and her NATO partners were to blame for the "preventive" invasion of Czechoslovakia went somewhat further than raising the level of military tension in Europe. Among other things, Soviet efforts to depict Bonn as the villain in the piece brought West Germany's policy of reconciliation toward the East to a virtual standstill. By interpreting Bonn's *Ostpolitik* as evidence of a hostile attitude toward the Soviet Union and demanding an end to Bonn's influence in the East,[80] Moscow all but throttled for the moment any German hopes of cultivat-

[76] See previous discussion of the successive Soviet attempts to justify the invasion, chapter XIV, pp. 381–85.

[77] See, in particular, Iurii Zhukov, "The Black Dog Will Remain Black," *Pravda*, September 5, 1968.

[78] The notion that the Bundeswehr, an army of twelve divisions without nuclear weapons, would march through Czechoslovakia to take on the massive armed forces of the Soviet Union was clearly ridiculous, and merely served to point up the threadbare character of the Soviet claim that the intervention had been a justifiable response to a military threat from the West. On the other hand, the Soviet Union doubtless was motivated to intervene partly out of concern that its own forward military position in East Europe would be jeopardized should Czechoslovakia prove to be an unco-operative partner (see p. 390 above).

[79] One of the reported fourteen provisions of the August 26 Moscow Agreement was that outside forces would remain permanently in Western Bohemia to secure the frontier facing the Federal Republic. See *New York Times*, August 28, 1968. For Soviet statements on conditions for partial withdrawal of occupation forces, see E. Grigor'ev, B. Dubrovin, and V. Zhuravskii, "Prague: Everyday Life and Contrasts," *Pravda*, September 6, 1968; Georgii Ratiani, "Imperialism's Forfeited Stakes," ibid., September 22, 1968.

[80] The Soviet propaganda campaign against West Germany, aimed in the first instance perhaps at justifying the invasion of Czechoslovakia, grew into a full-fledged attack on Bonn's *Ostpolitik* following delivery of a Soviet note to Chancellor Kiesinger on September 3, 1968, by Soviet

ing normal relations with the Soviet bloc. Although the Bonn coalition government declined to regard its eastern policy as bankrupt, and soon offered to reopen a dialogue with Moscow on improvement of relations in the East,[81] it could be presumed that the Soviet Union, having reaffirmed its military rule over East Europe, was not likely to countenance fresh *Ostpolitik* overtures unless they involved more extensive concessions than any Bonn had ever been willing to make.[82]

For a brief interval between the end of the July crisis and the invasion, it had seemed that the Soviet Union might be toying with a shift of tactics toward West Germany, designed perhaps to play upon the promise of improved relations with the Soviet Union and the German Democratic Republic, in order to sidetrack the development of a special West German relationship with Czechoslovakia. One sign of such a conciliatory approach to Bonn was Ulbricht's rather surprising offer, on August 9, to open talks on a renunciation-of-force agreement without making full-scale recognition of his regime a precondition.[83] While this gesture may have come at Ulbricht's own initiative, it seems unlikely that he would have turned abruptly from a hostile to a co-operative stance without agreement from Moscow. But, if Ulbricht's move was to have been the opening step in a concerted effort to isolate Bonn from Prague by conciliatory tactics,[84] it was overtaken by events and not followed up.

On the contrary, an even tougher Soviet line toward West Germany emerged after the invasion. Not only did Moscow express its disapproval of Bonn's *Ostpolitik*, but—more ominously still—the Soviet Union reasserted the claim that, under Articles 53 and 107 of the UN Charter as well as under the Potsdam agreements, it was entitled to intervene unilaterally in West Germany, by force if necessary, to prevent the "renewal of aggressive policy" by a former enemy

---

Ambassador S. K. Tsarapkin. The note warned the German government that it must give up attempts to exert influence in East Europe or "face the consequences." See David Binder, "Moscow Cautions Bonn on Policies," *New York Times*, September 4, 1968. Among subsequent Soviet attacks on the Federal Republic's Eastern policy, see Nikolai Gribachev, "Prophets and Lessons," *Pravda*, September 4, 1968; V. Mikhailov, "What Kind of Bridges Is Bonn Building," *Pravda*, September 17, 20, 23, 1968.

[81] Both Kiesinger and Brandt made clear their view that a peaceful understanding with the Soviet Union remained the key to hopes for solving the problem of Germany's division. See David Binder, "Kiesinger Offers Soviet New Talks To Insure Peace," *New York Times*, October 7, 1968; Juan de Onis, "Brandt Cautions on East Europe," ibid., October 11, 1968.

[82] See Ermarth, *Internationalism, Security, and Legitimacy*, pp. 121–22.

[83] David Binder, "Ulbricht Offers Talks With Bonn; Eases Conditions," *New York Times*, August 10, 1968. The Federal Republic, in turn, indicated its willingness to explore the prospects for a compromise of various differences. A Bonn spokesman on August 16 also indicated that the Federal Republic was prepared to make a long-demanded conciliatory gesture to Czechoslovakia by declaring the 1938 Munich Pact "null from the outset." This may have sharpened Soviet suspicions that the ground was being prepared for restoration of diplomatic relations between Bonn and Prague. See David Binder, "Bonn Ready To Invalidate Munich Pact as of 1938," *New York Times*, August 17, 1968.

[84] Perhaps the possibility ought not to be overlooked that a Soviet–GDR conciliatory ploy toward Bonn after the Cierna–Bratislava meetings may have been intended to lull West Germany —and incidentally, to throw the Czechs off guard—while the invasion preparations were being completed.

state.[85] Warnings from the Western powers that any Soviet attempt to test this thesis would lead to an "immediate allied response" under the North Atlantic Treaty helped perhaps to allay anxiety in West Germany,[86] while in most other quarters in the West the tendency was to regard the Soviet claim as a propaganda ploy rather than a prelude to a power move against Germany.[87] After what had happened to Czechoslovakia, however, there remained a lingering concern that the Soviet Union might find a pretext for a power squeeze against Berlin designed to demonstrate that it was not in retreat because of its difficulties in East Europe.[88]

Although the effect of the Czechoslovak invasion in spiking West Germany's conciliatory approach to the East doubtless was regarded in Moscow as an appreciable gain, both in terms of traditional Soviet interest in the maintenance of a divided Germany and as a reminder to Bonn that the keys to any future German settlement remained firmly in Soviet hands, it also involved certain political costs. An important part of the Soviet Union's political capital in Europe had always been the contention that Germany was the inveterate trouble-maker against whom stern Soviet policies were necessary and justifiable. Now the shoe was on the other foot, and it was a trouble-making Soviet Union which sought to depict West Germany's desire for normal relations as a warlike provocation and uttered veiled threats of military intervention. Henceforth, the Soviet Union could hardly expect to trade quite so freely as before on the image of an ever-delinquent Germany.

But the Soviet Union's position with respect to West Germany suffered still further damage from the invasion of Czechoslovakai. The use of East German

[85] As noted in chapter XIII, p. 322, the Soviet Union had specified in a memorandum to Bonn on July 5, 1968, that it reserved the right to intervene unilaterally in West Germany even if a renunciation-of-force agreement were signed. After the Czech invasion put Soviet intervention proclivities in a new light, Bonn prevailed on the tripartite powers to warn Moscow against exercising its claimed right under UN Articles 53 and 107 to intervene in Germany as a former "enemy state." This Western warning was issued on September 17. The following day, the Soviet Union reasserted its right to intervene in West Germany to suppress "a rebirth of German militarism and Nazism," citing as sanction the Potsdam Agreement as well as the UN Charter. See Vladlen Kuznetsov, "Far-Reaching Aims," *Pravda*, September 18, 1968; L. Volodin, "Apropos the Revanchists," *Izvestiia*, September 20, 1968.

[86] See Benjamin Welles, "Soviet Is Warned on West Germany," *New York Times*, September 18, 1968.

[87] See, for example, editorials "Soviet Ploy" and "New Heat on Germany," *Washington Post*, September 19 and 22, 1968; Benjamin Welles, "NATO Allies Doubt Russians Will Move into West Germany," *New York Times*, September 20, 1968; George Sherman, "Soviet Bloc Unity Is Goal of Anti-German Drive," *Washington Star*, September 21, 1968.

[88] Although Soviet warnings that steps would be taken against "illegal encroachment on West Berlin" were no novelty, in this case they took on a more forbidding aspect by being linked to the contention that the Soviet Union had a right to intervene under the UN Charter. The psychological effect of Soviet warnings concerning Berlin was reflected in public opinion polls showing a rising level of concern among the population. See "West Berliners Reassured by Mayor on Soviet Threat," *New York Times*, September 21, 1968; Crosby S. Noyes, "Bonn Jittery as Soviet Threats Unanswered," *Washington Star*, September 26, 1968; Drew Pearson, "Jittery Berlin: Western Part of City Is Afraid that Russia May Miscalculate Again," *Washington Post*, September 29, 1968.

forces in the invasion, for example, gave a cynical twist to Moscow's long-standing animadversions about the "menace" of German militarism, not only casting doubt on the sincerity of the Soviet Union's professed alarm about revived German militarism[89] but pointing up the contrast between the international conduct of the two German governments in a manner distinctly unfavorable to the Communist regime. Bonn's delay in ratifying the nuclear non-proliferation treaty (its ratification having been an objective avidly pursued by the Soviet Union) was another by-product of the intervention in Czechoslovakia. The violation of Czechoslovak sovereignty gave Bonn both a plausible excuse to postpone approval of the treaty and a fresh opportunity to press for stronger American nuclear guarantees in return for its signing.

Finally, one of the invasion's more significant effects on the Soviet Union's German policy was the crimp it put in Moscow's prospect of either isolating West Germany or weaning her away from the Western alliance. In either case, the key to attainment of the objective lay in separating Germany from the United States; in the first instance, by prevailing upon Washington to place Soviet–American collaboration ahead of Germany's interests; in the second, by convincing Bonn that a bilateral understanding with Russia would bring greater rewards than a close tie to NATO. Although neither avenue toward undermining the US–German relationship was necessarily closed to the Soviet Union by its action in Czechoslovakia, the temporary effects of the invasion were hardly favorable to Moscow,[90] for both Washington and Bonn had been given fresh reason to look to the preservation of firm US–German ties, the foundation upon which the Western alliance rested.

Spur to the Mending of American Relations with West European Countries

Apart from putting a new premium on the maintenance of firm bonds between the United States and its West German ally, the Soviet invasion of Czechoslovakia also brought home to Washington the need for greater attention to its relations with other West European countries. In the larger sense this meant that the United States was again being drawn more actively into Europe, a development obviously detrimental to the Soviet aim of detaching the United States from its European partners. At the same time, however, it was apparent that the Czechoslovak crisis had injected a certain asperity into US–West European relationships, from which Moscow might derive some satisfaction. Complaints were raised in several European capitals, for example, that the

---

[89] The tripartite powers, noting that the real show of German militarism during the Czechoslovak crisis had come from Pankow, not Bonn, indicated in September that, if Soviet complaints against West Germany continued, they would charge the Soviet Union with violation of the Potsdam Agreement for having used East German troops in the invasion. See "Big-3 Allies To Protest Use of E. German Army," *Washington Post*, September 24, 1968.

[90] Obviously, there is some contradiction between this statement and the previously made point that the Soviet Union's position toward Bonn was strengthened by the invasion's having cut the ground from beneath Bonn's *Ostpolitik* (see pp. 415–16 above). However, temporarily at least, Moscow was unable to play the stronger cards it had acquired; whether it would manage to do so in the future would depend not only on the suppleness of Soviet policy but on the character of US–German relations and a host of other factors.

United States reacted "insensitively" to the invasion, showing unseemly haste to resume the pursuit of détente with the Soviet leaders and thereby appearing to give symbolic approval to the Soviet Union's breach of morality and standards of decency in international conduct.[91] Some European critics of American diplomacy, including de Gaulle, saw in the situation a cynical understanding between the two Great Powers on "spheres of influence,"[92] while others went so far as to assert that it was "obvious that the Americans gave the Russians carte blanche to invade Czechoslovakia."[93]

Although critics tended to ignore such things as the lead taken by the United States in seeking a UN Security Council resolution of condemnation,[94] some of their reproaches, particularly those suggesting that there should be "a decent interval" before any meeting between top Soviet and American leaders, appeared well warranted. In any event, the agitation over Washington's initial reaction to the Czechoslovak crisis subsided after the United States began to manifest a sterner attitude toward the Soviet Union, beginning on August 30 with President Johnson's warning to Moscow not "to unleash the dogs of war." Shortly afterward, among other manifestations of disapproval, the United States also indicated that it was no longer in a hurry to get on with strategic arms talks with the Soviet Union, although still hopeful of salvaging them later at an "appropriate time."[95]

Whether or not postponement of these talks left Moscow seriously dis-

[91] See, for example, Edwin L. Dule, Jr., "U.S. Will Pursue Arms Limit Talks," *New York Times*, August 21, 1968; Anthony Lewis, "Hope For Détente Wanes in Europe: Soviet and American Actions Both Assailed Anew," ibid., August 30, 1968; Peter Grose, "U.S. Reassessing Policies in Wake of Prague Crisis," ibid., September 5, 1968; Anthony Lewis, "Europeans Upset by U.S. Reactions," ibid., September 9, 1968; Murrey Marder, "U.S. 'Haste' To Continue Talks Bewildering to Allies in NATO," *Washington Post*, September 7, 1968.

[92] On de Gaulle's reaction, see fn. 55 above. De Gaulle's version of postwar European history, blaming the United States and Russia for arriving at a "spheres of influence" agreement at Yalta, was challenged by W. Averell Harriman, who argued that Soviet domination of East Europe came about not because of the Yalta agreements but because they were broken. See Donald H. Louchheim, "Harriman Answers de Gaulle," *Washington Post*, September 12, 1968.

[93] "Dishonour Among Thieves," *New Statesman*, London, September 6, 1968.

[94] It was no surprise to anyone that the Soviet Union cast its 105th veto in the Security Council to kill the censure motion on the invasion of Czechoslovakia. However, the debate, especially that between George W. Ball of the United States and Iakov A. Malik of the Soviet Union, served to put US condemnation of the Soviet action before the world. It also gave Czechoslovakia's representatives an opportunity to deflate the Soviet Union's claim that it had been invited to intervene. See "UN Council Votes To Discuss Crisis," *New York Times*, August 22, 1968; Drew Middleton, "Czechs Send 2 Protests to UN; Troop Withdrawal Demanded," ibid.

[95] Just prior to the Czech invasion, US–Soviet agreement reportedly had been reached on a time and place for the strategic arms talks that were to begin in the near future. (Peter Grose, "Progress Made on Missile Talks," *New York Times*, August 23, 1968.) Announcement of the agreement was held up by the invasion, however, and as pressure grew for the United States to demonstrate that it was not prepared to overlook the Soviet use of force in East Europe, the opening date for the talks was deferred. Secretary of Defense Clark H. Clifford gave public notice of the delay in a speech at the National Press Club on September 5, when he said, "We can continue to hope that, at an appropriate time, these talks can take place." See excerpts from Clifford's speech, *New York Times*, September 6, 1968. Reported Soviet suggestions that the talks be opened in Geneva at the end of September likewise met with apparent coolness in Washington. See Benjamin Welles, "U.S. Cool to New Soviet Bid on Nuclear Talks," *New York Times*, September 19, 1968.

appointed was an open question. However, the fact that the United States, despite its manifest interest in pursuing the talks, felt obliged to set them aside for the time being attested to Washington's new, postinvasion responsiveness to European concerns that the United States might put collaboration with the Soviet Union ahead of its alliance obligations to Europe. To the extent that this development narrowed the Soviet Union's opportunity to play upon differences between the United States and its European partners, still another debit could be chalked up to the misadventure in Czechoslovakia.

Embarrassment of Communist Parties in Western Europe

A further effect of the Soviet move against Czechoslovakia was the somewhat unhappy plight in which it left the various West European Communist parties. Were they to condone the Soviet action, their chances of winning public support and of promoting Popular Front movements in the West were bound to face decline, while disapproval would not only offend the Soviet Union but would widen the fissures in the international Communist movement. Most of the West European parties, including the two major ones in France and Italy, chose to dissociate themselves from Moscow's move;[96] nevertheless, it appeared that they had been badly damaged both in their appeal to domestic constituencies and as instruments for the support of Soviet policy in Europe.

Tangible evidence of the adverse impact of the invasion upon the fortunes of a West European Communist party came first from Sweden, where in the parliamentary elections of mid-September the Communists lost substantial ground, despite having denounced the Soviet action against Czechoslovakia.[97] The Finnish Communists suffered a similar electoral setback in early October. Internal dissension within the various European parties, especially bitter in France and Italy, arose also over the issue of how far to go in criticizing the Soviet Union.[98] Although threats from Moscow to cut off subsidies and other help to the West European Communist parties led some of them (particularly the French party) to soften their criticism,[99] the divisive effects of wrangling

[96] The only West European parties which expressed approval of the invasion were the Luxembourg party and the illegal wing of the West German Communist party. For accounts of the adverse reaction of most West European Communist parties to the invasion, see Henry Tanner, "Reds Throughout West Europe Condemn Moscow for Invasion," *New York Times,* August 22, 1968; John L. Hess, "Criticism Joined by Communists," ibid.; "Italians To Shun Party Talks," *Times,* London, September 7, 1968; Leo J. Wollemborg, "Czech Issue Shakes Italian Red Party," *Washington Post,* September 11, 1968; Jean Riollot, "World CP Reactions to Invasion of CSSR," Research Report, CRD 311/68, *Radio Liberty,* Munich, August 27, 1968.

[97] The Swedish Communist party slipped from 6.4 per cent of the vote to 2.9 per cent and lost five of its eight seats in parliament, a defeat which the Soviet Union attributed to "the fierce anti-Communist propaganda unleashed by the Swedish press on the eve of the elections, particularly in connection with the events in Czechoslovakia" ("The Ruling Party's Success in Sweden," *Izvestiia,* September 17, 1968). See also Wilfred Fleisher, "Swedish Socialists Triumph in Voting," *Washington Post,* September 16, 1968.

[98] See Henry Tanner, "French Red Party Hardens Position," *New York Times,* October 24, 1968; Robert C. Doty, "European Reds Are Torn by Dissent over Czechs," ibid., November 10, 1968.

[99] Threatened loss of financial support was not the only factor inducing West European Communists to soften their criticism of Soviet policy. Once the Soviets had restored a façade of Soviet–

between pro- and anti-Soviet factions seemed likely to persist for some time. Besides creating difficulties between Moscow and the Western party leaderships, the invasion also brought a challenge to Moscow's influence over the two largest Communist-led trade unions in Western Europe, those in France and Italy, with the further possibility that revolt against Soviet control might spread to the Communist World Federation of Trade Unions.[100]

Perhaps one of the principal setbacks to Communist interests in Western Europe could only be measured in terms of a "lost alternative." Had the development of a "democratized" national Communist system in Czechoslovakia been permitted to continue, its example might have gone far toward convincing social-democratic and neutralist elements in Western European countries that it was safe to get into bed with their domestic Communist parties without fearing the loss of national integrity. As it was, however, the Soviet suppression of the Czechoslovak experiment demonstrated that any country in which Communists came to office would find its sovereignty in jeopardy, which hardly improved the domestic standing of the Western parties.

Just as Moscow's disregard for Czechoslovak sovereignty had prejudiced the domestic influence of the West European Communist organizations, so it tended also to reduce the attraction of neutralist positions in the European political spectrum. Austria, sharing a border with Czechoslovakia, was a case in point. A perceptible cooling of Soviet–Austrian relations set in after the invasion, and concern was evident in Vienna that Austrian neutrality might not be respected should the Soviet Union at some point decide that military measures were needed to suppress criticism of Soviet policy in Rumania and Yugoslavia.[101] On the other hand, as the initial shock of the invasion wore off, it became evident that neutralist sentiment in some parts of Europe would revive. Finland provided a pertinent example. There, after a nervous interval during which a few anti-Soviet demonstrations were staged, the Finns returned to a carefully neutral stance, professing to see no alternative to this position for a small country living at the Soviet Union's doorstep.[102]

Setback to the Prospects for East–West Reconciliation

Although much of the political capital accumulated in Western Europe by the Brezhnev–Kosygin regime had been dissipated at one stroke by the invasion

Czech harmony under the Husak regime, much of the ground for open opposition was cut from under the West European Communists. The tendency of the French party to toe the line once more was illustrated by the expulsion in early 1970 of Roger Garaudy, a ranking party figure and severe Soviet critic.

100 See Joseph A. Loftus, "Invasion Assailed by Red Labor Unit," *New York Times*, October 2, 1968; David Binder, "European Unions Challenge Soviet," ibid., October 28, 1968.

101 See Paul Hoffman, "Austrian Socialist Warns of Pressure by Moscow," *New York Times*, September 4, 1968. Public concern in Austria about the country's neutrality reportedly included not only the fear that the USSR might, under a "spheres of influence" arrangement, reoccupy the eastern part of Austria in a possible military move against Yugoslavia but also the possibility that the United States might react by reoccupying the western half of the country. See Paul Hoffman, "Austria Seeks To Allay Fears," ibid., September 19, 1968.

102 See David Binder, "Finns See Policy Proved Correct," *New York Times*, September 25, 1968.

of Czechoslovakia, the Soviet Union could probably expect to regain some of it gradually as time softened outraged sentiment and the intolerable again became the normal state of affairs. There was, after all, the precedent of Hungary, also a traumatic case of armed intervention which the Soviet Union had rather quickly managed to live down. But in some ways Hungary was not an apt parallel, for there one could recognize that the Soviet Union had acted to restore a Communist regime that had been thrown out of power and to bring back into the Soviet camp a country that had left the Warsaw Pact. Neither of these extenuating conditions applied in the case of Czechoslovakia, where the issue was the right of an incumbent Communist regime to experiment with a modified, "humanized" form of Communist rule.

The difference was crucial. Indeed, the implications which flowed from this distinction between Hungary in 1956 and Czechoslovakia in 1968 would have perhaps a more fundamental bearing on Western Europe's future relationship with the Soviet Union than any other effect of the Soviet intervention. For, in trampling Czechoslovakia underfoot, the Soviet Union laid bare the melancholy truth that Communist orthodoxy remained a formidable obstacle to the reconciliation of a divided European continent and to genuine East–West coexistence.

Despite having leaned over backwards not to "meddle" in the Czechoslovak reform experiment, the West learned that the Soviet leaders could not abide even the mild breath of freedom promised by "reform Communism," but on the contrary felt that communism could only survive by continuing to employ such weapons as strict press censorship, monopoly party rule, secret police controls, and, ultimately, armed repression. What this meant, in effect, was that so long as the defenders of orthodox communism remained fearful of liberalizing reforms from within, they also were likely to feel threatened by contaminating ideas from without. By mere force of example, the West was cast as a constant "subversive" threat against which tighter barriers must be erected.

After Czechoslovakia, the renewed jamming of Western broadcasts and attacks on bridge-building concepts as alleged weapons in the West's subversive arsenal reflected this fear of outside contamination, if indeed the resumption of these practices did not testify to a deeper need for an external enemy against which the Soviet leaders could mobilize their subjects in order to keep their totalitarian system running.[103] Moreover, the Czechoslovak case also marked the rebirth in Moscow of the pernicious doctrine that the Soviet Union enjoys the right to impose orthodox rule within its sphere by using its military and police power, regardless of "abstract" notions of national sovereignty and self-determination. In this climate, the prospects for bridge-building and freer East–West traffic in ideas hardly looked promising, much less the attainment of genuine reconciliation between the rival systems in a divided Europe.

Whither Soviet European Policy?

To be sure, there was no fatal inevitability that a new Iron Curtain would be rung down around the Warsaw bloc, nor, if so, that it would remain long intact.

[103] See Michel Tatu, "The Soviet Union," *Interplay* (November 1968): 2.

The subterranean evolution of the Communist order within the Soviet bloc might prove stronger than efforts to hold it back. The dogmatists and defenders of orthodoxy themselves might lose their hold upon the machinery of decision within the Soviet leadership, opening the way for more flexible accommodation to the process of change in East Europe and to the notion of bridge-building in both directions between East and West.

For that matter, even if the Soviet Union were to remain preoccupied with staving off "subversion" of its system from the West, the situation was not necessarily altogether bleak from the West European viewpoint. For, in a sense, this could mean a diversion of Soviet energies, with Moscow giving less attention to altering the status quo in Western Europe and more to defending it in East Europe.

But, at best, any such shift of attention promised to be only a relative matter, unlikely to keep the Soviet leaders so absorbed that they would cease to interest themselves in the affairs of the Western half of Europe, the more so as the Brezhnev–Kosygin regime showed no disposition to abandon the tendency—common also to its predecessors—to obstruct the emergence of a united Western policy front toward the Soviet Union. This tendency, perhaps consistent enough to be called a basic principle of Moscow's European diplomacy, reflected several apparently deep-seated convictions: (1) that a united Europe would represent a threat to Soviet security and, conversely, that a divided or fragmented Europe would enhance Soviet security and provide a better environment for the pursuit of Soviet interests; (2) that a prospering and reasonably cohesive Western Europe would prove a powerful attraction for the East European countries in Moscow's orbit, thus threatening the Soviet Union's hegemony in a region it deemed vital to its security; and (3) that a unified Western Europe, or a reconciled East-and-West Europe, would come to be dominated by Germany, a prospect that made it necessary to keep Germany divided in a divided Europe.

Given this bias against European unity long characteristic of Soviet policy,[104] it might be assumed that the Soviet leadership would be loath to sit by and forgo recurrent opportunities to exploit fissures among the Western allies. Indeed, by early 1969, there were already signs that despite an obvious desire to tighten the Soviet bloc against ideological penetration from the West the Kremlin leadership had begun to reactivate a stalled diplomatic effort toward Western Europe, where the unifying effects of the Czechoslovak invasion appeared to be wearing thin.

The renewal of a more active Soviet diplomacy toward Western Europe was centered on the general theme that Soviet–West European relations should be put back on the track on which they had been prior to the Czechoslovak "interruption." France, perhaps considered the country most prone to resume cooperative relations with the Soviet Union, became the initial target of overtures

---

[104] The chief exception to this bias, intermittently manifested under all postwar Soviet regimes, was, of course, Moscow's advocacy of various pan-European collective security schemes. However, since these proposals generally implied also a reduction of Amerian influence in Europe that would leave the Soviet Union the predominant power in the area, they were perhaps not wholly an exception to the rule.

for a return to preinvasion "normality,"[105] in contrast with Moscow's distinctly cool attitude toward Britain.[106] Toward West Germany, the customary harsh Soviet line was tempered by several amicable gestures in early 1969,[107] while with respect to NATO itself the Soviet line reflected a certain ambivalence, varying from a renewed and somewhat conciliatory appeal in March for an all-European security conference to a vitriolic denunciation of NATO on its twentieth anniversary in April.[108]

Meanwhile, in the early months of 1969, the Brezhnev–Kosygin regime evidently found it expedient also to weigh its moves in Europe with a particular eye to their impact upon Soviet relations with the new Nixon administration in the United States. As suggested by the Kremlin's disinclination to press the issue of West Germany's election of a new federal president, in Berlin on March 5, beyond the dimensions of a temporary mini-crisis,[109] the Soviet Union's interest in preserving an atmosphere suitable to conducting strategic arms talks and other negotiations with Washington seemed to counsel a diplomacy in Europe that would keep tensions within bounds.[110] In addition to the matter of Soviet–US relations, there were, of course, other incentives for Soviet

[105] Soviet overtures to France were signaled by a request for the rescheduling in early January 1969 of a postponed meeting of the Grande Commission to discuss further economic co-operation, to which the French agreed. See Donald H. Louchheim, "De Gaulle Accepts an Early Date as the Soviet Suitor Returns," *Washington Post*, December 5, 1968.

[106] The Soviet Union voiced particular displeasure over a British move in late 1968 to limit the size of the Soviet Embassy Staff in London. See Anthony Lewis, "Soviet Criticizes Britain Harshly," *New York Times*, December 4, 1968.

[107] These gestures included an offer to reopen negotiations on a civil air agreement, and talks between Tsarapkin and Brandt in January at which the resumption of a dialogue on a renunciation-of-force treaty reportedly was explored. In early February 1969, a relatively mild Soviet note to Bonn broached the possibility of easing Soviet pressures on West Germany in exchange for her signature on the nuclear nonproliferation treaty, while in March, after an incipient crisis over Berlin had subsided, it was rumored that Soviet thinking about a rapprochement with Bonn had reached the point of causing strain in Soviet–GDR relations. See Ralph Blumenthal, "Bonn and Moscow Seek Closer Ties," *New York Times*, January 11, 1969; David Binder, "Moscow Offers Generosity if Bonn Signs Nuclear Pact," ibid., February 8, 1969; Anatole Shub, "E. German, Soviet Ties Show Strain," *Washington Post*, March 28, 1969.

[108] The renewed call for a European security conference was made at a Warsaw Pact meeting in Budapest on March 17, 1969. See "Message from the Warsaw Treaty States to All European Countries," *Pravda*, March 18, 1969. On NATO's anniversary, the Soviet government repeated the security conference proposal, but coupled this with a statement denouncing NATO as the "main source of the danger of war," "the patron of West German militarism," and "the organizer of subversion and . . . counterrevolutionary coup attempts in socialist countries." See "Statement of the Soviet Government," *Pravda*, April 10, 1969.

[109] The Bundesversammlung that was to meet in West Berlin to elect a federal president there for the third time (the previous such elections were held in 1959 and 1964) caused an incipient crisis in early 1969, with threats of "dire consequences" from the GDR. The Soviet Union blew hot and cold in backing up the Ulbricht regime's threats of retaliation, and at one juncture joint Soviet–GDR maneuvers were mounted along the Berlin access routes, reminiscent of tactics employed in July 1965. Following President Nixon's visit to West Berlin on February 27, and reported advice from American to Soviet officials that a major Berlin crisis would prejudice the climate for Soviet–US talks, the election came off on March 5 without precipitating an East–West confrontation.

[110] Another example of this interest came later in the summer when, despite its resentment over President Nixon's visit to Rumania in August 1969, the Kremlin refrained from open criticism of the visit. Rather, Soviet displeasure was expressed indirectly by cancellation of a projected trip by Brezhnev and Kosygin to Bucharest.

interest in lowering tensions on the European front, such as new difficulties with China in the Far East and economic problems at home.[111]

Whatever the reasons, Soviet diplomacy now stepped up its efforts to promote an atmosphere of détente in Europe. Among moves in this direction were further proposals for a European security conference, advanced at Warsaw Pact meetings in October and December 1969, along with the suggestion that such a conference might be held in Helsinki in the first half of 1970.[112] Incidentally, though the Soviet Union seemed hopeful that a security conference would have the effect in Western Europe of putting a tacit stamp of approval on its occupation of Czechoslovakia, it also had the problem of keeping its own East European allies from seeking greater freedom of action under the guise of discussing security arrangements with the West.[113]

But perhaps the principal, and at the same time the most ticklish, European negotiatory moves by the Soviet Union had to do with West Germany, where the new Brandt government, which had won office in October 1969, expressed a willingness to go farther than any of its predecessors toward meeting the terms for normalization of relations with the Warsaw bloc, including East Germany.[114] Apart from the fact that Soviet efforts to foster an air of détente in Europe would carry little conviction if Bonn's conciliatory initiatives were again spurned, a new dialogue with the Brandt government may have seemed, from the Soviet viewpoint, to offer several promising opportunities: (1) the possibility of loosening West German ties with NATO and the United States; (2) a chance to seal the recognition of a separate East German state; and (3) the prospect of obtaining technical-economic benefits from West German industry.

In any event, after voicing guarded approval of the new Bonn government at a Warsaw Pact "summit" meeting in Moscow in mid-December 1969,[115] and despite reported negative reactions from the Ulbricht regime, the Soviet Union began bilateral talks with West Germany later in the month on a renun-

---

[111] See chapter XI.

[112] "Declaration of the Meeting of Foreign Ministers of the Warsaw Treaty States," *Pravda*, November 1, 1969; "Meeting of Leaders of the Fraternal Countries," ibid., December 5, 1969. At the first of these meetings, which took place in Prague, a previous Finnish offer of Helsinki as a conference site was "accepted." The conference agenda proposed at Prague and endorsed at the second meeting in Moscow was briefer than earlier proposals, calling only for renunciation of force and economic–scientific co-operation. Soviet interest in an early target date for a security conference of governments apparently declined somewhat in January 1970, when it was suggested in Moscow that a "people's congress" should first be held in the latter half of the year, ostensibly to rally popular support for a governmental conference.

[113] The Poles, in particular, showed signs of taking the bit in their teeth, advancing their own version of a draft treaty on European security in the spring of 1969, and inviting Western delegations to Warsaw to discuss the subject.

[114] See David Binder, "Brandt Makes Bid for Improved Ties With East Europe," *New York Times*, October 29, 1969, and "Brandt Revises Position on East," ibid., January 15, 1970.

[115] The "positive" appraisal of the new Brandt government was no doubt due in part to Bonn's signing of the nuclear nonproliferation treaty on November 28, 1969. The communiqué of the Moscow meeting was also notable for putting formal recognition of East Germany by Bonn in the "desirable" category, rather than making it a precondition of negotiations, a nuance to which the East Germans reportedly objected. *Pravda*, December 5, 1969.

ciation-of-force agreement and other matters.[116] Concurrently, the Soviet Union sanctioned the opening of Polish–West German political talks in Warsaw in February 1970, while shortly thereafter the East German leadership, apparently fearing that further obstructive tactics might leave it isolated, also entered into what might prove to be historically significant conversations of its own with West Germany at the Brandt–Stoph level.[117]

Meanwhile, in February 1970, the Soviet Union agreed to reopen four-power talks on Berlin, long the symbolic focal point of East–West differences in Europe.[118] Together with other Soviet diplomatic moves in Europe in early 1970, the opening of the four-power Berlin talks on March 26 had the effect of buttressing Moscow's contention that East–West diplomacy in Europe need no longer be encumbered by the memory of Czechoslovakia. Beyond this, it was yet to be seen what course Soviet diplomacy might pursue in Europe. Optimists might hope that the Kremlin leadership was prepared to so modify its past positions on Berlin[119] and other unresolved European issues as to offer some prospect of better East–West relations and perhaps even of ending the division of Europe. Skeptics could answer that twenty-five years of postwar history argued against a substantive shift of Soviet policy sufficient to bring a new European settlement within reach. But, at the very least, it did appear that Moscow's European diplomacy had again set out to encourage the gradual erosion of NATO, a process which had been underway before the Czechoslovak "interruption" and which had represented one of the major, though perhaps largely unearned, successes of Soviet policy in Europe.

[116] The bilateral talks in Moscow on renunciation of force were conducted by a special West German emissary, State Secretary Egon Bahr, and Soviet Foreign Minister Gromyko. Concurrently, another Bonn delegation was received in Moscow to discuss technological-scientific exchanges, while a third step in Soviet–West German co-operation was the signing of an agreement for supply of large-diameter gas pipe to the USSR in return for future pipeline delivery of Soviet natural gas to West Germany.

[117] The first in what was intended to be a series of conversations between West German Chancellor Brandt and East German Premier Willi Stoph took place in Erfurt on March 19, 1970, after a period of wrangling over the site for the meeting. Stoph reportedly insisted that Bonn must yield to East German demands for formal diplomatic recognition and other conditions of a draft treaty proposed by the GDR in December 1969. At the same time, Brandt's enthusiastic reception by the East German populace raised some question that the GDR might get cold feet about continuing this historic exchange between leaders of the two estranged halves of Germany, an exchange which might conceivably mark a pivotal moment in the postwar history of a divided Europe. See "Stoph's Report Stresses Differences with Brandt" and "The Two Germanys Meet, and a Cry Goes Up," *New York Times*, March 22, 1970; editorial, "The Road from Erfurt," *Washington Post*, March 23, 1970.

[118] Soviet agreement to four-power talks on Berlin—the first since the Big Four Foreign Ministers discussed the subject in Geneva in 1959—came in response to Western urging in December 1969 that talks on Berlin's status and other concrete issues in Europe should precede any general conference in European security. See Chalmers M. Roberts, "Russia Agrees to Proposal for Talks on Berlin," *Washington Post*, February 11, 1970.

[119] The brief communiqué on the first session of the four-power Berlin talks on March 26, 1970, gave no information on the position taken by the Soviet Union, stating simply that views had been exchanged. Prior to the meeting, however, it was reported that the Soviet position would call for turning West Berlin into a "separate political entity" and severing its ties with Bonn, while leaving the status of East Berlin unchanged. The outcome of the second Berlin session, scheduled to take place on April 28, 1970, was not known at this writing. See David Binder, "West Is Hopeful on Berlin Parley," *New York Times*, March 25, 1970; Laurence Fellows, "West Eases Curb on Travel as Big 4 Open Berlin Talks," ibid., March 27, 1970.

XVI

SOVIET MILITARY POLICY UNDER THE
BREZHNEV–KOSYGIN REGIME

Like Khrushchev, his successors apparently discovered after taking office that the task of creating and maintaining a modern military establishment was costly and often in conflict with their domestic goals. Nevertheless, the Brezhnev–Kosygin regime saw fit to go ahead with a large arms build-up, which by early 1970 had put the Soviet Union in a much stronger military position than that in which Khrushchev had left it some five years earlier. This build-up was aimed largely at improving the Soviet Union's global power position, suggesting that, while the new Kremlin leadership may have had no great fault to find with the military power left at its disposal on the European continent, it was by no means pleased to have inherited a situation in which for two decades the United States not only enjoyed marked strategic superiority over the Soviet Union but also went virtually unchallenged in its capacity to intervene locally in contested trouble spots around the globe.

In the present chapter, we shall examine the broad trends which marked the over-all evolution of Soviet military policy during the first half-decade of the Brezhnev–Kosygin regime; in the next, we shall deal specifically with developments affecting the Soviet Union's military posture in Europe.

Change and Continuity in Soviet Defense Policy

Before taking stock of the main trends in Soviet defense policy and posture in the 1965–70 period, it may be useful to make a few general observations on change and continuity in this field. Soviet military policy can be seen, at least in part, as reflecting the differing conceptions that have informed Soviet foreign policy under successive leaderships from Stalin to the present day. Under Stalin, for example, the Soviet Union pursued a foreign policy of essentially continental dimensions, and its military policy remained largely oriented in a continental direction. In the Khrushchev era, by contrast, the Soviet Union was transformed into a global power, breaking out of its continental shell to assert its influence and interests in every quarter of the world. However, Khrushchev never succeeded in fully reshaping Soviet military power to support a political strategy of global dimensions. His successors, in effect, picked up this task where Khrushchev left it. The common denominator in all three leadership periods was the maintenance of a strong military stance toward Europe—a point brought home once more in August 1968 by the Soviet move against Czechoslovakia, which, among other things, increased the forward deployment of Soviet forces in East and Central Europe.

It may oversimplify matters to suggest that Khrushchev's successors set out in systematic fashion to correct various shortcomings in the Soviet military posture in order to match it more precisely with their foreign policy objectives. Military power and foreign policy can seldom be kept neatly in phase, for many contingent factors tend to intrude. In the Soviet case, such factors include the organizational habits of the bureaucracy; the bargaining interplay among various elite groups; the constraints of resources, technology, geography, and tradition; and the pressures exerted on Soviet decisions by allies and adversaries. Nevertheless, the general direction of Soviet military policy under the Brezhnev–Kosygin regime seems to have stemmed from the regime's attempt to bring the Soviet Union's military posture more into line with its growing global obligations and interests.

In a more specific sense, the governing assumptions and priorities upon which the military policy of the present leadership has appeared to rest are: (1) that general nuclear war must be avoided; (2) that deterrence based on Soviet strategic-nuclear power, both offensive and defensive, offers the best guarantee against nuclear war; (3) that the Soviet Union must maintain its traditionally strong continental military position, both to back up its interests in the crucial political arena of Europe and to cope with the problems created by the rise of a rival seat of Communist power in Peking; and (4) that the Soviet Union must also continue to develop more mobile and versatile conventional forces—including Soviet naval and maritime capabilities—to support its interests in the Third World and to sustain its role as a global competitor of the United States. In essence, much the same set of assumptions underlay Khrushchev's military programs. What has distinguished the Soviet military preparations of the Brezhnev–Kosygin period from those of the Khrushchev decade, therefore, has been not their general direction but their more substantial scale.

Khrushchev's successors probably were prompted to increase the scale of Soviet military preparations by the belief that the USSR must provide itself with a wider range of military options and divest itself of the political liability of having a markedly second-best strategic posture in any future confrontation with the United States—liability that was dramatically driven home by the Cuban missile crisis toward the end of the Khrushchev decade.[1] The war in Vietnam and a general Soviet belief that US military power was being increasingly committed to the suppression of "national liberation" movements in the Third World, doubtless served also to persuade the Brezhnev–Kosygin regime that further measures were needed to improve the Soviet Union's ability to project its military presence into areas like the Middle East, Africa, and the Indian Ocean.

In any event, despite the high priority they had set upon major investment

---

[1] For discussion of factors which apparently persuaded the new regime that remedial measures were required to restore the credibility of Soviet military power as a backstop for Moscow's declaratory policies, see Roman Kolkowicz, *The Dilemma of Superpower: Soviet Policy and Strategy in Transition* (Arlington, Va.: Institute for Defense Analyses, October 1967), p. 10.

programs and various reforms to stimulate economic growth and performance, the Soviet leaders found it expedient to make successive annual increases in the military budget. The Brezhnev–Kosygin regime's first military budget, for 1965, was 12.8 billion rubles. Thereafter, the figure mounted each year: 1966—13.4; 1967—14.5; 1968—16.7; 1969—17.7; while for 1970 the announced budget rose to 17.9 billion rubles.[2]

This steady upward trend in Soviet military outlays represented a diversion of resources hardly calculated to help the new regime meet its domestic economic goals. As suggested by Kosygin's observation at the Twenty-third Party Congress, in April 1966, the need for strengthening Soviet defenses to meet the threat posed by a deteriorating international situation had prevented the Soviet Union from making "a substantial reduction in military expenditures and a correspondingly greater capital investment in peaceful sectors of the economy."[3] Later, the cumulative effects of favoring the defense industry sector of the Soviet economy[4] were to contribute to a lagging rate of economic growth.[5]

Not surprisingly, the pressure of rising military costs under the Brezhnev–Kosygin regime helped to revive a certain amount of policy controversy over the perennial issue of economic and defense priorities. This first took the form of doctrinal articles in the military press, arguing that one-sided emphasis on deterrence, as practiced under Khrushchev, could lead to neglect of the all-round strengthening of the armed forces and to doubt about "the need to spend large resources on them."[6] Subsequently, however, after the party leadership gave its sanction to increases in the military budget, the issue of civil-military competition for resources shifted to new grounds, centering on the problem of meshing

[2] These figures are for the publicly announced military budgets. They take into account neither additional expenditures for defense generally thought to be buried in other parts of the state budget, nor the problem of converting ruble figures into a meaningful measure of the real resources devoted to defense. According to the Institute for Strategic Studies, the real resources for 1969, calculated in equivalent American prices, would come to between $42 billion and $53 billion. See *The Military Balance, 1969–1970* (London, 1969), p. 5. See also Abraham S. Becker, *Soviet Growth, Resources Allocation, and Military Outlays*, The RAND Corporation, P-4135, June 1969, pp. 7–10.

[3] "Directives of the Twenty-third CPSU Congress on the 1966–1970 Five-Year Plan of the Development of the National Economy," speech of the chairman of the USSR Council of Ministers, Comrade A. N. Kosygin, *Pravda*, April 6, 1966.

[4] The defense industry sector of the Soviet economy consists, in addition to a Ministry of Defense Industry, of seven other ministries concerned with various kinds of machine building, aviation, shipbuilding, and electronics. These industries, though producing for civilian as well as military uses, have received first call on resources, skills, and new equipment in order to meet their military production goals. According to a Soviet economist, A. G. Aganbegian, around 40 per cent of the Soviet economy is tied directly or indirectly to the defense industry sector. See John P. Hardt, *Economic Insights on Current Soviet Policy and Strategy*, Research Analysis Corporation, McLean, Va., December 1969, p. 28. See also Richard Armstrong, "Military-Industrial Complex—Russian Style," *Fortune*, August 1, 1969, p. 124.

[5] See chapter XI, p. 246. An analysis of the effects of defense production on Soviet economic growth may be found in Hardt, *Economic Insights*, pp. 37–48.

[6] Colonel I. Sidel'nikov, "V. I. Lenin on the Class Approach to Defining the Character of War," *Krasnaia zvezda*, September 22, 1965. For details of the revival of controversy over economic-versus-defense priorities, see Thomas W. Wolfe, *The Soviet Military Scene: Institutional and Defense Policy Considerations*, The RAND Corporation, RM-4913-PR, June 1966, pp. 62–69.

economic planning more effectively with the procurement of weapons for the armed forces. In general, military spokesmen conceded the need for strict party control over the "complex tasks" of co-ordinating civilian and military production, but they also expressed reservations about the wisdom of allowing purely economic criteria to outweigh military requirements.[7]

The possibility that this issue had provoked internal argument for a major alteration of the traditional organization of the Defense Ministry along more civilian-oriented lines arose after the death of Marshal Malinovskii, the Defense Minister, in March 1967. At that time, there was a spate of rumors in Moscow that his successor might be Dmitri Ustinov, a party civilian with a long career in the management of defense industry.[8] Had Ustinov taken over the post customarily occupied by a military professional with command prerogatives over the armed forces, it seems likely that rather sweeping organizational changes would have followed, perhaps with the effect of further reducing the influence of the professional military on resource decisions, a development as radical as some of the reforms with which Khrushchev was associated. As it turned out, the regime shied away from such an innovation, if it had in fact seriously contemplated it, and after a brief delay Marshal A. A. Grechko was appointed, leaving undisturbed the role of military professionals in the defense hierarchy.

In 1968 the tendency of the Soviet leadership to seek resolution of its political dilemma in Czechoslovakia through military pressure—first in the form of threatened intervention and then by actual invasion—raised anew the question of military influence upon the Soviet decision-making process. Military professionals played an important instrumental role in the invasion and in the confused early days of the occupation, which clearly enhanced their prestige, and, in 1969, the threat of new repressive measures against Prague in the wake of anti-Soviet demonstrations again underscored the active role which had devolved upon military men like Marshal Grechko as the executors of Moscow's East European policy.[9] Meanwhile, as will be brought out later in this chapter, there was a renewal of internal debate over Soviet strategic doctrine and military

---

[7] An emphatic statement of the need to work out a co-ordinated "military-economic policy" to insure weapons production in "properly substantiated proportions" appeared in an April 1967 article by Colonel A. Babin, "The Party—Leader of the USSR Armed Forces," *Krasnaia zvezda* (Red Star), April 6, 1967. Another treatment of the question, with emphasis upon "correct and effective use of resources" to "insure solution of all military-economic tasks," was offered by Colonel Ia. Vlasevich, "Modern War and the Economy," *Kommunist Vooruzhennykh Sil* (Communist of the Armed Forces), no. 12 (June 1967): 27–33. See also N. Ia. Sushko and T. R. Kondratkov, eds., *Metodologicheskie problemy voennoi teorii i praktiki* (Methodological Problems of Military Theory and Practice) (Moscow: Voenizdat, 1966), p. 79; P. V. Sokolov, ed., *Voennoekonomicheskie voprosy v kurse politekonomii* (Military-Economic Questions in the Course of Political Economy) (Moscow: Voenizdat, 1968), pp. 279–95.

[8] See Stephen S. Rosenfeld, "Kremlin Looking for a McNamara To Rule Its Brass," *Washington Post*, April 23, 1967; Raymond H. Anderson, "Soviet Affirms Party Rule over the Military Forces," *New York Times*, April 7, 1967.

[9] For discussion pertinent to this question, see chapters XIV, pp. 380–81, and XVII, pp. 464–65 and fn. 16. Some Western observers credited Marshal Grechko with having succeeded where Soviet political leaders had failed in forcing Dubcek out of office, and suggested that this betokened a real shift in political power to the Soviet marshals. See, for example, Anatole Shub, "Czech Backdown Laid to Efforts of Grechko," *Washington Post*, April 18, 1969.

preparations, some aspects of which suggested an assertive bid by the military hierarchy for a larger voice in the decisions affecting the country's security. Although it remained to be seen to what extent the Soviet military leadership might succeed in translating its instrumental and advisory role into a more potent and direct influence within the top councils of the regime, so far as could be judged from the outward evidence available up to early 1970, the traditional grip of the Soviet political leadership on the machinery of decision-making was still intact.

Viewed as a whole, the stewardship of the Brezhnev–Kosygin regime over Soviet military affairs in the five years following Khrushchev's ouster yielded some rather impressive accomplishments. True, a number of perennial problems remained unresolved, such as that of reconciling defense requirements with economic demands, while the new leaders also found that the task of translating military might into tangible political gains was hardly less intractable than it had been in Khruschev's day. Nevertheless, the military policy and programs of the new regime produced notable changes in the Soviet armed forces, contributing to a gradual shift in the American–Soviet strategic balance and to the transformation of the USSR from an essentially continental military power into a more truly global one. Neither the precise nature nor the ultimate effect of this emerging pattern of power in the international system is as yet predictable, although any substantial shift in the previously recognized power balance could well have a far-reaching impact upon world politics and upon the international rivalry between the Soviet Union and the United States. This is a matter to which we shall return later in this study. Meanwhile, let us look at the main features of the military programs undertaken by the Brezhnev–Kosygin regime, considering first its efforts to strengthen the Soviet Union's strategic posture.

Programs Affecting the Soviet Strategic Posture

Under the Brezhnev–Kosygin regime, programs in the strategic field have fallen largely into two categories: those aimed at a build-up of the strategic delivery forces, and those directed toward strengthening the Soviet Union's strategic defenses, including the initiation of ABM deployment. These efforts have reflected the concept that a complementary "mix" of offensive and defensive forces should be sought, a concept more congenial to orthodox Soviet military thinking than giving preference to either offense or defense alone.[10]

When Khrushchev's successors first came to office, however, it was by no means clear how vigorously they would seek to improve the Soviet Union's

---

[10] As noted earlier, one of the sources of friction between Khrushchev and some of his more conservative-minded marshals had been their belief that he was putting "one-sided" emphasis on the importance of ballistic missiles. Although Khrushchev's successors apparently managed to still such criticism by sanctioning a more balanced force concept, it should be noted that this did not put an end to professional debate over the relative value of active strategic defense versus the offense. See fns. 57 and 58 below. For a relevant discussion of this issue during the Khrushchev era, see chapter IX, pp. 199–201, especially fn. 18.

strategic posture vis-à-vis the United States. Their initial approach did indicate, if nothing else, a determination to strengthen the technological base upon which any effort to alter the strategic balance would ultimately depend. Appropriations for scientific research were stepped up, and, as made evident by the public display of new families of offensive and defensive weapons, the Soviet military research and development program was pushed even more energetically than before.[11] Only after the new leaders had been in power a year or two did it gradually become apparent that they had committed themselves to a substantial build-up of Soviet strategic delivery forces.

Build-up of Strategic Offensive Forces

As indicated by informed accounts which began to appear in the US press in the summer of 1966, an accelerated program of Soviet ICBM deployment had been set in motion in the USSR.[12] Given a lead time of around eighteen months for construction of a typical ICBM launcher site, it was apparent in retrospect that the decision to go ahead with accelerated deployment of new launchers, which began to show up in increasing numbers in the summer of 1966, must have been taken not long after the new regime came to power. By October 1966 the number of ICBM launchers stood at about 340, and a year later the operational ICBM total reached 720, representing a deployment rate of more than one new launcher per day.[13]

Although the pace of deployment began to slow down in 1968, the Soviet ICBM build-up did not taper off at this juncture to the extent expected in some Western quarters. By September 1968 the ICBM total had edged up to 900,[14] while a year later it came to 1,060, giving the Soviet Union a slightly larger ICBM force than the United States for the first time since the earliest days of the missile age.[15] Upon completion of additional launching silos under construction in early 1970, the Soviet Union was expected to have almost 1,300 opera-

---

[11] Published Soviet allocations for scientific research, of which a substantial share goes to support military research and development, have risen as follows: 1963—4.7 billion rubles; 1964—5.2; 1965—5.4; 1966—6.5; 1967—7.2; 1968—7.9; 1969—9; 1970—11.

[12] Among representative early accounts of this buildup, see William Beecher, "Soviet Increases Buildup of Missiles and Deploys a Defensive System," *New York Times*, November 13, 1966; Richard J. Whalen, "The Shifting Equation of Nuclear Defense," *Fortune*, June 1, 1967, p. 87; and an annual publication of the Institute for Strategic Studies, *The Military Balance, 1967–1968* (London, 1967), p. 5.

[13] See *Statement of Secretary of Defense Robert S. McNamara Before the Senate Armed Services Committee on the Fiscal Year 1969–1973 Defense Program and 1969 Defense Budget, January 22, 1968*, Government Printing Office, 1968, p. 55 (cited hereafter as *McNamara Statement, 1968*).

[14] See *Statement of Secretary of Defense Clark M. Clifford: The Fiscal Year 1970–74 Defense Program and 1970 Defense Budget*, Department of Defense, January 15, 1959, p. 42 (cited hereafter as *Clifford Statement, 1969*). Clifford noted in this statement that the rate of Soviet ICBM deployment in 1968 had been "somewhat greater than estimated a year ago."

[15] See *Statement by Secretary of Defense Melvin R. Laird Before a Joint Session of the Senate Armed Services and Appropriations Committees on Fiscal Year 1971 Defense Program and Budget, February 20, 1970*, Government Printing Office, 1970, p. 103 (cited hereafter as *Laird Statement, 1970*). Compared with the Soviet force of 1,060 ICBMs attained by September 1969, the United States had a land-based ICBM force of 1,054 launchers (1,000 Minutemen, and the remainder Titan-2 missiles).

tional ICBMs by the end of the year, with no upper limit as yet in sight.[16] These figures on the Soviet ICBM build-up under the Brezhnev–Kosygin regime may be compared with a total deployment of around 200 ICBM launchers in Khrushchev's time.

Along with this quantitative build-up of ICBMs went qualitative improvements, such as the introduction of new types of missiles in dispersed and hardened sites, in contrast with the ICBM force of the Khrushchev period, much of which consisted of early-generation missiles of "soft-site" configuration.[17] The principal new missile types added during the rapid expansion of the ICBM force from 1966 to 1970 were the SS-9 and the SS-11, both liquid-fueled and emplaced in dispersed concrete silos, together with the SS-13, the Soviet Union's first ICBM in the solid-fuel category.

The SS-9, the largest missile in the Soviet arsenal, with a warhead variously estimated at 10 to 25 megatons, became the object of widespread attention after it was singled out by US Secretary of Defense Melvin R. Laird in March 1969, during debate over the Safeguard missile defense system, as a weapon which posed a first-strike threat against the American land-based Minuteman deterrent force.[18] Laird indicated that there were then about 200 SS-9s in the Soviet inventory, a figure which he later said had increased to 275 by February 1970.[19] The smaller SS-11, with a warhead of about one megaton, was deployed in greater numbers than any of the new missiles, accounting for well over half of the Soviet build-up.[20] In early 1970, it became known that this ICBM was being provided with a new, more accurate warhead,[21] and that it also was being installed at medium-range launch complexes in the southwestern USSR [22]—a move which promised to give the Russians a flexible dual-purpose delivery system against targets either in Europe or the United States. The SS-13, the Soviet ICBM most comparable to the US Minuteman, played a relatively minor role

---

[16] According to Secretary Laird, the Soviets were expected to have about 1,260 operational ICBMs by mid-1970, but the future upper limit of the force, he said, could not be estimated "with any high confidence." Ibid. The projected figure of 1,290 Soviet ICBMs by the end of 1970 was given in President Nixon's report, *United States Foreign Policy for the 1970's: A New Strategy for Peace,* text as published in *New York Times,* February 19, 1970, p. 24M (cited hereafter as *Nixon Foreign Policy Report*).

[17] In the Khrushchev period, the Soviet ICBM force consisted of two types of liquid-fueled missiles, designated SS-6 and SS-7 by Western officials. The SS-7 made up the bulk of this force, only part of which was in hardened silos.

[18] See testimony by Secretary of Defense Melvin R. Laird before the Senate Armed Services Committee on March 20, and the Senate Foreign Relations Committee on March 21, 1969, as reported in *New York Times,* March 21, 22, 1969. See also John W. Finney, "SS-9 Helps Administration Score Points in Missile Debate," ibid., March 24, 1969. About two weeks later, Mr. Laird and Secretary of State William P. Rogers, in separate press conferences, both denied having imputed first-strike intentions to the Soviet Union on the basis of the SS-9 build-up. Mr. Laird said he had been talking about "capability," not "intentions," in referring to a first-strike threat. See *Washington Post,* April 8, 1969.

[19] *Laird Statement, 1970,* p. 35.

[20] See William Beecher, "Soviet Missile Deployment Puzzles Top U.S. Analysts," *New York Times,* April 14, 1969.

[21] *Nixon Foreign Policy Report,* p. 24M.

[22] See William Beecher, "U.S. Satellites Detect Soviet ICBM's in Medium-Range Missile Complexes," *New York Times,* February 11, 1970.

in the strategic build-up, becoming operational in small numbers only during 1969.[23]

In addition to strategic missiles emplaced in fixed sites, the Soviet Union also accorded "special importance" to the development of mobile land-based missiles, as emphasized by the late Marshal Malinovskii in 1966 and subsequently reiterated by other military spokesmen.[24] Mobile missiles, it was stressed, would lend themselves to concealment from "enemy reconnaissance" and thus reduce their vulnerability to attack. The actual deployment of such missiles apparently lagged behind Soviet claims;[25] however, Western authorities in 1968 confirmed that a mobile, solid-fuel ICBM was in the works, together with mobile strategic missiles of shorter range in the MRBM or IRBM class.[26]

While the expansion and qualitative improvement of the land-based ICBM force stood first among measures to strengthen the Soviet strategic delivery capacity, other delivery means also received attention. A high priority, for example, went to missile-launching submarines, as was made evident in 1968 by the introduction of a new class of nuclear-powered submarines with a ballistic missile-launching capacity—16 tubes—comparable to the US Polaris-type submarine.[27] Appearance of the new Y-class submarine, after a pause in the nuclear sub construction program, suggested that the Soviet Union intended to expand its missile-launching submarine force, which then numbered about 75 submarines, or about one-fifth of the total underseas fleet.[28] By early 1970, thanks to a Y-class construction program estimated at seven to eight boats per year,[29] the Soviet Union appeared likely to have about 300 submarine-launched ballistic missiles at its disposal by the end of the year.[30]

As Soviet military leaders pointed out, the USSR also continued to count

[23] *Laird Statement, 1970*, p. 103.

[24] "Speech of Comrade R. Ia. Malinovskii," *Pravda*, April 3, 1966. For other Soviet claims relating to mobile, solid-fuel ICBMs, see Lt. Colonel V. Bondarenko, "Military-Technical Superiority: The Most Important Factor for Reliable Defense of the Country," *Kommunist Vooruzhennykh Sil*, no. 17 (September 1966): 9; Colonel S. A. Tiushkevich, "The Modern Revolution in Military Affairs: Its Sources and Character," ibid., no. 20 (October 1966): 23; Marshal K. Moskalenko, TASS interview, Moscow radio broadcast, February 19, 1969; Marshal M. Zakharov, "On Guard over Socialism and Peace," *Partiinaia zhizn'* (Party Life), no. 9 (May 1969).

[25] A mobile, solid-fuel missile displayed in the annual Red Square parade on November 7, 1967, was said by Soviet commentators to be already operational, but the size of the missile in question suggested that it was probably a medium- or intermediate-range weapon, rather than an ICBM. See A. Sgibnev and A. Shichalin, "Mobile, Strategic . . .," *Krasnaia zvezda*, November 11, 1967.

[26] See George C. Wilson, "U.S. Worried by Strides in Soviet Strategic Arms," *Washington Post*, February 20, 1968.

[27] See David Hoffman, "Navy Warns of Improved Russian Subs," *Washington Post*, March 14, 1968.

[28] Before introduction of the new Y-class in 1968, the Soviet missile-launching submarine force consisted of about thirty-five submarines (ten of which were nuclear-powered) capable of firing an average of three ballistic missiles each, and another forty submarines (of which about twenty were nuclear-powered) equipped to fire about four cruise-type winged missiles each. Although the cruise missiles could be used against land targets, their primary mission was against naval and merchant vessels. See *The Military Balance, 1967–1968*, p. 7; *McNamara Statement, 1968*, p. 54.

[29] *New York Times*, March 24, 1969; *Laird Statement, 1970*, pp. 36, 104.

[30] *Nixon Foreign Policy Report*, p. 24M. As noted in *Laird Statement, 1970*, p. 105, a new naval ballistic missile was under development in the Soviet Union in 1969. The statement did not indicate, however, whether this new missile was expected to enter service in the near future.

on manned aircraft as an element of its strategic striking power, this contribution being provided chiefly by a holdover force of long-range bombers equipped with air-to-surface missiles for "stand-off" attacks against enemy targets.[31] Heavy bomber training flights to northern coastal areas of the American continent in 1968–69[32] testified to the Soviet Union's interest in maintaining a manned-aircraft strategic delivery system, as did the discovery, in the fall of 1969, that the Soviet aircraft industry had produced a new prototype medium bomber of advanced variable-wing design.[33]

Apart from the various delivery systems mentioned above, the research and development effort fostered by the Brezhnev–Kosygin regime yielded a number of other strategic delivery projects. One of these was an orbital bombardment system of some sort. It first came to public attention in 1965, when Soviet commentators described a large missile paraded through Red Square as an "orbital" vehicle that could "deliver a surprise blow on the first, or any other, orbit around the earth";[34] a claim which immediately raised the question whether the USSR intended to comply with the October 1963 UN resolution against placing nuclear weapons in orbit.[35] In 1967, US defense officials identified the Soviet project as a "fractional orbital bombardment system" (FOBS) designed to deliver its weapon payload from a satellite before completing a single orbit;[36] later, it was also accorded a dual role as a depressed trajectory

[31] See Marshal Malinovskii's speech, *Krasnaia zvezda*, April 2, 1966, and his article, "October and the Building of the Armed Forces," *Kommunist*, no. 1 (January 1967): 34; see also speech by his successor, Marshal Grechko, *Pravda*, February 24, 1968. According to Western estimates, the Soviet Union in 1969–70 possessed about 150 heavy bombers (M-4 BISON and TU-95 BEAR), together with about 50 similar types used as tankers. The Soviet strategic air arm also included a force of about 800 jet medium bombers (TU-16 BADGER and the newer TU-22 BLINDER), considered more suitable for striking Eurasian targets than for long-range intercontinental missions. See *The Military Balance, 1969–1970*, p. 9; *Laird Statement, 1970*, p. 105.

[32] As announced by the Canadian Defense Department in March 1968 (see *Washington Post*, March 15, 1968), Soviet long-range bombers conducted at least seven flights in early 1968 close to the North American continent: in the vicinity of Greenland and Labrador off the Atlantic coast and around the Aleutian Islands chain in the Pacific. Such flights were reported to be continuing on a routine basis in 1969. In the Khrushchev period, flights of Soviet bombers at such distances from the Soviet Union were unknown. See "Soviet Bombers Patrolling around North America," *New York Times*, April 9, 1969.

[33] The new Soviet aircraft came as a surprise to many Western observers, since it had been widely assumed that the USSR had written off further development of strategic bombers. See George C. Wilson, "Russia Testing New Bomber," *Washington Post*, October 19, 1969.

[34] G. Grebennikov et al., "Mighty Unity of Party and People," *Pravda*, November 8, 1965; interview with Colonel General V. F. Tolubko, *Trud* (Labor), November 17, 1965. Several months before the public display of the "orbital" missile (Western designation—SCRAG), Brezhnev had boasted of the Soviet Union's possession of orbital missiles. See *Moscow News*, July 10, 1965.

[35] In reply to an American diplomatic inquiry, the USSR in December 1965 denied any intent to evade the nonorbiting resolution (which subsequently was incorporated in the Space Treaty of January 27, 1967). The Soviet press took the position that the UN resolution barred, not the development or production of orbital missiles, but only the actual placing of warheads in orbit, which in a strict sense was true. See "Moscow Abjures A-Arms in Space," *New York Times*, December 11, 1965; Observer, "False Doubts," *Pravda*, December 9, 1965.

[36] See Secretary McNamara's statement and comments at a press conference dealing with Soviet development of FOBS, *New York Times*, November 4, 1967. See also testimony of Paul H. Nitze, Deputy Secretary of Defense, and Dr. John S. Foster, Jr., Director of Defense Research and Engineering, Hearings Before the Subcommittee on Military Applications of the Joint Committee

ICBM.[37] Although uncertainty persisted as to the military significance of the project,[38] the effort invested in frequent flight-testing of FOBS[39] would tend to suggest that the Soviets hoped to derive dividends from it, perhaps of a political-psychological as well as a military nature.[40]

Another project that might appreciably increase the Soviet strategic delivery potential came to light in September 1968, when it became known that the Soviet Union was developing a multiple warhead for the SS-9. Soviet interest in multiple warheads of either the MRV or the MIRV variety[41] had been inferred for some time; the fact that as early as 1963 Soviet military leaders had made reference to the "future possibility" of degrading Western defenses by means of "maneuverable warheads,"[42] together with the obvious advantages the Soviet Union would derive from adapting its large missile payloads to MIRV,[43] suggested that sooner or later the Soviets would unveil a multiple-warhead program of their own. This they did by first testing their version of a multiple warhead about one week after the initial American tests of MIRV for Minuteman and Poseidon had taken place, in late August 1968.[44] Whether the Soviet project would include an independently targetable feature similar to the US MIRV was apparently not known. It was at least clear, however, that the Soviet Union had not been idle in the multiple-warhead field.

---

on Atomic Energy . . ., *Scope, Magnitude, and Implications of the United States Antiballistic Missile Program*, November 6 and 7, 1967 (hereafter cited as *Hearings, Antiballistic Missile Program, November 1967*), 90th Congress, 1st Session, Government Printing Office, Washington, D.C., 1968, pp. 21–29.

[37] *Clifford Statement, 1969*, p. 42; *Laird Statement, 1970*, p. 103.

[38] When Secretary McNamara first discussed FOBS in November 1967, he noted that it might be intended to reduce the warning time available through conventional radar, but he stated that US development of "over-the-horizon" radar would make it possible to recapture any lost warning time. Secretary Clifford, in his January 1969 posture statement, said that the Soviets might be trying to develop the system for delivery of weapons against soft targets either via orbit or by depressed trajectory. Secretary Laird, in his statement on March 19, 1969, before the Senate Armed Services Committee, mentioned the possibility of using the FOBS against bomber bases, but later noted that there were still "uncertainties concerning the characteristics and purposes of this weapon system." *Laird Statement, 1970*, p. 103.

[39] Between September 1966 and October 1968, FOBS was flight-tested thirteen times, according to US officials. Testing of the system was resumed in September 1969, after a hiatus of about eleven months in the test program. See George C. Wilson, "Russia Resumes Testing of Orbital Bomb System," *Washington Post*, September 17, 1969.

[40] For some speculative comments on possible military and political reasons for Soviet interest in an orbital delivery system, see the author's testimony, *Hearings, Antiballistic Missile Program, November 1967*, pp. 91–92.

[41] MIRV, which stands for "multiple, independently targetable reentry vehicle," and MRV, an acronym for "multiple reentry vehicle," both have the effect of multiplying the number of warheads deliverable by a single booster, but MIRV, with its capacity for separate guidance of each warhead in the reentry package, is the more versatile and complex system.

[42] Major General I. Baryshev, "Nuclear Weapons and PVO," *Krasnaia zvezda*, November 13, 1963.

[43] For example, a Czech writer in September 1967, citing the large payload capacity of Soviet missiles, said: "With the introduction of multiple warheads, the change in the number of warheads which can be transported by American and Soviet rockets will alter the balance of forces from the now claimed American superiority of 3 to 1 to a Soviet superiority of 4 to 2." Jiri Hochman, "Rockets, Antiballistic Missiles, and Politics," *Rude Pravo*, September 23, 1967.

[44] See George C. Wilson, "Soviet Test of Warhead Is Reported," *Washington Post*, September 4, 1968; "USSR: Closing the MIRV Gap," *Newsweek*, September 9, 1968.

These then were some of the steps taken under the Brezhnev–Kosygin regime with respect to both deployed strategic delivery systems and R&D projects. To sum up, several points seem important.

First, the Soviet programs were evidently intended not only to increase the weight of strategic firepower but to diversify the Soviet strategic delivery potential and to reduce its vulnerability. Whether an intent to acquire a first-strike capability lay behind these programs was by no means self-evident, but at least some aspects of the strategic build-up were sufficiently ambiguous to lend themselves to such an interpretation, as was, indeed, Soviet targeting doctrine itself.[45]

Second, as matters stood in early 1970, the Soviet Union had several new strategic delivery systems which were either in the very early stages of deployment or in a preoperational testing stage. A critical policy decision facing the Soviet leaders at this juncture, therefore, was whether to go ahead with the procurement and deployment in meaningful numbers of some or all of these new delivery systems, or to hold back until they saw what came of the strategic arms limitation talks.

A third and closely related policy question was whether, having attained slightly better than numerical parity with the United States in ICBM launchers, the Soviet Union should next attempt to establish definite superiority in strategic delivery capacities or forgo for at least the time being another strategic arms build-up. In the final chapter of this study we shall return to considerations bearing on these policy choices. For the moment, let us take up the programs sponsored by the Brezhnev–Kosygin regime in the field of strategic defense.

Strategic Defense and the Deployment of ABM

Parallel to measures for improvement of Soviet strategic delivery capabilities, another significant move by the new regime to bolster the Soviet strategic posture was its decision to go ahead with the deployment of anti-ballistic missile defenses. As discussed in an earlier chapter, it is still not entirely clear whether the tentative deployment of a first-generation ABM complex employing the GRIFFON missile had begun in Leningrad in 1962 and then been halted for technical, economic, or other reasons.[46] At any rate, only after the Brezhnev–

[45] The growing Soviet inventory of SS-9 missiles with a counterforce capability against US land-based ICBMs was, as previously noted, the principal basis of the first-strike threat pictured by Secretary Laird in early 1969. The FOBS, with its reduced warning time against such soft targets as bomber bases, also lent itself to interpretation as a potential first-strike weapon. On the other hand, the SS-11 missiles, outnumbering all other types in the Soviet ICBM inventory, had characteristics making them more suitable for use against cities or nonhardened military targets than for counterforce first-strike purposes. Soviet targeting doctrine itself did not serve to clarify all the ambiguities in the Soviet force posture. For example, a dual targeting doctrine—calling for both counterforce strikes against the adversary's nuclear delivery means and for attacks upon civil targets such as economic-administrative centers—had long been preached in Soviet military literature and continued to be expressed during the period of strategic build-up under the Brezhnev-Kosygin regime. As for the first-strike issue, Soviet pronouncements ascribed intentions of striking the first nuclear blow exclusively to the "imperialist camp," but Soviet doctrine also continued to harbor an ambiguous injunction to "break up" and "frustrate" such an attack, which bordered on advocacy of pre-emption. See Wolfe, *The Soviet Military Scene*, pp. 77–80.

[46] See chapter VIII, pp. 187–88.

Kosygin regime assumed power did it become unmistakably evident that the Soviet Union had taken the historical first step of deploying ABM defenses. The first official US cognizance of the Soviet deployment program was given in an interview by Secretary McNamara in November 1966.[47] According to his and subsequent accounts, the Soviet Union had installed a second-generation ABM defense system around Moscow,[48] employing the so-called GALOSH missile displayed on several occasions in Red Square parades.[49] This system was credited with providing limited area defense to the Moscow region against Minuteman firings from North America or Polaris missiles launched from northern waters.[50]

The extent to which additional ABM defenses of the GALOSH type or different design might be scheduled for deployment elsewhere throughout the Soviet Union remained, however, a matter of continuing conjecture. As widely noted in the US press, the installation of ABM defenses around Moscow was accompanied by construction of another new defensive system—the so-called "Tallin" system—deployed over an extensive geographic area, including the northwestern approaches to the Soviet Union.[51] Initially, the Tallin system was thought in many quarters to be a third-generation ABM deployment program, but in early 1968 Secretary McNamara stated that the majority of the US intelligence community had come around to the view that the system "most likely" was designed "against an aero-dynamic rather than a ballistic missile threat."[52] Should the future bear out this judgment, then obviously the Soviet ABM program as it developed during the first few years of the Brezhnev–Kosygin regime represented a much more modest start toward coping with the formidable problems of missile defense than was originally thought to be the case. Incidentally, the addition of the new Tallin system to an already massive array

[47] *New York Times*, November 11, 1966.

[48] See, for example, Henry Gemmill, "U.S. Ponders Response to Soviet Installation of Antimissile System," *Wall Street Journal*, December 14, 1966; interview with Secretary of Defense Robert S. McNamara, "Defense Fantasy Now Come True," *Life*, September 29, 1967, p. 28c; *The Soviet Military Technological Challenge* (Washington, D.C.: Center for Strategic Studies, Georgetown University, September 1967), pp. 90–91. See also this author's statement on the Soviet ABM program, *Hearings, Antiballistic Missile Program, November 1967*, p. 65.

[49] The GALOSH missile (Western designation), first paraded in Moscow in November 1964, was described by Soviet commentators as capable of intercepting ballistic missiles at long distances from defended targets, suggesting that it was an exo-atmospheric weapon designed to take on incoming missiles several hundred miles above the earth. See *Pravda*, November 8, 1964. See also *Krasnaia zvezda*, November 10, 1965. Although GALOSH has always been sheathed in a protective cannister when displayed in public, demonstration firings of the missile have been shown on Moscow television.

[50] *The Military Balance, 1968–1969*, p. 6.

[51] The "Tallin" system takes its name from the former Estonian capital, presumably because part of the system is deployed in the Baltic area which guards the northwestern approaches to the USSR. See *McNamara Statement, 1968*, p. 55. See also Hanson W. Baldwin, "Soviet Antimissile System Spurs New U.S. Weapons," *New York Times*, February 5, 1967; Anne M. Jonas, "Strategic Deterrence in the 1970s—Five Problems for U.S. Policy," *Air Force and Space Digest*, July 1967, pp. 32–33.

[52] *McNamara Statement, 1968*, p. 55.

of air defenses—together with Soviet development of new long-range interceptor aircraft[53]—also would imply that even in the missile age Soviet planners have continued to place a high priority on improving their strategic defenses against bomber attacks.

Whatever the uncertainties attending Western estimates of the status of Soviet ABM defenses, it can be said that Soviet spokesmen themselves failed to express unmitigated confidence in their country's ABM program. Soviet claims of ABM progress during the first years of the Brezhnev–Kosygin regime varied from outright assertions that the Soviet Union had "solved" the missile defense problem to more guarded statements like those of Marshal Malinovskii at the Twenty-third Party Congress to the effect that Soviet defenses could cope with some but not all enemy missiles.[54] In early 1967 several prominent Soviet military leaders voiced notably conflicting views on the state of the country's missile defenses,[55] which again suggested that professional military opinion in the Soviet Union was by no means agreed on the effectiveness of an ABM program in which something on the order of $4 to $5 billion in resources had already been invested.[56]

Although Soviet military men differed occasionally as to the capabilities of the country's ABM system, none questioned publicly the desirability of building such defenses.[57] Indeed, many military spokesmen continued to emphasize the

[53] The FIDDLER was the first of the new long-range interceptors introduced into the PVO (Air Defense) inventory, which in 1968 was estimated to number about 3,700 fighters of all types. Another improved interceptor in this force was the FLAGON-A, while the long-range FOXBAT was reported in 1969 to be still in the development stage. See *The Military Balance, 1968–1969*, p. 6; *Clifford Statement, 1969*, p. 44.

[54] *Pravda*, April 3, 1966.

[55] General (later Marshal) P. F. Batitskii, commander of the Soviet air and missile defenses, and General P. A. Kurochkin, a deputy defense minister, in interviews in connection with the forty-ninth anniversary of the Soviet armed forces, took the optimistic position that Soviet ABM defenses could reliably protect the country against missile attack; two other senior officers, Marshal A. A. Grechko, soon to be defense minister, and Marshal V. I. Chuikov, head of Soviet Civil Defense, offered the more sober assessment that the Soviet Union did not yet possess defenses capable "in practice" of intercepting all incoming enemy planes and missiles. General Batitskii interview, TASS International Service, Moscow, February 20, 1967; "General Kurochkin's Press Conference," *Soviet News*, February 24, 1967, p. 98. Marshal A. A. Grechko, "October Army," *Izvestiia*, February 23, 1967; Marshal Chuikov's television speech, TASS International Service, Moscow, February 22, 1967.

[56] According to estimates attributed to American officials in early 1967, the Soviet Union had spent up to that time from $4 to $5 billion on development of its ABM system, compared with something over $2 billion spent by the United States on development of the Nike-X missile defense system. See Hedrick Smith, "Soviet Spending on Antimissiles Put at $4 Billion," *New York Times*, January 29, 1967.

[57] Neither Soviet civilian nor military spokesmen have engaged in the kind of open debate about the pros and cons of ABM that has taken place in the West. Negative attitudes toward ABM generally have been expressed only obliquely in the Soviet Union. Thus, one may infer from the statements of some Soviet officers on the advantages of strategic offensive missiles that they hold a low opinion of the usefulness of investing in ABM defenses. For example, the commander of the Soviet Strategic Rocket Troops, Marshal N. Krylov, writing in July 1967, asserted that the "great speed" of ballistic missiles, "together with variable trajectories, especially upon approach to target, practically guarantees the invulnerability of missiles in flight, the more so when they are employed en masse." See "The Strategic Rocket Troops," *Voenno–istoricheskii zhurnal* (Military–Historical Journal), no. 7 (July 1967): 20. A rare example of more outspoken Soviet denigration of ABM

important role that ABM was expected to play in the strategic defense system, an example being the strong case made for ABM in a March 1967 article by a Soviet general, who stressed the value of both active defense and of a powerful offensive posture.[58] Likewise, the third edition of the widely-known Sokolovskii treatise *Military Strategy*, issued in early 1968, repeated without change an assessment offered five years earlier to the effect that modern defense resources would make it possible to insure "the complete destruction of all attacking enemy planes and missiles, preventing them from reaching the targets marked for destruction."[59]

While in Soviet military circles there was thus general advocacy of a vigorous ABM program, tempered perhaps by professional debate over the technical and operational potential of available defense systems, it remained unclear what the policy preferences of the Soviet political leadership itself might be with regard to the pace and extent of ABM deployment. As noted in a previous chapter, American suggestions in early 1967 for an ABM moratorium apparently touched off a policy debate within the Kremlin on this and the associated question of strategic arms limitation talks.[60] For a period of almost eighteen months neither the American moratorium proposal nor the US decision of September 1967 to go ahead with a "thin" ABM deployment in the United States elicited a response from Moscow.[61] Then, in June 1968, the Soviet Union finally agreed to enter talks with the United States on ABM and other strategic arms levels. Precisely how the future of the Soviet ABM program might be affected by the Kremlin's belated decision to explore the prospects of an ABM moratorium was, however, not clear.

On the one hand, in late 1968, work on the GALOSH anti-missile system around Moscow apparently came to a standstill about two-thirds of the way toward

---

defenses was provided on March 23, 1969, in a *Pravda Ukrainy* article by G. Gerasimov, who said that it was impossible to achieve 100 per cent interception, without which an ABM system could not be considered effective, and that in any case "investments in ABM can be neutralized by much smaller investments in additional offensive means."

[58] Lt. General I. G. Zav'ialov, "On Soviet Military Doctrine," *Krasnaia zvezda*, March 31, 1967 (second of two articles). For arguments by other Soviet military writers that new methods of strategic defense like ABM, combined with powerful offensive forces, would give the Soviet Union a military posture capable of inflicting "speedy defeat upon the aggressor" and minimizing damage to the USSR, see Lt. Colonel E. Rybkin, "On the Essence of World Missile-Nuclear War," *Kommunist Vooruzhennykh Sil*, no. 17 (September 1965): 55; Rear Admiral V. Andreev, "The Dialectics of the Correlation of Forces," *Krasnaia zvezda*, December 13, 1967.

[59] Marshal V. D. Sokolovskii et al., *Voennaia strategiia* (Military Strategy) (3rd ed., Moscow: Voenizdat, 1968), p. 362. This volume, sent to the press in late 1967, appeared in print not long before Sokolovskii's death in May 1968. For a discussion of the treatment of the ABM question in the previous editions of this work (published in 1962 and 1963), see Thomas W. Wolfe, *Soviet Strategy at the Crossroads* (Cambridge, Mass.: Harvard University Press, 1964), especially pp. 190–93.

[60] See chapter XI, pp. 270–71, 273–74, and fns. 137 and 149.

[61] Initial Soviet commentary took the line that the US decision on ABM was meant to appease pressure from political "hard-liners" and from the US arms industry, but that it would not satisfy those in the United States who advocated a "heavy" deployment costing $40 to $50 billion. For details on the response in the Soviet Union and East Europe to the US announcement, see the present author's remarks, *Hearings, Antiballistic Missile Program, November 1967*, pp. 68–69.

completion,[62] suggesting that despite the Soviet Union's modest headstart in ABM deployment there was doubt in Soviet leadership circles about the feasibility of acquiring effective missile defenses. On the other hand, the Soviet Union continued throughout 1968–69 to pursue a high level of research activity in the ABM field,[63] and by early 1970 some Soviet military authorities were again claiming that the USSR possessed defenses "capable of reliably striking both enemy aircraft and missiles."[64] Moreover, Soviet commentary on the controversy in the United States over the Nixon administration's plans for deployment of the Safeguard missile defense system included notably few arguments against the merits of missile defenses as such,[65] which also tended to suggest that the Soviet leaders were not yet ready to write off further ABM deployment, but preferred to leave their hands untied in this field, at least pending the outcome of the SALT talks.

Efforts to Improve the "Reach" of Soviet Conventional Forces

If nothing else, the large investment of effort and resources devoted to building up the Soviet strategic posture seemed to testify to the determination of the Brezhnev–Kosygin regime to erase the image of a Soviet Union strategically inferior to its major adversary. At the same time, the regime's military preparations involved what might be described as a parallel attempt to improve the reach and mobility of Soviet conventional, or general purpose, forces. Although this undertaking did not match in scope and priority the effort that went into strengthening the Soviet strategic posture, it represented a significant advance beyond the steps taken toward the end of Khrushchev's tenure to enlarge the capacity of the country's naval forces for both blue-water and amphibious landing operations and to improve the mobility of its conventional military power in general.[66]

[62] See *Clifford Statement, 1969*, p. 7; John W. Finney, "Laird Sees 'Rapid' Soviet Missile Gains," *New York Times*, February 21, 1969.

[63] See *Clifford Statement, 1969*, p. 7; *Laird Statement, 1970*, pp. 37, 107. In a press conference on March 14, 1969, President Nixon also took note of continued Soviet ABM activity, suggesting that some of it seemed related to defense against China. "Transcript of the President's News Conference on Foreign and Domestic Affairs," *New York Times*, March 15, 1969.

[64] See, for example, article by Marshal A. A. Grechko, "Born in Battles," *Pravda,* February 23, 1970.

[65] The Soviet Union treated the US domestic debate over plans for deployment of the Safeguard ABM with considerable circumspection both before and after the opening of the initial round of SALT talks in November 1969. Although alleging that the Nixon administration hoped to use the Safeguard program as a "trump card" in negotiations with the USSR, Soviet commentators generally steered clear of arguments directed against ABM on technical or strategic grounds. A rare exception to this rule was the critical statement by G. Gerasimov cited in fn. 57 above. For more typical Soviet commentary, see V. Matveev, "Armaments and Disarmament" and "The Road Ahead," *Izvestiia*, March 13 and 27, 1969; V. Paramonov, "Missiles and Business." *Sovetskaia Rossiia* (Soviet Russia), March 26, 1969; B. Strel'nikov, "Dangerous 'Safeguard'," *Pravda*, March 31, 1969; article by Observer, "A Serious Problem," ibid., March 7, 1970. For pertinent Western observations, see Murrey Marder, "Russians Reserved on ABM," *Washington Post*, March 16, 1969; Johan J. Holst, "The Russians and 'Safeguard'," Paper H1-1176/3-P, Hudson Institute, Croton-on-Hudson, N.Y., April 2, 1969.

[66] For previous discussion of the initiation of such steps in the latter part of the Khrushchev era,

Developments in Naval Policy

The policies of the Brezhnev–Kosygin regime carried further the process of transforming the Soviet navy from its traditional role as a mere adjunct to land power into an instrument for the global support of Soviet interests, although the naval program failed to create "balanced" naval forces in the Western sense. Primary emphasis continued upon improving the fleet of more than 350 submarines, the world's largest underseas force, whose mission includes both strategic delivery of sub-launched missiles and interdiction of seaborne supply lines. According to a major article on Soviet sea power by Admiral S. G. Gorshkov, head of the Soviet navy, the submarine fleet and the naval air arm (a land-based force of some 850 aircraft[67]) had been given "the leading place" in the build-up of Soviet naval power.[68]

While the surface forces in this scheme of things thus did not enjoy top priority, as had been the case also in Khrushchev's time, there was a significant renewal of surface-ship construction under the new regime. In addition, many existing surface units in cruiser and destroyer classes were modernized to fire surface-to-surface and anti-aircraft missiles,[69] the latter suggesting an interest in preparing the surface forces to operate in waters beyond the protective range of land-based Soviet air cover. These forces in 1969 included some 20 cruisers; about 170 vessels classed as destroyers, frigates and destroyer escorts; upward of 100 amphibious ships; and a fleet of several hundred fast patrol boats, some of which were armed with missiles of the so-called STYX type, used by the Egyptians to sink an Israeli destroyer in October 1967.[70]

In the maritime field, meanwhile, the steady growth of the Soviet merchant fleet continued, bringing its tonnage up from about 6 million deadweight tons at the close of the Khrushchev period to about 11 million by 1969, according to Soviet shipping officials.[71] Along with this expansion of cargo capacity went a proliferation of trawler and oceanographic activities, providing useful logistics

see chapter VIII, pp. 190–94. See also Thomas W. Wolfe, "Russia's Forces Go Mobile," *Interplay* (March 1968): 28–33.

[67] About 300 of the aircraft in the naval air arm in early 1969 were TU-16 BADGER medium jet bombers, many equipped to fire air-to-surface missiles. The remainder included some TU-95 BEAR turboprop aircraft for long-range reconnaissance missions, together with a miscellaneous assortment of flying boats, helicopters, torpedo bombers, and transport aircraft. See *The Military Balance, 1968–1969*, p. 8.

[68] "Development of Soviet Naval Art," *Morskoi sbornik* (Naval Collection), no. 2 (February 1967): 20. A condensed version of this article by Gorshkov may be found in *Soviet Military Review*, no. 7 (July 1967).

[69] *The Military Balance, 1968–1969*, p. 7.

[70] Ibid. See also "Russia: Power Play on the Oceans," *Time*, February 23, 1968, pp. 23, 24; "The Soviet Navy," *Military Review* (April 1969): 11–17.

[71] V. G. Bakaev, Minister of the USSR Merchant Fleet, "The Soviet Flag on the Maritime Routes," *Morskoi sbornik*, no. 7 (July 1969): 33; report of interview with Nikolai Bykov, *New York Times*, October 14, 1969. By mid-1969 the Soviet shipbuilding program together with the purchase of commercial vessels abroad had placed the Soviet merchant fleet among the five largest in the world, with more than 1,500 vessels. For a well-informed analysis of merchant shipping as well as naval advances in the Soviet Union, see *Soviet Sea Power* (Washington, D.C.: Center for Strategic and International Studies, Georgetown University, 1969).

and intelligence adjuncts to Soviet sea power. It is worth noting, incidentally, that a large Soviet merchant fleet without global naval forces to protect it would tend to offer hostages to Western naval power in the event of a crisis, an inhibiting factor for Soviet policy, which may have been among the incentives for extending the blue-water reach of the naval forces.

The selective character of the Soviet naval program, particularly the failure to build a force of attack aircraft carriers, has led some to doubt that Soviet naval advances should be interpreted as evidence of an effort to lay down a worldwide offensive challenge to Western sea power.[72] Whatever may be the ultimate verdict on this score, a number of noteworthy innovations and departures from past Soviet naval practice did become evident under the Brezhnev–Kosygin regime. With increasing frequency after 1964, for example, Soviet submarines conducted regular patrols in distant ocean areas, including a much-publicized round-the-world cruise by nuclear-powered submarines in 1966[73] and the maintenance of full-time patrols within missile range of the Atlantic and Pacific coasts of the United States.[74] These demonstrations of a Soviet capacity for blue-water operations were not confined to the submarine fleet. As pointed out in April 1966 by Paul H. Nitze, then US Secretary of the Navy, Soviet surface ships were also "developing the capability for high seas operations away from their confined home waters, replenishing at sea, as our navies long ago found advantageous."[75]

Perhaps a more striking example of the Soviet navy's departure from past practice—if only because of its greater visibility—was the establishment during the 1967 Arab–Israeli conflict of what appears to have become a permanent naval presence in the Mediterranean. Actually, the Soviet Union had begun to establish such a presence on a modest scale at the time of the Cyprus crisis of 1964.[76] However, it was only after Brezhnev demanded withdrawal of the US Sixth

[72] Among those who argued that, until the Soviet Union creates more balanced naval forces by building up carrier aviation, its sea power will essentially remain fitted for a traditional defensive role is Robert W. Herrick, a retired US Navy officer. See his book *Soviet Naval Strategy: Fifty Years of Theory and Practice*, published by the United States Naval Institute, Annapolis, Md., in 1968. A somewhat similar view, apparently intended to caution against overreaction to Soviet naval advances, was expressed by Secretary of the Navy Paul R. Ignatius, who said in a speech on March 29, 1968: "Soviet sea power has been long in developing and no precipitate action on our part is required to maintain the strategic balance. Our fleet is far larger, stronger and more versatile than theirs and we intend to keep it so." See "Books Deprecating Soviet Navy Power Delayed for Disclaimer," *New York Times*, March 31, 1968; "Ignatius Seeks To Allay Fears on Soviet Navy Gains," ibid., March 30, 1968.

[73] See Malinovskii speech at the Twenty-third Party Congress, *Krasnaia zvezda*, April 2, 1966.

[74] Michael Getler, "Soviet Missile Subs Patrol Off U.S.," *Missiles and Rockets*, April 4, 1966, p. 2; William Beecher, "Soviet Missile Submarines on Patrol Off U.S. Coasts," *New York Times*, May 10, 1968.

[75] "Remarks by the Honorable Paul H. Nitze, Secretary of the Navy," Azalea Festival Luncheon, Norfolk, Va., April 21, 1966.

[76] Although Soviet surface naval units began to appear in the Mediterranean only in 1964 during the building up of tension over Cyprus, submarines and intelligence-collection vessels had operated in small numbers in Mediterranean waters prior to that time. Before the Soviet break with Albania in 1961, it may be recalled, a few Soviet submarines had been based at the Adriatic port of Valona.

Fleet, in April 1967, on the eve of the Arab–Israeli confrontation, that the dispatch of additional Soviet naval units to the Mediterranean attracted widespread notice.[77]

The augmented Soviet detachment of some forty combat and auxiliary vessels which stationed itself in the eastern Mediterranean at the time of the June war was, of course, clearly inadequate to taking on the Sixth Fleet,[78] and doubtless was not intended to challenge the latter directly. What drew particular attention to the Soviet presence was the inclusion in the naval force of a tank-landing ship—a type of amphibious vessel only recently introduced into the Soviet navy[79]—together with a couple of troop-landing ships carrying black-bereted troops of the reconstituted naval infantry forces.[80] Although the peak of the crisis had passed before these landing ships arrived on the scene, the unprecedented display of an amphibious capability well away from the home waters no doubt was meant to convey the impression that the Soviet Union was prepared to intervene with local landing parties if necessary.

Soviet reluctance to become involved militarily in the Arab–Israeli fighting and thereby risk triggering a Great Power confrontation actually took much of the edge off any implied threat of intervention by Russian naval forces in the area. Yet Soviet spokesmen contended that both during and after the June war the naval units served an important deterrent function in "frustrating the adventurous plans" of the Israelis and their alleged "imperialist" backers.[81] Whatever degree of credence such claims might warrant, the establishment of a naval presence in the Mediterranean,[82] together with the initiation in 1968 of goodwill

[77] See, for example, "Soviet Is Sending 10 More Warships to Middle East," *New York Times*, May 31, 1967; Hanson W. Baldwin, "Soviet Naval Power," ibid., June 2, 1967.

[78] The US Sixth Fleet, by comparison, represented a balanced naval force of some sixty warships, built around two large aircraft carriers. In addition to the Sixth Fleet, Italian and French naval forces, as well as British, operated in the Mediterranean.

[79] It was only after the initial transit of a Soviet tank-landing ship from the Black Sea to the Mediterranean during the June Arab–Israeli crisis that photos of such vessels began to be published in the Soviet press. For example, Admiral Gorshkov's article in the July 1967 issue of *Soviet Military Review* included a picture of a tank-landing operation, although a lengthier illustrated version of the same article in another publication six months earlier did not.

[80] As noted earlier (chapter VIII, pp. 192–93), the naval infantry, or *morskaia pekhota*, had been revised in mid-1964, after a long period of deactivation. Its training for special landing operations was given a good deal of publicity during the last years of Khruschchev's rule and under the new regime. At the Red Square parade of November 7, 1967, contingents of these troops, described as the "Black Berets," were singled out for laudatory comment. For a typical article describing the rigorous training and versatile qualities of the naval infantry, see Captain 2nd Rank N. Belous, "The Naval Infantry Is Taught To Win," *Kommunist Vooruzhennykh Sil*, no. 7 (April 1968): 50-55.

[81] See chapter XIII, pp. 326–27, 339–40. The claim that the Soviet naval presence was needed to protect the Arab countries from the US Sixth Fleet remained a theme in Soviet statements thereafter. See Vice Admiral N. Smirnov, "Soviet Ships in the Mediterranean Sea," *Krasnaia zvezda*, November 12, 1968.

[82] Up to early 1970 the size of the Soviet Mediterranean force reportedly fluctuated from around thirty to sixty vessels, as units were rotated in and out from the Black Sea via the Dardanelles and from the Baltic via Gibraltar. In addition to one or two guided missile cruisers, the force included destroyers, submarines, landing ships, and supply auxiliaries. For about a month in the fall of 1968 and again in 1969, the new helicopter carrier *Moskva* maneuvered with the Mediterranean naval force. It also was reported that Egypt-based TU-16 medium jet bombers flown by Soviet pilots

naval visits to the Indian Ocean and the Persian Gulf,[83] clearly meant that the Soviet Union had acquired a new diplomatic tool for support of its interests in this part of the world.[84]

Another notable innovation in Soviet naval policy was the decision to build helicopter carriers, the first two of which were completed after the Brezhnev–Kosygin regime took office.[85] This development came as the climax to a long and evidently frustrating internal debate over the pros and cons of adopting aircraft carriers. As mentioned earlier, the World War II head of the Soviet navy, Admiral N. G. Kuznetsov, revealed in his memoirs, in 1966, that proposals for carrier construction in the late thirties had been vetoed by Stalin.[86] After World War II a carrier program was again proposed, but it too was

carried out reconnaissance flights for the Soviet naval units in the Mediterranean during 1968. See Basil Gingell, "Russian Buildup in Mediterranean," *Times*, London, October 1, 1968; Neal Ascherson, "Soviet Mediterranean Buildup Fits World Rather than Local Strategy," *Washington Post*, October 26, 1968; Robert H. Estabrook, "Soviet Navy Stirs Concern at UN," ibid., November 15, 1968; *Soviet Sea Power*, pp 67–72; "Soviet Deploying Big Fleet Abroad," *New York Times*, August 21, 1969.

[83] See chapter XIII, pp. 340–41. In addition to Soviet goodwill naval cruising, the year 1968 saw the increased presence in the Indian Ocean of Soviet vessels involved in the recovery aspects of the Soviet space program, especially the lunar program. During the Soviet Zond-6 lunar shot in November 1968, Soviet vessels converging on the recovery area included several warships which later made a flag-showing call at Mombasa in Kenya.

[84] For previous discussion of Soviet military and political interests in the Mediterranean and Middle East, see chapter XIII, pp. 325–27, 336–47. As therein noted, one effect of the Soviet naval presence in the Mediterranean was the growth of disquiet in NATO, which led among other things to the establishment in November 1968 of a new NATO air reconnaissance command, Maritime Air Forces Mediterranean, designed to keep Soviet naval activities in the area under surveillance. There was sharp verbal reaction from Moscow to this step and to accompanying NATO warnings against Soviet military intervention in Europe or the Mediterranean area. In its reply to NATO, the Soviet Union made known its intention to maintain a permanent naval presence in the area, repeating earlier statements by Gromyko and other spokesmen that the Soviet Union was "a Black Sea power, and consequently, a Mediterranean power," and that as such it had an "irrefutable right" to station warships in the Mediterranean to "promote stability and peace" in a part of the world "which is in direct proximity to the USSR's southern borders." See TASS account of Gromyko's May 12, 1968, interview with *L'Unità, Soviet News*, May 14, 1968; L. Kolosov, "Mediterranean Problems," *Izvestiia*, November 12, 1968; Admiral Smirnov, in *Krasnaia zvezda*, November 12, 1968; Drew Middleton, "NATO Bids Soviet Avoid Stirring Up a Crisis in Europe," *New York Times*, November 17, 1968; V. Ermakov, "American Billyclub in the Mediterranean Sea," *Pravda*, November 27, 1968. Among other effects of the Soviet Mediterranean naval presence, incidentally, was the issuance of hints by Spanish officials that a higher price would be required of the United States for political and military co-operation from Spain, and even that Spain might move toward a position of East–West neutrality. See Benjamin Welles, "Soviet Sea Moves Disturbing to U.S." and "U.S. Cool to Spain on Fleet Proposal," *New York Times*, April 17 and November 22, 1968, respectively; Richard Eder, "Move Perplexes Diplomats," ibid., November 22, 1968. For a good general analysis of the political-military implications of Soviet maritime developments, especially for NATO, see Martin Edmonds and John Skitt, "Current Soviet Maritime Strategy and NATO," *International Affairs*, Chatham House, London (January 1969): 28–43.

[85] The first two Soviet helicopter carriers, named the *Moskva* and the *Leningrad*, reportedly can handle about thirty helicopters each. The decision to build these ships evidently was made before Khrushchev left office, but construction and fitting out of the first one was not completed until sometime in 1966 or early 1967. Initial Western disclosure that the Soviets were building such vessels came in October 1967 (see *New York Times*, October 23, 1967), and there were later, unconfirmed reports that construction of a third helicopter carrier was about to begin. See William Beecher, "3d Soviet Carrier Believed On Ways," *New York Times*, February 14, 1968.

[86] See chapter III, pp. 46–47, and fn. 47.

turned down, in part because catching up with the West evidently posed too great a burden on Soviet resources, and in part, according to the incumbent head of the navy, because the advent of the nuclear age had underscored the vulnerability of carriers and marked the beginning of their "irreversible decline" as the "main striking element" of modern naval power.[87]

In the end, the decision to invest in helicopter carriers was a compromise representing, not a belated bid to compete with the United States in carrier attack aviation[88] (although such an effort in the future cannot be ruled out), but rather a step toward improving the Soviet potential for landing operations and anti-submarine warfare. Which of these two purposes might stand higher in Soviet plans for the new helicopter carriers had not yet been made clear in Soviet military literature by the end of 1969. However, the fact that efforts to overcome the Soviet lag in anti-submarine warfare had already involved the use of helicopters suggested that the carriers were likely to be employed as ASW platforms, an impression strengthened by the carrier *Moskva*'s reported ASW training activity in the Mediterranean in 1968–69.[89]

Understandably, Soviet naval authorities have spoken with great satisfaction of the trends which culminated in their navy's breaking out of its traditional confinement to closed seas around the Soviet littoral. Speeches marking the observance of Soviet Navy Day in July 1967, and again in 1968 and 1969, were notable for their frequent sounding of the theme that Soviet sea power had extended its reach to "remote areas of the world's oceans previously considered a zone of supremacy of the fleets of imperialist powers," and that henceforth its mission would include "constantly cruising and patrolling wherever required in defense of the state interests of the Soviet Union."[90]

Such utterances by Soviet admirals, though doubtless colored by pride of service, reflected an assessment of the changing role of Soviet sea power that was without precedent in Soviet history. Certainly, the notion that the navy's

---

[87] Admiral Gorshkov, in *Morskoi sbornik* (February 1967): 18–19.

[88] The United States in 1968 had fifteen attack carriers in active commission, plus three others under construction or in conversion, representing a formidable lead should the Soviet Union wish to compete in this category of carrier aviation. In addition, the United States had eight ASW carriers, which, unlike the Soviet helicopter carriers, were suited to accommodate patrol aircraft and fighters in addition to helicopters. Perhaps the nearest US equivalent to the Soviet carriers was the LPH amphibious assault ship (Landing Platform, Helicopter), a type of converted carrier accommodating thirty to thirty-five helicopters and about 2,000 marines. In early 1968 the United States possessed eight LPHs, some of which were to be replaced by a larger and more versatile type (LHA). See *McNamara Statement, 1968*, pp. 119, 122, 129.

[89] Although the *Moskva* participated primarily in ASW activities in the Mediterranean, this does not, of course, rule out other types of missions, including landing operations. As pictures of the *Moskva* indicate, the vessel is equipped with an array of guided missile launchers, in addition to a helicopter deck. For such a photograph, see "U.S. Plane Watches a Soviet Carrier," *Washington Post*, November 4, 1968. See also William Beecher, "U.S. Fears Threat to Polaris Craft in Soviet Buildup," *New York Times*, November 20, 1968; "Soviets Seen Increasing Fleet in Mediterranean," *Washington Post*, August 20, 1969.

[90] See, for example, articles by Fleet Admiral V. Kasatonov, "On Battle Watch," *Krasnaia zvezda*, July 30, 1967, and Admiral N. Sergeev, *Sovetskaia Kirgiziia*, July 30, 1967; interview with Admiral N. Kharlamov, "Guarding Our Country's Maritime Boundaries Reliably," *Moscow News*, no. 30, August 3–10, 1968, p. 3; Fleet Admiral S. G. Gorshkov, "Oceanic Guard of the Fatherland," *Pravda*, July 27, 1969.

task was to look after the worldwide "state interests" of the USSR was new to the Soviet political vocabulary. The increasing incidence of harassment at sea between Soviet and US naval units,[91] the intrusion of Soviet intelligence-gathering ships into US waters,[92] the entry of a Soviet screening force into the Sea of Japan after the *Pueblo* incident,[93] and the first appearance of Soviet warships in the Gulf of Mexico during a naval visit to Cuba in 1969,[94] all seemed to reflect this new conception of the role of the Soviet navy.

Other Trends Bearing on Soviet Global Mobility

Apart from the naval and maritime trends noted above, the period following Khrushchev's ouster was marked by other developments bearing upon the Soviet Union's capacity to project conventional military power into distant areas. The improvement of airlift potential, for example, went forward under the Brezhnev–Kosygin regime, which like its predecessors looked to the airplane to help satisfy the civil and military logistics demands of a vast country with a thinly developed road and rail net. Among the more celebrated products of Soviet air transport technology unveiled in the early years of the new regime was the AN-22 heavy transport, an aircraft which went into production in the fall of 1966 to provide a means for long-range, large-load airlift previously unavailable to the Soviet Union.[95] One of its potential military uses was displayed in July 1967 at the Moscow air show, where AN-22s took part in a simulated combat landing of airborne troops with several types of missiles and self-propelled guns.[96] Presumably, these aircraft could also be used to ferry troops and equipment to distant theaters of contention.

[91] In addition to stalking US carriers, submarines, and other warships by long-range reconnaissance aircraft and naval vessels, the Soviet navy's new and bolder pattern of harassment at sea included maneuvering into the midst of US naval formations in the Mediterranean and elsewhere. A particularly dramatic example of this activity occurred in May 1968, when one of two Soviet TU-16 jet bombers making a low pass close to the US carrier *Essex* crashed into the Norwegian Sea. See "Soviet Hazard," *Washington Post*, February 14, 1968; *Time*, February 23, 1968, p. 27; William Beecher, "U.S. and Soviet Craft Play Tag Under Sea," *New York Times*, May 11, 1968; Fred Hoffman, "Soviet Jet Buzzes Ship, Falls into Sea," *Washington Post*, May 26, 1968.

[92] Following the *Pueblo* incident, a US spokesman in February 1968 disclosed that a series of intrusions into US territorial waters by Soviet intelligence ships had taken place during the previous three years, and that the ships had not been seized but had been told to move on. A Soviet spokesman, Marshal M. V. Zakharov, denied shortly afterwards that the USSR operated such ships near foreign shores, although he also added: "We will sail all the world's seas. No force on earth can prevent us." See "Mansfield Asks Caution on Spy Ship Questions," *Washington Post*, February 7, 1968; "Soviet Aide: No Spying Near Coasts," ibid., February 17, 1968.

[93] See "Soviet Vessel Stalking Enterprise," *New York Times*, January 27, 1968; Ambassador Goldberg's remarks at UN Security Council Debate on the *Pueblo* incident, ibid., January 28, 1968; and *Time*, February 23, 1968, p. 24.

[94] G. Zafesov, "Soviet Sailors in Cuba," *Pravda*, July 23, 1969; speech by Fleet Admiral S. G. Gorshkov, ibid., July 27, 1969.

[95] The AN-22 has a payload of about 45 tons at a range of 6,000 miles and about double that capacity at half the distance. See "Holiday Panorama," *Nedelia* (Week), October 30–November 5, 1966, p. 4; Lt. Colonel E. Simakov, "Antaeus Rises Above the Earth," *Soviet Military Review*, no. 7 (July 1966): 30–31.

[96] See "Soviets Demonstrate Vertical Envelopment Capability with AN-22 Heavy Transport," *Aviation Week & Space Technology*, August 14, 1967, pp. 52–53.

The quick seizure of Prague by Soviet airborne troops on the night of August 20–21, 1968, provided what was doubtless the most graphic demonstration of Soviet combat-landing capabilities,[97] although this operation was conducted in Central Europe, within easy range of Soviet base areas, and was therefore not wholly representative of the Soviet Union's airlift potential to more distant regions. A geographically more extended effort, illustrative of the Soviet logistical, rather than combat-landing, capacity beyond the borders of the Soviet Union was the massive air-resupply operation mounted promptly after the June 1967 Arab–Israeli war to replenish Nasser's forces.[98] The airlift to Yemen later in 1967 and in 1968 was a repeat performance on a smaller scale. Vietnam provides the best general example of the lengthening of the Soviet Union's logistical reach far beyond its borders. Although airlift has played a minor role there, partly because of Chinese restrictions on overflights, the supplying of North Vietnam by sea and rail in the 1965–70 period furnished creditable evidence of the Soviet Union's capacity to conduct a major and sustained logistical effort over long lines of communication,[99] at least under conditions where it does not have to face military interdiction.

Deficiencies in the means of protecting lines of communication distant from the USSR against determined interdiction doubtless remain among the more serious handicaps yet to be overcome, although it is worth pointing out that under the "rules of the game" which have thus far grown up around Third World conflicts the problem of interdiction has not arisen for the Soviet Union.[100] A related problem, bearing on the Soviet Union's ability to lend logistical support or make its military presence felt on various distant fronts in the Third World, is that of geographic and political access. The Soviet Union's traditional unwillingness to acquire overseas bases may remain a barrier to setting up military shop in some regions, just as appropriate access routes to areas of contention may be blocked by the unco-operative attitude of intervening states. In this respect, however, potential base arrangements and "calling privileges" have been one legacy of Soviet military aid programs in some areas, of which the Middle East is currently a prime example, and Soviet diplomacy seems capable of softening the attitudes of a number of states that sit astride

[97] See chapters XIV, p. 380, and XVII, pp. 473–74.

[98] The air resupply operation on Nasser's behalf, which involved several hundred flights by Soviet transport aircraft, was quickly organized and set in motion. Although Tito's co-operation in permitting overflight and staging through Yugoslavia facilitated the mounting of this operation, it was nevertheless an impressive demonstration of prompt airlift resupply capability. The principal aircraft employed was the AN-12, an older aircraft than the AN-22, but by the same designer, Oleg Antonov. The AN-12, a four-engine turboprop transport is widely used for Soviet military airlift, as well as by the civil airline organization, Aeroflot.

[99] Sea routes from both Soviet Black Sea and Pacific ports have been used for shipment of bulk cargoes, transport equipment, and the like to Vietnam, but rail transport across China also has been used for military supply items, partly to reduce the risk of confrontation at sea with US naval forces. See Paul Wohl, "How the Soviets Ship Arms Aid to North Vietnam," *Christian Science Monitor*, January 1, 1966.

[100] The author is indebted to a colleague, Fritz Ermarth, for this reminder. A notable exception to "rules of the game" under which the United States has not sought to impose military interdiction on Soviet logistical operations was the brief embargo against certain types of Soviet military shipments to Cuba at the height of the 1962 missile crisis.

strategic access routes beyond the Soviet borders. The improvement of Soviet relations with Turkey, whose co-operation has been an essential factor in Soviet naval access to the eastern Mediterranean, comes to mind in this connection.

With respect to the ability of the Soviet Union to project its military influence into distant limited war situations, experience is also a relevant factor. Soviet forces as such have not been openly engaged in Third World military hostilities, although there is a rather lengthy list of occasions, from Indonesia in 1962 to the Middle East in 1967–70, not to mention Vietnam, where Soviet personnel in the guise of military advisers and technicians found themselves to some extent involved in active combat.[101] It may be assumed that such exposure to limited war situations is no substitute for the experience of organized unit activity, particularly in the complex problems of employing co-ordinated ground and tactical air power. Nevertheless, the observation of, and twilight participation in, various conflicts undoubtedly has brought home many useful lessons in the conduct of local war. The Soviet role in Vietnam, for example, not only has yielded experience in dealing with problems of logistics support and technical backup but has afforded the opportunity for combat-testing of air defense and other weapons systems in a limited-war environment. At the same time, Soviet military professionals apparently have kept an attentive eye on the development of new US technology and techniques as applied to the war in Southeast Asia; indeed, judging from the Soviet military press, there seems to have been some concern lest Soviet military thought and practice fail to keep pace with innovations spurred by the American effort in Vietnam.[102]

Interest in the improvement of airborne and amphibious assault capabilities, a trend already in evidence toward the close of the Khrushchev period,[103] became more pronounced under the Brezhnev–Kosygin regime. Besides the development of new air-landing methods and equipment, increased emphasis was given to airborne operations and airlift reinforcement in connection with various Warsaw Pact field exercises.[104] Although these training operations—

101 With respect to Indonesia, A. I. Mikoyan disclosed in a speech in 1964 that Soviet military personnel on training duty in that country were prepared to take part in 1962 in fighting over West Irian, had the issue not been settled. Prior to that, some Soviet personnel were involved in the Korean war in the early fifties and in the 1956 Suez affair. In Cuba in 1962, the organized Soviet strategic missile units sent there saw no action, but some Soviet technicians presumably lent a hand in manning the then new Cuban air defense system, which shot down a US reconnaissance plane. Again, in the Vietnam war, Soviet advisors and technicians were at some stages closely involved, under fire, in helping the DRV get its air defenses in operation. The June 1967 war in the Middle East produced widespread rumors that some Soviet military advisors were taking part in combat operations, especially on the Syrian front. In early 1968 a Soviet pilot was reported to have been shot down on a combat mission against the royalists in Yemen, while in early 1970 the Soviet Union was rumored to be on the verge of introducing air defense personnel into Egypt.

102 The bulk of Soviet military commentary on the Vietnam war has emphasized the difficulties encountered by US forces, but occasional accounts of such new US tactics as employment of air-mobile units betray a professional Soviet awareness that the war has produced developments in military technology not matched by the USSR. In this connection, see Colonel M. Belov, "Helicopters and Tactics of Combined Arms Combat," *Krasnaia zvezda*, August 7, 1969.

103 See chapter VIII, pp. 192–93.

104 Joint Soviet–GDR exercises in the spring of 1965 featured the deployment of Soviet airborne troops into East Germany, while in October 1965 a larger Warsaw Pact maneuver in the GDR, "October Storm," also involved bringing airlifted reinforcements into the maneuver area, including Polish troops lifted in Soviet transports. A much publicized airlift training operation also was part

like the actual air-landing assault during the invasion of Czechoslovakia—were Europe-centered and of restricted geographical scope, the lessons learned were doubtless not without some application to the problems of conducting operations in more distant areas. Likewise, the potential for amphibious assault was enhanced, not only by the addition of helicopter and landing ships but also by an increase in the size of Soviet marine forces, or "naval infantry." These forces, which grew from about 6,000 to 12,000 men in the 1966–69 period,[105] were distributed among the several Soviet territorial fleets and trained for special landing operations.

One can by no means identify all of the developments sketched above as well-meshed parts of a purposeful long-range plan to acquire capabilities for active use in local conflicts beyond the USSR's borders. Some of these developments probably were improvised responses to particular crises rather than the fruits of long-range planning; others were by-products of Soviet military and economic aid programs; still others, the outgrowth of efforts to improve the mobility of Soviet forces in the European theater and to achieve a more balanced general war posture. However, despite their varied origin, they did seem to suggest, as a Yugoslav strategic writer put it in 1967, that the Soviet Union had begun to embark upon "a policy of countering the strategy of local and restricted wars" by providing itself with the kinds of military capabilities necessary to conduct "that selfsame local and restricted war."[106]

The implication here that the Soviet Union under the Brezhnev–Kosygin leadership began moving toward a more active role for military power in support of its commitments and interests in distant areas of contention can only be tested with the passage of time, for not only the availability of the requisite forces is involved but also the willingness of the political leadership to take on the military and political risks that recourse to limited war might entail. To the extent that doctrinal considerations are relevant to this critical policy question, it can be said that Soviet military preparations during the first five years of the Brezhnev–Kosygin regime were carried out against the background of a military doctrinal discussion which—while by no means representing a sharp break from the previous orientation of Soviet doctrine toward the problems of general nuclear war—nevertheless tended to place more emphasis than before on the possibility of having to deal with non-nuclear and limited warfare situations

---

of the "Vltava" exercises in Czechoslovakia by joint Warsaw Pact forces in October 1966. See Thomas W. Wolfe, "The Warsaw Pact in Evolution," in Kurt London, ed., *Eastern Europe in Transition* (Baltimore, Md.: The Johns Hopkins Press, 1966), pp. 225–26; Benjamin Welles, "New Soviet Arms Viewed as Increasing Military Threat to West Europe," *New York Times*, November 6, 1966. See also the more detailed discussion of joint Warsaw Pact exercises in chapter XVII, pp. 477–80.

[105] *The Military Balance, 1967–1968*, and *1969–1970*, pp. 8, 9, respectively. See also fn. 80 above.

[106] Andro Gabelic, "New Accent in Soviet Strategy," reprinted from *Review of International Affairs*, November 20, 1967, in *Survival*, The Institute for Strategic Studies, London (February 1968): 46–47. The Yugoslav author of this article, it should be added, also expressed the view that the Soviet Union would find it a difficult and lengthy task to marshal the resources necessary for acquiring such military capabilities.

in various potential theaters of conflict, including Europe. A brief review of pertinent developments in Soviet military doctrine may therefore be appropriate at this point.

Doctrinal Developments

Although toward the end of Khrushchev's tenure some attention had been given to the need for improving conventional as well as nuclear warfare capabilities,[107] it was mainly after his ouster that Soviet military theorists recognized more explicitly the importance of having Soviet forces prepared for a wide range of operations below the level of general nuclear war. Besides departing from the monotonous cliché that any hostilities involving the nuclear powers would almost automatically bring their strategic arsenals into play,[108] some Soviet military men soon began to voice other ideas that were at variance with standard doctrinal positions on limited warfare.

Thus, for example, General S. M. Shtemenko stated in early 1965 that Soviet military doctrine did not "exclude" the possibility of non-nuclear warfare or of warfare restricted to tactical nuclear weapons "within the framework of so-called 'local' wars."[109] Later the same year, another military man, General N. Lomov, carried this thought a step further by applying it to the situation in Europe. Noting that the American strategy of "flexible response" meant that local wars might "take place in Europe," Lomov said that such wars "are fought, as a rule, with conventional arms, though this does not exclude the possibility of employing tactical nuclear weapons."[110] Lomov's observation that one might envisage a local war limited to conventional means or to tactical nuclear weapons even in Europe was promptly qualified by the caveat that "the probability of escalation into a nuclear world war is always great and might under certain circumstances become inevitable." But in any event, he wrote, Soviet forces should be prepared not only for general nuclear war but also for operations "with conventional arms alone" or with "limited employment of nuclear weapons."[111]

Other military writers subsequently expanded on this theme, stating that

---

[107] See discussion in chapter IX, pp. 206–11.

[108] One of the first military leaders to suggest after Khrushchev's removal that hostilities in Europe might not automatically involve nuclear weapons was Marshal P. A. Rotmistrov. In December 1964, while criticizing a proposal in NATO for a belt of atomic land mines along the German border, he declared that the proposal would preclude the possibility of any hostilities remaining non-nuclear, which seemed to indicate a belief that conventional warfare was otherwise possible. See Rotmistrov, "Dangerous Plans of the Bonn Militarists," *Krasnaia zvezda*, December 29, 1964. Marshal Malinovskii, too, suggested on several occasions that the Soviet Union might find itself involved in wars without use of nuclear weapons, although he did not specify Europe as the locale. Marshal R. Ia. Malinovskii, "The Soldier in Modern Warfare," Radio Volga broadcast, September 8, 1965, also appearing in *Sovetskaia armiia* (Soviet Army) of the same date.

[109] Colonel General S. M. Shtemenko, *Nedelia*, no. 6, January 31–February 6, 1965. See also similar comment by Colonel V. Karamyshev, "The Principles of Soviet Military Development," *Krasnaia zvezda*, February 12, 1965; Colonel V. Glazov, "Laws of Development and Changing Methods of Warfare," *Kommunist Vooruzhennykh Sil*, no. 11 (June 1965): 50.

[110] Major General N. A. Lomov, "The Influence of Soviet Military Doctrine on the Development of the Military Art," *Kommunist Vooruzhennykh Sil*, no. 21 (November 1965): 16, 18.

[111] Ibid., p. 22.

current Soviet military doctrine called for the armed forces to "be prepared to conduct world war as well as limited war, both with and without the use of nuclear weapons."[112] This prescription for a doctrine of multiple military options bore a rather close resemblance to the American doctrine of flexible response; indeed, Soviet writers sometimes employed essentially the same language in describing the one as the other.[113] It is worth noting, however, that Soviet military literature acknowledged in only the most oblique fashion any debt it may have owed to the US version of flexible response.

The typical Soviet treatment of the subject presented the United States as having been driven to adopt a doctrine of flexible response, with its associated "concept of limited wars," after the Soviet Union's attainment of powerful strategic forces made it too dangerous for America to bank any longer on waging a preventive general nuclear war against the USSR.[114] According to the Soviet exegesis, US advocacy of limited wars antedated the birth of flexible response in the early sixties, but the limited war concept took on new importance for the "imperialist aggressors" when the United States, in its role "as the world gendarme, was forced to resort to the use of arms with increasing frequency" to suppress "the stormy national liberation movement in the countries of Asia, Africa, and Latin America."[115] Furthermore, according to the Soviet argument, as US and NATO planners also began to apply the doctrine of flexible response to the European theater, they hoped to work out principles for conducting limited war in Europe without risk of its being transformed into general war.[116] Although Soviet military writing thus continued to condemn the Western doctrine of flexible response as reflecting merely a persistent search for "safe" paths of "imperialist aggression,"[117] at least some Soviet military men apparently concluded that it was time to overhaul their own doctrine.

[112] Colonel N. Kozlov, "The Armed Forces of the USSR in the Period of the Building of Communism," *Kommunist Vooruzhennykh Sil*, no. 4 (February 1967): 80. See also Colonel I. Prusanov, "Party Activity To Strengthen the Armed Forces under Conditions of the Revolution in Military Affairs," ibid., no. 3 (February 1966): 10; Colonel V. Morozov and Lt. Colonel E. Rybkin, "Problems of Methodology in Military Affairs," ibid., no. 4 (February 1967): 93; Sushko and Kondratkov, eds., *Metodologicheskie problemy voennoi teorii i praktiki*, pp. 107–8.

[113] Compare, for example, the above-cited description of Soviet doctrine with the words of a Soviet general who wrote that "flexible response . . . the official U.S. doctrine since 1961 . . . envisaged preparations for waging any war—a world or a local war, nuclear or conventional, large or small." Colonel General M. Povalii, "The Strategic Concepts of Imperialism: The Doctrine of the Aggressor and International Gendarme," *Krasnaia zvezda*, March 12, 1968.

[114] Ibid. A more complete exposition from the Soviet viewpoint of the genesis and development of US flexible response doctrine along lines similar to the Povalii article appears in the third edition of the Sokolovskii treatise *Military Strategy*, published in early 1968 before Sokolovskii's death. See *Voennaia strategiia*, 3rd ed., pp. 66–95. This edition expands somewhat the treatment of flexible response in the 1962 and 1963 editions.

[115] Povalii, in *Krasnaia zvezda*, March 12, 1968.

[116] Ibid.; *Voennaia strategiia*, 2nd ed., p. 89.

[117] The published Soviet literature in the Brezhnev–Kosygin period continued to take a similar view of American concepts for limiting and controlling the use of strategic nuclear weapons. As a Soviet writer put it in a chapter on "The Theories of 'Limited Strategic War'," American theoreticians adopted a "doctrine of 'limited strategic war' [in] an attempt to apply the rules of 'limited' local nuclear war to a 'big war' involving the use of strategic nuclear-missile weapons." The purpose behind American efforts to develop "mutual rules" for "limiting nuclear-missile war,"

Among the more emphatic proponents of a broad-gauged Soviet military doctrine that would accord an enhanced value to conventional forces and would allow for a less rigid reliance on strategic nuclear weapons alone was Marshal I. I. Iakubovskii. In July 1967, shortly after being appointed commander of the joint Warsaw Pact forces, Iakubovskii wrote an article in which he argued that nuclear weapons should not be treated as "absolutes," especially in theater force operations.[118] He also noted with some satisfaction on this occasion that the efforts of party and government in the past few years had improved "the capability of the ground forces to conduct military operations successfully with or without the use of nuclear weapons."

Such comments by Soviet military leaders, together with the kind of doctrinal discussion alluded to above, certainly suggested the recognition, under the Brezhnev–Kosygin regime, that general purpose forces should be placed in a posture that would enable them to deal with situations in which it might not be expedient to bring Soviet strategic nuclear power to bear either militarily or politically. However, it did not follow that the new regime had abandoned reliance upon Soviet nuclear arms in either a military or a political sense, as some Western observers were tempted to conclude from such articles as that by Marshal Iakubovskii.[119] Not only did the large Soviet investment in a strategic force build-up testify to the contrary, but even Soviet proponents of better-balanced forces continued to concede priority to capabilities for conducting general nuclear war.[120] For example, not long before his death in 1967, Soviet Defense Minister Marshal Malinovskii stated categorically that in Soviet defense planning "first priority is being given to the strategic missile forces and atomic missile-launching submarines—forces which are the principal means of deterring the aggressor and decisively defeating him in war."[121]

The late Marshal V. D. Sokolovskii was another well-known military authority who consistently upheld the view that the responsibility of Soviet

according to the writer in question, was "to untie the hands of the nuclear aggressors and to whitewash such a war from the moral point of view." See G. A. Trofimenko, *Strategiia global'noi voiny* (The Strategy of Global War) (Moscow, 1968), pp. 128–45. In short, if private Soviet military thought became at all receptive to the idea of mutual "rules of the game" for limiting the use of strategic nuclear weapons, this was not reflected in open doctrinal writing. For a discussion of Soviet thinking on this subject during the Khrushchev period, see chapter IX, pp. 212–13.

[118] Marshal I. I. Iakubovskii, "Ground Forces," *Krasnaia zvezda*, July 21, 1967. For a similar line of argument, see Major General Iu. Novikov's review of the book *Iadernoe oruzhie i razvitie taktiki* (Nuclear Weapons and the Development of Tactics) in *Krasnaia zvezda*, June 28, 1968. The reviewer criticized the book's authors, P. M. Petrus', P. V. Shemanskii, and N. K. Chul'skii, for "overestimating nuclear weapons, absolutizing their role in close combat, and underestimating the potential of conventional arms."

[119] See, for example, Victor Zorza's interpretation (later modified), "Soviet Defense Shift Seen," *Washington Post*, July 22, 1967.

[120] See Sushko and Kondratkov, eds., *Metodologicheskie problemy voennoi teorii i praktiki*, p. 299; Major General V. Reznichenko, "Trends in the Development of Modern Battle," *Krasnaia zvezda*, June 28, 1967; Marshal A. A. Grechko, "October Army," *Izvestiia*, February 23, 1967; Vice Admiral V. Cherokov, "The Navy's Striking Force," *Krasnaia zvezda*, December 19, 1967; Marshal I. I. Iakubovskii, "The Great Deed," ibid., May 9, 1968.

[121] Marshal R. Ia. Malinovskii, "October and the Building of the Armed Forces," *Kommunist*, no. 1 (January 1967): 34.

strategy was to plan for the use "above all of missile nuclear weapons as the main means of warfare."[122] Sokolovskii's last contribution to Soviet military literature, the third revised edition of *Military Strategy*, issued under his editorship in early 1968, gave increased space to discussion of the Western doctrine of flexible response, but on the whole it showed much the same preoccupation with the problems of nuclear war and the paramount danger of surprise nuclear attack as the previous editions.[123] In this Sokolovskii was not alone, for most Soviet military literature of the Brezhnev–Kosygin period likewise remained centered on questions concerning the "revolution in military affairs" brought about by nuclear weapons, missiles, and other technological advances.[124]

Indeed, this period witnessed a revival of the doctrinal argument about nuclear war as an instrument of policy, with the lines drawn between those asserting that it was theoretically and politically unwise to succumb to the notion that "victory in nuclear war is impossible" and those warning that theorizing on the prospects of nuclear victory should not be carried too far.[125] A related theme upon which Soviet doctrinal writing continued to dwell dealt with

[122] Marshal V. D. Sokolovskii and General M. Cherednichenko, "On Contemporary Military Strategy," *Kommunist Vooruzhennykh Sil*, no. 7 (April 1966): 59–66.

[123] *Voennaia strategiia*, 3rd ed., especially pp. 216–55. The 1968 version of the Sokolovskii work omitted (cf. p. 344) several passages from the 2nd edition (p. 374) which had discussed rather large-scale conventional operations in a theater environment resembling Europe. At a press conference on December 2, 1966, Sokolovskii also had stressed the view that any war involving the great powers would "immediately become thermonuclear." TASS International Service broadcast, Moscow, December 2, 1966.

[124] Characteristic examples of this literature include the following: Colonel P. M. Derevianko, ed., *Problemy revoliutsii v voennom dele* (Problems of the Revolution in Military Affairs) (Moscow: Voenizdat, 1965), especially pp. 1–132; Colonel A. A. Strokov, *Istoriia voennogo iskusstva* (History of Military Art) (Moscow: Voenizdat, 1966), pp. 590–638; Major General K. Bochkarev, "The Character and Types of Wars in the Modern Epoch," *Kommunist Vooruzhennykh Sil*, no. 11 (June 1965): 8–17; Colonel V. Glazov, "Laws of Development and Changing Methods of Warfare," ibid., pp. 43–50; Colonel S. V. Malianchikov, "The Character and Features of Nuclear War," ibid., no. 21 (November 1965): 69–74; Major General V. Voznenko, "Dialectics of Development and Change in Forms and Methods of Armed Conflict," ibid., no. 11 (June 1966): 41–48; Colonel N. V. Miroshnichenko, "Changes in the Content and Nature of Modern Combat," *Voennyi vestnik* (Military Herald) (October 1966): 26–29; Lt. Colonel V. Bondarenko and Colonel S. Tiushkevich, "The Contemporary Stage of the Revolution in Military Affairs and Its Demands on Military Cadres," *Kommunist Vooruzhennykh Sil*, no. 6 (March 1968): 18–25. A useful collection of translated articles, including some of the above, may be found in William R. Kintner and Harriet Fast Scott, *The Nuclear Revolution in Soviet Affairs* (Norman, Okla.: University of Oklahoma Press, 1968).

[125] See Lt. Colonel E. Rybkin, "On the Essence of World Missile-Nuclear War." *Kommunist Vooruzhennykh Sil*, no. 17 (September 1965): 50–56; Colonel I. Grudinin, "The Question of the Essence of War," *Krasnaia zvezda*, July 21, 1966; editorial, "On the Essence of War," ibid., January 24, 1967; Sushko and Kondratkov, eds., *Metodologicheskie problemy voennoi teorii i praktiki*, pp. 33–34. This debate in 1965–67 seemed to center on the argument, not that the then-existing "correlation of forces" would offer a good prospect of Soviet victory if war should occur, but that future changes in the power relationship between the Soviet Union and its adversaries might do so. In effect, those challenging the "fatalistic" notion that nuclear war had become "obsolete" were arguing for further build-up of modern Soviet arms and especially for imaginative exploitation of the "military-technical revolution," whereas the contrary view apparently remained skeptical of the chances of salvaging victory in a nuclear war—a view which led among other things to questioning the desirability of additional large resource expenditures on preparation for such a war.

the need to achieve military-technological superiority, and here, too, the emphasis was on nuclear missile technology. As one Soviet military theorist put it in 1966:

> Despite the fact that conventional arms, as before, have an important place in the technical equipping of armies, the decisive means of combat in modern war is the nuclear weapon, which is new in principle. Therefore, it is precisely the quantity and quality of nuclear munitions and their means of delivery which provide the basis for the military-technical superiority of one side over the other.[126]

Some two years later, the same writer, Lt. Colonel V. Bondarenko, asserted that it was wrong to suppose that because conventional arms retained their usefulness under certain circumstances this meant the end of the military-technical revolution. Rather, he said, new opportunities for traditional arms arose precisely because of the presence of nuclear missile weapons provided by the ongoing military-technical revolution, a process with "its own logic of development."[127] (Besides contributing to the debate on conventional versus nuclear arms, which included the argument that it would be a "more serious" mistake to overemphasize the importance of conventional arms than that of nuclear weapons, Bondarenko in this article also raised questions which seemed to bear on even broader issues of Soviet military policy and civil-military relations.[128]) Another

[126] Lt. Colonel V. Bondarenko, "Military-Technical Superiority—The Most Important Factor for Reliable Defense of the Country," *Kommunist Vooruzhennykh Sil*, no. 17 (September 1966): 9. See also Colonel A. Chegrinets and Lt. Colonel N. Dovbnia, "Scientific-Technical Progress and the Defense Capability of the Country," ibid., no. 4 (February 1968): 53–59.

[127] Lt. Colonel V. Bondarenko, "The Contemporary Revolution in Military Affairs and the Combat Readiness of the Armed Forces," *Kommunist Vooruzhennykh Sil*, no. 24 (December 1968): 24, 29.

[128] The Bondarenko article was notable, not only for its restatement of the thesis that the Soviet Union must pursue the race for military-technical superiority but also for its blunt assertion that "political organizations and their leaders" might "fail to use the emerging possibilities" offered by the revolution in military affairs. Coming at a time when strategic arms talks with the United States were pending, this article appeared to put the Soviet political leadership on warning not to entertain agreements that the military deemed prejudicial to the defense of the country.

In addition to the Bondarenko article, there were other thinly veiled warnings from military writers against utopian "illusions" that one can eliminate the danger of war and achieve security through disarmament agreements. See, for example, review article by Colonel E. Rybkin, "Critique of Bourgeois Conceptions of War and Peace." *Kommunist Vooruzhennykh Sil*, no. 18 (September 1968): 89–90. Another line taken up by military spokesmen in early 1969, in a series of articles devoted to Lenin's thinking on war and military affairs, also seemed part of a concerted campaign for maintaining a high level of Soviet military preparations and, by implication, against relying on arms control negotiations for Soviet security. These articles uniformly stressed Lenin's teaching that "imperialism" would remain implacably hostile to the Soviet state and that the danger of a war to restore the capitalist system would continue to exist until the historical transition from capitalism to communism was complete. For pertinent examples of such statements see Marshal A. A. Grechko, "V. I. Lenin and the Building of the Soviet Armed Forces," *Kommunist*, no. 3 (February 1969): 15–16 ff.; General A. Epishev, "Leninism—Foundation of the Training of Soviet Troops," ibid., no. 6 (April 1969): 61, 68; Major General K. S. Bochkarev, "V. I. Lenin and the Building of the Armed Forces of the USSR," *Morskoi sbornik*, no. 2 (February 1969): 4–5; Colonel M. Vetrov, "Problems of Revolution, War, and Peace in the Remarks of V. I. Lenin at Comintern Congresses," *Voenno-istoricheskii zhurnal*, no. 3 (March 1969); 11; A. Galitsan, "For a Leninist Line," ibid., 12–13.

writer, taking note of concern about the increasing cost and complexity of modern weapons systems, conceded that it was essential to make optimum use of resources, but argued that in the last analysis the maintenance of technical-military superiority required that the quality of advanced weapons systems and not their cost should be the governing consideration.[129]

From all this one could gather not only that there was a continuing internal debate under the Brezhnev–Kosygin regime over the broad issue of developing the Soviet armed forces in such a way as to enhance the prospects of meaningful "victory" in the event of nuclear war but also that those in the Soviet Union who favored greater emphasis on preparation for limited wars and a corresponding shift of resources in this direction had not managed to make their case fully persuasive. Especially interesting in the context of the present study may be the fact that Soviet thinking with respect to theater warfare in Europe appeared to have emerged from the doctrinal debate of 1965–69 without having shifted radically from its position at the close of the Khrushchev period.

This is not to say, of course, that there were no changes in the Soviet outlook. As we have seen, it had been recognized that limited conventional or tactical nuclear operations in Europe ought not to be "excluded" from the realm of possibilities, especially in light of the flexible response doctrine adopted by NATO. This admission, if not a *radical* break from the doctrinal assumptions of the Khrushchev period, marked at least a noteworthy trend in a new direction. Also, several joint Warsaw Pact exercises now included an initial phase of conventional operations which apparently took into account the possibility of delayed resort to nuclear weapons on both sides.[130] And at least one large non-Warsaw Pact exercise within the Soviet Union itself, the "Dnepr" maneuvers of September 1967, to which we shall give attention in the next chapter, appeared to be primarily a test of Soviet conventional warfare capabilities.

For the most part, however, the basic features of the Soviet outlook on warfare in the European theater persisted with little change. Thus, Soviet opinion remained largely skeptical with regard to the chances of keeping any East–West military hostilities in Europe within bounds. This skepticism was typified early in the Brezhnev–Kosygin period by a Soviet military writer who dismissed the notion of "waging a local nuclear war" in Europe with these words: "It is obvious that a war in Europe, which is saturated with nuclear weapons and

---

[129] Major General M. Cherednichenko, "Economics and Military-Technical Policy," *Kommunist Vooruzhennykh Sil*, no. 15 (August 1968): 11–13.

[130] The "October Storm" exercise in East Germany in October 1965, for example, began with a phase of conventional operations, but later included simulated nuclear strikes by the joint Warsaw Pact forces after the assumed "Western aggressor" had used nuclear weapons. The "Vltava" joint exercise in Czechoslovakia in the fall of 1966 also began with conventional operations, including an airlift of Soviet troops into the maneuver area. As a Czech general engaged in this exercise noted, the maneuvers were staged, "not only from the aspect of our own military doctrine, but also from the aspect of the military aims of the adversary. It is well known that the strategic military concept of the United States—the theory of flexible response—recognizes the possibility of wars with limited use of nuclear weapons or with conventional arms only." See the more detailed discussion of Warsaw Pact joint exercises in chapter XVII.

missiles, would immediately assume the broadest dimensions."[131] Even later, as Soviet military literature gave more attention to NATO's doctrine of flexible response, the general view was that efforts to hold the line at conventional operations or the selective use of tactical nuclear weapons would prove unavailing.[132] In fact, as noted in an earlier chapter, when the NATO Council in December 1967 formally endorsed a flexible response strategy, the Soviet Union denounced the concept on the grounds that it might "raise false hopes that a military conflict in Europe can be kept within local bounds and not allowed to develop into a big war with use of all means of extermination."[133]

Just as there apparently was no basic revision of the belief that any military conflict permitted to arise between the opposing blocs in Europe would pose great danger of escalation to general nuclear war, so there was no essential change in the thinking of the professional military on how theater warfare in Europe would be fought in the event that war should occur. Soviet military literature continued to prescribe the familiar principles for theater operations, cast largely in a context in which the early use of nuclear weapons by both sides was assumed. These principles included prompt seizure of the initiative, use of surprise and rapid offensive exploitation through the depth of the theater, with even more stress than previously on tank and airborne operations.[134]

Soviet theater warfare doctrine having been described at some length in an earlier chapter,[135] we need not dwell on its features here. But before leaving the subject of doctrine it may be worth noting that the persistence of a nuclear orientation in Soviet thinking on theater operations in Europe looked somewhat less anachronistic in 1969 than it may have appeared in the early and middle sixties, when efforts were underway within NATO to sell the concepts

---

[131] Major General Zemskov, "The Escalation of Madness," *Krasnaia zvezda*, August 3, 1965.

[132] This was the view taken in the 1968 edition of the Sokolovskii work *Military Strategy*. Although expanded treatment was given to Western conceptions of limited war and to NATO's efforts to work out theories of flexible response in Europe "to diminish the risk of limited war being transformed into general war," the conclusion offered "with certainty" was that such theories were unlikely to work. See *Voennaia strategiia*, 3rd ed., pp. 82–89.

[133] See chapter XIII, pp. 327–28.

[134] The points generally stressed in the Soviet literature on tanks are that they provide "one of the main means for rapid exploitation of missile strikes," and that they offer a high degree of protection against the effects of nuclear weapons as well as conventional weapons. Another routine claim is that Soviet tanks are superior to Western models in armor, firepower, and endurance. The literature on airborne forces generally singles out their ability to exploit quickly the results of nuclear strikes as their "most important role" in combined arms operations. The ability of the airborne forces to create a "second front" by landing well-armed contingents in the enemy's rear is another factor frequently stressed, and the experience of several maneuvers in East Europe is cited in this connection. For a sampling of this literature, see Colonel V. Petrukhin, "Powerful Arsenal of Victory," *Kommunist Vooruzhennykh Sil*, no. 4 (February 1968): 22–23; Marshal P. P. Poluboiarov, "Tankmen," *Krasnaia zvezda*, February 29, 1968; Colonel I. Vorob'ev, "Maneuver," ibid., September 20, 1967; Colonel General V. Komarov, "Main Striking Force," ibid., September 10, 1967; Marshal P. Rotmistrov, "Time and Tanks," *Izvestiia*, September 10, 1967; Lt. General I. Taranenko, "Winged Transport of the Soviet Army," *Krasnaia zvezda*, January 25, 1968; General V. Margelov, "Attackers from the Skies," ibid., February 20, 1968. For a useful Western account of Soviet tank doctrine, see Colonel Charles G. Fitzgerald, "Armor: Soviet Arm of Decision?" *Military Review* (March 1969): 35–46.

[135] See chapter IX.

of graduated response and larger conventional forces. Those efforts, as we have seen, had begun to have an impact on the thinking of Soviet military leaders, some of whom urged that more attention be given to preparing Soviet forces for conventional theater operations. But by the time NATO officially adopted a flexible response strategy, in December 1967, there were new pressures to reduce NATO's conventional force levels. This meant that, despite its formal commitment to flexible response, NATO in effect was left in a position in which it would be compelled to resort to nuclear weapons rather early in the event of war. In light of this, the nuclear-oriented Soviet theater doctrine carried over from the Khrushchev period had, as it were, acquired a new lease on life.[136] Moreover, the situation arising out of the invasion of Czechoslovakia in August 1968 seemed more likely than not to perpetuate this state of affairs. For, unless NATO responded by bolstering its conventional force posture substantially— a doubtful prospect at best[137]—the forward deployment of additional Soviet theater forces in Central Europe promised to make it all the more necessary for NATO to count on early resort to nuclear weapons in the event of an East– West military clash in Europe.

[136] An interesting sidelight on nuclear doctrine was provided in November 1968 by the East Germans. A featured article in Ulbricht's press stated that the GDR's current military doctrine, worked out in agreement with the Soviet Union and other Warsaw Pact countries, envisaged that any war in Europe would be promptly transformed into an all-out nuclear conflict "from the very beginning or after a few days of conventional warfare," and hence that intensified training of the GDR's armed forces for warfare under nuclear conditions was necessary. The extent to which this may have represented lobbying by the GDR for nuclear-sharing on the part of the Soviet Union (a subject we shall take up in the next chapter) is difficult to say. Nevertheless, the article would seem to reflect some tendency in Soviet bloc military circles to return to the thesis of early escalation to nuclear use. See Wolfgang Wuensche, "For the Joint Defense of Socialism: On the Principles and Tasks of the GDR Military Doctrine," *Neues Deutschland*, November 23, 1968. See also "A-War Stressed by German Reds," *New York Times*, November 24, 1968.

[137] For a discussion of response in NATO to the invasion of Czechoslovakia, see chapter XV, especially pp. 407–12.

XVII

THE SOVIET MILITARY POSTURE TOWARD EUROPE

The maintenance of the Soviet Union's power position in Europe was one traditional feature of its military policy which continued to receive undiminished attention under the Brezhnev–Kosygin regime. Neither the Vietnam conflict and friction with China in the East nor the Soviet Union's interest in promoting an atmosphere of relaxation in the West that might hasten the demise of NATO seemed to counsel any significant redisposition of the military power deployed against Europe. Not only were strong formations of Soviet combined-arms theater forces kept in place in East Europe and the Western USSR, but a large force of Soviet MRBM–IRBM missiles remained targeted against NATO Europe, thus perpetuating the redundant capabilities built into the Soviet military posture toward Europe in Khrushchev's day.[1] Indeed, developments growing out of the Czechoslovak invasion in 1968 saw larger Soviet combined-arms forces temporarily deployed in Central Europe than at any time since the years immediately after World War II, laying the Soviet Union open to the charge that it had disturbed the customary balance of forces in the European arena.

With respect to the role of the Warsaw Pact in Soviet policy, the Brezhnev–Kosygin regime initially saw fit to continue Khrushchev's policy of closer military co-operation with the East European members of the Pact, aimed both at improving the collective military capabilities of the Warsaw alliance and at tightening its political cohesion in the face of polycentric tendencies in East Europe. Later, with the onset of the crisis over Czechoslovakia, the Soviet aim of improving the collective military efficiency was overshadowed by the need to employ the Pact as an instrument for restoring Soviet political control over Prague. Because Czechoslovakia happened to be a key link in the Northern Tier of the Warsaw Pact's military structure, its occupation could be presented as a necessary move to ensure the security of the Warsaw bloc against alleged military threats from the West.[2] Whether, in fact, the naked police action against a member state of the Warsaw bloc would ultimately prove to have strengthened the Pact as a military coalition against NATO remained to be seen, for the resentment bred by the invasion might well leave Czechoslovakia a grudging and unreliable ally at best. For the short term, however, the forward deployment of additional Soviet forces upon Czech territory was doubtless regarded in Moscow as having stiffened the military posture of the Pact toward the West.

[1] See previous discussion of the question of redundancy, chapter VII, pp. 154–56.
[2] See chapter XV, pp. 390–91.

In this chapter we shall be concerned with developments affecting the Soviet Union's military posture vis-à-vis NATO Europe, as well as with those germane to its management of military affairs within the Warsaw Pact. To begin with, let us examine several considerations bearing on the evident resolve of the Brezhnev–Kosygin regime to keep substantial Soviet forces positioned in the European theater, despite various circumstances that might have seemed to argue for reducing them.

Conditions Affecting the Soviet Military Presence in Europe

Although the Brezhnev–Kosygin regime proved unwilling to depart from the past Soviet practice of keeping a large military presence in Europe, several considerations suggested that under some circumstances the Soviet leaders might find it expedient to alter this policy. One of these was the perennial problem of holding down defense costs, especially at a time when measures to strengthen the Soviet Union's strategic posture and to improve the global reach of the general purpose forces were driving the demands upon Soviet resources upward. If the Soviet leadership were to find it possible to lay aside such political preconditions as a German settlement, this might open the way for mutual troop reductions in Europe, which could reduce for both sides the costs of maintaining the military standoff there,[3] and which might, in any case, be a by-product of future negotiations aimed at a freeze or a lowering of strategic force levels.

A second consideration arguing for a more flexible attitude on the forward deployment of Soviet forces in Europe was the inconsistency between these forces and the Soviet Union's policy of cultivating co-operative relations with the countries of Western Europe. While it might be argued, as Soviet propaganda frequently did, that few West Europeans believed any longer in the "old myth" of a Soviet military threat and that the time was ripe, therefore, for the European states jointly to work out new pan-European security arrangements,[4] so long as the Soviet military presence in the center of Europe loomed as large as ever, European members of NATO were likely to be reluctant to jeopardize their protective ties with the United States. In short, if a Soviet policy of reassurance toward West Europe were to be made credible, a few gestures in the direction of Soviet troop reduction would certainly be of some help.

---

[3] An indication that NATO was thinking of new initiatives in this direction came in early 1968, when it was announced after a meeting between President Johnson and Manlio Brosio, Secretary General of NATO, that the Western allies would seek to devise a new program for mutual East–West troop reductions and then try to "find a way to submit it to the Russians." Later, at the NATO Council meeting in Iceland in June 1968, a declaration was issued favoring "mutual and balanced force reductions" and calling upon the Soviet Union and the countries of East Europe to "join in this search for progress toward peace." See Peter Grose, "NATO May Offer East a Troop Cut," *New York Times*, February 20, 1968; Robert C. Doty, "NATO Council Urges an East–West Troop Cutback," ibid., June 26, 1968. Following the invasion of Czechoslovakia, NATO noted that a serious setback had been dealt the prospect of mutual troop reductions, but by early 1970 the subject had again been revised.

[4] For previous discussion of Soviet collective security proposals, see chapters XIII and XV.

Third, there was the problem of China, which had potential military as well as political dimensions for the Soviet Union. Although an outright military collision between the two Communist powers was perhaps not a matter of immediate concern to Moscow during the early years of the Brezhnev–Kosygin regime, it gradually became a less remote possibility. In the spring of 1966, for example, the Soviet leadership felt obliged to castigate Peking for telling the Chinese people that it was "necessary to prepare themselves for a military struggle with the USSR."[5] During 1967, amid increasing rumors of border incidents, the Soviet Far East was visited by several top leaders, including Kosygin, who in a speech at Vladivostok on January 10 advised Soviet military officials in the area that the "anti-Soviet policy of Mao Tse-tung has entered a new, dangerous phase."[6] By the end of 1969, after widely publicized frontier clashes earlier in the years along the Ussuri and in Sinkiang had given rise to what Moscow described as a "war psychosis," the two sides chose a momentary truce by entering into negotiations on the border issue.[7]

In view of these developments, one may assume that the Brezhnev–Kosygin regime found it prudent to conduct a running reappraisal of its military planning to take into account a potential "two-front" threat in Europe and in the Far East.[8] While such a reappraisal would have been likely to confirm the wisdom of proceeding with the build-up of Soviet strategic nuclear power as insurance against China's developing atomic capability,[9] it no doubt would have raised also the question whether Soviet theater forces in the regions bordering China should be permanently strengthened, and if so, whether this requirement might best be met by shifting some forces from the European theater to the Far East. The answer apparently was that the Soviet Union should indeed bolster its military garrisons in Asia, but not at the expense of the general purpose forces deployed in Europe.

Finally, in addition to the economic burden of maintaining large Soviet general purpose forces in Europe and the possibility of being able to transfer some of them to Asia, there was still another consideration that might have argued for down-grading the traditional theater role of these forces in Europe. In light of a Soviet foreign policy line looking toward the break-up of NATO, the emergence of a new European collective security system, and the military

[5] This statement appeared in a letter of the CPSU Central Committee circulated privately in early 1966 to "fraternal" parties, the text of which was first published on March 21, 1966, in the Hamburg newspaper *Die Welt*. See *New York Times*, March 20, 24, 1966; *Washington Post*, March 22, 1966.

[6] "Mao Policy Peril Cited by Kosygin," *Washington Post*, January 11, 1967. On January 9, in Magnitorgorsk, Kosygin also condemned Maoist policies. Moscow Radio "Peace and Progress" broadcast, January 9, 1967.

[7] See chapter XI, p. 259.

[8] For an analysis which puts emphasis on the revival of a "two-front" threat in Soviet thinking see John R. Thomas, *U.S.–East European Relations: Strategic Aspects* (McLean, Va.: Research Analysis Corporation, April 1968), p. 6.

[9] See Nikolai Ya. Galay, "The Changing Nature of the Soviet Army," *Analysis of Current Developments in the Soviet Union*, no. 490, Institute for the Study of the USSR, Munich, February 20, 1968, p. 6.

disengagement of the United States from the European continent, the future need for a Soviet theater force posture of past dimensions in Europe might appear to be of declining importance. In effect, if the Soviet–American competition were envisaged as shifting gradually toward the Third World and becoming essentially extra-European, then Soviet military policy would require strong strategic forces and more mobile conventional capabilities to hold up the Soviet end of the global competition, but there would be a correspondingly lesser role for the once dominant ground-air theater forces deployed mainly against Europe.

Obviously, however, none of these arguments carried sufficient weight with Khrushchev's successors to prompt a reduction of the Soviet Union's traditionally strong military foothold in Europe. Besides such general factors as the simple inertia of two-and-a-half decades and the long-time priority attached to the Soviet Union's ability to keep Germany in check, a number of other considerations may have persuaded the Brezhnev–Kosygin regime to sit tight with respect to the Soviet military presence in Europe. For one thing, any substantial change in deployments in Europe, even if carried out in the context of mutual troop withdrawals, would have left the Soviet leaders vulnerable to Chinese allegations that they were in "collusion" with the United States to ease the European situation and permit the transfer of American troops to Vietnam.[10] Moreover, quite apart from Chinese criticism, to which the Soviet leaders may have been inured, an unreceptive attitude toward American suggestions for troop reduction in Europe gave Moscow a way of making felt its opposition to US policy in Vietnam.

Second, the Soviet view of the appropriate path to new security and disarmament arrangements in Europe apparently presupposed the political settlement of the German problem, requiring, at a minimum, West Germany's recognition of the German Democratic Republic and acceptance of existing frontiers in Europe.[11] So long as such a settlement remained as elusive as ever, insistence upon linking it with any new security arrangements involving military disengagement in Europe was tantamount to saying that Soviet troops would stay put. To the Soviet leaders this probably made more sense as West Germany's weight within the Western alliance continued to grow, especially after France's military withdrawal from NATO.

A third factor, related to the gradual erosion of NATO's posture, also may have had a bearing on the Kremlin's resolve to keep the Soviet Union's own military posture toward Europe essentially intact. In the face of recurrent evidence, from about mid-1966 on, that political and economic pressures upon American policy might be leading toward a substantial unilateral reduction of US forces in Europe,[12] the Soviet leaders may have thought that by simply

[10] See chapter XII, p. 295.
[11] See chapter XIII, pp. 317–18.
[12] The issue of troop reductions in Europe (see previous discussion, chapter XII, pp. 294–95) sharpened with presentation in the Senate on August 31, 1966, of the Mansfield Resolution, which was proposed again on January 19, 1967, with growing senatorial support. Despite warnings from administration spokesmen against unilateral troop withdrawals, the balance-of-payments question

sitting tight they could watch their relative military position vis-à-vis West Europe grow stronger without having to offer a major quid pro quo. Under such circumstances, the chances of their being able to engineer a European political settlement to their own liking may well have looked promising enough to the men in the Kremlin to make them decide to outwait the other side.

A fourth impediment to Soviet troop withdrawal was probably the belief that it would produce immediately deleterious effects on Soviet disciplinary efforts in East Europe while offering only uncertain long-term political benefits in West Europe. The 1966 Bucharest declaration was revealing of this caution on the issue of troop reductions. In it, the Soviets proposed phased and gradual reductions by both East and West Germany, but where their own troops were concerned they offered only the ultimate and more remote goal of "withdrawal of forces from foreign territories."

Finally, whatever thought may have been given to paring down the Soviet military presence in Europe during the first two or three years of the Brezhnev–Kosygin regime, the clinching argument against doing so undoubtedly came when the reform movement in Czechoslovakia gathered momentum in early 1968. Until this ferment within one of the key Northern Tier countries of the Warsaw Pact subsided or was otherwise resolved, the Soviet Union was hardly in a position to consider reducing its military foothold in the East European countries ringing Czechoslovakia. As it turned out, the resort to arms in August 1968 to crush the Czechoslovak reform experiment and the ensuing occupation

---

and other pressures appeared to be leading to steps in this direction. On May 2, 1967, following tripartite talks by US, British, and German representatives, it was announced that beginning in early 1968 some 35,000 US troops and four fighter squadrons would be returned to the United States on a "dual basing" plan expected to reduce the balance-of-payments deficit by about $75 million annually. This move, which had been preceded in 1966 by the temporary withdrawal of 15,000 US military specialists for Vietnam training duties, would, when completed, bring American strength in Germany down to some 220,000 men. While welcoming this step, Senator Mansfield indicated that it did not go far enough and said that the issue of further "substantial" cuts would be kept on the "front burner." On March 23, 1968, in a speech in Chicago, Senator Henry M. Jackson, a proponent of maintaining a strong US military presence in Europe, cautioned that pressures for further reduction were growing and that continued maintenance of large American forces in Europe would depend on whether West Europeans believe "they are still needed there." On May 17, 1968, a somewhat similar sentiment was voiced by the new US Defense Secretary Clark M. Clifford, who told the Senate Foreign Relations Committee that he had advised the NATO defense ministers "not to expect the United States to maintain the present level of its forces in Europe." Toward the end of June 1968, Senator Stuart Symington joined Senator Mansfield in urging a major unilateral cutback of American forces in Europe, proposing that the United States place a ceiling of 50,000 on these forces without expecting the Soviet Union to reciprocate. This, in brief, was the background against which the Soviet leadership might judge the utility of not responding to proposals for mutual troop reductions in Europe.

Among relevant sources see "Text of Mansfield's Statement to Senate on Resolution To Reduce Forces in Europe," *New York Times*, September 1, 1966; Murrey Marder, "Mansfield Moves To Cut U.S. Troops in Europe," *Washington Post*, January 20, 1967; John W. Finney, "Europe Troop Cut Fought in Senate," *New York Times*, March 6, 1967; *The Atlantic Alliance: Unfinished Business*, A Study Submitted by the Subcommittee on National Security and International Operations, Committee on Government Operations, U.S. Senate, 90th Congress, 1st Session (Washington, D.C.: Government Printing Office, 1967); Finney, "U.S. Will Cut Its Forces in Germany by 35,000," *New York Times*, May 3, 1967; "Jackson Cautions Europe on Troops," ibid., March 25, 1968; John Maffre, "Troop Cut Likely, U.S. Warns NATO," *Washington Post*, May 18, 1968; Peter Grose, "Two Senators Again Ask a Troop Cut in Europe," *New York Times*, June 26, 1968.

created a new situation in which the prospect for any significant dilution of Soviet military power in East Europe seemed to have been indefinitely postponed.

Soviet Theater Forces and Their European Role

If the invasion of Czechoslovakia conveyed primarily the political lesson that the Soviet Union would not shrink from applying raw force to preserve its hegemony in East Europe, it also told something about the military capacity of the ground-air theater forces which had been employed to conduct the police action against a member of the Warsaw bloc. These forces—illustrative of the general-purpose theater forces with which Western Europe would have to contend in the event of a conflict between NATO and the Warsaw bloc—acquitted themselves well in the swift surprise invasion of Czechoslovakia. Their performance, about which we shall have more to say later, doubtless brought satisfaction to those military leaders who, from the outset of the Brezhnev–Kosygin regime, had lobbied against any tendency to downgrade the theater forces and their continental role in Europe. Indeed, it might be said that the employment of the theater forces in the Czechoslovak crisis, first as a major instrument of pressure and ultimately for intervention, capped a series of steps through which these forces regained a firmer footing in the Soviet scheme of things than they had enjoyed at the end of the Khrushchev period.

Developments Boosting the Status of the General Purpose Forces

Among steps relevant to the improved status of the theater forces was the restoration, in 1967, of a separate command for the Soviet ground forces, the service which accounts for the bulk of the manpower in the theater forces. This command headquarters had been abolished in 1964, at which time the ground forces were subordinated directly to the General Staff in the Ministry of Defense as part of Khrushchev's effort to streamline the military establishment.[13] An article in *Krasnaia zvezda* on December 24, 1967, which identified General of the Army I. G. Pavlovskii as commander-in-chief of the ground forces, provided the first official indication that the command of the ground forces had been restored, although its re-establishment may have taken place sometime earlier, after Pavlovskii's elevation to the post of deputy defense minister in April 1967. According to *Pravda* of January 20, 1968, Pavlovskii's recent military assignments had included a tour as commander of the Far East Military District, which gave him first-hand knowledge of an area of growing sensitivity

---

[13] Abolishment of the ground forces command in September 1964, just before Khrushchev's ouster, was perhaps the last of a long list of measures which had not endeared Khrushchev to leaders of the ground forces in the Soviet military hierarchy. The date of this action became known only in 1968 with publication of a volume edited by Marshal M. V. Zakharov, *50 Let Vooruzhennykh Sil SSSR* (50 Years of the USSR Armed Forces) (Moscow: Voenizdat, 1968), p. 510.

in Soviet military planning.[14] The reintroduction of the ground forces command under him could be interpreted not only as a boost in prestige for these forces but also as a practical reflection of their increased weight in the Soviet military picture.[15] Much the same could be said when, some months later, Pavlovskii turned out to be the Kremlin's choice as commander of the invasion forces and, temporarily, the chief occupation authority in Czechoslovakia.[16]

Another, earlier development suggesting that the general purpose forces had gained status under the Brezhnev–Kosygin regime was the recognition of their long-term requirements for a generous supply of trained manpower, as made evident by a new military service law adopted in October 1967. Under the new law, the length of service for conscripted personnel was reduced by one year and compulsory retirement was prescribed for some high-ranking military grades.[17] Apart from the latter provision, which allowed for a much-needed rejuvenation of the military high command,[18] this measure appeared to trade off certain short-term military disadvantages for long-term advantages particu-

[14] For a detailed discussion of the ground forces command issue, see J. L. (John Long), "Army General I. G. Pavlovsky Becomes Land Forces Commander-in-Chief," Research Document CRD 41/68, *Radio Liberty*, Munich, January 24, 1968.

[15] See *Strategic Survey, 1967* (London: The Institute for Strategic Studies, 1968), p. 21; Petr Kruzhin, "The Restoration of the High Command of the Soviet Land Forces," *Bulletin*, Institute for the Study of the USSR, Munich (March 1968): 20–27.

[16] Apart from boosting the prestige of the theater forces within the Soviet military establishment, the invasion and occupation of Czechoslovakia also may have contributed to an increase in the influence of the Soviet military command generally within the Soviet leadership. Owing to the inept handling of the political aspects of the intervention, Soviet military men almost by default were thrust into a combined military-political role as the only effective representatives of Soviet power in Czechoslovakia during the first days of the confused post-invasion period. Whether a permanent accretion of greater military influence in high Soviet councils was among the effects of the invasion remains a debated question. See chapter XVI, pp. 430–31.

[17] The new military service law replaced one in force since 1939 (amended in 1950), under which terms of service in the army and air force were three years and in the navy, four, with call-up on an annual basis. Besides lowering these terms by one year, the new law reduced the draft age from nineteen to eighteen, scheduled two annual call-ups in place of one, and provided for extensive premilitary training of seventeen-year-olds through the DOSAAF paramilitary organization. The latter provision presumably would alleviate part of the short-term proficiency problem, since under the old system a good part of the recruit's first year was spent in basic training, which DOSAAF's expanded program is intended to take care of. For Soviet materials and explanations concerning the new law, see "Decree of the Presidium of the USSR Supreme Soviet on the Terms of the Implementation of the USSR Law 'On Universal Military Duty'," *Pravda*, October 25, 1967; "Fifty Years of Guarding the Achievements of the Great October," speech by Marshal A. A. Grechko, ibid., February 24, 1968; General A. Getman, "The Law on Universal Military Duty and the Problems of DOSAAF," *Krasnaia zvezda* (Red Star), January 13, 1968; and interview with General I. G. Pavlovskii, "Always Combat Ready," *Pravda*, January 20, 1968. For a detailed Western analysis of the new military service law, see Geoffrey Jukes, "Changes in Soviet Conscription Law," *Australian Outlook* (September 1968).

[18] The officer retirement portion of the new service law prescribed compulsory retirement at age sixty for grade levels of colonel general, marshal of arms, and full admiral, but allowed for a five-year extension by the Council of Ministers. Marshal of the Soviet Union, the highest rank, remained exempted from the law. Despite these loopholes, the law did seem likely to spur retirements among the notoriously overage high command to make way for younger blood. In fact, a considerable speed-up in advancement of younger officers (mostly in their fifties) to responsible positions in the Ministry of Defense and military districts did occur, although not necessarily as a direct result of the new law.

larly relevant to the general purpose forces—the principal user of military manpower in the mass.

By reducing the term of service, the measure promised to lower temporarily
the technical proficiency of conscripted personnel,[19] but by increasing the
number of youths inducted annually by 30 to 40 per cent it would also create
a far larger trained reserve to be called upon should it become necessary to
expand the size of the Soviet conventional military establishment so as to match
a prospective adversary who possessed massive conventional military power. It
was this aspect of the new service law which doubtless led some Western experts
to regard it in part as a long-range precautionary and warning measure aimed
at China,[20] although it would also have an obvious bearing on the Soviet
Union's ability to meet the manpower requirements of any "two-front" situation
calling for the simultaneous use of theater forces in Europe and the Far East.

Size and Deployment of the Theater Forces

While attention was thus given to broadening the long-term manpower base
of the general purpose forces, there was no apparent move on the part of the
Brezhnev–Kosygin regime, at least up to the Czech crisis of 1968, to boost the
standing size of these forces. Throughout the period from Khrushchev's removal to mid-summer 1968, for example, the over-all strength of the ground
forces remained at an estimated level of about 2 million men out of a total of
slightly more than 3 million in the armed forces, and the number of ground
force divisions was kept at about 140.[21] No substantial change in the categories
of combat readiness and the personnel strength of these divisions was reflected
in published Western estimates.[22] Tactical air strength available to the combined-arms theater forces likewise remained fairly constant, at an estimated
figure of nearly 4,000 aircraft.[23]

Whether the permanent strength level of the theater forces would be somewhat higher as a result of the mobilization of reserves which occurred in connection with the intervention in Czechoslovakia was not clear at the time.
Various units participating in and supporting the invasion apparently were

[19] See fn. 17 above. A further point to be noted is that the general purpose forces would be
somewhat less affected by a shorter service period than some of the other elements of the military
establishment, such as the air and missile forces, the navy, and the technical branches, in which
there is a higher concentration of specialized skills.

[20] See, for example, *Strategic Survey, 1967*, pp. 21–22. Other implications of the new law were to
free young men for productive labor sooner and thereby ease the industrial manpower shortage, and
also to provide patriotic socialist indoctrination for a larger segment of Soviet youth in answer to
the regime's concern about the ideological slackness of the younger generation. See previous discussion of the latter point, chapter XI, p. 249.

[21] The over-all manpower strength of the Soviet armed forces went up from about 3 to 3.2
million men, according to Western estimates, but apparently this small increase in the period
preceding the Czech crisis went mainly to the rocket forces and the navy rather than to the ground
forces. See *The Military Balance, 1966–1967* (London: The Institute for Strategic Studies, September 1966), pp. 2, 4; ibid., *1967–1968*, pp. 5, 6; ibid., *1968–1969*, pp. 5, 6.

[22] For a description of the three categories of combat readiness which apply to Soviet divisions, see
chapter VIII, p. 169.

[23] *The Military Balance, 1967–1968*, p. 8; ibid., *1968–1969*, p. 8.

brought up to combat strength by the call-up of reserves during July and August 1968, but there were no reports that the over-all number of around 140 divisions in the theater forces had been increased. However, if the tensions growing out of the Czechoslovak episode produced no increase in the standing size of the theater forces, the situation in Asia during 1969 apparently did have such an effect. As figures published by the Institute for Strategic Studies indicated, the total number of Soviet divisions rose to 148 in 1969, presumably as a result of mobilizing additional forces to face China in the Far East.[24]

With regard to the territorial distribution of the theater forces, the over-all pattern of deployment was left much the same under the Brezhnev–Kosygin regime as it had been at the time of Khrushchev's ouster, with two notable exceptions. One of these had to do with steps taken to bolster the Soviet posture in Asia; the other was the influx of additional theater force elements into East Europe in connection with the invasion of Czechoslovakia.

In the first case, so far as the public record permits one to judge, the Brezhnev–Kosygin regime began gradually, in 1965 and 1966, to shift some Soviet forces to the Asian military districts of the USSR,[25] and the stationing of Soviet troops in Outer Mongolia was reported in 1967.[26] During the next two years the movement of Soviet reinforcements to the Far East was stepped up, particularly in the summer of 1969, when the Trans-Siberian railroad was closed to foreign travel for several months. The result was a substantial increase in Soviet troop strength and supporting air and missile units in the area, representing, according to some accounts, almost a doubling of the forces deployed there at the outset of the Brezhnev–Kosygin period.[27]

[24] See *The Military Balance, 1968–1969,* and *1969–1970,* pp. 6, 7, respectively.

[25] The Soviet military districts bordering China from Manchuria to Sinkiang were, from East to West, the Far Eastern, Transbaikal, Siberian, and Turkestan districts. In November 1969 it became known that a new Central Asian military district had been set up opposite Sinkiang, taking over part of the territory of the Turkestan district. See "Soviet Army Area Set Up Near China," *New York Times,* November 19, 1969.

[26] Soviet troops had garrisoned Mongolia from 1937 to 1956, but were withdrawn for a period of about ten years until after signing of a new Soviet–Mongolian People's Republic defense treaty in January 1966. In September 1967 Western press dispatches from Moscow reported that Soviet troops had reentered Mongolia "within the last few months," while at a holiday parade in November 1967 Soviet tank troops were paraded publicly in the Mongolian capital for the first time. It also was reported later that Soviet missile units had been deployed to Mongolia. See AP dispatch, "Soviet Troops Protecting Mongolia from Chinese," *Washington Star,* September 14, 1967; Harrison E. Salisbury, *War Between Russia and China* (New York: W. W. Norton & Company, 1969), pp. 152–53.

[27] Published Western estimates give a rather imprecise chronology of the Soviet build-up in the Far East, but it can perhaps best be reconstructed as follows. At the beginning of the Brezhnev–Kosygin regime, there were 12 to 14 divisions east of Lake Baikal, where in the early fifties, during the Korean war, about 30 divisions had been deployed. Up to 1967, Soviet strength in the Far East increased only slightly, by perhaps 2 or 3 divisions; by mid-1969, however, it had grown to around 25 to 27 divisions, representing about 300,000 troops, together with supporting air and missile elements. In addition to these forces, an undetermined number of divisions to man the new Central Asian military district could bring the total to 30 or more divisions facing China along the 4,000 mile border. See *The Military Balance, 1967–1968,* and *1969–1970,* pp. 6, 7, respectively; *The Economist,* March 22, 1969; Harrison E. Salisbury, "Soviet Expands Airfields in Far Eastern Build-Up," *New York Times,* May 24, 1969; Leonard Beaton, "Soviet Military Dominance over China," *Times,* London, February 4, 1970.

However, this strengthening of the Soviet posture in Asia was accomplished by the internal deployment and mobilization of additional forces and not by any significant withdrawal of forces stationed in East Europe or immediately adjacent western areas of the USSR. Rumors of Soviet plans to withdraw sizable numbers of troops from East Germany were heard in 1966–67, but Western sources noted that there was no evidence to confirm them.[28] What is more, Moscow itself made no claim that Soviet forces had been withdrawn from East Europe; had they been, it seems unlikely that the Soviet Union would have passed up the opportunity to seek political credit from such a move. Even after the serious flare-ups along the Sino–Soviet border in 1969, there was no indication that Soviet troops were being shifted from Europe to stiffen the Soviet position in the Far East. On the contrary, at the same time that the Soviet Union was shoring up its forces in Asia, it also apparently was on the verge of sending more occupation troops into Czechoslovakia.[29]

With respect to the deployment of theater forces in East Europe, the picture remained essentially stable from the end of the Khrushchev period until the onset of the Czech crisis, with a total of 26 Soviet divisions outside the Soviet Union, supported by about 1,200 tactical aircraft. Most of these forces—20 divisions and about 800 aircraft—were stationed in East Germany; the remainder in Hungary and Poland. At the same time, Western estimates placed the number of Soviet divisions in the European USSR at about 60, of which 25 divisions were credited with being capable of commitment to theater operations in Europe within two weeks of the outbreak of war.[30] As for the strategic missile units deployed in the Western USSR for employment against targets in the European theater, their strength, too, remained where it had leveled off during the Khrushchev period, at about 700 MRBM and IRBM launchers in fixed sites.[31] As mentioned previously, there were indications pointing to the development of mobile missiles in the MRBM–IRBM category, but it was not clear whether these mobile types were meant to replace or to augment the existing MRBM–IRBM force targeted against Europe.

With the unfolding of the Czech crisis in the summer of 1968, the Soviet Union began a series of maneuvers and troop movements which had the effect of substantially increasing the forward deployment of theater force elements in East Europe. As noted earlier, there was considerable confusion as to how many Soviet troops were involved in the several field maneuvers (in which allied Warsaw Pact troops also took part) prior to the August invasion.[32] The size of the invading forces, as well as the number of troops that stayed on into

[28] See chapter XII, pp. 294–95. See also "Soviet Troop Cut in Germany Seen," *New York Times*, February 10, 1967; AP Berlin dispatch, "No Soviet Troop Shift?" *Christian Science Monitor*, February 11, 1967; "Troop Cuts: Russia's Move?" *New York Times*, May 1, 1967; *Strategic Survey, 1967*, p. 22.

[29] See fn. 41 below.

[30] *The Military Balance, 1967–1968*, p. 6. See also Benjamin Welles, in *New York Times*, November 6, 1966.

[31] Ibid.

[32] See chapter XIV, pp. 372–75, 378–80, and fns. 121, 130.

the occupation period, also remained subject to rather widely varying estimates. For the number of troops directly involved in the invasion of August 20–21 and the peak build-up which took place within the next few days, the estimates began at 250,000 to 300,000 and ran up to 650,000 with the number of divisions ranging from around 20 to 35.[33] The bulk of these were Soviet forces, padded by an estimated 2 to 4 Polish divisions, elements of 2 to 3 East German divisions, and contingents of less than division-size from Hungary and Bulgaria. Furnishing tactical support for these forces were an estimated 400 to 700 combat aircraft, plus about 250 transport aircraft that landed a divisional force of Soviet airborne troops in Prague on the night of the invasion.[34]

Precisely where, within the range of estimated figures, the size of the invasion forces actually fell can only be surmised. Taking it as a rule of thumb that Soviet military planners would have sought a force superiority of about two to one over the 14 potentially opposing Czechoslovak divisions in order to ensure the quick suppression of any resistance, one might hazard a guess that roughly 22 Soviet divisions plus 4 or 5 other Warsaw Pact divisions were introduced into Czechoslovakia.[35] Given a presumed Soviet division "slice" of 15,000 to 20,000 men, this would come to between 400,000 to 500,000 troops. Some of the rear support elements included in this troop total, as already noted, may have remained outside the country in adjacent border areas.

Since part of the invasion force was assembled from Soviet units previously stationed in East Europe (East Germany, Poland, and Hungary), it was not immediately obvious what the deployment of additional forces from the USSR itself may have been. However, according to various accounts based on NATO sources,[36] it would appear that at least 10 to 11 additional Soviet divisions plus supporting elements—a net increment of perhaps 150,000 to 200,000 men—were

[33] The lower estimates were those given by NATO spokesmen; the higher ones were attributed to Western observers in Prague and to various Czechoslovak officials, including General Martin Dzur, the defense minister. Part of the large difference of around 300,000 between the low and high estimates may have grown out of differing distinctions drawn between combat formations and logistic-administrative supporting elements; some of the latter may have remained outside Czechoslovakia in adjacent "rear" areas. See Charles Douglas-Home, "Czech Army Seen as Russia's Weak Link," *Times*, London, September 25, 1968; William Beecher, "U.S. Aides Expect Soviet Union To Cut Force in Czechoslovakia," ibid., October 4, 1968; Orr Kelly, in *Washington Star*, October 6, 1968; Alfred Friendly, "Czechs, Soviets Open Troop Pullout Talks," *Washington Post*, October 15, 1968.

[34] See chapter XIV, p. 380, and fn. 154.

[35] As a matter of comparison with this arithmetic, figures given to the North Atlantic Assembly in November 1968 by Senator John Sherman Cooper, who said that his information came from NATO and US Defense Department sources, indicated that twenty-two Soviet divisions and three allied Warsaw Pact divisions had moved into Czechoslovakia. See Clyde H. Farnsworth, "Brosio Says NATO Could Not Act on Invasion of Czechoslovakia," *New York Times*, November 12, 1968.

[36] The defense correspondent of the *Times* of London, Charles Douglas-Home, in the edition of September 25, 1968, reported a NATO assessment that "11 new Soviet divisions were brought into Eastern Europe from the Soviet Union" in connection with the invasion. The figures disclosed by Senator Cooper on the occasion cited in fn. 35 above gave the following breakdown of the origins of the twenty-two Soviet invasion divisions: Eleven came from the Western USSR; eight moved in from East Germany; two from Hungary; and one airborne division was flown from the Soviet Union. In addition, according to Cooper, ten Soviet reserve divisions were upgraded to replace those sent from the USSR to East Europe.

deployed from the USSR to augment the 26 divisions already in place in East
Europe prior to the invasion.

How large a share of this incremental theater force would remain in Czechoslovakia to occupy the country and man its borders against the West was left
an open-ended question during the first two or three months after the invasion.
In the unequal negotiations between Dubcek and the Soviet leaders in October,
as well as in the one-sided treaty "legalizing" the occupation which the Czechs
were obliged to sign on October 16,[37] the Soviet Union declined to commit
itself on how many troops it would keep in Czechoslovakia or how long their
"temporary" stationing would last. This gave rise to anxious speculation in
Prague about the intended size of the occupation force, ranging from hopeful
Czech comments that it might soon be whittled down to two divisions to more
pessimistic appraisals that it would remain at least three or four times that size.[38]

But by early December 1968, following the first announced withdrawal of
some occupation units several weeks earlier,[39] reports from Prague indicated that
the bulk of the Soviet troops had been removed, leaving behind a force estimated at between 60,000 and 100,000 men in four to five divisions, which
presumably would constitute the garrison "legalized" by the status-of-forces
treaty signed in Moscow the previous October.[40] Although the Soviet Union
itself remained silent on its long-term occupation plans for Czechoslovakia,
doubtless having made them contingent upon that country's progress toward
"normalization," it appeared, as winter set in, that Moscow had settled for an
occupation force representing perhaps about one-third of the troops brought
from the USSR during the invasion.[41] Thus, the forward deployment of Soviet
theater forces in East Europe remained only marginally greater than the

[37] See discussion of this treaty in chapter XV, p. 399.

[38] On August 28, for example, President Ludvik Svoboda had expressed the view that perhaps two
Soviet divisions would remain in Czechoslovakia after a withdrawal process of several months.
See Tad Szulc, "Soviet To Leave 2 Bloc Divisions on Czechs' Soil," *New York Times*, August 29,
1968. In September and October, however, Western newsmen were being told by "highly placed
informants" in Prague that the Russians would probably leave six to eight divisions, a minimum
of around 100,000 men, in Czechoslovakia. See Szulc, "Czechs Are Told Most Soviet Units Will
Go by October 28," ibid., September 24, 1968; "Soviet Exit Seen in Weeks," *Washington Post*,
October 6, 1968.

[39] The first publicized exodus of invasion troops was on October 21, 1968, when some
Hungarian units left the country. The first announced withdrawal of a Soviet unit came on
October 24, when the Soviet press reported that troops returning to Kaliningrad via Poland had
been welcomed home with roadside slogans proclaiming: "The Motherland Is Proud of You" and
"You Have Fulfilled Your International Duty." See Clyde H. Farnsworth, "Hungarians Begin
Leaving Slovakia," *New York Times*, October 22, 1968; Lt. Colonel B. Briukhanov, "True Sons
of the People," *Krasnaia zvezda*, October 24, 1968.

[40] Prague news dispatch, "Czech Sees Soviet Pullout by Dec. 15," *Washington Post*, November
10, 1968; Karl E. Meyer, "Soviet Pullout Reflects New Czech Normality," ibid., December 3, 1968.

[41] In April 1969, in connection with threats of new Soviet intervention to bring about changes
in the Czechoslovak leadership and to demonstrate that anti-Soviet outbursts of the kind that
followed a Czech ice hockey victory in March would not be tolerated, there were reports that
Moscow was on the verge of sending additional troops into Czechoslovakia. On April 12 the
Prague government actually made an announcement to this effect, which was rescinded the same
day without explanation. See Alvin Shuster. "Prague Retracts Word that Soviet Is Sending Troops,"
New York Times, April 13, 1969.

level traditionally maintained in that region. To some extent, the withdrawal of the bulk of the Soviet invasion force may have been spurred by Western charges that the Soviet Union had upset the postwar military balance in Central Europe by introducing large forces into Czechoslovakia. But this is a separate question, to which we shall return presently. First, let us review briefly various measures taken under the Brezhnev–Kosygin regime to improve the capabilities of the Soviet theater forces.

Measures to Improve Theater Force Capabilities

Concurrent with doctrinal trends during the first years of the Brezhnev–Kosygin regime which had given renewed emphasis to the need for enabling the theater forces to cope with a broad range of operational conditions, various measures were taken to improve their capabilities for operating in both a nuclear and a conventional environment. In the ground forces these measures included the provision of more tubed artillery to increase conventional firepower; the incorporation of a motorized rifle division in tank armies; the further introduction of new equipment such as the T-62 medium tank, mobile anti-aircraft weapons, and modified tactical missile and rocket launchers; the increased application of cross-country fuel supply techniques; and attempts to improve command and control through wider automation.[42] As the new commander of the ground forces and other Soviet officials occasionally pointed out, even if one did not take into account the nuclear weapons at the disposal of these forces, their firepower had been greatly increased by improvements in both the quality and the quantity of conventional weapons available to them.[43]

In tactical air units, replacement of older aircraft with MIG-21 and Su-7 fighter bombers and the Yak-28 supersonic light bomber continued; meanwhile, several new aircraft types, including a variable-wing aircraft resembling the American F-111, were displayed at the Moscow air show in July 1967, indicating that further modernization of tactical air units was in prospect.[44] In training

[42] Kruzhin, in *Bulletin*, Institute for the Study of the USSR (March 1968): 27; *The Military Balance, 1967–1968*, pp. 6–7. With respect to command and control, Soviet military writers frequently made the point that technical innovations in this field made possible through wider use of computers and associated equipment represent the third major stage in the military-technical revolution of modern times, the first two being the introduction of nuclear weapons and missiles, respectively. See N. Ia. Sushko and T. R. Kondratkov, eds., *Metodologicheskie problemy voennoi teorii i praktiki* (Methodological Problems of Military Theory and Practice) (Moscow: Voenizdat, 1966), pp. 69, 243–65, 279; Lt. Colonel V. Bondarenko and Colonel S. Tiushkevich, "The Contemporary Stage of the Revolution in Military Affairs and Its Demands on Military Cadres," *Kommunist Vooruzhennykh Sil* (Communist of the Armed Forces), no. 6 (March 1968): 18–21.

[43] Interview with General I. G. Pavlovskii, "Always Combat Ready," *Pravda*, January 20, 1968; speech of Marshal A. A. Grechko, "On the Draft Law of General Military Service," *Pravda*, October 13, 1967. The favorite illustration offered by these military leaders was that in comparison with a standard infantry division of 1939 the Soviet motorized rifle division of today has thirty times the artillery-mortar firepower, sixteen times more tanks, thirteen times more automatic weapons, and thirty-seven times more armored personnel carriers. It is not, of course, the Soviet habit to give absolute figures which would make such comparisons more meaningful.

[44] *The Military Balance, 1967–1968*, pp. 8–9. For photos and description of the various new aircraft displayed at the July 1967 air show, see the three-page section of *Krasnaia zvezda*, July 11, 1967, devoted to this subject under the rubric "The Power and Might of Soviet Aviation."

exercises, as previously mentioned, emphasis was also put on quick airlift reinforcement for theater forces, although, according to some Western studies of
the Soviet threat against NATO, these forces remained deficient in the balanced
support elements that would be needed for any lengthy, large-scale operations
in Europe.[45]

With respect to preparations for possible operations in local areas outside
Europe or the Eurasian mainland, some elements of the general purpose forces
were, of course, involved in what we described in the preceding chapter as
an effort by the Brezhnev–Kosygin regime to extend the reach of Soviet conventional power. But, although the improvement of amphibious landing,
airborne, and naval capabilities helped to broaden the prospective operating
zones of the theater forces, and perhaps foreshadowed the day when a stronger
Soviet military presence might be projected into the Mediterranean basin on the
southern flank of NATO, the main share of resources and energies devoted to
the general purpose forces still went largely into preparing them for their long-
standing theater role in Europe proper.

Among the training activities illustrative of the continued European orientation of the theater forces was the highly publicized "Dnepr" exercise held in
the western USSR in September 1967 and billed as the largest of its kind in
recent years.[46] This exercise, intended to test the preparedness of the theater
forces for their continental role in Europe, included tank and motorized infantry penetrations up to 500 miles, helicopter landings and airlift reinforcement,
as well as supporting tactical missile and air strikes. Although some Soviet
accounts mentioned the participation of strategic missile units, no explicit reference was made to the simulated use of nuclear weapons, suggesting that the
Soviets were interested in underscoring the conventional warfare aspects of the
maneuvers.[47]

An additional point of some interest was that other Warsaw Pact military
personnel did not participate in the "Dnepr" exercise except as observers. Inasmuch as for several years previously the Soviet Union had habitually given wide
publicity only to theater exercises involving joint collaboration with other

[45] See reference to one such Pentagon study by Chalmers M. Roberts, "Can NATO and Dollar
Both Be Sound?" *Washington Post*, October 30, 1966. For earlier, more detailed discussion of Soviet
capabilities for support and reinforcement of theater forces in Europe during the Khrushchev
period, see chapter VII, pp. 157–59. Many of the same limitations evidently continued to apply
under the Brezhnev–Kosygin regime, although it must be presumed that some improvement took
place, especially with regard to airlift reinforcement.

[46] Among Soviet accounts of the "Dnepr" exercise, see daily coverage in *Krasnaia zvezda*,
September 23–October 1, 1967; speech by Minister of Defense Marshal A. A. Grechko, ibid.,
October 3, 1967; Colonel S. Aleshin, Colonel V. Grinevskii, and Lt. Colonel N. Vasil'ev, "Dnepr—
Forces on the Move," ibid., October 4, 1967; "Dnepr Exercise—Combat Report of the Defenders
of the Fatherland," *Kommunist Vooruzhennykh Sil*, no 21 (November 1967): 59–63.

[47] By way of contrast with the playing up of the conventional warfare aspects of the "Dnepr"
maneuvers, when an exercise of similar scope was held in the western USSR in March 1970, under
the command of Marshal Grechko (the "Dvina" maneuvers), Soviet accounts dwelt on the
simulated battlefield employment of nuclear weapons by both sides, as well as on the conventional
features of the maneuvers. S. Borzenko, G. Buravkin, Ia. Makarenko, "Mastery and Maturity,"
Pravda, March 11, 1970; V. Gol'tsev, "Mastery," *Izvestiia*, March 12, 1970; K. Retinskii and G.
Shevelev, radio broadcast from the "Dvina" exercise area, March 12, 1970.

Warsaw bloc forces, this departure from custom might be taken to mean that Moscow was again envisaging circumstances in which Soviet forces might find themselves operating in the European arena outside the framework of the Warsaw Pact. If this were so, it not only would imply that by 1967 Soviet relations with the rest of the Pact members had deteriorated more than was apparent on the surface; it might also suggest that Soviet military policy toward the Warsaw Pact was beginning to shift away from the principle of greater reliance on East European forces, which had been adopted during the Khrushchev period. As we shall see presently, the merits of this principle were again to be tested by the events in Czechoslovakia in August 1968. For the moment, however, we are interested in what the military operation against Czechoslovakia revealed with respect to the capabilities of the Soviet theater forces.

Czechoslovakia: The Theater Forces in Action

The Soviet-led invasion of Czechoslovakia lacked one essential ingredient of a realistic test of theater forces in action: organized armed opposition. Nevertheless, the operation provided an opportunity unparalleled since World War II to observe the performance of a large force of combat-ready Soviet armored and motorized rifle formations, together with rear echelon and air support elements. The invasion brought together, under Soviet command, forces from five countries in a massive co-ordinated operation—on a scale almost as large as would be involved in a major military thrust against NATO's central front in Europe. By contrast, the military suppression of the Hungarian revolution in 1956 had involved the active use of only seven Soviet divisions.

Western accounts (the only ones to provide any military details of the Czechoslovak invasion) are generally agreed that the operation was impressive.[48] Meticulous planning and advance preparations were manifest in the assembly of forces for the operation and in the high degree of tactical surprise achieved, in keeping, incidentally, with Soviet doctrine that a theater attack is best launched under the cover of field exercises. The operation itself was conducted without an observable hitch, almost with field-manual perfection. In particular, the seizure of Prague by airborne forces, quickly backed up by night-time armored penetration from the country's borders was faultlessly executed in the brief period of about four hours.

[48] See Tad Szulc, "Soviet Army in Action Impresses West," *New York Times*, September 10, 1968. In a speech to the Association of the US Army in Washington on October 28, 1968, General Lyman L. Lemnitzer, NATO's military commander, emphasized that the invasion not only was a highly skilled military effort but was accomplished "without any tactical warning whatsoever." See "Bolstering of NATO Is Urged," *Washington Post*, October 29, 1968. See also Raymond J. Barrett, "The United States and Europe," *Military Review* (December 1968): 4. Although the Soviet Union devoted its full propaganda resources to justification of the invasion and occasionally cited Western sources to the effect that it was "faultless from the viewpoint of military science," there was little professional treatment of the operation in Soviet military literature. For some typical Soviet accounts of the manner in which Soviet fighting men carried out their "international duty" in Czechoslovakia, see editorial, "In Defense of the Achievements of Socialism," *Krasnaia zvezda*, August 23, 1968; editorial, "True Sons of the People," ibid., August 31, 1968; editorial, "Fidelity to International Duty," *Kommunist Vooruzhennykh Sil*, no. 18 (September 1968): 9–12; Viktor Shragrin's commentary, "For the Soldiers of the Soviet Army," Moscow radio broadcast, September 14, 1968.

In the wake of this performance by the forces which in effect constituted the core of the Soviet Union's conventional striking power in the European theater, several points stood out. First, even though the ground-air combat units had been put through their paces under conditions much less severe than on a live battlefield, the size and co-ordinated nature of the operation had nonetheless imposed exacting demands on communications and logistic support elements. Although some logistic shortcomings were evident, it appeared on the whole that this test had been met efficiently.[49]

Second, the theater forces had been raised to a higher level of combat readiness than at any time in recent years, and they had demonstrated a capacity for a quick initial strike and mobile penetration that seemed to meet the prescription of Soviet theater warfare doctrine for rapidly unfolding offensive operations. To the extent that some in the West, especially in West Germany, still felt concern about a possible Soviet attempt to carry out a swift action against an exposed objective, such as Hamburg or Berlin, and thereby present the West with a fait accompli, this was hardly reassuring. At the same time, however, despite the tactical surprise achieved by the invasion forces, their build-up and positioning had required several weeks of preinvasion maneuvering, which gave NATO strategic warning and thus provided at least an opportunity to put Western defenses on the alert.

A third point relevant to the capabilities of the Soviet theater forces was that some of the combat-ready formations introduced into Czechoslovakia had come equipped with tactical missiles that customarily are allotted a nuclear role. According to Western reports, Soviet tactical missile units moved into a closely guarded military area vacated by the Czechoslovak troops at Mlada, north of Prague.[50] Although it was not known whether these units actually brought along nuclear warheads, their inclusion in the invasion order-of-battle was a tacit reminder that the Soviet theater forces could call upon nuclear as well as conventional firepower. Inasmuch as the establishment of Soviet control over Czechoslovakia was hardly a task requiring nuclear arms, this reminder presumably was meant to put NATO on notice that the Soviet forces had come prepared to fight a nuclear-equipped adversary, if necessary.

[49] Contention has arisen over how to appraise the Soviet logistics performance in the invasion. Some analysts contend that although Soviet airlift performed surprisingly well, many weaknesses showed up in ground supply services, due partly to shortage of organic transport, which required mobilization of trucks from the Soviet civilian economy. See, for example, Leo Heiman, "Soviet Invasion Weaknesses," *Military Review* (August 1969): 38–45. A different view has been expressed by General Lyman L. Lemnitzer, former NATO commander. In an interview with the author on February 28, 1970, General Lemnitzer said that Soviet logistics services not only performed creditably, but that the mobilization of motor transport reserves from the economy, in accordance with standard Soviet practice, testified to careful advance planning. Soviet accounts, incidentally, stress that the rear area maneuvers which preceded the intervention were intended to test the mobilization of "reservists as well as motor vehicle equipment from the national economy," and that the rear services "passed a stiff examination" successfully. See editorial, "The Rear Service Troops Take an Examination," *Krasnaia zvezda*, July 25, 1968; interview with General S. S. Mariakhin, chief of the rear services, ibid., July 31, 1968.

[50] See Tad Szulc, "Czech Army Unit Evacuates a Base for Russians," *New York Times*, October 1, 1968.

Finally, perhaps the principal and most contentious point to emerge in a military context in the immediate aftermath of the invasion was whether the introduction of additional combat-ready Soviet theater forces into Czechoslovakia had upset the European military balance and adversely affected the stability of deterrence in Europe. During the first three postinvasion months, while the bulk of the Soviet forces remained in Czechoslovakia, it was widely asserted in the West that the new lodgment of Soviet military power opposite West Germany's southern flank in Bavaria had altered the long-standing balance of power.[51] While not necessarily indicating that the Soviet Union intended to take military action against Western Europe, its entry into Czechoslovakia and the resultant forward concentration of Soviet theater forces in Central Europe were seen as a destabilizing element in the European military environment. Not only were these forces so positioned as to give the Soviet Union certain military advantages in terms of territorial access and reduced warning time for a potential jump-off against southern Germany or Austria, but their forward deployment could compel NATO planners to lower the threshold for employment of nuclear weapons in defense of the NATO area.[52]

On the other hand, different views also were advanced in the West as to the net effect of the Soviet theater forces build-up in the Northern Tier of the Warsaw Pact. Some observers held, for example, that the forward deployment of additional Soviet forces was offset by the probable unreliability of the Czechoslovak armed forces, thus leaving the over-all military balance between the two alliances essentially unchanged.[53] As for the impact of the Soviet military presence in Czechoslovakia upon the stability of the European military environment, it could be argued that the very build-up of Soviet forces in Central Europe, by making it likely that NATO would be obliged to seek earlier recourse to nuclear weapons in the event of an attack, might serve as a further deterrent to any intemperate Soviet action against the West.[54] Nevertheless, until about mid-November of 1968, following a series of internal NATO studies and reviews in the wake of the invasion, the prevailing opinion within NATO seemed to be that the European military balance had been, in General Lemnitzer's words, "significantly altered to the disadvantage of the West" by the influx of Soviet forces into Czechoslovakia, and that future NATO political and

[51] A US statement of August 31, 1968, gave the first official appraisal in the West that the invasion had altered the long-standing military balance in Europe. See Statement of the US State Department, "U.S. and NATO Allies Review East-West Military Situation," *Department of State Bulletin*, September 16, 1968. See also David Binder, "Kiesinger Urges Defense Step-Up," *New York Times*, September 20, 1968. For a representative marshaling of arguments that the balance had been upset in Central Europe by the Soviet action, see Harry B. Ellis, "NATO's Defense Strategy Outdated," *Christian Science Monitor*, September 11, 1968. For discussion of Soviet Counterstatements on the military balance issue, see chapter XV, pp. 409–10.

[52] See "Lemnitzer Foresees Quicker Atom Defense," *Washington Post*, October 16, 1968; "Schroeder Sees Quick A-Response," ibid., October 18, 1968.

[53] For a representative view arguing that there had been little shift if any in the military balance, see R. T. Rockingham Gill, "Europe's Military Balance After Czechoslovakia," *East Europe* (October 1968): 17–21. See also Charles Douglas-Home, in *Times*, London, September 25, 1968.

[54] See Gill, in *East Europe* (October 1968): 19.

military planning should be based on the assumption of the "unpredictability" of Soviet behavior.[55]

In November, however, with the accretion of evidence that most of the Soviet forces were being withdrawn from Czechoslovakia, the argument that the August invasion had unhinged the European military balance began to lose conviction. Whereas the deployment of eleven added Soviet divisions and supporting elements in Central Europe certainly could be considered to have tipped the previous fine balance of conventional arms,[56] the same could hardly be said about the presence of only four or five additional divisions, which were less likely to be poised against the West than preoccupied with keeping the Czechoslovaks in line. Indeed, at the ministerial session of the NATO Council in Brussels on November 15–16, 1968, the issue of the military balance no longer was emphasized;[57] rather, the Soviet action against Czechoslovakia, together with Moscow's new doctrine of intervention (the "Brezhnev doctrine"[58]), was said to have given rise to uncertainties in the face of which the NATO allies were obliged to reassess and improve the state of their defenses.

Although at the time it remained to be seen what responsive measures NATO

[55] Bernard Gwertzman, "Lemnitzer Urges Stronger Forces for NATO," New York Times, October 29, 1968. The assessment that Soviet "unpredictability" must be given new weight in NATO planning was among a number of conclusions reportedly reached within NATO by mid-October 1968. Two others were that the new territorial deployment of Soviet forces along the Bavarian and Austrian borders had in fact had an important effect on the security balance in Europe, and that the Soviet naval build-up in the Mediterranean posed a growing strategic threat of concern to NATO. See Tad Szulc, "NATO Council Urges New Policy Principles in Wake of Czech Occupation," New York Times, October 17, 1968.

[56] Precisely how the conventional balance in Central Europe stood prior to the Czech invasion was, it may be noted, a much-disputed issue in the West, with the answer depending on the way the opposing forces were measured. On the NATO side, available for use in Central Europe was a standing force of 24 divisions and around 2,000 tactical aircraft. On the Warsaw Pact side in Central Europe were 26 Soviet divisions and about 1,200 Soviet tactical aircraft, plus whatever portion of the ground-air strength of the East European countries in the central area might be deemed eligible for inclusion. The four relevant countries (the GDR, Poland, Czechoslovakia, and Hungary) had a total of about 35 to 40 divisions and 1,700 combat aircraft. On the face of it, NATO was therefore considerably outnumbered in conventional forces in the central area, though generally conceded to have a substantial edge in tactical nuclear strength. However, after adjusting the conventional force figures to take into account numerous factors, such as the 60 per cent higher manpower and equipment levels of NATO divisions and the greater bomb load and endurance of NATO aircraft, and leaving the majority of the East European divisions out of the reckoning of combat-ready forces, some estimates concluded that "an accurate picture of all factors indicates rough equality" between the two sides. One such appraisal, which received wide attention, was given by Dr. Alain Enthoven, a US Assistant Secretary of Defense, at a NATO briefing in February 1968. For an outline of Dr. Enthoven's briefing, together with a critical dissection of it by a US congressional subcommittee, see Review of a Systems Analysis Evaluation of NATO vs Warsaw Pact Conventional Forces, Report of the Special Subcommittee on National Defense Posture, of the Committee on Armed Services of the U.S. House of Representatives, September 4, 1968 (Washington, D.C.: Government Printing Office, 1968). See also Dr. Enthoven's "Letter to the Editor," on the same subject, Survival (September 1968): 308. For a fuller discussion of problems involved in appraising the conventional balance in Europe, see chapter VIII, pp. 166–73.

[57] On this point, the communiqué of the meeting simply stated: "The use of force and the stationing in Czechoslovakia of Soviet forces not hitherto deployed there have aroused grave uncertainty and demands great vigilance on the part of the allies." See "Text of Communiqué Issued by NATO Ministers," New York Times, November 17, 1968.

[58] See discussion of the Brezhnev doctrine in chapter XIV, pp. 383–85.

would prove willing to carry out and how painful the Soviet Union might find them, it did appear that the Soviet leaders had been somewhat embarrassed by charges that the USSR was upsetting the balance of forces in Europe. At least, by choosing to pull back most of the forces they had sent into Czechoslovakia, they conveyed the impression that they were more interested in returning to something like the status quo in East–West military power in Europe than in bolstering the Soviet military posture against the West by leaving substantially greater conventional firepower deployed at NATO's doorstep. For its part, NATO had been made freshly aware of the mobile capabilities of the Soviet theater forces and of the Soviet Union's potential for tipping the conventional arms balance on the European continent at short notice should it once again elect to increase the forward deployment of these forces in Central Europe.

The Warsaw Pact and Soviet Military Policy

Soviet policy with respect to the Warsaw Pact initially bore much the same features under the Brezhnev–Kosygin regime as in the Khrushchev period. Thus, the Warsaw Pact was called upon to play two basic, though sometimes rather incompatible, roles in Soviet policy: first, as a military coalition to counter NATO and augment the Soviet Union's own military capacities against the West; second, as an internal mechanism for promoting political cohesion within the bloc and, when necessary, enforcing Soviet control over potentially errant bloc members.

Although reconciling the Pact's internal policing function with the task of improving its collective military efficiency against the West was to become increasingly troublesome for the Soviet Union, especially after the 1968 crisis over Czechoslovakia, the Brezhnev–Kosygin regime for a time appeared to be making reasonably good progress in building up the military potential of the joint Warsaw Pact forces. Among steps contributing to this end were joint field exercises, commanders' conferences, and Soviet military mission activities in the various Warsaw Pact countries, all aimed at a more thorough integration of the East European armed forces into Soviet operational plans. At the same time, the Soviet Union also went ahead with programs for the re-equipment and modernization of the Pact forces, particularly those of the Northern Tier countries, in order to bring their capabilities better into line with their enlarged theater responsibilities.

Joint Warsaw Pact Training Exercises

Perhaps the most conspicuous feature of Soviet military policy toward the Warsaw Pact under the new regime was the practice of holding multinational field maneuvers of Pact forces in various parts of East Europe, with at least one major joint exercise a year and one or more of smaller scope. Between the time of Khrushchev's removal, in the fall of 1964, and August 1968 about seventeen such joint theater maneuvers took place, compared with nine during the Khrushchev period. As the detailed listing of these maneuvers in Table 1 (pp. 478–80) indicates, the Pact forces most frequently involved along with Soviet

TABLE 1—Joint Warsaw Pact Maneuvers, 1961–68*

Date	Participation and location (location in italics)	Remarks
1. Oct–Nov 61	SU, *GDR*, *Poland*, Czechoslovakia	First publicized multilateral WP maneuvers for "show of force" during Berlin crisis. (Some previous unpublicized Soviet–GDR bilateral field training had taken place.)
2. Apr 62	SU, *Hungary*, Rumania	Minor exercise with token Rumanian participation, but attended by Marshal Malinovskii to observe Hungarian performance.
3. Sep 62	SU, GDR, *Czechoslovakia*	Well-publicized exercise in Northern Tier area employing standard scenario frequently followed thereafter, with NATO attack, WP counterattack, and simulated nuclear exchange.
4. Oct 62	SU, *GDR*, *Poland*	Partial Northern Tier exercise, with nominal Polish commander. (Unless otherwise noted, all exercise commanders presumed to be Soviet.)
5. Oct 62	SU, *Rumania*, Bulgaria	First joint maneuvers in Southern Tier, with nominal Rumanian commander.
6. Jun 63	SU, Rumania, *Bulgaria*	Low-key maneuver in Southern Tier.
7. Sep 63	SU, *GDR*, Czechoslovakia, Poland	Major Northern Tier exercise employing standard scenario. Named "Quartet," with nominal GDR commander.
8. Jul 64	SU, GDR, *Czechoslovakia*	Low-key maneuver, with nominal Czech commander.
9. Sep 64	SU, Rumania, *Bulgaria*	Major Southern Tier exercise, including airborne, amphibious landings. Simulated use of nuclear weapons. Nominal Bulgarian commander.
10. Apr 65	SU, *GDR*	Used as excuse to close Autobahn temporarily. Included airlift from SU.
11. Oct 65	SU, *GDR*, Poland, Czechoslovakia	Highly publicized "October Storm." Largest exercise to date. Standard Northern Tier scenario, plus Soviet airlift of Polish airborne troops. Simulated nuclear exchanges.
12. Jul 66	SU, *GDR*, *Poland*	Coastal and naval exercise with landings in Baltic.
13. Aug 66	SU, *GDR*	Ground-air exercise with GDR commander.
14. Sep 66	SU, GDR, *Czechoslovakia*, Hungary	Highly publicized "Vltava" exercise, which advance billing claimed to be larger than "October Storm." First participation of Hungary with Northern Tier countries. Soviet airlift reinforcement. Simulated nuclear strikes.

TABLE 1—Joint Warsaw Pact Maneuvers, 1961–68*—*Continued*

Date	Participation and location (location in italics)	Remarks
15. Mar 67	SU, *GDR*, Czechoslovakia	Standard scenario of NATO attack, with nuclear resort after conventional phase.
16. May–Jun 67	SU, *GDR*, Poland	Similar to March 1967 exercise.
17. Jun 67	SU, *GDR*, Poland	Combined naval exercise in Baltic.
18. Jun 67	SU, *Czechoslovakia, Hungary*	Apparently small-scale, with token participation by Hungary.
19. Aug 67	SU, *GDR*, Poland, Czechoslovakia	Standard Northern Tier exercise, attended by new WP commander, Marshal Iakubovskii.
20. Aug 67	SU, Rumania, *Bulgaria*	First Rumanian participation since similar Sep 1964 exercise. Amphibious and airborne landings. Nominal Bulgarian commander.
21. Mar 68	SU, *GDR*	This exercise, not officially acknowledged by Soviet sources, was reported in the Western press to have taken place on short notice in the southeastern part of the GDR opposite the Czech border during the Dresden meeting of Pact leaders. Ostensibly, its purpose was to bring pressure on the Dubcek government.
22. May 68	SU, *Poland*	Small joint Soviet–Polish maneuvers, announced as taking place "in accordance with the training plan" of the Warsaw Pact, following Western reports of Soviet troop movements along the Czech–Polish border.
23. Jun 68	SU, GDR, Poland, Hungary, *Czechoslovakia*	These maneuvers, originally announced as a limited staff exercise, were expanded to a field exercise under the command of Marshal Iakubovskii, the Pact commander. They played a controversial role as a device to influence the policies of the Dubcek reform government in Czechoslovakia. (See chapter XIV.)
24. Jul 68	*SU, GDR, Poland*	Joint naval exercises, the most ambitious undertaken by the Pact up to this time, in the Baltic, Barents, North, and Norwegian Seas. Soviet, East German, and Polish bases were used. These maneuvers, code-named "Sever" and commanded by Admiral Gorshkov, head of the Soviet navy, were given more publicity than any previous naval exercises.

TABLE 1—Joint Warsaw Pact Maneuvers, 1961–68*—*Continued*

Date	Participation and location (location in italics)	Remarks
25. Jul–Aug 68	*SU, GDR, Poland Hungary*	Originally announced as the "largest logistical exercises" in Soviet history, these maneuvers at first involved only Soviet forces operating along the western frontiers of the USSR under General Mariakhin, but were subsequently extended to include troops of all the Warsaw Pact countries bordering on Czechoslovakia. These maneuvers, in connection with which the Soviet Union announced the call-up of reservists, were also part of the pressure on Prague during the July crisis. (See chapter XIV.) Simulated nuclear operations and the "Sky Shield" air exercises were tacked on in the course of these maneuvers, to which the Soviets gave the code name "Nemen."
26. Aug 68	*SU, GDR, Poland, Hungary*	These maneuvers, which began the day the "Nemen" logistical exercises ended on August 10, were part of a continuing effort to apply pressure around the border areas of Czechoslovakia. It was originally announced that they involved primarily communications troops, but later it became known that they amounted to a dress rehearsal for the invasion of Czechoslovakia. (See chapter XIV.)

* Among the sources from which this table was compiled are the following: *Izvestiia*, September 26, 1961, October 21, 22, 1965, July 23, 1968; *Pravda*, April 21, 1962, September 15, 1963, September 21, 1964, September 21, 23, 25, 1965, October 23, 1965, January 20, 1968, May 14, 1968; *Krasnaia zvezda*, July 2, 1964, April 11, 1965, October 23, 24, 26, 1965, September 18, 20, 22, 24, 27, 1966, January 25, 1968, July 13, 25, 31, 1968; *Neues Deutschland*, October 6, 1961, October 6, 15, 1965, June 6, 1967, July 12, 1968; *Kommunist Vooruzhennykh Sil*, no. 8 (April 1964): 80; no. 9 (May 1964): 86; no. 19 (October 1964): 81; no. 8 (April 1965): 70; no. 9 (May 1965): 14; no. 17 (September 1968): 5; *Soviet News*, September 23, 1966, p. 120; *New York Times*, October 14, 15, 1961, April 21, 23, 1962, October 2, 10, 11, 1962, September 22, 27, 1963, September 19, 1966, August 28, 29, 1967, May 10, 25, 1968, June 2, 5, 6, 16, 19, 1968; *Washington Post*, September 25, 1966, May 10, 11, 16, 23, 1968, July 1, 1968; *Soviet Military Review*, no. 11 (November 1967): 14–19; no. 9 (September 1968): 22; East Berlin ADN radio broadcasts, August 24, 26, 1966, July 12, 1968; East Berlin radio broadcast, August 27, 1966; *Ostsee Zeitung* (Rostock), August 23, 1966; *Christian Science Monitor*, July 26, 1967. See also fn. 68 below for reference to subsequent maneuvers.

troops in East Europe were from the countries of the Northern Tier: East Germany, Poland, and Czechoslovakia. In keeping with her pivotal role and location, East Germany took part in nineteen joint exercises—more than any other Soviet ally—and was the host territory on fourteen occasions.

The trend toward emphasis on the Northern Tier countries grew much more pronounced after the advent of the Brezhnev–Kosygin regime; only one of the seventeen exercises held after the autumn of 1964—that involving Rumanian and Bulgarian participation with Soviet forces, in August 1967—took place in the Southern Tier area. The two largest and most highly publicized of the joint exercises prior to the Czechoslovak crisis of 1968—"October Storm" in October 1965 and "Vltava" in September 1966—both occurred in Northern

Tier territory, although the "Vltava" maneuvers in Czechoslovakia drew Hungary into association with the Northern Tier for the first time.[59] The majority of the maneuvers were staged in a land battlefield setting, occasionally with co-ordinated naval exercises and coastal landings in the Black Sea or Baltic areas. Joint exercises involving only naval units of some of the Warsaw Pact countries also were held from time to time, but usually without the publicity accorded the combined ground-air maneuvers. The same was true of periodic joint air defense exercises.[60]

The scenario followed in most of the exercises had hostile forces launching the first attack, being contained, and then destroyed by a counterattack of Pact forces. In most of the larger exercises, including "October Storm" and "Vltava," there was a simulated nuclear exchange initiated by hostile forces. (By contrast, in the non-Warsaw Pact "Dnepr" exercise in the Soviet Union, in September 1967, attention was given primarily to the conventional character of the operations.[61]) From the fall of 1964 on, airborne and amphibious landings also were more frequently demonstrated in the combined exercises. Soviet officers directed the majority of the joint maneuvers, but at one time or another each East European country, except Hungary, was accorded the well-publicized honor of furnishing the nominal exercise commander.[62] The size of the larger annual maneuvers ranged from about 40,000 to 60,000 troops, and their active duration—not counting assembly period, post-exercise ceremonies, and so on—was three or four days. The smaller exercises involved fewer troops and generally had an active phase of one or two days.

In assessing the maneuvers that took place during the first year or so of the Brezhnev–Kosygin regime, some Western experts argued that the military value of the joint Warsaw Pact exercises was clearly secondary to their political function of demonstrating the unity and common purpose of the bloc.[63] This view rested partly on the propaganda character of the extensive Warsaw Pact literature on the joint maneuvers, and partly on the argument that the welding of the several armies of the bloc into a single, integrated military force was not likely to be served by maneuvers involving, for the most part, only relatively

[59] In the "Vltava" exercise, Poland, although a Northern Tier country, did not participate directly. However, Polish forces conducted well-publicized national maneuvers at about the same time. Some Soviet ground and naval forces may have had a role in the latter.

[60] With a few exceptions which received wide public attention, such as the "Sever" exercise in July 1968, purely naval exercises are not included in the listing given in Table 1, nor are periodic air defense exercises, which often involved co-operation among the various Pact countries.

[61] See fn. 47 above.

[62] The East European officials assigned nominal command were the defense ministers of the countries concerned, who are, within the Warsaw Pact command structure, considered deputies to the supreme Pact commander, a Soviet officer. The GDR defense minister, General Heinz Hoffman, was twice given the prestige assignment of exercise director, as was the Bulgarian defense minister, while the others each received one turn, except for Hungary, which was left out altogether.

[63] For a well-argued example of this view, which applies, however, only to the first eleven joint maneuvers, conducted between October 1961 and October 1965, see Stanley Dziuban, *The Warsaw Pact Maneuvers: Proof of Readiness or Psychological Warfare?* N-369(R) (Arlington, Va.: Institute for Defense Analyses, August 1966).

small formations of selected Pact forces, in contrast with the NATO practice of wide-scale unit participation in annual exercises.[64] In particular, it was questioned whether the modest scale and short duration of most of the maneuvers provided an adequate test of the logistical support capabilities of the Pact forces for extended, theaterwide campaigns.[65]

Although such criticism probably was valid until about 1966, it would appear somewhat dated in light of later developments. The frequency and scope of the joint maneuvers not only increased substantially in 1967 and 1968, but—as suggested by the series of exercises that culminated in the invasion of Czechoslovakia—the forces of at least the five participating Pact countries doubtless gained much collective military experience in operational co-ordination, logistical support, joint field and staff activities, and the like. To be sure, the "integrated" military enterprise which unfolded against Czechoslovakia was largely dominated by Soviet forces, emphasizing once more that the main burden of any Warsaw Pact military undertakings in Europe was still on the Soviet Union. Indeed, the very concept of joint Warsaw Pact forces unified in a common cause was severely shaken by the military intervention in Czechoslovakia.

Despite the fact that the joint exercises of 1968 were linked much more intimately with Soviet efforts to halt unfavorable internal trends in the Warsaw bloc than with the task of improving the Pact's collective military capability against an external foe, there was no indication that the Soviet Union was writing off the chances of achieving better integrated Pact forces through the medium of joint maneuvers. On the contrary, after the invasion, in urging the countries of the "socialist commonwealth" to strengthen their military alliance against the "growing aggressiveness" of NATO,[66] Soviet spokesmen stressed that joint maneuvers would continue to have "an important place" among various "practical measures for improving collective defense."[67] At the same time, the circumstances in which joint military exercises were resumed in 1969 suggested that the Soviet Union was also quite prepared to perpetuate the use of such exercises for the purposes of internal Warsaw bloc politics.[68]

[64] Dziuban pointed out, for example, that only about 15 per cent of the field forces of the East European countries were involved in joint exercises through 1965, except East Germany, where he estimated the figure at 25–35 per cent. Subsequent exercises would have boosted these percentages, however, especially for the Northern Tier countries. Ibid., p. 14.

[65] Ibid., pp. 16–17. It may be noted that the first large exercise to stress logistical capabilities was the "Nemen" exercise in July 1968, which was also in part a political-military demonstration aimed at Czechoslovakia.

[66] See, for example, editorial, "To Strengthen the Peace in Europe," *Pravda*, September 20, 1968; Colonel P. Karpenko and Lt. Colonel V. Gavrilov, "Indoctrination of Troops in the Spirit of Internationalism," *Kommunist Vooruzhennykh Sil*, no. 16 (August 1969): 69–70.

[67] "Armed Forces of Warsaw Treaty Member Countries," *Soviet Military Review*, no. 9 (September 1968): 22-23.

[68] Four well-published joint exercises were held in 1969. The first, from March 25 to April 11, took place in Bulgaria under the command of Marshal I. I. Iakubovskii and, according to the Soviet announcement, involved joint activity by Bulgarian, Soviet, and Rumanian "operational staffs." The second, named "Vesna 69," ran from March 30 to April 4. It was held on Polish, East German, and Czech territory, and involved communications troops of those countries and of the USSR under the nominal command of a Polish general. The third, April 14–16, was a bloc-wide air defense exercise commanded by Marshal P. F. Batitskii. The fourth, named "Oder-Neisse

Modernization of the Pact Forces with
Emphasis on the Northern Tier

Parallel with the practice of holding periodic joint maneuvers, the Soviet Union under the Brezhnev–Kosygin regime also continued the programs instituted under Khrushchev to re-equip and modernize the East European armed forces.[69] This activity became more selective, however, with the flow of new ground and air equipment from the Soviet Union tending to favor the Northern Tier countries. Polish, Czech, and East German divisions, for example, were the main recipients of such Soviet matériel as T-55 tanks, self-propelled AA guns, and amphibious personnel carriers, and their tactical air units were strengthened by additional deliveries of advanced aircraft like the MIG-21 and the Su-7. The Northern Tier countries also apparently were encouraged and assisted in placing their own defense production industries on a more nearly self-sufficient basis, using standard Soviet specifications to insure compatibility of weapons and equipment.[70]

The chief exception to this sharing of arms production technology lay in the nuclear and missile fields, which the Soviet Union manifestly intended to reserve to itself. Tactical missile delivery systems, the first of which had been furnished to the East European countries under a program started by Khrushchev in 1964,[71] continued to be supplied in modest numbers by the Soviet Union, as were air defense missile systems of the SA-2 type employed in North Vietnam. Nuclear munitions, however, remained in Soviet hands, as had been the case from the beginning. As we shall see presently, however, the problem of nuclear sharing and control within the Warsaw Pact evidently was a source of some difficulty for the Brezhnev–Kosygin regime.

From the standpoint of size, the East European components of the Warsaw Pact—like the Soviet Union's own forces—remained fairly stable during the first years of the new regime, although here, too, some differentiation was apparent between the countries of the Northern and those of the Southern Tier.

69," was the largest Pact exercise ever held in Poland. It took place in late September, with participants from Poland, East Germany, Czechoslovakia, and the USSR. The first two of these exercises had pronounced political overtones, for they came at a time when the Soviet Union had sent Marshal A. A. Grechko and Deputy Foreign Minister V. S. Semenov to Czechoslovakia to demand that Prague restore orthodox, pro-Soviet leaders to power. In the first case, Rumania's participation in a joint exercise for the first time since August 1967 was also presumably a symbolic bow to bloc unity and a partial concession to Soviet pressure for military reintegration of Rumania into the Pact. In the second case, the "Vesna 69" exercise not only had the obvious political function of backing up new Soviet demands on Prague, but by involving Czechoslovakia's territory and troops it also constituted a test of Prague's adherence to the process of "normalization." See, "Joint Exercise," *Pravda*, April 2, 1969; "Joint Exercise of the Armed Forces of the USSR, GDR, Czechoslovakia, and Poland," *Krasnaia zvezda*, March 30, 1969; "PVO Exercise of Warsaw Treaty States," ibid., April 15, 1969; interview with Marshal I. I. Iakubovskii, "From the Scene of the Joint Troop Exercises," ibid., September 28, 1969.

69 See chapter VII, pp. 150–51.

70 In some cases, the East European countries became suppliers of military items to the Soviet Union. Poland and Czechoslovakia, for example, both produced light aircraft, helicopters, and jet trainers, of either Soviet or domestic design, for use by other Pact members, including the Soviet Union. Production of advanced combat aircraft, however, remained in the Soviet Union.

71 See chapter VII, p. 151.

Rumania, for example, reduced the level of its armed forces by some 30,000 men in the mid-sixties, and Hungary also apparently cut its forces slightly; but in the other Pact countries there were no appreciable changes. By mid-1968 the over-all number of men under arms throughout East Europe stood at between 850,000 and 900,000, of which the three Northern Tier countries had supplied some 600,000. Of the total of about 62 East European divisions, the Northern Tier countries accounted for 35, and their air forces owned some 1,700 of the 2,400 combat aircraft in the East European inventory. In naval forces, Poland and East Germany together continued to overshadow the remainder of the East European Pact members. Czechoslovakia, the landlocked member of the Northern Tier trio, had no navy, of course, but her army and air force strength was close behind that of Poland, the strongest military power of the Warsaw Pact apart from the Soviet Union itself.[72]

The August 1968 invasion of Czechoslovakia produced at least a temporary change in the Warsaw Pact strength in East Europe, although most of this was due to the forward deployment of additional Soviet theater forces. Whether the four East European Pact countries that took part in the invasion mobilized some of their reserves was not made clear, but Rumania—the notable abstainer from the intervention—was prompted to bolster her regular forces and militia during the postinvasion period, when rumors were rife that Rumania might be the next target of disciplinary action.[73] The most significantly affected armed forces, of course, were those of Czechoslovakia herself. Although no formal cutback in their size was announced, they were effectively neutralized until the outcome of the Soviet–imposed "normalization" process had become clear. In October 1968, according to some reports, the Soviet Union was insisting on a housecleaning within the Czech armed forces that was to include a one-third reduction in their size—a step which the Prague government itself might have welcomed in view of its economic difficulties and the fact that its forces were virtually immobilized by the occupation anyway.[74]

[72] Czechoslovakia's armed forces prior to the invasion of August 1968 came to about 225,000 men, with an army of 14 divisions and an air force of 600 tactical-type combat aircraft. Comparable figures for Poland were 270,000 men, with 16 divisions and around 800 combat aircraft, plus a navy of modest size. East Germany, the third Northern Tier member, had a total of about 126,000 men under arms, with an army of six divisions, an air force of 270 combat aircraft, and a navy slightly smaller than that of Poland. For detailed estimates of the military forces available to the various East European members of the Warsaw Pact in this period, see *The Military Balance, 1966–1967*, pp. 6–8; *1967–1968*, pp. 2–4; *1968–1969*, pp. 2–4. See also L.J.M. van den Berk, "After the Biggest Maneuver in German History: Military Developments in Poland, Czechoslovakia and East Germany," *NATO's Fifteen Nations* (June–July 1966): 102–4. It should be noted that, in addition to the regular military establishments of the Warsaw Pact nations, these countries continued to maintain paramilitary forces, such as border and security troops and people's militias, which in East Europe came in the aggregate to about 225,000 to 235,000 men.

[73] See, for example, Harry B. Ellis, "Romanian Jeopardy Spotlighted," *Christian Science Monitor*, August 30, 1968; Hans Benedict, "Rumania Citizens in Drills," *Washington Post*, September 1, 1968.

[74] See Alfred Friendly, "Soviet Design on Czech Army Seen," *Washington Post*, October 16, 1968. With respect to the size of Czechoslovakia's armed forces, it has been conjectured that prior to the invasion the Dubcek regime may have sought to reduce its armed forces by several divisions, both because of the country's economic plight and because of a re-evaluation of the

In terms of the over-all military posture of the Warsaw alliance, it may be presumed that the process of training and modernization of the East European forces which went forward under the Brezhnev–Kosygin regime in the three-and-a-half years before the Czech invasion had helped to bring these forces, especially the Northern Tier group, somewhat closer to the standards of combat capability and readiness governing the Soviet Union's own theater forces in the European arena. Whereas in 1964, toward the end of Khrushchev's rule, no more than half of the East European forces had been considered fit for fairly early commitment to combat operations, during the next couple of years, according to some Western estimates, the proportion crept up to about two-thirds.[75] However, this picture of steady progress toward improvement of the Warsaw Pact's military potential was not without its negative aspects. Even before the policing operation against Czechoslovakia, whose effects might well damage the integrity and military effectiveness of the Northern Tier regional structure upon which Moscow had previously bestowed a great deal of attention, a variety of problems in the management of Warsaw Pact military affairs had confronted the Soviet leadership. At least some of these problems were likely to make the attainment of a well-integrated military posture difficult and uncertain.

Management of Warsaw Pact Military Affairs

Several of the issues which faced the Moscow leadership in the management of military relations with the other Warsaw Pact members were essentially carry-overs from the Khrushchev period; others emerged after his departure. Among the first category was undoubtedly the question of how to share the economic burden of Warsaw Pact military activities. One aspect of this problem —the question of who should pay for the maintenance of Soviet occupation forces—went back to the early days after World War II when Soviet troops were first stationed in East Europe. In the course of time, according to the limited data available on this question, the Soviet Union gradually reduced the charges for Soviet troop maintenance in East Germany from $900 million annually in 1949 to $350 million in 1957, and reportedly lifted the obligation entirely in 1959.[76] After status-of-forces agreements were signed with Poland and Hungary in 1957, these countries, too, presumably were freed from direct support of Soviet garrison costs. However, as suggested by Rumanian complaints in 1966 about the expense of maintaining Soviet troops in East Europe,[77] the question apparently had not been laid to rest. As no Soviet troops had been

---

West German threat, and that this contributed to Soviet displeasure with Dubcek's policies. That after the invasion the Soviets would themselves demand a cutback does not on the surface seem logical, unless Moscow by then regarded the Czech army as too unreliable to contribute much to Pact defense. See R. T. Rockingham Gill, *East Europe* (October 1968): 19.

[75] See, for example, Benjamin Welles, "A New Look at NATO" and "New Soviet Arms Viewed as Increasing Military Threat to West Europe," *New York Times*, October 27 and November 6, 1966.

[76] See Marshall I. Goldman, *Soviet Foreign Aid* (New York: Frederick A. Praeger, Inc., 1967), p. 5.

[77] See chapter XII, p. 307.

stationed in Rumania itself since 1958, the complaint suggests the expenses of
Soviet troop maintenance may have been prorated within the Warsaw Pact.

A second aspect of the cost issue, on the other hand, seemed to cut the other
way, to judge by occasional hints from Moscow that a large and perhaps undue
share of the overhead for collective Warsaw Pact defense was being borne by
the Soviet Union.[78] In particular, the Soviet Union emphasized that it was carrying the burden of resources for the nuclear "shield" behind which the rest of
the Eastern bloc took shelter. One may suppose that the Soviet leaders were not
enthusiastic about helping to foot the additional bill for the procurement and
training programs designed to bring the various national forces of the East
European countries up to a common level of modernization and integration.
Unfortunately, little information is available on how these costs may have been
distributed, but the chances are that each country was expected to pay its own
way.

In this connection, the military budgets of the various East European Pact
members tended to follow the upward curve of Soviet military expenditures in
the period after the Brezhnev–Kosygin regime came to power. As the size of
their forces remained essentially unchanged, this suggests that the budget increases were meant to absorb the costs of re-equipment and modernization. The
sharpest of these annual budgetary hikes came after the Soviet announcement,
in October 1967, of a 15 per cent increase in Soviet military outlays for 1968.
In the next few months, all but two of the other Pact countries boosted their
military budgets by 10 to 15 per cent. The exceptions were East Germany,
which in December 1967 announced a surprising increase of more than 50 per
cent, and Rumania, which acted last with a mere 4 per cent increase.[79]

Another Soviet step which some of the East European countries appeared
ready to emulate was the reduction in terms of service prescribed by the new
Soviet military service law in the fall of 1967. Early in 1968, East Germany,
Hungary, and Czechoslovakia indicated that they would follow suit. Rumania
had anticipated the others by several years, having cut back the term of service
for draftees from twenty-four to sixteen months in 1964. At the time, this move
had not been welcomed by Soviet officers concerned with improving the military
efficiency of the Warsaw Pact forces.[80] Nor were they likely, in 1968, to regard
the reduction of compulsory military service in other East European countries
as a useful contribution to the collective efficiency of the Pact, but by then it had
become a matter of East Europe's following the Soviet example, and they were
in a poor position to complain.

---

[78] See chapter XII, p. 299. See also Colonel V. Alekseev and Lt. Colonel O. Ivanov, "Reliable
Shield of Socialism," *Krasnaia zvezda*, March 30, 1968.

[79] "East European Overt Military Appropriations, 1967 and 1968," *Radio Free Europe*, January
19, 1968; "Situation Report—Rumania," ibid., December 27, 1967. See also *The Military Balance,
1967–1968*, pp. 2–4, and *1968–1969*, pp. 2–4.

[80] Marshal A. A. Grechko, then the Warsaw Pact commander, made trips to Bucharest in
November 1963, and again in May–June 1965, which were evidently prompted by Rumania's
foot-dragging in military affairs, including the cutback in terms of service. See *New York Times*,
June 5, 1965; "Current Developments," *East Europe* (July 1965): 32.

Nuclear Policy Issues

Among other Warsaw Pact policy problems that the Brezhnev–Kosygin regime inherited from Khrushchev was the issue of nuclear access and control within the alliance. Although this issue came to the surface in the Warsaw Pact less frequently than did the comparable question in NATO, the preservation of the Soviet Union's jealously guarded nuclear monopoly evidently was not without troubles for the Soviet leadership. Perhaps the first development that had posed at least potential problems of nuclear policy for the Kremlin was the decision under Khrushchev to provide the East European forces with the means of nuclear delivery in the form of tactical missiles and advanced fighter-bomber aircraft.[81] This step raised a series of policy questions concerning the arrangements, both in peace and in war, under which nuclear warheads for these delivery systems might be made available to the Soviet Union's allies.

However, Moscow cast little light on such arrangements. Despite the fact that East European forces were given training in nuclear warfare methods during joint exercises, and although there were some indications that "joint nuclear forces" had been formally established,[82] the Soviet Union repeatedly declined to comment on its procedures for controlling nuclear access within the Warsaw alliance,[83] in contrast to the detailed disclosure of nuclear safeguards and controls within NATO. In the absence of evidence to the contrary, it was generally assumed (and, in the opinion of the author, rightly so) that the Soviet Union had seen to it that nuclear warheads were kept well out of reach of its allies, an impression bolstered by the occasional informal remarks of Soviet officials.[84]

Whether its partners were altogether satisfied with the nuclear situation within the Warsaw Pact was far from clear. From time to time, there were hints that some of the East European countries were finding the Soviet formula for management of nuclear matters in need of revision. At least two separate issues seem to have been involved: that of East European access to nuclear weapons, or nuclear sharing; and that of participation in nuclear planning and

---

[81] See chapter VII, p. 151.

[82] A rare Soviet comment indicating that some kind of formal joint organizational arrangement for nuclear purposes may have been set up within the Pact was made in May 1965 by Marshal Grechko. In a speech celebrating the tenth anniversary of the Warsaw Treaty, Grechko employed the term "the joint nuclear forces of the Warsaw Pact" in stating that these forces "are always ready to rebuff any aggressor." Moscow radio broadcast, May 14, 1965. Articles and statements dealing with the various Pact armies also mentioned from time to time that they were prepared to fight if necessary with nuclear missile weapons. Among the more specific statements of this kind was one by General Heinz Hoffman, the GDR defense minister, who said in November 1966: "The armed forces of the GDR are also ready and able to fight under the conditions of a nuclear-rocket war and to achieve victory." East Berlin ADN domestic broadcast, November 9, 1966. See also *Kommunist Vooruzhennykh Sil*, no. 8 (April 1965): 70; and previous reference to 1968 GDR doctrine on nuclear training, chapter XVI, fn. 135.

[83] See comment on this point by Secretary of State Dean Rusk, *New York Times*, November 6, 1965.

[84] The author has discussed this question informally with various Soviet representatives at international conferences and elsewhere. Their attitude almost invariably has been that the Soviet Union will permit no erosion of its nuclear monopoly, with emphasis on not allowing the East Germans to have access to nuclear weapons.

strategy. With respect to the first issue, there was some suggestion that the question of East European access to nuclear weapons was raised at the Pact consultative meeting in Warsaw in January 1965, which had been convened to consider new Warsaw Pact defense measures in the event that the West's MLF project—with its supposed granting of nuclear access to West Germany—were to be carried out.[85]

Presumably, any discussion of countersteps by the Warsaw alliance would have touched on the question of opening similar "access" to its members, especially East Germany, upon whose initiative the January meeting apparently had been called. However, pointed Soviet reminders after this meeting that "the security of the socialist countries is guaranteed by the nuclear missile might of the Soviet Union"[86] could be interpreted as a rebuff to any East European pleas for some form of nuclear sharing.[87] If the Warsaw Pact partners did indeed bring serious internal pressure to bear against Moscow on the access issue, it was probably well deflated by 1968, when the nuclear nonproliferation treaty provided the Soviet Union with a handy instrument to formalize permanently its nuclear monopoly within the Warsaw alliance.

On the issue of broader consultation within the Warsaw Pact on nuclear strategy and the use of nuclear weapons, Rumania appears to have taken the initiative in questioning the Soviet Union's right to decide such matters for itself. As previously noted, Rumania had taken constitutional steps as early as mid-1965 to insure against being committed to war by a Soviet decision; and in May 1966, there was a deliberate leak of a proposal, of apparently Rumanian origin, for reform of Warsaw Pact procedures, including a demand for prior consultation on nuclear employment.[88] This challenge to the Soviet Union's prerogative of nuclear decision-making came to the surface after a private session of Pact leaders in February 1966 in East Berlin, where the Soviet spokesmen reportedly had balked at Rumanian insistence on a larger East European role in Warsaw Pact military planning.[89] Later, as differences arose between Bucharest and Moscow over the proposed terms of the nuclear nonproliferation treaty,[90] a further dimension was added to Rumanian criticism of the Soviet nuclear monopoly. By siding with those states that were questioning the adequacy of guarantees offered by the nuclear powers for the defense of non-nuclear coun-

[85] See "Communiqué on the Meeting of the Political Consultative Committee of the Member States of the Warsaw Treaty," *Krasnaia zvezda*, January 22, 1965; report of Kosygin's speech in Leipzig, *Pravda*, March 2, 1965.

[86] Marshal A. A. Grechko, "Military Alliance of Fraternal Nations," *Pravda*, May 13, 1965. See also Grechko, "Reliable Shield of Peace and Security of Nations," *Kommunist Vooruzhennykh Sil*, no. 9 (May 1965): 13; General P. Batov, "Reliable Shield for the Security of Nations," *Soviet Military Review*, no. 5 (May 1965); Marshal R. Ia. Malinovskii, "Powerful Guardian of the Security of Nations," *Krasnaia zvezda*, May 13, 1965.

[87] See Fritz Ermarth, "The Warsaw Pact on the Bloc Agenda," *Radio Free Europe*, September 16, 1965, p. 5.

[88] See chapter XII, p. 307.

[89] See Stephen S. Rosenfeld, "Warsaw Pact Nations Called to July Summit," *Washington Post*, May 3, 1966.

[90] See chapter XIV, pp. 356–57.

tries, Bucharest seemed not only to be challenging the Soviet Union's right to use nuclear weapons without consulting the other Warsaw Pact members but also to be implying that Moscow might prove reluctant to employ its nuclear arsenal in their defense.

That Rumania was not alone in harboring such doubts was suggested by the remarks of a Czech radio commentator in early 1968. Discussing the problems facing the Warsaw Pact consultative meeting in Sofia in March, the Czech spokesman took note of Rumania's attitude on the point that "nonnuclear states will not have access to the great powers' nuclear weapons," a point which, he said, "also concerns the other members of the Warsaw Pact."[91] The nature of this concern, he indicated, had grown in part out of "certain changes" in Soviet military doctrine, especially as pertained to the concept of local wars, according to which "it is, in fact, very probable that the other countries of the Pact would become a theater of war, without sufficient guarantees of nuclear defense." Although the commentator held out hope that "differences of opinion between the socialist countries" on such matters could be "successfully bridged," he also left the impression that other Pact members might join Rumania in raising potentially divisive questions about Soviet nuclear strategy. In his words, "If the creators of Soviet strategic concepts today no longer consider it necessary to reply to an attack on one of the socialist countries with a nuclear strike causing wholesale destruction, the Warsaw Pact member countries might ask some questions similar to those which some time ago caused de Gaulle to quit NATO."

Pressures for Reform of the Pact's Military Command Structure

In a sense, nuclear policy issues were but one aspect of a broader set of problems relating to command and decision-making within the Warsaw Pact with which the Brezhnev–Kosygin regime found it necessary to deal. Although the need for changes in the Pact's organizational and command structure was publicly recognized almost from the outset of the new regime,[92] the views of some of the East European Pact members concerning the nature and the purpose of such changes evidently differed widely from those of the Soviet Union. Indeed, the reforms advocated by some of the Soviet Union's partners called for a new command machinery, and a new balance of power in decision-making, which implicitly challenged the traditional structure of Soviet authority within the Pact.

As it stood when the Brezhnev–Kosygin regime took office, the Warsaw Pact command structure was such as to allow little room for East European influence upon the operational and strategic leadership of the Pact forces. The supreme commander and the chief-of-staff of these forces were Soviet officers, with control over all national units assigned to them, and a special branch of the Soviet General Staff was known to serve as the planning and co-ordinating center for

[91] Lubos Bobrovskii, Prague domestic service broadcast, March 6, 1968.
[92] See chapter XII, pp. 304–6. See also chapter XIII, p. 312.

Pact military activities.[93] The head and the majority of officials of the Joint Secretariat, an administrative body located in Moscow, were likewise Russians.[94] Extant Soviet literature on the direction of joint Pact operations in wartime suggested that Soviet military men would exercise command on the major fronts,[95] and control over the integrated air defense system of the bloc countries rested in Soviet hands.[96] Moreover, the Soviet military missions maintained in the various Warsaw Pact capitals apparently exercised influence over the national military establishments outside formal Pact channels as well as through them.[97]

Although the Soviet Union showed some deference to its Warsaw Pact partners by such palliative devices as placing East European defense officials in nominal charge of occasional joint military exercises, it took no steps in the early years of the Brezhnev–Kosygin regime that promised to cut into the substance of Soviet control. When key posts in the Warsaw Pact command structure fell vacant, for example, they invariably were refilled with Soviet officers.[98] In the military planning and strategy of the alliance, the Soviet Union likewise yielded little to any pressures for change from its allies.

Pressures for reform of the Soviet-dominated command structure had first been publicly reflected, in 1966–67, in the Rumanian proposals for nuclear consultation and for rotation of the supreme commander's job among non-Soviet officers.[99] Again in early 1968 it became known that the March meeting of the Pact's Political Consultative Committee in Sofia had debated "certain

[93] See Raymond L. Garthoff, "The Military Establishment," *East Europe* (September 1965): 13; Richard F. Staar, "The East European Alliance System," *U.S. Naval Institute Proceedings* (September 1964): 35.

[94] The chief of staff of the Warsaw Pact forces also served as chairman of the Joint Secretariat. See *The Military Balance, 1967–1968*, p. 1.

[95] See Thomas W. Wolfe, *Soviet Strategy at the Crossroads* (Cambridge, Mass.: Harvard University Press, 1964), pp. 211–12.

[96] For example, Air Marshal V. A. Sudets, then commander of the Soviet Union's air defense forces, was publicly referred to in 1964 as being also commander-in-chief of Air Defense of the Warsaw Pact. See Garthoff, in *East Europe* (September 1965): 14. Sudets' successor, Marshal P. F. Batitskii, inherited the same dual roles.

[97] Apart from their training and advisory functions, little is known of the role played in the East European countries during the past few years by the Soviet military missions, which were a holdover from Stalin's day before Warsaw Pact machinery came into existence. In one sense, the military missions may represent an alternative bilateral instrument for Soviet influence and surveillance over the national military establishments, either as a backstop to the Pact machinery or as a potential substitute for it if the Pact should ever be dissolved. Another purpose of the missions may be to cultivate pro-Soviet lobbies within the various defense establishments, on the theory that such interest groups would offset any nationalistic tendencies within East European military circles.

[98] For example, when Marshal A. A. Grechko gave up command of the Warsaw Pact forces, he was succeeded in July 1967 by Marshal I. I. Iakubovskii. At about the same time, when General P. I. Batov was relieved as chief of staff, his place was taken by another Soviet officer, General M. I. Kazakov. Again, just two weeks before the invasion of Czechoslovakia, Kazakov's place was taken by General Sergei M. Shtemenko, also a Russian. Though the sixty-eight-year-old Kazakov's retirement was attributed to ill health, there was speculation later that he stepped down to make way for a more vigorous officer in light of the upcoming invasion. Shtemenko, a prominent Soviet strategist and ground forces leader, was seven years his junior. See Peter Grose, "Command Change in Bloc Recalled," *New York Times*, September 4, 1968.

[99] See chapter XII, p. 307, and chapter XIV, p. 353.

problems connected with the work of the headquarters of the Warsaw Pact."[100] The conferees had failed to agree on measures for reform of the Pact command structure, but, according to Rumania's Ceausescu, they undertook to "draw up proposals for improvement of the activity of this command," to be submitted within a six-month period.[101] Less than three weeks later, however, Pact leaders were convened in Dresden in connection with the Czech crisis. Rumania was not invited.

According to the communiqué of the Dresden meeting, "the determination was unanimously confirmed to carry out practical measures in the immediate future to consolidate the Warsaw Pact and its armed forces."[102] On the face of it, this suggested that the Soviet leaders had tired of trying to reach an accommodation on Pact reforms with Rumania, and had seized the opportunity presented by the latter's exclusion from the Dresden meeting to wrap up a set of reform measures more to their own liking. Precisely what "practical measures" were to be carried out in the immediate future to consolidate the Pact's command structure was left undisclosed. It might be presumed, however, that at this particular time the Soviet Union was interested in measures that would permit tighter centralized military control within the alliance and that would help Moscow to deal more effectively with any member states it might regard as prone to shirk their Pact commitments, such as Rumania and Czechoslovakia.

The fact that Czechoslovakia had been pressing privately for substantial Pact reforms along lines espoused more publicly by Rumania came into the open during the July phase of the Soviet–Czech crisis of 1968, largely as a result of disclosures by Lt. General Vaclav Prchlik, then chief of the Czechoslovak Central Committee's department of military and security affairs. In a memorable press conference on July 15, at a time when Soviet troops were still on Czech soil after a joint Warsaw Pact exercise in June, General Prchlik called for basic revision of the Warsaw Pact to insure "the real equality of the individual members of this coalition."[103] Stating that non-Soviet representatives on the Pact's joint command had been relegated to liaison roles, Prchlik said: "This is why our party presented proposals in the past for the creation of the prerequisites for the joint command to competently discharge its functions." Such prerequisites, he said, should include arrangements to permit non-Soviet representatives "to participate in the whole process of learning and deciding, in the whole command system. So far the proper conclusions have not been made."

Prchlik's remarks touched also on several other areas of needed reform:

[100] The first disclosure to this effect came from Zenon Kliszko, a secretary of the Polish Central Committee in an interview on Polish television, March 9, 1968. Cited in Stanley Riveles, "Prague, Moscow and the Warsaw Pact," *Radio Free Europe*, May 21, 1968, p. 3.

[101] Speech in Bucharest by Nicolai Ceausescu, Agerpress, April 27, 1968, cited in Riveles, "Prague, Moscow and the Warsaw Pact," p. 3.

[102] TASS, "Information Communiqué," *Pravda*, March 25, 1968.

[103] The full text of Prchlik's press conference was given in a Prague radio broadcast on July 15, 1968. For an account of the press conference, see Henry Kamm, "Czechs Demand a Basic Revision of the Warsaw Pact," *New York Times*, July 16, 1968. See also earlier discussion of the Prchlik case in chapter XIV, p. 375, and especially fn. 132.

guarantees to prevent use of the Warsaw Treaty by a group of its members against another member; strengthening of the Pact's Political Consultative Committee; reaffirmation of the principle that no Pact member has the right arbitrarily to station forces on another partner's territory; and creation of appropriate conditions for an individual state to contribute its own views on military doctrine. Most of these criticisms were endorsed in somewhat more diplomatic language the next day by the Czechoslovak Defense Minister Martin Dzur.[104]

In a harsh rejoinder to Prchlik, the Soviet press accused him of distortion and slander, refusing to concede that officers of "the Czechoslovak and other fraternal armies" had been treated as other than "equals among equals," and charging that his "irresponsible statements about the Warsaw Pact" were directed against "the interests of the socialist community."[105] Nevertheless, it is reasonable to suppose that the critical attitude toward Soviet domination of Pact arrangements that was voiced, first, by the Rumanians and later by Czech spokesmen was in some measure shared by other East European members of the alliance. At any rate, though the Czechoslovak intervention temporarily pushed the issue of reorganization into the background, it was soon to re-emerge again along with other questions bearing on the Soviet Union's future military relations with its Warsaw Pact partners.

Postinvasion Trends Affecting the Pact's Future Military Role

Before we examine the effects of the Czechoslovak experience upon Moscow's military arrangements in East Europe, it may be useful to recall that during the first few years of the Brezhnev–Kosygin regime the Soviet Union had tended to accord the East European armed forces growing weight in both peacetime and potential wartime contributions to Warsaw Pact defense. Several factors helped to account for this. First, the reliability of the East European forces, with the probable exception of Rumania, could be regarded by Moscow as reasonably good, even though there may have been some residual doubt about how the East European armies might conduct themselves under adverse circumstances. Second, the military effectiveness of the East European forces, especially those of the strategically situated Northern Tier countries, had steadily improved, and though these forces still fell somewhat short of the capabilities of the best Soviet units, they represented nevertheless a respectable share of the Warsaw bloc's theater warfare potential in Europe. Third, the Soviet Union's military dependence on the East European countries also seemed to grow gradually in keeping with the policy of closer military integration pursued since Khrushchev's day.

---

[104] General Dzur's comments in *Rude Pravo* of July 16, 1968, stressed Czechoslovakia's adherence to the Warsaw Pact, but at the same time cited various articles of the Warsaw Treaty itself to make the point that Prague's reform proposals were consonant with the purposes of the Pact. That Prague also may have been making trouble on the reform issue during the Novotny regime was suggested by an anniversary article in *Krasnaia zvezda*, May 15, 1966, in which Dzur's predecessor, General Bohumir Lomsky, stated that bloc security must be approached in a "new manner" and that individual countries of the Warsaw Pact should have "larger responsibility."

[105] "Whom Is General V. Prchlik Serving?" *Krasnaia zvezda*, July 23, 1968.

True, this dependence on the Warsaw bloc allies had in one sense been reduced by such factors as the sizable Soviet strategic missile forces trained on Western Europe from the USSR itself, forces which could serve either deterrent or war-waging functions without much regard for the belt of Warsaw Pact territory that lay in between. Other considerations, however, suggested that on balance the Soviet Union's need for the military co-operation of its Warsaw allies had tended to increase. For example, in the event of war under nuclear conditions, the difficulty of deploying large Soviet reinforcements from the USSR would place a premium on having effective Warsaw Pact forces already in position close to the arena of European conflict. In the event of non-nuclear hostilities, large East European forces trained and equipped to supplement Soviet conventional theater capabilities also would be a valuable asset, the more so if renewed doctrinal speculation on the possibility of conventional operations of substantial scale should prove right.

Even in the more likely event that no major East–West military conflict broke out in Europe, there were other things to be said for a Soviet policy of greater military dependence on the East European members of the Warsaw Pact. For example, the presence of competent and reliable allied forces in East Europe could give the Soviet Union considerable flexibility in managing local crises where it might wish to avoid direct involvement of its own military power. Or, should the Soviet Union find it expedient to withdraw some of its troops from East Europe in connection with new collective security and arms control arrangements, the existence of viable East European armed forces again would serve as a useful prop for Soviet policy. Finally, close military co-operation with East Europe could prove an important symbolic, if not a direct military, asset for Moscow in any confrontation with Maoist China which might arise.

From the early part of 1968, however, developments in East Europe began to call into question many of the assumptions underlying a Soviet policy of placing greater reliance on the East European armed forces. In particular, the turn of events in Czechoslovakia ran increasingly counter to Moscow's hopes of improving the military cohesion of the Warsaw alliance by bringing the Northern Tier countries into tighter association with the Soviet Union. Although in March 1968 Czechoslovakia went along in principle with the findings of the Dresden meeting and disavowed any intention of cutting back her Warsaw Pact commitments, the Dubcek regime's policies offered little promise that the country was prepared to accept more binding military and political links with its Northern Tier neighbors. On the contrary, the more independent direction in which Czechoslovakia appeared to be moving threatened to undermine even the existing military arrangements in the Northern Tier.

From a strategic standpoint, Czechoslovakia occupied perhaps a slightly less critical position in the Northern Tier area than did either East Germany, where the lodgment of Soviet military power was vital to the Soviet Union's security and political interest in maintaining a divided Germany, or Poland, through which passed the Soviet line of communications with the German Democratic

Republic. Nevertheless, the forward location of Czechoslovakia, and particularly the possibility of losing military access to her territory, doubtless influenced Moscow's decision to intervene in August 1968.[106]

Should Principle of Integrated Forces Be Scrapped?

If, in an immediate sense, the intervention enabled the Soviet Union to plug a potential breach in the Northern Tier by introducing substantial forces into Czechoslovakia, it could hardly have failed to raise anew some fundamental questions concerning Soviet military relations with the other Warsaw bloc countries, including the extent to which the Soviet Union would henceforth be able to count upon the military contributions of the East European members of the Pact. In one form or another, perhaps the central military policy issue for Moscow was whether to continue in the direction of integrated forces and closer multilateral co-operation with the other Warsaw alliance members or to scrap this principle in favor of other military arrangements in East Europe, possibly outside the framework of the Warsaw Pact.

A number of considerations suggested that the Soviet Union was likely to pursue the first alternative, continuing its efforts to improve the military potential of the East European armed forces and their capacity for joint action. Militarily, the doubtful status of Czechoslovakia's forces gave added significance to those of neighboring East European countries as a supplement to Soviet conventional theater capabilities. Soviet access to East European territory was still required, for the same military reasons as before: to provide a defensive cushion against any armed incursion from the West and to put Soviet forces in a position to launch offensive operations against Western Europe on short notice, should such a move ever seem necessary. This requirement, too, would be served by a policy of close military co-operation within the bloc. Moreover, the disciplinary action against Czechoslovakia did not necessarily mean that the basis for collaborative military planning and preparation within the Warsaw Pact had been irreparably damaged. Leaving aside the armed forces of Czechoslovakia and Rumania, the other East European forces still were ostensibly amenable to Soviet direction; indeed, their co-operative role in the invasion may have enhanced their apparent reliability and given Moscow cause to feel that the East European military elites remained favorably oriented toward the Soviet Union despite the Czechoslovak episode.[107]

On the other hand, it was quite obvious that Moscow's co-operative allies had been useful mainly to provide window dressing, and that Soviet military

---

[106] See chapter XV, pp. 390–91, 415.

[107] It is a controversial point whether the military elites of the East European countries were generally sympathetic to the Soviet action in Czechoslovakia, or whether they regarded it as an affront to national sovereignty. This writer would tend to assume the latter, but also would note that, in the view of such close observers of East European affairs as J. F. Brown, the senior officer corps in most of these countries had exhibited more solidarity with their counterparts in the Soviet Union than perhaps any other professional group in East European societies except the secret police. If so, it may well be that there was less censure of the Soviet Union among East European military elites than customarily assumed.

power was the reality which counted in the disciplinary action against Czechoslovakia. To Soviet troops, moreover, had fallen the task of reinforcing the sector of Warsaw Pact defenses thinned by the temporary neutralization of Czechoslovakia's armed forces. As for the reliability of the East European armies in general, and of the Czechoslovak national forces in particular, some question concerning their wholehearted dedication to Soviet interests must certainly have crossed a few minds in Moscow. It might, therefore, be supposed that in some Soviet quarters there were second thoughts about going ahead with a policy of greater dependence on the collective contributions of the East European Pact forces. The Czechoslovak experience, for example, may have fortified sentiment within the Soviet defense hierarchy in favor of giving forthright priority in planning and resources to the Soviet Union's own theater forces. If so, there was a ready-made argument at hand that the requirement for forward deployment of Soviet forces in vital areas of East and Central Europe could be met through the bilateral defense treaties which had been renegotiated with various Pact members in 1967,[108] without further diversion of effort and resources to the multilateral Warsaw Pact organization, which in any real military emergency would at best serve only as a façade for essentially autonomous Soviet action.

But even though on purely military grounds the Soviet Union might get along without serious inconvenience if it were to de-emphasize the multilateral contributions of the East European Pact members, this course entailed other drawbacks. It would, for example, call for an increase in expenditures for the Soviet theater forces and would undercut the argument for having the other Pact partners share more of the economic burden of collective bloc defense. Above all, the question remained whether Moscow could find an acceptable institutional substitute for the political-integrative and policing functions of the Pact, which obviously were still of acute interest to the Soviet Union in the wake of the Czechoslovak experience. A few signs appeared in the fall of 1968 that, at the urging of East German leaders, the Soviet Union might be toying with the idea of a new, selective grouping in East Europe that would in effect relegate Rumania and Czechoslovakia to secondary status within the Warsaw Pact.[109] Such a grouping of Moscow's hard-core supporters could be envisaged as the organizational instrument to accompany the Brezhnev doctrine of inter-

---

[108] As pointed out earlier (see chapter XIV, p. 350), one purpose of the renewal of the Soviet Union's bilateral defense treaties with the various East European Countries in 1967 may have been to prepare a fallback position under which the Soviet Union would retain the right to keep a strong military presence in the region in the event that the Warsaw Pact arrangements, for one reason or another, were altered. For an argument that Soviet preferences from a military viewpoint alone had long run to the system of bilateral defense arrangements, see Bela K. Kiraly, "Why the Soviets Need the Warsaw Pact," *East Europe* (April 1969): 11.

[109] According to Walter Ulbricht and other East German leaders, the idea of a new organizational grouping giving selective status to the Soviet Union and its four hard-corps supporters within the Pact was explored immediately after the Czech invasion. GDR statements also indicated—without Soviet corroboration—that Moscow and Pankow were to have the guiding role in such a grouping. See David Binder, "Soviet Is Seeking New Red Grouping," *New York Times*, October 31, 1968. See also chapter XV, p. 394.

vention in a "socialist commonwealth" with no institutional form of its own, whose perimeters would be both defined and defended primarily by the Soviet Union.

However, the Soviet leadership gave no indication that it was seriously prepared either to take up the East German suggestion for a restructuring of the Pact along more selective lines or to fall back upon a strictly bilateral pattern of military relationships in East Europe, either of which alternatives would put further strain upon the already damaged fabric of bloc unity. Rather, by early 1969, Moscow appeared again to be looking mainly toward the multilateral machinery of the Warsaw Pact (and of CEMA[110]) as a basic means of exercising its control in East Europe and restoring unity within the alliance system. Toward this end, the Soviet Union seemed prepared to accept organizational reforms in the Warsaw Pact which, on the surface at least, would give the East European members a larger role in the management of joint military activities. This became evident at the Warsaw Pact political consultative session in Budapest on March 17, 1969, the first full meeting of the Pact's top political and military leaders since the Czechoslovak intervention seven months before.

Organizational Reforms and Moscow's Call for Bloc Solidarity against China

The Budapest meeting, notable for an unsuccessful Soviet attempt to rally Warsaw bloc support against China as well as for the attention given to organizational reforms, saw the adoption of new measures to "further perfect the structure and command bodies" of the Warsaw Treaty Organization. These measures consisted of the formal establishment of a Committee of Defense Ministers, and of a Military Council of the joint armed forces; the setting up of a more integrated joint staff structure; the creation of a joint committee to co-ordinate weapons development; and a new provision for appointing a national deputy to the Soviet commander in each country in which Soviet troops were stationed.[111] Although the organizational changes adopted at Budapest could be interpreted primarily as Soviet concessions to Rumania and other Pact

---

[110] The post-Czechoslovak revival of Soviet efforts to promote closer integration of the Warsaw bloc through the Council for Economic Mutual Assistance was heralded by Brezhnev in a November 1968 speech in Poland, where he announced that a CEMA summit meeting would soon take place for the purpose of "strengthening" the organization. A session of the CEMA Council in East Berlin on January 21–22, 1969, apparently failed to produce much enthusiasm for tighter economic integration from most of the East European countries, including, surprisingly enough, the GDR. However, Soviet and Polish propaganda continued to push the idea prior to the opening of the CEMA summit meeting in Moscow on April 23, 1969. See *Pravda*, November 12, 1968; Tad Szulc, "Soviet Economic Bloc Stalled by Two Key Problems," *New York Times*, February 2, 1969; I. Ikonnikov, "CEMA's Role in Cooperation Between the Socialist Countries," *International Affairs*, no. 4 (April 1969): 65–70; "On the Opening of the Session of the Council of Economic Mutual Assistance," *Pravda*, April 24, 1969.

[111] The brief official communiqué ,of the Budapest meeting (*Pravda*, March 18, 1969) was vague as to the details of these organizational changes, but further information later became available in accounts circulated by some of the participants and in statements by Soviet officials, including General Shtemenko and Marshal Grechko. Perhaps the most significant effect of the changes was to remove each national defense minister from direct subordination to the Soviet commander of the Pact, as called for in the original Pact statutes, and to provide a senior national commander in charge of his country's Pact forces who was to be accountable both to his own

members for a more meaningful voice in joint activities rather than as steps permitting the USSR to tighten its control over the national armed forces of the East European countries, their practical effect might be to satisfy the Soviets more than the Rumanians. By drawing Rumania into participation in various joint bodies, for example, Moscow could make it more difficult for the Rumanians to maintain independent positions against a presumed majority of Soviet supporters. The hint in Communist commentary on the Budapest meeting that the price of more equal participation in Pact activities would include taking on a larger proportionate share of the joint expenses also suggested that perhaps the Soviet Union salvaged more from its concessions to the Rumanian viewpoint than met the eye.[112]

Subsequent to the Budapest consultative session, several meetings of the new "directing bodies" of the Warsaw Pact forces took place amidst publicity stressing that they conformed to "the new statute on the joint armed forces and the joint command" adopted in March 1969.[113] A further statement calling attention to the implementation of the Budapest reforms and emphasizing their contribution to the "collective" defense might of the "socialist military coalition" appeared in January 1970 over the signature of General Shtemenko, chief of staff of the Warsaw Pact forces.[114] Despite such efforts to suggest that the Budapest reforms had reconciled national interests with collective defense and produced a "common viewpoint" on military policy, the ever-troublesome Rumanians again entered their reservations. In an apparent response to the Shtemenko article, Ceausescu delivered a speech on February 5, 1970, in which he coupled assurance that Rumania would observe the "spirit of the Budapest agreements" with a declaration that only Rumanian officials "can give orders to our army."[115]

In thus reasserting Rumania's right to autonomous military decisions, Ceausescu was taking a stand which seemed to rule out the use of his country's forces in any conflict involving Soviet action against another socialist country such as Yugoslavia or China. This issue had arisen at the Budapest meeting in March 1969, where Rumania not only blocked a Soviet move to obtain Pact condemnation of China as the aggressor in the Ussuri incident but also reportedly opposed an appeal from Brezhnev that each member country send "sym-

defense minister and to the Soviet Pact commander. Neither the precise functions nor the membership of the new "Military Council of the joint armed forces" were specified, although it was mentioned that Marshal Iakubovskii, the Pact commander, chairs this body. See "On the Joint Armed Forces of the Warsaw Treaty States," *Krasnaia zvezda*, December 11, 1969; Marshal A. A. Grechko, "Born in Battles," *Pravda*, February 23, 1970.

[112] See account by Anatole Shub, *Washington Post*, March 18, 1969.

[113] One of these meetings was a five-day conference of Pact military officials in Prague in November 1969, which overlapped with a foreign ministers meeting. It was chaired by Marshal Iakubovskii, the Warsaw Pact commander. Another was the first publicly announced meeting of the new Committee of Defense Ministers in Moscow, December 22–23, 1969. *Krasnaia zvezda*, November 4, December 24, 1969.

[114] General of the Army S. Shtemenko, "Combat Brotherhood," *Krasnaia zvezda*, January 24, 1970. This article was at first interpreted by some Western observers to mean that new organizational steps were being taken beyond those adopted in March 1969, but subsequent Soviet commentary indicated that Shtemenko was not breaking new ground. See Colonel A. Leont'ev, "Story of a 'Canard'," *Krasnaia zvezda*, February 5, 1970.

[115] Speech to Rumanian armed forces cadres by Nicolae Ceausescu, *Scinteia*, February 6, 1970.

bolic military detachments" to the Sino–Soviet border area to demonstrate
Warsaw bloc backing of the Soviet Union.[116] Brezhnev's call for such support
presumably fell by the wayside because the East European delegations were
reluctant to override Rumanian objections that the Warsaw Pact was a Euro-
pean-oriented alliance with no charter to interfere in relations between the
Soviet Union and China.[117]

The Budapest meeting and various developments growing out of it in 1969
and early 1970 seemed to have several important implications for future Soviet
military relations with East Europe. For one thing, even though the Czechoslovak episode had made clear once more the Soviet Union's authoritative role
in the Warsaw alliance, it was apparent that Moscow meant to hold fast to the
multilateral principle in Warsaw bloc military affairs. Second, the Soviet
Union had demonstrated a willingness to make some concessions to national
sentiments through organizational reforms, even though the actual latitude
allowed the East Europeans might prove to be less than the rhetoric suggested.
Third, despite renewed emphasis on "proletarian internationalism" and a
"common viewpoint" among members of the Warsaw Pact,[118] it was obvious
that some members, particularly the Rumanians, were still out of step with
Moscow on certain issues.

Not the least of these was the question of engaging the Warsaw Pact in the
Soviet Union's quarrel with China. Although the Budapest meeting had rebuffed Brezhnev's appeal for backing against China, there were occasional
rumors later in 1969 that the Russians had succeeded in persuading at least the
Poles and Bulgarians to send "symbolic" air detachments for maneuvers along
the Sino–Soviet border.[119] All of this suggested, in turn, that the need for a show
of Warsaw bloc solidarity against China had become a factor of some consequence in Moscow's shaping of its Warsaw Pact military policy. Should the
Soviet Union persist in efforts to enlist East European military co-operation
against Peking, even on a symbolic basis, this would amount to a significant
shift in the original conception of the Warsaw Pact, widening its scope from
an alliance facing westward against the NATO countries to one that also
faced eastward against another major Communist power.

[116] See Anatole Shub, "Rumania Thwarts Soviets" and "Chinese Threat Obsesses Table-
Pounding Brezhnev," *Washington Post*, March 18 and 19, 1969; "Red Bloc Chiefs Meet for First
Time Since Invasion of Czechoslovakia," *New York Times*, March 18, 1969.

[117] See article entitled "Blitz Conference" by Miodrag Marovic in the Belgrade weekly *Nin*,
March 23, 1969, as translated by Slobodan Stankovic, *Radio Free Europe*, March 25, 1969.

[118] See, for example, Karpenko and Gavrilov in *Kommunist Vooruzhennykh Sil*, no. 16
(August 1969); Shtemenko in *Krasnaia zvezda*, January 24, 1970.

[119] "Sinkiang: Where It Could Happen," *Economist*, September 20, 1969, p. 36. Although these
rumors remained unconfirmed, an indication that Poland might have responded to Soviet requests
for co-operation against China was given by Polish Defense Minister Jaruzelski during a visit to the
USSR, in April 1969. In a speech at Volgograd, he noted that in view of "the anti-Soviet madness
of Mao Tse-tung's group," each "fraternal socialist state" should make its own contribution to
"the arsenal of political weapons and armaments which consolidate our combined strength." See
"Polish Soldiers Are Ready to Perform Their Duty of Defending the Security of the Peoples and
the Cause of Peace and Socialism," *Zolnierz Wolnosci*, Warsaw, April 23, 1969.

XVIII

SOVIET POLICY AND A CHANGING POWER BALANCE

In previous chapters of this study of Soviet power and purpose in Europe, we deferred discussion of a number of questions relating to the changing military balance between the Soviet Union and the United States and to its effects upon both the European and the wider, global aspects of the relationship between the two countries.[1] We take up these matters in this concluding chapter.

Trends in Soviet military policy and programs under the Brezhnev–Kosygin regime up to early 1970 contributed, as we have seen, to a perceptible shift in the Soviet–American strategic balance—a shift which could perhaps best be regarded as part of a larger historical process, still underway, marking the Soviet Union's emergence as one of the world's two global superpowers. Needless to say, though its ultimate effects upon world politics were scarely predictable, the narrowing of the margin between Soviet and American power promised to have significant implications for the future. It not only gave "new bite"—to use Carl Kaysen's apt expression—to the immediate question of whether the United States was losing its long-held strategic superiority over the Soviet Union,[2] but it also raised other far-reaching questions concerning such matters as the course of the global competition between the superpowers, the stability of mutual deterrence, and the conduct of the Soviet Union on the international scene in the decade ahead.

Before we venture into some of the implications of a changing power balance, however, several considerations bearing upon the future strategic power relationship between the Soviet Union and the United States merit attention. First, an admonition should be sounded concerning the contingent and precarious nature of today's assumptions about tomorrow's military balance. The precise character of any new correlation of forces that may emerge in the coming decade is unpredictable. It will depend in part upon what the United States chooses to do about its own defense posture and in part upon the willingness of the Soviet leaders to raise the ante still further and the capacity of their economy to stand the strain. Our inability to say what sort of strategic posture will satisfy the Soviet leaders is another source of uncertainty: Is their aim "parity" with the United States or "superiority" for the Soviet Union? And, obviously, any arms limitation agreements that may be reached in the strategic arms talks or other negotiations also will help to determine the emerging Soviet–American strategic balance.

Even the measurement of the strategic power relationship in terms of "parity"

---

[1] See in particular chapter XI, p. 264, and chapter XVI, pp. 431, 437, 440–41.
[2] Carl Kaysen, "Keeping the Strategic Balance," *Foreign Affairs* (July 1968): 669.

or "superiority," one must emphasize, is in itself an exercise fraught with ambiguity. These are elusive concepts, and the mere arithmetic of totting up the forces on each side does little to clarify the relative balance.[3] Indeed, controversy has flourished over how to identify the level at which it becomes militarily—or, for that matter, politically—meaningless to exceed a major nuclear adversary in numbers of weapons, megatonnage, deliverable warheads, and other attributes of strategic forces.[4] It was perhaps the need to find a less controversial concept that brought into vogue the term "sufficiency," used by President Nixon at a press conference in early 1969, and again in his February 1970 foreign policy report, to describe an appropriate level of strategic arms.[5]

Nevertheless, difficult though it may be to define what would constitute a meaningful shift in the power balance, it remains evident that the Soviet Union under the Brezhnev–Kosygin regime dedicated a substantial and costly effort in the 1965–70 period to improving its relative power position vis-à-vis the United States. Among the pivotal questions to be asked, therefore, as the Soviet Union and the United States entered the Vienna round of their strategic arms talks in the spring of 1970,[6] were these: Would the Soviet leaders prove to be essentially

[3] For a caustic view of the inadequacy of the "numbers game" in appraising relative strategic forces, see Leonard Beaton, "Recounting the Missiles," *Times,* London, November 1, 1968. Though a satisfactory formula for describing parity and superiority may be lacking, there are some definitions which avoid simple numerical comparisons. For example, parity may be defined as mutual possession of "assured destruction"; superiority as the capacity to inflict assured destruction upon an enemy while denying the same capacity to him through such "damage-limiting" means as active defense and/or a first strike. Even so, such a definition probably raises more questions than it answers.

[4] The literature on this question in the United States is very extensive. For an example of the controversy prompted by trying to define the elements of strategic superiority, see *New York Times,* July 12, 1967, for a study by the American Security Council sponsored by the House Armed Services Committee, together with an answering statement by the Department of Defense. For a later expression of the view that criteria of relative strategic "advantage" have become largely irrelevant in the case of the two superpowers, see McGeorge Bundy, "To Cap the Volcano," *Foreign Affairs* (October 1969): especially pp. 3–14. On the Soviet side, there has been far less tendency to debate the issue of strategic criteria or to question publicly the long-standing shibboleth that for the Soviet Union quantitative and qualitative superiority would be a good thing. However, an occasional Soviet writer, such as Gennady Gerasimov, has said that among major nuclear powers "superiority has become a concept which has no bearing on war." The anonymous Soviet author of a *Pravda* editorial in early 1970 also ventured the view that it was "unrealistic" for the West to count on victory in a nuclear war through attainment of strategic superiority. See Gerasimov, "Pentagonia, 1966," *International Affairs,* no. 5 (Moscow: May, 1966): 28; also his letter on the same subject, "A Russian Replies," *Washington Star,* July 16, 1968; Observer, "A Serious Problem," *Pravda,* March 7, 1970.

[5] See "Transcript of the President's News Conference on Foreign and Domestic Affairs," *New York Times,* January 28, 1969; "United States Foreign Policy for the 1970's: A New Strategy for Peace," as published in ibid., February 19, 1970, p. 24M. Prior advocacy of the notion of "sufficiency" in preference to "parity" or "superiority" was advanced by Professor George W. Rathjens in his pamphlet *The Future of the Strategic Arms Race: Options for the 1970's* (New York: Carnegie Endowment for International Peace, 1969), p. 10. Initial Soviet comment on President Nixon's "sufficiency" formula generally treated it as a step in the right direction, though one commentator, D. Kraminov, in *Za rubezhom* (Life Abroad), no. 6, February 7–13, 1969, said that it merely allowed the generals to decide the extent to which nuclear weapons are "insufficient or sufficient for defense needs."

[6] Unlike the first exploratory round of SALT talks at Helsinki, which had consisted mainly of feeling out the attitudes of each side (see chapter XI, p. 277), the second round beginning in Vienna on April 16, 1970, was expected to bring negotiation on substantive issues.

content to rest on the strategic gains they had made in five years of strenuous effort, or were they disposed to press actively for a still more favorable power position? And how, in any event, might the strategic arms limitation talks fit into the picture of Soviet policy?

Soviet Strategic Aims and the Arms Talks

Although categorical answers were hardly possible, one might identify three separate sets of views as to the aims of the Soviet strategic build-up and its relationship to the SALT talks. The first tended to explain Soviet strategic policy primarily in terms of a catch-up effort oriented toward stabilizing the strategic balance at a level of parity with the United States. The second saw the Soviet Union aiming more or less purposefully toward attainment of strategic superiority, in accordance with a long-term strategic plan. The third ruled out neither lasting Soviet acceptance of strategic equality nor a bid for military-technical superiority; however, in this view, which was somewhat more elastic than the others, it was assumed that the Brezhnev–Kosygin regime had entered the SALT negotiations to "hold and explore" without having settled upon any fixed strategic objective. Let us examine briefly each of these explanations.

View A—Stability through Parity

Holding that the principal impulse behind the Soviet strategic build-up was simply a desire to catch up with the United States, this explanation found many adherents among those once persuaded that the Soviet Union was reconciled to living indefinitely in a status of strategic inferiority, counting upon a "minimum deterrent" posture to restrain the United States and maintain stability. According to this view, the traumatic Cuban missile crisis had a great deal to do with convincing the Soviet leadership that stability must rest on strategic equality; any past stability based on US predominance not only was politically undesirable to Moscow but strategically precarious, since the United States could always threaten to upset it. With regard to internal alignments within the Soviet leadership on strategic policy, it was granted that real differences had arisen from time to time, especially between "stabilizers," whose chief spokesman was reputed to be Kosygin, and various party hard-liners backed by the military. However, by the time the first SALT talks began in late 1969, a working consensus had come to prevail within the leadership, according to View A, with the stabilizers tending to be dominant in shaping Soviet policy.

Economic considerations were credited with having played an important part in persuading the Soviet leaders to settle for a situation of approximate strategic parity with the United States. The main economic argument was that growth investment needs, satisfaction of rising consumer demands, the need for technological innovation in nondefense industrial sectors, and other claims on Soviet resources were such that the Soviet Union would be hard put to it to meet an additional major round of strategic arms procurement.[7] The necessity

[7] Signs of a slowdown in the rate of industrial growth in both 1968 and 1969 (see chapter XI, p. 246) lent some support to the argument that the Soviet economy was hurting from the large

to fix the parameters for the next Five-Year Plan (1971–75) also was held to be a compelling reason for stabilizing the strategic competition. Still another economic argument rested on the assumption that within the Soviet military establishment itself, pressure groups for nonstrategic forces were interested in capturing more defense resources for their purposes,[8] and therefore would be amenable to parity with the United States on the strategic level.

Politically, the leading argument in support of View A was that the Soviet leaders would find a climate of acknowledged parity favorable to the pursuit of many of their more important foreign policy objectives, while at the same time they could avoid new uncertainties stemming from unrestricted strategic competition which might impair mutual deterrence and give the arms race a steep upward boost. Besides the general satisfaction of being able to deal with the United States as a strategic equal, the Soviet leaders could expect a parity situation to provide several attractive political opportunities.

In Europe, for example, the effect of parity might be to undermine the remaining European faith in America's pledges to defend Europe even at the risk of nuclear war. Possible dividends from such doubt about the US commitment could include a weakening of NATO and increased West European receptiveness to Soviet collective security proposals aimed at sealing the division of Germany. By achieving a stable equilibrium at the strategic level, the Kremlin might also hope to reap greater political returns from its conventional military power outside Europe, especially by gaining more freedom of action to deal with the China problem.

How actively the Soviet Union might seek to operate in the Third World against the backdrop of a stable Soviet–American strategic relationship was left a moot question by the expositors of View A. Some saw the Soviet leadership tending toward recognition of a duopoly situation, possibly based on a tacit "spheres-of-influence" understanding, with political give-and-take between the two powers being kept within reasonable bounds. Others saw the possibility of more active Soviet support of "national liberation" movements in the Third World, with the Soviet leadership acting on the assumption that Washington was likely to be reluctant to intervene militarily against such movements without the backing of a superior strategic posture to deter Soviet countermoves.

The thesis that the Soviet leaders, after five years of effort to catch up, were ready and willing to rest on their strategic oars, involved two further political suppositions. The first was that the Kremlin leadership probably entertained considerable doubt—born of past experience with American response to bomber and missile "gap" situations—that any margin of superiority attainable by the Soviet Union would last long enough to yield political gains significantly greater than those to be derived from a parity position. The second was that

---

military programs of the Brezhnev–Kosygin regime. Slippage of previously planned investment for long-term economic growth in both nondefense industry and agriculture was similarly regarded as an adverse effect of high military priorities.

[8] Among the purposes competitive with a larger strategic force build-up were improvement of Soviet capabilities for naval and conventional operations in distant areas, and bolstering of the posture of the ground-air theater forces in a continental environment complicated by the Czechoslovak problem in Europe and difficulties with China in the Asian borderlands.

.

even if the Soviet leaders happened to believe that a lasting reversal of the strategic balance was within reach, they probably had learned their lesson from the experience of the United States itself, which, despite its long period of strategic superiority, had not managed to extract vital political concessions from the Soviet Union. In weighing the costs of striving for superiority, might not the Soviet leaders ask themselves whether they could expect to do better?

The SALT talks, in View *A*, thus came at a time when majority sentiment within the Soviet leadership was "ripe" for reaching genuine agreements with the United States on strategic arms limitations. Not only were the Kremlin leaders thought to feel that nothing significant could be gained from a new cycle of strategic competition, but for the economic and political reasons noted above—plus fear that US response to a further unilateral build-up might cancel out the relative improvement of their position already attained—they were presumed to welcome the opportunity provided by the next round of SALT talks to stabilize the strategic balance at a parity level.

View B—Purposeful Pursuit of Superiority

This variant view of Soviet strategic aims rested for some time mainly on two grounds: technological and doctrinal. As regards the first, it could be noted that the Soviet Union under both Khrushchev and his successors had chosen to undertake an expanding research and development effort in the strategic field, marked by the orderly phasing of successive generations of offensive systems and parallel development of defensive systems. The systematic nature of these programs, paced according to the growth of basic technology over an extended period, seemed consonant with an over-all process of strategic planning aimed at eventual superiority. In a doctrinal context, proponents of this view could point both to general Communist doctrine on the "historically inevitable" superiority of the Communist system over other socio-political-economic systems, and to a Soviet military doctrine calling for qualitative and quantitative superiority in military power, as evidence that the concept of superiority stood high in Soviet thinking, even though its attainment had been regularly thwarted by stubborn realities. However, so long as the goal of superiority appeared to remain largely in the realm of doctrinal commitment, it could be written off as rhetoric without serious content.

The Soviet strategic build-up of the 1965–70 period tended, of course, to put a good deal more substance into the rhetoric. It could now be argued, for example, that the Brezhnev–Kosygin regime, having finally managed to draw close to the Soviet Union's major adversary in most elements of strategic power, was likely to have sensed an opportunity to forge ahead of the United States, particularly since the latter—unlike its previous responses to strategic gap alarms—had stood by during the rapid Soviet strategic build-up of the late sixties without lifting the fixed ceiling it had set for its own strategic forces in the early sixties.[9] Indeed, evidence that the USSR's missile expansion programs

[9] Early in the Kennedy administration, the United States set ceilings for its strategic delivery forces (around 1,050 land-based ICBMs, 650 Polaris SLBMs, and 600–700 heavy bombers); these levels, which had been substantially attained by the end of 1965, were not increased as evidence

were continuing unabated in early 1970, after having passed a previously assumed leveling-off point,[10] together with the fact that Soviet development of
follow-on strategic systems showed no signs of slackening, served to buttress
the view that the strategic build-up had gathered a momentum which the
Kremlin leadership, or at least its hard-line elements, were loath to check before
seeing whether it would in fact bring the Soviet Union a clear margin of
superiority over the United States. As seen by the proponents of View B, incidentally, there was little cleavage within the Soviet leadership over strategic
policy, at least not after authoritative decisions to go ahead with the strategic
build-up had been taken.

In the economic field, although conceding that competing claims upon resources continued to represent a vexing problem and that the Soviet leaders
probably were averse to allowing military allocations to increase faster than the
economic growth rate, it was held that economic constraints upon Soviet
strategic competition with the United States were less compelling than formerly
for at least two reasons: first, because Soviet industrial output, despite a slight
decline in growth rate, was still increasing at a respectable rate of about 7 per
cent annually; and second, because the United States itself—beset with meeting
domestic economic needs, the costs of the Vietnam war, and a rising tide of
anti-military criticism at home[11]—appeared reluctant to restore its own strategic
arms expenditures to the levels it had been willing to accept in the past.[12]

In considering the political incentives behind the Soviet strategic build-up,

---

became available that a rapid Soviet strategic build-up was underway. The basic US rationale
evidently was that a stable strategic posture held at the long-established levels was preferable to an
upward response that could stimulate a new round in the strategic arms race. The Soviet Union
apparently attributed the leveling off in the US strategic force effort primarily to the increased
defense burden of the Vietnam war. With respect to budgetary effort, US spending for strategic
forces was at the level of about $11 billion in 1962, declined to about half that amount by 1966,
and began to climb back up to about $9 billion in 1968 and $9.6 billion in 1969. This rise reflected
mainly an expanded R&D effort and not an increase in the established force levels.

[10] In remarks to the Aviation-Space Writers' Association on May 12, 1969, Dr. John S. Foster,
Jr., the Pentagon's Director of Defense Research and Engineering, stated that Soviet missile
deployment was "moving even faster than anticipated and . . . having passed the assumed leveling-
off point, their expansion programs are continuing unabated." This, according to Dr. Foster, had
given the American intelligence community reason to "doubt most seriously" its earlier assumption
that the Soviet Union was merely trying to draw even with the United States in ICBMs. Secretary
of Defense Melvin R. Laird similarly noted in early 1970 that it had been necessary to revise
intelligence projections "upward in each of the past five years." See *New York Times*, May 13,
1969; *Statement by Secretary of Defense Melvin R. Laird Before a Joint Session of the Senate
Armed Services and Appropriations Committees: Fiscal Year 1971 Defense Program and Budget,
February 20, 1970* (Washington, D.C.: Government Printing Office, 1970), p. 34.

[11] For a Soviet expression of the view that internal pressures in the United States and the
Vietnam war had demonstrated that the American economy could no longer provide "guns and
butter simultaneously," see the review article by Georgii Arbatov, director of the new American
Institute of the USSR Academy of Sciences, "Complex Problems, Difficult Solutions," *Izvestiia*,
January 11, 1969. See also his lead article in the Institute's journal, *USA—Economics, Politics,
Ideology*, no. 1 (January 1970), 21–34.

[12] Supporters of the view that the Soviet Union was more willing to raise the strategic ante than
Washington could cite estimates—as given in speeches by Secretary Laird on February 25 and
August 26, 1969—that Soviet expenditures for strategic arms were running twice as high in
1968–69 as those of the United States.

adherents of this view tended to cite some of the same foreign policy objectives as those posited in View *A,* such as weakening NATO's ties with the United States and decoupling the US strategic deterrent regionally from areas like Europe and the Middle East. However, according to this interpretation Moscow would feel more confident of achieving such objectives in a setting of recognizable Soviet superiority than in one of mere parity. With occasional exceptions, those espousing View *B* stopped short of asserting that the Soviet leaders might expect to achieve a strategic posture so predominant that it would permit the Soviet Union to initiate war with impunity; rather, it was argued that they might have set their sights on reaching a position in which they could approach any crisis confrontations with the United States confident that the latter would swallow diplomatic defeat rather than risk a military showdown. The Soviet Union's need to calculate its strategic requirements in terms of an emerging nuclear rival in China, as well as with an eye to America, was another probable incentive for aiming at something more than parity with the United States.

In so far as the Soviet leaders might be interested in "stability" as an end-product of their strategic policy, it was argued that their prime interest lay in creating an environment in which their own power sphere would remain inviolate to destabilizing influences from without, while they were free to encroach upon the political preserve of others. A Soviet quest of superiority would contribute toward this end, according to View *B,* but it would not necessarily mean that the Soviet leaders were bent on throwing caution to the winds; in fact, the men in the Kremlin might feel as fully qualified to exercise "responsible" political custody over strategic superiority as any group of Western leaders had ever been.

In expressing skepticism about the Soviet Union's readiness to accept strategic parity on a permanent basis, proponents of View *B* held that the Soviet leaders not only continued to see potential political advantages in superiority, but that they still saw important military reasons for superiority also. Chief among these was the desire to hedge against the possibility that deterrence might fail. In such an event, Soviet doctrine called for having offensive and defensive forces, including civil defense, capable of ensuring "victory" over the enemy and permitting survival of Soviet society in any nuclear war that might occur. Because the Soviet strategic build-up reflected a systematic effort to acquire forces to fit this doctrine,[13] it thus indicated that the Soviets were practicing what they preached.

[13] Although the analysis of the Soviet strategic posture upon which this view rested cannot be reconstructed in detail here, some of its salient points were as follows: Soviet strategic delivery forces were configured for both "counterforce" and "countervalue" attacks, and were in the process of acquiring greater capability for attacks upon hard targets (primarily by means of the SS-9 ICBM) to match their already potent capability against soft targets. These attributes of the Soviet strategic offensive forces—together with hardening and concealment measures to protect the delivery forces and both active and passive (civil) defenses to limit damage to the country itself and its national control center in Moscow—all were in keeping with a doctrine of preparing the Soviet Union to fight and survive a nuclear war in which either side might strike the first blow. For a study which makes these points in greater detail, see William T. Lee, *Rationale Underlying Soviet Strategic Forces* (Menlo Park, Calif.: Stanford Research Institute, June 1969).

The Soviet attitude toward the SALT talks, according to View *B*, was conditioned by the same political and military incentives which lay behind the strategic build-up. In this view, the Soviet Union was not prepared to settle for a lasting strategic and political standoff with the United States when it agreed to enter the talks; therefore, any professed Soviet interest in a stabilizing agreement via the SALT negotiations was to be seen primarily as a holding stratagem, designed to inhibit new US programs while the Soviet Union pursued a further technological effort intended to produce conditions for a breakthrough to superiority.[14] The growth of antimilitary and anti-arms-race trends in the United States was, in this view, a bonus factor upon which the Soviet Union would attempt to capitalize through the SALT talks in order to make the most of a "historical opportunity" to gain a major strategic advantage over its principal Western adversary.[15]

View C—Mixed Motives: No Fixed Blueprint

This view might best be described as the refuge of those who were not prepared to accept either View *A* or View *B* as a binding explanation of Soviet strategic aims and interests in the SALT talks, but who could find elements of plausibility in both. The basic premise of this view was that the Soviet leaders probably embarked upon the strategic build-up without a fixed blueprint for the future and without having settled among themselves precisely what sort of strategic relationship with the United States would prove satisfactory to future Soviet policy needs. Rather, a broad spectrum of preferences might be found within the leadership, probably all starting from the proposition that nothing less than Soviet-American strategic equality would be acceptable any longer. Some segments of the leadership, for example, may have preferred to seek a stable and low-cost strategic relationship with the United States in order to channel resources to domestic purposes; others perhaps deemed it desirable to peg parity at a high level in order to sustain a duopoly of power in interna-

---

[14] This argument implied that the Soviet leaders were relatively confident that the Soviet Union could escape early and unequivocal detection if it chose to make major unannounced changes in its strategic posture. Whether this could actually be done without detection is a moot question, though it is generally conceded that new technology would complicate the task of keeping track of Soviet strategic programs. Some programs, such as the installation of missile silos, the building of ABM sites, and the construction of missile-launching submarines, doubtless would be difficult to conceal, but others, such as deployment of mobile missiles and refitting of emplaced missiles with multiple warheads, could well escape detection for a rather long time. For comment on this subject, see Rathjens, *The Future of the Strategic Arms Race*, pp. 28, 39.

[15] The following logic underlay the thesis that the Soviet leaders would be aiming at large stakes in trying to inhibit US strategic programs while pushing on with unilateral measures of their own: A Soviet maneuver of this sort could be explained on grounds of short-term advantage, such as improving the Kremlin's bargaining power or leaving the Soviet strategic posture temporarily stronger if the talks should break down; however, it would certainly involve the risk of provoking a major renewal of the US strategic effort, not to mention the damage it might do to the prospect of negotiations in other areas. Therefore, any transient advantage to be gained would hardly make sense unless the Soviet leadership were, in fact, prepared to engage in an unrestricted contest for strategic superiority.

tional politics; still others may have set their sights on attaining general strategic superiority over the United States in the belief that only thus could military and political freedom of action requisite to Soviet needs be assured.

The economic burden of arms competition with two rivals the size of the United States and China was regarded by proponents of View C as a serious concern for all elements of the Soviet leadership, but not an overriding consideration in the shaping of Soviet strategic policy.[16] As for other motivations behind this policy, it was felt that general agreement probably existed on a number of points among all leadership groupings. For example, there was doubtless agreement that the strategic build-up, however burdensome, had strengthened the image of the Soviet Union in world affairs and opened a range of political opportunities in Europe, the Middle East, and elsewhere. There was probably also a generally shared belief that Soviet military programs should not be solely oriented toward deterrence, but should try to provide both a strategic nuclear posture and conventional forces adequate to wage war successfully if deterrence should fail.

Beyond such areas of agreement, however, there were in View C, some basic issues on which no firm consensus obtained. For example, as argued by View A, the Soviet leaders were persuaded that the strategic race had already been run now that they had substantially caught up with the United States, and that nothing significant was to be gained from further competition. On the contrary, as argued by View B, the Soviet leaders were convinced that exploitable concerns in the United States about the dangers of an unrestricted arms race would provide an opportunity to transform a duopoly relationship into one in which Soviet freedom of action progressively widened while that of the United States gradually shrank. In View C, both arguments probably had strong supporters within the Soviet hierarchy, but it remained an open question which would prevail.

Similarly, although recognizing that the continuity and systematic character of Soviet research and development programs in the strategic field testified to a broad measure of agreement on long leadtime technical decisions, proponents of View C did not take this to mean that firm commitment to large resource-consuming procurement and deployment programs necessarily had been agreed upon concurrently. Rather, the research and deployment effort was regarded primarily as the foundation for a strategic build-up whose scope and pace probably had been subject to continuing internal leadership debate. In any event, whether the build-up grew out of a well-meshed strategic plan or a somewhat more haphazard series of developments, it clearly had the effect of narrowing the strategic margin between the two superpowers and had put the Soviet leadership in a position where it was obliged to ask itself, in effect:

---

[16] In this view, the fact that the Brezhnev–Kosygin regime had chosen to emphasize military over economic priorities, even after the Soviet Union had virtually caught up with the United States, suggested that the economic strain of the strategic competition, however painful, remained secondary to other considerations.

Where do we go from here? Unlike those who would contend that the Soviet leaders had already made up their minds—to halt the build-up at parity in the one case or to pursue it further in search of superiority in the other—adherents of View C tended to assume that no solid consensus in either direction actually prevailed when the SALT talks began.[17]

Given this assumption, it could be supposed that the Soviet leadership entered the talks with a range of possible objectives in mind: at one extreme, to curb further strategic arms competition through agreements which would serve to stabilize the strategic balance at existing levels or perhaps at some lower level of parity; at the other extreme, to use the talks mainly as a device to slow down a new cycle of US strategic programs while the Soviet Union pressed ahead with an accelerated technological effort aimed at achieving eventual superiority. However, in View C it seemed more likely that a compromise between these two approaches might emerge, with the Soviet Union tending to look for agreements, either tacit or formal, that would on the one hand validate Soviet strategic equality with the United States, and on the other, permit stretching out military programs to relieve pressure on Soviet resources. Such a formula could be expected to minimize internal Soviet policy differences while allowing the Kremlin leadership to mark time to see what might turn up in the way of new political and technological opportunities.

[17] This assumption rested on a series of indications that the Soviet leadership had found it difficult to piece together a position for the opening round of exploratory talks in Helsinki. Signs of internal controversy over the country's strategic policy and its stance toward strategic arms talks with the United States had continued after the initial Soviet decision to enter such talks was made known on June 27, 1968. One form in which internal disagreement showed up was editorial tampering with official statements on arms control policy. For example, the military newspaper *Krasnaia zvezda* of October 4, 1968, in reporting Foreign Minister Gromyko's October 3, 1968, UN address, deleted his remarks on the subject of strategic arms negotiations, even though it mentioned other arms control proposals. Likewise, the Soviet press omitted reference to the same subject in a UN speech of November 13 by Iakov Malik, the Soviet UN representative. The November 6, 1968, anniversary speech of Politburo member Kirill Mazurov in Moscow also received press treatment differing from the live version; the effect of the change was to censor out a statement expressing the Soviet Union's readiness to negotiate on "the whole complex" of questions involved in the strategic arms issue.

A second form in which apparent opposition to the SALT talks manifested itself was the publication of a number of thinly disguised polemical articles by military writers in late 1968 and 1969. Among other things, these articles voiced doubt about the utility of arms agreements to assure peace; they reiterated the familiar theme that Soviet military policy should aim at the attainment of superiority and cited Lenin's works to make the point that "imperialism" would continue to seek the military destruction of the Soviet Union until the worldwide triumph of communism.

A third indication that enthusiasm for launching the talks was by no means universal in Soviet leadership circles came after Kosygin had taken pains in mid-November 1968 to assure several American visitors, including former Defense Secretary Robert S. McNamara and Senators Claiborne Pell and Albert Gore, that the Soviet Union was eager for an early start on the talks. Shortly thereafter, Washington officials were said to have learned that Moscow was no longer pressing for negotiations, which seemed to suggest that Kosygin's attitude was not shared by some of his peers. See Bernard Gwertzman, "U.S. Said to Notify Soviet It Is Ready for Missile Talks," *New York Times*, December 7, 1968, and "U.S. Sees a Delay on Missile Talks," ibid., December 15, 1968. For previous discussion of signs that the Soviet approach to strategic arms negotiations was a discordant issue within the leadership, see chapter XI, p. 273; chapter XVI, fn. 128.

Although, needless to say, only the passage of time would show which of the above alternative explanations came closest to the mark, each case was lent some support by events prior to the opening of the second round of SALT talks at Vienna. In the first instance, the nonpolemical and "business-like approach" adopted by the Soviet delegation at the initial Helsinki session,[18] together with public Soviet statements that the existing "correlation of forces" would not be changed by "a new spiral in the arms race,"[19] could be construed as further evidence that the Soviet Union was seriously bent upon reaching a parity agreement. In the second case, the resumption—after Helsinki—of Soviet polemics questioning US sincerity,[20] together with unabated deployment of Soviet missiles, could be taken to mean that the Soviet leadership was more intent upon strengthening its own political and military position than upon reaching an accommodation with the United States. In the third instance, the continuing ambivalence exhibited toward the SALT talks by the Soviet Union, together with Moscow's caveat that it was interested in steps toward limitation of strategic arms but *no more so* than the United States, could be interpreted as reflecting something less than a consensus within the leadership on its strategic objectives.[21]

It might well turn out that the process of negotiation itself and the interaction between the two sides would help to shape the Soviet policy stance as the SALT talks unfolded. From Moscow's viewpoint, no matter how explicit or how diffuse its negotiating position might prove to be, there were certainly reasons for avoiding an open collapse of the talks, for not only would such a breakdown run counter to the Soviet aim of encouraging détente in Europe, but it might also play into China's hands by increasing the chances of a rapprochement be-

---

[18] See chapter XI, p. 277.

[19] The most noteworthy of these statements was a *Pravda* editorial of March 7, 1970, which, though expressing doubt as to US sincerity with regard to limiting strategic arms, also made the point that the Soviet Union saw no profit for either side in a new round of strategic competition. See fn. 4 above.

[20] Soviet charges that the United States was insincere and was trying to put obstacles in the way of the SALT talks began to appear in early January 1970, after plans for expansion of the Safeguard ABM system were announced in Washington, and grew in intensity following the disclosure on March 10 that the United States would begin to equip a small number of Minuteman missiles with MIRV in mid-1970. See TASS broadcast of press conference by Leonid Zamiatin at the USSR Ministry of Foreign Affairs, January 13, 1970; Observer article in *Pravda*, March 7, 1970; Lev Tolkunov, "America Today," *Izvestiia*, March 14, 1970; V. Berezin, "Sticks in the Wheel," *Krasnaia zvezda*, March 14, 1970.

[21] Soviet ambivalence toward SALT was apparent in several respects. For example, some Soviet spokesmen continued to insist that Moscow was hopeful of reaching agreement for "ending or at least restricting" the strategic arms race. Although such statements generally were qualified by the admonition that "it must not be inferred" that Soviet interest in agreement "is greater than that of others," the impression given was that the Soviet Union did not want to prejudice the prospect of useful negotiations in advance of the second round at Vienna. On the other hand, however, the Soviet Union also resorted to polemical attacks on American intentions and sought increasingly to influence the US domestic debate on arms policy. If the United States were to reply in kind, the result would hardly have been to improve the atmosphere for the next round of SALT. Without putting too fine a point on it, this perhaps was what at least some factions within the Soviet leadership were aiming at. For pertinent commentary, see William Beecher, "Soviet Criticism on Arms Dismays Top U.S. Aides," *New York Times*, March 9, 1970; Chalmers M. Roberts, "U.S., Russia Maneuver for Positions at SALT," *Washington Post*, March 10, 1970.

tween Peking and Washington. But whatever direction the SALT talks might take before running their course, they could hardly be expected to reverse the process by which the Soviet Union had gradually whittled away the strategic margin of its main Western adversary. At the least, the talks were likely to register a transition from the long-standing inferiority of the Soviet Union to putative parity with the United States.

Implications of a Shift in the Soviet–American Power Relationship

It is by no means a foregone conclusion, of course, that a change in the power relationship of the Soviet Union and the United States will necessarily have deeply disturbing effects upon the stability of mutual deterrence and upon their global political rivalry. One may well argue that so long as each nuclear power retains the capacity to inflict upon the other retaliatory destruction of "unacceptable" dimensions—a variously defined criterion, to be sure[22]—deterrence will continue to operate as before and shifts in the strategic power balance are likely to have relatively little political impact. Even though changes—especially rapid ones—in technology, weaponry, force levels, and other aspects of the strategic environment generally are conceded to introduce many elements of uncertainty into the situation, it can also be argued that uncertainty itself may contribute to mutual restraint and discourage any political maneuver that might upset the deterrent balance.

Comforting as it may be to view matters in this light, however, one can hardly dismiss the possibility that in a new setting of either strategic parity or Soviet superiority many of the familiar assumptions of the past about the stability of deterrence and the political conduct of the Soviet Union in the international arena will no longer hold good. This applies especially under conditions where changes in the strategic balance have been accompanied by the Soviet Union's growing capacity to project naval forces and other nonstrategic elements of its military power into distant areas. The development of such capacities not only has been a notable factor in reshaping the over-all power balance and in giving the Soviet Union, for the first time in its history, the credentials of a global military power; it also has opened up the prospect that the USSR and the United States—pursuing their differing interests in the dynamic environment of Third World instability—may have to reckon with a new order of problems arising from the "overlapping" of their military presence in trouble spots around the world.[23]

The question of a possible breakdown in the system of mutual deterrence

---

[22] For descriptions of the criteria for effective deterrence, see Kaysen, in *Foreign Affairs* (July 1968): 664–68; "Strategic Forces and Related Issues," remarks by The Hon. Townsend Hoopes, Under Secretary of the Air Force, before the Commonwealth Club, San Francisco, September 13, 1968; Franklin A. Long, "Strategic Balance and the ABM," *Bulletin of the Atomic Scientists* (December 1968): 2–3.

[23] See Zbigniew Brzezinski, "Peace and Power: Looking Toward the 1970s," *Encounter* (November 1968): 8–9.

that has operated in the past does not center on the spectre of a deliberate resort to nuclear war. Although, in theory, one can devise scenarios in which an aggressor with an appropriate combination of offensive and defensive forces might hope, by striking the first blow and dealing with only disorganized residual counterblows, to escape effective retaliation, it is generally assumed that in the real world of decision no rational leadership will care to put such a case to the test. Rather, threats to the stability of deterrence may lie in the possibility of the two powers stumbling into war because of a reassessment of the risks involved in trying to translate a changed correlation of forces into political advantage.

A cardinal feature of the past structure of deterrence was its asymmetry, both military and political. Superior American nuclear power coincided with a political posture oriented mainly toward defense of the international status quo; the Soviet Union's inferior strategic power went along with political-ideological aspirations to reshape the world order along Communist lines.[24] In this setting, the one-sided weight of American strategic power, together with Western superiority in globally mobile forces, set definite limits to the range of risks the Soviet Union was willing to run in pursuing its political ambitions. Perhaps one of the prime questions to be asked, therefore, is whether the novelty of no longer laboring under a markedly unfavorable power balance may tempt the Soviet leaders to embark on more militant policies and to accept a wider range of risks than hitherto.

Historically speaking, it is perhaps more accurate to say that Soviet foreign policy behavior has reflected a combination of caution and militance;[25] but as suggested by our discussion of alternative explanations for the Soviet strategic build-up, there are still quite disparate opinions as to which of these elements can be expected to predominate in the future. Some students of Soviet affairs find it prudent to assume that the Soviet leadership may indeed accept greater risks in the process of trying to extract political gains from a changed strategic equation, thus introducing new elements of turbulence into international relations.[26] In Europe, which still constitutes in Soviet eyes a focal arena of world politics, the strain on deterrence might increase considerably in a situation

[24] Ibid., pp. 7–8.

[25] For an interesting analysis of Soviet behavior in twenty-nine postwar crises from 1945 to 1963, intended to test empirically whether the Soviet Union was reckless or cautious, see Jan F. Triska and David D. Finley, *Soviet Foreign Policy* (New York: The Macmillan Company, 1968), pp. 310–49. This analysis, which included a survey of the Western literature on Soviet risk-taking, concluded that the Soviet Union showed mixed tendencies toward militant and cautious behavior, with the latter predominating. It was also found that the Soviet risk-taking propensity was higher with respect to action against other members of the Communist system than when potential conflict with the West was involved.

[26] See, for example, statements by Philip E. Mosely and Thomas W. Wolfe, in Hearings Before the Subcommittee on Military Applications of the Joint Committee on Atomic Energy, Congress of the United States, *Scope, Magnitude, and Implications of the United States Antiballistic Missile Program*, November 6 and 7, 1967 (Washington, D.C.: Government Printing Office, 1968), pp. 54–55, 72–73. See also Walter Laqueur, "What Do They Want?" *Survival* (November 1968): 362.

where preponderant Soviet conventional strength was no longer checkmated by superior American strategic power; this could be all the more true in the event of a strategic arms limitation agreement, which in a sense would serve as a substitute for an American pledge of no-first-use of nuclear weapons.[27] Under these circumstances, the caution characteristically displayed by every generation of Soviet leaders toward the risk of military conflict in Europe might decline, possibly to the point where the Soviet Union would try to effect political changes by the threat of direct military pressure. Alternatively, of course, Soviet leaders might go no further than attempting to persuade Europeans that, in the absence of yesterday's American nuclear guarantee, they had best work out tomorrow's security arrangements along lines proposed by Moscow.

In trouble spots elsewhere—such as the Middle East—where the presence of US and Soviet military power may tend to overlap, even a slight propensity in the Kremlin to press for political gains commensurate with the Soviet Union's stronger military posture could aggravate existing instabilities and even lead to a Great Power confrontation. Moreover, a Soviet Union advertised as the strategic equal of the United States and possessing an improved capacity to intervene in local situations would probably find itself under new pressures to come to the help of clients in other continents, where previously it was excused from becoming directly engaged because it obviously lacked the means to do so. If the United States were to enter on a period of neo-isolationism, or at least what might be described as a Vietnam-induced mood of withdrawal from extensive global commitments, the resultant situation might seem to offer the Soviet Union an added invitation to break out of its erstwhile containment onto a wider global stage.

The Soviet Union's internal economic problems and the apparently waning attraction of Marxist–Leninist ideology both to the Soviet people and as a model for the outside world may also have the effect of persuading the Kremlin leadership to call increasingly upon its growing military power for extension of Soviet influence abroad through classical modes of power politics. At the least, the asymmetry between the expansion of Soviet military power and the Soviet system's declining appeal as an example of modern societal growth and progress could tend to nudge the leadership in this direction.

None of this is to argue that Soviet leaders would be likely to step so far out of character that they would court a confrontation with the United States. But the combination of a stronger military posture and the more vigorous asser-

---

[27] Soviet proposals of one kind or another for banning the use of nuclear weapons were for many years a central feature of Soviet efforts to inhibit the United States from deriving political advantage from its superior nuclear posture. In particular, a ban on first-use of nuclear weapons was closely linked to Moscow's European diplomacy, for it would in effect cancel out the guarantee of US nuclear protection to Europe. The Soviet position outlined in advance of the strategic talks (see, for example, Pravda, July 2, 1968, and Izvestiia, January 21, 1969) continued to call for a ban on nuclear use. But even if such a ban were not to be specifically adopted, it seems likely that any agreement on strategic arms levels marking the end of the historical US strategic advantage would be regarded as tantamount to a no-first-use pledge.

tion of what they regarded as the Soviet Union's global interests would probably raise the incidence of dangerous situations and the possibility that in some major crisis, believing themselves in a position to make the other side back down, the Soviet leaders might blunder into actions with imaginably unhappy consequences. The impression of an incumbent regime prone to act unpredictably under the pressure of the Czechoslovak crisis does little to increase confidence in the collective judgment of Soviet leaders.[28]

In contrast with the picture drawn above, let it be said that many competent observers of Soviet leadership behavior tend to doubt that Soviet risk-taking propensities will rise appreciably in the foreseeable future. Rather, engrained caution toward the risk of war is considered likely to continue to dominate the Kremlin's outlook, even though the power balance may look much more favorable to the Soviet Union than before.[29] In this view, the desire to avoid dangerous confrontations, coupled with concern about diversion of resources to sustain a highly competitive military situation, would probably discourage risky probing against Western political positions. Although more militant, hard-line tendencies in the Soviet leadership have coincided with the strengthening of the country's relative power position, these elements have thus far had their way only with regard to such intra-bloc issues as Czechoslovakia; it remains open to question, in this view, whether there will be any appreciable extension of militancy to Soviet conduct outside the bloc. The need to mend fences in the West while girding for possible enlargement of border conflicts with China is another factor deemed likely to temper militant anti-Western tendencies in Moscow.

Whichever of these contrasting appraisals may come closer to the mark, the whole question of future Soviet conduct turns, of course, on many considerations other than those pertaining to a newly emerging power balance that have been touched upon here. At bottom, perhaps, what is chiefly involved is the direction in which the Soviet system itself is moving. Although one can offer only a vastly oversimplified comment on this complex issue, it would seem that there are at least two broad possibilities.[30]

The first of these is that, despite the regressive, neo-Stalinist tendencies that have emerged in the past few years, the Soviet Union may basically be evolving in a direction that will find its leaders prepared to play a more responsible and stabilizing role in international politics. Internal changes at work in Soviet society as well as external factors may be helping to reshape the outlook of the

28 See chapter XV, pp. 412–14.

29 See, for example, Marshall D. Shulman, "Relations with the Soviet Union," in Kermit Gordon, ed., *Agenda for the Nation* (Washington, D.C.: The Brookings Institution, 1968), pp. 380–84. A somewhat similar view, holding that the Soviet leaders are likely to prove "unwilling to run major risks on behalf of militant causes," and to find themselves instead engaged in "an uneasy pattern of both rivalry and accommodation with the United States," has been expressed by Zbigniew Brzezinski, "Meeting Moscow's 'Limited Coexistence'," *New Leader*, December 16, 1968, p. 2.

30 See chapter X, pp. 221–24, for a more detailed discussion of alternative views on the process of change in the Soviet system which was set in motion during the Khrushchev period.

ruling elite, bringing its influential elements around to a view that favors lasting accommodation with the ongoing world order over ambitious attempts to reconstruct it in accordance with an outworn dogma. Graceful adjustment to reform and liberalizing tendencies at home and within the Soviet bloc might, in this case, be facilitated by a new military power balance with the West which convinced Soviet leaders that they were at least secure from external danger.

Though it is not to be supposed that the Soviet leaders could easily shed their habitual suspicion of the Western world, various "imperatives" for a Soviet–American rapprochement might increasingly make themselves felt; they would include such needs as the avoidance of nuclear war, containment of Communist China, and tackling the worldwide problems of overpopulation, food supply, pollution of the biosphere, space and underocean exploration, and the like. Thus, in spite of continuing ideological conflict and unresolved political issues, the Soviet Union in this climate might exhibit a growing receptivity to the idea that the two nuclear superpowers should extend their groping search for co-operation and accommodation. The moderation of military competition, in particular, might in this instance become increasingly attractive to both sides. Just as their apparent mutual interest in heading off an unrestricted strategic arms race had led gradually toward strategic arms limitation talks, so the two superpowers might find it expedient to seek new "rules of the game" to mitigate the prospects of explosive entanglements in various global zones of contention.

On the other hand, however, there is the alternative possibility that the Soviet Union may be moving in a direction that is far more grim, backing into the future on the basis of old policies and habits more likely to promote global ferment and discord than world stability. Its leaders, grown old in their ways and perhaps still prisoners of a rhetoric of class struggle rooted in the past, may find it impossible to set the Soviet Union on a new track at home and abroad. Instead, fearful of a threat to monopoly party rule from discontents within the Soviet bloc and fancied ideological subversion from outside, the Soviet governing elite may revert increasingly to the suppression of internal societal change and to a hostile external stance toward the West.

In this environment, there not only would be a premium on the further strengthening of the Soviet military posture, but the influence of orthodox hard-line elements who argue that Soviet security can only be assured by gaining the upper hand in military power would probably grow within the leadership. Although some recognition of mutual interests, such as the avoidance of nuclear war, would doubtless remain, the area of potential collaboration between the Soviet Union and the United States could be expected to shrink, and there might well be much less disposition in the Kremlin to believe that the Soviet Union ought to co-operate closely with the other nuclear superpower in reducing the sources of international tension and instability.

One would prefer, of course, to conclude on a hopeful note, suggesting that the present generation of leaders has every good reason to seek the security and prosperity of the Soviet people by generally guiding the country in the first of the alternative directions sketched above. This, however, would presuppose a rather marked transformation of the world outlook of the ruling elite, and would call for what the Soviet leaders might well regard as too drastic a re-orientation of the internal and external policies to which they have been dedicated. Whether the incumbent leadership or the next generation of leaders that steps into the shoes of the Brezhnev–Kosygin regime will prove capable of breaking with the past and setting out upon a more enlightened course remains therefore a question to which the answer—be it hopeful or discouraging—can only be furnished by the future.

INDEX

SELECTED RAND BOOKS

BECKER, ABRAHAM S. *Soviet National Income 1958–64*. Berkeley and Los Angeles, Calif.: University of California Press, 1969.

BERGSON, A. *The Real National Income of Soviet Russia Since 1928*. Cambridge, Mass.: Harvard University Press, 1961.

BRODIE, BERNARD. *Strategy in the Missile Age*. Princeton, N.J.: Princeton University Press, 1959.

DAVISON, W. PHILLIPS. *The Berlin Blockade: A Study in Cold War Politics*. Princeton, N.J.: Princeton University Press, 1958.

DINERSTEIN, H. S. *War and the Soviet Union: Nuclear Weapons and the Revolution in Soviet Military and Political Thinking*. New York: Frederick A. Praeger, 1959.

FAINSOD, MERLE. *Smolensk Under Soviet Rule*. Cambridge, Mass.: Harvard University Press, 1958.

GARTHOFF, RAYMOND L. *Soviet Military Doctrine*. Glencoe, Ill.: The Free Press, 1953.

GEORGE, ALEXANDER L. *Propaganda Analysis: A Study of Inferences Made From Nazi Propaganda in World War II*. Evanston, Ill.: Row, Peterson and Company, 1959.

GOURÉ, LEON. *Civil Defense in the Soviet Union*. Los Angeles, Calif.: University of California Press, 1962.

GOURÉ, LEON. *The Siege of Leningrad*. Stanford, Calif.: Stanford University Press, 1962.

GURTOV, MELVIN. *Southeast Asia Tomorrow: Problems and Prospects for US Policy*. Baltimore, Md.: The Johns Hopkins Press, 1970.

HALPERN, MANFRED. *The Politics of Social Change in the Middle East and North Africa*. Princeton, N.J.: Princeton University Press, 1963.

HITCH, CHARLES J., and ROLAND McKEAN. *The Economics of Defense in the Nuclear Age*. Cambridge, Mass.: Harvard University Press, 1960.

HORELICK, ARNOLD L., and MYRON RUSH. *Strategic Power and Soviet Foreign Policy*. Chicago, Ill.: University of Chicago Press, 1966.

HSIEH, ALICE LANGLEY. *Communist China's Strategy in the Nuclear Era*. Englewood Cliffs, N.J.: Prentice-Hall, 1962.

JOHNSON, JOHN J. (ed.). *The Role of the Military in Underdeveloped Countries*. Princeton, N.J.: Princeton University Press, 1962.

KECSKEMETI, PAUL. *The Unexpected Revolution*. Stanford, Calif.: Stanford University Press, 1961.

KOLKOWICZ, ROMAN. *The Soviet Military and the Communist Party*. Princeton, N.J.: Princeton University Press, 1967.

KRAMISH, ARNOLD. *Atomic Energy in the Soviet Union*. Stanford, Calif.: Stanford University Press, 1959.

LEITES, NATHAN. *A Study of Bolshevism*. Glencoe, Ill.: The Free Press, 1953.

LEITES, NATHAN. *The Operational Code of the Politburo*. New York: McGraw-Hill Book Company, 1951.

LEITES, NATHAN, and CHARLES WOLF, JR. *Rebellion and Authority: An Analytic Essay on Insurgent Conflicts*. Chicago, Ill.: Markham Publishing Company, 1970.

LUBELL, HAROLD. *Middle East Oil Crises and Western Europe's Energy Supplies*. Baltimore, Md.: The Johns Hopkins Press, 1963.

PINCUS, JOHN A. *Economic Aid and International Cost Sharing*. Baltimore, Md.: The Johns Hopkins Press, 1965.

QUADE, E. S., and W. I. BOUCHER, *Systems Analysis and Policy Planning Applications in Defense*. New York: American Elsevier Publishing Co., 1968.